Management Information Systems

Readings and Cases

A Managerial Perspective

Management Information Systems

Readings and Cases

A Managerial Perspective

Andrew C. Boynton
University of Virginia

Robert W. Zmud
Florida State University

The Scott, Foresman Series in
Computers and Information Systems
Thomas H. Athey, Consulting Editor

SCOTT, FORESMAN/LITTLE, BROWN HIGHER EDUCATION
A Division of Scott, Foresman and Company
Glenview, Illinois   London, England

Library of Congress Cataloging-in-Publication Data

Management information systems : readings and cases : a managerial perspective /
[edited] by Andrew C. Boynton and Robert W. Zmud.
    p.   cm.
  ISBN 0-673-38859-X
  1. Management information systems. I. Boynton, Andrew C.
II. Zmud, Robert W.
T58.6.M3518 1990
658.4′038−dc20   90-8046
                                                                    CIP

1 2 3 4 5 6−KPF−95 94 93 92 91 90

PREFACE

ANDREW C. BOYNTON is Assistant Professor of Business Administration at the Darden Graduate School of Business, University of Virginia, where he teaches information systems and business policy. Dr. Boynton is interested in the topics of information technology management and information systems and their relationship to organizational design. His work has been published in MIS Quarterly *and* Sloan Management Review. *Dr. Boynton holds a B.S. degree from Boston College, and an M.B.A. and a Ph.D. degree from the University of North Carolina, Chapel Hill.*

ROBERT W. ZMUD is Professor and Thomas L. Williams, Jr., Eminent Scholar in Management Information Systems at the College of Business, Florida State University. Dr. Zmud holds a B.A.E. degree from the University of Virginia, an S.M. degree from the Sloan School of Management, Massachusetts Institute of Technology, and a Ph.D. degree from the College of Business and Public Administration, University of Arizona. His research interests include the impact of information technology on organizations and organizational efforts to plan, manage, and diffuse information technology.

One of the most important recent business trends is the use of information technology (IT) resources in flexible and innovative ways. Popular business magazines are full of stories about exciting new IT applications that change the very nature of how companies compete.

In addition to this trend, many companies are moving the responsibility for IT implementation and management away from MIS departments to all departments and their managers. Current and future business managers must be as prepared to understand and manage information technology as they are to manage human, capital, and financial resources.

Because managers tend to respond to opportunities, problems, and threats by using skills and actions drawn from their personal "tool kits," educating them to draw upon IT resources as a tool is a key responsibility of management educators. *Manage-*

ment Information Systems: Readings and Cases—A Managerial Perspective will help educators carry out this responsibility. It provides readers with the latest concepts and the most important management trends regarding IT resources, and also illustrates effective, thoughtful, and creative uses of IT resources in a variety of business settings.

This book is targeted at current and future managers of any business area. The focus is on management issues; there is little discussion of esoteric notions such as "bits and bytes" or how a manager can use a particular type of software or hardware. We assume only that readers have an understanding of basic business concepts.

The readings come from a variety of leading magazines and journals such as *Business Week, Forbes, Sloan Management Review, MIS Quarterly, Datamation,* and *InformationWeek.* They address the forefront of thinking across a variety of IT issues. The cases in Part 5 of the book—from the Harvard Business School and other sources—provide in-depth descriptions of how companies are managing and using IT resources. They offer readers comprehensive examples to illustrate the ideas and concepts put forth in the readings. All the readings and cases provide excellent material for classroom discussion and show the exciting ways in which IT resources can be used in a variety of businesses.

The book is organized into five parts. The first, "Waves of Change," contains articles on emerging trends in the use and management of IT resources, including discussions of the following topics:

- The increased IT-management role of line managers
- Technology changes for the year 2000
- Emerging organizational structures
- The strengths and limitations of IT as a competitive weapon
- The changing role of IT in successful companies

Part 2 of the book is titled "The Bottom Line: Payoffs from Information Technology Investments" and provides short, but powerful, examples of companies using IT for a variety of business applications. The articles illustrate how companies can gain competitive advantage by using the following tools:

- Expert systems
- Decision support systems
- Executive information systems
- Electronic data interchange
- Image processing
- Global networking

A discussion of effective uses of IT resources would be incomplete without a discussion of the ways in which companies are implementing these applications. To address issues associated with the design and construction of information systems, Part 3 of the book, "Beating the High Costs of Building Information Systems," includes articles on the following topics:

- Prototyping
- Software engineering
- Reusable software
- Buying application packages
- Computer-aided systems engineering
- Critical success factors and information requirements
- Organizational change associated with new information-system implementation

Part 4, "Managing Waves of Change," is a series of articles highlighting issues that are critical to effective IT management. The articles cover the following topics:

- The future role of the MIS function in organizations
- The changing roles of "Chief Information Officers"
- The management of decentralized and centralized information technology
- Techniques to conceptualize IT management from an overall organizational perspective
- The relationship between IT architecture and organizational structure and strategy
- Ways to justify the costs of new technologies
- Effective methods for information technology planning

Articles in Part 5, "Information Technology Management: In Depth Studies," give detailed information from the "real world." The case studies included in this part examine the histories of successful information systems and provide important background on the following issues:

- Managing IT resources from a corporate perspective
- Establishing an effective end-user support structure
- Designing and implementing effective decision support systems
- Recognizing the role of IT in the 1987 stock market collapse
- Understanding the behavior principles of systems design

This collection of readings and cases addresses the most important trends in IT management and will, we believe, prove topical, informative, and interesting to students from a variety of backgrounds. Nevertheless, we could not include everything; we recognize that many readers will have their own favorite readings that we have either omitted for space reasons or simply overlooked. We encourage readers to recommend articles or cases to us for future editions of this book.

Andrew C. Boynton
Robert W. Zmud

CONTENTS

PART THREE   **Beating the High Costs of Building Information Systems**   *171*

PART FOUR   *Managing Waves of Change*   *259*

JOHN F. ROCKART is a Senior Lecturer and Director of the Center for Information Systems Research at the Sloan School of Management, Massachusetts Institute of Technology. Dr. Rockart holds an A.B. degree from Princeton University, an M.B.A. degree from Harvard University, and a Ph.D. degree from M.I.T. His current interests are in the areas of the critical success factors concept, top management information use, linking business and IS strategy, managing end-user computing, and executive support systems.

After 20 years of sleep, Rip Van Winkle awoke to a world that was quite unlike the one he had known. Although a few things seemed the same, his surroundings were, for the most part, very different.

Managers in the information systems world are in a similar situation. If data-processing managers from the 1950s, the 1960s, or even the early 1970s were transported to 1990, they would find themselves in a vastly different environment. For such managers, the world would be new, unreal, and replete with challenges.

The transported managers would find themselves surrounded by personal computers with more power than many of the largest mainframes they had utilized. Their department's name would have changed from "Data Processing" or "MIS" to "Information Technology," in recognition of the now widespread understanding that telecommunications and computers are inseparable. The department staff would be talking about establishing telecommunications standards, data-driven design, and a host of other practices that had been only concepts for the transported managers.

The Rip Van Winkle managers would be staggered to find that information technology is now heavily intertwined with the strategy of the firm. Senior executives in the organization are major users of terminals for something called "executive support systems"; likewise, "expert systems" are now more than just the dream of a few people in computer science laboratories. Above all, as these managers walked the halls of their organizations, they would be surprised to hear some line managers talking seriously about information technology and their responsibilities for its effective use.

For those of us who have been involved with information technology for part or all of the past four decades, continual change has become almost routine. In the 1980s, however—especially in the last five years—a quantum change has taken place: information technology has become inextricably intertwined with business. Information technology is now the province not only of information systems professionals, but of business managers at every level.

For a business to be successful in the 1990s, it is not enough to merely do a good job of purchasing, manufacturing, selling, and financing a steady stream of well-designed, new products. A firm must also utilize information technology in all functions. In particular, it must use information technology to coordinate among departments and between organizations. Finally, a business must manage the information technology function exceedingly well—an extremely difficult task.

Boynton and Zmud focus their book of readings on this changed business environment. Several key messages emerge from the articles, such as the "competitive advantage" gained by using technology effectively; the benefits of technical and managerial integration of systems; and the need for leadership in the creative use of information technology by all business managers (not just information technologists). The readings examine many other issues as well, and provide some of the best thought available on the problems and goals of today's management information systems. In short, this is a valuable set of readings put together by two professors who, more than most, have both a theoretical and a pragmatic perspective on the field of information technology.

PART ONE

Waves of Change

To learn how to manage information technology (IT) resources effectively, managers must understand the way in which these resources are currently being used in organizations, the rate at which they are developing technologically, and their ultimate effects on organizations. In a relatively short period of time, fundamental changes have occurred in each of these aspects of IT management. IT experts expect changes to accelerate in the future. The nine articles in this section enhance the knowledge of current and future managers regarding these "waves of change," and help them anticipate how these changes will continue to affect organizations.

Part 1 begins with a selection by John F. Rockart from *Sloan Management Review* that establishes a major theme of this book—the changing nature of IT management in today's learning organizations. Rockart's message is clear and powerful: YOU—current and future managers—are ultimately responsible for ensuring the effective use of IT resources. The second reading, "The Withering Away of the IS Organization," raises questions about the necessity of central information systems functions dedicated to managing these resources. Gene Bylinsky's article (Reading 3) then provides insight into continuing developments as well as future applications. In Readings 4 and 5, contemporary views of emerging organizational forms and critical business success factors are articulated. Both of these readings demonstrate that IT resources will play key roles in the success of organizations in virtually all industries.

The final four articles in this section examine how IT can be used for competitive advantage. Michael Hammer and Glenn Mangurian discuss how communications technologies can be used to change a company's competitive position in Reading 6, "The Changing Value of Communications Technology." "The Myths and Realities of Competitive Advantage" (Reading 7) and "Information Technology as a Competitive Burden" (Reading 8) point out the potential drawbacks to a reliance upon IT to enhance a firm's competitive stance. The final reading—"A Hard Look at Strategic Systems"—is from *Indications,* a publication by The Index Group, a leading consulting firm. It provides a pragmatic approach to identifying opportunities for using IT to gain competitive advantage.

The Line Takes the Leadership— IS Management in a Wired Society

John F. Rockart

When George David conceptualized an approach to elevator maintenance based on a centralized computer communications network, he had no idea it would become a notable example of the use of information technology to gain competitive advantage. Yet the story of the major improvement in customer service made possible by OTISLINE, the Otis system, has been told and retold from the lectern and in the trade press. David, formerly head of Otis North America and now CEO of Otis Elevator Company, was something of a trailblazer: an executive outside the IS function proposing and implementing a major change in how the company used information systems.

The system itself is striking. Previously, loosely coordinated, decentralized maintenance efforts were carried out in more than one hundred local offices; now Otis centrally coordinates the efforts of its nationwide repair force. Trouble calls are taken by highly trained, often multilingual operators who work from a computer screen to record all data concerning the problem elevator. Repair personnel are dispatched via a telephone/beeper system. Upon completion of the maintenance, all relevant information is once again recorded in the computer.

The advantages the system provides to Otis are manifold. Perhaps most important is senior management's increased ability to view the status of maintenance efforts nationwide. A specialist can quickly be directed to a particular customer with a difficult problem. Frequent trouble from a specific type of elevator or a geographic locale can be observed as the pattern develops, and corrective action taken. The quality of telephone response to anxious customers can be closely monitored. And fault data, available both to management and the company's engineers and designers, is more precise, more copious, and more accessible than the information that previously worked its way up through the five-level chain of command.

Although many elements of this now rather well-known story are fascinating, one often overlooked factor is particularly significant. The system was conceptualized and its implementation driven not by information systems personnel, but by George David himself. Ed Burke, Otis's director of MIS, asserts, "It was and is George's system. He saw the need. He saw the solution. I helped, but he made it happen."

Even a few years ago, executives like George David would have been almost unique. Today, however, there is a small but rapidly growing number of senior line and staff executives taking responsibility for significant strategic projects centered on computer and communication technology in their companies, divisions, or departments. A pattern of emerging line responsibility for such projects is now becoming clearer. This paper presents some conclusions derived from a study of line executives in fifteen companies who have been proactive in their use of information technology. (The word "line" is used to encompass all managers—whether line or staff—having responsibility for a major segment of an organization.)

For the first three decades of the computer era, the key figures in information technology use were the information systems professionals. Today, for a number of reasons noted below, the shaping of information systems' direction is passing to line managers. No longer willing to delegate the strategic or tactical uses of this technology to the information systems department, these managers are taking the lead in applying information technology to the most important areas of their businesses. Many are using the technology as a core element in aggressive new approaches to the marketplace or to enhance control of internal operations, as Otis did.

Including information technology as a significant component in business planning and, thus, in the process of conception of new business strategies and tactics, is only one part of an emerging senior executive role. The other, and equally important, element of this role is the active direction of the implementation of new systems. I will examine the logic underlying the need for both parts of this role later in this paper. First, however, let us look at a few other examples of "the line taking the leadership."

- Three years ago Bob Campbell, president of the Refining and Marketing Division of the Sun Corporation, identified crude oil trading as perhaps the key business activity in his organization. He gave Woody Roe the job of improving Sun's efforts in this area. Roe quickly realized the trading process was dispersed to a large number of groups located worldwide, each acting relatively independently. Some reported to the management of other Sun divisions.

  Although he had no information technology background, Roe envisioned a central trading room supported by information from Reuters and other trade data sources. He turned to Sun's information technology department for the technical design of the system, but then set out himself, with Campbells' support, to initiate the process and organizational changes needed to make the system effective. Today centralized, on-line trading is recognized by Campbell and other Sun executives as a major weapon in Sun's fight for increased revenue and profit in its very competitive industry.

- Dick Kennedy, while president of the Vitrified Products Division of the Norton Company, developed a strategic plan heavily based on the use of information technology. Realizing that his division (which manufactured grinding materials) was in a mature business, Kennedy focused on two critical success factors—low cost and excellent service. His business strategy was to make the division the international leader in both areas. To do so, he initiated a set of major information technology projects. These ranged from the "Norton Connection" (a computer-based telecommunications link between Norton and its distributors), to a more effective order-processing system, to a series of manufacturing technologies ultimately targeted at flexible manufacturing and automated materials control. Implementing several large, extremely complex systems at the same time is far from simple. But Kennedy had accomplished much of this, with considerable bottom-line impact, before Norton executive management combined his division with several others in a sweeping organizational realignment.

- In a similar manner, Jerome Grossman, president of the New England Medical center (NEMC), took the initiative in using information technology to help him manage this 450-bed teaching hospital in Boston. Drawing upon his knowledge of the technology, he designed a "product-based" planning and control system of which any industrial manufacturing manager would be proud. The system, built with a relational database, now provides a wealth of information for future planning, day-to-day management, and retrospective analysis of operations.

   The system is simple enough in concept. Each "product" the hospital delivers (e.g., a heart bypass operation) has a list of the resources (nursing hours, X rays, etc.) that will be used to help the patient. This product/resource list (or bill of materials) is used in three major ways. First, for annual planning purposes, the expected number of patients in each category can be multiplied by the resource requirements for each, and the institution's total resource needs in X ray, laboratories, and so on, can be roughly estimated. Second, as patients are treated, the institution can monitor the use of resources by resource category, by department, by product, or by physician. Third, comparisons can be made between expected and actual resource use by case type to help set prices in the future.

   A sweeping change of this type, from simple year-to-year budgeting processes to much more specific, detailed resource management using state-of-the-art information technology, was conceptually innovative. But the real work had just begun. Implementing this new management system, which smacked of uncaring industrial practice, took significant education and persuasion on Dr. Grossman's part of the management team, the medical staff, and the trustees. Only a senior executive strongly committed to this strategy could possibly implement such a system. It is now in place at NEMC.

   If war is too important to leave to the generals, the deployment of information technology is far too important, in 1988, to be left to information technologists. For many reasons, a growing number of line managers have realized this and are taking charge of information technology use in their organizations.

   Line involvement with information technology is increasingly evident in the development of major new projects and systems such as those described above. The new role of the line, however, has not diminished the influence of information systems executives. In fact, as the final section of this paper notes, their role has actually expanded.

THE FOURTH ERA OF INFORMATION
SYSTEMS MANAGEMENT

Each of the managers mentioned above has explicitly or implicitly realized that, in the past few years, information technology has gone through a radical change: both the applications and the effective management of information technology look very diffrent than they did just a few years ago. In fact, this is the fourth major wave of information technology; each new type of technology has, in turn, led to a different era of applications and managerial processes. These eras can be called — after the applications each enabled — the accounting era, the operational era, the information era, and the "wired society."

The Accounting Era: IS Dominance

In the 1950s and early 1960s, with only batch-processing technology available, commercial computer use centered on the applications of the accountant who, conveniently, carried out payroll, accounts payable, and other operations in batches. In those early days, the information systems staff was in charge of all systems efforts. The computer professionals were responsible for conceptual design, programming, implementation, and operation of the system. In many cases the relevant manager (in charge of payroll or accounts receivable, for example) was more a "subject" of the new system than a contributor to it. The information systems staff swept into the department, interviewed the clerks, and designed the systems — most of which were barely understandable to anyone outside the computer hierarchy. Operating managers stood to the side; they provided some assistance and guidance, but the responsibility for system design and implementation rested clearly with the information systems people.

The Operational Era: Line Involvement

As on-line systems and direct access files became available and computers grew faster and were made more reliable, it became feasible to computerize the firm's key logistical (operational) systems. Since these systems required continual real-time updates (e.g., withdrawals from and additions to inventory files) and direct access to their current status, they could be effectively implemented only in an on-line environment. IS dominance worked reasonably well for a few of the era's simpler systems, but more complex systems, such as manufacturing scheduling, proved very difficult to implement. It became clear that complex systems were not workable unless line managers helped to define their objectives and functionality. Thus began an era of line management involvement in the conceptualization, design, and implementation of systems. Despite good intentions, however, the degree to which line managers understood and were involved in these systems varied widely. In most instances, there was little doubt among the participants as to who was ultimately responsible for the system's success. It was still the information systems department.

The Information Era: Individual Decision Support

The availability of improved, "fourth generation" user languages and relational databases, as well as the personal computer, ushered in a new era in the late 1970s and early 1980s. The focus changed from transaction processing, which epitomized the first two eras, to the use of information. Able at last to access and manipulate data and text, individual users reveled in the ability to "do their own thing." Many analytically oriented decision support systems were created. Staff worked hard to understand and exploit the new opportunities for information acquisition and manipulation. Information systems managers set up information centers and other end-user support organizations and turned much of the responsibility for end-user programming and information access over to the users. Yet information systems management retained its responsibility for developing and maintaining databases, setting computer and telecommunications standards, and other aspects of information technology. The seeds for line leadership in all aspects of computing were sown. What emerged from this era was a partnership between the users of information (who decided what they wanted to do and also did some programming) and the information technology organization (which provided networks, access to data, and so forth).

The Wired Society: Line Leadership in Strategic Systems

Vastly improved communications capability has been the key technology change driving the most recent era. Combined with ever more cost-effective computer hardware and software, cheaper, higher band-width communications have led to the fourth era, perhaps appropriately characterized as the wired society. The label is relevant because a significant aspect of this era's applications is the wiring together of suborganizations within a single firm and, more strikingly, of firms to each other. At Sun, crude trading information flows from around the world to one location. At Otis, the geographically distributed repair offices are no longer as independent; they are logically and physically wired to the corporate office. At Xerox and Hewlett-Packard, design, engineering, and manufacturing functions are now closely intertwined in the development of new products. Norton and a number of other companies are closely attached to their customers through terminal-based order entry systems.

It is this multiorganizational, multifunctional aspect of fourth era systems that makes line leadership imperative. Significant business understanding, which exists primarily at senior levels, must go into system conception. Equally important, implementation of these systems most often requires significant organizational change. Information technology management cannot effect these changes. Only line management can. The next sections develop this idea more fully.

LINE LEADERSHIP IN CONCEPTION AND IMPLEMENTATION

An entirely new level of opportunity, complexity, risk, and reward has been opened up by the new, communications-intensive information technology. Vastly greater managerial attention to the use of the technology is now demanded. The exact form of a system that, for instance, links a business to its customers is (or now should be) the result of a strategic managerial decision. Line managers must ensure that appropriate features within the system support the chosen strategy. The exact data to be gathered by salespeople with portable computers, for example, as well as the functionality of the system and the periodicity and rapidity with which data is gathered, is most appropriately dictated by line management.

As information technology becomes increasingly significant in business operations, its use should be shaped by the managers running the business. More significantly, if they are to be operated effectively, today's systems almost always require major, sometimes radical, alterations in an organization's structure, personnel, roles, and business processes — sometimes even in the culture of the corporation itself. Thus the economic, behavioral, and political consequences of today's information technology applications should be well thought out and the requisite change processes effectively managed by those responsible for the management of the business itself. As Dudley Cooke, Sun's general manager of information systems, notes, "All the information technology people can do is provide the appropriate technology platform, program the system, and install the equipment. It is the task of line management to make the extremely difficult, but very necessary, changes in personnel, roles, allied systems, and even organization structure required to make today's uses of information technology pay off for the company."

THE ORGANIZATION AS A DYNAMIC EQUILIBRIUM

The fact that major changes in information technology can profoundly affect the people, processes, structure, and strategy of an organization was documented in the pioneering theoretical work done by Harold Leavitt at Carnegie-Mellon University and by Alfred Chandler at M.I.T. Although they came from different academic backgrounds and were doing research in different fields, these two men independently developed compatible points of view.

Interested in comparative business history, Chandler investigated the changing strategy and structure of large industrial organizations in the United States.[1] He found that changes in an organization's structure followed changes in the firm's strategy and that organizational structure often had to be modified continually until it effectively supported the strategy. Chandler also focused on individuals and their roles in organizations and in organizational changes. He found that particular individuals played unique and crucial roles in developing the fit between the organization's evolving strategy and an appropriate structure. In addition, he noted that many structural changes and shifts in strategy were caused by changes in the technology. For example, Du Pont took advantage of new chemical processes to move from munitions supply into industrial chemicals by broadening its strategy and opening up that new field. (One can readily recast Chandler's "structure follows strategy" paradigm into four of the five interacting elements portrayed in Exhibit 1.1.)

Coming from an entirely different direction, Leavitt concluded that any organizational analysis should include four components: task, technology, people, and organizational structure.[2] He saw one of management's key functions as maintaining

Exhibit 1.1
Leavitt's Balancing Act (Adjusted)

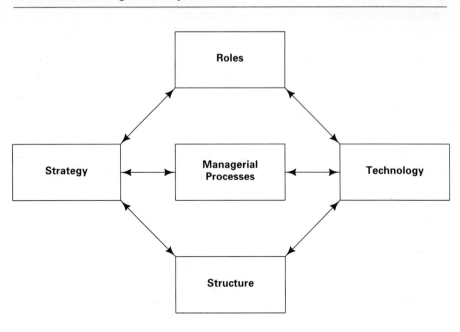

a "dynamic equilibrium" among these four elements. Although Leavitt's main interest was in the individual and that person's fit with the organization, he came up with the same four factors as Chandler did. The theoretical underpinnings of Leavitt's work came largely out of the social psychology field and drew on the work of Chapple and Sayles, Argyris, and others.[3]

In a paper that discussed the impact of information technology on corporate strategy, Michael Scott Morton and I modified Leavitt's approach.[4] First we changed his generic "task" into the broader concept of the organization's strategy (see Exhibit 1.1). This does not violate Leavitt's conceptual structure, since "strategy" represents a summing of an organization's tasks. Second, we included an additional box for "management processes." This is in the middle of the diagram because we see management processes as part of the glue that holds the organization together. Here we include such processes as strategic planning; meetings, discussions, and evaluations that result in the annual or the capital budget; compensation; and personnel management. Every organization has such processes, and they represent a good deal of what is done in an organization.

Exhibit 1.2
Four Major Stages of Applications of Development:
Leadership in Stages of Project Management

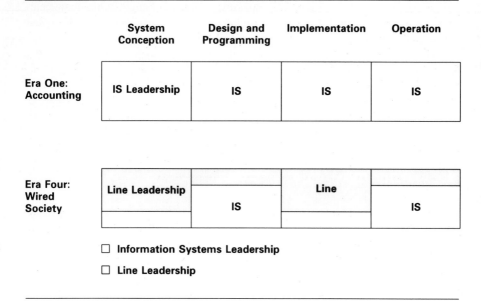

	System Conception	Design and Programming	Implementation	Operation
Era One: Accounting	IS Leadership	IS	IS	IS
Era Four: Wired Society	Line Leadership	IS	Line	IS

☐ Information Systems Leadership

☐ Line Leadership

IMPLEMENTATION AS TRANSFORMATION

Leavitt's conceptual structure, as modified in Exhibit 1.1, aids in understanding the necessity for line leadership in information technology's fourth era. Exhibit 1.2 notes four major stages of applications development. In era one, the accounting era, the data-processing people carried out all of the functions—system conception, design and programming, implementation, and operation. Today, in era four, while the bulk of design, programming, and operation remains the domain of information technologists, conception and implementation need to be line dominated.

The logic behind the need for line management involvement in system conception is straightforward. The people who run the corporation, the division, or the department are the people who must envision the direction in which they plan to drive their organization. Appropriate use of information technology can be a major factor in the accomplishment of that vision. Just as effective leaders plan to deploy key people for significant tasks, so too must they guide the most effective use of information technology.

The need for line involvement in implementation is more complex but equally compelling. Exhibit 1.1 suggests why. Any change in the technology will lead, as Leavitt notes, to changes in all or most of the other four elements. In fact, the systems described earlier have all changed organizational roles, processes, and structures. The changes have not been minor. At Otis, the roles of branch managers and district and corporate executives were all affected. The number of organizational levels was questioned. Several processes allied to maintenance, such as engineering data gathering, were also affected. Similarly, Sun's system caused more centralization of a major business process. Comparable proposed changes in the major elements shown in Exhibit 1.1 can be traced in each of the other companies discussed here and in almost all of the organizations we studied.

These changes are so significant that the term "implementation" is too weak a word to describe what takes place when systems such as these are integrated into the organization's functioning. John Henderson at M.I.T. prefers the word "transformation" for the third stage of project management noted in Exhibit 1.2, and he is right. When implementation is carried out with strong line direction (as it is at Otis, Norton, NEMC, and Sun), it becomes a transformation that cuts across previously independent divisions, functions, or other organizational subunits. It affects aspects of most (if not all) organizational elements noted in Exhibit 1.1. That is why this step of application development must now belong to the line. Only line management has the power to initiate and execute an organizational transformation of any magnitude. (See Levinson for an excellent description of the change process involved.[5])

A MAJOR NEW RESPONSIBILITY

What results from this emerging pattern of line direction of fourth era information technology applications? Quite simply, the line managers we interviewed believe they have merely added another item to their list of significant responsibilities.

It can be argued that most managers have traditionally accepted three major responsibilities (see Table 1.1). First, they have always been responsible for the operations of their organization. For an accounts receivable supervisor, this means ensuring that the cash is collected. For a transportation manager, it means seeing that the trucks run on time and that deliveries are made. As one moves up from functions to divisions and from there to the organization as a whole, the "operations" job becomes one of managing lower-level managers.

In addition, line managers have always been responsible for control of two major resources, money and people. Although corporate staff groups may assist in these areas, the responsibility of a line manager to meet budget and revenue goals is clear, as is the responsibility to deploy, develop, and manage human resources.

About three decades ago, an additional major responsibility was added to each line manager's agenda. In the early 1960s, when it became increasingly evident that "planning" (beyond one-year budget projections) was vital, corporations attempted to meet that need using a central planning staff. Unfortunately, this did not work. When it was realized that the planning process needed to be integrally connected to each line manager's actual competitive environment, the primary responsibility for planning was shifted from staff planners to line managers. In most organizations today, line managers are responsible for annual, long-range, and strategic planning to ensure that their resources are used effectively to meet their goals.

Table 1.1
Significant Line Management Responsibilities

Traditional
Operations
Financial management
Personnel management

Added in the 1960s
Long-range and strategic planning

Added in the 1980s
Strategic use of information technology

In 1988, an increasing number of line managers are taking on an additional responsibility—that of actively exploiting information technology resources. For some, proactive management of information technology is as critical as the management of other resources, if not more so.

THE GROWING ROLE OF THE INFORMATION TECHNOLOGY MANAGER

Given the state of the technology and many line managers' lack of expertise about that technology, the line cannot develop strategic uses of infomation technology by itself. In every case we have seen, IS staff has been involved in system conception and implementation. This interaction ranges from simple education or consulting to serious involvement in translating ideas into systems or designing and assisting during implementation. For major new systems, a full partnership between the line and the IS group has most often been evident.

In fact, as the line role grows, the information systems group role is also expanding.[6] This is not a zero-sum game. While several traditional functions remain, the role of the senior information technology executive is a far more significant one today than ever in the past, along five major dimensions (see Table 1.2).

First, with regard to system development, even those systems in which the line is heavily involved require greater competence and skills on the part of the IS organization than ever before. To effectively play the helping role noted above, IS personnel need significant knowledge of the business. Equally important, the technical design, programming, and operation of these business-critical, often highly complex, systems present a far greater challenge than did earlier-era systems. Today's systems require database, project-management, telecommunications, and a host of other skills not previously demanded of IS personnel.

Second, today's systems require the development and implementation of a general, and eventually "seamless," information technology infrastructure. The challenge to IS management of providing leadership for this profoundly important set of "highways" in the "wired society" cannot be overstated.

Table 1.2
The Information Systems Leadership Role

Traditional Major IS Functions
Technical (sometimes business) design and programming
Project management
Operations
Staff activities (consulting, planning, education, etc.)

Newly Critical Functions in the Late 1980s and 1990s
Design and programming of increasingly complex "mission critical" systems
Infrastructure development and maintenance (computers, network, software, data)
Education of line management to its responsibilities
Education of IS management concerning the business
Proactive use of business and technical knowledge to "seed" the line with innovative ideas
concerning effective uses of information technology

Third, there is a need to educate line management about its new responsibility. The line executives noted above are an intentionally biased sample. Not many like them exist today. The need now is to get all line executives to take on this new role, and it can only be done through formal and informal education, sometimes over an extended period of time.

Fourth, IS executives must educate themselves and their staffs about the business itself. Otherwise they will not be able to help line managers create systems that facilitate strategy implementation. Nor will they be able to carry out their fifth newly critical function, that of "seeding" line managers with ideas about effective applications of each new technology.

In short, the role of the information systems executive has also expanded. He or she is now a business executive—increasingly responsible for providing the line with knowledge about applicable technology and with the tools and infrastructure that allow development and implementation of innovative business systems. The ingredients of this leadership role were clearly expressed by Ed Schefer, previously the senior information executive at General Foods. Before his promotion to a senior line position, Schefer noted that he spent one-third of his time running the IS organization, one-third communicating with General Foods executives (both learning about the business and educating them about the technology), and one-third of his time outside of General Foods—learning about advances in the technology and business conditions in the industry.

Thus, in the "wired society" there is a need for a significant line leadership role, but there is also a need for growth and expansion of the IS leadership role. With the increasing importance of information technology in industry today, these developments are far from surprising.

NOTES

[1]A.D. Chandler, Jr., *Strategy and Structure: Chapters in the History of the Industrial Enterprise* (Cambridge: MIT Press, 1962).

[2]H.J. Leavitt, "Applied Organizational Change in Industry," in *Handbook of Organizations*, ed. J.G. March (Chicago: Rand McNally, 1965).

[3]E.D. Chapple and L.R. Sayles, *The Measure of Management* (New York: Macmillan, 1961); C. Argyris, *Personality and Organization* (New York: Harper & Row, 1957).

[4]J.F. Rockart and M.S. Scott Morton, "Implications of Changes in Information Technology for Corporate Strategy," *Interfaces.* January–February 1984, pp. 84–95.

[5]E. Levinson, "The Line Manager and Systems-Induced Organizational Change" (Cambridge: Sloan School of Management, M.I.T., Management in the 1990s comment draft, August 1985).

[6]J.F. Rockart and R. Benjamin, "The Unique Role of Information Technology Organization" (Cambridge: Sloan School of Management, M.I.T., draft working paper, April 1988).

The Withering Away of
the IS Organization

John Dearden

Yet another revolution has begun in the field of information systems (IS). When it is over, IS departments as they are currently constituted will be dismantled. Independent software specialists will dominate the development of systems, programming and other software. Users will completely control individual information systems. Sophisticated systems will be practical for medium-sized and even small companies.

The development of centralized IS departments over the past twenty-five years was the product of the economic limitations of an evolving technology. It was not a natural separation of responsibilities. It never worked well, but until recently there was no alternative. The economics of information technologies are changing, and as a result the centralized IS department is rapidly becoming obsolete. The problem facing senior managers is this: There will be a stubborn rearguard action to maintain a powerful IS group. The resistance will affect the speed with which improved information technology is adopted. This paper describes the developments that made this revolution possible and explains why it is necessary to change the locus of responsibility for information systems.

One substantial caveat is necessary before we proceed. Companies with large IS capabilities—financial service firms, insurance companies, airlines, and automobile manufacturers—will not dismantle their information systems departments. Instead, they will establish independent IS profit centers or independent subsidiaries that will compete both inside and outside the company. Such subsidiaries' viability will depend on having a significant specialized base from which to compete. For example, automobile companies have large, complex programs for production scheduling and control. Airlines have sophisticated reservation systems, and financial institutions have an assortment of specialized financial systems. Furthermore, these companies have large numbers of competent IS staff members with specialized expertise. Some companies will doubtless acquire independent software companies — as General Motors acquired Electronic Data Systems. These software subsidiaries will constitute an important part of the entire software market. As far as users are concerned, though, dealing with subsidiaries should be no different than dealing with independent suppliers.

TECHNOLOGICAL DEVELOPMENTS AND COST REDUCTIONS

Developments in hardware are well documented: micro and personal computers have already made users largely independent of mainframes. Future developments in software will enable users to be independent of IS departments for software support, as well. If users can get both hardware and software support from another source, then there is no reason why they should not exercise complete control over their information systems. I believe that within the next five years companies specializing in software will largely replace in-house resources in U.S. companies because the cost will be far lower and the quality far higher than that which can be developed internally.

It is difficult to conceive of a more inefficient method for developing software than the one used for the past twenty-five years. Literally hundreds of companies have developed systems and written programs for the same types of applications. The duplication of effort has been enormous, and the quality and cost of the software have varied widely.

The solution to this problem, of course, is for users to buy or lease programs prepared by companies that specialize in creating software that could be used by a variety of companies. Unfortunately, for many years that was not a practical alternative. Few such programs were available, and those that did exist were frequently not satisfactory. They tended to be inefficient in both the amount of memory they used and in the time required to run the programs. The relative expensiveness of computer capacity became a dominant consideration in software design. There were other problems, as well. The programs often had to be modified extensively. In some instances, the documentation was inadequate, so that, if something went wrong while a program was running, the problem would be difficult to correct. Not enough programs were available, so a company needed in-house capability in any event.

That need to develop systems and write programs in-house is changing, and it is changing fast. Most companies will soon find it uneconomical to do this work in-house. As I see it, the following factors will create an economic advantage for software specialists:

• The most obvious factor is that more than one company will be able to use a given program. Once a program is written, the cost of each additional user is relatively small. Consequently, the cost per user will decrease rapidly as the number of users increases. As more companies use software packages, the unit cost will continue to decrease almost indefinitely. I believe that the cost of software will decrease as dramatically as did the cost of hardware.

- Software companies will be able to specialize by type of application and by type of industry, whereas an IS department must be a jack-of-all-trades.
- The systems and programming personnel will be more capable, on average, than the people currently working in industry because the selection, training, and evaluation will be better. The difficulty in evaluating information systems personnel has plagued businesses since computers were introduced. Even today, many senior managers are unable to evaluate the quality of their IS department. Software specialists will be much better able to handle the personnel function—their workers' skills will not be unfathomable, and competitive pressure will ensure that excellent performance is required.

What this boils down to is that the factors that made in-house capability an economic necessity have now been overcome. Less expensive hardware has tremendously reduced the economic disadvantage of the software packages. The increased availability and lower costs of software have presented businesses with a realistic alternative to internal development.

THE COMPLEXITY OF SYSTEM DESIGN

Assessing and directing the flow of information to managers is one of the most complex aspects of information systems creation. Consequently it calls for specialized knowledge both of the individual system and of the manager's need for information.

The creation of an automated management information system can be divided into three steps. The first is to develop the basic system. That is, to decide what information is required by management, how much information is available, how it is to be processed, and what the nature and format of the output should be. That step is crucial because it determines the usefulness, reliability, and relevance of the information management receives. Accomplishing this step requires different skills for each important management information system. The development of the system requries an intimate knowledge of management needs and of the information available to meet those needs. It also requires an understanding of computer capability.

Once the necessary information is decided upon, the second step is to develop procedures and flow charts for processing the information. The third step is to write the computer programs to automate the procedures created in step two.

The problem is that step one requires different expertise for each type of system. The more important the system, the more likely it is to require expertise not available in the typical IS department. As a result, many automated systems are nothing more than a manual system transmitted onto a computer.

For example, most manual cost accounting systems I have observed do not provide sufficiently meaningful information to management, and many provide no useful information at all. When these systems were automated, they should have been updated to correct the deficiency of the manual system, as well as to incorporate improvements made possible by the technology. The problem is that few, if any, IS specialists understand cost accounting well enough to do this. As a result, deficient manual cost accounting systems become deficient automated cost accounting systems. The IS specialist is knowledgeable only about steps two and three.

In some applications, such as payroll or routine data processing, steps two and three are sufficient. The skills required to automate these systems are reasonably consistent among applications. In many important applications, however, the initial design of the system is critical and can only be done by specialists in the particular system. Yet today such specialists may not even exist in a company. As a result, systems development has been inadequate.

Software companies are, even now, specializing in particular types of information systems such as cost accounting, logistics, manufacturing, marketing, planning, and financial forecasting. As this process develops a user will be able to acquire a software package that includes state-of-the-art developments in the particular type of system. (Software companies will also specialize by industry, e.g., banking, insurance, or brokerage houses.) Consequently, purchased or leased software will not only be dramatically less expensive than internally generated software — even more important, it will also be dramatically better.

DECENTRALIZATION: A MAJOR BENEFIT

Lower costs and superior products are not the only benefits arising out of these changes. The software revolution will also enable senior managers to assign responsibility for information systems to the system user. When computer hardware was expensive and capacity limited, and when systems analysis and programming were unique and specialized skills, it was not economically feasible to delegate responsibliity for computer applications to each functional manager. But centralization is no longer an economic requirement, or at least it will not be in the near future. I believe that this new arrangement will be a real improvement. Giving responsibility for part of the management information system to an independent group was never a natural arrangement, because the goals and priorities of IS departments were almost invariably different from those of most users. Yet the users had no alternatives to dealing with the IS departments.

Decentralization will therefore also correct many user dissatisfactions that have plagued information systems for as long as I can remember. Other benefits of decentralization are:

- The user is in the best position to react quickly to competitive threats that result from the installation of superior software systems. Since most companies will be adopting improved systems, the ability to take prompt and effective action could be the difference between success or failure.
- The user is in the best position to judge and assess the importance and priority of applications.
- The user is in the best position to control the interface between computerized and noncomputerized information systems.

- When users are given complete authority for their information systems, they are also given complete responsibility. If the systems prove inadequate, the blame cannot be placed on someone else.

In summary, the primary argument for decentralization is that managers should be responsible for their own information systems because their ability to function effectively is dependent on the quality of those systems. The factors that once necessitated centralization no longer exist. Consequently, the authority and responsibility for managing information systems should revert to the user.

DECENTRALIZATION: POTENTIAL PITFALLS

There will, of course, be a great deal of resistance to decentralizing computer information systems. Even if it is generally acknowledged that hardware and software control could be given to the functional manager, four principal reasons will still be given for maintaining centralized control. These are:

- To maintain computer linkage between different users.
- To ensure compatibility of hardware and software.
- To prevent duplication of systems and programming.
- To ensure integrity and consistency of information.

Linkage

For at least twenty-five years, many experts have advocated integrating all information systems. That concept has gone by a number of names: integrated data processing, total systems, management information systems, and database systems. Instead of accepting the partial centralization of information systems as an economic necessity, these experts believed that centralization itself was desirable. They now propose that independent computer installations be integrated through networking, providing the users of decentralized hardware with access to each other's systems.

The concept of a single integrated information system has never made sense to me, and I have so stated on a number of occasions.[1] It now makes even less sense. Networking is expensive. It complicates the installation of systems and, in some cases, reduces the number of hardware and software options available. Clearly, there must be distinct benefits from these networks in order for them to be defensible. I have yet to see evidence that those benefits exist.

Any benefits from networking must result from the instantaneous access of one user to information in another user's system. But how much common data really exists? A recent *Wall Street Journal* article estimated that "on average, 80 percent of corporate information isn't needed elsewhere in the company."[2] This estimate is consistent with my own experience. More important, however, most or all of the remaining 20 percent is not needed on-line and, therefore, need not be linked. For example, the same *Wall Street Journal* article noted that one financial service unit in a company could "sift out new prospects from another unit's customer list." How often would a user need to do this? Certainly not more than once a month. Why, then, could not the different services agree to trade new customer lists every month? Most of the information used in more than one system is not required on-line. For example, little or no accounting information is even useful on an instantaneous basis, because accounting information measures the financial effects of events that occur over a long period of time.

Some common information, principally in manufacturing and logistics systems, may be required on-line. I see no reason, however, why users cannot work this out between themselves. Responsibility for networks can be delegated to the parties involved. I do not see what a central IS department adds to the process.

Electronic mail is also cited as an important benefit of networking. In fact, however, most information received through the mail will not gain from being delivered in any other fashion. And there are satisfactory methods for delivering urgent messages. If electronic mail is the excuse to maintain centralized control of hardware, then it is of questionable value.

Compatibility

It is in a user's best interest to have compatible equipment if it must interface directly with other users' equipment. (Certainly, users must have better information on the interfaces to their systems than IS personnel.) In any case, the problems of compatibility are already being reduced by manufacturers and I believe that this trend will continue.

Duplicate Programs and Consistency

The same considerations apply to duplicate programs and consistent information. The first does not appear to be a problem, because most software will be purchased; specialized programs would probably apply only to the particular system. If there are interfaces, why can't the managers involved work out the consistency of data preparation? If there are no interfaces, what difference does it make? My point here is that coordination was necessary when the company had a mainframe that everyone used and a department that was responsible for the operation of the mainframe and the related equipment, programming, and systems. Only the IS group understood these operations. Consequently, the group was involved in all decisions affecting computer use. When the responsibility for computer systems is decentralized, only the users will have the knowledge needed for decision making about their own information systems. To require that these decisions be reviewed and approved by a central computer group assumes that the users do not have the ability to make a rational decision or that the IS group has knowledge not available to the users.

THE TRANSITION PERIOD

The process of decentralizing systems responsibility has, of course, been under way for some time. But inevitably the early stages of the process are slow. For more than twenty-five years most systems have been influenced strongly, if not controlled completely, by in-house IS groups. This pattern cannot be quickly reversed. There are, however, indications that the reversal has begun.

In a recent article, University of Virginia professor Brandt Allen described the process whereby IS departments are being made into profit centers. His thesis is that they must compete for business and that the users are responsible for decision making. Allen writes, "Users can better evaluate and acquire new systems, software, and information processing technology than can a centralized IS Department." He also describes several sophisticated companies that have made their IS departments into profit centers.[3]

Although Professor Allen does not envision the demise of information systems departments in the same way that I do, we are probably disagreeing only about timing. These groups will not be gone next week, but making them into profit centers is the first step in an inevitable journey to oblivion. With the exception of companies with large IS capabilities, there is no way in-house departments will be able to compete against software companies in the long run. This conclusion is not based on an assumption that in-house staff are any less competent than software company specialists — although, for the reasons stated earlier, I believe that in many cases they are. Even with the best people, IS departments will not be able to compete because their client base is too small and too diversified. They cannot specialize in a limited number of applications, nor can they use the same or a similar program with a number of different clients.

In many companies the decentralization of information systems will be resisted — in some cases, adamantly. That will occur because decentraliztion is entirely contrary to the longstanding goals of many IS experts. They have pursued increased centralization even though its result is increased user dissatisfaction.

The concept that information systems are homogeneous is a fallacy. The concept that it is necessary for all or most information to be available instantaneously, or even that it is most useful instantaneously, is also a fallacy. Different information systems vary widely in purpose, content, and required availability. For any given user, there are many more interfaces between automated and nonautomated information than between automated information and other user systems. Also, an expert in one information system is not necessarily an expert in other systems. No one is an expert in all systems. Consequently, decentralization of information systems is logical, while centralization was logical only for as long as it was dictated by economics.

NOTES

[1] J. Dearden, "MIS Is a Mirage," *Harvard Business Review*, January–February 1972, pp. 90–99.

[2] D. Keale, "Computer Caution," *Wall Street Journal*, 28 January 1986.

[3] B. Allen, "Make Information Services Pay Its Way," *Harvard Business Review*, January–February 1987, pp. 57–63.

Technology in the Year 2000

Gene Bylinsky

All is vanity, said the Preacher, and there is nothing new under the sun. Well, maybe there wasn't in the time of King Solomon, and anyway the author of Ecclesiastes was pondering the human condition, not man's evolution as toolmaker and healer. In these high-tech last days of the second millennium A.D., something new whizzes by practically every minute. In just the past dozen years the personal computer has transformed offices; videocassette recorders and compact discs have revolutionized home entertainment; and biotechnology has conferred genetically engineered vaccines and a host of other benefits on mankind. The next dozen years will bring the world to the year 2000. What further wonders are lurking in the labs today that will be commonplace when the next century begins?

"We'll see a minimum of ten times as much progress in the next 12 years as we've seen in the past 12," exults John Peers, president of Novix Inc., a Silicon Valley company that recently put a computer language on a chip to give new zip to communications-signal processing. He adds, "I wouldn't want to be a science fiction writer today because reality is leaping ahead of fantasy." Quite soberly Peers and his peers on the high-tech frontiers say that by the year 2000:

- Computers that don't look and act like computers will surround you—shirt-pocket and notebooklike devices that respond to handwritten and spoken queries and commands, maybe even gestures.
- In corporate research centers, supercomputers 1,000 times more powerful than today's will calculate electron interactions in molecules in order to create materials that never existed before.
- When you travel, you may carry along an electronic book that opens up to display text on two facing screens. The book's memory will contain as many as 200 novels or nonfiction volumes; you just write the name of the one you want to read—and up it pops.

- Your doctor will check your heart by having you walk through a diagnostic machine rivaling Dr. McCoy's on *Star Trek*.

That's just a glimpse of the year 2000, when "we'll have capabilities no humans ever had," says Ralph E. Gomory, senior vice president for science and technology at IBM. Gomory, 59, adds, "When my father was young, he used to take a horse-drawn carriage to the railroad station. There were no automobiles, no telephones, no movies. No airplane had ever flown. There was no television, no atomic bomb, no man on the moon. But by the time he died, he had flown in a jet and had seen all those other things happen. No generation had ever been through a transformation like that."

With all that has happened already, why are today's high-technologists so superconfident that the next 12 years will lead to a technological as well as a chronological millennium? What could possibly top all that has gone before?

The answer is that now, in contrast with earlier decades of invention, man stands at the dawn of the Age of Insight—a new era of understanding how things work and how to make them work better. In both electronics and biotechnology, the two principal fountainheads of new products, the immediate future holds not just the compilation of more and more data but also some startling new visions. In the view of many scientists, the computer is being transformed from a number cruncher into a machine for insight and discovery. It will become an instrument even more revolutionary than the microscope or the telescope. Unlike those fabulous and stil evolving tools, the computer can look into the future. Supercomputers do it already by forecasting weather a few days ahead. As they leap forward in power, by the year 2000 they will be forecasting the structures of new materials and simulating such cosmic phenomena as the evolution of stars and galaxies.

The new Age of Insight will also offer views of the workings of the human body never before attainable. Deciphering the interactions of the body's own healing substances and the underlying causes of disease will allow researchers to develop novel drugs and methods of treatment. They will increasingly tap the body itself as a new pharmacopeia, an almost inexhaustible trove of medications that genetic engineers can copy and improve on.

Converging with these new insights and new computing power is the rapid emergence of telecommunications networks. It is as if—for a change—high powered cars and sleek highways to accommodate them were arriving at the same time. Telecommunications experts see nothing less than a world linked by great computerized networks that process voice, data, and video with equal ease. The first ISDNs—integrated service digital networks—are just going into service in the U.S., Japan, and Western Europe. In a few years they are expected to yield billion-dollar annual savings to corporations in increased productivity and lowered communications costs.

The certainty of these advances makes the experts drool. "I've never been as excited about the future and about the speed with which we're making progress," says Gordon Bell, vice president for research and development at Ardent Computer of Sunnyvale, California, a maker of supercomputers. Bell is one of the world's top computer designers and visionaries: He led the development of Digital Equipment's landmark VAX computer systems. Now he is pioneering the new insight and discovery machines.

Most of the underlying technologies for products that will be on the market by the year 2000 are already in the labs or just entering them. Walter Utz, Hewlett-Packard's manager of advanced engineering, notes that it takes about 12 years to translate a new technology into useful products. Since the turn of the century is only 12 years away, many of the directions have already been set.

This article is based on an assessment of the future as a framework of the possible—as helicopter pioneer Igor Sikorsky once described it—by some 100 experts in industry, universities, federal agencies, and venture capital firms in the U.S., Western Europe, and Japan. Forty of these experts make up FORTUNE's Probability Panels, offering their predictions about the likelihood of specific innovations as shown in the accompanying tables. Surprises are bound to emerge along the way that may throw some of the predictions off track: Witness the recent surge in high-temperature superconducting materials. But, says IBM's Gomory, "forget the unexpected—the unexpected will just accelerate the progress. Believe me, we're having a revolution without superconductivity or anything like that."

A tour of what's coming by 2000:

The experts agree that progress in both consumer electronics and computers will continue to be led by advances in semiconductor chips. These advances have been nothing short of spectacular, and they will continue to be so. Just 18 years ago Intel Corp. pioneered a 1,024-bit, or one-kilobit, DRAM (dynamic random access memory) chip, which held about 4,000 transistors and related components. Today, four-megabit—four-million-bit-DRAMs with about 16 million components are already in use.

"A one-billion-transistor chip by the year 2000 is not inconceivable," says Robert N. Noyce, vice chairman of Intel and co-inventor of the silicon chip. He thinks that a hundredfold, perhaps even a thousandfold, improvement is still possible with conventional technology, including so-called wafer-scale integration—building hundreds of different chips into a single system. Greater chip density makes chips cheaper and computers smaller and more reliable.

Along the way a new kind of information storage and processing technology may possibly emerge. One intriguing candidate: an optical liquid-crystal medium that would allow information to be stored in three dimensions, instead of the two dimensions of today's chips. This would permit the equivalent of thousands of memory chips to be jammed into a device the size of a coffee cup, says Caltech chip designer John Hopfield.

It's already clear that the galloping extension of today's technology will give computers of the year 2000 an electronic punch that will startle today's users. Desktop workstations will pack the power of what we now know as supercomputers. Supercomputers themselves will soar into the numerical stratosphere—as will their cost. Supercomputers of the future are expected to do at least four trillion complex calculations a second—1,000 times more than today. The biggest may cost as much as $1 billion, but that will represent a vast improvement in computing bang for the buck. A whole corporation might be built around a single supercomputing system.

One big challenge: devising appropriate software to run these supercomputers, which will likely consist of hundreds or even thousands of individual computers running in parallel. If that type of programming can be mastered, and most experts believe it will be, supercomputers will emerge as great vision- and intellect-extending engines by the year 2000. Kenneth G. Wilson, a Cornell University Nobel Prize winner in physics and an expert on supercomputing, predicts that the machines "will open vast new domains of scientific research—domains that are inaccessible to traditional experimental or theoretical modes of investigation." Supercomputers, he explains, will enable scientists to "see" objects on a smaller scale than microscopes can—a vital contribution to chemistry, chemical engineering, molecular biology, and other fields. Supercomputers could also describe lightning-fast events, such as the chemistry involved in photosynthesis, in greater detail than today's instruments permit.

The supercomputer of the year 2000 will emerge as an indispensable industrial tool, because its enormous capacity will make possible mathematical modeling of complex phenomena that are influenced by huge numbers of variables. Among other things, it is likely to serve by then as a full-fledged electronic wind tunnel. Where today only portions of airplanes can be tested in computers, complete airframes will be "flown" inside supercomputers at supersonic and hypersonic speeds. Better cars will be designed in computers because an engineer will be able to "feel" how a car handles before it is built. On the screen the designer could repeatedly crash his computer-model car into barriers or other cars to see how well it withstands the damage.

The design of new materials should benefit spectacularly from the new supercomputer power. "Scientists have so far explored only an infinitesimal fraction of possible forms of matter," says Wilson. Since the properties and structure of molecules are ultimately determined by the interactions of the electrons within them, Wilson says, sufficiently powerful supercomputers should theoretically be able to "predict everything about a material with no experimental information whatsoever" by calculating those interactions. He adds, "The potential importance for both basic research and industry applications is beyond anything one can imagine today, if reliability could be achieved."

The discovery capabilities of computers of all sizes will be enhanced by the great leap in computing power by the year 2000. The reason: the advent of what scientists have begun to call "visual computing," which in effect reproduces reality mathematically within a computer so that objects can be both seen and manipulated in all sorts of ways. The nature and behavior of an object or phenomenon can be described in equations and presented visually; the objects simulated can include anything from the steering mechanism of a car to the interior of a star. This kind of computing will open up new areas to scientific inquiry and bring products to market at unheard-of speeds by allowing the rapid testing of almost infinite product variations.

Visual computing makes seeing become believing. It gives engineers and scientists a new window into complex realities. As Donald P. Greenberg, director of the computer graphics program at Cornell, explains it: "I don't care whether we're traveling down the bloodstream and inside the heart, or looking at a building shaking in a simulated earthquake, or at an interior design of a house, or at a demographic projection with six variables. I just want to see what's happening so that if my model does not yield the results I anticipate, or if the interrelationships between the variables are incorrect, I can go back and change the simulation."

Another great benefit of soaring computing power will be the arrival of the truly "user friendly" computer. A great gap still separates man and machine. Despite their computational brilliance, which dwarfs man's, machines have horrendous difficulty with speech recognition because people speak in unstructured and inconsistent ways. Computers have comparable problems identifying visual patterns and recognizing objects from varying angles.

To the rescue, by the year 2000, may come neural circuits, simplified analogs of much more complex human auditory and visual nerves and related structures. One of those unpredictable twists in the high-tech road to the future may be a $2,000 board for PCs that will allow them to understand several hundred words of continuous speech. The board, which Digitech Inc., a small Missouri company, says it will deliver by the end of this year, uses chips that try to imitate some of the ear's sound-processing functions. Similar work is in progress in vision. Caltech's noted microchip designer, Carver Mead, for instance, has already built a chip that imitates some of the eye's information processing.

By putting some of these ideas into practice, says Jean-Louis Gassée, Apple Computer's senior vice president for research and development, "by the year 2000 computers will seem magic to my wife, who really doesn't like computers." The day may well have come when machines respond readily to spoken commands — and even answer back, just as the strong-willed HAL-9000 computer did in the 20-year-old film *2001: A Space Odyssey*.

By the year 2000 most computers will have lost their familiar boxy shapes. The idea is to make them more compatible with people by making them look less like machines. Says Gomory: "One way to make computers easy to use is to pretend there is no computer. Instead, you reproduce on the screen whatever you're used to. If you want to write a letter, you reproduce a piece of paper on the screen and you write on it. The computer translates your handwriting into type. If you want to file the letter, a picture of a filing cabinet appears and you stick the letter in."

Handwriting as a means of entering data into computers, in fact, tops the list of many experts' predictions. They feel it is a more natural way to interact with

---

Table 3.1
A FORTUNE Probability Panel: Computers

Ten experts in industry, universities, and government agencies rate on a scale of 1 to 10 the likelihood that each item listed will be available by the year 2000.

	Ten Experts										Consensus
Computers that recognize handwriting	7	9	9	8	8	9	9	4	9	7	7.9
Instant access to all available information on a subject	9	9	7	8	10	8	3	9	4	4	7.1
Voice-controlled computers	5	3	1	3	10	9	9	10	8	9	6.7
Gesture-controlled computers	3	8	8	6	10	1	9	10	7	3	6.5
Flat desktop computers	8	6	2	5	10	5	9	7	5	5	6.2

computers than using keyboards, even though some people can type faster than they write and others have messy handwriting. The writing would be done on thin flat screens placed on desks, much like blotters.

Companies are hard at work on putting these concepts into practice. IBM, for one, is developing components of an electronic book that would contain the text and illustrations from hundreds of volumes on a small diskette, with an easy-to-read liquid-crystal screen instead of pages. "We could even give it to you in a leather binding, if you prefer," says Gomory. In addition, it could be used as a computerized workbook, a small machine for word processing and other applications that a traveler could carry along and communicate with in longhand instead of using a keyboard or a mouse. Texas Instruments is also exploring the idea.

Mitchell Kapor designed the Lotus 1-2-3 spreadsheet programs and is now chairman of On Technology Inc., a Cambridge, Massachusetts, software company. He sees almost all PCs assuming the shape of hard-cover books in the year 2000. He predicts the appearance of a computer-based reference book, a cross between a dictionary and an encyclopedia, that answers questions about people, places, and events. Gassée of Apple envisions computers of many sizes—from a 3-by-5-inch card to a blackboard tapped into a database. Noyce of Intel expects to see a personalized electronic file by the year 2000. He describes this device as "a filing system that will read and recall every piece of information that comes across my desk, or that I deal with in my daily activity." The device, furthermore, would have "instant communication with every other computer." The function of computers will also change dramatically. They will, in essence, become instruments of access to a network over which desired information flows rapidly on demand.

Telecommunications are converging with computers at an opportune time. Just as computational capabilities are beginning to soar, the telecommunications industry is rapidly switching from analog to digital transmission of signals—the "bit" language of computers. Furthermore, the industry is greatly enhancing the transmission capacity of existing telephone lines to allow simultaneous transmission of voice, data, and video. A few years further in the future is wide use of capacious fiber-optic cables in business and at home. Gassée calls such a cable "a data hydrant."

The telephone of the year 2000 will evolve into what Bell Labs' vice president for research, Arno A. Penzias, refers to as "an integrated information appliance." This would be a sleek device with a large flat screen that would allow picture-phone conferences in full color as well as offer all the other accoutrements of the information age: the ability to send and receive documents and messages, act as a full-size computer, and provide access to many information sources.

Roland C. Moreno, president of Paris-based Innovatron and inventor of a "smart" credit-and-charge card equipped with a chip, sees counterparts of the French Minitel system in wide use in other countries by the turn of the century. (West Germany's Bundespost, the federal postal service, is now expanding its version of the system.) Minitel replaces telephone books with a small computer terminal. Besides finding addresses, it can buy theater, plane, and train tickets, send bouquets of flowers with notes translated if need be—albeit clumsily—and find girlfriends or boyfriends, the machine's most popular service. Minitel is now in use in nearly four million French households and offices as a government-subsidized experiment.

Table 3.2
A FORTUNE Probability Panel: Telecommunications

Ten experts give all these possible products a good chance to be on the market in 12 years except the instantaneous-translation telephone, a Japanese dream machine.

	Ten Experts										Consensus
Voice controlled telephones	5	8	8	10	7	8	9	10	5	8	7.8
Color fax	8	8	4	10	7	6	6	10	10	8	7.7
Combined telephone/computer/TV	9	5	8	4	8	7	8	8	2	9	6.8
Picture phones	3	4	6	7	5	6	9	10	8	8	6.6
Instantaneous-translation telephones	4	4	5	3	3	3	3	5	1	6	3.7

Japan's entry in the future-telephone derby is likely to be an instantaneous translation telephone that will work at least in English and Japanese, for openers. NEC, the Japanese electronics giant, began research on the project in 1983. Akihiro Kitamura, a NEC vice president, says it will take at minimum another five to ten years to complete the device—assuming the problem of recognizing continuous speech will have been mastered by then.

The Age of Insight is also revolutionizing both medical diagnosis and treatment by making them far quicker and more specific. An imposing array of new tests and instrumentation—from antibodies that seek out harmful viruses and bacteria to vastly improved body-scanning technologies—are opening the interior of the body to a new view. All this should allow doctors to diagnose infections in minutes instead of days and heart attacks in seconds instead of hours. They should also be able to detect tumors before symptoms appear, permitting treatment to begin earlier and drastically improving the chance of success.

New insights into human diseases would spur the creation of elegant new treatments. For instance, Leroy Hood, a brilliant Caltech immunologist, says that by the year 2000 it should be essentially possible to prevent such autoimmune diseases as rheumatoid arthritis, multiple sclerosis, and insulin-dependent diabetes, in which the body mistakenly attacks its own tissue. Clones of immune system cells gone haywire do the damage. Hood and his associates are already designing ways to remove such undesirable cell families in mice.

One of the experts' most startling predictions is that by the year 2000 it should be possible to regrow whole organs, or parts of them, in the body instead of replacing them with transplants. This could come about in at least two ways. First, scientists could decipher the remarkable biological program that leads to the growth of a new heart in an embryo, for example. Second, they could repair sections of a heart that had been damaged by a heart attack, say, by administering such tissue-restoring substances as the fibroblast growth factor that the body makes to regenerate blood vessels. California Biotechnology Inc., of Mountain View, the first company to clone the factor, has shown that it significantly accelerates the healing of wounds in animals; tests on people start next year. The growth factor also appears to repair nerve cells such as those destroyed in the brains of Alzheimer's victims.

Table 3.3
A FORTUNE Probability Panel: Biotechnology & Medicine

The medical experts give an AIDS vaccine by the year 2000 less than an even chance, but quicker diagnosis and better treatment should limit damage from heart attacks.

	Ten Experts										Consensus
Defeat of heart disease	7	10	6	7	8	0	4	3	6	2	5.3
Defeat of AIDS virus	5	2	3	5	8	10	1	5	7	2	4.8
Defeat of rheumatoid arthritis and multiple sclerosis	8	5	5	5	2	6	5	0	6	3	4.5
Defeat of leukemia and lung cancer	6	5	5	5	4	2	3	0	2	1	3.3
Defeat of Alzheimer's and Parkinson's	3	2	4	1	1	2	0	2	0	0	1.5

By extracting such healing substances from the human body and duplicating them through genetic engineering, scientists are cashing in on—and enhancing—the body's remarkable ability to heal itself. Genetic engineers have hit a potential bonanza: The body makes about 100,000 proteins. Says David Botstein, vice president for science at Genentech, the biggest U.S. biotech company: "Suppose 1% of them have the potential of being turned into pharmaceuticals. That's 1,000 new drugs." Other drugs of the year 2000 should include inexpensive and highly specific molecules tailored to fit receptors for hormones, peptides, and other substances that regulate physiological events in the body from hunger to the sex drive. These precisely targeted drugs will replace chemicals discovered by the historical trial-and-error method. Genetically engineered vaccines, such as the recently introduced hepatitis killer, could eradicate many infectious diseases, including malaria.

This century's crowning achievement in biology could well turn out to be the deciphering of the human genome—the determination of the order, content, and location of the genes on the human chromosomes that control the body's growth and well-being. Broken down to the most basic chemical level, says Hood of Caltech, those instructions would fill 500 volumes, each 1,000 pages long, each page containing 1,000 words, each word consisting of six letters of the DNA language. The mapping of the genome would open broad new avenues of medical diagnosis and treatment. In basic biology, comparative analysis of the genomes of mice, fruit flies, and people would allow scientists to break the other two still undeciphered DNA codes—one that dictates steps in cell differentiation and development, another that governs the structure of chromosomes.

Cracking the remaining codes, Hood suggests, would raise the spectacular possibility of creating entirely new types of biostructures for medical and industrial uses. A molecule might be designed, for instance, that would connect with cancerous cells and make them revert to normal. Deciphering the genome would also allow doctors to prepare a genetic printout of a baby at birth to spot susceptibility to various diseases and to start early treatment.

Surprisingly, FORTUNE's Probability Panel [see Exhibit 3.4] doubts that the most talked-about recent scientific breakthrough—superconductivity—will contribute much

Table 3.4

A FORTUNE Probability Panel: Superconductivity

These experts thing the technology is likely to improve magnets and motors, but doubt that such things as magnetically levitating trains will soon be a commercial reality.

	Ten Experts										Consensus
Magnets	5	7	8	4	7	7	7	6	1	7	5.9
Motors and generators	5	7	7	6	7	7	8	5	0	5	5.7
Energy storage	4	7	4	4	8	4	4	5	0	5	4.5
Power transmission	4	2	4	5	2	4	5	4	0	5	3.5
Levitating transportation	4	2	6	2	1	2	2	2	0	2	2.3

by the year 2000. The phenomenon greatly speeds the flow of electrons by cooling the conductors they pass through—to the point where they lose resistance. But Ian Ross, president of Bell Labs, says that while superconductivity is of great interest in instrumentation, working at extremely low temperatures in computing and signal switching is "too irksome." Chairman Gordon Moore of Intel adds that he is always suspicious of new technologies "where everybody seems to be excited about it for somebody else's application. You know, 'My view is that it doesn't impact the kinds of things we do much but the power generation people will find it great.' "

At IBM, Gomory draws a sharp distinction between new superconducting materials as scientific discoveries and their possible technological applications. He says, "A door has been opened into the unknown and we don't know what's on the other side. We're in a whole new world of materials. History has shown us that over time that tends to amount to something." But he guesses that most of those breathless forecasts about superconductivity powering 300-mile-per-hour trains and carrying electricity cheaply over long distances probably won't come true.

The impact of new technology on everyday work and life in the year 2000 will be more subtle than the dramatic transformations wrought in the lifetime of Gomory's father by automobiles, airplanes, movies, antibiotics, television, spaceflight, and other marvels. Some of the changes computers will bring about will be more intellectual in content, while in biotechnology the great advances in diagnostics and treatment will be readily apparent. Says George H. Heilmeier, chief technical officer at Texas Instruments: "In the medical field alone, the ability to bring the best medical care in the world to any local hospital will represent as big a jump as going from the horse-drawn cart to the automobile."

There are limits, of course. None of the technological possibilities that scientists and engineers are pursuing today suggest that man will soon decipher such fundamental mysteries as the workings of the human mind or the fate of the universe. Ecclesiastes also declared, "No man can find out the work that God maketh from the beginning to the end." The Preacher may not have been right about new things under the sun, but on this one he hasn't been proved wrong—yet.

4

Organizations: New Concepts for New Forms

Raymond E. Miles and Charles C. Snow

These are turbulent times in the world of organizations. Following a decade of declining productivity and failed organizations, many U.S. companies in the eighties have been forced to rethink their competitive approaches. Rapid technological change, as well as shifting patterns of international trade and competition, have put intense strain on these organizations' ability to keep pace with a set of new and often unpredictable competitors. One prominent executive, describing the current business landscape, says, "Not only is it a competitive jungle out there, new beasts are roaming around that we can't even identify."

Two major outcomes of the search for new competitive approaches are already apparent:

- First, the search is producing a new organizational form—a unique combination of strategy, structure, and management processes that we refer to as the dynamic network. The new form is both a cause and a result of today's competitive environment: The same "competitive beast" that some companies do not understand has been the solution to other companies' competitive difficulties.

- Second, as is always the case, the new organizational form is forcing the development of new concepts and language to explain its features and functions and, in the process, is providing new insights into the workings of existing strategies and structures. In the future, many organizations will be designed using concepts such as vertical disaggregation, internal and external brokering, full-disclosure information systems, and market substitutes for administrative mechanisms.

In the following sections, we describe these new concepts and the dynamic network forms. We then examine their implications for management practice, organizational redesign, and government policy in trade and industry issues.

BUILDING BLOCKS OF CURRENT THEORY: STRATEGIC CHOICE AND FIT

Based on research conducted during the late sixties and seventies, there is now widespread agreement that most industries can contemporaneously support several different competitive strategies. Sociologists, for example, have described "generalist" organizations that are able to survive in a variety of environments alongside "specialist" organizations that thrive only in narrower segments or niches.[1] Economists have shown that in a given industry some firms compete primarily on the basis of cost leadership, some differentiate their product or service in the eyes of consumers, and others simply focus on a particular market segment.[2]

The most common competitive strategies, sometimes referred to as generic strategies, have been labelled Prospectors, Defenders, and Analyzers.[3] Prospectors are "first-to-the-market" with a new product or service and differentiate themselves from their competitors by using their ability to develop innovative technologies and products. Alternatively, Defenders offer a limited, stable product line and compete primarily on the basis of value and/or cost. Analyzers pursue a "second-in" strategy whereby they imitate and improve upon the product offerings of their competitors. Thus, they are frequently able to sell widely because of their ability to rationalize other firms' product designs and methods of production.

The Prospector-Defender-Analyzer typology, besides indicating overall strategic orientation, also specifies the major organizational and managerial features needed to support these competitive strategies. Defenders, for example, rely heavily on the functional organization structure developed around the turn of the century and its accompanying managerial characteristics of centralized decision making and control, vertical communications and integration, and high degrees of technical specialization.[4] Prospectors, on the other hand, use more flexible structures such as autonomous work-groups or product divisions in which planning and control are highly decentralized. These structures, pioneered in the twenties and thirties and refined in the fifties, facilitate market responsiveness but at the expense of overall specialization and efficiency. Finally, Analyzers often employ a "mixed" structure such as the matrix wherein project, program, or brand managers act as integrators between resource groups and program units. Matrix structures, which were widely adopted in the sixties, blend features of both the functional and divisional structures and thus are designed to be simultaneously efficient and flexible.[5]

Current theory in the area of strategy, structure, and process is founded largely on the twin concepts of strategic choice and fit. Managers make strategic choices based on their perceptions of the environment and of their organizations' capabilities. The success of these choices rests on how well competitive strategy matches environmental conditions and whether organization structure and management processes are properly fitted to strategy. Historically, strategy and structure have evolved together. Each advance in structural form was stimulated by the limitations of the previous form, and, because each new form built on the previous form, it helped to clarify the strengths and limitations of its predecessor. Also, each development in structure permitted new competitive strategies to be pursued. Saying all of this in different language, ways of doing business traditionally have been highly contingent on ways of organizing, and major competitive breakthroughs have been achieved by firms that invented, or were quick to apply, new forms of organization and management.[6]

BUILDING BLOCKS OF NEW THEORY: DYNAMIC NETWORKS AND INDUSTRY SYNERGY

New organizational forms arise to cope with new environmental conditions. However, no new means of organizing or managing arrives full-blown; usually it results from a variety of experimental actions taken by innovative companies. The competitive environment of the eighties is pushing many companies into this innovative mode, and the United States is on the verge of another breakthrough in organizational form. In order to describe this emerging form, illustrate its distinctive competence, and discuss the contributions it makes to the understanding of previous organizational forms, we must broaden the current theoretical framework summarized above to include new ways of looking at individual organizations and how they interact with each other in their respective industries.

Signs of the new organizational form—such as increased use of joint ventures, subcontracting and licensing activities occurring across international borders, and new business ventures spinning off of established companies—are already evident in several industries, so the realization of this new form simply awaits articulation and understanding. As noted, we have chosen to call this form the dynamic network to suggest that its major components can be assembled and reassembled in order to meet complex and changing competitive conditions.[7] Briefly, the characteristics of the dynamic network are as follows (see Exhibit 4.1):

- Vertical Disaggregation—Business functions such as product design and development, manufacturing, marketing, and distribution, typically conducted within a single organization, are performed by independent organizations within a network. Networks may be more or less complex and dynamic depending on competitive circumstances.

- Brokers—Because each function is not necessarily part of a single organization, business groups are assembled by or located through brokers. In some cases, a single broker plays a lead role and subcontracts for needed services. In other cases, linkages among equal partners are created by various brokers specializing in a particular service. In still others, one network component uses a broker to locate one or more other functions.

- Market Mechanisms—The major functions are held together in the main by market mechanisms rather than plans and controls. Contracts and payment for results are used more frequently than progress reports and personal supervision.

- Full-Disclosure Information Systems—Broad-access computerized information systems are used as substitutes for lengthy trust-building processes based on experience. Participants in the network agree on a general structure of payment for value added and then hook themselves together in a continuously updated information system so that contributions can be mutually and instantaneously verified.

Exhibit 4.1
A Dynamic Network

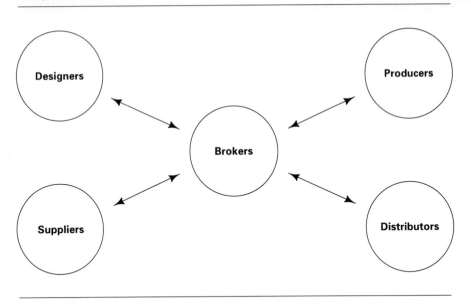

In order to understand all of its ramifications, the dynamic network must be viewed simultaneously from the perspective of its individual components and from the network as a whole. For the individual firm (or component), the primary benefit of participation in the network is the opportunity to pursue its particular distinctive competence. A properly constructed network can display the technical specialization of the functional structure, the market responsiveness of the divisional structure, and the balanced orientation characteristic of the matrix. Therefore, each network component can be seen as complementing rather than competing with the other components. Complementarity permits the creation of elaborate networks designed to handle complex situations, such as international construction projects, which cannot be accomplished by a single organization. It also permits rapid adjustment to changing competitive conditions such as those found in many consumer goods industries (such as apparel or electronics).

Viewing the network as a whole, each firm's distinctive competence is not only enhanced by participation in the network, it is held in check by its fellow network members. That is, if a particular component performs its role poorly or somehow takes unfair advantage of another component, then it can be removed from the network (due to the independence that allows the network to reshape itself whenever necessary). However, removal of a component means that the initiating component and/or the responsible broker must find a replacement part or encourage one of the remaining components to perform the missing function. In either case, the network as a whole is likely to operate temporarily at undesirable levels. Thus, there is complementarity present in every well-conceived network that encourages each participant, singly and in combination, to perform capably and responsibly.

With this grasp of the means and motivation underlying the dynamic network form, it is possible to create a theoretical analog that enhances understanding of the role played by existing organizational forms within their own industries. We refer to this phenomenon as industry synergy. This concept comes from our belief that there is symmetry between the characteristics and operations of the dynamic network and the features and behavior of the firms within an industry (or major industry segment).

As noted earlier, most industries are able to support companies pursuing different competitive strategies. Each strategy type both contributes to, and benefits from, the demand for goods and services in the industry, shaping its contribution around its own distinctive competence. Each firm, according to current theory, competes symbiotically with other firms in the industry for a share of the total market. However, when viewed from the industry perspective, each firm also has a synergistic role to play that might be described as implicit interdependence among competitors. For example, in order to maintain its long-run viability, the total industry must meet the dual objectives of innovation and efficiency, suggesting that there may be an ideal mix of competitive strategies required by every healthy industry.[8] Using the language introduced earlier, every industry to some extent requires the presence of Prospectors, Defenders, and Analyzers. Prospectors generate the technological and product innovations that push the industry forward, Analyzers rationalize some of these innovations for marketability and ease of manufacture, and Defenders lower costs to the minimum in certain product areas to facilitate mass consumption. In a manner analogous to the complementarity of the network form, each of these strategy types requires the presence of the others in order to perform its own role to the fullest. In turn, the industry's long-run aggregate performance is better than it otherwise would be if any one of the generic competitive strategies was missing.

DYNAMIC SYNERGY

Although no definitive research can be cited as evidence, it appears from case studies and observation that the mix of strategic roles required for industry synergy changes as the industry evolves. Several different patterns can be ascertained. First, and perhaps most obviously, embryonic industries are heavily populated with firms pursuing the Prospector strategy. A current example is the bioengineering "industry," in which many relatively small firms are experimenting with different technologies and product-service configurations. Less obvious is the claim that such industries are likely to remain latent until firms begin playing Analyzer and Defender roles. In the early days of the automobile industry, growth was not especially dramatic as various companies experimented with steam, electric, and internal combustion technologies, as well as various distribution methods. Rapid growth occurred only after Henry Ford played a Defender role by installing an assembly-line for manufacturing a single type of car on a standardized basis and by forming a distribution network of franchise dealers that sold cars to the mass market. Similarly, one would predict that in today's bioengineering industry, growth gains will be greatest when some large established company acquires one or more small R&D firms and begins to produce standardized products in large volume.

A second pattern of strategic mix involves mature industries. Here one would expect fewer participants than in new industries and a much greater proportion of firms using the efficiency-oriented Defender strategy. However, in order to prevent the industry from heading into decline, a few firms must behave as Prospectors (probably in limited areas). An example is the major home appliance industry. Over the last 15 years, dramatic gains in market share have been made by White Consolidated Industries, a company that relies exclusively on the Defender approach. Although much of the industry appears to have the characteristics of a commodity business, with advanced automated production systems churning out standardized products on a cost-effective basis, portions of the industry deal with innovative products and technologies (e.g., the "smart" kitchen). In these innovative areas, the leadership role is played by companies such as General Electric. To maintain its health, a mature industry requires the successful performance of both kinds of strategic roles.

Finally, there are industries in transition, for which the desired mix of competitive strategies is more varied and changing. One example is the electronics industry (including computers and semiconductors). Neither a new nor a mature industry, electronics is in the growth stage, but its segments are growing at much different rates. Consequently, over the next several years, there is the potential for this industry to achieve great success if it develops a comprehensive mix of competitive strategies. However, there is also the possibility that this industry will not realize its potential if the strategic mix becomes too narrow.

Consider the following scenario. Hewlett-Packard, a company that has traditionally competed as a Prospector across most of the markets in which it operates recently has attempted to play an uncustomary role in its computer business. Within its Business Computers Group, Hewlett-Packard has tried to achieve the standardization, coordination, and integration most characteristic of the Analyzer, and it is having difficulty grafting this approach onto its present organization and management culture. If the approaches taken in the reorganization of its computer business are forced onto other HP businesses, then it is possible that across the entire company Hewlett-Packard will dilute its strength as both a Prospector and an Analyzer. Similarly, Intel, which has traditionally prided itself on its high-technology production competence, has recently begun to design, produce, and market business computer network systems. It, too, must be careful not to dilute its primary distinctive competence as it moves into new businesses requiring different technical and organizational abilities. If, as these examples suggest, certain companies do not maintain their primary distinctive competence, then the industry as a whole may not exhibit the comprehensive mix of competitive strategies needed to achieve long-term success.

In sum, a healthy industry's needs for innovation and efficiency are met through the complementary efforts of firms pursuing different strategies, each of which is based on a primary distinctive competence. By regularly being "first-to-the-market," Prospectors sustain technological innovation and are the principal contributors to the design of new products and services. By competing primarily as efficient producers, Defenders uphold quality levels while driving down the costs of standardized goods and services. The most important role played by Analyzers is that of transferring information throughout the industry, especially as it concerns the standardization of technology and product design. By sorting through the experiments conducted by Prospectors to determine those technologies, products, and services most amenable to rationalization, Analyzers establish a new plateau from which the next round of innovation can be launched. Subsequently, by developing successful approaches to mass production and marketing of new products, the Analyzer sets broad efficiency targets that Defenders try to surpass.

DIFFUSION OF THE DYNAMIC NETWORK FORM

Returning to the dynamic network shown in Exhibit 4.1, it can be argued that Prospectors essentially play the designer role within an industry, Analyzers play the marketing/distribution role (and also contribute as information brokers), and Defenders perform the producer role. By relating the components of the network form to the synergistic roles played by firms within an industry, it is possible to forecast where and how rapidly the network form may emerge.

Aspects of the new form can be identified even in capital-intensive industries where large investments, relatively indivisible production functions, and other factors make it difficult for companies to move toward the network structure. Often firms in these industries have a limited range of distinctive competence even though they may perform all of the activities associated with a given business. In the petroleum industry, for example, most of the major firms have sought vertical integration as a means of assuring an uninterrupted flow of operations, ranging from the acquisition of raw materials to the sale of consumer petroleum products. Yet, these companies are not all equally skilled at performing each step of the exploration (supply), refining (production), product development (design), and marketing/distribution process. Thus, even though vertical disaggregation may be feasible in this industry, it is unlikely to occur in the short run. Presumably, if vertical disaggregation were easier to implement, some of the major firms would divest their less central functions and focus only on those value-added activities most closely associated with their abilities. Our prediction is that Defender companies would choose to perform the producer role, Prospectors would select the designer role, and so on.

In labor-intensive industries, where vertical disaggregation is less costly and easier to administer, the network form is gaining in popularity much more rapidly. In fact, one of our studies uncovered the partial use of the network structure over twenty years ago.[9] During the sixties and seventies, developments in the college textbook publishing industry caused many of the major firms to reevaluate their publishing activities and to modify their organization structures. For example, virtually every publishing company got out of the printing and binding business and simply contracted for these services as needed. Also, several companies allowed key editors to form their own publishing firms which then became subsidiaries of the parent companies. These subsidiaries usually engaged in new publishing approaches, thereby developing an expertise that the parent company could tap into whenever appropriate. Lastly, some publishers drastically cut back their in-house operations in art, graphics, and design, choosing instead to subcontract this work to smaller, specialized groups that comprised a cottage industry around the major publishers. Thus, in the space of ten years or so, several of the major college textbook publishers in effect developed networks in which portions of the producer and designer roles were moved out of the original companies into smaller specialty firms. The major companies simply retained those functions that were closest to their traditional distinctive competence (such as McGraw-Hill in product development and Prentice-Hall in sales).

As the United States continues to become more of a service economy, the case of textbook publishing (and many other examples) may well suggest the pattern by which other labor-intensive industries move toward the dynamic network model. The rationale for "people" and service businesses to adopt this structure is clearcut. The dynamic network is a far more flexible structure than any of the previous forms, it can accommodate a vast amount of complexity while maximizing specialized competence, and it provides much more effective use of human resources that otherwise have to be accumulated, allocated, and maintained by a single organization. The practice of leasing entire workforces, already in use in construction, hotel management, and retail sales, is a network characteristic that will become even more prevalent in the future. As managers gain experience and confidence in these network designs and practices, the dynamic network form will spread accordingly.

IMPLICATIONS

A new organizational form is both a cause and a result of the changing nature of competition. As organizations formulate new strategies to meet new competitive conditions, they find that their structures and management systems also require modification. Simultaneously, as new organizational forms become better understood and more widely used, new competitive strategies are easier to implement. The dynamic network form, as indicated earlier, has appeared as a means of coping with the business environment of the seventies and eighties. Its arrival now has implications for the way managers view the future directions of their companies, for the approaches used to manage existing structures, and for the way in which public policy is used to restore competitive vigor.

Strategists

Strategic planners have a growing literature to call upon as they formulate objectives and strategies for their companies. Frameworks are available to help strategists determine their companies' distinctive competence, generate strategic options, analyze competitors' behavior, and so on. However, all of these frameworks ignore or underemphasize the concept of industry synergy and the key industry roles defined by the network model. From these concepts, several recommendations for the strategic decision maker can be derived. First, the strategist must examine the industry's current mix of competitive strategies as a means of forecasting the industry's prospects for long-term viability. A healthy industry must at a minimum have firms with the ability to perform the designer and producer roles. Next, the strategist must try to anticipate how the industry's strategic mix might change over time. All firms are generally aware that as an industry matures, the mix of competitive strategies is likely to shift from a high proportion of Prospectors to a high proportion of Defenders. Therefore, the astute strategist can develop moves within this overall scenario that are not obvious at first glance. For example, it might be advantageous to become the first Defender in an embryonic industry. Or it might be desirable to be the last Prospector in a mature industry. Basically, the strategist can be prepared to offer "nonobvious" strategies by thinking in terms of strategic roles and synergies at the industry level. Finally, the strategist must be ready to show the organization how it can change directions in order to take advantage of new opportunities or counter competitive threats. The logic of the dynamic network model indicates that this flexibility can be achieved largely through vertical disaggregation. Thus, an organization may be able to obtain competitive advantage by performing only those activities closest to its distinctive competence, contracting with other components of a network for goods or services on an ad hoc basis, and perhaps serving as a broker in yet other areas. IBM used this approach in developing its personal computer (the PC jr.). Initially lagging behind its competitors, IBM quickly assembled a network of designers, suppliers, producers, and marketers to put together its first product offering. Later, after it had established itself in the market, IBM reintegrated portions of the network into its primary operating system.

Policymakers

The concepts of industry synergy and dynamic network can be used to examine aspects of international competition and their implications for public policy. The U.S. economy is becoming increasingly connected to world markets, so dynamic networks in many industries now operate across national boundaries. This fact complicates the recommendations made above to strategists. For example, in the case of a purely domestic industry, long-term viability rests on member firms playing a heterogeneous set of roles such as designer, producer, and marketer/distributor. In the case of an international industry, however, one or more of these roles may be best suited to foreign firms. Presently, some large U.S. industries have the bulk of their manufacturing and assembly operations located overseas. The domestic portion of the industry is quite homogeneous, with a few firms performing the designer role and the remainder performing the marketing/distribution role. In these situations, long-term industry health is an international concern, and individual firm strategists must take this into account as they try to anticipate the industry's strategic mix over time. Further, calls for a national industrial policy to revitalize declining industries will fail, according to the logic of the dynamic network model, if they implicitly rely on an improper role for American firms. The realities of international competition indicate that many American "producers" should rethink their industry role and attempt to find a more valuable location in an international network. Apparently, this is happening in the steel industry. Several American firms have achieved recent success by reorienting their plants toward customized products and applications instead of commodity products.[10] These companies cannot compete well in most commodity steel markets, so it is to their advantage to play a designer role in the industry and leave the producer role to foreign competitors.

Managers and Organization Designers

The final set of implications applies to managers, especially those in a position to redesign their organizations. Executives who perceive the network form as a competitive advantage for their companies now have an explicit model to guide their redesign efforts. On the other hand, some companies cannot or will not vertically disaggregate and completely adopt the new form. Nevertheless, these companies desire the benefits of the network approach. Managers of these companies need ideas for, and the means of, altering their existing organizations so as to simulate desirable features of the dynamic network.

In companies whose distinctive competence is best served by traditional organization structures, there may still be pressure to demonstrate more flexible, innovative behavior. The network model suggests that these companies can be more innovative by setting up special units focused on innovation in which brokers bring resources together and later transfer results to the larger operating system. A number of mechanisms for supplementing existing structures are available, including internal venturing or "intrapreneurship," external coventuring, idea markets, and innovator roles such as idea champions, sponsors, and orchestrators. Taken together, these structures, processes, and interpersonal roles comprise an innovating organization that operates parallel to the main system.[11] Developed and used in companies such as IBM, Texas Instruments, Minnesota Mining and Manufacturing, and others, these innovating mechanisms can be employed by more traditional firms to keep pace with developments in their industries. Some companies may choose to internally generate more ideas and innovations, while others may rely on external coventuring schemes to create needed innovations. In either case, advances made by the innovating system are integrated into the larger organization only after their utility has been clearly demonstrated.

CONCLUSIONS

Current "merger mania" notwithstanding, it seems likely that the eighties and nineties will be known as decades of largescale disaggregation and redeployment of resources in the United States and of a reshaping of strategic roles across the world economy. By the turn of the century, we expect U.S. firms to be playing producer roles primarily in high-technology goods and service industries (agriculture may be regarded as a high-tech industry). These industries are characterized by sophisticated products and delivery systems for which the United States has a worldwide competitive advantage. In more mature industries, especially those containing a large proportion of commodity products or services, we would expect U.S. firms to play primarily designer and distributor roles, with production limited to special-needs products and prototype designs to be licensed for production abroad. Of course, the United States will play a major marketer/distributor role in most industries throughout this period.

These shifting alignments will create both competitive challenges and opportunities for managers and policymakers. The greatest barrier to success will be outmoded views of what an "organization" must look like and how it must be managed. Future forms will all feature some of the properties of the dynamic network form, particularly heavy reliance on self-managed workgroups and a greater willingness to view organizational boundaries and membership as highly flexible. We anticipate, ultimately, that key business units—such as a design engineering group or prototype-production team—will be autonomous building blocks to be assembled, reassembled, and redeployed within and across organizational and national boundaries as product or service life cycles demand.

NOTES

[1]Michael T. Hannan and John H. Freeman, "The Population Ecology of Organizations," *American Journal of Sociology,* vol. 82 (March 1977): 929–964; and Howard E. Aldrich, *Organizations and Environments* (Englewood Cliffs, NJ: Prentice-Hall, 1979).

[2]Michael E. Porter, *Competitive Strategy* (New York, NY: Free Press, 1980).

[3]Raymond E. Miles and Charles C. Snow, *Organizational Strategy, Structure, and Process* (New York, NY: McGraw-Hill, 1978).

[4]Alfred D. Chandler, Jr., *Strategy and Structure* (New York, NY: Doubleday, 1962).

[5]Stanley M. Davis and Paul R. Lawrence, *Matrix* (Reading, MA: Addison-Wesley, 1977).

[6]Raymond E. Miles and Charles C. Snow, "Fit, Failure, and the Hall of Fame," *California Management Review,* Vol. XXVI (Spring 1984): 10–28.

[7]Ibid.

[8]Economists do not agree on a single definition of industry health. Classical equilibrium theory states that firms in a competitive industry should not make profits in excess of the normal bank rate of return. Another economic theory, however, says that excess profits are required for industry innovation. Yet another theory maintains that excess profits may be rightfully earned by firms that minimize buyers' search and information-processing costs (by consistently offering high-quality products, etc.). Our criteria of long-run industry health are taken from Paul R. Lawrence and Davis Dyer, *Renewing American Industry* (New York, NY: Free Press, 1983).

[9]Miles and Snow, *Organizational Strategy, Structure, and Process,* op. cit., Chapter 10.

[10]Joel D. Goldhar and Mariann Jelinek, "Plan for Economies of Scope," *Harvard Business Review,* Vol. 61 (November/December 1983): 141–148.

[11]See Jay R. Galbraith, "Designing the Innovating Organization," *Organizational Dynamics* (Winter 1982), pp. 5–25; and Gifford Pinchot, III, *Intrapreneuring* (New York, NY: Harper and Row, 1985).

5 The Winning Organization

Jeremy Main

American executives feel a sense of vast impending change, and they ought to. Take a look at what they can already foresee in the Nineties. Companies will be forced to develop products and make decisions faster. They will adopt fluid structures that can be altered as business conditions change. More than being helped by computers, companies will live by them, shaping strategy and structure to fit new information technology. They will engage in even more joint ventures, gaining access to techniques and markets they might not have developed on their own. And they will have to cope with a work force made more demanding by a scarcity of labor.

The Nineties will be tougher than the Eighties, which have seemed pretty tough. American companies did much to raise productivity and quality in the current decade; they will have to do even more in the next. Says Ray Stata, chairman of Analog Devices: "What the electronics industry has to do to stay competitive in the next five years is incredible. It almost seems impossible." GE Chairman Jack Welch told his stockholders recently that "the Nineties will be a white-knuckle decade for global business . . . fast . . . exhilarating."

The gurus who think about such things are floating their visions of the corporation of the Nineties. The Hudson Institute's William Johnston, a former assistant secretary of transportation, sees companies becoming "increasingly unstable collections of people." They will resemble firms in the toy industry today, which expand rapidly when they have a hit and shrink fast when a fad passes. In a flight of imagination in the *Harvard Business Review* earlier this year, Peter Drucker envisaged the business organization of the Nineties as being less like today's model and more like "the hospital, the university, the symphony orchestra." In Drucker's vision, employees in the new information-based company will know what they have to do without a flock of vice presidents feeding them information and orders. One conductor—the chief executive—will be enough to keep the oboes and cellos on the same beat.

In interviews with business school professors, consultants, and executives, FORTUNE found the issue of change much on their minds. Business school deans are worried that they may be preparing students for the wrong world (see page 45). Of the many ideas and visions these experts expressed, the following are anchored in reality—and already visible.

SPEED

Speed has become a competitive weapon. Citibank has introduced as many as three new financial services a week. The Limited rushes new fashions off the design board and into its 3,200 stores in less than 60 days, while most competitors still order Christmas apparel the previous May. IBM's development time for mainframes has dropped from three years to 18 months. Honda and Toyota can take a car from concept to market in three years, vs. five for General Motors. Ford has already cut its new-car cycle from five to four years and is shooting for three. David Cole, director of the University of Michigan's center for automotive studies, thinks the Big Three can get it down to a year in the Nineties.

Better technology is one reason things can happen faster. Improved simulations allow IBM to skip two of the usual three generations of prototypes in making new integrated circuits. That cuts development time by 70%, says William Rich, IBM's corporate secretary. Simplified designs are another help. IBM has been making five medium-size computers, each available in three cabinets, for a total of 15 different boxes. The new medium computers, this year's AS/400 and last year's 9370, use only three cabinets between them.

Speed also calls for a new attitude among managers, who, like most people, tend to resist change. Paul Hirsch, a professor at the University of Chicago business school, says that managers must learn to see change as it occurs. That sounds simple enough, but it turns out to be an enormous challenge. Hirsch suggests that companies may have to promote oddballs who might not normally fit at the top. Example: Gerald Tsai Jr. The unpredictable, Shanghai-born Tsai hardly fitted into the manufacturing culture of the old American Can Co. But as the company, now called Primerica, tried to get out of the declining packaging industry, he was the right man to lead it into financial services and a planned merger with commercial credit.

How fast is fast enough? The Limited tracks consumer preferences every day through point-of-sale computers. Orders, with facsimile illustrations, are sent by satellite to suppliers around the U.S. and in Hong Kong, South Korea, Singapore, and Sri Lanka. Within days clothing from those distant points begins to collect in Hong Kong. About four times a week a chartered 747 brings it to the company's distribution center in Ohio, where goods are priced and shipped to stores within 48 hours. Says Chairman Leslie Wexner: "That's not fast enough for the Nineties."

Exhibit 5.1
Coming Surprises

- **Far more subordinates will report to each manager**

- **Overseas duty will be vital to an executive's advancement**

- **Jobs will grow faster than the labor force (below)**

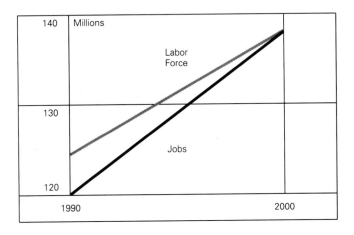

INFORMATION

The technology of information will alter the legal and physical boundaries of companies—in ways that may well give the lawyers heartburn. You might allow a supplier access to your computer so he can see what you need and reorder it for you. But you will also risk giving an outsider too much information about your operations. Computers can let customers look into your company too. Pacific Intermountain Express, a big trucking firm, is already giving customers access to its computers so they can check the status of their shipments.

Roger Samuel, manager of a five-year study of information technology at MIT's Sloan School of Management, suggests that vertical integration becomes less necessary when companies use information systems imaginatively. A company that once might have acquired a key supplier to get more control over raw materials may now feel it can do better simply tracking the supplier's performance by computer.

It's not that computers will invade chief executives' offices in the Nineties; they are already there. What will change is how the top man uses his terminal or PC. Until now, according to Samuel, he set strategy and then told the computer people to support it. In the future, Samuel says, strategy and information technology will

With so much change ahead in the Nineties, business school deans—and managers who hire MBAs—worry that U.S. schools at best have slipped off the leading edge and at worst have become irrelevant. Says Xerox vice chairman William Glavin: "They are developing middle managers, but we are not hiring or promoting very many of them."

J. Brian Quinn, a professor at Dartmouth's Tuck school, is blunter. He says business schools—including his own—are turning out graduates who are ignorant of technology, especially information technology, and who know little about America's growing service economy.

The top schools are only beginning to adjust to such criticism, adding a course in quality here and a course in manufacturing there. The University of Pennsylvania, in response to the need for globally minded executives, offers a dual master's program, combining the full requirements of its Wharton business school with international studies at its Lauder Institute.

Glavin is one of a number of businessmen helping Wharton figure out how it needs to change by the year 2000. Dartmouth has begun a full-blown review of its curriculum. MIT's Sloan school has nearly finished a five-year study of information technology, financed by $6 million in grants from ten large companies plus the Army and the Internal Revenue Service.

Professor Jerry Wind, who heads the Wharton study, says business schools have always been good at teaching specific business functions, such as accounting or marketing, but not so good at turning out the rounded person who understands business. In the Nineties even well rounded may not be enough. The task is to train managers to deal with constant, rapid change. Nobody yet has any idea how you go about doing that.

be considered together. You can't decide to go to just-in-time inventory controls or automatic ordering unless you have the technology to back it up. Says professor J. Brian Quinn of Dartmouth's Tuck business school "Very few companies have an integrated information strategy."

With a good management information system, says Daniel Valentino, president of the consulting firm United Research, an executive can see where everything stands and who has made what decisions. He can put a spreadsheet on his screen and "drill down," as computer buffs say, to get at what's behind a particular figure that interests him.

ORGANIZATION

Managers have been reading for years that the hierarchical model adapted by business from the military nearly a century ago will fade. But they may not have imagined how extensive the changes could be. With the help of information technology, managers can increase by several magnitudes the number of people reporting to them. "Corporate staffs will virtually disappear," says Jewell Westerman, a consultant with Temple Barker & Sloane who specializes in organizational issues. He says some of his clients have gone from a dozen layers of managers between the chief executive and front-line supervisors to six, and he thinks maybe one more layer could go.

IBM has cut its payroll by 16,000 since 1985, mostly through early retirement. The company shifted many remaining workers out of headquarters and manufacturing into marketing and sales. But the company wants to be leaner still. "We haven't done as well as we should have," says corporate secretary Rich. "We will have to be structured differently in the Nineties."

The major reorganization last January was a start. The company decentralized into seven largely autonomous business units, including six product lines and one support group to serve the others. The new units, says Rich, no longer have to suffer the "insidious delays of excessive staff reviews." The company was also split into four worldwide geographic regions.

Since taking over Franklin Mint three years ago, Stewart Resnick has cut management layers from six to four while nearly doubling sales, to about $500 million. He has also doubled the number of people reporting to him to 12. Professor Quinn of Dartmouth thinks that in general the number could be much larger than that. He argues that so-called spans of control—the number of subordinates one executive can effectively command—are giving way to "spans of communications," the number of people an executive can reach through a good information system. Ultimately, he says, one manager could have as many as 200 people reporting to him. Just like that symphony orchestra!

These trimmed and flattened companies will occasionally find themselves short-handed. Instead of rebuilding staffs, they will create temporary task forces to address particular problems, such as a quality glitch. They will also hire outside consultants and specialists. IBM has signed up a new Pitney Bowes service to run mail rooms, stockrooms, and reproduction operations in two locations on a trial basis.

Engineering design shops like the Troy Pioneer Group, which has ten branches in Michigan, are busier than ever helping the Big Three develop new cars. Troy Pioneer can build prototypes, clay models, and show cars, and can design many of the pieces that go into a car—work that used to be done mostly by the automakers' staff designers. Troy Pioneer's revenues reportedly reached $135 million last year. President Gerald Mahoney was director of specialty vehicles—such as limousines and convertibles—at GM until last August.

ALLIANCES

To enhance their competitiveness, U.S. companies will form more strategic alliances—through partnerships, joint ventures, or other agreements. Kathryn Harrigan, a Columbia University business professor, says the number of such ventures began to pick up in the early Eighties, from a growth rate of some 6% a year to around 22%. She looks for much faster growth in the next few years. IBM, which once felt strong enough to go it alone, today has 40 active alliances, including several major partnerships in Japan. It is also cooperating with ADP to provide Merrill Lynch with software and hardware that enable brokers to call up displays of data about their clients.

IBM is also one of 14 companies supporting Sematech, the new research consortium in Austin, Texas. Sematech, which gets half its funding from a $100 million appropriation from Congress, is designed to help the U.S. semiconductor business become competitive again.

GLOBALIZATION

"The root cause of change in the Nineties will be globalization," says Noel Tichy, business professor at the University of Michigan. "You'll have to have global standards for quality, for pricing, for service, for design. You will have to have global leadership." The decade will see upheavals and opportunities in world markets, most dramatically in 1992 when the European Economic Community removes most of the remaining barriers between member states, and in 1997 when China takes over Hong Kong.

The U.S. has many multinational companies, of course, but Tichy argues that few are truly international. Most are what he calls multidomestic—companies with a string of relatively unconnected operations in various countries. Many top executives, Tichy says, don't have a global grasp. For managers, time spent overseas has meant time off the career ladder.

In the Nineties, says Tichy, overseas experience will be crucial to executive advancement. Many non-Americans will climb high in U.S. companies. Already half the recruits who go through Morgan Guaranty's management training program in New York are foreigners.

GE is a prime example of a company that is developing a global strategy. The company sold its consumer electronics business in Europe to Thomson SA of France, then bought Thomson's medical equipment business, Thomson CGR, to strengthen its own medical unit. Together with GE Medical Systems Asia, CGR gives GE a global organization that can compete against Siemens, Philips, and Toshiba in the world market for X-ray, CAT scan, magnetic resonance, and other medical equipment. Just 13% of GE Medical Systems' sales came from outside the U.S. in 1985. John Trani, the GE group executive who runs the unit, says the figure will be 45% for 1988.

Trani is using a few other Nineties techniques. He wants what he calls a loose, flexible organization with no rigid chain of command. And he has formed leadership groups of managers from three continents to work on matters like shortening the product development cycle.

PEOPLE

Now that virtually all the baby-boomers hold jobs, growth of the work force will slow way down—from 2.4% a year in the Eighties to 1.2% in the Nineties. The Bureau of Labor Statistics estimates that the number of jobs will grow a bit faster than the labor force. To attract workers, companies will have to develop new appeals, especially to women, who will make up two-thirds of the new workers.

IBM personnel vice president Walton Burdick says, "Basic economics are still important. But other things are emerging, such as the company's response to societal issues." Four years ago IBM helped finance and set up a referral network for day-care centers for its employees. The service now lists 7,500 around the U.S. Like a growing number of companies, IBM is offering other innovative family benefits, such as care for elderly relatives and takeout dinners that working spouses can pick up at the company cafeteria on their way home.

Companies will have to hustle to hang on to employees. "In the waves of restructuring, the long-term contract has been ruptured," says Harvard business school professor Howard Stevenson. "The commitment will always be tentative." The University of Chicago's Hirsch points out that the task of rebuilding trust is especially difficult because restructuring is still going on in many companies.

Higher pay is an obvious answer. Another is to help skilled people keep abreast of their specialties by sending them to professional meetings or paying for additional education. If engineers and scientists, for instance, think their talents are highly marketable, they will worry less about being restructured out of a job.

MOTIVATION

The new buzzword in employee motivation is "ownership," which can mean either an equity share or just a worker's sense that he counts. Says Harvard business school professor J. Richard Hackman: "If you want me to care, then I want to be treated like an owner and have some real voice in where we're going." The concept grows out of the "employee involvement" of the 1980s, which got off to a shaky start with quality circles that never amounted to much, then grew stronger as workers were brought into decision-making. Rochester Products in Coopersville, Michigan, which makes fuel injectors for GM, solicits advice from workers on who should be promoted to supervisor. The company also asks them to help evaluate potential suppliers.

Ownership goes a step further by seeking to put employees in the shoes of entrepreneurs. Xerox, 3M, and Honeywell help finance startups by employees who have promising ideas in return for a minority share. Alfred West, founder and chairman of SEI Corp., a $123-million-a-year financial services company in Wayne, Pennsylvania, is planning a more radical experiment with his 1,100 workers. He intends to divide his company into entrepreneurial units, each led by a so-called champion who has been particularly effective in promoting whatever the unit does. West will give each group of employees a 20% interest in their unit. After a suitable period, he will invite an investment bank to put a price on the unit. Then West will pay members for their 20%. If the unit flops, the members get nothing beyond their salaries. Says West: "I'm an entrepreneur, and I want more people like that here."

ACCOUNTING

The elaborate U.S. accounting system, designed for clerks of a generation ago, has a lot of catching up to do. Says Robert Kaplan, professor of accounting at Harvard: "It just isn't giving managers the information they need to run a business." While the system may provide useful information for regulators and stockholders, Kaplan says, it is too cumbersome to help managers react fast enough.

Kaplan even suggests that some U.S. companies have abandoned the low end of their product lines to Asian competitors because accountants gave them a false picture of costs. He argues that simple, moderately priced items have low overhead costs. But as a company adds higher-priced models with more options, it spends relatively more on capital goods and administration. Overhead costs rise disproportionately. But accountants take what Kaplan calls the peanut butter approach, spreading costs according to the amount of direct labor involved in each product line. The low-end items get loaded up with high overhead costs created by high-end items and soon appear to be too expensive to produce.

To know how a company is really doing, says Kaplan, you need some physical performance figures, such as defect rates or delivery numbers, in addition to financial figures. Kaplan has hardly started a corporate rebellion against present accounting methods, but one chief executive has independently begun doing what he wants. Ray Stata of Analog Devices this year is dropping all but four or five of the 20 financials in his quarterly and annual reports. He is replacing them with nonfinancial numbers on quality, deliveries, and output. Analysts and stockholders always want to focus on the dollar numbers, says Stata, but "if they had any sense they wouldn't look at the quarterly financial numbers." They'd learn more from production data.

A few pessimists think that even if U.S. business takes all these steps, it may not remain competitive globally. Quinn of Dartmouth, for one, thinks that American companies, burdened by what he considers a preoccupation with high and rapid rates of return, will always trail Asian companies that presumably will continue making more modest demands. That view underestimates the creativity of U.S. business. The fact that business organization is the subject of so much thought, talk, and experiment today is a promising sign. Daniel Valentino of United Research says that in the companies he studies he usually finds room for a 30% to 50% improvement in productivity. With innovative force applied to that potential, there is no reason American business should not be a world leader indefinitely.

6

The Changing Value of Communications Technology

Michael Hammer and Glenn E. Mangurian

It is no longer meaningful to talk about information processing and communications as independent activities. Parallel technological advances in both of these domains have given rise to a new generation of distributed information systems involving both processing and transmitting information. In these systems, the roles of computing and communicating are so intertwined that their business value depends on the total system, rather than on the separateness of the communications or processing function.

In this paper, we focus on the business opportunities made possible by these new synergistic systems, which we call communications-intensive information systems (CIIS). Made up of processors, intelligent work stations, and terminals, the systems are interconnected by means of wide- and local-area networks. Although they may come in many forms, all communications technology systems are capable of rapidly transmitting information, in electronic form, between geographically dispersed sites and/or among separate organizational entities. In fact, the capabilities of these systems are becoming so widely recognized that many firms are now aggressively using them to improve their market positions, or to transform their products, services, and the industries in which they compete.[1] What managers lack, however, is a conceptual framework in which they can structure their search for, and subsequent evaluation of, such opportunities.

With this in mind, we present a framework that we believe will help managers understand the benefits and applications of CIIS technology in the context of their organizations. We also provide some basic guidelines for those companies that wish to exploit the opportunities made available by this technology. The model, which is technology independent and applications oriented, identifies three primary areas of impact for communications technology: compression of time, overcoming the restrictions of geography, and the restructuring of relationships. It also characterizes the business value of an information system in terms of increased operating efficiency, improved business effectiveness, or a basic transformation of a firm's business functions. Each impact-value pair defines a particular type of communications technology application and considers an attendant set of implementation issues (see Exhibit 6.1).

THE POTENTIAL IMPACT

Time compression is the most immediate impact that a CIIS may have on an organization. Through clear communications links, information can be transmitted quickly between sites or organizational units. Consequently, the time required to perform a larger business process, of which information transmission is a part, may be reduced. For example, filling an order can be expedited by transmitting the order information from the field to the warehouse: or, management decision making can be made more efficient by electronically transmitting data directly from headquarters to a manager at a remote location.

Communications technology can also enable an organization to overcome limitations imposed by geography. Traditionally, extending an organization's activities into a new geographical area first required that the firm establish a major physical presence there. Doing so, however, can be expensive, cumbersome, and time-consuming. A CIIS that links a new territory to existing locations is an alternate way of expanding the firm's reach.

Exhibit 6.1
Impact Value Framework

IMPACT	VALUE		
	Efficiency	Effectiveness	Innovation
Time	Accelerate Business Process	Reduce Information Float	Create Service Excellence
Geography	Recapture Scale	Ensure Global Management Control	Penetrate New Markets
Relationships	Bypass Intermediaries	Replicate Scarce Knowledge	Build Umbilical Cords

Finally, information technology can alter the structure of organizational relationships—both within the firm and between the firm and other entities.[2] Since relationships are, in effect, defined by lines of communication, a CIIS can establish new relationships or dissolve old ones. For instance, a brokerage firm that allows customers to directly access a computerized database and order-placement system can lessen customers' dependence on a particular broker: the customers then become the firm's customers, not the broker's.

THE POTENTIAL BUSINESS VALUE

The business value of information systems can be manifested in various ways, depending on the kind of value the firm seeks to provide its customers. Generically, a communications technology provides business value in three distinct areas: efficiency (increased productivity), effectiveness (better management), and innovation (improved products and services).

Increased efficiency is the application most familiar to managers, and the one with which organizations have the most experience. Most of the traditional applications—from payroll to order entry—are implemented to increase the efficiency of some internal processes. The resulting benefit is increased productivity, with either lowered costs for the existing level of transaction processing or avoided costs for increased volume processing.

Increased productivity, however, is not the only benefit that can be realized. Improved information access, resulting from better communications systems, can improve management effectiveness. For example, information technology can help ensure the availability of customer accounts information needed to support effective management decision making. While availability does not by itself guarantee management effectiveness, it is rapidly becoming a necessary competitive prerequisite.

Finally, information systems can bring about an innovation or enhancements to the quality of products and services, thereby improving the company's competitive position. A manufacturer, for instance, may allow its customers access to a work-in-process database to determine the status of their orders. Similarly, a distributor can give its customers systems that will allow them to manage their inventories more efficiently. In both cases, companies distinguish themselves from their competitors by means of the additional product/service quality made possible by this technology.

IMPACT/VALUE FRAMEWORK

The two critical dimensions of impact and value can be used to define a framework for organizing and analyzing CIIS applications. Without this framework, the growing collection of well-known information technology cases simply represents folklore that won't help managers identify their own opportunities for exploiting this technology. The grid in Exhibit 6.1 provides a means of conceptualizing a wide variety of applications. The rows of the grid correspond to the three primary forms of impact; the columns correspond to the three distinct classes of value.

A grid entry represents a unique kind of business change, that is, a vehicle by which impact is translated into value. Because a single CIIS may have multiple impacts on an organization and thus yield more than one kind of value, an application will seldom be described by a single entry (see Exhibit 6.1). In the following section, we consider specific applications in terms of their impact and business value to an organization.

MAKING USE OF TIME COMPRESSION

Accelerate the Business Process

When communications technology accelerates a business process, the result is typically an increase in efficiency by decreasing the time required to perform a particular business process. Here, the firm's main objective is to reduce the labor costs incurred by information transactions and the costs of the business process itself.

A CIIS can also yield indirect efficiency improvements by increasing the accuracy of those business processes that require heavy information exchange, but which do not have quick communication feedback. Such processes are often susceptible to recording and transcription errors, which can either introduce delays when the errors are discovered or entail expensive and time-consuming error elimination controls. A CIIS can forestall such errors, and so contribute indirectly to process efficiency.

Opportunities for process acceleration may be found in those activities that are labor intensive, time critical, or correlated with business volume. Rand McNally & Company is a case in point. The company's 1983 acquisition of Infomap quickly became the focal point of Rand McNally's development of computer-based products. The customer provides the company with information to be mapped, and Rand McNally's system generates the customer map without further intervention.[3]

Reduce Information Float

Time compression can also improve management decision making. In many firms, managers must base their decisions on incomplete and often obsolete data. Information technology can alleviate this problem by making data more rapidly available to decision makers. Here, time compression yields effectiveness rather than efficiency.

This phenomenon has been referred to as "reducing the information float."[4] Often because the user of some information in an organization is not the producer of that information, significant time may elapse between the production of the information and its communication to the user. Because of this float, the user may be employing inappropriate data. This occurs especially when data is of far less relevance to the producer than it is to the consumer. By linking the site that originates the information with the one that utilizes it, a CIIS can reduce, or even eliminate, the float. In doing so, an organization increases its potential to become information intensive and feedback sensitive.

Opportunities for reducing information float may be found in situations where key decisions depend on diffused data (e.g., information coming from multiple remote sources), or where quick feedback is essential. For example, the marketing management of a consumer products firm used to base its advertising and promotion strategies on historical sales information. Management's actions, however, were frequently inappropriate because of delays in gathering and disseminating the information. A communications technology system solved this problem. With the use of this system, the salespeople entered orders at the customer site (or at the branch office shortly after their return). The orders were then communicated immediately to a headquarters system for processing, and the sales data was aggregated and distributed through work stations made accessible by the marketing staff. Consequently, marketing managers could quickly assess the results of a promotion or an advertising campaign, determine its effectiveness, and decide how it should be altered.

Another example is Boehringer Ingelheim. The company uses a computer-based call reporting system that dramatically reduces the time needed to collect and analyze marketing data from the field.[5]

Create Service Excellence

Communications technology can also increase the speed of the firm's operations as perceived by its customers, thereby improving customer service. A major international bank, for example, installed a worldwide communications system that allows loan applications originating in East Asia to be transmitted electronically to New York for analysis and approval. This resulted in a significant reduction in the time required to respond to loan requests. The bank used the responsiveness perceived by customers to establish an advantage over competitors who still used conventional, paper-based communications.

Superior service can also apply to increasing the speed of product delivery. By using a CIIS to speed order processing or to manage inventories in a way that leads to fewer out-of-stock situations, a manufacturer or distributor can quickly deliver to a customer the product that has been requested. An actual example is Inventory Locator Service. This service allows air carriers to specify the parts they require for aircraft maintenance. When requested, the system automatically generates "request for quotation" letters to potential suppliers.[6]

A CIIS can improve service quality not only by responding more quickly to customer inquiry but also by streamlining communication between the firm and the customer. Customers can use a single point of contact and obtain precise and current information. Such an arrangement can help eliminate, or at least diminish, confusing and frustrating communication problems that can destroy the relationship between firm and customer.

Clearly, opportunities for creating service excellence are found at key points of customer interaction, where responsiveness has high business value.

OVERCOMING GEOGRAPHICAL RESTRICTIONS

Recapture Scale

One of the major problems with geographically dispersed organizations is that individual sites may not operate at a sufficiently high volume to benefit from economies of scale. By using a communications technology system, however, a collection of small, individual offices can operate as though they were one large organization. Such a system allows information to be transferred between remote units as readily and efficiently as can be done within a single physical site. The firm is thus able to lower its operational costs and still realize the benefits derived from geographically dispersed operations.

Target opportunities for scale recapture may be found in remote business processes that are susceptible to sudden increases in transaction volumes or that require specialized skills in order to provide full service. Warehouses, for instance, often maintain high contigency reserves because of uncertain demand. Moreover, it is difficult and time-consuming to determine what items are at other warehouses. A CIIS that links the inventory data-bases of a collection of warehouses allows a distributor to share more readily reserves among them; the result is a lower aggregate inventory level in the warehouse system as a whole. Chrysler is one such example. All of its manufacturing and assembly plants are tied into an information system that provides a fully interactive look at inventory on hand, material in transit, and upcoming material needs. The company claims that this dynamic inventory analysis system has helped cut inventory costs by more than $700 million.[7]

Ensure Global Management Control

Another drawback of geographical dispersion is that management may have difficulty ensuring quality consistency across dispersed units. In other words, when an organization decentralizes its operations and resources, central quality control may become a problem. By means of a CIIS, however, rapid access to information on the performance of remote units can help corporate management monitor and redirect the activities of dispersed units. In this way uniformity and quality consistency are maintained throughout the organization.

Another problem arises because of local suboptimization. Remotely located units tend to operate within the domain of their own physical and psychological boundaries, which often leads to actions aimed at satisfying their own needs. A CIIS can help to realign the goals of local units with those of corporate headquarters by providing remote subgroups with information about, and quick feedback on, the broader set of corporate concerns and objectives.

Target opportunities for global management control may be found in situations where a company's success requires the interdependent contribution of all its organizational entities, and where local parochial actions need to be balanced against broader corporate goals.

Take, for example, General Electric's Materials & Plastics Division. The division developed ERIS (Engineering Resins Information System), which provides handbook information on all commercially available resins (not just GE's), helps the company's design engineers select materials, determines optimal processing conditions, and predicts manufacturing costs. In 1984 the system was also made available to outside customers, mostly to original equipment manufacturers (OEMs). Customers, however, cannot access ERIS directly; they work with trained GE marketing and technical personnel and use portable computers at the customers sites.[8]

Penetrate New Markets

The costs of geographical expansion can inhibit market penetration for many firms. Here again, a CIIS can help overcome these limitations and facilitate entry into new markets. A manufacturer can quickly open a new field office with only a skeleton staff; most of the support is received electronically through an information system at corporate headquarters. Similarly, for the customer who demands that all of his or her dispersed sites be serviced by a single vendor, an information system can create a logical presence by extending the capabilities of a field office, and thus qualify the firm with the customer. In both cases, geographical conquest by an information system translates into improvements in marketplace position.

Often, it is not physical limitations that restrict market entry, but rather legal or regulatory issues. A CIIS can be used to establish an electronic presence; therefore, regulatory restrictions — although changing laws may complicate this situation — can be overcome. In particular, financial service organizations have shown great ingenuity in projecting themselves into environments from which they might otherwise be barred. ATM networks also make it easier for firms to penetrate new markets.

Communications technology also enables a firm to enter new markets by expanding the time window during which it is allowed to do business on a national or international basis. A worldwide communications system allows a brokerage firm to operate in multiple trading markets effectively on a twenty-four-hour basis, thereby permitting its customers to place and execute orders at any time of the day.

Target opportunities of this class may be found in situations where customers require reporting and service nationally or globally; where physical presence is not economical or legal; or, where extending business hours across time zones would increase revenues. Citibank, in particular, has a global communications network that is used in its mergers and acquisition business. When the unit has a prospective seller, it frequently transmits data on the client to some 7,000 Citibank officers around the world. By the time a brochure announcing the sale is published, the company may already have some prospective buyers.[9]

RESTRUCTURING BUSINESS RELATIONSHIPS

Bypass Intermediaries

A CIIS can widen the span of management control within a firm, thereby reducing the number of management layers. From the customer's perspective, such a system can obviate the need for "translator" or "expeditor" intermediaries by permitting direct communication between originator and servicer. One such example is a customer who uses an on-line system to check the status of a previously placed order instead of asking the sales representative, who must then ask the plant manager.

Target opportunities for bypassing intermediaries may be found in cases where the cost of intervention or information handling is high (e.g., middle management in a hierarchical structure, or information brokering within a value-added chain). Here, the process is restructured and made more efficient. USAA illustrates this point. Since 1969, this San Antonio-based insurer has developed an extensive sales and marketing system that allows the company to conduct sales and service over the telephone. This eliminated the use of agents, who boost premiums. As a result, *Consumer Reports* ranked USAA at or near the top in customer satisfaction for its auto and homeowner claims handling.[10]

Replicate Scarce Knowledge

Communications technology can have the effect of distributing knowledge within an organization, especially to remote locations. The effect may be expressed in terms of changes in relationships within the organization since knowledge no longer becomes the exclusive preserve of only a few individuals. The result is not greater process efficiency, but rather a more effective organization.

Replicating and distributing knowledge can also have a profound impact on the structure and culture of a company. Senior managers typically have access to scarce information, and so are presumed most capable of deciding critical issues. When such information is made more widely available to the entire organization, people at lower levels may more aggressively set their own directions. This leads to a revived entrepreneurial spirit within the firm: individual managers feel empowered by information access to resolve issues on their own.

For example, in an industrial products firm, sales information traditionally had been available only to senior, headquarters-based management (and even to them on a less than timely basis). The implementation of a CIIS led to the on-line availability of a sales database to branch sales managers. This provided them with an overall perspective, which had been previously unobtainable, on both salesman performance and product experience. They were now able to use this information to develop successful sales strategies explicitly targeted to their local markets; they did so with little guidance from corporate headquarters.

The exchange of knowledge made possible with communications technology leads to an interesting duality: regaining global control and moving power down an organization's hierarchy. This simultaneous centralization and decentralization may represent the best of both worlds.[11] Through the distribution of information and knowledge, decision making is widely dispersed and driven down to levels closest to operations, customers, and their associated problems. Conversely, information technology also allows senior executives to monitor the performance of these semi-independent decision makers. This enables them to identify problems at an early stage and to intervene where appropriate. In addition, a CIIS gives smaller and more dispersed units enough responsibility and autonomy without an organization jeopardizing its centralized control.

Target opportunities for this class may be found in situations where dispersed individuals require access to scarce knowledge or experience in order to respond to local markets. A case in point is Medicare-Glaser Corp. This company implemented an information system that warns a customer of potentially dangerous effects caused by the interaction of certain prescription drugs.

Build Umbilical Cords to Customers

The most celebrated communications technology applications are those that have been used to establish closer ties with customers. For example, a distributor placed order-entry terminals in the premises of small pharmacies. To be sure, one intent of this action was to increase the efficiency of the order-entry process, from which both vendor and customer would benefit. However, it also strengthened the bond between the customer and the distributor by raising the customer's switching costs and tightening the distributor's hold. Once the link is established, this system can also serve as a distribution channel for additional products and services, which, in turn, can further tighten the vendor/customer bond.

An example of this is PIE Nationwide, Inc. The firm developed an information system for tracking shipments from origin to destination. Consequently, a customer may check on a shipment by accessing the PIE system, using his or her own terminal. Senior executives report that this system brings competitive advantage to PIE, because the company "stands out technologically in the trucking field."[13]

GUIDELINES FOR ACTION

The combination of communications and information processing offers a powerful vehicle for achieving critical business goals. However, many companies are ill equipped to exploit these opportunities. Following are basic actions that a firm must be willing to take in order to reposition itself and meet the communications technological challenge.

Reeducate Applications Staff

Applications planners should reorient their analysis activities to identify communications-intensive opportunities that have high business value. This reorientation requires quick learning about advances in information systems, as well as about the synergistic effects made possible by integrating communications and computing technologies.

Create a Technology Architecture

To support future information transport and connection needs, CIIS applications require a reliable technology infrastructure. To be effective, however, this infrastructure must provide compatibility among differing component technologies. The danger here is that, in light of the increasing rate of technology and business change, it may be unreasonable and risky to configure a network based purely on today's known needs. Similarly, extensive analysis aimed at anticipating all future requirements and constructing the "ideal" solution may just as easily result in paralysis and inaction.

Consolidate Communications Responsibilities

Identification and exploitation of leading-edge applications presuppose the effective deployment and management of communications technology. However, many organizations are still organized on the basis of historically distinct islands of information and communications systems management. Leadership responsibilities should be realigned under an "information services director" to establish a critical mass of internal technical expertise, to provide a focal point for vendor management, to assimilate emerging technologies, and to ensure technical compatibility.

NOTES

[1]*Business Week,* "Information Power: How Companies Are Using New Technologies to Gain a Competitive Edge," 14 October 1985, p. 108; J.I. Cash, Jr., and B.R. Konsynski, "IS Redraws Competitive Boundaries," *Harvard Business Review,* March–April 1985, p. 134; B.B Jackson, "Build Customer Relationships That Last," *Harvard Business Review,* November–December 1985, p. 120; F.W. McFarlan, "Information Technology Changes the Way You Compete," *Harvard Business Review,* May–June 1984, p. 98; G.L. Parsons, "Information Technology: A New Competitive Weapon," *Sloan Management Review,* Fall 1983, p. 3; M.E. Porter and V.E. Millar, "How Information Gives You Competitive Advantage," *Harvard Business Review,* July–August 1985, p. 149.

[2]Cash and Konsynski (March–April 1985); Jackson (November–December 1985).

[3]"Rand McNally & Company" (Cambridge, MA: Index Systems, Inc., case study, 1985).

[4]P.G.W. Keen, *Competing in Time: Using Telecommunications for Competitive Advantage* (Cambridge, MA: Ballinger Publishing, 1986).

[5]"Call Reporting Made Fast and Easy," *Medical Marketing and Media,* September 1985, pp. 22–27.

[6]Database Keeps Aircraft Service Firms Afloat," *Computerworld,* 29 August 1983, p. 34.

[7]"The Role of Information Systems in Chrysler's Resurgence," *Information Strategy: The Executive's Journal,* Winter 1986, pp. 4–7.

[8]"GE Materials & Plastics Division: ERIS" (Cambridge, MA: Index Systems, Inc., case study, 1985).

[9]"Commercial Banks Beef Up Merger Arms," *Wall Street Journal,* 9 April 1986.

[10]"Rand McNally & Company" (1985).

[11]Keen (1986).

[12]"Safety Prompts Computer Use in Drugstores," *Wall Street Journal,* 9 September 1983, p. 31.

[13]C. Wiseman, *Strategy and Computers* (New York: Dow Jones-Irwin, 1985).

7

The Myths and Realities of Competitive Advantage

Michael Miron, John Cecil,
Kevin Bradicich, and Gene Hall

Information power! Legions of consultants, academicians, and vendors have been preaching the gospel of information technology — how its transforming power will create "strategic systems" that will propel business to new heights of success. The faith in technology has created what has almost become an admonition — if your company doesn't get on board quickly with the latest technology, it will be left behind.

While information technology is often essential to maintain competitiveness, it may not be capable of achieving competitive advantage where none existed before, and its most common application — as a tool for automating a process — is least likely to yield that advantage. When IT is used to leverage existing business strengths, such as economies of scale or unique institutional skills, however, it is more likely to result in competitive gains. But the most strategic IT breakthroughs occur in industries where the continuing rapid rate of technological change, as well as other industry changes (government regulation, evolving customer needs, etc.) lead to new business approaches and opportunities to substantially change competitive position.

It is in these situations that early mover companies that are among the first to understand and use IT can create new advantages and even change the industry structure.

However, most IT investments today involve standalone applications. They generally take the form of specific initiatives — such as image capture technologies or automated calling systems — that reduce costs or improve service. While these applications are often critical to remaining competitive, they generally do not provide an edge because most of these technologies are available from vendors to all comers.

Even internally developed systems can be copied by competitors. Because the underlying technology is widely available, the application can be replicated by those with comparable scale. Smaller players can often gain access to comparable appli-

How One Company Rode Information Technology to Success

One firm that used IT to ride a wave of industry change is an East Coast investment firm. Since the early '80s, the tide of competition has been steadily rising in the mortgage industry. With increasing securitization of mortgages, interest rate volatility, and overcapacity in the industry, competition has been intensifying, placing a greater premium on risk management. Since the mortgages acting as collateral in mortgage securities can be prepaid at any time, assessing and managing prepayment risk is crucial.

While many investment banks involved in structuring mortgage securities invested in information technology to track and analyze prepayment rates, this firm correctly anticipated the need to analyze the prepayment rates of the specific pools of loans backing collateralized mortgage obligation (CMOs). When the CMO market was small, the firm began to construct a system that takes publicly available data on the economic performance of each geographic area in the United States, default delinquency data, mortgage pool characteristics, and prepayment rates from the Federal National Mortgage Association, Government National Mortgage Association, and Federal Home Loan Mortgage Corporation. A computer-based analytic/decision-support system gives traders improved pool-specific pricing capability, which has led to a preeminent position for the firm in pool-specific trading. The system helps salesmen assist customers in valuing their portfolios, which strengthens customer relationships, and provides the firm with additional information about the location of specific securities. The system also allows the firm's underwriters to structure CMO payments more accurately, which has allowed them to obtain superior pricing by being among the first firms to construct innovative new securities that more closely meet investor needs.

The key to this firm's success has been the experience it derived from being

cations through independent software vendors that can spread the development and maintenance costs across a number of users. Since the minimum efficient scale for single-user, internally developed systems based on widely available technology is typically much higher than for externally acquired systems, the cost of these internally developed systems will generally put their developers at a disadvantage.

Because standalone IT investments can be copied, they do not lead to competitive advantage. In fact, the nonexclusive nature of the applications will often allow competitors to meet or exceed the service levels of existing market leaders at substantially lower costs. As a result, technology will tend to homogenize competitive positions by driving the cost and service quality of broad sets of competitors toward similar levels. The net impact is typically a reduction in total industry cost and profitability, because in a competitive industry, cost savings will not be captured by the company applying the technology (except in the short term before others copy the application), but instead will be passed on to customers.

The overall homogenization of competition tends to intensify price competition an early adopter—not only of the relevant technologies but also of ongoing, wholesale changes in the way it does business. These changes did not occur all at once: they represent the cumulative learning and refinement of business approaches over a period of years. For example, the experience of building and refining the system taught the firm what capabilities were required—but the firm also realized that whatever it might achieve, it would be useless unless customers recognized its value. That led the firm to conduct customer education seminars, which provided valuable feedback to refine the system.

Meanwhile, customers began to use the firm's capability to execute trades, allowing it to build market share. This translated into increased understanding of the marketplace and generated ideas for refining the system and making more adaptations to its business procedures. The firm then began efforts to link other functions into the system and expanded its training efforts by producing videotapes on the benefits of the system, making it possible to gain an additional share of the trading. This created opportunities to underwrite innovative new securities, resulting in greater placement volume, which increased commissions further, and generated funds to invest in ever-greater capabilities.

While competitors could duplicate the technology and information this firm uses, they could not easily duplicate the real source of advantage—the tremendous experience gained by the firm in adapting virtually all of its operations to the new business environment, coupled with the hundreds of refinements and enhancements made to the system itself since its inception. As a result, the firm has recently overtaken many of its traditional competitors and is now uniquely positioned to exploit additional information on specific loans within the pools as it becomes available.

by minimizing other forms of differentiation. The benefits will only be captured directly by companies that have a competitively defensible position in other areas, such as strong customer loyalty, which will allow those companies to avoid competing solely on the basis of price. Thus, standalone information technology-based cost reduction or service enhancement initiatives by themselves will not create competitive advantages, and can erode industry profitability. In these situations, the best strategy is one of superior execution. Investments in new applications should be selective and well timed.

LEVERAGING BUSINESS STRENGTHS

Developing a secure edge is more likely when IT is combined with existing nontechnology-based strengths. Scale, unique institutional skills, and customer loyalty are strengths that most often can be exploited.

IT can be used to enhance scale economies by increasing the volume through an existing process that has a scale advantage. This can be accomplished by implementing tailored business approaches through the use of large-scale sources of information. Opportunities to use IT to enhance scale can be found in unexpected aspects of the business, as a major retailer that developed a credit model for each store location in its large customer base discovered.

These models permit superior credit control (lower credit losses, without overly restricting credit to creditworthy customers) over competitors with lower scale. This type of tailoring using a large-scale base of information is often very powerful in consumer mass market businesses.

Another way to use information to leverage scale is to schedule and coordinate complex but predictable demand more effectively. The management of a leading consumer packaged goods manufacturer with nationwide distribution faced a problem of how to distribute enough of its perishable food products to meet highly volatile consumption patterns. Since the worst possible problem they could create would be to run a promotion and find themselves without product, they had established multiple facilities around the country and overstocked them with inventory to avoid being caught short.

Although overstocking in this fashion caused waste, they were afraid to attempt any consolidation for fear of losing sales. Recently, however, they constructed a system to improve sales forecasting, scheduling, and production planning using historical information to analyze these complex demand swings under different kinds of marketing plans. They found that the demand was actually quite predictable. This allowed a significant reduction in inventories and a consolidation of facilities with scale economies, which lowered branch operations costs by 20% and improved capacity utilization without the risk of stockouts. This kind of application is most effective in businesses with large demand swings and wide geographic distribution, such as in the consumer products field.

Another way to exploit existing strengths is to use IT to leverage unique institutional skills. Routine activities can be automated to allow a company's highly skilled employees to concentrate on higher value-added tasks. Alternatively, expert systems may be used to share expert knowledge across a broader labor force. Such applications are quite powerful when truly unique and valuable skills exist and are sustainable, but these conditions occur only in select situations, where the skills are not likely to be rapidly replicable by many competitors.

IT can be used to provide new, tailored features to strengthen product differentiation. A major airline provides IT-based services that are tailored to meet the needs of specific segments. It provides mileage awards to all of its frequent flyer program members and maintains a customer preference database for use in making reservations. For the top 2% to 3% of its customers, who account for half of their business travel volume, it identifies the person as a valued customer on all customer service screens and reports, gives those customers the ability to overbook, offers them larger mileage awards, automatically blocks off seats next to them if the plane is not full, and gives them free first-class upgrades at the gate whenever seats are available.

Opportunities to provide tailored features occur commonly in businesses with proprietary customer information, but in most cases they do not significantly strengthen competitive advantage, since such tailoring often increases the customer benefit of the basic product only marginally.

Many companies fail to exploit opportunities to leverage strengths with IT because most of the ways to enhance such strengths require them to integrate various aspects of their businesses. Integration opportunities are often unrecognized or underexploited because of organizational barriers and systems limitations. Many companies are structured around strong organizations defined by product lines, functions, or geographic customer segments. Accordingly, such cross-cutting opportunities are difficult to identify and typically are not exploited due to divergent priorities and a lack of coordination across the organization. Systems often have been developed as a series of ad hoc applications and add-ons, so it is extremely difficult to link across customers, products, functions, or markets because of incompatible data structures, applications, or operating environments. In addition, the data are typically nonstandardized and dedicated to specific applications.

CREATING STRUCTURAL ADVANTAGES

Thus far, IT initiatives that deal with existing business approaches have been addressed. However, in certain businesses, opportunities may exist to create structural competitive advantages with IT. Merrill Lynch's Cash Management Account and American Airlines' SABRE reservation system are perhaps the best known examples of this kind of structural advantage. Structural changes with IT can be achieved through switching costs, sharing information with an existing business, introducing and controlling a new distribution channel, or gaining power over suppliers.

Switching costs are created by automating the interface between customer and supplier so that either the customer can make low-value purchases more conveniently or the supplier can become an important part of the customer's business system, locking in the relationship. IT-based switching costs can be important in businesses that have customers who make frequent repeat purchases of low-value items because the potential savings from competitive products are likely to be very small relative to the customer's total costs.

Alternatively, where there is a complex interface, switching costs are also likely to be significant. However, these situations are infrequent since there are a limited number of cases where sourcing from a very few number of vendors is acceptable.

Companies can enter new product markets with superior cost positions by sharing information costs with an existing business, since the cost of the customer acquisition often is very high. Businesses with large-scale proprietary customer information are in the best position to exploit information sharing, as Merrill Lynch did. Banks can cross-sell other financial products, such as checking and savings accounts to mortgage applicants, by sharing information captured in a mortgage application. The potential profitability of such cross-sell opportunities may be almost as high as making the original mortgage loan.

Information technology may also allow companies to create and control new distribution channels that provide advantages over traditional delivery methods. In the mortgage industry, for example, changes in IT are contributing to the trend of banks packaging individual mortgage loans into securities for sale to investors instead of holding on to them until they are paid off. This process, known as securitization, breaks up the traditional business system into discrete roles that are played by different firms, rather than having all the roles taken by the firm that first created the mortgage.

CHANGING THE BASIS OF COMPETITION

This IT-supported trend has changed the basis of competition and has facilitated the entrance of nontraditional competitors into the industry. A major insurance company has entered the mortgage origination business with a highly automated centralized direct mail/telemarketing approach. The new approach has cut application processing to 10 days from 23 and saved the expense of branch offices and loan officers, allowing the company to offer lower rates to customers.

Opportunities to create and control a new distribution channel may be found in businesses where customers have grown sophisticated enough to reduce or remove direct human contact in product delivery. Companies that correctly gauge whether customers are indeed ready can gain a powerful cost advantage over existing competitors who are saddled with higher cost operations that they cannot easily alter.

Finally, information technology can sometimes be used by customers to shift power away from suppliers. In the consumer packaged goods industry, most major retailers are beginning to integrate data obtained from checkout scanners on item-specific performance to increase power over manufacturers through better purchasing, more control over shelf management and direct store delivery sales forces, and improved understanding of promotions. Customers must capture unexploited information that is produced as a by-product of their businesses in order to gain power over suppliers.

There is an alternative way to create new sources of competitive advantage with IT, which may not be as rare as the creation of the kinds of structural advantages discussed above. Companies that develop new business approaches using technology in conjunction with aggressive changes to every other aspect of their businesses may be able to build up significant advantages if they can leverage institutional experience. The strategy demands early implementation of IT applications and a significant commitment and ability to make organizational and other nontechnology changes to the business.

These advantages can be sustainable because competitors would have to copy more than just the technology. They would have to go through the same learning and adapting process with their organizations, while the innovator stretches its lead.

ADAPTING TO EVOLVING ENVIRONMENTS

To succeed in these situations, companies must continually adapt to the evolving business and technological environment. When change creates an opportunity, further changes could give future opportunities to competitors that move early. Thus, the firms that will be most successful will typically perform the following:

- reexamine all elements of the business system and understand the importance of organizational change, as well as new technology;
- commit substantial technical and nontechnical resources to development early in the game; and
- recognize that the ultimate application cannot be identified beforehand—the application and supporting organization will evolve as the company sees new enhancement opportunities, and as the new business approach takes shape.

These principles contrast greatly with the appropriate approach to standalone applications, where rigorous economic analysis is the proper way to select technologies and determine the optimal point of adoption.

In creating new experience-based advantages, companies must commit resources early on, without knowing the magnitude of the total investment, the end product, or the scope of the impact. They must have the vision and unwavering commitment, especially of top management, to invest early enough to enable the company to make thousands of evolutionary adjustments and refinements to both the technology application and its organizational capabilities.

Let us not forget that all of the roles of IT we have described should be considered strategic. Omitting or failing at any one could cost a company its competitive position, even if it does not enhance or create advantages by itself.

Ultimately, the strategic use of IT is a business decision, not merely a technology choice. The winners in any industry will be those players who first understand that, and then take the necessary steps to carefully assess the information technology potential for their own business situations.

8   *Information Technology as a Competitive Burden*

Timothy N. Warner

A major electronics manufacturer establishes an automated warehouse for incoming components. Robots glide up and down the high-rise bays, selecting bins of components under computer control; the bins are passed to a conveyor system; they move around on a path determined by bar code scanners that identify each bin and route it to a stock picker. The stock picker removes items for dispatch to the factory floor as instructed by a computer workstation. An automated guided vehicle rolls off to the factory along a track painted on the floor.

At a cost of many millions of dollars, the system epitomizes the technology of the "factory of the future." But it is now idle. The firm now delivers the bulk of its supplies directly to the factory floor, bypassing the automated warehouse.

Perhaps the managers of this firm thought that information technology was a competitive weapon; perhaps they thought that advanced manufacturing technologies incorporating microelectronics were the key to manufacturing cost reduction. At least, finally, they recognized an organizational design alternative to the use of information technology. Had they not done so, information technology would have continued to be, for them as for many others, a competitive burden.

The purpose of this paper is to review the role of information technology in manufacturing enterprises and to point to alternative strategies for achieving the results that information technology promises. It will also argue that the proper role of information technology in a production system cannot be correctly assessed until the system has been restructured for maximum efficiency using conventional means.

INFORMATION TECHNOLOGY IN MANUFACTURING

When we consider the use of information technology in manufacturing, we find three main components. The first is the use on the shop floor of devices containing some level of intelligence—robots, numerically controlled machines, flexible manufacturing systems, automated guided vehicles, and the like—and falling under the rubric of flexible automation, or advanced manufacturing technologies. The second is the use of computer-aided design techniques, and the third is the use of computerized manufacturing information and control systems. Together these components are capable of becoming computer-integrated manufacturing systems (CIM). Businesses most affected by them tend to be from the aerospace, automotive, electrical equipment, electronics, machinery, and metal-fabricating industries. Many observers see these technologies as truly strategic in impact. For example, rapidly shifting consumer tastes and increased global competition necessitate short product design cycles and responsive manufacturing facilities; economies of scope replace economies of scale. Indeed, some observers see in these information-technology-based approaches the solution to the problem of North American competitiveness.[1]

INFORMATION TECHNOLOGY AND ORGANIZATIONAL DESIGN

Information systems, whether they incorporate "information technology" or not, serve a coordinating function in the firm, allowing it to cope with complexity and uncertainty. Jay Galbraith's work provides a framework for understanding how this occurs.[2] He starts with the issue of how to organize for a task that grows in complexity and uncertainty, and considers the problems of coordination. As soon as the task becomes so large that several persons are engaged in it, they face a management problem. This can be resolved in a variety of ways. For example, a hierarchy of authority is more or less essential, as are agreed-upon rules, programs, and procedures. If the task to be performed is known and standardized, little more needs to be done. But uncertainty in the task creates problems because, to resolve the issues created by uncertainty, more and more information passes up the channels of authority, ultimately overloading them. Galbraith suggests a number of generic strategies for dealing with this problem, which he divides into two broad categories.

Reduce the need for information processing:

- Give organizational units more discretionary authority so that the need for upper-management intervention is diminished. Doing this is associated with redesign of tasks into larger, firewalled modules that are carried out by craft or skilled workers.
- Manage the environment to reduce the amount of uncertainty.
- Create slack resources, often in the form of inventory or order backlogs.

Increase information-processing capacity:

- Increase vertical-channel capacity in the hierarchy.
- Increase information-processing capacity of selected nodes in the hierarchy.
- Increase the amount of lateral coordination, not involving higher levels of management.

These strategies are not so much mutually exclusive as they are complementary. The important thing to realize is that sometimes one can meet an apparent information-processing problem not by throwing computer power at it, but by removing the conditions that caused the need for information processing in the first place. The example with which I opened this paper demonstrates this possibility well. The control of raw materials inventory and of its movement within the factory are such complicated jobs that advanced computer systems, and computerized devices, are needed to cope with them in an efficient manner—that is, in an analysis comparing manual and automated systems, the automated system would appear more efficient. A better alternative (ignored if one focuses on the use of information technology) might be to remove the conditions that cause inventory to be held.

The Japanese have taught us to regard inventory as "waste." Galbraith's analysis shows us that, if inventory is waste, then information-processing capacity that serves the same function as inventory is also waste.

Information-processing capacity is used to cope with uncertainty and complexity, but much of the uncertainty and complexity faced by a firm is created by the firm itself, because, for example, the product is too complex, contains components from too many suppliers, and is produced by systems of high variability. Let us examine four cases where dealing directly with these conditions replaces attempting to compute one's way around them.

DESIGN FOR MANUFACTURABILITY

Complex products are reflected in complex production systems. It is instructive to analyze examples where sophisticated companies have taken a hard look at their production systems, intending to raise the level of manufacturing efficiency, perhaps to become the industry's low-cost producer. Generally there are three elements in their strategies: product design, automation, and manufacturing control systems. While it is hard to disentangle the relative benefits of each, a strong case can be made that much of the gain in efficiency comes from a process of change that may well have been precipitated by the adoption of automation but is otherwise unrelated to it.

Consider the example of Northern Telecom, a major multinational corporation in the telecommunications industry that was faced with the challenge of low-cost telephones produced in Pacific Rim countries. The company's response was to redesign the telephone and reduce its labor content through automation. The redesign is especially interesting because it succeeded in reducing the parts count from 325 to 156.[3] The original labor content was twenty-three minutes per handset. A crude computation shows that if labor content were proportional to parts count, then manual assembly of the revised product would take eleven minutes. Actual labor content, after automation, was nine minutes. It is clear where the major leverage was achieved.

A similar analysis could be conducted with another well-documented automation success—the IBM Proprinter.[4] Redesign for manufacturability reduced the parts count by 60 percent (the printer has 60 parts, compared to 150 in a competitor's product), and the product was simplified for robotic assembly. A similar emphasis on product design at Ford Motor Company reduced the number of pieces in a car-body side panel from 15 to 2. What these examples tell us is that product redesign has tremendous leverage to reduce complexity and its concomitant variability. The important thing is to manage what we might call the internal environment; automation is secondary.

GROUP TECHNOLOGY

A second example, from the secondary manufacturing sector, is the job shop—a production system in which jumbled flow dominates. Scheduling problems in job shops are severe. The result is that the typical machined part spends 95 percent of its total time on the factory floor waiting, and only 5 percent on a machine, being cut. A machine tool might spend only a small fraction of its time cutting metal, the bulk of its day being taken up waiting for work or being set up. The consequent waste of resources has motivated considerable research into job-shop scheduling, and the development of shop-floor data acquisition systems to aid in managing the flow of work through the shop. With few exceptions the North American solution has been to throw computer power at the problem.[5]

Information processing is not the only, or necessarily the best, solution. People who didn't have the luxury of computers established the concept of "group technology," which in essence is the classification of parts produced by the job shop in terms of similar fabrication sequence, shape, and size.[6] Suppose we can, via such a classification scheme, allocate 80 percent of the shop's volume to families of like parts. Then we can process each family through a manufacturing cell whose machines are placed in the correct sequence and are tailored for the family. The job shop starts to look like a flow shop; scheduling problems are reduced; the prospect for dramatic reductions in work-in-process inventory is enhanced. (As it happens, information technology can play a key role in the application of group technology concepts, and is perhaps essential to that process, but at least when this is the case we know that the technology is being applied reasonably.) In Galbraith's terms, we have redesigned the task into self-contained modules, as opposed to finding the information-processing capacity to schedule the more complex task.

MANUFACTURING CELLS

Jelinek and Goldhar have pointed out that the new technologies of flexible automation—particularly the use of numerically controlled machine tools, robots, and flexible manufacturing systems—give rise to new production system possibilities based on short production runs and rapid switching (at near-zero cost) from one product to another.[7] These provide economies of scope, contrasted with economies of scale. The essential component here is the programmable device, say the NC machine or industrial robot, that can switch immediately from performing one kind of task to another under program control. Once switching costs are zero, then small lot sizes become feasible, indeed optimal. Combining the concepts of rapid change-over through programmability, and group technology, one arrives at the flexible manufacturing cell—the first step toward CIM.[8] It may consist of an integrated multifunctional NC machining center, or a circle of NC tools with automatic tool-changing and raw-material loading and unloading, perhaps with automated guided vehicles moving the pieces from one machine to the next. Its purpose is to produce, in small lot sizes, the components in a particular family.

It is incorrect to think that only programmable multifunctional machines are capable of instant zero-cost switching. The Japanese have shown us that conventional technology can be used in the same way.[9] The trick is to reduce setup times to very small amounts through ingenious engineering and the application of what is, in retrospect, common sense. The "multifunctional" machine can be created from an assemblage of low-cost conventional machines in a manufacturing cell. Hence a concept—economies of scope—that appeared to depend on the advent of high technology on the factory floor is applicable in a much more modest manufacturing environment.[10]

In its simplest form a manufacturing cell is a line (or U-configuration, or circle) of simple machine tools, say, for the production of a family of parts. In order to produce a part, a worker starts with the raw material piece and walks it down the line, performing each operation sequentially, until he or she reaches the end. Note, lot size equals one, and setups must be one-touch, not involving other workers. To speed up the line one simply adds another worker; each takes roughly half the work of the cell. One can keep adding workers until the physical ability of the cell to accommodate them is exhausted.

The conventional manufacturing cell achieves flexibility with slack machine resources (which can be cheap, because the machines are simple) and multifunction workers. (Galbraith suggests that a function of "craft" workers is to reduce the costs of coordination.) The cell is a low-fixed-cost increment to a firm's manufacturing capacity, a feature not shared by the information-technology-intensive flexible manufacturing cell, which achieves flexibility through machine-based intelligence.

There is a further consideration—the flexibility of the fully automated "flexible manufacturing cell" is deceptive, because of the extent to which inflexible materials-handling equipment is integral to its operation. This factor limits the number of different items that can in fact be processed by the cell, rather undermining the notion of flexibility.[11]

JUST-IN-TIME SYSTEMS

Another complementary approach to uncertainty and complexity arises out of the problem of management control in repetitive discrete manufacturing (of cars, airplanes, computers, or lawnmowers, for example). In this situation, an information-technology approach (material requirements planning) contrasts strongly with a non-information-technology approach (continuous flow manufacturing).

The manufacture of such goods is information intensive. It is said, for example, that the engineering documentation for a Boeing 747 weighs more than the plane itself. The manufacturing process involves many separate suppliers, spread across the globe, whose activities must be coordinated. The production system for these goods is an industry, not a single enterprise. The sheer volume of transactions required to manage such a production system makes it a natural target for information technology.

Material requirements planning (MRP) is an approach to the management of fabrication and assembly of products of this type. The key concept is that the demand for low-level components derives from the production of an end product whose production level is planned. Traditionally a component of, say, a lawnmower (a particular blade, perhaps) is manufactured in an economic lot size, stored in a warehouse, and used as needed until a reorder point is reached, at which point another batch is fabricated. The inventory of blades constitutes slack in the sense that it exists because nobody bothered to figure out exactly when the blades would be needed based on the production schedule for end-items, or perhaps because the number of end-items required could not be accurately forecasted or determined.

Clearly, if we know the precise production schedule of all the lawnmowers into which this particular blade goes, then we can establish, by back scheduling, when to produce or order the blades, so that inventory never builds up much in excess of requirements. MRP, then, substitutes information processing for slack in the way that Galbraith envisions. But MRP systems are notoriously difficult to implement and consume substantial resources in the form of computing power and indirect manufacturing labor.[12] Further, although they deal with the slack created by the earlier inability to back schedule production, they trap and institutionalize other slack that is generally more significant. In order to back schedule you have to estimate lead times for production. As mentioned earlier, 95 percent of the manufacturing lead time in a job shop is wasted, and building this exorbitant lead time into a computer system merely institutionalizes waste. In addition, the buffering function of inventory—allowing for variations in lead time or quantity delivered—is generally handled by artificially inflating the lead time or the quantity produced, which again casts inefficient organizational processes in stone. A final point is that the occurrence of stockouts on the shop floor can be ascribed to "the computer" rather than to some individual who could take corrective action. The system does not contain the levers that would motivate the work force to more efficient behavior; standing apart from the system on the shop floor, the MRP system introduces a fatal bifurcation of responsibility for overall performance.

Contrast this with what has been called Just-in-Time (JIT) or Stockless Production, or Continuous Flow Manufacturing.[13] Suppose for a moment that production of all components could be accomplished instantly. Then back scheduling from the number of different lawnmowers required to the number of blades required in a given period is simplified. But even this is unnecessary. If there is almost no work-in-process inventory (WIP), then replacement of the components required for a particular lawnmower must occur soon after its production. All we need is a signaling system that lets the blade production worker know when to produce. This is accomplished through the well-known kanban system. No computers are necessary to accomplish job-order release and dispatching, since these happen because of the pull system in place.

But there is a radical change in the organization of production. Setup times must be very low; lot sizes are correspondingly small—otherwise a machine would be occupied running large lots at the time it is required to produce a component "on demand." The flow of work might be reorganized so that travel times between successive workstations are minimized, and so that visual signaling methods (kanban squares, colored golf balls, etc.) can be used. There can be absolutely no defective parts passed along the system, because there is little WIP to absorb the discrepancies between planned and actual production.

Because there is so little WIP, it can all be located on the factory floor. No elaborate materials-handling or inventory control systems are required. The benefits are legion, well documented, and persuasive to the increasing number of U.S. manufacturers adopting these techniques.

In Galbraith's terms, the firm adopting JIT seems to be doing the impossible—lowering the information-processing requirement and removing slack from the system. This is not a complete picture, because the JIT firm plans slack resources in the form of machinery running more slowly, people working less than complete shifts, heavy maintenance, and idle equipment. In addition, the JIT firm eventually manages the uncertainty in its external environment by negotiating supply and delivery schedules to which all parties firmly adhere.[14]

We see here the competitive use of information systems, to be sure, but the use is not necessarily based on high technology. We also see whole industries being transformed by the impact of JIT methods, and corporations such as Hewlett-Packard and IBM relying on the cost and quality benefits of JIT to achieve a competitive edge.[15] One authority at IBM, which has reportedly invested $22 billion in manufacturing in the last five years, comments, "Of all the aspects of IBM's investment in manufacturing . . . the least expensive—Continuous Flow Manufacturing—is the most significant."[16]

I do not intend to give the impression that JIT systems are universally applicable in place of MRP systems. A balanced view might be that each has its place, or that some blend of the two is appropriate.[17] Certain conditions (long lead times for production, uncertain reject rates, fluctuating demand, high setup costs) favor MRP systems.[18] The tragedy is that an information-technology approach treats these conditions as immutable, whereas in many cases they are not. Rather than reducing waste, an information-technology approach adds to it by burdening an already inefficient system with the cost of computation.

CONCLUSIONS

Just as piles of work-in-process inventory can signal inefficient production, so also can the elaborate information system, or the machine tool with more axes than it needs, or the automatic storage and retrieval system. The paradox here is that some of the finest examples of manufacturing efficiency incorporate the most advanced computer control systems and factory automation. For example, comparing North American to Japanese manufacturers, we find in North America a lower rate of adoption of NC machines and robots, the building blocks of flexible automation. The reason is that for the well-organized production system the benefits of automation are clear. The Japanese, having paid more attention to basics than the North Americans, are in a better position to evaluate new technologies and have production systems into which devices such as robots and NC machines more readily fit.

The analysis presented above suggests that the twin strategies of product design and production system design around conventional technologies can achieve the lion's share of the benefits associated with moving from an unexamined, poorly organized production system to a world-class manufacturing facility. The issue is one of timing — a firm should forego information-technology-based approaches to solving production problems until it has exhausted conventional approaches, and then move forward into flexible automation. At that point it can examine the benefits of flexible automation relative to the best alternative practice.

Information technology is seen as a new competitive weapon; "strategic systems" take their place alongside decision support systems and traditional data processing;[19] and the "chief information officer" commands a seat at the table where strategic decisions are made.[20] Indeed, in the five years or so since early work on information technology as a competitive weapon appeared, the topic has achieved the status of cliche. Cliche or not, many firms look to information technology as a key weapon in their strategic arsenal.

When one considers what kinds of competitive advantage firms hope to achieve using information technology, one finds a depressingly high proportion of firms hoping to reduce competition through raising switching costs, reducing the amount of information available to the customer, and so forth — that is, using information technology to secure a local monopoly.[21] Depressing, because innovations in the service sector, or in the distribution, marketing, or purchasing functions of manufacturing enterprises, do little to counter the concern that North American enterprises are becoming "hollow corporations."[22] Meanwhile, a naive faith in technological silver bullets diverts manufacturers from the hard work of rebuilding North America's industrial base, and tempts them into alarming, high-risk forays toward the factory of the future. A recent report describes the experience of Deere and Company:

> The giant farm equipment manufacturer broke fresh ground a decade ago with factory automation that was then regarded as the model for all others to emulate. FMS technology worth $1.5 billion was designed to provide a choice of 5,000 process changes on ten basic tractor models.
>
> As Deere had to weather a depressed farm equipment market and then a strike, it became apparent that the company had invested too much in its state-of-the-art FMS without regard to the process being automated. . . .
>
> Billion-dollar losses were followed by rationalization of the production process, and today automated manufacturing at Deere is a much more organized, simplified affair. John Lardner, a company vice-president, said: "The FMS was a retrofit to a production design problem that shouldn't have existed in the first place."[23]

Manufacturing competitiveness is the only enduring base for a viable modern economy. Information technology will play a key role in transforming manufacturing. But not now, not for most firms. For them it is the hard road of conventional process improvement and production system organization that will lead to manufacturing competitiveness.

NOTES

The author wishes to thank I. A. Litvak for his comments on this paper.

[1]R.I. Benjamin, J.F. Rockart, M.S. Scott Morton, and J. Wyman, "Information Technology: A Strategic Opportunity," *Sloan Management Review,* Spring 1984, pp. 3–10; R.M. Cyert, "The Plight of Manufacturing: What Can Be Done?" *Issues in Science and Technology* 1 (1985): 87–100.

[2]J.R. Galbraith, *Organization Design* (Reading, MA: Addison-Wesley, 1977).

[3]R. McClean, "Quality and Productivity at Northern Telecom," in *Proceedings of the Fourth Annual Operations Management Association Meeting,* 1985, pp. 1–9.

[4]"Less Is More in Automation," *IBM Engineering/Scientific Innovation,* Fall 1986, pp. 4–5.

[5]W.K. Holstein and W.L. Berry, "Work Flow Structure: An Analysis for Planning and Control," *Management Science* 16 (February 1970): B324–B336.

[6]N.L. Hyer and U. Wemmerlöv, "Group Technology and Productivity," *Harvard Business Review,* July–August 1984, pp. 140–149.

[7]M. Jelinek and J.D. Goldhar, "The Strategic Implications of the Factory of the Future," *Sloan Management Review,* Summer 1984, pp. 29–37.

[8]P. Huang and B. Houck, "Cellular Manufacturing: An Overview and Bibliography," *Production and Inventory Management,* Fourth Quarter 1985, pp. 83–92.

[9]S. Shingo, *A Revolution in Manufacturing: The SMED System* (Stanford, CT: Productivity Press, 1985).

[10]U. Wemmerlöv and N.L. Hyer, "Research Issues in Cellular Manufacturing," *International Journal of Production Research* 25 (March 1987): 413–431.

[11]R. Jaikumar, "Postindustrial Manufacturing," *Harvard Business Review,* November–December 1986, pp. 69–76.

[12]J.C. Anderson, R.G. Schroeder, S.E. Tupy, and E.M. White, "Material Requirements Planning Systems: The State of the Art," *Production and Inventory Management,* Fourth Quarter 1982, pp. 51–66.

[13]R.W. Hall, *Zero Inventories* (Homewood, IL: Dow Jones-Irwin, 1983); R. Schonberger, "Applications of Single-Card and Dual-Card Kanban," *Interfaces,* August 1983, pp. 56–67; "Integrated Manufacturing: Nothing Succeeds Like Successful Implementation," *Production Engineering,* May 1987, pp. IM4–IM32.

[14]S. Chapman and M. Schimke, "Towards a Theoretical Understanding of Just-In-Time Manufacturing," *Operations Management Review,* Summer 1986, pp. 32–36.

[15]R.C. Walleigh, "What's Your Excuse for Not Using JIT?" *Harvard Business Review,* March–April 1986, pp. 38–54.

[16]"What Did IBM Buy for $22 Billion?" *Computerworld,* 15 June 1987, pp. 69–83.

[17]Schonberger (August 1983).

[18]L.J. Krajewski, B.E. King, L.P. Ritzman, and D.S. Wong, "Kanban, MRP, and Shaping the Manufacturing Environment," *Management Science* 33 (January 1987): 39–57.

[19]M.E. Porter and V.E. Millar, "How Information Gives You Competitive Advantage," *Harvard Business Review,* July–August 1985, pp. 149–160.

[20]"Management's Newest Star: Meet the Chief Information Officer," *Business Week,* 13 October 1986, pp. 160–172.

[21]G.L. Parsons, "Information Technology: A New Competitive Weapon," *Sloan Management Review,* Fall 1983, pp. 3–14; B. Ives and G.P. Learmonth, "The Information Systems as a Competitive Weapon," *Communications of the ACM,* December 1984, pp. 1193–1201; J.Y. Bakos and M.E. Treacy, "Information Technology and Corporate Strategy: A Research Perspective," *MIS Quarterly,* June 1986, pp. 107–119.

[22]"The Hollow Corporation," *Business Week,* 3 March 1986, pp. 56–78.

[23]T. Davis, "Manufacturers Review Their Strategy on Factory Automation," *Globe and Mail,* 4 July 1987, p. B7.

9

A Hard Look at Strategic Systems

Robert F. Morison and Kirtland C. Mead

If American Hospital Supply and American Airlines could do it, why couldn't we? In essence, that's what the senior vice president of sales and marketing at a large U.S. industrial company asked just a few years ago. Seeing the sizable competitive advantage those two companies gained after furnishing customers with terminals for booking orders, the marketing executive decided he, too, could electronically bind his company to its customers.

After 1½ years of developing the "channel" system, the executive installed more than 300 PCs in customer offices in the U.S. But they would have little effect. Customers could only view information about products—they couldn't order electronically. To the customers, the system was only slightly more helpful than catalogs. It was barely used.

After the executive transferred to Europe to try the idea there, the support for the American system waned; nobody was willing to take over the project and make the necessary system enhancements. The effort stalled and eventually was discontinued.

Welcome to the world of strategic systems. While press reports sing the praises of American Hospital Supply's (now Baxter Healthcare's) ASAP and American Airlines' SABRE channel systems, scarcely a word of caution has been issued about the difficulty, much less the risk, in creating and building strategic systems. In fact, failures are common, and probably outnumber successes.

THE MYTHS

Failures have more to teach us about strategic systems than many of the success stories. Drawing on PRISM research[1] and our consulting experiences, we have found that, while information systems indeed have played an important role in the success of many companies, many of the popular stories of strategic systems are largely oversimplified, mistaken, or even fictitious. After in-depth investigation into several well-known examples of strategic systems and numerous systems initiatives among Index clients and PRISM sponsors, we came to several myth-breaking conclusions:

- The system itself isn't strategic. Simply put, there is no such thing as a strategic or competitive information system; rather, an information system may support (or enable) an important change in the way business is done, and it is this business change that is strategic. The ASAP system, which links the health care products supplier to numerous hospitals, was part of a larger and concerted business program to help customers manage materials effectively. Thus, looking for corporate salvation through a "hot systems concept" is self-defeating. Instead, technology and business managers need to identify important changes in key business processes, changes that may well depend on new information systems.

- The competitive advantage often is fleeting. It is rarely possible to make a "first strike" that is so devastating that competitors cannot retaliate equally or better. Attempting to sustain an edge while your competitors strike back with their own strategic systems can be enormously expensive and sometimes fruitless.

- The nature and extent of the advantage gained from these systems are often unanticipated in the beginning. Many strategic systems were partly accidental, evolving from much humbler roots. They seldom were built from scratch: usually they stood on top of existing systems built for traditional automation purposes.

- The success stories almost always involve powerful suppliers (e.g., American Airlines) distributing product directly (not through distributors) to small customers—very often small businesses like travel agents. There are very few examples of big industrial customers which were "locked up" by suppliers. Indeed, the large customer is often using information technology to dominate its suppliers.

- Systems development and implementation are usually prolonged, difficult and expensive. In the early 1970s, American Hospital Supply used education, consulting, and computer systems to promote modern materials management among its hospital customers. ASAP, however, did not appear until 1976, and the system did not begin making major market share gains until 1978. It took six years and $350 million before American Airlines' SABRE travel agency reservation system started paying off. And the technical challenges were just as formidable: The company lived on the frontier of very large systems technology, constructing custom operating and database management systems to handle millions of transactions a day.

SIX ISSUES TO ADDRESS

Our research shows that companies must address six issues for an information system to result in a major marketplace edge: change in business processes, degree of market power, sustainability, industry structure, customer viewpoints, and risk.

Change in Business Processes

The greatest advantage from an information system accrues when it supports a fundamental change in the way business is conducted. A truly strategic system is likely to be large and complex, supporting major changes in business practices, and entailing significant effort and investment. Information systems that merely automate existing manual procedures are easy to imitate and unlikely to convey major business advantage.

PRISM research has found four business changes that are typically attempted during a major systems effort: positioning the business to deliver a new product or service; confronting a difficult strategic imperative, such as responding to deregulation; opening a new marketing channel; and reconfiguring core business processes along more flexible and productive lines.

Business changes of this magnitude entail enormous amounts of time, effort, investment, technical challenge and corporate commitment. Even systems implemented quickly eventually require major effort to solidify and prolong the competitive advantage. Thus, companies serious about promoting competitive advantage through information technology must live by the "no pain, no gain" credo. They must be ambitious, willing to invest, and able to expend systems and other resources on dramatic (not incremental) business change.

Market Power

Index research indicates that developers of strategic "channel" systems often already had substantial power in their marketing channels. Thus it was the largest American air carriers, American Airlines and United Air Lines, that locked up the channel to the small, much weaker travel agents. It is the powerful customers in retailing and automaking that are using electronic data interchange (EDI) to gain influence over their smaller, weaker suppliers.[2]

In channel systems, success is most likely to occur when the company attempting the system deals with weaker business partners. Thus, a supplier stands a better chance by aiming its system at, say, mid-sized customers rather than its largest ones.

Furthermore, a supplier's channel systems opportunities are greater when its product is complex, possessing high "information content" (that is, the customer requires a lot of information from the supplier to decide whether to buy it), or requires customization. In contrast, commodity products, sold on price and quality, provide fewer opportunities for channel lockup.

In France, a major beverage supplier had big problems with a customer order-entry system. Targeted at the restaurant market, the system allowed the customer to order all his food and beverages by standard meal menus. Deliveries were made by independent distributors who assembled supplies from various vendors.

While customers loved the system, the distributors' sales forces saw their order-taking function being taken over by a computer. In addition, the distributors were reluctant to see one of their suppliers "going around them" and direct to the customer. In the end, the beverage supplier had to withdraw the system in face of this resistance.

The lesson is that companies should focus their channel systems initiatives on their most powerful products and on small and mid-sized customers to whom they have direct distribution.

Sustainability

The advantage arising from strategic systems are often short-lived. Many companies make major investments in information technology designed to achieve a lasting marketplace edge, only to find their competitors caught on early and quickly responded with the same, or even better, systems. This raises the cost of doing business for everyone, with the only benefactor being the customer — and suppliers of computer equipment.[3]

There are three potential sources of sustainability: pre-emption, intimidation, and synergy with corporate strengths. The first mover enjoys the advantages of time, surprise, and the respect that follows innovation. Intimidation results when would-be duplicators are scared off by the sheer scale, risk or complexity of an information system and the business change involved. And information systems that leverage a company's strengths or proprietary capabilities usually maintain a lead over competing efforts that go against the corporate grain or do not exploit their advantages. A competitor to American Hospital Supply had a difficult time answering ASAP because its highly decentralized and autonomous business units hampered the building of an integrated order processing system (while AHS's structure and culture facilitated it).

In most cases, however, an information system does not provide lasting competitive advantage. What it can provide is the base and environment for ongoing innovation that creates a moving target for would-be imitators. Advantage can be sustained by continual enhancement and development.

Industry Structure

Strategic systems must be built with their intended market effects — on the competition and the structure of the industry — in mind. A major distributor that implemented an extremely successful customer order-entry system wasn't targeting its major competitors (who later implemented similar systems) but rather the many small distributors, which did not have the technological resources to fight back. In a similar vein, the American textile industry has banded together to install a system linking clothing retailers with manufacturers and mills to speed the delivery of orders. In this cooperative effort, the target of the system is clear — offshore makers of cheaper clothing — and so is the system's major objective: to fight the price disadvantage with service levels logistically impossible for the overseas competition to match.

To position a strategic system in the overall industry structure, some key questions must be asked:

- Who are the targets, and what are we trying to do to them?
- How and how soon will they react?

- Will we affect the balance of power in the industry, and how?
- If our initiative is taken to its logical extreme (e.g., everyone has such a system), will it be good for the industry as a whole? Or will it create more efficient markets, more price sensitivity and lower margins?

For success with these systems, a company must understand its environment and focus its objectives accordingly, pick the right targets, and anticipate competitive responses.

Customer Viewpoints

Just as companies must carefully consider whom their system is designed to hurt, they also must be clear about whom they want to please and what relationships they want to foster. Many efforts to build strategic systems fail because they do not take into account the perspective and concerns of customers or suppliers who must embrace the system for it to succeed.

Lock-in to a single supplier is usually inimical to customer interests. Moreover, developments benefiting the customer (such as industry-standard networks) come at the expense of a supplier trying to maintain a unique position.

Rather than thinking of the customer as victim, an organization should look to offer the customer value: improved delivery times and customer service, new products and services, customized products and services, lower product service or administrative costs. Sometimes, these customer benefits must come at the short-term expense of the system provider. Helping the customer manage inventory better means lower stock levels and less waste for the customer, but a potential dip in sales for the supplier. However, for the sake of longer-term market share, it may be better to wield the knife than to let an innovative competitor do it.

Risk

Strategic systems are highly risky and an advantage won at great costs is sometimes transitory. In addition, these major systems initiatives often lead to surprising destinations. Competitors come back with their answers to the systems, resulting in a heated race for marginal market share to cover larger fixed costs.

If the race to stay competitive becomes a technology race, the basis of competition may shift: Instead of the pecking order determined by who sells, markets, or manufactures the best, the game may become one of technical ability.

Furthermore, power may shift away from the company or industry as a whole. For instance, the airline industry faces the prospect of a truly efficient market for airline fares, in which customers have easy access to everyone's prices. In theory, this depresses prices and airline profits.

Technological risks also loom large: picking the wrong technology vendor, implementing a new technology too early in its life, being rendered obsolete by the introduction of new or cheaper technology, or being stuck with proprietary technology when standards emerge. Technological risks are highest when an organization pushes the current limits of technology, which usually happens with specialized, hardware-intensive systems.

Finally, strategic systems come with the risks associated with any large change in the business or a major systems project. People and departments may resist changing the way they operate. For example, many industrial and consumer goods companies are afraid to tamper with arcane pricing structures and "old boy" sales forces, even though information systems could help simplify pricing, tighten customer relationships, and boost profitability. A system that fails to convince a company's stakeholders is bound to be derailed.

Implementing strategic systems successfully requires understanding the risks, then assessing, assuming and managing them.

THE CHALLENGE AND ROLE FOR THE I/S FUNCTION

From these observations we deduce two conditions essential for success with strategic systems: a champion for the system in upper management and a strong I/S organization.

The first is an absolute necessity. The champion can't be the information systems executive. The reason: These systems entail major business change, which in turn entails risk and uncertainty. The natural organizational response is resistance and inertia. The I/S organization is rarely, if ever, in a position to implement a system over these obstacles.[4]

Instead, the champion must be a senior business executive who supports the system and is willing to fight for it. He or she must have a vision of the system. The champion is salesperson, educator, and change agent, with organizational respect, clout, and access to resources.

The capability of the I/S organization is just as important. Contrary to conventional wisdom, technology, and not just an innovative idea, plays a major role in strategic systems. Major strategic systems/business initiatives cannot be implemented without the movement and manipulation of information in new and complex ways. Re-engineering the way business is done often requires new information, applications and technology.

In this game, the I/S organization must have a solid track record in implementing systems, rapidly deploying innovative concepts, conducting farsighted analyses of new technologies, and building robust technology "platforms." Such platforms are often the basis upon which strategic applications are built. For instance, a worldwide engineering system evolved from a parts database, and a major banking product began as an internal financial control system.

In the companies where information technology has made a major contribution to corporate success, this "platform" phenomenon is not surprising. Many organizations would not attempt a major systems effort based on a highly uncertain payback.

The platform effect has several implications for major systems efforts. First, systems should be justified not only on their immediate benefits but also on their platform potential. Second, these systems should be built with their eventual use as a platform in mind. Third, companies should carefully examine existing systems for their platform potential.

As important as strong platforms is the ability to develop systems faster and at lower cost than the competition. A manufacturing and distribution company fended off a rival by building a better system and making better technology selections. And two financial services firms are able to bring new financial products and services to market faster because they can integrate information systems and critical data on products and customers better than the competition.

In the strategic systems arena, the I/S organization must be ready to play an often uncharacteristically aggressive and visible role. I/S must act as a catalyst, helping business people recognize the strategic potential of information technology. Broadly experienced I/S people often are in a position to look across functions, to step back and see linkages, synergies, and systems-based opportunities that business people do not.

For the I/S organization to be a full and active partner in these initiatives, it must have a deep understanding of the business and its requirements, so that it can build strategic systems that match the company's unique needs and market context, rather than imitate the strategic systems "successes" attributed to the competition.

NOTES

[1]PRISM research report, "A Hard Look at Competitive Systems," July 1988.

[2]For more on the market power issue, see John M. Thompson and Kirt Mead's March/April 1988 Indications, "Boost Your Market Power With Information Technology."

[3]John Thompson examines how an information technology initiative can start an arms race in his October 1987 Indications. "Winners and Losers in Channel Warfare."

[4]For more on the organizational requirements to implement strategic systems projects, see Adam D. Crescenzi's August 1987 Indications, "Implementing Strategic Information Systems."

PART TWO

The Bottom Line:
Payoffs from Information
Technology Investments

The increasing variety of IT applications is one of the most exciting and important developments in the American business community. The best way to illustrate this trend is through real-world examples. This section of the book is thus composed of articles illustrating innovative applications. The goal of these readings is to make the phrase "competitive use" meaningful through a series of short, thought-provoking articles.

One of the more important IT developments is the application of a broad spectrum of technologies that integrate computers with telecommunications. The first six readings in this section (Readings 10–15) illustrate the application of these technologies. The common theme among these six articles is that it is the *integration* of IT resources that enables firms to remove barriers of time and distance.

Reading 16, "McDonald's ISDN Troubled," is a reminder of the complexities that can arise in implementing large-scale IT applications. "Look Who Is Sabotaging CIM" (Reading 17) examines behavioral as well as technical factors underlying the successful use of IT resources to automate manufacturing processes.

The next two articles examine two technologies that hold special promise for business. Reading 18, "Top Drug Firms to Digitize Documentation," discusses image processing and its application in pharmaceutical firms. Expert systems are the focus of Reading 19, which describes the American Express Company's success in developing an expert system that automatically performs credit checks on credit-card purchases.

The increasing use of expert systems raises a number of interesting questions for today's managers. Reading 20, "Expert Systems and the Law," discusses the legal implications of delegating important decision-making tasks to machines.

The last three articles in this section show how work stations that enable effective information management and analysis can help business professionals to "work smarter." Reading 21, "The Battle for the Broker's Desk," illustrates how professionals in financial services firms are being supported by IT. Readings 22 and 23 demonstrate how IT resources can provide strategic information to a firm's senior executives.

10

FedEx: America's Warehouse

Charles von Simson

"The end of this century will be marked by fundamental industrial change," forecasts Jim Barksdale, chief operating officer of Federal Express. "In the same way that railroads changed industry at the turn of the last century, jet transportation will completely change distribution. Our systems will allow jet speeds to be matched with customer needs."

Barksdale's tight-lipped remarks give a visitor the sense that if the conversation lags he will simply stand and leave. He's not press shy. But his impatience is understandable. The information and tracking systems that drove FedEx to the top of the overnight courier heap are now driving the 15-year-old company into a new area — one with extraordinary potential to change the way American corporations do business. In the process, FedEx may realize growth that'll make its accomplishments in overnight mail look small.

Basically, FedEx seeks the title of "America's Warehouse." No longer will FedEx just whiz by to pick up packages. Using the Parts Bank distribution management system, FedEx's hubs become warehouses, storing parts until a corporation's customer calls for them. Think of the DC-10 as a flying warehouse for corporations encumbered with delivering material to customers in 50 states. Given this activity, maybe what adds to Barksdale's impatience is that people still ask, more than a year after Federal's ZapMail blunder, if he is worried about competition from fax machines. He's not. The fax was heralded as an overnight express killer. What few realize is that only about 30% of Federal's overnight business comes from letters. The balance of the volume is in package delivery.

FedEx's expertise lies in inventory management, both as a technology developer and a logistics guru. Now FedEx aims to transfer the shipping and routing expertise that routinely moves 800,000 packages through Memphis in four hours. The first taker: IBM. Sources say that Big Blue ships mainframe parts to Memphis. When the parts are needed in an emergency, they are routed by IBM through FedEx distribution management systems. FedEx pulls the parts and gets them to the customer overnight. That pulls IBM out of one aspect of the warehouse and distribution game. And it puts FedEx much deeper into IBM, taking over its operations, not just speeding its deliveries.

While neither IBM nor Federal will offer details on the parts distribution business, it's been the subject of industry scrutiny. Sources at rival companies say that Federal is handling time sensitive parts, such as mainframe components, that have to be shipped at a moment's notice to revive down systems, using the Federal Parts Bank system. If industry supposition is correct, the IBM contract is significant not only because of the sheer weight of Big Blue, but because of the sensitive responsibility it has entrusted to Federal. "We are a large distribution facility for IBM," says Chris Demos, one of the people most directly responsible for the success of the Cosmos system. "They would not be able to do these things for themselves."

"The old notions of distribution are disappearing," says Barksdale, the corners of his eyes narrowing as he speaks. "Good companies are becoming aware that the management of time is just as important as the management of money; they are able to react more quickly and capitalize on change." FedEx, he adds, plans to deliver faster reaction times.

Where Barksdale bridles under a reporter's questions, his partner, Ron Ponder, senior vice president for information systems, is expansive, and the challenge is not to keep him in his seat, but to keep up with the pace of his thinking. His office is populated by a number of model Federal jets, a constant reminder that his real business is not data processing. Federal's IS chief is the steward for the engines that will drive the company's changing course, and an integral player in strategic planning. "Traditionally, the reason to have warehouses is that you can't trust the distribution chain," says Ponder. "You need to know where things are. But with the right control, why can't an airplane be a warehouse? A lot of us feel that the concepts of JIT and time-based competition coincides directly with the direction of our company."

MANUFACTURING A SERVICE

As much as trucks and airplanes, the ability to deliver packages anywhere in the country overnight is based on the continual updating of handling and routing information. "You have to see service as a product," says one Federal technology manager. "Our systems are measuring and recording information about the manufacturing of service." The tracking of packages is as important to the production of Federal's service as process control is to a discrete manufacturer. In fact, the two are analogous. "If you can't measure it, you can't do it," the manager continues.

Big customers have FedEx terminals in their offices and can access the much-heralded Cosmos package tracking system. The Cosmos system absorbs information from Federal's remote tracking equipment and provides constant, "custodial" information about the whereabouts of packages. Those terminals are a trojan horse, which enables FedEx to begin to supply what it calls "logistics management." "We will go upstream with customer terminals, and handle more logistics," says Barksdale. By upstream, he means deeper into the company.

FedEx's strategy is to take existing shipping terminals, install greater functionality, and string them into a network. "Most of our customer workstations today are standalone," says Ponder, "but we are moving. The move from PCs networked together to inventory management is not a long way to walk."

MATURING MARKET

Federal's evolving focus is partly a result of the changing low end of the air-express market, the overnight delivery of letters. The willingness of smaller couriers such as Airborne Freight to offer slashed prices to large accounts has gained them several large customers, including IBM. At the same time, fax has been shrinking FedEx's document delivery volume. "Seventy percent of our business is boxes," says Barksdale. "Fax will not hurt our growth rate. Letters are not Federal Express's most important business."

But the relentless price war has cut Federal's operating profit margin from 16.9% of revenue in fiscal 1981 to around 11% last year. These and other pressures made Federal strategists realize that the market was maturing and that the company did not enjoy the insurmountable technical advantages that it had in its early years. It was time to look to a new market. "Three-to-five years ago it became obvious where the market was going," says Ponder. "Growth rates aren't the same forever." The competition was going to school on Federal's tracking systems, and Ponder readily acknowledges that technology can always be emulated. "Everyone gets better," he says. "The next step is obvious—try to build systems to add value. The last three-to-five years have seen us add layer upon layer of functionality to Cosmos."

Different interpretations of the same question speak reams about the partnership between Ponder and Barksdale. "The market is not maturing; it is running at a growth rate in terms of pieces that is unprecedented," chafes Barksdale. "We will add the 1982 volume of Federal Express this year." Taking pure numbers of pieces handled, rather than a percentage of the existing market, growth in the air express industry is moving at an accelerated rate. Barksdale is addressing the role of systems from the point of view of managing expanded capacity rather than product differentiation.

Certainly Barksdale's view is an important part of the story. Federal's system acted as a sponge for demand throughout the booming early 1980s. Without the technical infrastructure, the company wouldn't have been able to handle the mushrooming volume of pickup requests. In 1981, Federal was a $400 million company, as was its largest competitor, UPS's air express operation. Federal closed the last fiscal year at $3.2 billion, with UPS collecting an estimated $1.7 billion from overnight delivery.

EXECUTIVE PARTNERS

Barksdale's fluency in the issues surrounding technology management is not simply a sharp boss parroting the insights of a manager. Ron Ponder succeeded Barksdale in Federal's top technology seat in 1982, and as a result the two share a perspective on the use and value of information that creates unique opportunities, and demands, for each. "The reason we have come so far is that I have a boss who understands technology," says Ponder. "There is no room for bluffing; it makes my job doubly difficult."

A hint of a smile crosses Jim Barksdale's face at the mention of Ponder's complaint. "Don't let Dr. Ponder give you the impression that I'm too tough on him," Barksdale says, his smile widening. In truth, Ponder's stature in the organization is second only to that of Barksdale and Federal's founder and chief executive officer, Fred Smith. His input is clearly central to the company's strategic direction. "Fred Smith looks over the hills," says Barksdale, "and Ponder and I take them. When we get there, Smith better be right."

That sort of profile leads to an obvious question: Is chief technical officer enough for Ron Ponder? He ducks the question, instead talking about the rising fortunes of corporate MIS directors. "If you look at where the world is going, it is becoming more dependent on logistics management," he says. "That's all the world is, beside cost and quality. That is based on information systems. One might sense that the requirements of corporate leadership are going to need to include the requirements of MIS leaders."

Barksdale concurs. "People outside systems don't understand what a marvelous crow's nest it is. In IS you touch all systems, know about how they work," he says. "People in that background understand the organization; they gain a good detailed knowledge of how things work."

THE COMPETITION

Federal is not alone in the emerging market. Airborne Freight's Stock Exchange system for storing and moving time-sensitive merchandise will not highlight technology—where many industry observers acknowledge Federal has a clear lead—but will capitalize on their rural Ohio hub. "We're out in the middle of nowhere," says Jeanne Gwazdouskas, Airborne's director of customer automation. "We can provide customers with a range of distribution options based at our hub." Gwazdouskas points out that since Airborne runs its own airport, it has many more options for customizing customer shipping facilities. This increases warehousing options.

Airborne's approach will be closely watched by critics who claim that Federal's custodial tracking capability is lost on customers who simply want their packages to arrive overnight. While Airborne is an able technology company, they lack the level of systems integration that allows Federal's Cosmos to anticipate routing bottlenecks and assorted distribution problems, a capacity that Federal calls "pro-active customer service."

Airborne may well rely on the aggressive pricing that was successful in luring IBM away from Federal Express in the overnight letter business. Airborne slashed rates (many claim the company took a loss on IBM) to get their business at the low end, but IBM has stayed with Federal in the more sensitive parts-distribution portion of an increasingly segmented air express market. While part of the situation has to do with the timing of bids, IBM must be comfortable with Federal's formidable tracking prowess.

It is still too early to tell whether Barksdale and Ponder can sell their view of the future to a corporate America still struggling with the barcode reader. It is, however, certain that as industry adopts such technologies as electronic data interchange and computer-integrated manufacturing, it will begin to demand that goods flow as quickly as information. It is an awakening that Federal Express is banking on.

And their technological muscle will make it very difficult for their competitors to follow. "We're expanding our focus as much as we can," says Ponder. "The ultimate aim is that we are everyone's warehouse."

11   *In the Chips*

Jon Pepper

Don't try to tell the folks at Frito-Lay that a bag of chips is just small potatoes. All those Doritos, Ruffles, Lay's and other snack foods the company produces add up to some staggering numbers. Frito uses one percent of the annual U.S. potato crop and four percent of the corn, and it contributes about 38 percent of the profit of parent company Pepsico—an $11.5 billion corporation.

So when the people at Frito-Lay Inc. in Dallas began to think about equipping their route sales staff with hand-held computers and making some major changes in the way the company gathered data on product sales, the project turned into an effort of enormous proportions. It not only involved the task of computerizing 10,000 salespeople; the corporate database had to be modified to take advantage of the greater flexibility made possible by the hand-held units as well.

To the casual observer, Frito-Lay might not appear to be the type of company that would be heavily vested in technology. But Charles Feld, vice president of management services, explained that some compelling reasons made the company move in that direction. "To the extent that technology gives you productivity in terms of cost margins, we have put major systems in place that are very pinpointed to doing more with less for manufacturing and distribution," said Feld. "And that has given us a direct impact on the marketplace."

The company found that paper simply wasn't flexible enough to "allow us to react to changing market conditions," Feld said.

Feld is responsible for the development, processing and function of the company's considerable computer network. He was intimately involved in the hand-held computer project, which serves as both an object lesson in successfully implementing technology and a demonstration of how the use of IT in a traditionally "non-technology" business can pay big dividends.

Feld referred to the 10,000 route salespeople who service Frito-Lay's tens of thousands of accounts as "pretty much the lifeblood of the company." Consequently,

Helping Hands

Hand-held Computers Have Changed the Way Frito-Lay Sales Staff Serves Accounts

Under Frito-Lay's old account-management system, salespeople had to fill out masses of pricing forms, calculate special promotions and sales, and do all the math by hand. Hand-held computers now do all of that work.

With the units now in the hands of Frito-Lay's roughly 10,000 route salespeople, the job now entails going into a store and calling up the customer account, which appears on a small liquid crystal display. Then the salesperson enters numerical quantities for product names that appear on the LCD screen in the order they are racked (the standard arrangement of Frito products on store shelves) — so many bags of this item delivered, so many coming back, and so forth.

The salesperson then goes to the truck, puts the hand-held into a cradle in a printer, and prints out a physical sales ticket. The hand-held performs all the calculations, which take account of sales tax, special promotions and discounts. This system also benefits the store manager, who now only needs to check the quantity of items coming in. The supply link between the salespeople and their accounts is thus greatly simplified.

The other half of the process is the link between salespeople and Frito-Lay headquarters. Every day, salespeople put their hand-helds in communications cradles at the distribution centers (or in their homes, if they happen to be on rural routes). Data from the hand-helds is telecommunicated to an IBM 8100 at the area distribution center. That information is then uploaded to the IBM mainframe in Dallas. At the same time, all new pricing and promotion information and any changes to the individual accounts are down-loaded to the hand-helds.

The benefits are obvious. The salesperson has more time to devote to sales and service activities and also has consistently accurate sales tickets. Frito-Lay collects precise information on a daily basis as to what products are selling in which regions of the country. And with most of the machines now carrying 552K bytes of memory, salespeople can wait as long as five days between transmissions in the event of some problem.

---

anything that makes them more productive tends to reflect pretty directly on the bottom line. The hand-held computer project is unique, according to Feld, in that it "is an application . . . that really puts the technology in the hands of the people who are making the business run — not the people who are keeping score."

The project was fueled by numerous internal and external pressures and events. These included an expanding product line, slowed growth of Frito-Lay's profit margins, increasing competitive pressures and, ultimately, management's need to find a better way to monitor product movement and control costs.

According to Feld, as far back as the late 1960s the company felt the need to deal more effectively with the number of transactions it had — which at that time included about 5,000 route salespeople selling about 30 or 40 different products. "Even though they may have been 25-cent items, you have to sell a lot to make money, and we needed to monitor those transactions," he said.

Frito-Lay began keypunching the handwritten sales tickets and data from the sales force, but as the number of salespeople and products grew, "there wouldn't be enough keypunch operators you could hire to handle the billing," explained Feld.

Although Frito-Lay looked at putting mobile devices in the trucks at that time, the technology simply wasn't ready yet. So the company settled on OCR – optical character reader – technology in the mid-1970s, said Feld. The sales staff would fill out forms that would be mailed to headquarters in Dallas and scanned using the OCR system. This worked fine until the number of line items began to increase and it became more difficult to fit everything on the forms. "Plus, the cycle to print up forms takes time, and [as we began to have] different prices in different parts of the country, it just looked like it was getting too complex," Feld said.

Hand-held technology began to appear at the time, but it was too expensive and didn't offer the storage that Frito-Lay needed. They continued to work with the OCR system, but the salespeople were beginning to lose patience. "It's not just that they spent a significant amount of time doing paperwork," Feld said. "But . . . when you are standing in a truck in Minnesota and it's 20 below zero outside, it gets a little more difficult to get the marks in the right place on the OCR forms."

Then, in the early 1980s (with the company's product line growing increasingly complex), the appearance of the desktop computer created a breakthrough that rippled down to the hand-helds. "The PC was the real turning point," said Feld. "There was similar technology involved in terms of miniaturization, and we began to see some real leverage in terms of [lowered] prices." As a result, Frito-Lay began an active prototyping process, putting the units out on a portion of the routes to learn how the sales staff could use them and how the store managers would respond.

The project was also driven by an additional factor. "IBM stopped making [OCR] scanners," said Feld, "and we couldn't buy another one if we needed it, so we knew that we had to do something."

Feld's department was the continuity link that held the project together over its long duration. "Going back to 1975, we were simply looking for better ways to solve the data-capture problem," explained Feld. "However, at that time it wasn't particularly high on the list for the sales department."

That changed in the '80s as Frito-Lay's sales managers began to realize how the technology could help boost productivity. And in 1982–'83, with a growing need for more detailed information on products, the marketing department got involved.

Selling the project to top management was difficult mainly because it would require a substantial investment. "You either make this investment or build a plant or do something else," said Feld, "and this had to compete with some fairly big issues – they didn't just approve this because they liked me."

However, the years of prototyping had taught Feld a lot about actual costs and benefits, the sales staff's acceptance of the technology, the mean time between failure rate (MTBF) of the hand-held units, and retail customers' acceptance – all of which information was valuable both in securing corporate approval and in the implementation and training processes.

Frito-Lay wrote its own hardware specs and sent them out to a number of major vendors, including IBM, Hewlett-Packard, Norand and Fujitsu—everyone that Feld considered could possibly make the hand-held computers.

While all the vendors that offered bids came in at about the same price with basically the same functions, Fujitsu led the pack because its proposal solved two MTBF issues. First, Fujitsu created a rubberized keyboard that was resistant to contamination. Second, it created an optical connector—an infrared light-beam connection equivalent to a pin connector—that lasted longer than pin connectors for printer or battery charger hookups.

According to Feld, those two solutions drove the MTBF rate up from one year to over three years—a significant difference. "With 10,000 hand-helds, 10,000 printers, 10,000 battery packs and so on, if everything only breaks once a year you have 30,000 or 40,000 repairs," said Feld. "It's really pretty phenomenal when you think about all those machines out in a truck breaking only once a year—and that wasn't good enough for us."

The project was justified to management largely on the basis that it would cost no more than continuing with the OCR system. The straight-up justification did not count the benefits of the new system. But the benefits, it turned out, were manifold.

While Feld refused to disclose the overall cost of the project, the company's sales department estimates savings for Frito-Lay are on the order of $20 million a year. With the hand-helds freeing up three to five hours a week of a route salesperson's time, sales personnel have more opportunities to look for new accounts or to better service existing ones.

In order to make a smooth interface with Frito-Lay's main computer system, Feld said that his group totally re-examined its database setup. "We took this all the way back into our accounting, manufacturing and distribution systems, so that it is very well connected," he said. For example, the product code data is all held in one database, which feeds information to the hand-helds and supplies data to the manufacturing and accounting divisions. "So if we want to change the price of a product in a certain part of the country," he said, "we change it in one database and it flows through everything else."

To accommodate this flexibility, every system in the company that carried product code had to be modified because the product codes grew from six to eleven digits to handle the added intelligence needed. "It was really massive in terms of integration," Feld said, "but it gives us some very good control."

As an example of that control, he explained that if the company wants to run a regional promotion, the promotional data is put into one database, from which it flows into the hand-helds for the appropriate part of the country. "Each hand-held can have its own footprint [unique identity code] so that we are absolutely disconnected from having to print things up," he said.

Frito-Lay is working with trade associations to try to build an electronic connection between hand-helds and major store systems in order to eliminate paper completely. However, Feld said, "it will take years to get [the technology] to a full working level."

One of Feld's major concerns in implementing the new computers was people- rather than technology-based. He had worried that rolling out the computers to the sales force and handling the training and support needs would be difficult. "These are salespeople, not technical people," said Feld. "They are in sales because they like to sell products, and we wanted to put a very disciplined type of technology into the hands of people with a different goal in life than to make the numbers come out right."

As it turned out, Feld's fears were largely unfounded. Acceptance on the part of the sales force was "phenomenal," he said.

A tutorial that resided on the hand-held was developed to lead the new user through all of the principal functions, and hands-on training was given at Frito-Lay's 210 distribution centers. A support phone line in Dallas is manned around the clock to help hand-held users with procedural matters as well as hardware and software problems.

According to Feld, all the training and support was overkill. For one thing, he said, "there was so much good feeling about [the hand-helds] that we didn't have to overcome any negative feeling. And as the word spread during the rollout, route salesmen heard that it was easy to use and fun.

"It keeps their inventory straight, it keeps their books, and they don't have to sit down at the end of the day and spend an hour doing their reconciliation," Feld said. "It really takes a lot of the stress out of the job."

He added that from his viewpoint, the biggest success of the entire project was not the software or hardware, but the acceptance on the part of the sales force. "It's not only a productivity boost; it's a morale boost for them. It's a quality-of-life boost — there's really no bad news anywhere," said Feld.

In fact, he added, the Frito-Lay project is the only implementation of technology he knows about where there is no bad news at all. The stores are more comfortable with the new professionalism on the part of the sales force, and the sales force is a lot happier in general. "And there's nothing wrong with having 10,000 people who like their jobs."

In some ways, the rollout of the hand-held computers marks the end of a certain direction in terms of information management at Frito-Lay. Feld said that in a general sense, they have pretty much closed the loop now on transaction processing.

"We know pretty much what is going on with every bag moving through every store, and [we] have similar kinds of systems for our manufacturing and distribution side so we can follow the sequence from raw material through [to] the store shelf," he said. "We are really pretty well tied together now and automated."

The focus for the next few years will be on developing a decision-support system, Feld said. "Now that we have the data, how can we get it into a presentable form so that people at every level can take action on it: that's our challenge." The company is working on a prototype DB2 database on its IBM mainframes to get feedback from managers on which data they need and how they want it presented. "I don't see that as being a long, hard pull," said Feld. However, the technology to deliver complex data is just emerging. "With the 386s, the PCs are really just coming into their own," he said, "and we have a lot of connecting up to do, so we are really architecting our own environment there."

Feld sees technology as being a balance between productivity and offensive flexibility. He cited three factors that he believes place Frito-Lay at about a seven on a scale of technology advancement—"if you rate a company like American Airlines probably being a 10"—even though technology is clearly not the main engine of Frito-Lay.

First, the company's tremendous number of transactions have to be accounted for at different stages of the product cycle. Second, the perishability of its products demands accuracy and speed in ordering and distribution. "You have only a certain number of days, and if you make too many of a certain size bag, you have to throw it away."

Finally, the company needs technology to deal with complexity. "We have different manufacturing and distribution systems and different approaches to regional preferences for products—it's not just one set of national products," he said.

The role of the data center has been to better position the company in the market. The hand-helds are a prime example of the company's success in using technology to achieve a competitive edge. "If we weren't this far along, we either wouldn't be able to do the business we do, or we couldn't execute it as well," said Feld. "There would be a lot more cases where we just couldn't get the products to the right place at the right time—and it would be a lot harder to be doing as well as we are without technology."

12

Carriers Land Profits by Empowering DP Units

Elisabeth Horwitt

Airline carriers are squeezing their information systems for all they're worth.

Industry leaders have discovered they can leverage their systems to raise the bottom line in two important ways. They can turn a profit from reselling internally developed software and services, which eventually evens out the cyclical earnings of air transportation.

They can also improve the effectiveness of internal operations and support value-added services that generate more business.

As a result, airlines are counting on their computer systems more than ever to help them stay aloft in today's turbulent, deregulated market.

"The purchase of Eastern Airlines and its information services subsidiary System One was a crucial part of [Chairman and Chief Executive Officer] Frank Lorenzo's strategy" for growth and for developing products that differentiate Texas Air from its competitors, says David Hultsman, staff vice-president of technology planning for System One Corp., now Texas Air's information processing subsidiary.

Texas Air effectively tripled the MIPS power of its major data processing facility and turned itself into a third-party networking provider in order to ensure virtually unlimited bandwidth for networking applications in the past year, Hultsman says.

That airline company is not the only carrier with large MIS and communications expenditures.

Airlines increased their communications budgets an average of 26.2% from 1986 to 1987 — the largest jump by any industry, according to a recent survey by the International Communications Association.

"Carriers are right up there with insurance companies as far as MIS outlay goes," says William Maybaum, a vice-president at DMW Group, Inc., an Ann Arbor, Mich., consulting firm. "All the major airlines are building systems to meet upcoming requirements and to supply services, and it's all roll-your-own code."

Airlines have moved in three directions to accommodate today's market pressures:

- Travel reservation systems. Ever since United Airlines and American Airlines developed their reservation systems in the late 1970s, carriers have been using computer systems to lure customers away from the competitors.
- Independent MIS subsidiaries. Major airlines have broken their DP departments into separate subsidiaries that are expected to be profitable in their own right.
- Competitive in-house operations for customer service. Even the traditional DP role of supporting in-house operations has taken on a competitive edge, with carriers racing with each other to recover from bad press on their customer service and safety records.

But is the expense of these new systems and networks worth the price?

In a competitive market such as this one—yes. That is, if the development of a new product allows a carrier to recoup development or installation costs through resale, like the Texas Air network, or bring in additional business and profits, like many of the airline reservation systems currently in use.

And the profits can be significant. According to an American Airlines spokesman, operating earnings for its Sabre reservation system were $107 million in 1987. Operating earnings for AMR Corp., American's parent company, according to a preliminary unaudited report, were $196.4 million. That means Sabre's revenue was 54% of total company revenue.

THE KEY TO SERVICE

Computer systems have spearheaded campaigns by Texas Air and its rivals to restore customer confidence in airline safety and service levels.

"We want people to see Continental and Eastern as the most reliable systems going in terms of having baggage go to the right place and finding your seat assigned when you get on a flight," System One's Hultsman says.

"It would be a real competitive advantage to provide this in a shorter time frame than anyone else," he adds.

Airline spokesmen admit that deregulation and the spate of mergers that followed have made it increasingly difficult for computer systems to track and coordinate various key operational areas.

American, for instance, has had to steadily upgrade its IBM mainframe capacity, beginning in the late 1970s, "to get us over the deregulation hump," says Joseph Selman, a senior representative for corporate communications at AMR.

"The big impact [to American's systems] came a couple of years back, when you had volatile fares and a vast number of airlines flying to places they never had before," Selman says.

Today, American's Sabre system handles as many as 1.5 million fare changes overnight "when a price war kicks off," Selman adds.

Recently formed conglomerates, like Texas Air, Northwest Airlines-Piedmont Aviation and Delta-Western, are all still in the process of merging their MIS operations.

For example, Texas Air has had to set up high-speed communications links between Continental Airlines and Eastern data centers to keep track of "flights in the air, on the ground, preparation for new flights — it's a very complex situation," Hultsman says.

"We've had to link Data General, Unisys and IBM computers and integrate [acquired subsidiaries] old applications into the system, since we don't have the time to develop new ones," he adds.

AIRPORT OF THE FUTURE

Both Texas Air and United hope to bring about quick, visible improvements to customer services by revamping airport terminal systems that customers deal with directly.

United, for example, has spent 680,000 man-hours converting its new terminal at Chicago's O'Hare Airport into "a just-in-time facility," interconnecting various departments and hosts "so that a lot of things happen automatically now," says Richard Pemberton, senior technical support design analyst for United's data processing subsidiary, Covia Corp. [CW, Jan. 18].

Formerly, one set of terminals accessed Apollo, United's IBM-based reservation system; a second set provided links to the airline's Univac-based flight operations and crew management system.

Today, United's terminal and public information operations at O'Hare are handled on IBM Personal System/2 Model 50s linked over an IBM Token-Ring network.

A remote gateway ties the PS/2s to United's reservation and operations systems. Users can hot-key between the two systems, or they can call both up at once via a Microsoft Corp. Windows interface.

The ability to interact in real time with different operational areas has significantly increased operators' ability to juggle airport resources effectively and, in turn, has increased the number of flights the terminal can safely and efficiently take on, Pemberton notes.

A year and a half ago, the terminal handled 330 to 350 flights a day; today, it manages more than 400 flights.

Texas Air is prototyping an airport terminal system in Houston that would distribute as much functionality as possible, steering it away from the carrier's centralized computing facility, Hultsman says.

For example, customer services such as baggage handling, boarding pass distribution, charge account handling and some gate assignment operations at Texas Air would be handled on Tandem Computers, Inc. systems at individual airport terminals.

The Tandem computers would use IBM's Systems Network Architecture protocols in order to communicate back to the data center's IBM host machines for basic operations, such as flight coordination.

The fault-tolerant computers are one component of System One's drive for more reliable customer service, Hultsman says.

The company also plans to set up a fault-tolerant packet-switched network with redundant high-speed lines, which would ensure reliable communications among the firm's various carriers and data processing facilities.

STRAYING OFF RESERVATION

The travel reservation service market is another focal point for carriers' strategic deployment of computer systems.

American and United, which pioneered such systems in the late 1970s, faced no serious challenge to their dominance until the last year or so.

What changed the market from a two-horse race into a free-for-all was the realization by all major carriers of how large a return reservation services offer, says Peter Zegan, a professor of MIS at Miami's Florida International University and a consultant for several airlines.

American, for example, reportedly receives $1.70 for every transaction on its reservation system and gets about 20% more business from agencies that use Sabre than from those that do not, Zegan says.

Given that travel agencies generate approximately 70% of all airline ticket sales, according to Zegan, it is not surprising that American and United's market share is being threatened by Texas Air, Delta and a partnership consisting of Transworld Airlines and Northwest.

The combatants seek to gain and keep customers by enhancing their reservation systems to be more reliable and easy to use and by introducing turnkey systems that are designed to make travel agents' jobs easier.

A large portion of carriers' telecommunications outlays have gone into faster, more reliable pipelines to deliver their services to the various travel agencies.

System One recently installed a high-speed pipeline between Continental and Eastern data centers, enabling agents to make and confirm reservations without having to log off one system and on to another.

Most of the major competitors now offer to replace an agent's IBM 3270 terminal with a PS/2 workstation, which, in addition to calling up reservation data on the airline's host, can practically perform travel agents' jobs for them.

American's Sabreworks, for example, provides word processing, data base and spreadsheet capabilities as well as a fill-in-the-blanks menu to guide inexperienced agents through the reservation making process.

United's Focal point is said to provide both memos and an English-like command structure for agents intimidated by the complex code typically used to imput reservations.

The up-front development and installation costs of such systems can be high. When American sued Delta and Texas Air recently for allegedly persuading agencies to break their five-year contracts with Sabre, one of its principal complaints was of having to write off the installation, training and amortized development costs of turncoat agencies' PS/2-based systems, AMR's Selman says.

Carriers harbor few doubts that the potential paybacks are well worth the up-front costs and risks, however. Delta's quick pickup of 91 agencies in less than six months after introducing Deltastar exemplifies the return of such systems.

The PS/2-based systems offer another potential return, according to United's Pemberton. By providing agents with local intelligence, the systems cut back on the amount of computing power and communications bandwidth that the carrier must allocate to agency services.

Under "the old dumb-terminal mode," he says, the carrier's mainframes kept overloading as use of its reservation service grew.

Travel reservation systems are only one of a growing number of products and facilities that carriers are reselling to other companies — both for profit and as a way of boosting market share.

TAKING SYSTEMS TO MARKET

Major carriers are starting to look at their DP centers as profitable in their own right, according to DMW Group's Maybaum. AMR, for example, includes a travel services group that sells, among other things, a turnkey reservation system to hotels.

Former United/Allegis Corp. Chairman Richard Ferris set up Covia approximately a year ago to support both in-house operations and planned expansion into the travel services business, Selman says.

For several years now, major carriers have resold internally developed software and excess computing resources.

"Just about everything developed for Continental or Eastern is being resold to other airlines; the Continental reservation system does reservations for 35 to 40 other airlines," System One's Hultsman says.

"It's a small incremental cost to add another airline to your system," Florida International's Zegan says.

Demand for predeveloped maintenance, flight tracking, reservation and crew management computer systems is high among small airlines that cannot afford in-house software development costs — which are about the same for a small or large carrier, he adds.

The ability to recoup development or installation costs through resale has allowed some carriers' DP subsidiaries to undertake ambitious projects that ultimately win the carrier a bigger piece of the market pie.

In January, for example, System One purchased 10,000 route miles of fiber-optic cable, which supports 45M-bit/sec. voice/data transmission, from Lightnet and Williams Telecommunications Group.

The network will serve at least three purposes. First, it will support faster and more reliable communications between various Texas Air subsidiaries and internal operations, according to Hultsman.

Second, it will bring in profit: System One has become a telecommunications carrier with the right to sell voice/data transmission services to other businesses. And third, the network's "virtually unlimited bandwidth," coupled with major upgrades in distributed computing power, will give System One the leverage to quickly develop new applications and products that will "differentiate us from other carriers in a marketplace that is changing at the speed of light," Hultsman says.

He adds, "I agree with people who have been saying that deregulation would have been impossible without the technology to support it."

13

EDI: Putting the Muscle in Commerce and Industry

Willie Schatz

Getting in shape has become a cause célèbre across America. Adherents of this movement to tone up can be found practicing their discipline in homes, schools, dozens of competing health club chains, even in offices. This movement now seems to have spread into corporate management philosophy; a new high-tech rigor called electronic data interchange is building up many corporations and changing the way they do business.

EDI—the direct computer-to-computer exchange of standard business documents such as invoices, bills of lading, and purchase orders—holds out the promise of streamlined daily business routines. As a result, proponents claim, companies can save time and money.

"Doing business without EDI will soon be like trying to do business without the telephone," Edward E. Lucente, IBM vp and group executive in the U.S. marketing and services group, told attendees at the annual meeting of the Electronic Data Interchange Association (EDIA). "No EDI, no business."

According to Lucente, IBM's 37 worldwide plants will be doing EDI with over 2,000 of the company's largest suppliers by 1991. That represents 80% of Big Blue's production, which is a rather significant slice of the entire computer industry's output. Lucente says IBM believes that implementing EDI will save it $60 million over the next five years.

The cost savings and the speed of doing business are just two selling points that customers are hearing from suppliers. Sometimes, the message comes through loud and clear, as in General Motors' 1984 letter that gave its suppliers until 1987 to get on-line with EDI or go off-line with GM. More often, a company that has implemented EDI uses the carrot of more orders or the stick of less orders to convince a doubter that paper is out and EDI is in.

If the potential loss of business to a competitor isn't enough reason for a company to implement EDI, a quick glance at the numbers should settle the issue. Input

Inc., Mountain View, Calif., puts EDI's 1987 domestic market volume between $75 million and $90 million for network/processing services, software, and professional services. Aprés ça, le déluge: the consulting firm predicts a $1.3 billion domestic market by 1991.

EDI USER TOTAL EXPECTED TO JUMP 200%

On the international front, Input expects U.S. user expenditures for EDI network and processing services to rise to $220 million in 1992 from $2.5 million this year, for an average annual growth rate of 147%. Link Resources Corp., in New York, predicts the number of U.S. EDI user companies will leap to 10,500 by 1991 from the current 3,500.

We may not be talking megabucks here, but it's not chopped liver either. And there's money to be made throughout the EDI spectrum. As users kiss off traditional business practices, they'll save countless employee hours and several forests of paper. That may not translate into a quantifiable asset on the balance sheet, but it won't take very long for the positive productivity effects to be noticed. Companies can implement EDI in one of two ways, either through their own efforts or with the aid of a third-party provider (see "Should You Sign Up With a Third-Party Provider?").

CUSTOMER PRESSURE DRIVING INTEREST

"Breaking down the resistance to EDI is a function of the bottom line. EDI has become mandatory," says Dave Pond, manager of REDinet Services. REDinet is Control Data's entry in the EDI third-party provider sweepstakes. Other major systems include IBM's Information Systems Network, St. Petersburg, Fla.; EDI*Net from McDonnell Douglas, St. Louis; EDI*Express, of GE Information Services, Rockville, Md.; and Telenet Electronic Data Interchange from Telenet, Reston, Va.

"Customer pressure is creating the conversions to EDI," Pond explains. "The threat of losing business is really convincing companies that are hesitating."

"There's been a fundamental shift in attitudes in the last 12 months," says Steve Korn, GE's manager of EDI product marketing. "EDI is no longer just 'nice to have.' It's a 'must have.' Companies are no longer running pilot projects where they're trying EDI to see if it works and being very cautious about spending money for its implementation. EDI is no longer an option in corporate America.

"So the question now is not whether to do EDI," Korn concludes, "but how and when."

The "when" piece is a lock: yesterday if possible, today for sure. The "how" issue is tougher. If a company decides on Wednesday that it's going to implement EDI and expects to have the deal go down by Monday morning, then a hard rain's a-gonna fall. EDI is not an overnight panacea for all that ails the company's business procedures. Remember back to when you put that pc on your desk and assumed all your problems were history, then discovered to your horror that you actually had to put the disks in and program them? EDI works the same way.

"The whole problem is integrating the EDI software into the internal dp system," Pond explains. "You've got to revamp the in-house system to allow it to talk to an outside system. That requires a considerable mental leap that, until recently, businesses have been reluctant to take."

"People used to think that buying EDI was like buying a tv set," says Dick Norris, the practice leader for logistics at Arthur D. Little (ADL), Cambridge, Mass. Asked by the grocery industry in 1980 to study the feasibility of doing business electronically, Norris concluded that the grocers would save $333 million a year if only half of them implemented EDI. When that info hit the street, EDI took off.

"Now I think they know it's not something that you go and do and be done with," Norris says. "In the last few years, people have found that EDI's going to happen, it's inevitable, and it's something they're going to have to learn to do."

Most companies want to retain as much control as possible over any alteration to their in-house system, but they'll gladly have the EDI provider do the teaching. You don't learn EDI just by pulling an all-nighter. So, very few users have contracted the "Not Invented Here" disease. If EDI is to be implemented correctly, prospective users can expect to devote as much as a year in planning for its installation. And finally having reached that decision, there's no point in blowing the whole deal by keeping it to yourself.

BALL CORP.'S LONG INVESTIGATION

Take Ball Corp., for example. In 1987, when the consumer products division of the Columbus, Ind.-based, $1 billion manufacturer of containers and packaging materials began receiving monthly phone calls from its customers about using electronic purchase orders and invoices, the division thought it prudent to check it out.

A poll of the consumer products division's other customers found that 17 of the top 20 were using EDI. When other Ball divisions expressed interest in implementing it in the near future, that clinched the decision for the consumer products division to get started with EDI. The only question left was how to get EDI on-line.

"If a customer is transmitting electronically, it's an obvious benefit to us if we can do the same," says Cindy Jackson, a communications specialist for Ball. "I wouldn't say the consumer products customer gave us an ultimatum, but it made its position very clear. As a supplier, when your customer says it's doing EDI and would like you to do it, it's an added incentive. So, when consumer products came to us and asked us to look into EDI, it wasn't too hard to convince us to go EDI."

It wasn't too easy picking a company to implement EDI, though. Ball spent all of last year checking out third-party vendors before committing to Telenet. But signing on the dotted line in December doesn't guarantee implementation in January. There are weekly tests of demo tapes to make sure that everything's cool with Ball's 3083. The company hoped to be running in real time on March 1.

Even those companies that want to go their own way eventually decide to seek help. In mid-1984, when Muncie, Ind.-based Cummins Engine Co., the world's largest independent supplier of diesel engines, wanted to link up with its suppliers, it began on its own. It took six months before Cummins could meet with its top 50 suppliers. Nine months later, it had 25 suppliers on-line.

"That wasn't close to enough," says Dave Slimko, Cummins' manager of supply administration. "We weren't getting a whole lot of supplier pressure, but we could see that electronic linking was starting to be seeded into American business. We knew we didn't have the capability to implement EDI ourselves, so five of us went through six third-party presentations. We decided at the end of '85 that we would go with either GE or CDC. We picked CDC because we needed somebody to work for us, and we weren't sure GE would do that. In retrospect, the decision was as correct as could be."

The first CDC link occurred on Jan. 5, 1986. By the end of the year, there were 125 suppliers on-line at 225 locations. A year later, there were about 350 world-wide suppliers on the EDI line. Cummins has also linked its U.K. plants with their U.S. suppliers.

The company is so sold on EDI that it presents full-day seminars to suppliers. Cummins uses the sessions to outline its EDI expectations, one of which is that suppliers will get on board in 90 days. The quid pro quo is that Cummins will pay all the supplier's communications costs. "We don't give them ultimatums," Slimko says. "We just give them no reason not to get on with EDI." Two major suppliers, which Cummins declines to identify, continue to hold out, but the company hasn't stopped doing business with them.

Cummins hasn't forgotten the customer side. It trades electronically with only 10 customers, but those companies represent 90% of Cummins' volume. The partners use EDI for electronic funds transfer and evaluation receipt settlement, by which a company pays for materials received without an invoice.

"I think the feeling is that if you implement EDI, it solves all your upstream problems," Slimko says. "It doesn't. EDI is a lot of work and a lot of headaches. Change is very difficult for some people, which is why it sometimes takes much longer than it should to implement EDI. If a company thinks everything is fine, it's very hard to convince it to change its method of doing business.

"That's really what we're talking about. It's a new way to do business. We've only been doing it three years. But that makes me feel like an old-timer."

TRUCKING COMPANIES ARE PIONEERS

In that case, EDI practitioners at companies in the motor carrier industry must feel positively ancient. Members of that business segment have been committed to EDI for at least the last decade. The EDI concept was just beginning to see the light in those prehistoric times.

"We have had to try to sell the concept for the last 10 years," says Ken Jamison, manager of systems and programming for Yellow Freight Co., a major trucking company based in Overland Park, Kansas. Yellow Freight is one of about 60 major LTL companies with EDI capability (LTL is "less than truckload," meaning the carrier transports small shipments from many shippers). Those companies electronically trade freight bill and shipment status information and accept bills of lading from a shipper.

"Acceptance was very slow in the beginning," says Jamison, who's also the chairman of the American Trucking Association's EDI Task Group. "People saw EDI as a technical function that appeared to be significantly different from what they had done before. So they hesitated to spend money on what might be a pipe dream. But as EDI began to spread, the benefits were so great that everyone saw an opportunity for cost savings."

For those companies that seized the moment, we're talking megabucks. According to the *Journal of Petroleum Accounting,* 200 EDI users in the oil industry processed 7 million transactions in 1986 at a gross cash flow savings of $40 million. Not bad, even in an industry that doesn't want to know from millions. And that's droplets compared to what Arco, Amoco, Shell, and Exxon should save this year.

After running a pilot program last year using GE's EDI*Express, those companies will now perform joint interest billing electronically. What formerly consumed hours will now take minutes. Joint interest billing is the industry's method of allocating costs in a drilling consortium. Popular perception notwithstanding, no oil company drills its own wells. It's too expensive even for them. The lead partner in the consortium sends out monthly joint interest bills itemizing each partner's costs for that particular well. A lead partner – Amoco, for instance – usually spends 80 hours per week entering Shell's bills into its computer system.

Joint interest billing is "an economic nightmare," says Bill Cafiero, a senior EDI consultant for GE in Houston. "But EDI's going to change that. I think joint interest billing is an excellent example of how even the fiercest competitors are forced to have to trust each other to derive common economic benefits from EDI.

"It shows that EDI's not a fad. Competitive pressure won't allow it to disappear. It's here, and it's not going anywhere."

No lie. But seven years ago, not even a compulsive gambler would have put money on EDI sticking around. Most of the business community didn't know EDI existed.

Along came the ADL grocery industry study. Norris and his team analyzed the transaction requirements of the industry, evaluated alternative concepts, and compared the current costs of conventional intercompany processes with the potential that would result from going electronic. When the cost savings answer came out at a third of a billion dollars, companies trampled each other to get on the EDI bandwagon. The report also recommended that the companies use the standards developed by the Transportation Data Coordinating Committee (TDCC), a group of EDI users formed in 1968 (see "The Roots of EDI").

"The TDCC message format standard was specifically designed for the computer-to-computer exchange of routine information used in certain application areas in the transportation industry," the study found. "Because the scope is limited, the standard is easy to use and understand. Because the applications are varied, the standard includes an adequate variety of data typed for most business applications."

The grocery industry then signed up TDCC to help implement the Uniform Communication Standard, which governs intercompany computer-to-computer transmission of basic business applications.

"That report rescued the TDCC," Norris says. "It also really got EDI going. TDCC had the architecture for message syntax, but few places in the transportation industry were using it. Companies were losing patience at the lack of a standard. EDI acceptance was slowing down. But the grocery industry has so many customers that it had to bite the standards bullet."

Should You Sign Up with a Third-Party Provider?

EDI proponents hope that, someday, electronic data interchange will be as easy as dropping a letter in the corner mailbox. Until that day comes, however, the implementation of EDI will require at least a few more steps.

One possible step in the right direction might be along the third-party service route. There are 11 third-party providers out there trying their damnedest to convince users that their service will lead to EDI's promised land.

Why go with a third party? If your company is going one-on-one with a business partner, then you can probably handle EDI yourself. But if you're trading with many business partners, then it's a different ball game. Partners may have different communications protocols, line speeds, and hours of availability; the traders may have incompatible hardware or software.

Third-party providers also claim to have the experience to overcome problems and can help get your trading partners up much faster than your company ever could. The third parties also have the requisite backup hardware and communications equipment to get you up quickly when you go down.

According to Dave Pond, manager of REDinet Services, Control Data Corp.'s EDI network, most EDI networks provide standard mailbox services in which a user dials in and drops off a "mailbag." The network then distributes the enclosed documents—e.g., purchase order or invoice—to the trading partners' mailboxes.

The trading partners dial in to pick up the documents, usually the same day. Most networks also provide three reports: an audit of the user's most recent activity, a historical summary, and an open interchange, which tells the company what it has sent that hasn't yet been picked up.

There are several different methods of EDI network access, the better to suit a user's fancy. Users can go with async at several speeds; bisync 2780/3780 protocol; RJE connections; SNA capability; and X.25 availability. Most providers also offer international access, often through their private networks in other countries.

"There are six services users should look for in an EDI vendor," Pond says. "Reliability, capability to get the job done, reasonable costs, willingness and ability to interconnect (so that users don't have to worry about which network their trading partners use), value-added intangible services, and interest in the customer's EDI success."

In the end, EDI won't determine whether the business lives or dies. "You can do all the EDI work you possibly can and have the best EDI vendor in the world," says Doug Fisher, vp of marketing for Yellow Freight, a trucking company in Overland Park, Kansas. "But you're still selling your service. You're only selling EDI to the degree it helps your customers do better business. In our case, we're still selling where the rubber hits the road. If we don't deliver that, EDI won't matter."

As did each other industry segment. Trying to get a grocery company's computer to talk to one from an auto supply company was like trying to strike up a conversation between an Apple and a PC. Each group of companies or a single company within an industry had proprietary standards. There were no cross-industry purchase orders or invoices.

Enough already, cried the masses. Let us develop a common standard through which companies in different industry segments can communicate with one another.

SIXTY TRANSACTION SETS PLANNED

So they got together with the American National Standards Institute and thus was begat X12. That cross-industry, cross-functional standard has been a major factor in EDI's explosive growth in the past few years.

"There's been more awareness and acceptance of EDI in the last two years than in the first 2,000," Yellow Freight's Jamison says.

X12 expands the basic EDI architecture to accommodate general business documents, such as purchase orders and invoices. The X12 overseers develop transaction sets under which a purchase order is a purchase order is a purchase order. So far, X12 encompasses 20 transaction sets. When the standard is complete, there will be 60 transaction sets.

"There's no way the oil industry could have put joint interest billing on EDI without X12," GE's Cafiero contends. Before X12, there was no impetus to get people to do things the same way. Now there is.

"X12 has also eliminated the technical issue that made many people reluctant to commit resources to EDI," he adds. "X12 is just a data content standard. So now EDI is a pure business issue. Do you want to change the way you do business?"

EDI PARTNERS MUST TRUST EACH OTHER

More and more large companies are answering yes. In addition to the cost benefits, the supplier-customer-client relationships become less adversarial. That's not to say that competition decreases—this is America, remember? But an EDI relationship has no shot at effectiveness unless the partners trust each other. Otherwise, what's the point of exposing your previously proprietary and not state-of-the-art information system for the common good?

"We've seen a real market upsurge in the last year," says Michael Mansouri, Telenet's director of EDI. "The success stories in the grocery and transportation industries have helped. So has the progress in EDI technology and standards. But I think the major reason is the push by the Fortune 1000 to implement EDI."

Adds GE's Korn, "The technological standards have reached puberty. People aren't afraid to use them."

No lie. When GE went into the EDI business in 1985, it finished the year with 10 transactions flowing over its network. It finished 1986 with 500 transactions. When 1987 was history, there had been 1,700 transactions.

The Roots of EDI

It was only 20 years ago today that the question about electronic data interchange wasn't "when" or "how." It was "what."

The concept was created by Ed Guilbert, who, as director of traffic for the 1948 Berlin Airlift, found it terribly frustrating to cope with business transactions using paper. The documents describing the goods arrived days after the goods already had reached Berlin. During the Hungarian airlift eight years later, Guilbert improved the process and wouldn't let a plane take off unless the relevant information had preceded it.

It wasn't until 1966 that he could apply his international experience domestically. While working for the Department of Transportation, he established an Office of Facilitation to give businesspeople a chance to tell the government how business could improve its productivity if the government would ease up slightly on the bureaucracy. Impressed by the response, Guilbert thought it would be a decent idea if a group of business folk could practice what they preached. So, in 1968, he and a few colleagues formed the Transportation Data Coordinating Committee (TDCC) to support the standardization of tariffs for overseas shipments.

With a $50,000 budget and one full-time employee, the TDCC was hardly a high-powered Washington trade association. But it didn't need to be. Its mission was to convince business execs that it is far, far better to do business via computer than on paper. The TDCC established four ground rules, still valid, for EDI:

- It must provide generalized interface data standards and formats that will be responsive to users' needs for intercompany computer-to-computer transactions.

- Interface capability must be insensitive to internal computer equipment and programs of the interchange parties.

- EDI should leave to the using parties the selection of the option of communications speeds and services.

- It should have a capability of providing documents, when required, as a by-product of integrated database transactions.

Once the rules were on the books, TDCC needed to convince businesses to play by them. Guilbert established task forces of shipper and rail, shipper and motor, shippers/forwarders and ocean carriers, shippers/forwarders and airlines, shippers/carriers and banks.

"I had to weave commonality between each industry's code so the industries could interchange the information," says Guilbert, now an independent consultant in Washington, D.C. He wove his spell so well that TDCC released in 1975 the first EDI documentation: Rail Transportation Industry Applications. That document became the first of what are now 10 volumes of U.S. EDI Standards. There are also separate volumes for the EDI concept, the EDI general programming guide, and the EDI data segments and data elements.

"There were times when I thought we might not make it," says Guilbert, who more than once dug into his own pocket to keep TDCC from going under. "It takes time to turn around traditional practices. Now EDI has no place to go but up."

"The software has come a long way, too," Korn says. "It used to be that if you wanted to integrate EDI into an application, you had to develop your own software. Now there's software out there that will integrate EDI into whatever application you want.

"Of course, none of that would have been worth beans if business hadn't decided that EDI cuts costs and improves customer service. There's a real business imperative now that didn't exist before."

"It's not even clear to us that EDI will be a big revenue issue," says Linda Smith, a technical specialist in strategic marketing for McCormack & Dodge (M&D), Natick, Mass. M&D and GE Information Services, Rockville, MD., recently signed a joint EDI marketing agreement.

"The revenue isn't important right now," Smith explains. "This agreement is a starting place for us. We see EDI by 1990 as the major way businesses will interact with each other. We want to be ready."

What else can EDI do now? Is it the wave of the future, or what?

Well, EDI could make paper disappear. But it won't, at least not any time soon. And to make the impact on business practices that its supporters hope it will, the concept needs to take hold in smaller companies. No matter how enticing the prospect of eliminating paperwork is, is it really worth it for a trucking company with six trucks to invest the capital it takes to implement EDI? Hardly. But it may not have a choice.

CAN SMALL SUPPLIERS RESIST EDI?

As more large companies go with EDI, their small suppliers can refuse to go along, but at the risk of losing business. If a large company represents 90% of your business, it's just not that tough a call. Nevertheless, small companies aren't all that eager to make that call, and their reluctance is clearly preventing EDI from taking off even faster.

When most large companies look to the future, though, EDI looms large in their vision. Ed Guilbert, a Washington, D.C., consultant and the father of the EDI concept, says that there aren't any technical issues in the way of EDI, and he feels that "it's becoming a common way to do business for everybody, big or small."

"Getting into this is like learning to be fluent in Chinese," ADL's Norris says. "On the other hand, it can't be that difficult, because 1 billion people know how to do it."

There aren't that many EDI converts yet. But give it time.

14

Ford Jump Starts EDI

Jeanne Brokaw Iida with
Bruce Caldwell and
Charles von Simson

Ford has embarked on a $20 million project that will usher in the next wave of EDI, in which networks will further infiltrate corporations, tightening links among management, assembly plants, and suppliers. Ford's plan to link 70 manufacturing plants will save tens of millions of dollars a year, cut development time, improve quality, and bolster competitiveness.

"Other companies add EDI to the front or back end of their operations, but Ford is actually redesigning its system to put all of its production operation on the network," says Irv Chmielewski, associate director of the Auto Industry Action Group in Detroit, a trade organization that promotes standards for the auto industry. While smaller Chrysler has linked internal and external EDI networks, nothing compares to the scope of Ford's plan. When the project's effect on profitability becomes clear, other manufacturers, eager to emulate Ford's gains, will turn to connected EDI networks and drag EDI into the next century.

"Ford is the first case of a large-scale, totally redone EDI system [for managing production], rather than a patchwork on other systems," remarks Chmielewski. Also a systems engineer supervisor at Electronic Data Systems and a member of General Motors' EDI committee, Chmielewski says that GM is still looking at providing a common interface to suppliers. "We'll encourage them to provide EDI internally, but they're not doing it yet," he says.

Chrysler's EDI network links 11 plants and suppliers—compared with 70 plants at Ford—uses EDI to track shipping and receiving information, but not to coordinate purchase orders, invoices, shipments, components, and assembled cars in the way Ford envisions.

"EDI will make Ford a lot more responsive as a company—no question," says Keith Belton, an auto analyst with the Yankee Group. Ford's EDI project makes it possible, he says, to cut the design and manufacture time from four years to 30

The Issues

- Ford is building a unique $20 million EDI network that links internal and external operations.
- While EDI is a proven cost-cutting link between suppliers and customers, Ford's is the first application of the technology as a real management tool.
- Common Manufacturing Management Systems promises one-stop shopping for suppliers and dramatic productivity increases. This is the next wave of EDI.

months. S.I. Gilman, MIS chief at Ford, isn't one for grand predictions. Of his project, he says, "We want to improve quality, the timeliness of information, and reduce the costs of doing business."

EDI AS A MANAGEMENT TOOL

Using EDI to link suppliers with manufacturers is nothing new. Ford, GM, Chrysler, Levi-Strauss, K-Mart, International Harvester, Quaker Oats, and American Express all use EDI. Almost 80% of all drug orders made by pharmacies, for example, are done through EDI. The use of EDI is expected to grow 25% next year, according to Input, a market research firm.

But Ford is leading the auto industry charge in believing that the full potential of EDI will be realized with its use as a mechanism not for exchange of invoices, but for internal quality control and coordinating operations.

The project, dubbed the Common Manufacturing Management Systems, will be tried out early next year and completed by 1990. "We're searching for improved function and effectiveness," says Gilman.

For Ford, the linked EDI networks translate into better, more cost-effective manufacturing. According to Mark Winthers of Link Resources, an EDI market research firm, "EDI is increasingly seen as the foundation system" for just-in-time manufacturing. That means less inventory and lower overhead. Winthers adds, "Industry sources say EDI, fully implemented, could save $200 a car."

Before Ford can link internal and external EDI networks, however, it must build the former, which will string together 50 components plants and 20 assembly plants. The assembly plants and their hundreds of suppliers are already linked—that's the external aspect.

"In a business system sense, the heart of the manufacturing division is material control," says Gilman. "Many of [the older systems] are outdated, and haven't been changed for 15 years or so." Gilman says he's spending 2–3% of an MIS budget which outside estimates place at $2.3 billion on the project, and dedicating 35–40 programmers on Ford's payroll, with additional help from Arthur Andersen. The programmers are writing EDI software, based for the most part on the Ansi X.12 standard.

The bypassed processors in Ford's eight divisions may continue to be used for office automation or to spit out quality-control reports. That central computer makes for one-stop shopping for suppliers. The EDI network will act as a switch, so that if a supplier needs to communicate with six of seven different plants, he can do it in one shot. "Suppliers can get confused about where the information is, so it would be incredibly convenient to have one location [at Ford]," says Jim Shillito, senior analyst at Borg-Warner, a major parts supplier to the auto industry.

Gilman says one aspect of the project will be bar coding, which will make shipping orders obsolete. Suppliers and plants will bar code parts as they are loaded into a truck and then feed that information into the EDI network. The electronic invoice is read as the truck unloads, cutting down on errors. "You won't need people checking for shipment errors on the factory floor," says Gilman.

Gilman says the new system will also lead to better scheduling practices, because information on parts can be communicated through the network quickly. He estimates savings to be in "the tens of millions of dollars," the result of fewer people needed to do this scheduling.

Chrysler's MIS director G. Nichols Simonds agrees that EDI yields internal efficiencies. Says Simonds, "If you shorten the supply lines between yourself and your parts supplier, inventory doesn't get lost, and it doesn't get run over by a forklift."

THE NEXT WAVE

In the auto industry, EDI has already changed manufacturers' relationships with suppliers. Manufacturers are now looking at their suppliers and saying, "We as an industry must succeed," says Chmielewski. Some companies, such as Chrysler, are pushing more manufacturing out of their plants and into supplier companies. Ford spun off an internal steelmaking plant into an independent company. This is a worldwide trend: Dr. Ulich Sorgatz at Volkswagen in Wolfsburg, Germany, says, "There will be some type of restructuring on the supplier level," as the result of EDI. He predicts there will be fewer, more competitive suppliers.

Perhaps the greatest impact, however, will be on industry as a whole. The growth of EDI will force changes in most traditional business practices. Quaker Oats, for example, expects to make better use of its EDI network, and is basing an order processing system around it, something it says is possible now that the company has switched from Unisys mainframes to IBM. "With the Unisys systems we were forced to do a lot of translation and rely on third-party 'mailbox in the sky' vendors like Compuserve," says Ronald Brezinski, Quaker's information systems VP. That, in the end, could be the most important consequence of commitments to EDI such as Ford's: It may push MIS further into the welcoming arms of IBM.

15

McDonald's Serves Up Global ISDN Strategy

Richard Layne and
Cassimir J. Medford

The company that pioneered Big Macs, drive-thru windows, Chicken McNuggets, and headsets for counter help is pushing into another frontier: Integrated Services Digital Network (ISDN). McDonald's is the first business in the world to incorporate the full voice and data features of ISDN into its daily operations.

That's only the beginning. The company's goal is to rope all of its 10,000 stores into one network. Each of those stores around the world will feed sales and marketing information back to headquarters instantaneously. From that flow of information, McDonald's will be able to make faster, more informed decisions on what products to sell and how to sell them. In an increasingly competitive fast food market, that information carries the promise of increased profits.

But that worldwide network is ten years off. Its beginnings, however, are evident in simplified access over inexpensive telephone wire, one of the benefits of ISDN.

The ISDN strategy works like this: A professor at Hamburger University, McDonald's training ground for managers, wants to discuss how last month's promotional campaigns affected sales. He calls the Chicago regional sales manager in Oak Brook, Ill., a mile away. Both the professor and the sales manager can access the month's sales figures as they discuss them over the phone. Both the voice and the data flow over the same phone line. Without ISDN, achieving this simultaneous flow of data and voice is difficult. Each office would require a cluster of outlets and a knot of extra wires.

How does a purveyor of fast food become a technology trendsetter? McDonald's complex communications needs and tough competition pushed the company into ISDN, an as-yet poorly understood technology.

To uphold its image as a friendly neighborhood restaurant that efficiently serves 20 million customers daily, McDonald's has come to rely on technology, not advertising.

McDonald's is a multinational corporation with 137,000 employees in 68 offices and 10,000 restaurants in 47 countries. While the profusion of outlets would seem to make Big Mac attacks easy to cure, the $4 billion Oak Park, Ill., company is expanding at the rate of one new restaurant every 17 hours. Pushed by competition, McDonald's must keep abreast almost hourly on how its products are moving. While McDonald's has a large share of the market, the competition—notably from Wendy's—is fierce enough to prevent complacency from setting in.

Thirteen months ago, McDonald's began running the wires needed for ISDN around the campus of Hamburger U., which includes the new and old headquarters. That project was completed recently. Within ten years, it will have finished wiring all the stores and regional offices into the network.

"With ISDN we will have one network in and one network out and you can cross over and share databases with all of them without an extensive amount of work," says Bonnie Kos, vice president of facilities and systems at McDonald's.

The benefits are myriad. Details of a promotional campaign can be sent via data channels anywhere in the world. And the store managers can inform their regional sales offices of how the promotion is working immediately. The store managers and their regional bosses can access each other's files to check sales or inventory. They can share databases from anywhere in the world. New employees can be trained by computer on-site.

Without ISDN, McDonald's believes, it couldn't erect such a network. ISDN, which is nothing more than a set of interface protocols, gives corporations a blueprint for linking computer and communication devices. The standards include signaling protocol, interface standards, and bandwidth allocation.

"We are growing rapidly and that poses a serious challenge for our information systems," Kos says. "This system is designed to keep things simple as we grow. We want to free up store managers for the more important job of serving the customer."

An ISDN-based system would replace a mare's nest of networks. Currently, McDonald's subscribes to 21 networks to handle telephone and databases and links between headquarters and Hamburger University. "We can control, stabilize, and reduce overall communication expenses through a single network versus multiple networks," says Kos. "We avoid the cost of administrative overhead associated with supporting multiple unique networks, each of which uses different hardware, software, and premise distribution interfaces."

An ISDN network uses relatively inexpensive-twisted-pair cabling, dramatically lowering the cost of wiring buildings and offices. This appeals to the cost-conscious McDonald's: "We are a hamburger company of penny profits, with a penchant for details," explains Kos. "We make money by literally scraping the last ounce of catsup from each can."

ISDN is nothing if not inconspicuous. Next to every desktop in McDonald's new office building in Oak Brook, Ill., is one access outlet that can receive and carry integrated voice, data, image, and message signals on standard twisted-pair wire. Illinois Bell has more than 300 ISDN-based services from which McDonald's can choose. While McDonald's is interested in Centrex-related features like conference-calling, call-transfer, call-forwarding, and call pick-up, it also plans to fully exploit ISDN, using a computer in tandem with a phone.

A Network Built On The 5ESS Switch

Illinois Bell is staking much on ISDN, specifically the performance of AT&T's 5ESS switch located in the Oak Brook central office. The 5ESS switch is a computer that acts like a traffic cop. It directs calls and data to proper destinations and can handle up to 300,000 calls an hour.

McDonald's is tied into the switch through an ISDN line with three channels. Two are circuit-switched voice or data channels, the third is for carrying packet data, which is sent in bursts to a computer.

In a circuit-switched call, a switch sets up a path through the network and keeps it open for the duration of the call. When the call ends, the circuit is taken down.

For packet-switched calls, customer signals are assembled into discrete bundles of information or packets. Each is marked with an address and placed on a common transmission line with packets from other users. Packet switches in the network deliver the bundles of information to the proper destination as they arrive.

Those features unique to ISDN – like electronic directory, calling number identification, and message-waiting and retrieval – link together phone and computer. Electronic directory allows users to look up company telephone numbers and place calls at the touch of a button. Calling number identification displays the number of the person calling from within the company and, when used in conjunction with the electronic directory, can also display the caller's name. Message-waiting and retrieval gives users notice when a message has been left for them and allows them to retrieve or examine a series of waiting messages by scrolling through them.

McDonald's success with ISDN certainly paves the way for other companies. "It proves that ISDN is not a lab experiment anymore, it is now a product," says Timothy Bannon, Illinois Bell's assistant manager for media relations. "It's also a big boost to ISDN as an international standard." McDonald's high profile and global scope make it the ideal guinea-pig for Illinois Bell and AT&T – the two companies that cooperated on the project.

"The stakes in this partnership are immense," says Bob Carlson, AT&T's Network Systems vice president. "They're nothing more or less than the foundation for a new age in telecommunications."

Illinois Bell expects to make its ISDN service available to all customers in two weeks, after it files a tariff with the Illinois Commerce Commission. Likely candidates for this service include Deere & Co. in Moline, Ill., Sears & Roebuck in Chicago, and the University of Illinois at Urbana. Each of these firms has an Illinois Centrex and has contracted for a custom voice/data centrex package.

Illinois Bell isn't the only company offering ISDN. Pacific Bell, for example, has the first of three planned projects underway.

At Lockheed Missiles & Space Co. in Sunnyvale, Calif., which began installing the ISDN lines in September, ISDN will be used to improve voice and data communications, to aid file transfer between PCs and from PCs to a host, and for LAN applications.

Chevron in San Ramon will be the site of the second test, while a third test will take place with an as-yet unnamed San Francisco company.

Once the results of those tests are in ISDN will in all likelihood move several steps closer to becoming a commonly deployed IS tool. And McDonald's can say it got there first.

16 McDonald's ISDN Troubled: Telecom Manager Cites Lack of Network Management Tools

Karen Gullo

McDonald's Corp., one of the first companies to implement ISDN, is facing a grave lack of network management tools for ISDN that is threatening the viability of its corporate network.

"If something isn't done and done quickly, the basic service is in jeopardy," says Patrick Krause, manager of telecommunications at McDonald's. "We are extremely concerned about the current state of affairs."

Nearly all information and communications systems at McDonald's headquarters in Oak Brook, Ill., including mainframes, cluster controllers, personal computers, office automation equipment, telephones, and faxes are hooked into the ISDN network. The company has 1,300 digital subscriber lines serving 1,110 user stations. McDonald's began its first ISDN trials in December 1986, cutting over to full production in September of last year.

The complexity of the systems at McDonald's and the number of vendors supplying network equipment there have increased dramatically since ISDN implementation, says Krause. But there are no maintenance or management tools available to monitor and control faults in and performance of the network. Existing data network management products at McDonald's, such as NetView, don't address the lower layers of the network. "NetView can't provide a clue" about controller devices, Krause told a group of users and vendors last week at a session on network management at the North American ISDN Users (NIU) Forum meeting in Bethesda, Md.

The ISDN "trouble desk" at McDonald's takes an average of eight calls a day about network problems. The majority of problems are caused by wiring at the "U" interface, which resides between a line termination point and a network termination point.

SORRY STATE OF AFFAIRS

Half of the problems were undetected during network testing, says Krause. "That's a pretty good indication of the sorry state of affairs."

The lack of test equipment is driving up problem-resolution times to a critical level. After four hours, 55% of the network problems are unresolved, and 45% are still there eight hours after being reported. "We have to have better test equipment at both the switch and customer-premises level," says Krause. He cites loop-back and trace capabilities as the most crucial maintenance and management features needed.

"This affects all four players" in ISDN, says Krause: the switch-, service-, and customer-provided equipment (CPE) vendors, and end users. McDonald's suppliers—AT&T and Illinois Bell—are aware of the problem. "The issue has been on the table for a long time." He says AT&T has been working on improving trace capabilities.

Part of the problem is that the switch suppliers and the equipment suppliers only address network management in their segment of the network. "There has to be a fundamental change in attitude," he says. "Network management needs to be an end-to-end service."

Unless products and standards are forthcoming, the problem has grave implications for the further rollout of ISDN at McDonald's, adds Krause. The company will not extend the network out to its stores unless the problem is solved at headquarters, he says.

Other ISDN users at the NIU Forum said they were experiencing similar problems, although none wished to be quoted. After hearing about McDonald's, one user said there's "no way" a company would want to implement ISDN. And his company is conducting ISDN trials.

Alan J. Weissberger, a consultant at Data Communications Technology in Santa Clara, Calif., says there are ANSI and CCITT standards that address ISDN network management. But such standards focus on the switch level rather than the CPE level of the network. He predicts user-to-network maintenance services for data transfer devices will be based on proprietary switch functions recently proposed to ANSI by Northern Telecom and AT&T. Once switch-level ISDN network management solutions exist, then gateways to IBM's NetView and AT&T's UNMA can be built.

Users are concerned that standards set by service providers won't address their need for end-to-end network management and will lock them into one or two vendors. "We don't want to be solely dependent on service providers," says Krause.

17

Look Who Is Sabotaging CIM

Abner A. Layne

It's a mystery. If computer-integrated manufacturing is America's best hope for world market competition, why has it not been adopted with speed and alacrity? And where pioneers have begun to implement CIM, why are there still gaps? And the most painful question of all: Are some managers silently sabotaging CIM?

A succinct answer to the sabotage question from Michael Heschel, corporate vice president of information resources for Baxter Healthcare Corp. is: "That's true." And retired Deere & Co. MIS manager Robert A. Bulen answers all but the sabotage question by saying, "CIM is very hard to do and the last link may be the hardest." The last link is provably hardest to justify, as Fiat found out when its second-generation automation cut labor by only 20% compared with the first generation's 50%.

The twisted strands of cause and effect that result in slow progress are not easily separated or traced. But rounding up the usual leading suspect is a mistake— technology can be cleared of guilt, immediately. It is neither delaying nor obstructing the long-heralded advent of CIM and the factory of the future. Says Bulen: "We've recently installed about 25 automated cells in some units and technology was never a problem."

Technology might be innocent, but the not-inconsiderable cost of implementation can't be cleared out of hand. Neither can other suspects such as the lack of systems integrators and the lack of an industrywide standard. And slow change and foot dragging may, in fact, be inherent in the way CIM was born and is developing. Some 15 years ago, Joseph Harrington Jr. coined the term "computer-integrated manufacturing" as the title of his book. Nevertheless, to date, a universally agreed-upon definition for CIM is still to come.

Meanwhile, the newest and hitherto unsuspected "perpetrator" has been added to the lineup: lack of support at the management level.

In fact, "lack of support" may understate the mild form of guerrilla resistance to change at the middle management level. Some of it is covert, some of it is visible, but it seems to be at least partly to blame for slowing CIM's acceptance. Risk-shy managers tend to be conservative in taking on innovation. For example, managing a petroleum processing plant "is a tough job run on a no-mistake basis," says Dudley P. Cooke, who's starting a career as a consultant after being general manager of information systems at Sun Co. in Philadelphia. "For a risk-aversive manager, turning the job over to a new megasystem is no light step."

CIM HITS MANAGERS IN THE PSYCHE

Silently protesting managers can mount a subtle but often devastating form of resistance. One hidden reason for resistance, as some industry observers have recently learned: Automation lets low-level workers with access to a PC make important decisions. And many mid-level executives don't like that—those decisions used to be theirs to make.

They also have careers to justify. James F. Sutter, vice president and general manager of information systems for Rockwell International, points out that managers often take 20 years to reach middle level. After that long journey, he says, they have a strong "cultural resistance to change."

Mid-level executives also try to dodge close scrutiny from above, says Charles Eberle, a former vice president of manufacturing for Procter & Gamble and now a consultant in Cincinnati. Eberle recalls that when Procter & Gamble decided five years ago to build a manufacturing plant some distance from headquarters, the plans included so much electronic monitoring equipment that executives at HQ, 500 miles away, would have been able to check the plant's exact output at any time.

They would have—except for one purposeful glitch: Plant managers made sure the electronic hookup was not complete and headquarters ended up with only limited access.

Another information management consultant observes: "In the workplace, knowledge is power. Knowledge that used to be proprietary information is now available to anyone who knows how to call it up." Adds Baxter's Heschel, "As more control over production moves to the PC on the factory floor, apprehension grows at the mid-to-lower levels of management."

That power struggle continues to make industry an information battlefield. New information technologies and old management privileges find cohabitation a constant irritant. Specialists often find it hard to get management to introduce advanced technologies, such as CIM, that are needed to stay competitive—indeed, to survive. Many managers simply do not like the new order of accountability that technology has brought to their jobs.

The ramifications of that discontent—for companies and for American competitiveness in world markets—could be serious: Data shows that companies that have most successfully adopted information technologies have gained a significant edge over rivals.

In a 1986 study of 16 of the most advanced "factories of the future," Prof. Richard Walton of the Harvard Business School found that in companies with serious commitments to information technologies, corporate activities became more interdependent. Says Walton: "Now top levels of management know about problems at the lowest levels. At a number of modern highly automated plants, managers have told me that if they ran out of a minor part it would starve the whole system, shutting down the plant. In their old plants, a problem could simmer for weeks. Now it's only hours or minutes before everyone knows."

How threatening such a situation is varies from manager to manager, Walton points out. Nevertheless, technology makes many new demands on organizational realities. "In these early stages of automation and robotics, the effect may be muted," he says. "But linking it all together as in CIM creates problems for the organization." Says former Deere executive Bulen: "The technology changes, doubling the amount of computing in a plant every year; but people are harder to change."

Walton's colleague, Prof. Shoshana Zuboff, points out that productivity gains when management doesn't spend so much time on coordinating and controlling information. But most managers are unhappy when CIM loosens their hold on information. "It's an implied threat to the whole structure of authority," Zuboff says. "When a machine operator using his monitor discovered that expensive new steam hoods, bought to increase efficiency, were raising costs, the managers soon thwarted use of the monitor because they felt innovative cost decisions were their own prerogative; that was what a manager, not a machine operator, was paid for."

Paul A. Strassman, former computer systems vice president at Xerox, and now a writer on information technology in New Canaan, Conn., studied the uses of information technologies at 60 companies. He found that compared with the poorest-performing companies, top performers spent twice as much on information as rivals. Using advanced technology, top performers had less than four management layers; poor ones had about eight.

Strassman has no comparable conclusions about CIM: "The definitions [of CIM] are still too vague and ambiguous, and rigorous comparison studies haven't been made yet." Others disagree that definition of CIM is a problem. IBM, for example, gives credit to information technology. CIM, says an IBM spokesperson, "is an architecture for the integration of multiple technologies through information systems technology . . . based on the realization that when productivity tools can function as an integrated solution their benefits are multiplied." And David A. Bossen, president of Measurex Corp. in Cupertino, Calif., defines CIM as "the ability to link all phases of design, manufacturing, and automation into a computer-run communications and information network." Robert O. Carper, vice president of Pittsburgh-based American Cimflex Corp., succinctly emphasizes the information basis of CIM by pointing out that "most of the business of manufacturing is moving and manipulating information."

FIRMS GET HIT IN THE COST COLUMN

If the implementation of CIM puts mainly psychological pressures on mid-level management, cost is real and the pocketbook pressure is substantial. In fact, when CIM is first proposed to management, it usually runs into skepticism at the upper level of financial management – with some reason. Paul Haas, vice president of Kearney & Trecker, a leader in flexible manufacturing systems development based in Milwaukee, puts the average outlay for an FMS at $4 million. A single machinery workstation within an FMS can run to $800,000. The FMS at GE's Erie plant cost $16 million.

"The technology is not cheap," says Michael C. Mills, project manager of McDonnell Douglas Helicopter Co. in Culver City, Calif. "And implementation requires expensive changes up and down the organization."

An MIS chief with a firm in California points out that "automation changes the cost structure in areas other than the one being automated." Traditional cost-accounting systems can't predict or handle such cost tradeoffs, he adds.

PARTIAL CIM SPEEDS PRODUCTION

In consequence of cost and managerial resistance, the factory of the future has not yet been realized and no plant anywhere in the world can be truly said to be completely computer integrated. Nevertheless, a number of examples of partial integration demonstrate the cost effectiveness of going even part way:

Flexible Machining Cell

LTV Corp.'s Dallas-based Aircraft Products Group (APG), implemented a 40,000-square-foot Flexible Machining Cell two years ago. The cell – LTV's first building block of its master industrial modernization plan – has already proved itself. The integrated system is totally computer-controlled and consists of highly versatile machines, which direct the automated machining and inspection of more than 1,300 different military and commercial aircraft parts. The cell has reduced 200,000 hours of conventional machining time to 70,000 hours for a three-to-one productivity improvement and a cost reduction of more than $20 million on 60-foot-long fuselage sections of the B-1B bomber program alone. In September 1985, the APG installed a CAD system that allowed the engineers' designs to go directly to the cell's computer-controlled, shop-floor operation.

Robotic Welding Cell

This automated cell at APG began operating in 1983. It welds launcher structures for an Army rocket system at a two-to-one productivity increase over manual welding.

Automated Tape Laying Machine

Next-generation aircraft designs are likely to be 60% composite materials – mainly, reinforced plastics. An automated LTV tape layer cuts manual labor for a 10-to-one productivity increase.

Trends That Make CIM Irresistible

Disbursement
The spreading of production among ever-smaller manufacturing units is progressing remorselessly.

Labor Costs
They're becoming less important to companies because of modern automation plus a boost from the weak U.S. dollar.

Centralized Engineering
One characteristic of high-tech engineering is to bring the designers back to HQ. Their product blueprints, drawn using CAD at the head office, are now likely to be transmitted to CAM plants in the company's principal markets.

Manufacturing Flexibility
This rises dramatically as a result of applying the new techniques to machine tools. It permits a wider variety of products to be produced without raising costs, and allows CIM units to break even at low capacity utilization. One expert figures it at 30–35% of capacity compared with 65–70% for conventional plants.

Plug-in Servicing
This is a bonus. Faults in products made by CAD and CIM techniques can usually be diagnosed by plugging them into a computer.

Economies of Scale
Bigness alone is eroded by CIM in manufacturing and will have to be found elsewhere. R&D sales, and marketing are thought to be likely candidates for concentration.

Industrial Boutiques
Small independent operators using the latest CAD and CIM techniques are emerging as contractors to mainstream firms. Many mainliners may eventually off-load manufacturing units and buy tailor-made products.

Robotic Water-Jet Cutter

To cut aluminum, titanium, and composites, this device uses high-pressure water moving at about three times the speed of sound. It operates entirely under integrated computer control.

Voughtmatic

Automatic fastenings systems for large multicontour aircraft parts has increased the number of automatically installed fasteners from less than a million a year to more than three million. Quality discrepancy rates have dropped from 2% in the 1960s to less than 0.33%. Further development is expected to see large parts assembled by computer program with virtually no human intervention.

Robot Assembly

IBM automated the assembly process in its Lexington, Ky., facility. There, the same robot assembles typewriters, laser printers, and terminals. It goes from one to the other simply by changing computer commands and parts.

Metalworking

Sundstrand Corp. in Rockford, Ill., eliminated 100 conventional metalworking machines, replacing them with 10 machines linked together with a computer numerical control system. The new system processes five times as many different parts at twice the volume.

Axle Production

Rockwell International in Pittsburgh bought an 18-system FMS to produce differentials, as a first step toward fully automating the On-Highway Axle Division of its Automotive Operations unit in Asheville, N.C. "Plans call for our Asheville facility to be the hub for Rockwell's production of axles in North America upon scheduled completion of the expansion program," says Don DeFosset, vice president and General Manager of Rockwell's On-Highway Axle Division.

Starters Motors

The president of Allen-Bradley, J. Tracy O'Rourke, has a showcase operation in Bradley's 45,000-square-foot leading-edge facility in Milwaukee. There, Allen-Bradley builds starters motors and electrical contactors. Says O'Rourke: "In manufacturing our programmable controller, we have less than 1.5% of our total sales dollars in direct labor—down from 15% 10 years ago. There is so little direct labor in producing the high-volume product that it has become a non-issue even if I have to compete with someone who pays 32 cents an hour."

Electronics

At Texas Instruments' Defense Systems & Electronics Facility in Sherman, Texas, "we had simultaneously received two government contracts and we needed additional capacity," says Dave Oberholtzer, TI's manager of integrated factory systems. "If we had continued the existing production approach, we would have had to build additional warehousing and manufacturing space." Implementing CIM was a cost-saving measure at first. "Much less costly," he says, "based on a just-in-time/total-quality control concept. What happened was that integration also proved to be the source of improved quality and productivity."

Instrument Clusters

Ford Motor Co.'s newest CIM implementation is designed to reduce cost and increase quality. Installed by Carnegie, Pa.-based American Cimflex Corp. at Ford's Electrical and Electronic Division plant at Markham, Ontario, the system will produce digital instrument clusters for Taurus and Sable automobiles. Included are systems for quality management, manufacturing engineering, information management, and shop-floor control.

CIM IS AN IRRESISTIBLE FORCE

Thus, however slowly, CIM is moving to realization. A changing and embattled U.S. industrial economy militates for CIM. Certain trends appear to make CIM irresistible in the long run (see page 130).

Such trends as the spreading of manufacturing units are becoming known to industrial movers and shakers. A recent poll of top manufacturing executives demonstrates slow but inexorable progress: 64% say they know about CIM. But while they are favorably disposed, a little less than half (47%) think that top corporate management is positive toward CIM. However, over half believe their own companies will adopt CIM in the next five years, but that it will take two or three times as long for all U.S. industry to adopt it.

David E. Fyffe, who retired recently as associate director of the CIM program at Georgia Institute of Technology, confirms that estimate. His "time horizon is 15 to 20 years when at least half of all industry will be using CIM." For some industries, Fyffe thinks the inevitable is closer to hand. "I don't think electronics will be able to exist without CIM in the near future," he says.

Without CIM, it will be difficult, if not impossible, to bridge the gaps uncovered a few months ago by a Pentagon study. The time gap between the U.S. and Japanese response to an order and a shipment of machine tools, for example, was on average 4-½ months. That is, a Japanese manufacturer could get the order out the door nearly five months ahead of a U.S. company. In the electronics industry, the Japanese firms studied reworked less than 1% of the production run; U.S. firms, nearly 10%. And the final blow—the Japanese were more flexible and faster in turning new technology into marketable products. CIM is obviously needed now, but seems to be lingering on the way.

Optimists and innovators like Allen-Bradley's O'Rourke say, "Completely integrated plantwide automation is about to become reality. The technology already exists." Eric Teicholz, president of Graphic Systems Inc. in Cambridge, Mass., agrees that CIM can be achieved today. "There are no technological obstacles to overcome before we can build computer-controlled factories that run themselves," he says.

TREND SETTERS

In view of the technological state of readiness, CIM's slow growth appalls advocates like Unisys Corp.'s vice president Thomas G. Gunn, formerly national director of Arthur Young & Co.'s Manufacturing Consultant Group: "What I have seen of U.S. and European manufacturing plants is not encouraging. They are not responding well to change—change not only in the information technology underlying all of business today, but changes in materials, changes in manufacturing processes, and changes in people."

Says Albert B. Bishop, professor of industrial and systems engineering at Ohio State University in Columbus: "The main problem seems to be combining people and technology." To verify this initial impression, Bishop and his colleague, Prof. Robert I. Lund of Boston University, are now classifying and identifying the factors for success or failure in about 150 CIM implementations in metalworking companies.

However in Los Altos, Calif., Mark Ripma, director of advanced manufacturing systems for Ask Computer Systems, questions whether "at this time" CIM is, in fact, necessary for success or corporate survival. "Automation is indeed crucial now," he says. "And ultimately to make automation effective, CIM is necessary, but so are quality and just-in-time production systems."

Gunn, who urges U.S. manufacturers to aim at becoming "world-class," points out that the three pillars of achieving that status are total quality control (TQC), CIM, and just-in-time (JIT) production techniques. Until recently, however, companies have adopted various ingredients of this alphabet soup in isolation from one another. This always ends up with the free-floating "islands of automation" and a promise of integration.

Lately, this situation has begun to change. The technologies have begun to communicate with each other through local-area networks, and formerly isolated applications are being linked by CIM. With increasing integration, the closer a plant comes to CIM, the less tolerant of error it becomes, the more serious are the consequences of error, and the more everyone's performance depends on actions taken by nearly everyone else.

That means, says Baxter's Heschel, "The first priority must be simplification of the process or manufacturing system." Or as Graphic Systems' Teicholz points out: "Implementation of CIM requires an appreciation of the way things are, a vision of how they are to be, and a clear plan for getting from here to there, with minimal trauma to the manufacturing organization and its people."

Mills, of McDonnell Douglas Helicopter Co., says in the past year he has "integrated a couple of cells, one of them with 20 NC machine tools, with about 60 networked PCs for data collection and management control. Mills also warns that implementation requires a change in point of view. "Before a company can implement CIM technology successfully . . . it must view itself as interconnected networks of functions. All these functions require data to drive them and the data must be available at specific time intervals in order for the individual functions to be performed in a timely manner."

CLOSING IN ON THE DISCRETE

Says American Cimflex's Carper, "Factories of the future really do come in neat little boxes of such things as computers, vision systems, robots, conveyors, and software. Skillful integration is a necessary ingredient for success.

"Until recently, the concept was more closely tied to the continuous process industries that, by definition, had to have smooth and integrated process and infor-

The Evolution of Computer-Integrated Manufacturing

So far, the application of computers to manufacturing has occurred in bottom-up fashion; that is, its usefulness was applied to automation and was recognized at the production level long before it came to the attention of management. At the lower level, CAD/CAM was first applied to numerical control (NC) programming on the production side of the factory and to analysis on the engineering side. Later, it began to be used in detailed drafting and applied to design, where it could compress design times by factors of three to five. As a result, the factory is often broken up into unintegrated "islands of automation."

"We have a lot of bridging and tunneling to do between the islands," says Dave Fyffe, retired associate director of the CIM program at Georgia Institute of Technology. Many parts of organizations that use CAD/CAM rely on hard copies because other parts have no way to deal with digital information. This seems incredible in the face of a Harvard Business School study which shows that using computers instead of people costs 8,000 times less today than in 1950.

Other experts see CIM as the chief acronym in a virtual acronym soup named Advanced Manufacturing Technology. AMT, they say encompasses computer-aided manufacturing (CAM); which in turn encompasses CIM-dependent flexible manufacturing systems (FMS); robots, material handling devices, and numerically controlled (NC) machines, including computer numerical control (CNC) and direct numerical control (DNC).

Computer-aided design (CAD) and engineering (CAE) can vary in sophistication from computers that serve as electronic drafting boards to those that test alternative designs on the screen for stress, function, and other characteristics, and then translate the design into a program to produce the product. Manufacturing resource planning (MRPII) is software that translates demand for products into parts needed to produce them, and orders parts from inventory or from suppliers so they will be available when needed. Computer-aided process planning (Capp) is software that routes parts through the factory to maximize operating time and eliminate bottlenecks. With CIM, the savings in manufacturing times, costs, floor space, and manpower would range from 10% to 50%, according to Tom Gunn, a vice president at Unisys Corp.

mation flows," he continues. "Similarly, in the discrete parts manufacturing culture, the integrating function fell naturally to material-handling suppliers. Now, as CIM reshapes all manufacturing in the image of the process industries, systems integration becomes the necessary key that makes all the new technology work." Yet, he says, "Everyone thinks he knows what systems integration is, but more than likely he's like one of those proverbial blind men describing an elephant, each in terms of his own grasp."

It was quite natural for CIM to make early progress in the process industries where uniformity and continuous flow lent themselves to automation and control. But the process-industry suppliers are looking ahead.

Measurex, a factory-floor workstation vendor, for example, is very strong in the process industries, but says president Bossen, "We believe the discrete marketplace in total is about twice as big as the process industry marketplace. We intend to be in that from cell-level control through area-and plantwide control systems." He adds that "we decided the best market segment for us to get into was automotive.

"We signed a codevelopment contract with Ford Motor Co. a little over a year ago; it's about an $18 million contract. We have just shipped the first pilot program, which is for production monitoring of the Woodhaven, Mich., stamping plant. This is in the process of being installed. We will follow with a production-control update for that plant, and then in the Fall we will put a production monitoring system into the Wayne, Mich., assembly plant," continues Bossen. "Ultimately we will add device and diagnostic support and system support for those two plants. And, if they are successful, as we and Ford believe they will be, Ford will replicate them through its other 27 North American body and assembly plants, and perhaps in the rest of the world. The Woodhaven plant is about 2.8 million square feet, under a roof of about 60 acres. We have 250 input terminals and approximately 30 IBM PCs networked to a mainframe."

CIM TOMORROW

With so many cells and islands of automation in operation, it is easy now to imagine in some detail how a factory could operate if manufacturing areas were linked in interdependent modules by CIM. The factory floor would be divided into cells defined by their manufacturing function, such as a design cell, a flexible machine cell, a welding cell, and an assembly cell. Dozens of robots might be linked by a hierarchy of computers, much as direct-numerically controlled machine tools are today. Feedback to the manufacturing control systems from the robots, the machines, and the people in the factory would be immediate. And so the planned flow of products through the factory could be adjusted continuously to reflect changes in operating conditions. The design of the plant would emphasize flexibility, so that a variety of products would be made by the same machines; indeed, products might be made in unit quantity.

In that future time, CIM will make plants instantly responsive to the requirements of the enterprise of which they form a part. Investment in CIM, which was $10 billion in 1981, is expected to climb close to $60 billion by 1990.

However, fully automated factories are unlikely to become general before the late 1990s. And the achievement must come at a rate that both managers and workers can tolerate.

In fact, the projected rate is slow enough to accommodate the most conservative member of the workforce.

M. Eugene Merchant, of Metcut Research Association in Cincinnati, Ohio, reports conclusions based on the Delphi technique: By 1990, of all manufacturing industries, 25% will be using on-line inspection systems and 20% of industrial machine tools will be designed to eliminate the need for an operator at each workstation, through automatic part loading and unloading, automatic sensing of tool wear and changing of cutting tools, and completely computerized process monitoring.

Further into the future, Merchant says, we will see the advent of the factory of the future: "Design of a product will be done by iterative communication between humans and computers—the human creating the design and the computer the memory and calculations. During the procedure, the computer will use memory to compare costs and capabilities to find the design that costs least to manufacture and is most easily produced.

"At the same time, the production planning will proceed on the basis of the design parameters to choose equipment and processes, operations, conditions, and sequences. The operation will be self-diagnostic and capable of replacing defective machinery and tools. The product will be scrutinized at each stage of manufacture, corrected for deviations from tolerances. In the end, the product will be fully inspected and ready for shipment."

That's the future—perhaps the distant future. "It's sad," says Mills. "There's more technology out there than is needed to solve the problems. It's time to stop planning and execute! Execute!" Perhaps. But it's also time to stop preaching to the choir and start quoting chapter and verse to the non-believers.

18

Top Drug Firms to Digitize Documentation

Scott C. McCready

Fifteen of the top 25 pharmaceutical companies are poised to spend $23 million dollars over the next 18 to 24 months on the relatively new technology of digital document systems, according to recent research conducted by CAP International Inc., Norwell, Mass.

ICI Pharmaceuticals (Wilmington, Del.), Warner Lambert (Morris Plains, N.J.), Glaxo (Research Triangle Park, N.C.), and Pfizer (New York), have already taken the plunge. While the other 11 firms asked not to be identified for competitive reasons, they will all have optical storage-based document systems by the end of the year, at an average cost of over $1 million. The remaining 10 have committed to spending $17 million over the same period.

There are approximately 156 drug companies in the U.S., many of which are trying to speed the manufacture of new drugs by computerizing the new drug application (NDA) process with standard technologies (see "IS: the Best Medicine for Drug Monitoring," Aug. 1, p. 41).

What is it about optical-based document processing systems that is prompting the major pharmaceutical companies to assign it a large portion of their office automation budgets? They have discovered that digitizing document images and processing them electronically offers the greatest potential for shortening the R&D cycle, the time required for Food and Drug Administration (FDA) aproval, improving the effectiveness of label design and approval, and minimizing other administration expenses.

"Senior management is finally beginning to wake up. We process documents. That is the essence of this business. Because of the long R&D cycle and the strict regulatory environment, we need every tool available to improve the process and protect the integrity of our files," says a spokesperson for Ciba-Geigy, which is evaluating systems.

"This technology appears to be readily adaptable to the R&D environment," says David H. McCurdy, former ICI director of pharmaceutical research administration and an internal pioneer of its system, now a consultant to the firm. ICI Pharmaceuticals began investigating the use of electronic documentation as far back as 1984 and, after determining its existing costs of managing documentation, became the first pharmaceutical firm to employ optical disk technology with a pilot FileNet Corp. system in January 1986.

A spokesperson for Warner Lambert says, "This is the first technology in perhaps 20 years that will allow us to alter the basis of competition within this industry. Internal efficiencies stand to save us millions of dollars, while the impact on the FDA could amount to hundreds of millions."

Pharmaceutical firms, however, face a particularly cumbersome, paper-intensive process of bringing a new drug to market, a process that can take up to 10 years and $125 million to complete. Their health in the highly competitive industry is related entirely to their ability to innovate continually and bring those innovations to market first. Therefore, any investment in a technology—in this case, optical disk systems—that offers the potential to reduce radically the mountains of paper-based drug research information required by the FDA, while simultaneously offering significant economies for the R&D cycle, is money well spent.

The industry as a whole will spend in excess of $5 billion on R&D this year, but the average product will still take eight years to complete the cycle unless the means for accomplishing the process can be altered radically.

Both phases of the drug approval process, as they are conducted today, present overwhelming document processing problems. During the exhaustive clinical testing required by the FDA of any new drug, pharmaceutical firms have to manage not only internal R&D but a great deal of research that is performed, of necessity, by organizations outside the firm's control. It is not unusual for a pharmaceutical company to receive 600,000 case report forms per year from outside testing parties. Since these records are the "go or no go" evidence for the FDA to approve the drug, it is imperative that any incomplete case reports or patient records be clarified completely before being shipped to FDA evaluators. Today, clarifying the often incomplete case reports is done in batches, which usually are too large to be handled by phone and must be mailed back and forth between the pharmaceutical firm and the clinical testing site.

How to speed up the process of clarification? One answer: digitize the incoming documents and electronically route the report form to the appropriate department for review. Should further clarification be needed, those forms can be down-loaded overnight to the appropriate testing center. The clarification process can then be conducted by telephone and annotations made to the document in real time. This is no small investment on the part of the pharmaceutical manufacturer, but the potential financial return is relatively easy to discern.

In the second phase of the drug approval process, the FDA requires that each pharmaceutical company deliver the clinical test results to the agency in a strictly regulated format for evaluation by an assortment of physicians and medical experts. The net result is that the pharmaceutical company has to create new documentation that compiles and tabulates the statistical information contained in the case reports. The statistics must be classified to clearly show whether the drug caused any adverse reactions or reacted with other medications, and its overall effectiveness.

Since 1962, NDAs have been submitted on paper as the law requires, commonly delivered by tractor trailer. While the paper method of document presentation has yielded a remarkable level of safety for the U.S. population, the price it exacts is twofold: the great cost, which is eventually passed onto the consumer, and the lengthy approval process.

Using paper slows the process, not only because of the huge volume of documents involved, but also because paper documents do not allow simultaneous access by multiple users. Therefore, should an FDA inspector require a piece of unavailable documentation to continue an evaluation, he or she simply will go on to another NDA. The volume of documentation precludes the FDA from handling multiple copies were they even available.

Furthermore, should an inspector require clarification, the entire process must be conducted by mail to provide a record of the change for legal protection.

The FDA approval process is not likely to improve by streamlining the documentation itself. In fact, though the FDA, for the first time in its history, rewrote the requirements for drug filings over the past three years, the table "Technology Hasn't Helped Yet" shows this has not shortened the approval cycle.

Submitting NDA documentation via optical storage media is the most obvious solution to ultimately eliminating the paper glut, since one 12-inch optical disk can store approximately 50,000 pages. Unfortunately, until the law that requires NDA documentation on paper is changed, the drug companies will have to back up any optical disk-based NDAs with paper. The FDA has said it intends to change the law, though that could take years.

Using optical storage technology for NDAs would also allow immediate, multiple access to the same document and provide the benefits of on-line indexing techniques. Clarification requests would no longer have to be handled by mail, since sending images over telecommunications lines overnight is reasonably economical – if they are relatively few in number.

"The ability to rapidly introduce [this] technology to large paper-based files has been found to be possible, and integration into a computer-based information system is proven to be practical and readily implemented," says ICI's McCurdy. In June 1988, ICI was the first company to submit an optical NDA to the FDA. That NDA was backed up with paper documentation.

Once a drug has been approved, there is a step that represents another potential application for digital document systems: the design of an appropriate label and directions. To a greater degree than in the consumer products world, pharmaceutical companies have to be concerned about accuracy and safety in labeling.

The design of an appropriate label can become a nightmare of coordination to ensure that everyone is working with the latest version, and get the appropriate level of approval. The process can be streamlined and accelerated by digitizing the original draft and electronically routing it to the right people, along with the appropriate deadlines for changes and final approval. As with many applications for optical document systems, the net economic benefits are usually derived from being able to move the image around the office electronically and enforce discipline on the business system via work flow software.

MARKETING AND LEGAL

The introduction of any new technology always raises the issue of which departments should be able to access it and, perhaps, thereby contribute unforeseen benefits to the entire organization. Pharmaceutical companies could benefit by extending the system to the marketing and legal departments.

Marketing may be more of a hands-off proposition in the pharmaceutical industry than, for example, it is in the automobile industry, where marketing tends to set product direction and development.

Marketing's potential to contribute to the R&D process was demonstrated in the case of a pharmaceutical company that was developing a drug to control high blood pressure. The drug was successful in its primary goal, but marketing personnel noticed that it also caused weight loss. Therefore the drug had a potential secondary market that was missed by the original development team, but which could have provided a lucrative potential revenue stream sooner than it did.

Because the potential legal liability incurred by the introduction of a new drug is large, the legal staff must also be able to have access to R&D information to try to anticipate problems related to safety or effectiveness.

If optical document systems offer such improvements in the drug manufacturing process, given the hundreds of millions of dollars at stake, why aren't all pharmaceutical companies clamoring to have systems in place? Several issues have to be resolved prior to the optical NDA becoming a full-blown reality: FDA funding, system standards, and man's inevitable preference for homeostasis.

FDA FUNDING

Despite special congressional budget approval for a separate department to speed up approval of AIDS-related drugs, the FDA is severely underfunded. This year's FDA information systems budget, according to an official there, is "about $3.5 million, with $2.5 million of that scheduled to be spent on hardware, but this represents a figure much higher than the average funds available historically, and it is not certain that next year we will be able to spend as much."

Even if the FDA had the money to invest in digital document systems, a lack of standards makes its selection of a single system difficult. The issue is especially problematic, since the FDA must service the approximately 156 companies in the U.S. actively involved in the drug R&D process. Those pharmaceutical firms will undoubtedly purchase systems that reflect their individual methods of research and development. The dilemma arises in that the FDA cannot afford to invest in incompatible equipment or to train their examiners on a variety of systems.

The same standards problem arises within the pharmaceutical companies themselves. "Standards are an issue," says a Squibb spokesperson, "since there is certainly the need to have interoperability within the corporation, but we don't have that now, since departments use a variety of document creation programs and microfilm still remains lacking in the standards arena."

Issues such as file structure and media size standards, which would allow media interchangeability, are problems, but indexing, screen layout, and database query facilities are more pressing problems. In fact, says a high-level spokesman for the FDA Center for Drug Evaluation and Research, in Washington, D.C., "The issue is not media interchangeability. What is vital is a standard software to manipulate the data portion of the image."

One of the biggest problems in setting standards for digital image systems is their conflict with expected advances in the technology. Some of those improvements may include expert system-type logic for the database query facility that would translate queries between multiple vendor environments. A natural language interface to statistical test results would allow researchers and FDA reviewers to recombine data to obtain new statistical findings. Improved scanning technology will allow the data portion of the image to be converted into a form that can be manipulated.

Standards at the physical level, as defined by ISO, are not likely to exist for several years. Still, an advisory body made up of FDA officials, pharmaceutical manufacturers, the vendor community, and pharmaceutical associations could take the first step toward uniformity by separating data standards from image standards, which would pave the way to further progress. This is not an application of technology that can wait to be sorted by standards committees or de facto standards; getting drugs approved quickly involves the welfare of the nation.

Given man's tendency to perpetuate the status quo, it is relatively easy for end users to review digital document systems and decide that the technology is not quite there yet or that the system cannot be cost-justified. Cost-justifying any piece of office automation equipment is a large task since many of the benefits are difficult to quantify. Just ask IS managers to cost-justify upgrading a System/36 to an AS/400.

Table 18.1
Technology Hasn't Helped Yet
The average time required to get a drug approved has not shortened, although the worst-case situation has improved.

	1983	1984	1985	1986	1987
New Drug Applications	94	142	100	98	68
Average Approval Time*	14.7	18.7	22.1	21.6	27.0
Best Case	.9	1.5	2.6	1.2	2.9
Worst Case	93.3	131.3	121.0	127.5	87.3

Source: FDA, 1988
*Approval times are measured in number of months.

The cost-justification problem for image systems can be overcome, however, as the Upjohn Co. of Kalamazoo, Mich., has found. "We will have several systems in the near future, but they will have to use our existing workstations in order to keep cost down on a per-user basis," says an Upjohn spokesperson. Before Upjohn can use its pcs as image workstations, however, it will have to equip them with add-in boards to provide upgraded communications, image compression/decompression, and between 2MB and 10MB of extra RAM.

We all talk about technology as a competitive advantage but rarely do we take the time to classify technologies into those that provide a tactical advantage and those that offer a strategic pathway to success in an industry. Image processing is that technology pathway of the '90s.

Some companies have recognized image processing as such. "This is a highly knit community," says a representative of Hoescht-Celanese, New York, "and optical systems is the most frequently discussed topic at industry gatherings. Everyone is seriously looking at it, but the pharmaceutical industry is traditionally closed to outsiders, therefore no one wants to talk about what they're doing."

The fact is that the pioneers of this technology have a strategic advantage in an industry that has been traditionally reluctant to adopt any new technology. ICI Pharmaceuticals has a two-year lead over Warner Lambert, Glaxo, and Pfizer. The next tier of adopters are another 12 to 18 months behind those three. The question becomes, what further shot in the arm will it take for the rest of the industry to wake up? Or will they continue to behave like a child after a tetanus injection, thinking that, if they just sit on their hands, it won't hurt too much?

Up until now, pharmaceutical firms could have responded that way to a new technology with no ill effect, as success in the industry was predicated solely on the drug R&D and marketing efforts. As the spokesman for Warner Lambert indicates, however, the potential for image processing means that the most successful pharmaceutical companies will be those that take a leadership position in office systems technology.

19

Amex Builds an Expert System To Assist Its Credit Analysts

Don Steinberg

A computerized expert system that draws its conclusions from more than a dozen mainframe databases will soon make it easier for American Express (Amex) employees to live with one of the features that has made the American Express card famous worldwide.

Its lack of a preset spending limit has been critical to the success of the American Express charge card. Unlike bank-issued cards such as Mastercard and VISA, which impose a dollar limit on cardholders, Amex lets members rack up charges as high as they like—as long as they pay the entire bill every month.

However, while this policy is good for customer relations, it can be a headache for many Amex employees. Since there is no defined point at which credit should be denied to a customer, certain employees, called authorizers, must decide whether a purchase will be approved or denied.

Currently, some 200 to 300 authorizers, situated at four U.S. authorization centers, are devoted to the task of making these decisions. Sitting at IBM 3278 terminals, the authorizers receive basic information on a "purchase in progress" and must then toggle among a loosely organized group of mainframe databases, which hold customer credit histories, to determine whether to authorize the purchase.

The process may involve simply checking a customer's recent payment history or looking at the bank-account information given on the customer's original credit-card application. Either way, Amex guarantees its merchants that authorizers will make a decision within 90 seconds.

The cost of making wrong decisions can be huge. If an authorizer rejects an attempted purchase because the account has an unusually high balance or a history of frequent late payments, for example, Amex loses the revenue it would collect from the merchant for the transaction and also risks losing the insulted shopper as a member.

Conversely, if the authorizer approves a purchase that should not have been approved, the company faces the risk of never receiving payment. Losses from unpaid bills and credit-card fraud are staggering. "It's a nine-digit problem for them [In the hundreds of millions of dollars annually]," said Alex Jacobson, president and CEO of Inference Corp., the Los Angeles artificial intelligence (AI) software developer that Amex called upon to help develop its expert system.

WE'RE TALKING STRESS

Authorizers don't need to see such numbers to know that their job is rough. "This is a high-pressure job," said Ted Markowitz, director of technology strategy at American Express. "The burnout level is pretty high."

In 1984, Bob Flast, then manager of the credit-authorization department for Amex's American Express Travel Related Services Co. subsidiary in New York, devised a way to use information systems to try to relieve some of the pressure on his staff.

Mr. Flast presented a proposal to build a computerized expert system that would lighten the authorizer's load. The system would condense the array of customer data authorizers need to view during each transaction into a single screenful of data. Using rules garnered through interviews with the company's most experienced authorizers, the expert system also would formulate an approve-or-deny suggestion.

Once the company approved funding for the project, dubbed the Authorizer's Assistant, Mr. Flast recruited Mr. Markowitz to assist him in the system's planning and implementation.

From the beginning, the planners of the Authorizer's Assistant were confident that the project would succeed in the modest goals of increasing the productivity of human authorizers, Mr. Markowitz said. Still, the project did present risks, he said.

AI had never been used at American Express or anywhere else in a credit-authorization application, and the project was being carried out in an environment where success—or failure—would be obvious, according to Mr. Flast.

Not every American Express card transaction goes to a human authorizer. In fact, 95 percent of them are approved by the firm's Computerized Authorization System (CAS). But that still leaves human authorizers with a large number of decisions (American Express officials declined to provide an exact figure).

The authorization process begins whenever a consumer presents an American Express card to make a purchase, and the merchant contacts American Express to verify that the card is valid and the customer is credit-worthy (by checking with Amex, the merchant is relieved of responsibility for fraud), according to Mr. Flast.

Most merchants contact Amex for authorizations electronically through point-of-sale systems or credit-card readers. Others dial a toll-free telephone number and read the purchase and card information to Amex personnel.

Exhibit 19.1
American Express Purchase-Authorization
Process with Authorizer's Assistant

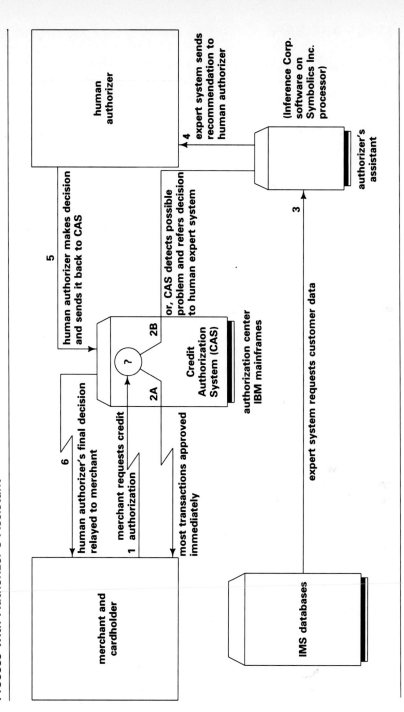

MOST ARE SAFE

In either case, the information is sent to an IBM mainframe at the company's data center, in Phoenix, Ariz., that runs CAS. CAS is a simple application that uses straightforward statistical analysis to separate normal transactions from those that might pose a problem. About 95 percent of the time, transactions are "system approved" by CAS within four or five seconds, according to Betsy Fearnow, project director of advanced technology at the Phoenix data center.

If CAS's statistical checks reveal potential problems with the transaction due to unusual account activity or a large account balance, Mr. Markowitz said, it refers the decision to human authorizers. Amex officials declined to reveal the parameters that would cause CAS to send a transaction to human authorizers.

At this point, with the old system, the human authorizer would be sent a screen of data from CAS on the current transaction, and would then need to access more than a dozen separate databases of customer records, synthesizing the information found there in order to make an authorization decision within 90 seconds. The expert system, which was prototyped in 1986 and pilot-tested early this year, is designed to simplify that process.

Authorizer's Assistant includes about 800 rules, some designed to condense customer data, others designed to formulate a recommendation, according to Mr. Markowitz. The expert system presents authorizers with a single screen of information that consists of an approve/reject recommendation and the data upon which that recommendation was based. It also produces a second screen that provides explanations of its decisions, he said. The final approval or rejection decision still rests with a human authorizer, however, he said.

PRODUCTIVITY'S UP

From its first test, the Authorizer's Assistant has been a boon to the productivity of Amex's credit authorizers, Mr. Flast said. In the testing that has been conducted with authorizers using the expert system—which now is scheduled to go live in Amex authorization centers beginning next spring—the company has seen a 20 percent increase in productivity, he said.

Based on those productivity gains, American Express expects Authorizer's Assistant to pay for itself in a little less than two years, he said.

"As the number of transactions grows, we won't have to hire as many new people," said Mr. Flast, who is now Amex vice president of corporate technology strategy.

American Express expects its transaction volume to increase significantly thanks to its recently introduced Optima credit card, which offers a revolving credit line similar to those offered by Mastercard and VISA.

There are also indications that other benefits of the new expert system will be much greater than anticipated, Mr. Flast said, with some gains directly affecting the millions Amex loses each year due to fraud and bad credit.

For instance, a recent test looked at 2,500 decisions made by authorizers with and without the expert system's help and then checked the quality of the cardmem-

Table 19.1
American Express Travel Related Services Co.

Problem: The American Express card is differentiated in the charge-card market by offering cardmembers no preset spending limit. This policy can be a back-office headache since there is no clear point at which credit should be denied. On questionable transactions, point-of-sale authorizers must pull together reams of data to make individual judgments on each case, and they must make each decision in no more than 90 seconds.

Solution: Backed by a research and development fund made available for high-tech projects, managers in the Amex credit-authorization department proposed to build a computerized expert system that would assist human authorizers in making decisions. The expert system was expected to support the no-credit limit policy, providing human authorizers with assistance, and to improve the overall quality of authorizers' decisions.

Tools: 3083 and other mainframes   3845 processor
IBM Corp.   Symbolics Inc.
Armonk, N.Y. 10504   Cambridge, Mass. 02142
(914) 765-1900   (617) 577-7500

Advanced Reasoning Tool
Inference Corp.
Los Angeles, Calif. 90045
(213) 417-7997

Prognosis: Scheduled to go live next spring, the Authorizer's Assistant expert system is expected to increase the productivity of human authorizers by 20 percent. This gain alone, officials expect, will pay for the system in less than two years. Officials also expect to reap gains by preventing loss through credit-card fraud and rooting out bad credit risks. They project that the system will cut the number of 90-day-overdue bills in half. The successful use of artificial intelligence in this system also has spawned other AI projects companywide.

ber accounts involved three months later. The study found that in cases where Authorizer's Assistant was used, far fewer accounts ended up in the collections department. Based on these tests, the company expects to cut its number of 90-day-overdue bills (the point at which accounts are referred to the collection department) in half. This benefit, said officials, would produce an additional five times the return on investment from the initial productivity gains.

Planners at Amex attributed success of the project to its use of AI techniques, which have allowed the firm to turn the amassed base of authorization knowledge among its senior authorizers into a hard and retained asset. The leap in performance created by Authorizer's Assistant could only have been brought about by an entirely new technical approach, they said.

Officials hope the expert system will improve consistency in authorizations among the firm's hundreds of authorizers, who vary widely in experience. They also hope the system will reduce the high burnout rate among authorizers.

The project has proven to be a springboard for new AI-related projects all across Amex.

"It was a proof of concept," said Mr. Markowitz. "There are 10 other AI-based systems now in place across the company."

20

Expert Systems and the Law

Edward Warner

The stock market crash of 1987 revealed the darker side of computer automation. According to a government commission, the October freefall was caused partly by computerized program trading, in which brokers' computer programs constantly compare the difference between the price of commodities futures and stocks. These price differences can change so fast that only computers can react quickly enough to take advantage of them. When stock prices started their dive, however, the system began feeding on itself, spinning the market out of human control and approaching what the chairman of the New York Stock Exchange later called a "meltdown."

The brokers of Black Monday readily delegated those buy/sell decisions to a computer program, but society at large is uneasy about using computers to make, or even give advice about, high-risk decisions. Nonetheless, software is becoming available which can do just that. These programs, called "expert systems," contain the knowledge of experts in a field and the logical rules those experts follow to solve a problem. Expert systems can advise a doctor on which medicine to prescribe for a patient's symptoms, tell an auditor how tax laws might apply to a budgetary line-item, or decide in seconds whether a radar blip is an enemy rocket or a meteor — a task they will tackle for the Star Wars program.

No one questions the utility of spreading expert knowledge, but what happens when an expert system makes a mistake? What will be the reaction when, for example, a glitch in the software causes a prescription program to specify the wrong medicine? Unlike program-trading software, which brokerage houses developed themselves, expert systems are being produced both for internal corporate use and for sale to third parties. Sales of expert systems leaves someone to blame, and some observers say the greatest obstacle to the spread of such systems is fear of litigation.

Nowhere is the concern over product liability stronger than among companies working on expert systems for medical applications, where malpractice suits already abound. "I know of interesting endeavors that never came to light because of liability problems," says Dr. Braxton Degarmo, owner of the Medical Software Consortium, a St. Louis supplier of medical software. Degarmo participated in a U.S. Army/NASA effort to develop an "intensive care stretcher," an unmanned emergency room for use on space vehicles. The stretcher would have monitored patients' vital signs and its expert system would have responded to changes in their condition with treatments such as drug injections. A medical-products company, he recalls, was ready to produce the stretcher's hardware, but balked at getting involved with the software because of concerns about the potential for lawsuits.

Expert systems consultant Tom J. Schwartz also knows of a medical expert system that was stalled because of legal doubts. The system's producer "sank a couple of man-years [of development time] into it and, when they looked at the cost for liability insurance, they said 'no way'," recalls Schwartz.

Litigation worries, says Degarmo, are particularly strong at universities, which are among the centers of medical expert systems development. A case in point: the Caduceus medical expert system at Carnegie-Mellon University in Pittsburgh, 17 years in development and still awaiting commercialization.

Despite these fears, the Health Industry Manufacturers Association predicts that, in the next 10 years, the biggest changes in health care will come from software. Expert systems "still haven't reached the capacity in the health-care system that their potential would indicate," says association president Frank E. Samuel, Jr.

Expert systems will also be widely used in the corporate sector. Boiler manufacturer Combustion Engineering of Stamford, Conn., for example, uses an expert system to collect the knowledge of its best designers, speeding the design process and easing the transition when designers leave the company (see "Success Story," September 1988). Coopers & Lybrand, the accounting firm, has a system that dispenses tax advice to its auditors, and Honeywell-Bull sales representatives use an expert system to configure customers' computers by simply entering the customers' needs. By one analyst's estimate, about half of the companies listed in the *Fortune* 500 are developing expert systems.

Expert systems will also be sold commercially. Louis Robinson, publisher of the *Spang Robinson Report on Artificial Intelligence* newsletter, believes expert systems will one day be so prevalent that computer companies will routinely include them with their hardware the way they bundle-in software today.

However, lawyers warn that before expert systems become commonplace they will probably become ensnared in the widening web of product-liability litigation. According to the Brookings Institution, the number of product-liability lawsuits increased eightfold from 1974 to 1986, when 13,595 such cases were filed. One reason is the increasing number of lawyers who specialize in computer-related issues, up from 100 in 1980 to 1,100 in 1985.

Mixing these numbers with a slug of hyperbole, consultant Schwartz warns, "There's 200,000 lawyers out there waiting for an expert system to kill a little old lady—and they're going to sue everybody in sight."

Of course, a suit does not automatically mean a loss in court. "The likelihood is that there would be many suits, but few judgments" against expert systems, predicts Richard Neely, a judge in the West Virginia Supreme Court of Appeals and an expert on product liability. But no expert-system producer wants to be the first to be saddled with a hefty judgment, and all expert systems producers worry that everyone's insurance rates will soar after the first company loses a suit. "A lot of people are waiting for that first test case," says Degarmo.

That first case is still over the horizon, so legal experts are looking closely at other lawsuits involving similar electronic products. In 1986, the U.S. Supreme Court upheld a $350,000 decision against Dun & Bradstreet, which provides credit information on U.S. companies, in a libel suit brought by a Vermont builder whose reputation was harmed by erroneous information from Dun & Bradstreet's computerized database. In 1982, NCR Corp. suffered a $2.3-million adverse judgment when a California court ruled that Glovatorium Inc., a dry cleaner, had been defrauded when NCR computers did not perform as promised.

Computer programs usually come with disclaimers that deny responsibility if the software fails to work as promised, but lawyers say these disavowals will offer little refuge when the summons hit the fan. Glovatorium's lawyer, Richard Perez, says he won his case despite several disclaimers in the NCR contract. One reason disclaimers carry little weight is that most software buyers never sign the enclosed license-agreement cards, notes Dan Shafer, editor of *Intelligent Systems Analyst,* a newsletter.

Eventually, something stronger than a disclaimer may be needed. In June, the House Energy and Commerce Committee approved a bill that would make companies liable if they fail to provide an adequate warning about hazards posed by their products.

Should an expert system user suffer damage, there will be no shortage of parties to blame. Experts say possible lawsuit targets may extend from the user to the programmer, the supplier, and even the expert whose knowledge went into the program. In determining who is at fault, lawyers say a great deal will hinge on whether the system lets the user make the final decision. Pointing to a case where an automatic radiation-therapy machine inadvertently dispensed lethal overdoses (see "Federal Rules on Expert Systems," p. 35). Ed Miller, director of the Food and Drug Administration's compliance division for radiological products, says "the reason [the overdose] could occur was an attempt to make the system more user friendly." Unfortunately, expert systems may be needed in situations where equipment is more sophisticated than the typical technician.

Another indicator of blame, lawyers say, is whether the software is found to have a "bug," or programming error. The prevalence of bugs, even in software involved in life-and-death decisions, is indicated by a recent FDA report that says bugs were behind 79 of the 84 computer-product recalls the agency initiated between 1983 and 1987. Judge Neely believes that bugs, not an expert's errors, pose the greatest potential for litigation against any type of software. Once customers come to expect a certain level of performance from any program—for instance, that it will add and subtract correctly—then a failure to meet that performance level "is like making a Buick with a wheel that falls off," he says.

No software company has yet lost a lawsuit brought over a bug, however. In 1986, Lotus Development Corp. was sued by a Florida construction company that claimed a bug in Lotus' 1-2-3 spreadsheet program caused the builder to overbid

Federal Rules on Expert Systems

While attorneys wait for lawsuits to clarify the legal risks of expert systems, the federal government is already enacting regulations to control the use of such programs.

In some cases, government agencies have applied the same measures they use to regulate human experts. In 1986, for example, the Internal Revenue Service began treating income-tax software the same way it deals with human tax preparers: If the program gives "substantive instructions" for completing a tax return and makes mistakes, it's liable.

Another agency, the Securities and Exchange Commission, short-circuited the development of an expert system proposed by Computer Language Research of Carrollton, Tex. The SEC refused to rule that the company's expert system would not have to register as a financial adviser—at least until the program was completed. Computer Language Research had wanted to create a version of its Financial Sense expert system that could make specific financial recommendations, not just generic ones, recalls product manager Steve Brown. The SEC, which draws the line at commercial computer programs that recommend specific stocks, left "the impression we might have some [legal] exposure there," Brown says.

The Food and Drug Administration has so far been the most aggressive expert-systems regulator because of its role in approving medical products. The FDA says the number of computerized medical products is increasing at an astronomical rate—so fast that this year the agency decided to specify what kind of software was not subject to review, a list that includes spreadsheets used in medical offices. Software that makes treatment decisions, however, still must receive FDA approval, and with good reason. In 1986, a software bug in a computerized radiation-therapy machine was blamed for the deaths of at least two patients undergoing treatment at a Texas hospital. The radiation machine in question was recalled by the FDA, and a lawsuit is now pending.

Ironically, the IRS, FBI, and Environmental Protection Agency are all developing or using expert systems on an in-house basis. Also, some law firms are using expert systems to judge when conditions are ripe to file a suit.

on a contract. Lotus blamed user error, and the case was settled out of court in Lotus' favor. But Boston-area lawyer Peter Marx, chairman of the New England Computer Law Forum, thinks the Lotus case is only the first in a wave of such suits. Marx warns that the courts will be increasingly inclined to hold programs to the strictest standard of liability.

Not only will expert systems need to be bug-free, they will also need to leaven their specialized knowledge with common sense. That may be very hard to do, says B. Chandrasekaran, director of the artificial intelligence research lab at Ohio State University. He points out that common sense consists of simple rules that everyone knows—such as the fact that two objects cannot occupy the same space—but also of other rules that have yet to be recognized. If we don't know all the rules of common sense, he asks, how can we program an expert system to think as intelligently as a human does?

Expert system vendors challenged in court will probably claim that their products are the equivalent of textbooks. Howard Kramer, assistant director for market regulation at the Securities and Exchange Commission, says computerized investment advisers are no different than any other research report. But consultant Schwartz disagrees. "Our society puts more stock into what a computer says than what a textbook says," he says. "Computers give interactive knowledge."

Software makers may also claim that expert systems are still an inexact science. But that defense is also not expected to hold water. Predicting the weather may seem equally inexact, but three years ago the courts ordered the U.S. government to pay $1.25 million to the surivors of four fishermen who perished in an Atlantic storm. The men had relied on an inaccurate National Weather Service forecast.

Software companies that make expert-system shells—the software used to develop an expert system—or that develop expert systems only for their own internal use, may think they don't have to worry about liability suits. But many lawyers say their sense of security may be illusory. If a product fails because it was built on a flawed structure, that structure may be held liable. Expert systems built by a company only for its own use are less vulnerable, provided they affect the company's operations alone. But corporations could be held accountable to their customers or employees. The federal government, for example, is required to maintain an accurate database of information on its employees; the Privacy Act of 1974 lets federal workers who lose out on a promotion or raise because of errors in the data sue for damages.

Apart from the liability issue, expert systems also raise the question of who owns the knowledge in them. Dennis Deutsch, a computer lawyer in Hackensack, N.J., represents a client who provided the expertise for an expert system as part of his job. The client has since lost that job, but wants to receive royalties on the system he created. "My client is claiming the system is owned by him in the absence of a contract" to the contrary, says Deutsch.

To avoid ownership challenges, Deutsch says, "the employer must have an adequate pre-employment contract," with the expert whose knowledge is written into the program. Other steps that could help reduce the risk of litigation include:

- accurately representing the system's abilities,
- creating a program that merely recommends particular actions, instead of acting on its own,
- avoiding software bugs,
- making sure disclaimers are legible, understandable, and likely to be signed, and
- obtaining liability insurance.

Despite the multitude of legal issues, few observers expect expert systems to wind up in the same dog house as nuclear power. Indeed, several expert systems are already in use.

For example, the Help system at Latter Day Saints Hospital in Salt Lake City assists doctors throughout the hospital in interpreting patient data, such as lab tests. According to Dr. Homer Warner, who led the system's development, the Help software is involved in approximately 80,000 decisions a day, and has improved the medical care of half a million patients in the 20 years since it came into use.

To reduce the risk of liability, the system was thoroughly tested and makes only recommendations, says Warner. In fact, Warner believes medical "expert systems are going to be the answer to litigation," by keeping doctors from making the errors that lead to suits.

Clearly, there are times an information-bearing product is so important that its utility must be recognized, litigation or not. This was the case with Jeppesen Sanderson Inc., a Denver company that converts government data into aircraft flight charts. After Jeppesen lost a major lawsuit in which its products had been blamed for an aircraft crash, the U.S. Congress took the unusual action of promising to indemnify Jeppesen if the government's data ever proved to be at fault. The action indicated the charts' value to the nation's air-traffic system, says company president Horst Bergmann.

Lawyer Marx believes a good next step would be for the courts to endorse the benefits of expert systems by subjecting them to a more forgiving liability standard. "We want to encourage people to innovate," he says.

The trade-off between benefits and risk will probably depend on how badly an expert system is needed. In poverty-stricken parts of the Third World, points out Ellen Staelen, a senior consultant at International Data Corp., a medical expert system could provide emergency advice, even for non-doctors. "When there's such a deplorable lack of resources," in these regions, she says, "one would hate to see the lawyers hold sway."

The public, not the experts, will ultimately decide the value and risk of expert systems, through lawsuits and regulations. Such decisions may involve a willingness to accept some level of danger. As a comparison, researcher Chandrasekaran wonders what would have happened to the automobile if, at its introduction, someone had warned, "Here's a technology that's going to kill 50,000 people a year."

21

The Battle for the Broker's Desk

Henry Fersko-Weiss

The financial-services industry is going through a major upheaval. As international markets become increasingly volatile and trading volumes expand, brokers and traders need additional data just to keep up, and information-service providers are locked in a battle to give it to them.

The weapons include new microcomputers and workstations, better analytical software, a decentralization of brokerage computer systems, and not-so-subtle psychological gamesmanship.

For companies that provide financial information, this is a fight for the future. The market positions of the first- and second-place players in the equities-information market—Quotron Systems and Automatic Data Processing (ADP)—are almost certain to be reversed. International heavyweight Reuters Holdings PLC has finally burst the contractual dam that kept it out of the U.S. market. As the top contenders struggle, smaller players such as PC Quote, Bridge Information Systems, and Knight-Ridder Financial Information will take advantage of the confusion to launch attacks on market niches.

The fallout of this battle will give brokers and traders faster access to more data, as well as new processing tools such as portfolio-management software, risk-management packages, and trading models. These tools give brokerage houses a way to lure top brokers, boost business, and give clients more focused help with investments.

The hottest systems are the most advanced equipment—microcomputers and workstations from companies such as IBM, Digital Equipment Corp., Hewlett-Packard, Sun Microsystems Inc., and Apollo Computer Inc. These machines offer superior speed and processing capabilities by using Intel 80386 and Motorola 68020 processing chips, and recently enjoyed a substantial drop in prices—partly due to economies of scale provided by opening up the financial market. These factors alone don't justify the purchase of hardware that can cost anywhere from $5,000 to more than $100,000 per box, but the growing complexity and competitiveness of the financial markets do.

"With the advent of 24-hour trading on global markets, institutions have to link their positions worldwide to allocate capital and determine risk," says Richard Caplis, director of the information-systems group at Coopers & Lybrand Management Consulting Services, a unit of the Big Eight accounting firm. "Positions are very large, the markets have become complicated, and changes come rapidly. Program trading [now mostly halted by securities firms], dreamed up by the people who do arbitrage between cash and options markets, was the beginning of the problem." The market competitiveness can be traced to the tremendous influx of investment dollars during the bull market of 1982 to 1987. As the market began to peak, trading activity hit a new level of volatility and stayed there.

To cope with these conditions, financial institutions spent $1.22 billion on information services in 1987, according to market researcher Link Resources Corp. Link predicts that the financial-information business will grow to $3.02 billion by 1991, topping credit and travel information to become the largest segment of the information industry.

The key information in this deluge of data are price quotations on stocks, bonds, foreign exchange, commodities, and other financial instruments. In the past, brokers got price quotes from "dumb" terminals connected by leased lines to the mainframe computer of a quotation provider. Today the terminals on a broker's desk are at least semi-intelligent, with some computing power of their own, and an increasing number are advanced workstations that pack more power than did the mainframes of a decade ago.

As terminals improved, so did the delivery path for information. In addition to standard leased telephone lines, today's systems use 56-kilobit land lines, satellites, and unused parts of the FM-radio and TV spectrums.

Presentation has also improved. Instead of a stream of hard-to-decipher digits, the new systems provide "multiwindow displays that might show different market data feeds in colors—let's say green for stocks and blue for foreign exchange," says Craig Symons, a vice president at the Gartner Group, a market-research firm. "Some of the price information may also be poured through an analytical program that then presents it in graphic form. These visual aids increase the immediate comprehension of the numbers."

Brokers equipped with workstations get more than price information. They can identify prospective clients through multi-layered database searches and analyze a client's position with risk management and portfolio management software—some with built-in artificial intelligence techniques. They can also communicate with each other via electronic mail. Most important, workstations let brokers use all of these functions at the same time.

Quotron now controls 60 percent of this world of flitting equities numbers and smart applications, according to George Sacerdote, a vice president at market-research firm Arthur D. Little. ADP is second with about 30 percent. The host of other providers split the remaining 10 percent.

ADP crashed the stock-quotation marketplace by buying Bunker Ramo in February 1986, and has kept pushing ever since. ADP originally provided back-office computing systems to many financial companies, so it understood the benefits of

Table 21.1
The Price-Quotation Leaders

Company	Worldwide Terminals	1987 Revenue	1987 Growth	Comments
Reuters Holdings Reuters North America 1700 Broadway New York, NY 10019 (212) 603-3300	145,000	$1.6 billion* (Reuters Holdings) $326 million* (Reuters North America)	39.6 percent 32.7 percent	Holds 80 percent of the foreign-exchange information market, forming the backbone of this international market. Reuters earns about 56 percent of its revenues from foreign-exchange, but also offers quotation and information services on fixed-income securities, commodities, and stocks. Now trying to penetrate the U.S. market for domestic stock data with its Equities 2000 system, which delivers real-time quotes on 100,000 instruments from 137 exchanges, Reuters' advanced technology, coupled with its enormous reach and financial power, should make it a third major force in that market.
Quotron Systems 5454 Beethoven St. Los Angeles, CA 90066 (213) 827-4600	95,000	Not available (subsidiary of Citicorp since 1986)	Not available	Holds 60 percent of the domestic stock quotation business, but is on the verge of losing its leadership to ADP. Quotron provides real-time price quotes from exchanges around the world, covering stocks, options, bonds, mutual funds, and commodities. The company's most advanced service, the Quotron 1000, uses minicomputers to serve the entire branch office and semi-intelligent workstations on the broker's desk to offer real-time price quotes, analytical programs, financial databases, and messaging facilities.
Telerate 1 World Trade Center New York, NY 10048 (212) 938-5200	67,000	$336 million	44.5 percent	Dominates the fixed-income information marketplace, offering real-time quotes on U.S. government and mortgage-backed securities. Telerate also covers worldwide money markets, foreign exchange, financial futures, and precious metals. In October 1987, it acquired Canada's CMQ Communications to try and crack the equities-information market.
Automatic Data Processing 1 ADP Blvd. Roseland, NJ 07068 (201) 994-5000	65,000	$1.4 billion	15 percent	In addition to real-time price quotes on stocks, bonds, commodities, and foreign exchange, ADP offers Videcom, a graphic technical-analysis service. Agreements with Merrill Lynch and Shearson to replace Quotron terminals with IBM PS/2s will make ADP the top domestic

Table 21.1 (cont.)

Company	Worldwide Terminals	1987 Revenue	1987 Growth	Comments
Knight-Ridder 1 Herald Plaza Miami, FL 33132 (305) 376-3838	19,750	$2.1 billion (corporate) $99.6 million (Business Information Services division)	8.5 percent 11.6 percent	equities-information provider. ADP's strength in back-office systems, coupled with advanced front-office technology, should continue to boost its market share. Dominates the commodities-quotes and news market with its CNS Data Quote service. Recently challenged Telerate in the fixed-income securities area with its Money Center service, which offers quotes on fixed-income, mortgage-backed, and government securities, plus fundamental news. Another service, called Trade Center, provides charts and analysis for all kinds of securities. Knight-Ridder has also set its sights on the fixed-income arena.
PC Quote 401 S. LaSalle St. Chicago, IL 60604 (312) 786-5400	Not applicable	$6,086,435	79 percent	Offers equity-quote information over a network of personal computers. This approach offers significant cost savings, and the company claims it has 1,200 customer locations. PC Quote lost $558,188 in 1987, but posted its first profitable quarter this year.
Bridge Information Systems 10050 Manchester Rd. St. Louis, MO 53122 (314) 821-5660	Not available	Not available	Not available	Provides last sale and historical information on more than 60,000 financial instruments. The system also offers computerized portfolio accounting packages, a brokerage office support system, electronic mail, and real-time news. Bridge, a private company, is noted for its use of graphics to make data clearer.
Data Broadcasting 8300 Old Courthouse Rd. Vienna, VA 22180 (703) 790-3570	1,600	Not available	Not available	Delivers price information and financial news over an unused part of a TV signal to individual investors and brokerage firms equipped with special decoders, TV tuners, and personal computers. Owned by Financial News Network, which is controlled by Infotechnology Corp., the company that publishes HIGH TECHNOLOGY BUSINESS.

*Based on an exchange rate of $1.89 to the pound on Dec. 31, 1987.
Source: High Technology Business Research/Information Industry Bulletin

integrating record-keeping with quotation and analytical functions. "ADP was very much aware of the need to increase the technological expertise used in information delivery," says Jim Settel, senior vice president of product development at Prudential-Bache Securities. "They made it easier for us to recognize the potential."

Prudential-Bache's system offers a good example of the benefits of financial-information products. ADP helped the company build an integrated system using Convergent Technologies minicomputers as branch-office processors and microcomputers as the brokers' window on the markets. The system combined data feeds from ADP, off-the-shelf software such as Lotus' 1-2-3 spreadsheet, and proprietary programs written by Prudential-Bache programmers. The new system lets brokers calculate bond yields to maturity by pressing a few keys, send personalized form letters to clients, and follow the New York Stock Exchange and bond markets. It was dubbed Boss 1, for branch-office support system. Three Prudential-Bache offices have already moved on to Boss 2, a distributed processing system that maintains branch-office data locally on the Convergent Technologies minicomputers.

"Brokers can create client or prospect profiles that include the data they think is important, such as income, objectives, product interests, even hobbies," says Settel. "There's also an electronic broker-book program that records every purchase, sale, profit, and loss, and maintains that information locally for 18 months. A query function lets brokers search for clients that fit certain criteria. For example, a broker could pull the records for all clients in a zip code who have municipal bonds in their portfolio, make more than $100,000, have a portfolio yield of less than 5 percent, and like to play golf. With this list, a broker could write a letter alerting the group to a special seminar on a new investment opportunity being held at the local golf club. Before this system, it would have been impossible to get so specific on a client search, and the information you could get would take much longer to stream down-line from our central mainframe."

The brokers at Prudential-Bache are so happy they are experiencing "techno-rapture," in Settel's words. "They can do things now they didn't dream of," he says. "Plus it reduced the professional overload."

"Workstations and proprietary software are becoming strategic weapons," says Mike Frank, group manager for the financial and commercial markets at Apollo Computer. "Once one firm sees the advantage of such systems, all the others jump on the bandwagon. Computers beget computers."

Merrill Lynch Pierce Fenner & Smith Inc. and Shearson Lehman Hutton Inc. have jumped after Prudential-Bache. Representatives from both firms visited Prudential-Bache to check out the new approach. "They were very impressed," says Settel. Both companies signed contracts with ADP to replace their present Quotron systems, a major blow to the market leader. Each of the new systems will use about 20,000 IBM PS/2 computers as terminals, a market-share shift of more than 50 points.

But George Levine, Quotron's executive vice president of customer relations and strategic marketing, doesn't accept the Merrill Lynch and Shearson deals as faits accomplis. "We are far from acquiescing," he says. "We continue to develop tools that would make replacing us more difficult. It's a moving target, and ADP has already missed some tentative delivery dates."

Still, Quotron has suffered for its emphasis on a dedicated system of semi-intelligent terminals rather than an open architecture that permits use of third-party personal computers or workstations. The dedicated system prevented brokers from using popular programs such as 1-2-3. Also, the terminals Quotron pushed lacked the sharp images and color available on personal computers and workstations.

The company is trying to fight back, and Levine insists that its new Q-1000 system is as capable as ADP's system, and as open. The Q-1000 has many of the same features: screen windows, multiple processing, a mix of client and market information, word processing, spreadsheets, portfolio management, and decentralized operation. In the future, the system will support workstations.

Quotron is converting customers with older technology to the Q-1000 and trying to attract business from regional brokerage houses. Regional successes include A.G. Edwards & Sons Inc. of St. Louis, and First of Michigan Capital Corp. of Detroit. On a larger scale, Quotron is in the process of converting all 285 of PaineWebber's offices.

PaineWebber approved its system shortly after Black Monday, in spite of general market pessimism and the talk of downsizing brokerage firms. Like managers at other major brokerage houses, PaineWebber's management decided that new information systems are essential to staying competitive; there has been no slowdown in computer purchases.

"We conducted a very extensive two-year evaluation of all the systems before we chose Quotron," says John Murphy, manager of consumer market systems at PaineWebber's New York headquarters. "We needed to upgrade our system because the branch offices had reached their capacity limits." One of the side benefits of upgrading the information system, according to Murphy, is that "it shows we are making a significant commitment to technology. This makes a difference in attracting and retaining brokers who have similar capabilities in other firms."

Aside from upgrading its technical capabilities, Quotron faces another challenge. Citicorp bought Quotron in November 1986, and brokerage firms often compete with Citicorp subsidiaries such as CitiBank. Many firms say they don't want to buy information from a rival.

While the two dominant players slug it out, Reuters is using its international strength to join the brawl. Last May, Reuters, the largest information provider worldwide, bought Instinet, an electronic trade-posting system that covers equities. Reuters has also developed a sophisticated digital network to deliver its information. One of the first offerings on the fast, 56-kilobit-per-second Integrated Digital Network (IDN) is Equities 2000, a worldwide quote system that offers real-time prices on more than 100,000 financial instruments traded on more than 137 exchanges.

Equities 2000 is Reuters' first foray into the U.S. equities-information market. An agreement with ADP kept Reuters out of the business until 1986, but the company is now trying to make up for lost time. Besides its acquisition of Instinet, Reuters bought several other companies in 1986 and 1987. One of these, Reveal Software Inc. of Roslyn, N.Y., has a package that helps brokers manage their clients' portfolios more efficiently. Another recent purchase, Toronto-based I.P. Sharp, markets 150 historical on-line databases, some of which carry financial and economic data useful to traders. In 1985, Reuters acquired Rich Inc. of Chicago, a manufacturer of complete trading-room systems. Rich gives Reuters a foot in the door at some of the largest equities-trading firms.

"We have two factors that will help us achieve an increasingly satisfactory market share," says Patrick Mannix, international technical manager for Reuters. "The first is our comprehensive coverage of international equities, which is of increasing interest to brokers. Second, we have a very good platform for trading in large institutions." Reuters got a big break last year when Prudential-Bache bought more than 1,000 Equities 2000 terminals for installation around the world—250 of them went into the company's New York headquarters.

Although Reuters hopes to become a major player in equities information, it does not see itself taking customers away from ADP and Quotron, says Mannix. "There is room for us to expand with the marketplace," he says. But A.D. Little's Sacerdote thinks that Reuters may have more dramatic long term ambitions. Reuters "is spending a lot of money to develop a U.S. position," he observes. "They clearly have designs on the market."

In the meantime, Reuters holds an impenetrable position in the foreign-exchange market, just as competitor Telerate dominates bonds and other fixed income securities. These markets are the special terrain of investment traders who work large blocks of instruments for their firms or for big accounts, such as pension funds.

"For the foreign-exchange and fixed-income markets, Reuters and Telerate essentially create the market," says Eugene McAuliffe, a senior analyst at First Albany Corp. "They are the equivalent of the New York Stock Exchange. This is very difficult to duplicate, so they have a virtual lock on [selling information about] these markets."

A number of smaller financial-information firms are eyeing the lucrative turf staked out by the major companies, but observers say their lack of economic clout will not be enough to crack the dominance of the top companies. Smaller players will have to be content with filling niches in the market.

PC Quote Inc., for example, offers quote systems based on networks of personal computers. But the company's chief advantage over ADP and Quotron is price, not technology. "The reason we chose PC Quote over ADP was cost," says Ernest Caruso, a Utica, N.Y., registered representative of Integrated Resources Equity Corp., a regional broker based in New York City. "I came from Tucker Anthony, where we were using ADP. But to get that same system in here would cost three times what we're paying for PC Quote." Caruso adds that he likes the flexibility of PC Quote, which allows him to see price data in several different formats.

Data Broadcasting Corp. (DBC) uses a hidden part of the Financial News Network's television signal to deliver market information and related news. DBC, an FNN subsidiary, inserts its information in the cable channel's vertical blanking interval—the black bar that appears when a TV picture rolls. The company provides quotes to some 1,500 customers, mostly individual investors who have personal computers, but the company plans to expand to brokerage houses as well.

Other niche players include Bridge Information Systems Inc., noted for its sophisticated graphics, and Knight-Ridder, which is playing off its success providing data to commodities brokers by offering statistical views of stocks, money markets, fixed-income securities, and other investment instruments.

Regardless of which companies ultimately win the information-services war, one thing is certain: Investment firms are shifting away from centralized data-processing systems and dumb quote terminals to distributed-processing networks that link corporate mainframes to branch-office minicomputers and intelligent desktop workstations. Brokers and traders benefit most from this transformation. Now they can maintain sophisticated client databases at their elbow, get access to a broader range of information, and use powerful analytical tools. As the major investment firms move quickly in this direction, the regional firms will have to follow suit. In an industry that depends on split-second decisions and complex supply-and-demand modeling, the better a company's technology, the sharper its competitive edge.

22

Strategy: Quaker Oats Co.— A New Information System Serves Up Instant Statistics for Top Executives

Patricia Mandell

After dinner, in the quiet of his home, Quaker Oats Co. President and Chief Operating Officer Frank Morgan switches on his PC. With a couple of keystrokes, he dials the company mainframe, logs on to the Executive Information system and calls up sales figures for the hot-cereals division.

Within 15 to 20 minutes, he has picked off the most up-to-date sales news available. Then he prints it out and tucks it into his briefcase, armed for an early breakfast meeting with one of the heads of Quaker's 50-odd business units, or perhaps with Chairman and CEO William Smithburg.

The progressive 49-year-old leader of this multinational $4.4 billion company, Mr. Smithburg was a prime catalyst behind the PC-based Executive Information System (EIS), which is now used by 23 top Quaker executives. Seven of them also have PCs at home, where they can use the system to their hearts' content, free from office distractions.

EIS puts key financial data at their fingertips—data they need to make important decisions quickly in the hotly competitive food industry. Interest and support from both the CEO and the president have helped shape EIS into the sophisticated, popular application it is today, as well as boost the use of technology throughout the entire company.

Before EIS was introduced in the spring of 1984, Mr. Smithburg was frustrated by how tough it was to quickly find out information he wanted to know. He wanted fast answers on financial statistics, broken down by the company's strategic business units—for example, hot cereals, ready-to-eat cereals and so on. Headquartered in Chicago, Quaker Oats is the country's No. 1 maker of oatmeal, and No. 1 or 2 with many of its other brands.

In addition to its flagship product, Old Fashioned Quaker Oats, Quaker manufactures such popular foods as Cap'n Crunch and Life cereals, Aunt Jemima syrups and pancakes, Quaker Rice Cakes, Gatorade, Van Camp products, and its newest entries: Oh's and Quaker Oat Squares. Quaker has also diversified with the acquisitions of Golden Grain, the Gaines pet-food business and Fisher-Price toymakers.

Mr. Smithburg's request for data seemed fairly simple, but it wasn't. "Unfortunately, the kind of information he was asking for was in the company, but it was in many sources," said Frank Hemmige, Information Center manager and one of two project leaders in the development of EIS. In those days, executives got financial reports by putting in a request to information services (IS), which would run a batch job on the mainframe. The executives would get hard-copy reports from several sources and do a lot of paper shuffling to arrive at comparisons.

Getting such reports to executives might take hours or days, often too late for a meeting.

Even worse, "In some cases, they decided they wouldn't even ask for the information . . . because they knew they wouldn't get it in time," said John Clements, manager of corporate planning and analysis, and the second project leader for EIS. Also, two executives might look to different in-house sources for the same numbers. Lo and behold, "The two executives come together in a meeting and they've got different numbers," Mr. Clements said.

It didn't take long to realize they needed a central source of easy-to-use summary data. Outside systems were reviewed and found to be as unsatisfying as lumpy oatmeal. So the information center (IC) was given a 6-month mandate to develop an on-line source. The IC came in under the wire with a system using IBM PCs in terminal-emulation mode to a Burroughs mainframe, and IFPS software, a financial-planning package from Execucom.

Project leaders hoped from the first to capitalize further on the PC's future capabilities as an intelligent workstation.

This original Executive Information System was quite slow, limited and hard to use, because it was command-driven. It gave only straight reports from the financial database, such as daily or current-month sales for a business unit. And it lacked the ability to do what-if analysis.

Although Mr. Smithburg and several other executives debuted the Burroughs system EIS, it wasn't winning any popularity contests. "I don't think we ever got more than 10 users," Mr. Clements said.

Today, Quaker's current EIS is a deluxe model. It was switched over to an IBM mainframe in March 1987, given a menu-based operation, what-if capabilities, on-screen color and many more options. It uses Comshare Inc.'s Information Gateway as a front end, which simplifies its use.

EIS's menu operation is truly user-friendly. "We should be able to take [any person] off the street, and if he knows how to read, we should be able to teach him the system," Mr. Clements said.

The system is so simple to use, he added, that executives are given only a half-hour training session. "We give them one sheet of information, and they don't even need to read that," he said.

As soon as they turn on the power, executives see the main menu, which offers five options: Financial Database, Dow Jones/News Retrieval (DJ/NR), Financial Worksheets, Daily Sales or Exit. They use the arrow keys to make a selection. When they choose the Financial Database or Daily Sales, they are automatically logged on to the mainframe and can access internal financial data regarding brands, strategic business units, corporate consolidated information and so on, related to 50 variables, such as sales, gross margin, advertising expenses, and so on.

The brand-level information is particularly crucial, because part of Quaker Oats' long-term strategy is to abandon poorly performing brands and intensify market-penetration efforts with those that do well.

Users who choose DJ/NR are automatically logged onto the on-line service, where they can review business and government news and stock quotes for Quaker Oats and many of its competitors.

Michael Beyers, unit manager of executive system support, has designed a front-end for DJ/NR that bypasses Dow Jones' complicated syntax and lets users search using simple English commands. "Financial Worksheets" starts local spreadsheets such as Lotus on the PC; spreadsheets can be customized so users "don't necessarily have to know Lotus at all," he said.

Mr. Beyers has also built simple English-language error messages into the Executive Information System, telling users how to solve problems themselves or directing them to the appropriate person who can.

Finally, EIS handles all the log-off procedures, too. "Executives can get in and get the information they need without having to know anything about computers and without having to do much work at all," Mr. Clements said.

The user friendliness of EIS was a key factor in its success. Although a number of executives had PCs at home, they were skeptical of the value of using one in the office, Mr. Beyers said. They had simply never seen any application they thought was worthwhile for them.

One of the biggest original skeptics was President Frank Morgan, who is now one of EIS's strongest advocates.

"I think what created the interest in EIS on the part of people like myself, who obviously didn't come up through the computer age, is that they made it extremely user-friendly," Mr. Morgan said.

He also gives EIS high marks for having fresh information. "It's kept up-to-date. Last night, something on an income projection didn't ring a bell with me. Today I came into work, and somebody reminded me that there was a reason for that aberration—and it had already been pumped into the system. I was impressed by that," Mr. Morgan said. "That keeps you confident that what you're accessing isn't last week's newspaper."

To persuade executives to use EIS, the information center did active marketing. "These kinds of systems have to be marketed—they don't just grow by themselves," said Mr. Hemmige, the IC manager.

The IC's tactic was to take a low-key, personalized approach, inviting each executive to a one-on-one demonstration.

Each demo was tailored to fit a particular executive's needs and questions, rather than served up as a canned speech. This approach also put executives more at ease.

"We don't have 20 people crowding around in the conference room," Mr. Hemmige said. Without an audience, "they feel more relaxed and more free to ask questions."

From the first, the support of the CEO and president gave marketing efforts a tremendous boost. The chairman himself offered to beta test the new IBM version of the Executive Information System. And the president was the first to start the ball rolling on enhancements: He asked for what-if capabilities back when EIS still ran on Burroughs.

"A lot of the requests we're getting now from vice presidents [to hook up to EIS] are because of his use. They're learning of things they didn't think he knew, and they wondered how he got that information," Mr. Clements said. Another dozen executives are waiting for demonstrations or installations, and there are potentially 100 users.

Besides user friendliness, the strongest selling points for EIS are its speed, accuracy and summary information—information that was never readily available before.

Now executives can find out in two minutes what previously took days to learn. The numbers are accurate, because they come from a central database. And the summary information enables them to make better decisions faster, which Quaker expects will improve its competitive position.

The value of EIS to the company as a whole is believed in wholeheartedly as a matter of faith. "It provides a lot of benefits to the organization which are very hard to measure," Mr. Hemmige said. Who can put a dollar value on better decisions?

One clearly perceived benefit is that EIS is helping to foster the use of technology at Quaker Oats, because an example has been set at such high levels.

"When people find out that somebody at a high level sits at a keyboard, that sends a message to lower levels," he said. This works both ways: When executives are using the technology themselves, they understand why it's important.

"People at higher levels sometimes have a hard time understanding the merits of technology. The benefit of EIS is, if they see the value, it propagates the use of technology in the organization," Mr. Hemmige said. One testament to this is that the IS budget has doubled in the last two years.

EIS has been enhanced every year of its existence, and many more enhancements are envisioned.

Already installed but not yet in use is a master controller for information on the mainframe, called W/Library, from Comshare. W/Library can target and distribute information to individual executives or lists of executives, much like electronic mail. It can also be used to update each PC with new changes to EIS.

Among other possible plans are graphics, windowing, touch-screen capabilities, exception reporting and customization. "It is possible that each user can have his own individualized menu," Mr. Clements said.

Another plan is building financial databases on the PC, where executives can access data much faster and bypass the typical communications problems involved in dialing the mainframe.

Meantime, the executives already using EIS are quite pleased with it. And every day, faster than you can whip up a bowl of Instant Quaker Oatmeal, they are getting data they need to make crucial decisions at the keyboards of their PCs.

23

GenRad's On-Line Executives

Donald G. Sundue

This paper describes a several year evolution of Executive Information Systems at GenRad, Inc. The objective of the system was to provide the senior management of the company with what our President calls a "Corporate Dashboard."

The development of this system has progressed through several iterations, including an all-mainframe approach built on top of a traditional DSS system, a stand-alone PC approach, and most recently an approach that integrates mainframe and micro technologies. The experiences and results in implementing each of these iterations will be presented, with emphasis on the present system's features and functionality.

BACKGROUND

The Company

GenRad, Inc. is the third largest manufacturer of automated test equipment (ATE) in the world, and is the number one producer of circuit board testers. Annual sales are approximately $250 million.

In recent years, the Company has undergone an expansion of its products into related areas such as field service testers, VLSI testers and integration of its products with the electronics design process and into the factory floor operations.

The organization is highly decentralized and is widely dispersed geographically. GenRad is headquartered in Waltham, MA and has manufacturing divisions in Massachusetts, Arizona and California. There are three R&D facilities in the U.K. The Sales and Marketing Division operates out of fourteen offices in the U.S. and Canada, six subsidiaries throughout Europe and two locations in the Far East.

"GenRad's On-Line Executives" by Donald G. Sundue, DSS-86 TRANSACTIONS, 1986, pp. 14–20. Reprinted by permission of GenRad, Inc.

GenRad's Corporate MIS Department is chartered with, among other things, developing and implementing information systems for senior management.

The Problem and Challenge

Effective information systems are critical to any company's success, particularly in an environment of changing organizational units, new products and multiple geographic locations.

From an executive information viewpoint, it became obvious that good communications and information flow among top management at each of the entities would be a key factor in controlling our business operations. This implied an integrated computer network for accessing and transmitting data between remote locations without delay.

Beyond the network issue, the major problem was how to improve the delivery mechanism for presenting the results of business operations as well as other executive information. One of the major formal reporting vehicles is a Monthly Operations Review (MOR) report containing numerous financial spreadsheets, pages of typed narrative and various tables of data. In addition to a growing number of financial reporting business units and their products, new metrics in such areas as quality, human resources, and customer support are constantly being added to this document. As a result, the increasing size and complexity of this report book decreases its effectiveness as a mangement information tool.

Thus, the challenge was developing an executive information system (EIS) that users would find more effective and could eventually replace the MOR book. Early discussions of the concept of an automated reporting system for driving the business from a top management perspective led our President, William R. Thurston, to coin the phrase "Corporate Dashboard" to describe the desired functionality.

OBJECTIVES AND STRATEGY

The initial objective was fairly straightforward:

> "To develop an information delivery system targeted to the needs of the executive user."

Executive, in this case, was loosely defined as a senior level person in the role of decision maker, rather than one whose primary function is to perform analyses and present alternatives.

Since there were no off-the-shelf EIS hardware and software packages at the time, we were obligated to use our own creativity and requirements definition. With the constant advances in computer technology, we accepted the fact that our efforts would be evolutionary and under continuous refinement. Our approach was to try to use current technologies that had become generally available and that seemed to have staying power.

Defining requirements and specifications at this stage was difficult. The users' creativity was constrained by the only system they knew, primarily existing printed reports. Common expressions of user requirements included:

1. "I'd like to have just one button to press and see anything I want. . . ."
2. "There are too many reports; make it all fit on two pages. . . ."
3. "I want instant access to all the relevant data. . . ."

Articles had started to appear on the subject of EIS and defining critical success factors (Rockart, 1979), but our first attempts at CSF analysis met with limited success. We decided on a strategy of doing a prototype or pilot project from an MIS perspective and directing further efforts based on user feedback.

EVOLUTION TO DATE

Phase I: The All-Mainframe Era

Approach   The first phase was started prior to the existence of IBM PC's and at a time when graphics terminals were limited and considered too CPU intensive. Our approach was to build the EIS on an office automation theme, thereby accomplishing other MIS goals at the same time.

The hardware consisted of dumb CRT terminals connected to DEC VAX computers. The computers in the various remote locations were networked together.

The software was DEC's ALL-IN-1 office automation offering. The benefits to using this package as an EIS foundation included:

a) Menu driven, for ease of use,
b) Customizable, to add our own EIS features,
c) Multi-node network support.

The main menu includes access to:

- Electronic Mail
- Decision Support (Spreadsheet and User Data Base)
- Dow Jones News Service
- Personal Calendar Management
- Company News/Events Calendar
- User Specific (sub-menus and applications)

From an EIS viewpoint, any financial or operational report previously delivered on a printout could now be retrieved on-line via CRT. Custom menus were constructed based on individual user's requirements.

Results   The demand for electronic mail was far greater than expected resulting in rapid implementation throughout all levels of the Company. Executives, many of whom were reluctant users at first, found the system indispensable in meeting their communication requirements and eliminating telephone tag.

Unfortunately, the EIS feature of delivering existing financial reports electronically was not a big success. Since the same information was already available in hardcopy, the CRT access provided no greater insight to the users' problems. The traditional DSS tools of spreadsheets and end-user data base systems were heavily used by analysts but avoided by most executives. The on-line access to Dow Jones, however, was used frequently by the senior managers with access privilege, providing a vital link to external information.

User feedback identified graphics as a key missing ingredient which would help provide greater insight to the existing information.

In this phase, we did achieve the objective of improving management communication and heightened the users' awareness of the potential benefits of the EIS concept. And of major importance, we overcame the hurdle of getting executives in front of terminals.

Phase II: The Standalone PC Workstation

Approach   When the era of the personal computer arrived, it initially seemed to be the appropriate vehicle for adding color graphics to our evolving EIS. A variety of graphics software packages were evaluated, but none specifically met our expectations of what would be appropriate for high level managers. At best, we could prepare a pre-recorded slide show of charts and data on a floppy disk, but timely media distribution would be a problem. We could periodically down load a data file to the PC to support slide-show software, but the process was slow and cumbersome for a busy executive to use. A central data base to support EIS was required, but the PC-mainframe links were still future promises.

Independent of the EIS efforts, many executives claimed to have a "need" for a PC, although in most cases the reason was unclear. However, there was general encouragement from top management that executives should gain a familiarity with the use of PC's both as a potential for aiding their own work as well as understanding the opportunities for productivity improvements in their organizations.

Results   The PC's ability to produce quality business graphics met our expectations, but the lack of software for easy access to a central data base kept the PC's in the realm of analysts. However, hard copy graphics began making their way more and more into management presentations and the MOR report, thereby enhancing the quality of executive information in general.

Of the executives who did acquire PC's, the primary interest was for word and document processing. As expected, very few seemed to have the time or inclination to become trained in a spreadsheet or other decision support tool. As a result, the most frequently used software was terminal emulation for access to electronic mail.

Phase III: Mainframe—Micro Connection

Approach When Pilot Executive Software announced their Command Center EIS software last year, it appeared to be the ideal solution for our needs. Its functionality overcame most of the shortcomings of our prior information delivery efforts.

Very briefly, the Pilot system can be described as:

Hardware
An IBM PC as the executive workstation providing high resolution color graphics, linked to a mainframe computer (IBM, DEC or Prime).

Software
A data base manager residing on the central computer.
PC software for accessing the data base and producing graphics on the PC screen or local printer.
A "fourth generation" development environment allowing programmers to quickly develop menus, reports, graphics, etc.

User Interface
Mouse-driven cursor for one-button operation and selection of menu items with ability to produce pop-up menus, windows, active cells, etc.

The next (and current) phase was to utilize the Command Center software to develop the "Corporate Dashboard" we had envisioned.

DEVELOPING THE CURRENT SYSTEM

Design Objectives

By this time, more literature had become available on the "How-To" of EIS. From our experience to date, we had concluded that to be truly effective for executives, the EIS should:

1. Produce insights and understanding not available in the standard MOR reports;
2. Provide an easy method to explore the information further, if and when desired, to the point of making simple ad hoc calculations;
3. Support tailoring to individual users, who may wish to view the same information in different formats or combinations or who require controlled access to sensitive information.

Design Criteria

Since the Command Center package is essentially an EIS software toolbox, we had to define our own architecture and user interface scheme. Our development guidelines were influenced by the graphics presentation principles suggested by Irwin M. Jarett (1983).

The design criteria included:

1. Heavy graphics orientation, with tabular reports of secondary importance
   Reason: To reduce the amount of time to see the problem;
2. Begin the first display of a business variable with key indicator variance chart(s), unless inappropriate
   Reason: Emphasis on exception reporting, i.e., no need to go further if on target;
3. Utilize the concept of aggregation/disaggregation of data in reporting various measures
   Reason: To support exploring the data on a layer-by-layer exception basis;
4. Standardize on the user mechanics of activating the displays. For example, clicking the cursor (mouse) over a number produces a graph of the data, while clicking the cursor over a word (e.g., "Sales"), brings up the supporting schedule or next level of the data
   Reason: Consistency is critical to user acceptance and training;
5. Standardize on a limited number of graphic formats for displaying financial and operational data
   Reason: Eliminate the need to study each chart before assessing the information depicted;
6. Standardize on graphic formats in terms of:
   - Color (e.g., black is always "actual", red is first comparative, and background is always off-white)
   - Layout (e.g., size and location on screen)
   - Legends and title (e.g., always in the same place on every chart)
   Reason: Artistic layout is a subtle factor but critical to the acceptance of reading data graphically.

Implementation

Specifications   The hardest part of the process, and certainly the most critical, is preparing the system specifications. The Command Center software is literally a set of powerful tools, requiring the system builder to decide every detail, including the item to be displayed, where it should be displayed and what techniques should be used to activate various screens. For example, should the name of a measure (e.g., Orders), when selected, retrieve a graph, a table of values, a graph and the table of values, several small graphs by sub-category, etc. The software has few limitations in its flexibility, thereby taxing the implementor's creativity.

A pre-printed specifications form was developed to aid in the process, and to provide a documented guide for subsequent coding. The form provides for a rough sketch of the desired graph, the data source and the rules for cursor activation control.

Data Base Architecture   The data base is optimized for time series data, although all types of information can be stored. A powerful feature is the built-in aggregation capability. This feature permits data to be stored non-redundantly at the lowest level. Subtotals of logical groupings of data, or roll-ups are computed on the fly as retrieved and are automatically maintained by the data base for future reference.

Since the bulk of our financial and operational measures are time-series oriented, there was no difficulty in defining the data base layout.

Program Code   The program code is essentially a set of high level one-word commands which create graphics, display reports or call menus. The commands are executed based on the mouse-driven cursor being activated. The command BAR SALES, for example, will produce a default bar chart of the data in the record labelled SALES. The editor for painting menus is itself mouse driven and a highly efficient utility.

Extensive programming skills are not required to produce reasonable results. However, our experience indicates that the use of professional programming techniques will produce a more efficient and maintainable system. For example, by making appropriate use of subroutines and reusable procedures, adding data records for a new product or division in our case does not require any programming changes to the system.

Data Load   The data must reside in the Command Center data base, as opposed to directly accessing existing data files.

New information is currently added monthly and we utilize several methods for loading it. Many of the existing Monthly Operations Review reports are spreadsheet based and already exist on the computer. Selected items from these spreadsheets are directly loaded using a simple procedure. Similarly, files containing data extracted from other transaction systems can be loaded automatically. Some measures and soft data are clerically keyed-in from a terminal which requires, at most, one hour per month. Although narrative is kept to a minimum, brief explanations of variances can be retrieved by the user. These files are simply the original word processed documents, already in machine-readable form on the system.

User Training   The training required for executives to use the system is minimal. Aside from a general description of the PC and mouse operation, the activation of menus and displays is fairly intuitive. Any item which lights-up when the cursor is over it is an active cell. Pressing the mouse button while the cursor is on an active cell causes a display action to occur. Experimentation is encouraged and the users have had no resistance to using the mouse. The users' intuition was most likely influenced by their exposure to the existing menu-based office automation system.

The limited training requirement permits more time for exploring and discussing the various graph formats and encouraging feedback for enhancements.

SYSTEM FEATURES AND FUNCTIONS

The EIS system is accessed from the main menu of the office automation system. The main categories of information are divided into two groups—internal and external sources. The formats are typically in actual vs. plan format as well as variance.

The menu items presently include:

Internal Information

Flash Report
Displays a four-graph snapshot of year-to-date orders, inventory, backlog and earnings.

Performance Summary
Displays a top-level variance report for orders, shipments, income, gross margin percentage and dollars and earnings, both current month and year-to-date. Also produces data and graphs for lower level supporting details and variances.

Financial Forecast
Revised monthly forecast by business entity and in total.

Division Operations
Under development, but planned to provide lower level supporting details for a variety of business variables within operating divisions.

Asset Management
Displays top level and supporting details for backlog, inventories and accounts receivable information.

Human Resources
Displays graphical measures of effectiveness in several areas including sales-per-employee ratios, workforce statistics, turnover and other available factors.

R&D/Technology
Under development, but planned to provide status on new product development activities.

Quality
Displays performance measures of:

- Cost of quality
- Late delivery ratio
- System installation time
- Warranty calls per installation
- Software performance reporting
- First pass board yield

Also retrievable are definitions of measures and variance analysis narrative.

External Information

Competitive Information
Displays a variety of financial measures on companies of choice. Retrieves data from an external data base via autodial sequence at scheduled times.

Dow Jones World News
Displays headlines and news stories based on user defined selection criteria. Retrieves data from an external data base via autodial sequence at scheduled times.

Economic News
Under development, but planned to access an external data base and retrieve data to support graphically displayed key economic indicators.

Stock Prices
Displays stock prices for companies of interest. Can be automatically downloaded from external source or keyed in manually.

Other functions include the ability to MARK certain displays, similar to a paper clip in a report, and then JUMP directly to the marked display rather than retracing previous steps.

A DATE function permits the user to change the default date of the current year to a prior year for historical analysis.

The WORKSHEET function permits a user to perform simple, ad hoc calculations and create graphs of the results by using just the mouse. The cursor is moved over the data of interest which is then selected by clicking the mouse. A menu of calculation capabilities and default chart types are available for operation on the selected data via the mouse. In addition, locally stored PC spreadsheets can be downloaded to this worksheet area for more sophisticated analysis.

Exiting from the EIS main menu returns the user to the office automation system.

CONCLUSION AND FUTURES

Our conclusion at this point is that we are definitely on the right track toward building an effective system targeted to the needs of executives. It appears that the acceptance of the system is due largely to the nature of the information delivery itself. The One-Button workstation is a reality through the use of the mouse. The rapid flash of color graphics has a tremendous appeal. And the patterns which can be visualized in the graphs can be read quicker and provide for greater insight than numerical reports alone.

The flexibility and power of the software enables rapid development and modification to suit changing user needs. The technical MIS support requirements are minimal.

Beyond this pilot phase, we intend to broaden the scope of information available on the system. Emphasis will be on tailoring the displays to individuals' critical success factors and their measures. We also plan to expand its use to middle level managers as an information tool for monitoring daily business operations.

REFERENCES

Jarett, Irwin M., *Computer Graphics and Reporting Financial Data,* John Wiley & Sons, New York, 1983.

Rockart, John F., "Chief Executives Define Their Own Data Needs," *Harvard Business Review,* March–April 1979.

PART THREE

Beating the High Costs of Building Information Systems

$\mathbf{A}$s can be seen from the articles in Part 2, the ability to apply IT resources to key business opportunities and problems is limited only by imagination and awareness of possibilities. Despite the success stories, however, firms continue to experience problems in their efforts to design, build, and implement effective IT applications. Striking examples of such problems are illustrated in Readings 24 and 25, "It's Late, Costly, Incompetent—But Try Firing a Computer System" and "Look Out Behind."

Developing a knowledge of the reasons that difficulties arise and of the techniques to overcome or prevent these difficulties are critical components of all managers' personal "tool kits." It is simply not enough for a manager to recognize how IT resources can be applied; the truly successful manager must develop insights into the way an idea for an IT application becomes a reality. The next five articles help to provide those insights. Reading 26, on prototyping, discusses how building information systems in an "experimental" fashion can, under certain conditions, be better than traditional "life cycle" system development approaches. Reading 27 discusses an approach to building information systems that combines traditional methods with prototyping to improve the quality and speed of the system development process. "Reusable Software" (Reading 28), and "The Off the Shelf Alternative" describe alternatives to custom-building new IT applications. Reading 30 examines how CASE (Computer Assisted Software Engineering) technology might provide the best long-term means for developing effective IT applications.

The next articles discuss some very useful techniques for resolving another problem associated with developing IT applications—identifying the type of information system to develop. Readings 31 and 32 provide how-to approaches to identifying managers and executives' information needs, an issue that has challenged information-system designers for years. Reading 33, "The Knowledge Engineers," describes how to learn from the masters in expert systems development. The section ends with Reading 34, in which Peter Keen combines theory and practice to explain how information systems change organizations, why employees tend to resist such changes, and what steps can be taken to overcome this resistance.

24

It's Late, Costly, Incompetent —But Try Firing a Computer System

Jeffrey Rothfeder

It's a project that, for Allstate Insurance Co., has redefined the concept of sparing no expense. The Sears, Roebuck & Co. subsidiary set out in 1982 to build the insurance industry's most sophisticated computer system, one that would make its competitors quake. The system was supposed to automate Allstate's office operations and shorten the normal three-year period needed to introduce new types of policies to one month. Allstate hired Electronic Data Systems Corp., the systems-integration company, to develop the software and help install it on the firm's hardware. The target date for completion was December, 1987; the target cost was $8 million. Some $15 million later, Allstate has a new project consultant, a new deadline, and a new cost estimate: $100 million.

The Allstate case is a classic example of a computer runaway, a system that's millions over budget, years behind schedule, and—if ever completed—less effective than promised. A recent Peat Marwick Mitchell & Co. survey of 600 of the accounting firm's largest clients highlighted the problem: Some 35% currently have major runaways. Indeed, experts say, such diverse systems integrators as the Big Eight accounting firms, computer suppliers, and even in-house data processing staffs are fast building a record of mediocrity. Says James A. Willbern, a management consultant at Peat Marwick: The industry's "ability to install systems is pretty crummy."

The problem is so acute that it has created a lucrative industry of its own. In 1986, Willbern set up a group at Peat Marwick to rein in runaways. Since then, he has had $30 million in revenues from nearly 20 clients, including Allstate.

BLOWN DEADLINES

Allstate's project ran on track for about a year before it went awry. First, deadlines for programming and for testing hardware started slipping by. Then Allstate technical staffers quarreled over the dimensions of the project and each other's roles. By

1987, the huge project had changed from savior to albatross, and Allstate had had enough. It started over with Peat Marwick, which helped revamp and train the in-house staff working on the system, now targeted for completion in 1993.

Although there are many explanations for the epidemic of runaways, there seems to be a common thread: Neither buyers nor builders of computer systems have adjusted their deadlines to reflect the increased complexity of computer projects. A decade ago, a $2 million computer system that took longer than a year to build was a rarity. Such systems were self-contained units with no interweaving of technologies and data bases. Connectivity was a foreign word. Today, although companies are developing systems of such magnitude that entire businesses are sculpted around them, many designers still use the old approach. Far better, consultants say, is to divide major projects into modules that can be finished one at a time.

"It's the difference between counting the number of people in a small room and doing a U.S. census," says Wayne Stevens, a leading systems-design theorist. "It takes two different skills, and when you go from the simpler to the more complex project, you'd better do things differently."

Tom Hefty learned this the hard way when a runaway carried Blue Cross & Blue Shield United of Wisconsin to the brink of disaster. In 1983, three years before Hefty became chief executive of the Milwaukee-based insurer, it hired EDS to build a $200 million system to coordinate all the services then being handled by five computers. The system was completed on time—in just 18 months. But it didn't work. One example: Because of an entry error, the computer sent out hundreds of checks to the fictitious hamlet of None, Wis. A month later the checks arrived back at Blue Cross for readdressing. During its first year, the system disbursed $60 million in overpayments or duplicate checks.

Before the runaway was stopped, Blue Cross lost 35,000 members—a setback it attributes to the computer problems. EDS contends foul-ups were inevitable because of the multitude of data to be converted from the old system to the new. But Blue Cross wants EDS to reimburse it for some of the lost revenues. The dispute is now in arbitration.

Inheriting this mess in 1986, Hefty immediately instituted tough quality-control measures. He found that the system's developers never adequately used checkpoints during the project to evaluate whether the system was on track. Only that, he says, would have ensured a more successful outcome. Others concur. "In larger projects, you should have a detailed review every 12 months," says Jack Epstein, a vice-president at the research firm International Data Corp. "In shorter-term projects, you could meet every six months." These meetings, Hefty adds, should include senior management. Most nontechnical executives are unwilling to take an active role in developing a computer system—until costs spiral out of control. "I let it slip, that's the problem," says the president of a medical diagnostic firm. "I kept hands off, and it hurt me in the end."

'PROMISING EVERYTHING'

This company experienced a nightmare last year when its new computer system, during its first day in operation, lost information pertaining to thousands of crucial medical tests. The software couldn't handle the volumes of data it had to deal with.

Table 24.1
A Sampling of 'Runaway' Projects

ALLSTATE INSURANCE   In 1982, with software from Electronic Data Systems, the insurer began to build an $8 million computer system that would automate it from top to bottom. Completion date: 1987. An assortment of problems developed, delaying completion until 1993. The new estimated price: $100 million

CITY OF RICHMOND   In 1984 it hired Arthur Young to develop a $1.2 million billing and information system for its water and gas utilities. Completion date: March, 1987. After paying out close to $1 million, Richmond recently canceled the contract, saying no system had been delivered. Arthur Young has filed a $2 million breach of contract suit against the city

BUSINESSMEN'S ASSURANCE   In 1985 the reinsurer began a one-year project to build a $500,000 system to help minimize the risk of buying insurance policies held by major insurers. The company has spent nearly $2 million to date on the project, which is in disarray. The new completion date is early 1990

STATE OF OKLAHOMA   In 1983 it hired a Big Eight accounting firm to design a $500,000 system to handle explosive growth in workers' compensation claims. Two years and more than $2 million later, the system still didn't exist. It finally was finished last year at a price of nearly $4 million

BLUE CROSS & BLUE SHIELD UNITED OF WISCONSIN   In late 1983 it hired Electronic Data Systems to build a $200 million computer system. It was ready 18 months later—on time. But it didn't work. The system spewed out some $60 million in overpayments and duplicate checks before it was harnessed last year. By then, Blue Cross says, it had lost 35,000 policyholders

Luckily, the loss was not permanent—but it took 30 days to reconstruct the records. At that point, the company's president decided to "take a clean look at this thing." He fired the data processing chief, hired a new technical staff, and announced that he would be closely involved with all future systems development. A new system is expected to be completed by the end of this year.

One problem with giving data processing professionals and outside suppliers free rein over a new computer system is that they tend to be overly optimistic: "They sell expectation, not reality," says Dave Elenburg, who last year led a group that cleaned up a multimillion-dollar runaway in the workers' compensation system in Oklahoma. "DPers feel they have to keep the executives happy by promising even what they can't deliver. And suppliers are out for sales."

One common gripe among customers is that after they hire a supplier to direct the development of a system, the work is frequently assigned to "students straight out of tech school," as Elenburg puts it. The more talented professionals who represented the supplier in the initial meetings are busy trying to bring in new business. Robert C. Bobb, city manager of Richmond, Va., was so incensed two years ago when Arthur Young sent inexperienced technicians to develop the management system for the city's utilities that he now writes into all consulting contracts the names of the people who must work on the project. Arthur Young says that its senior consultants were "heavily involved" in the Richmond project. But Bobb says that's not enough: "The partners have to begin to do the grunt work."

DISMAL PICTURE

So do the people who ultimately will use the system. Too often, a runaway occurs because during the planning stages the staffers who eventually will be operating the computers are not consulted for ideas about how the system should work. "User involvement cannot be casual," says George Hathaway, a runaway-buster at the Index Group, a Cambridge (Mass.) consultancy. "The mind-set has to be emphasized more to users that the computer works for you; you don't work for it."

As dismal as the picture is, there are glimmers of light. Many runaway consultants feel that the recent round of failures has taught buyers caution. "Corporate executives are becoming very wary about dropping millions of dollars into a bottomless bucket," says Phil Dressler, a Dallas-based runaway salvager. Moreover, Dressler adds, as such executives become more computer-literate over the next few years, they will be less afraid to take charge of technical projects. And data processing professionals are becoming better managers, increasingly using the modular approach to building systems. What's more, unyielding competition in the $5 billion-a-year systems-integration field will sooner or later force the companies in it to be more attentive to customers' needs or be losers in a booming market.

These trends are cause for hope. But until they spread, it seems inevitable that millions more will be squandered on computer systems that fail to work or even to see the light of day.

25   ***Look Out Behind***

Asher Yuval

What are the real problems in producing and maintaining software? Does MIS sometimes confuse essential problems with symptomatic ones? Can you put aside these symptoms – most probably the consequences of real problems – identify the actual problems and simply and coherently enumerate them?

If not, then in acquiring a computer-aided software engineering (CASE) tool, a methodology or any other software engineering technique, you may unknowingly be applying the right solution to the wrong need.

A symptom is a "problem" about which you may ask, "Yes, but why is it so? What causes it to occur?" A real problem, on the other hand, is one about which there is no further why to ask.

For example, software engineering problems have been described as goals not yet reached by Doug Bell, Ian Morrey and John Pugh in their book, *Software Engineering: A Programming Approach.* But those are probably symptoms rather than real problems, since you can simply ask, "Why haven't these goals been achieved?"

MIS' initial efforts in software engineering, therefore, should be to differentiate clearly between these two brands of difficulties. Then, after being identified and isolated, the real problems should be further divided into two subgroups:

- Environmental problems, which are especially relevant to information systems. These are real problems, insofar as our ability to change the environment is limited and, hence, asking why is practically useless.
- Fundamental problems, which, like natural laws, stem from the very nature of the software medium.

Ultimately, software engineering challenges can be properly broken down into symptoms, fundamental problems and environmental problems. All are identifiable. But whether or not identifying a problem is half a solution is left for you to decide.

SYMPTOMS

Once the symptoms are identified, then MIS can get to the real problems. Consider, for example, the following, which are more likely symptoms of larger challenges:

Software Cost and Schedule Estimation

After careful examination, you may discover that this problem isn't different from the more general problem of project management.

There are three classical approaches to project management in any engineering field: managing a project by its activities, by its intermediate products or by both. On the basis of the approach taken, schedule and budget estimates can be made. Project management is feasible only when either the activities or the intermediate products are fairly well known. If this is not the case, then even the most sophisticated project management system—using the latest PERT/CPM and Gantt techniques, an eight-color plotter and a dedicated 386 personal computer—simply won't help.

Consider, too, whether the activities or the products in software engineering projects are clearly defined before making a cost estimate. What methodology is being used to derive the activities and products? When and how is feedback from previous projects accumulated?

Cost and schedule estimates of software projects are never accurate unless the discipline that underlies the projects is clearly defined. The fact that project management isn't always a great success in other engineering fields should be a warning and not a comfort for software engineering.

In short, software cost and schedule estimates are not real problems; they undoubtedly result from a more fundamental problem—namely, the lack of a clearly defined software engineering discipline.

Lack of Experienced Professionals

Asking, "Why is there a lack of experienced professionals?" is quite natural in this case, and if the answer is "Because of a lack of experienced instructors," you may then ask, "Yes, but why aren't there experienced instructors?"

The answer might be "Instructors are underpaid," which is probably not true; or "Top professionals don't like to teach," which is probably not true; or "It's a young industry," which it isn't anymore.

Perhaps part of this problem is that the profession is not defined well enough. Can MIS precisely describe its different occupations and specify their requirements? Are there clear and meaningful titles for these occupations? Can a DP project manager who wants to staff a team point to the various craftsmen required, their exact titles and when and for what tasks they are required? Is the title "DP project manager" itself clearly defined?

While the situation differs from one MIS organization to another, on the whole, the issue remains serious. Since software engineering as a discipline is not defined, its different professions are not defined, either. And since the professions are not defined, how can they be properly taught and learned?

Be aware, however, that the lack of professionals is not an essential reason for the poor state of software engineering. Other problems prevent it from becoming a well-defined engineering discipline, thus making it difficult to teach and study.

Software Maintenance

This symptomatic challenge can be divided into two categories: the disturbing distribution of the cost between development (30%) and maintenance (70%); and the overall cost of maintenance in terms of money, morale and other factors.

Again, neither of these are real problems. First, as has been noted in Capers Jones' book, *Programming Productivity,* when maintenance is carefully analyzed and correctly split between defect repair and enhancement, the picture radically changes and the true figures become development (50%), defect repair (14%) and enhancement (36%).

Second, the high cost of maintenance, as most engineers will probably agree, is actually the result of incorrect design. Thus the question in this case is, "What is the cause of bad design?" Is it due to the failure to allocate enough resources for analysis and design?

Many MIS managers—backed by heavy experience and plentiful literature—deny this possibility, claiming that 50% of the development effort already goes into analysis and design with no major impact on maintenance.

Or perhaps bad design is the consequence of the rigid life-cycle model, which is unsuitable for dynamic, changing environments.

Whatever the reasons, software maintenance difficulties are the result of more basic problems in the software engineering discipline.

In a similar way, many other classical problems in software engineering—such as software reliability, software portability, performance, budget and schedule overruns and so on—are all symptoms of more essential problems.

So instead of dwelling on symptoms, MIS should address at least some of the real problems facing its software engineering professionals today.

ENVIRONMENTAL PROBLEMS

A handful of well-known problems are actually environmental problems, especially those related to information systems in which there exists a close interaction between the computerized system and the organization's strategic and intrinsic operations.

These problems can be characterized in terms of the interaction with the enterprise's functions and the interaction with other disciplines.

The DP field as a whole, and software engineering in particular, suffer from trying to fulfill expectations beyond their scope and capacity. In part, this is an artificial problem that stems from overselling DP as a solution to all of an organization's illnesses. At the same time, managing data in any organization is essential; it is almost like managing the organization itself. Thus, it is no wonder that building and implementing an information system requires talent, knowledge and power far beyond what software engineering alone has to offer.

MIS must make a major decision in this regard: Should it extend the software engineering discipline to cover topics outside its "natural" domain, or should it seek the cooperation of other disciplines (and if so, which ones?) and be ready to pay for such collaboration?

Another environmental problem deserves serious consideration, although it has received little attention. It can be called the transparency problem. "Transparency" in this case means the correspondence of the information system to the real world.

A software system with a high degree of transparency is one that truly reflects reality, whereas a system with a low degree of transparency is one that runs parallel to the real world without corresponding to it. Modern banking systems are good examples of high-transparency systems; one may even say that the real world— namely, the actual money—is in the system itself.

On the other hand, project management systems are examples of low-transparency systems—which may explain much of their operational difficulties.

MIS should try to categorize the following systems in terms of degrees of transparency: inventory, finance, reservation systems, command and control and electronic mail.

But why is the transparency issue important, and where exactly does the problem lie? In software engineering, the type of system we deal with is crucially important—as pointed out in *Programming Productivity*—and that is a fact MIS often disregards in the rush to build. Systems with low transparency are easy to build and maintain but may, in fact, be useless. Systems with high transparency may be difficult to build, and they are certainly difficult to enhance and modify, but they have high prospects for success.

How to identify and measure a system's transparency and how to raise the system from a low to a high degree of transparency are major environmental problems in software engineering.

FUNDAMENTAL PROBLEMS

The most fundamental problems in software engineering include the lack of physical properties, the flexibility-to-rigidity shift, the transformation issue and the informal-to-formal shift.

The Lack of Physical Properties

Or more correctly the lack of natural objective properties, is well described in E. R. Fairely's *Software Engineering Concepts.* Although somewhat hard to grasp when first posed, it is so fundamental that it probably forms the basis of many other problems.

Its main implication is that the gap between software engineering and other engineering disciplines is so wide that MIS should exercise caution before borrowing any idea from these disciplines.

Engineering disciplines throughout history have progressed as a result of the close interaction between natural science and practical engineering. At the very center of this fruitful interaction lies a shared body of knowledge to which many people have contributed and that has seldom been seriously challenged. And when someone does . . . well, such a person could only be an Einstein or a Newton.

Instead of physical properties, substituted soft(ware) properties emerge, such as structured programming rules, data normalization forms and so on. If this is the right trend, then software engineering is indeed a unique discipline, the first of its kind in history, in which human consensus—not nature—determines engineering properties.

The Flexibility-to-Rigidity Shift

Software is the most flexible engineering medium today. That's what makes it so easy to prototype. No wonder other engineering disciplines use software systems to simulate their systems. But somewhere along the development process the software medium becomes rigid and hard to modify. When exactly does this happen? What causes it to happen? Is it a matter of the system's order of magnitude? If so, in what terms is magnitude to be measured?

Our inability to explain the flexibility-to-rigidity shift in software engineering, let alone measure it, is certainly a fundamental problem.

The Transformation Issue

As a software system is being developed, it undergoes several transformations before finally becoming operational. It is first put into text format—the initiation stage; then data flow diagrams and data store diagrams are drawn up—the analysis stage; then structured charts and entity relationship diagrams are sketched—the design stage; then code is produced.

At the end of each stage the entire knowledge of the system must be transformed to a new medium.

Quite often this mapping is done verbally, passing from one professional mind—the analyst's—to another—the designer's. You can only pray that no information is spilt while being poured from one vessel to another. This problem has been intensified by all the structured methodologies that add more and more stages to the system's life cycle.

Still, it is a fundamental problem, since even the shortest path entails at least three transformations: from the user's mind to the professional's mind, from the professional's mind to a computer's symbolic language and from the operational system back to the user's mind.

One transformation, however, has been accomplished with remarkable precision ever since computers were invented: namely, good old compilers. There is probably much to gain by extending their power and introducing them earlier in the system's life cycle.

The Informal-to-Formal Shift

Another problem similar to both the transformation and the flexibility/rigidity problems is the informal-to-formal shift.

Informal, natural language is still the best vehicle for communicating. Without it no project ever gets off the ground. Most users prefer natural prose to technically sophisticated data flow diagrams.

But somewhere during a software engineering project, things must be formally defined or else they cannot be implemented in a machine. MIS must consider where the shift from the informal to the formal should be introduced and what impact this should have on the user's involvement in the project.

An interesting subset of this problem applies to non-English-speaking countries. The informal native language used at the beginning of the project is later converted to formal software engineering tools in English-like formats. A data entity, for instance, is first defined in a local language using analysis-stage tools or simply a text processor. This is essential in order to communicate with the user. Later on, that same data entity must be redefined and put into a database data dictionary in order to communicate with the application generator.

UNCLASSIFIED PROBLEMS

In addition to the fundamental and environmental problems in software engineering, there are several others that are more difficult to classify:

The "Small" Details Problem

Anyone who has ever analyzed a software system knows about those "small" nasty details that, if not defined to the very last bit, endanger the entire grand design. This is a severe problem not merely for topdown approaches but also for any implementation of ordered procedures, such as life-cycle models. This problem is unclassified because it could be considered a symptom or a real, fundamental problem in terms of the informal-to-formal shift.

The User Involvement Problem

User involvement is certainly crucial for a project's success. This may be regarded as a real environmental problem if only because it is difficult to identify the user throughout the entire life cycle. At the same time, it may be the result either of other environmental problems such as the interaction with the enterprise's functions or the fundamental transformation and informal-to-formal problems.

The Lack of a Computer Science

This problem is quite often cited as the problem in software engineering, and since it is an "academic" problem, it apparently is fundamental. But surely one may still ask: "Why isn't a science being built around software?" A possible answer may be that software lacks physical properties.

Psychological Problems

Various problems, such as professional egoism and reluctance to change, may be considered fundamental by some. But these problems may well be the result of the flexibility-to-rigidity shift or the lack of objective software properties.

PHILOSOPHIZING

Classifying software engineering problems may sometimes seem somewhat philosophical, but why not philosophize from time to time in our attrition-conscious profession? Furthermore, the classification of problems gives a yardstick by which to evaluate the different software engineering tools and methodologies.

The cost of implementing these solutions is very high and far exceeds their purchase cost. Also, as noted in 1986 by R. Goldberg in the *IBM Systems Journal,* technology transfer—particularly in software engineering—is very slow, and the implementation of new ideas can take years. Knowing in advance which problems a software engineering solution intends to solve is, therefore, extremely important.

For instance, a proposed software engineering solution that promises to reduce maintenance through CASE tools should comprise the following:

- Clearly defined and easily measured software characteristics.
- Flexible database and module definitions enabling changes as late as possible in the life cycle.
- A minimum number of stages in the life cycle and a straightforward transformation from one stage to another.

The differentiation between real problems and symptoms in software engineering does not necessarily mean that solutions should be applied only to real problems. As in medicine, remedies are often successfully applied directly to symptoms. Yet, also as in medicine, concentrating only on symptoms without trying to identify the real causes is certainly poor practice.

The decision to treat symptoms or real problems is perhaps also a function of time considerations. Applying solutions to symptoms can sometimes work quite well in the short run—for example, solving an immediate problem for a specific project.

But for companies where the production of software is an indispensable part of the business, and certainly for the software industry as a whole, the only effective and long-range solutions lie in attacking the real problems, not the symptoms.

26

Prototyping: Orchestrating for Success

Tor Guimaraes

At a multibillion-dollar transportation company, seven end users spent six months and $250,000 prototyping a 500-program carrier management system. The price was right. The system, which runs on a pc-based local area network, is returning profits by managing 5,000 trucks for two major clients.

A utilities company in the East used prototyping and fourth generation facilities to write 10 major high-volume applications in just two years. The productivity improvement in lines of documented, quality-assured, and user-accepted code written was 13-to-one over what they had ever been able to achieve using COBOL.

Prototyping as an "insurance policy for success" in systems development gained academic favor in the late '70s and early '80s. And as the cases above illustrate, the concept has been proven in practice. After nearly 10 years, the industry is discovering that there are a number of ways to make prototyping music. Not all of them, however, are right.

This was one major conclusion of a field study of 48 Fortune 1000 companies that was conducted by the Business Computer Information Systems Dept. at St. Cloud State University in Minnesota. Interviews with these firms, all of which have committed substantial resources to prototyping, revealed that users are just beginning to understand the best ways to use this systems development tool.

Increasingly, IS departments are employing a variety of approaches to prototyping, for a variety of reasons (see "Prototypes and Their Purposes" and Table 26.1). Our study found that firms generally practice one or more of eight different forms of prototyping. Two basic approaches—throwaway (i.e., the information is kept, but the coding is junked) or keep-it prototyping (the prototype is kept and maintained in a traditional manner)—are employed for four fundamental purposes:

- to define the user interface,
- to define the process or functional requirements,

- to model complex design configuration alternatives, and
- to develop a full-blown application.

It is rare that a company will limit itself to only one approach, although there are those with a very narrow view of prototyping. In such firms, it is often the case that politically powerful systems development groups with well-established development methodologies insist that prototyping is solely a vehicle for systems requirements definition, and that all such prototypes are to be thrown out and redeveloped through traditional means, despite the fact that enormous amounts of labor and money are sacrificed in the process.

Quick-and-dirty prototyping with no formal methodology is also creating trouble at some companies. Problems arise with this approach because undocumented prototypes that were intended to be thrown away are kept, and become the poorly planned bases for large, complex systems that are consequently difficult to use and maintain.

Another prototyping problem these firms have encountered is that all too often the end user has been left out of the equation. Prototyping is an iterative process for developing systems that first and foremost must involve and be controlled by the end user. And they've forgotten that it may take a few iterations to get it done right.

There are several apparent reasons for these prototyping problems: lack of awareness of alternative approaches to prototyping, a limited set of prototyping tools and personnel, lack of management support for prototyping experimentation, or systems developers who are unwilling to change or to try new ways.

As Table 26.1 indicates, all 48 companies use the throwaway approach for most purposes. But why do they practice such an expensive and inefficient policy? Many insist that prototypes are a quick way of establishing information requirements and are not an integral part of systems development, which should be done with tried-and-true methodologies that are oriented to quality and care.

AWAY WITH THROWAWAYS

Consider the fact that an end user or programmer spends anywhere from a few hours to a few hundred hours developing a prototype. He or she then passes it along to the systems development group, which extracts the information on user requirements, tosses out the code, and sits down to do development the traditional way. The wastefulness is clear.

The prototyping practice of one Chicago bank provides a good measure of throwaway losses. End users spent an average of 250 hours developing each throwaway prototype (primarily requirements definition) for a group of six large applications. They then invested an average of 45 hours more per prototype on working with systems developers to add other procedures. The systems development group itself expended between 75 and 225 hours repeating what had already been done in the prototype. Thus, the bank supported efforts that were between 30% and 90% redundant.

Table 26.1
Prototyping Ends and Means (by number of firms)

Operational Objectives	Throwaway Prototyping	Keep-It Prototyping
User Interface Development	48	33
Functional Development	48	33
Machine Performance Evaluation	23	26
Application Development	48	31

Prototyping Tools	Quick-and-Dirty	Formal, Enforced Methodology
End-user 4GLs	32	16
IS 4GLs	13	14
Autocode Generators	3	13
Embedded 4GLs	2	7

Through careful planning and discipline, prototypes can be integrated into the development process. The utility company in our example would not have been able to develop 10 major applications in two years with the throwaway approach. Teams of end users and systems developers evolved the major applications through multiple iterations. They planned and prepared to evolve the prototypes into final, documented, quality-assured programs. This cooperative, disciplined effort ensured that end-user requirements were defined and met, and all tenets of good systems development were followed.

Very few situations technically justify throwaways. In most cases, the reason for throwaways are due to basic underlying problems with computing in the organization, such as lack of integration of systems development resources, lack of cooperation between prototypers and traditional systems development groups, lack of training and support for prototypers, or incompatible software packages and development languages (e.g., the end-user prototype is done in Lotus 1-2-3, but the application is part of a mainframe system).

Despite the prevalence of quick-and-dirty, throwaway work, the study showed that a growing number of companies are doing keep-it prototyping (approximately two thirds of this group) and many are adopting formal, enforced methodologies for prototyping (approximately one third). More and more IS managers are learning to integrate prototyping effectively into their systems development life cycle (SDLC) methodology. It's not an easy process to adopt, requiring trade-offs between prototyping's fast approach to development and the long-term orientation of most SDLC methodologies.

Managers are also employng evolutionary prototyping for applications development. With this comprehensive method, the whole system—user interfaces, processing functions, error control and handling, documentation, etc.—is developed through prototyping and is cut over to operations as any system would be.

Prototyping proponents who thought the method would do away with documentation, project management, and the systems development life cycle itself are beginning to realize that just the opposite is true. But when systems development groups are too firmly entrenched in their old methodologies, change is more difficult. The transportation company mentioned earlier had a successful prototyping project, but it was an end-user project; IS people weren't involved. In fact, the firm's IS organization isn't using prototyping at all and two poles are developing: conservative IS and liberated end users.

The company was fortunate in that the seven end users developing its carrier management system were "paraprofessionals," proficient in the software tools they needed (dBase III for user interfaces and FORTRAN for process requirements) and aware of the quality and documentation requirements. They have in fact become a second MIS group within the company.

PROTOTYPING MADE EASIER

A wide variety of software development tools have contributed to effective prototyping. These tools may be classified under four basic types: fourth generation languages for end users (such as Focus, RAMIS, AS, and Nomad), fourth generation languages for information systems professionals (such as ADS/Online, Ideal, Mantis, and Natural), automatic code generation facilities, and embedded language facilities.

While the end-user facilities are easier to learn and much less procedural, their nonprocedural nature may ultimately restrict programming flexibility for systems developers. In addition, systems produced by means of these facilities are likely to be relatively slow at execution time and may cause severe response-time deterioration for other systems. But as we have seen, end-user participation in systems development is critical, and the limitations inherent in end-user tools must be complemented by other facilities.

Fourth generation facilities for IS professionals are not likely to be user friendly, but they provide much more programming flexibility and permit a great deal of intimacy with the machine. This intimacy is an important feature in the development of prototypes that are to be kept and executed often, thus making machine performance a major consideration. While some companies have trained end users in the use of these facilities for specific tasks such as screen painting and report generation, they are primarily used by IS personnel.

Automatic code generation facilities for COBOL or other third generation languages are exclusively in the domain of the IS pro. While they are valuable for rewriting some of the vast number of applications done in COBOL or for applications where coding represents a substantial part of the development effort, they are not useful for new prototype versions when requirements are unstable. Since automatic code generators need detailed systems design information to produce code, translating these shifting requirements into detailed design specifications becomes a cumbersome task.

Embedded 4GL facilities are also tools for IS professionals. These tools enhance programming flexibility by embedding nonprocedural or semiprocedural 4GL

Prototypes and Their Purposes

One of the most common reasons for prototyping is to provide a vehicle for more effectively defining systems information requirements. In the planning stage, many projects allow for a clear separation of the user interface (screens, reports, etc.) from the functions necessary to input data or to produce the data items for the screens and reports. Because of this, many companies develop prototypes to define the user interfaces for the system—which is called user interface development (UID) prototyping—or to define the processing or functional requirements—which is called functional development (FD) prototyping. Or they may develop prototypes with combined objectives.

The "silly empty shell" problem is one commonly associated with UID prototyping. For an end user, this means that a system's impressive-looking user interface lacks the processing needed to support it. Coordinating the completion of UID prototypes and their corresponding functions must be timed carefully to minimize this problem.

Provided this coordination is achieved, the major advantage of UID prototyping is that while end users or information center personnel are working on the user interface, IS professionals can be developing the functions concurrently. Thus, development is speeded up and people are deployed doing what they do best.

In FD prototyping, actual processing is done, producing information. The primary risk associated with this type of prototyping is that a prototype originally intended as a throwaway, quick-and-dirty solution is retained—often because of the will of a powerful user manager—and becomes the basis of a large, complex system that is expensive to operate and maintain. Such systems may contain incorrect algorithms and may process invalid data, with little provision for backup and recovery.

In situations where systems developers are unable to see through complex design alternatives, building a prototype to model particular design configurations can be a great advantage. The primary objective of this type of prototyping—machine performance evaluation (MPE)—is the determination of response times and/or memory requirements associated with various design alternatives that involve different numbers of files, file sizes, transaction processing approaches, physical database designs, or communications volume.

One of the few cases where throwaways are justifiable is MPE prototyping. It is less expensive to model the specific design aspects that are problematic than to develop alternative versions of the system. In MPE prototyping, the model is likely to be so incomplete that it will be discarded after the problem is resolved.

Applications development prototyping encompasses the user interfaces, the functions, and, in some cases, all other elements necessary to produce a full-blown system. In applications development, often a particular application cannot be easily decomposed into user interfaces and functional components. The prototypes for such applications actually represent combinations of the UID, FD, and MPE prototypes. In addition to employing applications of development prototypes for large, monolithic applications, prototypes for small systems also tend to be developed in this fashion, since there is little benefit to breaking down small systems into components.

statements in 3GL programs. For applications that are developed using substantial amounts of 3GL programming, however, systems development productivity usually suffers with this approach compared with what can be achieved through exclusive use of IS fourth generation facilities.

While our study found that firms are employing a variety of fourth generation facilities for prototyping, end-user and IS fourth generation facilities—when they are properly matched to the application at hand—are the most common, as well as the most effective, prototyping tools.

But beyond the right complement of tools, the firms achieving the greatest prototyping success are those that are discovering the right complement of end user and IS professional cooperation. The key to the utility company's success was to have teams of end users and developers working together closely.

Unfortunately, such consonance is still the exception, not the rule. But as the richness of the prototyping concept unfolds, more IS players will trade their johnny-one-note, throwaway tunes for harmonies with end users. The orchestrations invariably create more effective systems.

27

Accelerated Information Systems Development in the Army

Mary L. Cesena and Wendell O. Jones

For approximately 20 years, systems development in the U.S. Army adhered to a traditional model based on two implicit assumptions. One was the general suitability of a linear development strategy for all system types, and the second was that the developer could produce an effective system from predefined user specifications. Perhaps appropriate for structured transactions processing systems, these assumptions proved invalid in the contemporary age. Design and development of command and control, decision support, and other less-structured applications required a new strategy; and the rapid proliferation of distributed multi-user systems demanded accelerated development schedules. In the early 1980s, the U.S. Army progressed from the traditional methodology through prototyping techniques to a contemporary model. This paper describes the evolution of these accelerated approaches and explains the current methodology [4, 5].

PROBLEMS WITH THE TRADITIONAL METHODS

A typical systems development project in the 1970s took five to seven years with requirements definition alone consuming over two years. Development supposedly began when the functional proponent (user representative) delivered to the software developer a document asserted to contain clear, correct and complete definitions of user requirements. Instead of development initiation, this delivery typically triggered many rounds of revisions and cycles of frustration. Functional and detailed systems documents were passed back and forth over an invisible-but-real wall separating the functional proponent and software developer (See Exhibit 27.1). By the time physical design and development began, the Army's way of doing business and user requirements had inevitably changed. Consequently, a major challenge for the Army

Exhibit 27.1
Traditional Methodology

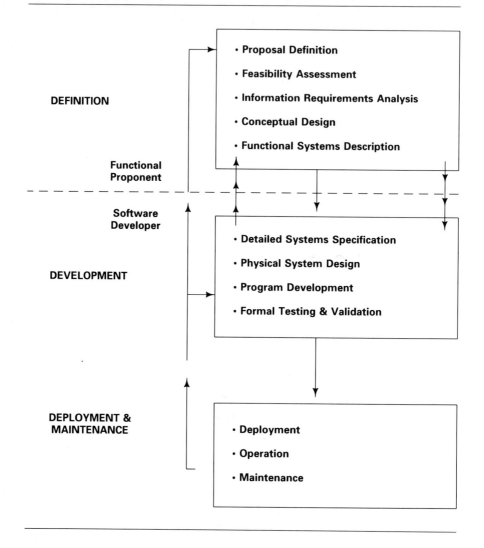

in the early 1980s was to devise a new methodology that accelerated information systems development.

At a time when prototyping was gaining acceptance as a new development paradigm, the U.S. Army Information Systems Software Development Center at Fort Lee, Va., began the design of four new systems. Because rapid development and deployment were required, the traditional methodology was abandoned in favor of rapid prototyping. The new method was called "Systems Through Evolutionary Prototyping with User Participation," or "STEP-UP."

SYSTEMS THROUGH EVOLUTIONARY PROTOTYPING WITH USER PARTICIPATION

In contrast to the traditional separation, STEP-UP co-located user representatives and software developers in the same office and applied prototyping techniques. As Exhibit 27.2 shows, STEP-UP emphasized construction of a working model as quickly as possible. The model, called a prototype, was developed with the user or user representative working side-by-side with the developer. Changes were made to each iteration until a final prototype was produced, tested and implemented. The proposition was that users could more easily express what they like or dislike about an existing application than explain the desired characteristics of an imagined, future system [3, 2, 6].

Along with prototyping and co-location, STEP-UP employed computer-aided design tools and fourth generation languages (4GL) — screen builders, report generators, query facilities and non-procedural languages. While prototyping and 4GL's improved development productivity, STEP-UP experience made it clear that prototyping and 4GL's were not a panacea. A number of potential problems and pitfalls were discovered.

Problems and Lessons Learned

One major pitfall of STEP-UP was inadequate system analysis. Teams with a high level of prototyping enthusiasm tended to perform inadequate system analysis. For example, three systems required integration, but due to insufficient up-front analysis, significant interface design errors were found during acceptance testing at a user site.

Another pitfall was the inclination of user management to embrace a premature prototype. A variety of factors seemed to encourage this. Dissatisfaction with an old system and need for an improved system that conformed to a pressing regulatory requirement were the two most common. These tendencies were present even though the premature system poorly used computer resources, inadequately interfaced with other systems, or delivered incomplete documentation. The importance of early analysis and strong project management controls was the lesson learned.

The opposite of fielding a premature version was overkill. If user management felt minimal pressure to implement a particular system, enhancements and iterations were almost without end. "Bells and whistles" were added, refined, deleted, and added again. Each end-user review led to further refinements. The "80/20 rule" was rediscovered; i.e., develop, test, and implement an initial baseline that includes 80 percent or so of the user requirements and delay "fine-tuning." In this way, developers were relieved of the expectation that endless changes would be requested.

STEP-UP also taught the importance of balanced teams. The inexperienced analyst and programmer found it difficult to provide technical guidance, and a novice user representative could overlook the broader implications of a new system, fail to appreciate management information needs, or ignore important system interfaces. Further, senior managers were inappropriate team members, for they were unable

Exhibit 27.2
STEP-UP Methodology

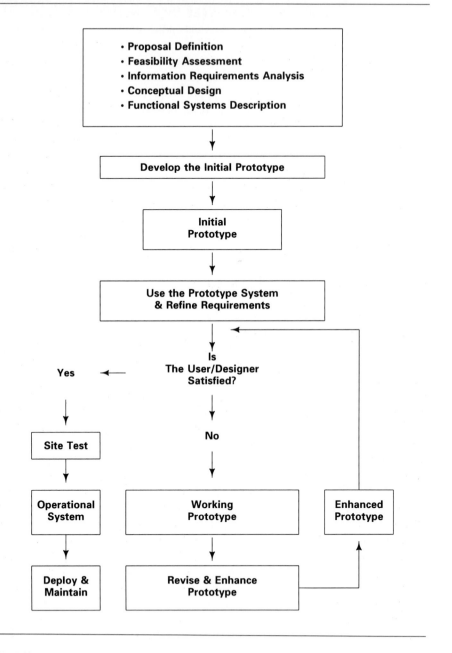

to devote the time for effective participation. The lesson learned was to assemble teams of experienced professionals and establish equal levels of responsibility for functional and technical team leaders.

In the early months of prototyping, a roadblock was resistance by some key functional and technical people. Co-location was perceived as a threat to established lines of authority and prototyping considered too different from conventional methods. Early resistance was lessened by the emphasis on prototyping as an extension of the familiar modeling process. Resistance gradually dissipated as prototyping successes were observed and the teams gained a sense of shared ownership.

Lack of project discipline was the most serious shortcoming of STEP-UP. Project control measures with structured phases, defined milestones, quality reviews, sign-offs and progress measures were proven more essential with the swings and roundabouts of the prototyping process.

STEP-UP produced four systems in record time with considerable savings, as shown in Exhibit 27.3. Average savings in development time, dollars and manmonths were 33 months, $1,460,000, and 467 manmonths, respectively. It was clear, however, that more than prototyping was required. Consequently, the Army refined STEP-UP and implemented a new methodology called Contemporary Life Cycle Development (CLCD).

Exhibit 27.3
STEP-UP Results
Development Time, Dollars and Manmonths (Traditional vs. Accelerated)

System	Estimates Using Traditional Method			Results Using Accelerated Method		
	Development Time (Months)	$$ (000)	Man-months	Development Time (Months)	$$ (000)	Man-months
Repair Parts Supply	36	1785	612	6	297	102
Property Accountability	60	875	300	22	245	84
Retail Supply Operations	60	3500	1200	7	408	140
Personnel Management	28	1775	225	18	1135	144

Average Savings:
Development Time   32.75
Dollars ($000)   1460
Manmonths   467

CONTEMPORARY LIFE-CYCLE DEVELOPMENT METHODOLOGY (CLCD)

CLCD emphasizes disciplined prototyping. STEP-UP encouraged invention and innovation, but was undocumented, unstructured and made it difficult to plan, budget, and control development. Formal quality reviews and checkpoints during the development cycle were also absent.

Major Features of CLCD

Quality assurance reviews, therefore, are an important aspect of CLCD. Design reviews mark the end of one phase and of the beginning of the next. The primary purpose of a design review is to allow all parties involved to review the development to that point and confirm that the data structures, design and system products meet user requirements. Standards, such as data elements and screen formats, are also verified during these reviews.

A key feature of CLCD is evolutionary requirements documentation. Development begins with only a broad functional description that defines system boundaries and interfaces. System boundaries delimit the system and identify known constraints. System interfaces, security, and communication requirements are also included. This broad description establishes a basis for dialog between the functional proponent and system developer and provides the skeleton for evolving detailed requirements. As each part of the system is produced, the functional analyst reviews the partial product. Development continues in this manner with the functional description continuously revised; ideas are encouraged and necessary changes made. An important question is when to "freeze" the functional description. STEP-UP experience showed that it is better to develop, test, and implement an operational prototype of essential "core" requirements that are initially firm but subject to later expansion. This approach decreases the expectation of last minute changes and provides a baseline for evolutionary functionality.

The broad description continuously evolves into a more detailed definition of user requirements as development progresses. The final definition of user requirements is documented following the end-user demonstration in the programming phase. Subsequent changes to system requirements are evaluated and approved by a configuration control board composed of representatives from user organizations, the software developer and the functional proponent.

The Army traditionally developed systems and specified data only in relation to one or a few systems without use of standard database formats or database management systems across functional boundaries. Several problems stemmed from this approach: new programs were difficult and costly to develop because of the need to build new files, redesign old files, or develop interfaces with existing data; information needed was often unavailable because no existing application provided the data; or data available for an application program was difficult and costly to access for ad hoc query. As a result of these problems in the past, the database approach is central to CLCD and key to achieving a future Army corporate database.

Overview of CLCD

Exhibit 27.4 is an overview of CLCD showing the four phases: requirements definition, design, programming, and test and validation. With the exception of the final test and validation, each phase is intentionally separated into data design and process design activities in order to promote independence of the data from the code.

The first phase begins with a system description that broadly describes the proposed system or application. The principal activity in the first phase is conceptual design. The second phase comprises logical database design and system/program design. From the logical design, the third phase includes physical database design, physical database implementation, and applications program development. Even though testing and end-user validation are performed throughout the development process, the fourth phase is a comprehensive systems stress/integration/performance evaluation.

Requirements Definition Phase

Requirements definition is separated into data (conceptual planning) activities and process (high-level functional decomposition) activities as shown in Table 27.1. Conceptual planning concentrates on the design of a conceptual data model that depicts a global, top-down view of system entities and relationships in the form of an entity-relationship chart. An entity-relationship chart shows the entities (places, persons, things, concepts, events) about which data is collected and the relationships and associations among the entities. Together, the entities and relationships express the information requirements outlined in the broad description. Process activities of the first phase decompose the broad description into boundaries that define the processes, sub-processes and events of the system, subsystem, and/or module. This phase culminates in a conceptual design walk-through. Requirements definition is complete if the key participants in this walk-through validate that the entities, relationships, and process activities fulfill the processing and information requirements of the broad description refined during this phase.

Design Phase

Shown in Table 27.2, this phase is also divided into design of data and the design of process. The objective is a data-oriented, not a procedure-oriented, system because "data-oriented techniques succeed if correctly applied where procedure-oriented techniques have failed [7]." Data modeling is applied to gain data independence, and user views are defined from the products of the system; (i.e., screens, menus, reports). It is critical that each data element be logically attributed to an entity or relationship in the entity/relationship model. If an element cannot be attributed, the entity/relationship model must be corrected by discovering the missing entity or relationship [8]. The design phase concludes with a logical database design walk-through "signed-off" by the key participants listed in Table 27.2.

Exhibit 27.4
Overview of Contemporary Life Cycle Development

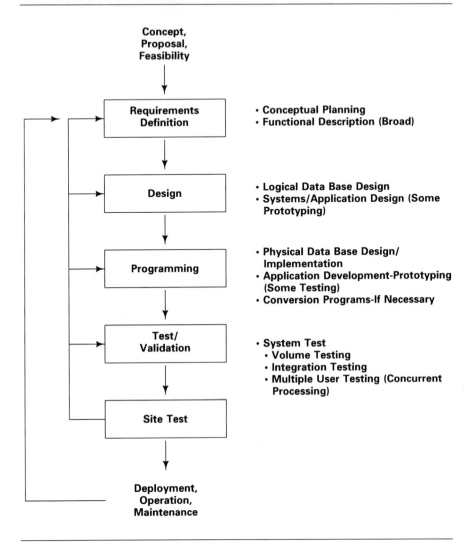

Data modeling for logical database design requires computer-aided design tools to synthesize process/entity matrices showing creators and users of data, user views, data element definitions, and normalization of user views for production of a logical data model. A logical design walk-through validates that user views are normalized, that data elements in each view use standard definitions and names, and that the logical design supports additions, deletions, and other modifications without loss of data or data integrity.

Process in the design phase encompasses decomposition and event analysis to produce diagrams of event sequences and process dependencies. System and pro-

Table 27.1
Requirements Definition Phase

Data	Process
Conceptual Planning	**Functional Description**
1. Identify all entities	Produce a broad functional description of all
2. Define Relationships/Associations	the activities/decisions required to manage
3. Resolve Many-to-Many Relationships	each entity. Include any boundaries/con-
4. Define Primary Keys	straints. These definitions will become your
5. Produce Entity/Relationship Chart	processes.
Conceptual Design Review	
Validate above with functional	
proponent (Walk-through)	
Participants:	
Developer	
Functional Designer	
Data Administration	

gram specifications are produced using definitions of the processes/sub-processes and linkages. Charts and matrices, created during development of the logical database design, are used to define data flow and data dependencies. The process and data dependencies are combined into process input/process/output diagrams, sub-process input/process/output diagrams, and program input/process/output diagrams. With the use of prototyping and 4GL tools, information requirements such as menus, screens, and reports are designed and formatted during this phase. A system design walk-through validates that all process diagrams, sub-process diagrams, program diagrams, specifications, and input/output formats (menus, screens, reports) support the functional description. An end-user review is also conducted to review system products. This important review allows early correction of formats; discrepancies are immediately corrected and redisplayed to the end user for validation.

Programming Phase

The programming phase (Table 27.3) consists of physical database design and applications program development. Physical database design includes software locks to insure security of classified data as well as considerations such as performance and optimization of the database. File maintenance procedures to load, back-up and restore the database are also identified. Hardware-dependent requirements such as storage capacity are applied during this phase. Once physical considerations are imposed on the logical model, the physical database is implemented and populated with test data. The programs written for the conversion are not minor; they must access a large number of files with redundant data. It is not a trivial job because time is needed to understand the conversion "from" and "to" and writing the application code, testing and revising it, and coordinating a number of programs [1]. A walk-through validates physical database design.

Table 27.2
Design Phase

Data

Logical Data Base Design
1. Process/entity matrix showing users/creators
2. Define user views (inputs, outputs, screens, reports, displays, etc.)
3. Establish names/definitions for each data-item
4. For each user view, identify which entities/data-items are used
5. Normalization
6. Add foreign keys
7. Canonical synthesis (combine logical models)

Logical Design Review
Confirm Accuracy of Conceptual Data Model

Participants:
  Developer
  Functional Designer
  Data Administration
  QA Standards

Process

System Design
1. Event analysis (sequence)
2. Data Flow (I/O) Diagrams
3. System/Program Specs
4. Begin Prototyping (develop screens, menus, reports, etc.)

System Design Review
Confirm accuracy of system diagrams, as well as screens, menus, reports design, etc.

Participants:
  Developer
  Functional Designer
  QA Standards

Inputs and outputs (menus, screens, reports, test data, etc.) designed in the previous phase are accessible in this phase. Logical views of the physical database are now available for each application since the logical model has been mapped to a physical model. The physical model is implemented and used by application programs. The users are presented with subsets of the logical model, called external models (also referred to as subschemas). External models are the views of the users from the logical model [1].

Unit testing of each individual program or module is accomplished using test criteria provided by the functional designer. Because the functional designer is physically located with the software developer, on-the-spot validation is possible. Once each individual unit is tested, modules are linked to form the necessary system tests. Again, discrepancies are quickly corrected and revalidated. A system/application design walk-through ensures a quality review to validate each logical unit as it moves through the system.

With a representative group of end users, a functional end-user demonstration is conducted with live demonstrations for end users who actually prepare input trans-

Table 27.3
Programming Phase

Data

1. Physical Database Design
   Using logical models, design physical files
   a. Add security
   b. Performance/optimization
   c. File maintenance: load, backup, restore, recovery procedures
   d. Hardware/environmental considerations.
2. Physical implementation—load database
3. Develop input data
4. Develop conversion programs

Physical Database Design Review
Evaluate physical database

Participants:
  Developer
  Hardware/Software Expert
  Database Administration
  Security

Process

5. Application Program Development
   a. Begin actual prototyping of applications using screens, menus, reports and database files.
   b. Develop JCL Procedures.
   c. Program Tests.—The programs & outputs are validated on-the-spot and corrections (refinements) made to broad functional description.

Systems/Application Design Review
Multiple validation points end of a logical unit of work (one function, one application, etc.)

Participants:
  Developer
  Hardware/Software Expert
  Functional Designer
  Communications

Functional End User Demonstration

actions. Problems uncovered during this demonstration are corrected and solutions revalidated.

Test/Validation Phase

Since much of the lower-level unit and program testing was completed in earlier phases, this phase concentrates on a total system test to include stresses placed upon the system. Volume tests, integration tests, multiple-user tests, and concurrent processing with two or more users accessing the system are the main evaluations (See Table 27.4). Successful completion leads to acceptance testing with live data at a selected user organization.

Table 27.4
Test & Validation

Full Blown Systems Test
- Volume Test (large volume test criteria provided by functional proponent)
- Integration Test (using interface files to/from other systems)
- Multiple User Testing (concurrent processing)

Systems Test Review
- Validate the above stresses upon the system

Participants:
  Developer
  Functional Designer
  Interface Developer
  Data Base Administration
  Hardware/Software
  Quality Assurance
  Standards
  Communications
  Security

RESULTS

The Army developed four systems using STEP-UP and is currently using CLCD for four new systems. Based on historical data for projects of comparable size and system complexity developed in earlier years, estimates of CLCD savings are summarized in Exhibit 27.5. The average reduction for four major systems is 19 months development time, $3,025,000 and 870 manmonths.

An example system in current development is a spare parts and vehicle maintenance management system designed for operation at thousands of repair shops. It is presently in the programming phase using Informix SQL and scheduled for completion much earlier than the Army can acquire and deliver the production hardware.

Another example, a system for management of real property and other facilities worldwide, is under development using a Sperry/5000 Unix-based environment with ORACLE/SQL. Software developers and functional designers are co-located with contract employees. With each phase structured and manageable, the level of effort and deliverables is easily identified and assigned to the three types of teams. Development using CLCD began in October 1986, and the project is scheduled for acceptance testing in February 1988.

Results of recent and on-going efforts show that faster development is the major benefit of CLCD. Techniques such as disciplined prototyping, co-location, and 4GL tools enhance productivity. Prototyping accelerates the development cycle and facilitates design changes. Co-location fosters cohesion and a feeling of partnership among developers, user representatives, and end-users. Quality walk-throughs permit validation of the conceptual, logical, and physical data design and the process design. Hardware, software, security, back-up, integration, and communications aspects of the system are addressed from the outset and at other critical points in the life cycle.

Exhibit 27.5
CLCD Projected Results
Development Time, Dollars and Manmonths (Traditional vs. Accelerated)

System	Estimates Using Traditional Method			Estimates Using Accelerated Method		
	Development Time (Months)	$$ (000)	Man-months	Development Time (Months)	$$ (000)	Man-months
Facilities Engineering	36	4800	1460	18	2100	396
Food Service Management	36	5300	1944	10	100	320
Ammunition Management	36	3700	1224	30	1700	576
Retail Supply Management	45	6200	348	21	4000	206

Average Savings:
Development Time   18.5
Dollars ($000)   3025
Manmonths   870

End-user demonstrations and reviews identify design errors early in the development process and 4GL tools permit easier modification of the software. Database design methodologies avoid data duplication and inconsistencies while improving data integrity. Moreover, decreased data redundancy reduces storage requirements.

Two anticipated advantages of the database approach are the development of systems compatible with the Army corporate database and reduced software maintenance costs. Unlike non-DBMS files with file definitions imbedded in the code, file changes for a DBMS-based system require only a data dictionary update to reflect the new logical view. Since all systems are being developed with a relational DBMS which conform to the Army standard, integration into the corporate database promises to be an easier task.

Finally, CLCD is a methodology which recognizes differences in project-related factors, in contrast to the traditional approach which forced all projects to use a single development strategy. For highly structured systems with requirements that can be determined in a straightforward process, a linear strategy with minimal iteration can be used. Where uncertainty is relatively high (large multiple-user systems or applications new to users or the developer), a life cycle structure with embedded prototyping is an available option. Systems or applications with high levels of requirements uncertainty can apply iterative approaches such as prototyping and systems simulation. Examples of high uncertainty are executive decision support, command and control and other unstructured applications for which it is difficult to specify requirements in advance (or requirements are expected to change significantly during development). CLCD is, in other words, a contingency model that permits the selection of a development strategy consistent with the level of uncertainty about user requirements or the technology [3, 5].

CONCLUSIONS

Because the traditional systems development approach was slow and inefficient, the Army implemented a new methodology. The first version essentially abandoned the life cycle method and associated project controls in favor of prototyping. While prototyping accelerated development and significantly reduced time and cost, problems were experienced. The major difficulties were: inadequate management of the development process due to frequent changes; an inclination to accept a premature prototype; and a tendency toward interminable iteration.

Based on experience developing four systems, the Army revised STEP-UP and implemented a new methodology for information systems development. The current methodology, called Contemporary Life Cycle Development, integrates 4GL tools, prototyping, and the database approach into a life cycle management structure with formal project controls. As the standard information systems methodology used throughout the U.S. Army, the contemporary method provides for alternative strategies and is producing new systems in less time with significantly reduced development costs.

REFERENCES

1. Atre, S., "Data Base: Structured Techniques for Design, Performance and Management," 1980, pp. 17, 18, 306.

2. Alavi, Maryam, "An Assessment of the Prototyping Approach to Information Systems," *Communications of the ACM,* 27:6, June 1984, pp. 556–563.

3. Jenkins, Milton, "Prototyping: A Methodology for the Design and Development of Application Systems," Working Paper, School of Business, Indiana University, 1983.

4. McKeen, James D., "Successful Development Strategies for Business Application Systems," *MIS Quarterly,* 7:3, September 1983, pp. 47–65.

5. Naumam, J. David, Davis, G. B., and McKeen, J. D., "Determining Information Requirements: A Contingency Method for Selection of a Requirements Assurance Strategy," *Journal of Systems and Software,* Vol. 1, p. 227.

6. Naumam, Justus D. and Jenkins, A. Milton, "Prototyping: The New Paradigm for Systems Development," *MIS Quarterly,* 6:3, September 1982, pp. 29–44.

7. Martin, James, "Strategic Data Planning Methodologies," 1982, p. 17.

8. Smith, William G., "The Fit Between E/R Modeling and Logical Data Modeling," *Data Base Newsletter,* Volume 14, Number 3, May/June 1986.

28 Reusable Software: Passage to Productivity?

Edward J. Joyce

If automobile technology had advanced at the same rate as computer technology over the past 30 years, a Rolls Royce would now cost $2.50 and get 2 million miles per gallon. Although it indeed may be a long, long way from the ENIAC to the Macintosh, advances in computer software that approach the stunning breakthroughs in hardware over this period have yet to be seen.

"The average software endeavor resembles the computer hardware of the 1950s in which many unique components were wired together for the first time. The over-all reliability of the finished product was predictably low," asserts Tom Love, chairman of Productivity Products International in Sandy Hook, Conn. "Manufacturers addressed the hardware reliability problem by relying on reusable, proven components," he says. "How many companies, for example, now build their own microprocessors from scratch? We as an industry must learn to build software from reusable components."

What does reusability mean in software development? According to T. Capers Jones, president of Software Productivity Research, Cambridge, Mass., it includes reusable data, designs, systems, programs, and modules or subroutines. Data, while appearing to be obvious candidates for reusability, are often isolated due to a lack of standard data interchange formats. The emergence of data interchange formats in spreadsheet programs and an awareness of the problems caused by dissimilar formats indicates that the "future will be better than the past," Jones says.

REUSABLE SOFTWARE MAY BOOST PRODUCTIVITY

Not even the most ardent supporters of reusability are predicting that the legendary achievements made in hardware will soon be duplicated in software, but a growing number of software pundits see carefully designed and documented reusable software as a way of breaking the bottleneck in programming productivity. Several companies are reaping significant increases in productivity through concerted reusability efforts. Toshiba Corp. realized annual productivity rates in excess of 20,000 lines of source code per person-year as a result of utilizing reusable designs.

One active proponent of reusability is Will Tracz, an advisory programmer at IBM's Federal Systems Div., Oswego, N.Y. A member of the company's Corporate Reuse Council, Tracz poses in his "alter ego" as a used-program salesman to draw attention to the issues surrounding software reuse. Tracz and other reusability advocates point to studies that show software productivity languishing at an increase of only 3% to 8% per year during the 1960s and 1970s. The processing capability of installed hardware, on the other hand, increased at a rate of 40% or better per year.

Studies also found that likely 15% of all programming code written in 1983 was unique, novel, and specific to individual applications. The remaining 85% was common and generic and theoretically could have been developed from reusable components. Typical examples include Gregorian date edit routines, Gregorian to Julian date conversions, and edits and validation of part, employee, and account numbers.

HIGHER FORMS OF REUSE SHOW PROMISE

The higher forms of reuse, namely designs and systems, show the most promise among researchers for future quantum leaps in productivity, but, by and large, these types of reuse have yet to have significant impact on the average programmer.

Since any program used by two or more users qualifies as reusable software, virtually all programming shops participate at this level through vendor-supplied and commercially purchased software. A large company's budget for off-the-shelf software, however, is typically dwarfed by spending for development of its own systems.

Commercial software can be disappointing in the reusability benefits it provides. One industry veteran gives the example of a client that bought a payroll package for $600,000 that was supposed to have been loaded with reusable, generic code. "Well, it took them one-and-a-half years and 20 people to make enough modifications just to install it. Why did it take 30 man-years to modify if you can just drop it in? Because you can't. And that was commercial code designed to be 'reusable.'"

In trying to control software development costs, some MIS managers are exploiting—with notable success—their existing software bases. Take, for example, the Hartford Insurance Group of Hartford, Conn. "Hartford started a reusability program in 1981 as part of a broad plan to increase applications development productivity by tenfold over 10 years," says Daniel R. Walsh, former director of the information management division, which has responsibility for software reusability at Hartford.

"The reusable products library, maintained on a Wang minicomputer, is available through an on-line network to a staff of 1,200 systems development people," he continues. "By reusing code in the library, we realize a savings of 250 person-days per month at a cost of 25 person-days in support and maintenance time."

Walsh, who recently left Hartford to head the consulting firm of Walsh and Associates in South Windsor, Conn., describes Hartford's reusable library as a collection of 35 documented and tested COBOL code modules consisting of 15 programs and 20 subroutines. Another 45 items reside in the "use as is" section of the library, which contains modules that have not undergone certification.

Programmers search through the reusable library using a function index, which can be searched from any workstation. The full inventory is indexed and cross-indexed according to data processing and business functions.

To track companywide reusability, Hartford's 14 applications development divisions are required to file monthly reports showing what percentage of reusable code comprises new systems. Based on these figures, which are reported to the vice president of information management, Walsh estimates that between 30% and 40% of the code in new systems comes from the reusable library.

Besides the mandate of upper management, the company relies on an incentive program to stimulate programmer interest in reusability. "Individuals who make submissions to the reusable library receive imprinted coffee mugs," explains Walsh, and, "the submissions are candidates for a $300 award the company issues for the best productivity suggestion of the month."

Token giveaways play a key role in getting programmers to participate in a reusability program, believes Steve Sposato, staff technology consultant, who initiated a giveaway program at Pacific Bell. "We promote the library by giving coffee mugs and screwdrivers to contributors. It's great publicity—just about everyone asks where they can get an official reusability coffee mug." A year ago, Sposato handed the program over to Mitch Che, staff manager in IS.

About 250 programmers at the firm's San Ramon, Calif., information systems department have access to an on-line library that contains "thousands" of C language components written for Unix and running on computers from Unisys, AT&T, and Digital Equipment Corp., among other manufacturers. The library also contains development tools and training guides.

EASE OF USE IS THE KEY TO SUCCESS

"The key to success in a reusable library, or any type of library for that matter, is giving your patrons a way of getting what they need with the least amount of trouble," explains Sposato. "We spent considerable time designing an easy and efficient user interface based on a hierarchical tree of function categories and subcategories, plus an extensive index of keywords."

Before the library was opened to users in October 1986, Sposato canvassed the company to collect a broad inventory of software. "You don't want to serve any library before its time," he cautions. "If people log-on to a library with little or no inventory, they'll think it's a waste of time. When the library eventually accumulates a decent collection, you'll then be faced with trying to convince those people to log-on again.

"Our overall philosophy is that you're either a consumer or a contributor," continues Sposato. "If a programmer is not using material from the reusable library when developing a system, then he should be contributing his code. In 1988, our management plans to set reusable quotas. Programmers will be expected to reuse a certain amount or contribute a certain amount."

Sposato notes that Pacific Bell's executive management has been a driving force behind reusability. "They learned about the concept from a presentation Capers Jones gave in November 1985. A month later, at Pac Bell's annual Pathfinder's Conference, management identified reusability as a corporate objective for the technical staff."

While recognizing the critical role management plays in a reusability program, Sposato believes that the ultimate success lies with programmers. "Programmers have the option of writing software from scratch or checking for a functional equivalent in the reusable library that is certified to work. But once they become accustomed to relying on the library, the behavior will be self-perpetuating. People who incorporate reusable code in their software will be more productive than those who don't."

Since the reusability library went on-line little more than a year ago, Pacific Bell has spent approximately $300,000 in hardware, software, and personnel support costs. Although it is "tough to measure" what that investment yields in savings, Sposato states emphatically, "There is no doubt in my mind that it's a worthwhile venture."

In Sposato's opinion, the difficulty with gauging return on investment in reusability is linked to the general problem of measuring programmer productivity. "How do you do software metrics? In some cases, 20 lines of code may be worth more than 20,000 lines. We have not found a way of correlating levels of reusability with lower head counts or decreased costs."

SPREADING THE WEALTH

Among the benefits of the reusable library he cites is the capability of spreading the wealth of the company's topflight programmers by making their code available to everyone. This factor helps train new personnel because they can browse through "role-model code" stored in a central repository.

While agreeing that software productivity is difficult to measure, another reusability pioneer, GTE Data Services, has devised a financial model for quantifying its investment. "Our model shows a savings of $1.5 million for 1987 based on a reuse factor of 14% [new systems containing 14% reused code]," states Mary Swanson, director of the company's information asset engineering group. "Our five-year business plan calls for 50% reuse, which will amount to a total savings in excess of $12 million."

Swanson points out that the 1987 figure, which exceeded projections, was achieved with a library of 136 components consisting of 168,000 source code lines available to 700 programmers. The contents of the library are published in paper form and distributed manually. In 1988, the library catalogue will be posted on-line and the user audience will be expanded to 1,100 software developers based in the company's Tampa, Fla., center. The Tampa group mainly develops centralized MIS applications for GTE's affiliated telephone companies.

Like the Hartford Insurance library, GTE's repository consists primarily of COBOL source code for a mainframe environment. The quality of candidate software components for the library are carefully screened for correctness, documentation, and potential application.

The final criteria examine how a component can be reused and how likely it is to be reused in light of the functional requirements of planned systems.

Swanson's staff of 17 engineers and analysts works closely with development groups in identifying components that are suitable for reuse. Swanson estimates that, on the average, 20 hours are spent to qualify each 1,000 lines of code accepted for reuse. To entice contributors, GTE pays authors a cash bonus of $25 each time a component is reused.

RAYTHEON REPORTS PRODUCTIVITY LEAP

When GTE management first studied the feasibility of reusability in 1985, recalls Swanson, she spoke at length to Robert Lanergan of Raytheon. In a widely quoted 1984 report, Lanergan describes how Raytheon achieved 60% reusable code in new development of COBOL applications for "a 50% increase in productivity" at Raytheon's Missile Systems Div. in Bedford, Mass.

Swanson says that "Raytheon's study proved the success of organized efforts to promote reusability. But the work was performed more than five years ago, and you don't necessarily want to replicate that exact model today." At GTE, she emphasizes, the library will eventually include reusable designs, architectures, user interfaces, and other items in addition to software components. The library's name reflects the diversity of its function; rather than a reusable software library, it's officially known as the Asset Catalog. Swanson's expectation of reusable designs points to a trend among those who have exploited the common nuts and bolts of programs and are now focusing attention on the generic subassemblies of applications.

Hartford Insurance is looking to a code generator-type product called CAP from Toronto-based Netron Inc., which allows a programmer to build software from reusable segments of COBOL code called frames. Walsh says that frame technology reduces program maintenance to a process of modifying a short engineering blueprint instead of changing pages of source code.

Netron announced in December that Westpac Banking Corp., Australia's largest banking group, chose the CAP product as part of a $A120 million automated banking project. A similar product, called Virtuoso, which was released last fall by Hewlett-Packard, also combines COBOL code generation and a reusable library for building applications.

IBM's Tracz believes that products such as these will help make widespread software reuse a reality. He sees momentum gathering in the form of industry and government financial incentives to foster the proper environment for software reuse.

The tools and technology emerging today, he predicts, can yield productivity "an order of magnitude over simple forms of reuse, such as subroutine libraries and code templates." In Tracz's opinion, it's about time that software developers agreed to stop reinventing the wheel.

29

Sotware Packages:
The Off-the-Shelf Alternative

Ed Praytor

The implementation of large applications software packages represents one of the most complex data processing projects likely to be encountered today. It is one of the least understood and most underestimated. Unrealistic expectations, marketing hyperbole, legal issues, limited management controls and a steep learning curve often combine to create mammoth cost overruns, time slippage and user discontent.

It doesn't have to be that way. Most application software packages provide an unparalleled opportunity to implement major information processing capabilities at substantially reduced costs. Where then do we go wrong?

First, we fail to realize that we have a problem. We all want quick and easy solutions. That's why we buy a package. Vendors often encourage a prospect's perception that, with a couple of signatures on contracts, a difficult problem becomes easy. Prospects want to believe this as well. This often results in a form of managerial and technical myopia that fails to plan for or to recognize serious project problems likely to occur.

Second, assuming we recognize the need to carefully manage the implementation process, we often fail to modify our management techniques to suit the unique project environment these large applications packages create.

By recognizing basic differences these packages and their vendors represent—and, more important, knowing what to do about them—we reduce the risk and cost of the project. By approaching implementation with a cohesive plan, we avoid many of the project-killing problems encountered so often in the past.

ENVIRONMENTAL DIFFERENCES

Some very basic differences exist between an in-house development project and package implementation. Perhaps the most troublesome is the great-expectations syndrome. Packages are often oversold and overbought. Consequently, the technical staff is surprised by and unforgiving of technical problems that appear. Convinced of the quality of the package, the user is similarly unprepared and unwilling to extensively test the system. As a result, the project is often understaffed and timeframes are grossly optimistic. As a general rule, peak staff levels may only be slightly reduced from the in-house alternative; testing time may be longer for a package. The primary savings to the technical staff is that the time-on-project may be reduced with the package approach.

Unlike in-house development situations where predecessor systems and the design process educate the technical and user staff, a software package often creates information shock. In order to become minimally competent on the new system, a great deal must be learned in a short time. Viable project plans build in special provisions for early education and documentation. Opportunities exist during the evaluation and acquisition phase to begin the learning process. Most project plans fail to allow for the decreased productivity of the staff in the early stages of the project.

The third major environmental difference is the presence of the software vendor. The integration of a vendor into the project is a complex subject beyond the scope of this article. It should be remembered, however, that the vendor is almost always on the critical path of the project. In addition to data processing (DP) and the user, the vendor is the third party with the ability to take unilateral actions which directly affect the quality and timeliness of the deliverables. An integrated project plan which includes vendor deliverables as critical items will be helpful. It illustrates that information systems (IS) is absolutely unable to commit to project dates until vendor deliverables are received and verified. Many a project has smashed on these rocks.

Related to the loss of control built into these projects are legal aspects. Complex documents are used for license, product support and professional service (consulting) agreements. Many articles and books advise on appropriate clauses. Most offer suggestions that will help your attorneys if the project fails.

Why not incorporate provisions and definitions that aid the project while underway? For example, the definition of minimum support levels and response times under product support agreements can significantly reduce your maintenance costs, even in the first year of the project. An area that is always too ambiguous is definition of base system error and the vendor's obligation to correct it. Both the vendor and the client benefit from specificity in those areas.

The last major factor of package implementation is the presence of other companies who use the system. Although there is often competition for vendor resources, cooperative arrangements between using companies are possible. Implementation techniques, task estimates, specific modifications and requests to the vendor may be shared in most cases.

Given that these differences exist, what should be done about them? A unified project plan is needed that defines the tasks and interrelationships of the process from cradle to grave. To do this, consider a phased implementation plan.

Consultants are fond of phases and methodologies. Sometimes this is to the exclusion of the client's needs, if they are imposed on an unsuitable project. As a basis from which to tailor a custom project approach, however, such methodologies have a place. A typical major application software package project has six major activity areas. These are dissimilar in their requirements, but very closely coupled. The areas are: needs assessment, search, acquisition, base system installation, tailored system implementation, and maintenance.

NEEDS ASSESSMENT

A determination is made that a systems solution is needed to a business problem; the need is sufficiently pressing to dedicate resources. The business requirement is often ill-defined at this point. An analysis is performed of the functions to be automated, the benefit and the relative priority of the need.

At this point, several options should be considered: in-house development modification of existing systems, processing services, and software-package acquisition. Care should be taken not to underestimate the true cost of the package or processing service option. A low estimate results in pursuit of a package solution when in-house development represents the best alternative. This phase is not a time to involve software vendors. They have strong conflicts of interest in evaluation of a processing need or in the estimation of cost.

SEARCH

The search begins once the needs assessment documents are complete. During this phase, available literature, consultants and vendor-supplied information are used to identify the most viable software options from a functional standpoint. Given a correctly done requirements model, the process is straightforward. It involves reviews of system marketing literature, system documentation, vendor presentations and checks with other users of the system.

Less obvious are those activities which cut through the usual vendor hyperbole to define the true functionality, reliability and resource requirements of the system. Also often overlooked are tasks which require a vendor to become specific about support levels during and after implementation. These performance issues form the basis of your company's future business relationship with the vendor.

ACQUISITION

The acquisition begins with the selection of a primary vendor. Once the field is narrowed to this point, two major activities begin. Contract negotiations are initiated for license agreements, product-support agreements and consulting agreements. At the same time, your DP and user staff should begin an in-depth evaluation of the product and produce a first-cut implementation plan. With this plan and the pricing information from the vendor, the eventual cost of the project can be estimated. Contract negotiations need to revolve around price, protection and performance.

PRICE

Price includes cost to acquire the product, cost of vendor supplied modification or installation services and cost of system maintenance services. Look at (and negotiate around) all of these. Protection involves legal provisions to ensure these disputes either never mature or are resolved outside the legal arena. The performance representations obtained during the search phase should be incorporated into the contracts as negotiations proceed.

INSTALLATION

Installation of the base system may be accomplished either on a trial basis or at purchase. In the latter case, acceptance criteria defined during acquisition should be passed before the system is formally accepted. Delivery of a magnetic tape is not delivery of a system by any reasonable measure. You have purchased logic and information that needs to be demonstrated, not magnetic media. When modifications must be made to the base system prior to your company meeting its automation objective, system acceptance may be an even more complex issue.

IMPLEMENTATION

Assuming you are implementing a system requiring modification, implementation — which includes tailoring, testing and introducing the product to the field — is the longest and most complex area. It is also during this phase that the consequences of the previous requirements analysis, negotiations and evaluations become clear. A detailed project plan that integrates user, vendor and data processing needs is your most effective tool. It should be more detailed than the one produced during acquisition.

MAINTENANCE

When does a software system enter the maintenance phase? There is no ironclad guideline. Often the rate of system change is higher after the product is introduced to production than before. This is particularly true with relatively new packages or ones still being completed by the vendor. Maintenance mode implies stability. It is important not to declare it too soon. Once in this mode, it is important to actively manage the vendor's product-support services. You must ensure that your previously negotiated performance standards are met. The effective use of vendor maintenance services is often misunderstood and beyond the scope of this article. The payback in reduction of the size of your own maintenance staff can be substantial, however.

As we stepped through the generic implementation process, there were several forward and backward references to other activities. Each activity provides the basis for subsequent tasks or builds on the basis of previous activities. This makes the implementation approach enormously powerful. Each project may be viewed as a set of key issues that thread through each phase. They are addressed continuously by tasks designed for the issue at each particular stage. Examples of those issues include requirements identification, business relationship with the vendor, understanding and developing system capability, user integration and staff development. To illllustrate how you can use this cohesive, issue-based approach, I will use the definition and installation of custom modifications to the package as an illustration.

MANAGING ENHANCEMENTS

The basis for identification of enhancements to tailor a package is built during needs assessment. As the package options are narrowed in the search, the functional priorities you established with the users are employed to estimate closeness of fit. By the time the primary vendor is selected, a laundry list of prioritized enhancements is available. During the acquisition, more detailed analysis is done to determine the cost and time required to accomplish modifications. Should vendor support to accomplish the modifications be under consideration, the cost of such support becomes a negotiating issue. The specifications of the modifications by the vendor and their timing generate contractual provisions.

During implementation and tailoring, the enhancement specifications become both control and working documents. They are used to manage the scope of the project, monitor vendor performance and provide guidance to the programmers, documentation and training specialists. During acceptance testing, the specifications generate acceptance criteria for the tailored systems.

Knowing the intended use of requirements information in each phase, you are able to reuse the work of your teams in several different tasks over the project duration. You also avoid repeating previous work. In this single area alone, careful management can reduce implementation time and cost as much as 35 percent. That's not a bad payback for a relatively small amount of planning.

With all of the complexity involved with a major software package, many top IS executives may question a package solution. Indeed, many IS divisions have developed a strong in-house bias because of previous bad experiences or an instinctive understanding of the complexity. Other equally qualified companies will consider in-house development only if no software packages are judged adequate. Why do these package-oriented shops take the plunge? The answer, of course, is the high potential cost savings and avoidance of technical risks that software packages offer.

Perhaps there is no other area in which careful IS project management can yield greater cost savings. Each of the risks and complexities of a software project has an effective management approach associated with it. The desirable solution is client management of the process from start to finish. In this way, your company can realize the potential benefits that these packages represent.

30

Corporate Programmers Lead the Way with CASE

Janet Mason

Conditions were critical at Ramada Inc. in Phoenix, Ariz. "We're a small DP shop and we found that, more and more, we were addicted to buying mainframe software applications," said programmer/analyst Alexander Ingram. Accompanying this addiction was expensive software support and maintenance.

It's the classic story of a mainframe software backlog, and it rings particularly true in such information-intensive concerns as the financial industry and the U.S. government. The widening gap between technically advanced hardware and beleaguered software has left institutions with a dearth of new applications. Compounding this are mounting maintenance costs on some software applications that were developed more than a decade ago.

Along with a small, but rapidly growing, number of companies, Ramada is solving this problem by using personal computer-and-mainframe-based computer-aided software engineering (CASE) tools.

CASE allows for more efficient development of software by automating routine analysis and programming tasks. Because it uses graphics, rather than the narrative style of traditional analysis, to demonstrate the data-flow diagram, users can more easily relate to CASE.

The basic concept of CASE is simple: It is software that assists in the development of software. Its finer details are more complex, however. There are two types of CASE. Front-end CASE aids in aligning the software strategy with business goals by analyzing the application. It also documents and designs the system with specifications residing in a dictionary or encyclopedia.

Back-end CASE takes the specifications and generates code to produce applications.

Both products run on a variety of hardware from PC to mainframe. Such vendors as Texas Instruments Inc. produce front- and back-end CASE tools. But many others, such as Index Technology Corp., produce one or the other, requiring interfaces to communicate with the other end.

While mainframes offer more memory and power, PC's present other advantages. "By using PCs we keep our development costs down because we don't have to tie up the larger VAX and IBM systems," pointed out Wayne Balmer, a senior systems analyst in the Information Engineering Association Division of E.I. du Pont de Nemours & Co.

"This keeps the software and hardware costs down considerably," added Mr. Balmer, whose Wilmington, Del., division is using CASE products to develop software for in- and out-of-house use.

Because CASE technology requires major changes in systems development and a substantial financial investment, many companies have hesitated to use it.

"It's really a cultural change from [the emphasis of traditional systems design on] writing code to doing analysis . . . and truly understanding the business problem," commented John Voss, systems development manager at Huntingdon National Bank, in Columbus, Ohio.

At first glance, the investment figures are far less than enticing. "The software alone can cost anywhere between $5,000 and $20,000 per workstation, depending on the CASE tool used and the size of the application," noted Darvis Cormier, director of advanced system development for Touche Ross U.S.A.

Added to this is the training costs, which were placed at $5,000 to $10,000 per analyst for companies "aggressively" using CASE.

Mr. Cormier noted that this is "insignificant" compared to the money being spent in large shops for software development and maintenance.

"A lot of our clients are interested in CASE," he said. "But a smaller subset are starting to use it. In the next couple of years, I expect to see a dramatic increase."

Mr. Cormier is also a line partner in the management consultant practice of the firm's Dallas office, which offers CASE services.

"In an eight-year period of developing and maintaining in-house software with CASE, we estimate that it will cost $60,000 for each application," explained Ramada's Mr. Ingram, as "Opposed to buying and maintaining commercial software for the same time period, which will cost us $180,000 for each application."

Mr. Ingram began his venture in CASE using Transform, a mainframe-based code generator from Transform Logic Corp., in Scottsdale, Ariz. After using Transform to generate hotel databases and on-line service applications, he found the applications to be "more sophisticated than if they had been coded by hand."

"Transform generated 95 percent of the code for our IBM 4381, and we did the rest," said Mr. Ingram. "By using the tool, we were able to provide help screens for every field, every screen and transaction. These are niceties when coding by hand we would add if we had some slack time, which, of course, we never had."

Even with the benefits of using Transform, the staff was still doing manual analysis and design. So Ramada started using Excelerator/IS, from Index Technology Corp. of Cambridge, Mass., on its IBM PC XTs and ATs.

The analysis tool provided much the same benefits to the analysts that computer-aided design offers to engineers.

"The first draft of the data-flow diagram on Excelerator takes as long as doing it manually, which is about one day," explained Mr. Ingram. "But on subsequent drafts, after we show it to the end-user and refine it, we save an inordinate amount of time. [Manually] redrawing the diagram usually takes another day, but with Excelerator, I can change it in 10 minutes—and that's using a dot-matrix and not a laser printer."

Ramada designed its first system using CASE in about five months. Without CASE, it would have taken twice the time and a third more resources, Mr. Ingram noted.

Using the CASE tools required the staff to focus more on analysis than programming. With traditional systems design, stated Mr. Ingram, "You spend 25 percent of your time on upfront analysis and 75 percent coding the program. With the CASE tools we spend about 65 percent of our time on analysis and design and the rest on programming."

Consequently, everyone involved in the application development had an opportunity to sit down and talk to the users.

"Everyone has the opportunity to learn more about how the business functions," continued Mr. Ingram. "We have had to start talking more like real people and less like computer people."

The CASE analysis forced the DP staff to standardize its practices. "We're all pretty much free spirits here and use different techniques for flow charting, program specifications and so on," Mr. Ingram said.

"Using Excelerator forced us to develop consistent standards, and we are finding that we're becoming much more productive," he added.

The lack of standards presents a major snafu for many other CASE users. Dupont's Mr. Balmer said the major problem facing CASE is the large number of systems with different infrastructures. He added that incompatibility is particularly a problem when using the tools on different hardware platforms.

STILL A YOUNG CASE

Because CASE is relatively new, all of the bugs have not yet been ironed out of the products. "The major drawback of CASE is its immaturity," said Hungtingdon National Bank's Mr. Voss, who has been using Texas Instruments' Information Engineering Facility to design customer information applications for the bank.

He added that he ran into a number of technical problems with the TI product that the vendor rapidly addressed. But since Mr. Voss is using a product that includes both front- and back-end CASE tools on a PC and mainframe, compatibility between products has not been a problem.

31

Critical Success Factors: Improving Management Effectiveness

Index Group, Inc.

The CEO of a large international corporation was called away from the office to conduct complicated business negotiations with another company. When he returned after a two month absence, he turned to his staff and asked a series of questions about the company's financial performance and execution of strategy. He was looking for quick, concise information which would rapidly bring him up to date with those things that had happened in his absence which were critical to the business.

Instead, the CEO merely received irrelevant data and apologetic shrugs from his staff. He was told that the information he requested was not immediately available, and that it would take weeks to extract what he wanted from the reports being produced. The CEO shook his head in frustration. This was not the first time he had met with this problem. He was reminded once again of the ineffectiveness of the company's management reporting system; in his view, this system was a disaster. There must be a better way, he thought.

Recognizing the seriousness of the problem, the Executive Vice President of the company asked the Financial Reporting and Control Department to improve the existing system for management information and reporting. The "hypothetical" system they devised after six long months of work addressed some of the needs of management, but the Management Committee and CEO were still not completely satisfied with its effectiveness. For the CEO it seemed like more of the same; it still didn't cut through to what was critical. The Financial Reporting and Control Department realized that what they really needed was a new approach to defining management information systems for the senior executives, since their own approach had proven to be so unsatisfactory.

Management's discontent with the company's current reporting systems was the result of a number of recent occurrences. Present systems were outgrowths of years of automated data processing of the clerical and operational transaction systems.

The corporation had expanded from its single product division to multiple lines of business. The management team, however, was composed of people who had run the business when it was concerned with only one product. Management was poorly equipped, therefore, to handle the demands of their new, much larger and more complex corporation; they also had trouble expressing their needs clearly and concisely. In addition, the information upon which these managers based their important decisions regarding the future of the business was generated from foundation information systems built in the days of the earlier, simpler organization.

This company's dilemma is typical of that faced by an alarming number of executives today. The decade has brought increased economic uncertainty, broadened competitive pressure, more frequent shifts in strategy and organization, greater stress on productivity and service, and a need for shorter decision times. Many of the existing financial and operational information systems created in the 1960s and '70s are outdated and inadequate for the growing needs of businesses today (see Exhibit 31.1a). Senior executives are frustrated and incapacitated by systems which leave them "data rich but information poor."

The effectiveness of managers is being seriously impeded by systems which merely produce a glut of unfiltered information. We have begun to hear a common refrain from senior executives who feel bound by the constraints of ineffective information systems: "We no longer know how to interpret the information we are getting. We're frustrated by systems which provide too much financial data, unfiltered data, irrelevant operational data, and no external environmental data. We need information about what really counts; just because data is easily generated doesn't mean it's important."

Executives who experience these and other frustrations often feel that they have lost the thread of the business, that a coherent strategic structure for their organization has been replaced or precluded by a furious shuffling of useless paper. The CEO of a large computer company complained, "My gross margin is eroding, and the volumes of reports I receive don't tell me why. Even more importantly, I should be able to find out what impact our strategic programs are going to have on gross margin—but I can't get that data when I need it!" These complaints are common to executives whose vision of their company's success has been obscured by the increasingly complicated and growing volume of available information. While executives have watched the cost of their systems rise rapidly, they have seen little improvement in the ability of these systems to pinpoint the critical information they need.

Information technology can improve management effectiveness, but before a company's management information system can be improved, senior executives should first determine the key business activities they want the system to serve. The process of improving management's effectiveness begins with the identification of those factors which are considered essential to the future success of the business. The Critical Success Factors (CSF) process is an important new tool which produces dramatic, positive results for senior management by linking key business activities to the information requirements of managers.

Developed by Dr. John F. Rockart of MIT's Sloan School of Management, CSF is primarily an interview technique that helps managers pinpoint the factors which

Exhibit 31.1
The CSF Process: Linking Key Information
Requirements to Business Objectives

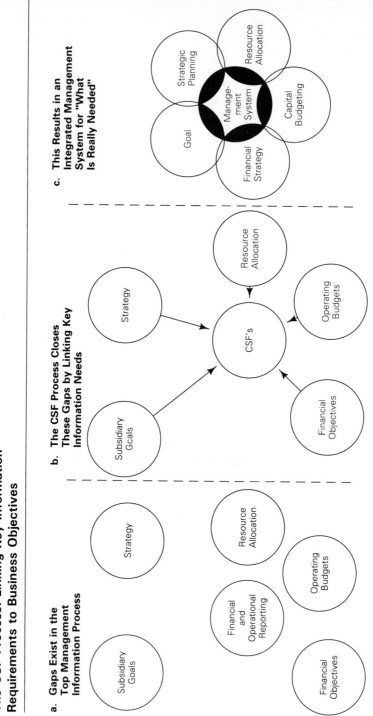

a. Gaps Exist in the
   Top Management
   Information Process

b. The CSF Process Closes
   These Gaps by Linking Key
   Information Needs

c. This Results in an
   Integrated Management
   System for "What
   Is Really Needed"

© Index Systems, Inc.

are most critical to the achievement of their business objectives. Using the CSF technique is a way of making the distinction between these objectives (or desired results) and the activities to which a company should be devoting its attention in order to accomplish those objectives. It is a way of realigning the company's management information systems with its business strategy and objectives by supporting what management does to achieve those objectives. The process also helps to communicate throughout the organization what information senior management considers important.

These CSFs are not end-products. They are activities which, when done well, will lead to the achievement of the primary business objectives. The process is the means of linking the critical activities of top management to the information systems which must support them. The CSF process takes place in several stages (see Exhibit 31.2).

First, an interviewer who is perceived as unbiased meets individually with the key members of the management team to identify what each person considers important for the company and for his part of the organization. The interviewer asks a series of questions: What is the company's mission? What are the objectives of the organization? Of your department? What has to go right, and what must not go wrong, in order for the company to meet these objectives? When you come back from vacation, what are the first three questions you ask?

The critical factors identified by individual managers are then compiled, and this data become the basis for discussion when management meets to thrash out their different perspectives on what is critical to the success of the business. The primary purpose of this second step, which takes the form of a management working session, is to uncover areas of alignment and nonalignment regarding both business objectives and the CSFs within the management team. This alignment is critical to focusing on the information needs required for management to achieve its business objectives (see Exhibit 31.1b). The session also produces a common vocabulary, consensus on responsibility, and a determination of further steps to be taken.

A high technology company that went through the process discovered that its vice president of operations thought the firm's objective was to be the low-cost producer in the markets it served. The marketing vice president, meanwhile, believed the objective was to diversify the company into new market niches. The end product of this alignment process was a set of common CSFs for the management team.

Next, top management must look at all of the information currently being provided to see how it supports the CSFs. Any information that is not focused on factors critical to the business should be discarded. This irrelevant information is a waste of management's time, and may convey a misleading impression of what is important to the organization.

Identifying information gaps in the company is the next step in the CSF process. What critical success factors are not being adequately supported by the current management information system? As a last step in the process, senior management must guide the development of an information reporting system to monitor and focus attention on performance which supports CSFs. The development of such a system gives executives a way of measuring effectiveness in those areas which are critical to the business; it also ensures that senior executives will talk about what

Exhibit 31.2
The Critical Success Factors Process

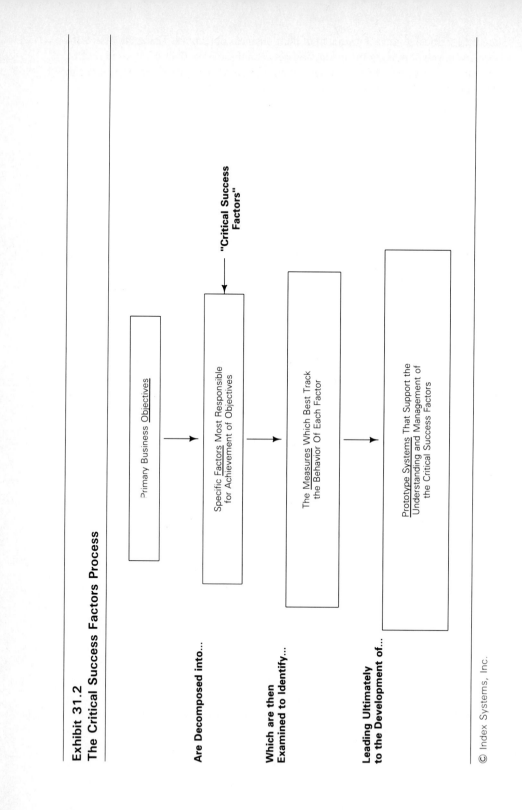

Primary Business <u>Objectives</u>

Are Decomposed into...

Specific <u>Factors</u> Most Responsible
for Achievement of Objectives

**"Critical Success
Factors"**

**Which are then
Examined to Identify...**

The <u>Measures</u> Which Best Track
the Behavior Of Each Factor

**Leading Ultimately
to the Development of...**

<u>Prototype Systems</u> That Support the
Understanding and Management of
the Critical Success Factors

matters to the company, and helps a business whose connecting threads may have begun to unravel to regain its vision and direction.

By focusing attention on the right activities and away from irrelevant or extraneous issues, executives can resolve the frustrating "data rich but information poor" dilemma. Executives will emerge from the CSF interviews with both a definition of the information systems requirements for managers and a focused, clear set of goals and objectives (see Exhibit 31.1c).

CSF SUCCESS AT ONE FIRM

The CSF technique has proven remarkably successful. At one of the nation's largest steel service centers, which was undergoing rapid growth, the CSF process provided dramatic results. In the early days, the business had been small and relatively simple for the original directors; having grown up with the business, they held much of its data and information in their heads. This first generation of directors had decided it was time to hand over the company to the next generation.

The new directors, however, faced certain problems which their predecessors had not: the business had become much larger and more complex, and its fast pace required quick decisions. It was essential to provide immediate response to customer inquiries on the availability and price of steel, as well as a half-day response to the steel mills' offers to sell secondary steel. New customer orders were accepted for processing on no more than 24-hour notice, and production schedules were revised at least once every 24 hours. Company policy was "Never turn down an order, and never fill an order late." Information technology was badly needed to help manage the business.

An initial data processing system, which used the traditional "bottom-up" development approach, was proposed by an outside firm. The estimated cost of the system was $2.4 million, with an implementation time of four years. Both dollar and time estimates came as a shock to management. If the system failed, the risk to the company was high both in dollars invested and in the company's ability to service its customers, since there was no guarantee that the functions included were feasible.

Management began a search for alternative approaches to the problem. The Vice President of Finance was dismayed by the original proposal, and was determined to find a better way. "I wasn't sure what I wanted," he said, "but I knew there had to be a more creative approach."

Index was consulted, and subsequently proposed a "top-down" approach, utilizing the Critical Success Factors process to identify information requirements of management, and a prototype approach to develop the new management system. It was estimated that this approach would require only six to nine months and cost less than $250,000, excluding new equipment. According to this scenario, the risk was well within the manageable limits, and management agreed to go ahead with the project.

Over the next two months, interviews were conducted with senior management and observations were made about the daily activities of senior and middle-level managers. Despite much skepticism on the part of many of the senior executives involved, a one-and-a-half day workshop with senior management resulted in a focused set of business goals and the alignment of the Critical Success Factors with those goals. As one senior-level manager noted, "The CSF process is the best focusing device I have ever been exposed to."

The twelve initial CSFs were then narrowed down to the following four factors:

- Maintaining excellent supplier relations
- Maintaining or improving customer relations
- Buying and selling available inventory in the best way possible
- Utilizing available capital and human resources efficiently and effectively.

Specific measures for these four CSFs were developed which provided the basis for the development of systems to support the targeted critical factors. The senior management team reviewed three options for prototypes, all three of which they wanted. These were a sales and marketing prototype, an inventory prototype, and a production control and delivery prototype. Within nine months, the sales and marketing and the inventory prototypes had been successfully implemented and were being used in day-to-day business operations, while the third prototype, the production control and delivery module, was completed three months later.

Instead of committing over $2 million and waiting four years before knowing whether the system would work, within nine months this management team was working daily with a new system that satisfied a large part of their needs at a cost of less than ten percent of the original proposal (see Exhibit 31.3). "We have achieved in nine months at far lower cost what we expected would take four years under the previously proposed plan," stated a key member of the management team.

"TOP-DOWN" APPROACH

The key to success in this case, as it is in most cases involving systems which support management, is using a "top-down" approach to the problem and a limited first attempt at implementation. Using the CSF technique to determine management's specific needs is the essential first step. Without determining what information is critical to managing the business, the systems that are developed run the risk of being irrelevant to management. According to the Vice President of Sales and Operations at the steel service center, one of the company's many early skeptics, "The CSF process took the concerns and assumptions that had previously been only intuitive and stated them explicitly . . . Systems were tied to what was critical, and there was a low risk factor. The Critical Success Factors concept sold us on Index."

In addition to steering management towards an information system that was appropriate to their needs, the CSF process provided some important, less tangible benefits. The process got senior managers talking to one another; it resulted in the development of a language which could be shared and understood by all senior executives in the company. It built a strong and cohesive management team, helped to align stated needs and goals, and resulted in a significant change in attitude on the part of many senior executives who had initially been wary.

Exhibit 31.3
CSF Versus Traditional Approach

Traditional "Bottom-Up" Approach:

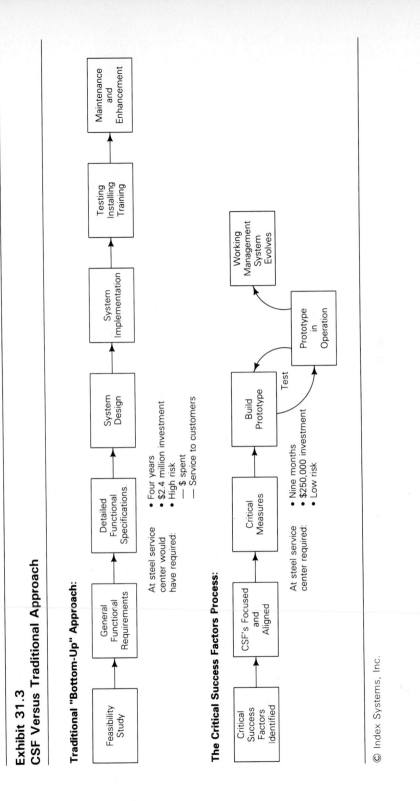

```
Feasibility        General          Detailed        System        System          Testing         Maintenance
Study        →     Functional   →   Functional  →   Design   →    Implementation  →  Installing  →  and
                   Requirements     Specifications                                  Training        Enhancement
```

At steel service
center would
have required:
- Four years
- $2.4 million investment
- High risk
  — $ spent
  — Service to customers

The Critical Success Factors Process:

```
Critical           CSF's Focused    Critical        Build
Success       →    and          →   Measures   →    Prototype
Factors            Aligned                            
Identified                                           
```

Test

```
Prototype
in
Operation

Working
Management
System
Evolves
```

At steel service
center required:
- Nine months
- $250,000 investment
- Low risk

© Index Systems, Inc.

The CSF process which is used to move the business towards success is concrete, clearly defined, and logical. It is not, however, simplistic or self-evident. The consultant or consultant team must be well versed in this particular process. The coordinator(s) of such a process must understand both the concrete requirements of the role (a working knowledge of the client's business, an ability to talk knowledgeably about the specifics of an executive's role, etc.) and its nuances (sensitivity to the issues and personalities involved, flexibility to move from one kind of industry to another and perform expertly, and an ability to listen well and analyze perceptively). With a trained coordinator and a cooperative client management team, the CSF process acts as a catalyst for change. It is a dynamic, customized process, an approach which is flexible enough to conform to the needs of each individual business and executive.

Before a business can meet its goals and fulfill its vision of success, senior management must know and agree upon the most important activities facing the organization. The Critical Success Factors process is a powerful tool for helping senior executives identify their needs and the needs of the company as a whole. It also leads to the choice and implementation of an information system which is tailored to meet the special requirements of the individual organization. The implementation of the information system, in turn, reinforces and measures the Critical Success Factors which have been targeted by management.

SUMMARY

It is apparent, then, that the CSF process is the dynamic and crucial first step in a company's movement towards greater management effectiveness. By generating clarity of vision, focus, and alignment—and by accomplishing these tasks in a fast, effective manner—the CSF process becomes the critical link between the recognition of a company's goals and the ultimate realization of corporate success. One senior executive who saw his company reap the benefits of the CSF process sums up the experience succinctly: "The organizational impact and change as a result of the systems has been profound. In a year when our marketplace is collapsing, we have been able to stay ahead, respond, and serve our customers better. This is a complete success story."

32

The Keys to Successful Executive Support Systems

Gary K. Guiden and Douglas E. Ewers

Executive support systems are a relatively new technique to address an age-old business problem: improving the quality of information that executives need to be effective.

Lately, there's been an outbreak of publicity on this tantalizing concept. The vision that's conjured up is one of a highly customized computer system that empowers a top executive to view crucial information unfiltered by management layers, to communicate and coordinate in lightning speed with anyone in the organization, to analyze business scenarios as never before, and, like a master puppeteer, to control and shape important decisions made in the far reaches of the corporation.

Behind the hype there is a considerable amount of substance. The technology available on executives' desktops today has the potential to allow them to:

- Simplify — sift through immense quantities of data and quickly extract relevant information
- Accelerate — eliminate the constraints of time and distance to the flow of information
- Expand thinking — widen the horizon of thinking and understanding of the business
- Motivate — affect people's attention and behavior

We have clients for whom ESSs have proven crucial to executives making major changes in business direction (such as shifting from a product to a market focus), organizational structure (especially flattening the organization and eliminating staff functions), and organizational communications patterns (as in moving to global product sourcing). But the majority of ESS efforts we encounter are on a course toward disappointment — destined to fall short of their potential impact.

THE OBSTACLES TO EFFECTIVE ESSs

While the benefits of ESSs may be evident, they tend to obscure the difficulties in building these information systems. The most powerful executive support systems we know of are not generic information and office automation utilities; rather they are highly customized solutions for executives or executive teams with specific business needs and desired effects on their minds.

Therefore, successful ESSs can't be designed assuming any one view of how an executive works or the kinds of information he or she needs (which is where organizations that rely solely on the commerically available software packages labeled "Executive Support" or "Executive Information Systems" fall short. These products are a good—but often incomplete—starting point or platform for architecting a custom ESS).

We believe there are two principal reasons why most executive support systems deliver less than they promise, or even fail. First is lack of clarity on the part of the sponsoring executive as to the purpose of the ESS, and second, the failure to incorporate the system into the "management processes" of the organization.

WHY ARE WE REALLY DOING THIS?

Disappointments arise most often because the executive sponsor's fundamental purpose for the ESS is vague or left up to the information systems staff to determine. Exhibit 32.1 lists a range of basic motivations we have seen for ESSs. Several points about this list:

First, it is surprisingly easy for a senior executive to articulate what is behind his or her request for an ESS once these options are spelled out this way. But unless an explicit conversation is held about motivations, they will almost always remain fuzzy.

Second, making clear distinctions between these various motivations is very important, since different motivations generally call for substantially different design and implementation approaches. A bland, general-purpose reporting, information retrieval and office automation system, developed with minimal executive involvement, might be adequate if the motivation were merely computer literacy. The same approach would be a miserable failure if the basic motivation were to support a strategic redirection or reorganization of the business.

Third, it is common for sponsors to have several motivations (e.g., "I want our ESS to be a learning experience first, but then I intend to use it to help drive a fundamental change in the way we do our business.") but to articulate only the first one. Being aware—up front—of this sense of direction or evolution is critical to avoid disappointment later on.

The CEO of a large energy company ordered that an executive support system be installed in the offices and homes of his management committee executives. His expressed rationale at the time was that the senior executive group needed to begin to move into the 20th century. The system provided electronic access to management reports already available in hardcopy, electronic mail, calendaring, word processing, spreadsheets, and an electronic news service. Usage of the new system was fairly active for a week or so, then it fell into disuse by all but the CEO. The CEO was sorely disappointed. When asked what his purpose was for creating the system, he replied, "Well, what I really wanted was for the management committee members to start looking at the business in new ways, and to think more strategically." Clearly a "lead the horses to water" approach didn't work.

Exhibit 32.1
Motivations for ESSs

MOTIVATIONS

Computer Literacy

"Send a Signal"

Work Efficiency

Improved Insights

Business Change
- Strategic Redirection
- Reorganization

Specific Problems
- Decisions
- Control

In contrast, a group of managers we worked with at Eastman Kodak Company quickly became active users of a customized information system that helped them implement a new business strategy. In this case, the motivation for the system was made clear by the group executive: A reorganization aimed at cutting manufacturing costs and boosting product quality required the adroit coordination of manufacturing facilities on a global basis. Manufacturing managers now needed information that never existed before, and it was stated at the outset that there was no way for this strategic move to be executed quickly and well enough in the absence of the new executive support tools.

ARE WE AFTER SUPPORT OR CHANGE?

Exhibit 32.2 addresses the issue of achieving clarity in a different fashion. The diagram first spells out what we believe to be the four primary areas of potential impact that an ESS can deliver. As with Exhibit 32.1, the question is: "Where on this picture is the intended emphasis of the ESS?" because different areas of emphasis call for different design and implementation strategies.

Exhibit 32.2
Types of Executive Support Systems

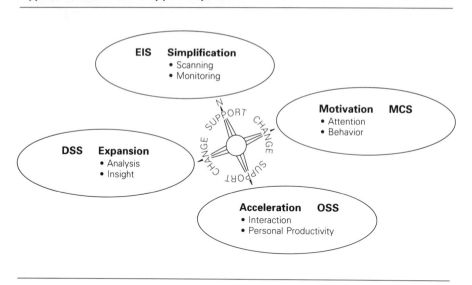

ESSs serve four general purposes, and either act as ''support'' tools or ''change'' tools.

At the top of Exhibit 32.2, the "Simplification" area addresses the need to quickly and easily maintain one's "feel" for the business by providing flexible access to, and formatting of, the wide array of operating information typically provided in piles of printed management reports each month. It is in this area, for example, that many of the "Executive Information System" (EIS) software packages excel.

At the bottom of the exhibit, the term "Acceleration" refers to the ability of electronic messaging, voicemail, calendaring, word processing, and other "Office Support Systems" (OSS) technologies to accelerate the flow of communication by removing time and location as constraints.

We characterize this North-South dimension of Exhibit 32.2 as "Support" in that these functions provide fundamental support to routine information and communications-handling tasks of management.

Some years ago, at the beginning of the personal computer revolution, we worked with a leading supplier of floppy disks whose management team was trying to cope with the transition from a company growing at a 30% annual rate to one growing at 300%! Prior to the explosion in demand for its product, printed management reports and the weekly management committee meeting in the headquarters conference room allowed the senior executives of this company to feel in control of their business. Once the growth hit, though, everyone was on the road setting up manufacturing and distribution around the world. The printed reports piled up in the "In" boxes, the conference room was nearly empty during the management committee meeting, and the valuable face-to-face exchanges that once took place in those meetings went away. An executive support system of the "North-South" variety was developed in order to provide electronic access, from anywhere in the world, to the previously printed management report information. And the reporting system was built around a "heart" of electronic mail and office automation so the executives could annotate and share the reports with each other, and resume their essential "face-to-face" conversations electronically.

ESSs THAT CREATE CHANGE

The East-West dimension of this diagram has a different flavor to it than the North-South axis. We call it the "Change" dimension.

The left side of Exhibit 32.2 is the area of "Expansion," referring to the capability of properly constructed and used ESSs to broaden executives' view, understanding, and insight into the business. This has been the traditional domain of decision support systems (DSS).

Finally, on the right side of the picture is the area of "Motivation." This refers to the potential for ESS to form a key ingredient in a management control system (MCS), affecting the focus of attention and behavior of executives in a management team.

"Change" was the name of the game for E.I. du Pont de Nemours & Company's Medical Products business a few years ago. The group's new chief operating officer was leading a transition from a product to a market orientation. Where once there were business units organized by product, he put into place business units focused on specific health care markets whose needs spanned the full line of Du Pont's product offering—and beyond. The management teams of these new business units needed to radically change the way they looked at and understood their marketplaces, and were being measured by new standards, such as customer segment market penetration and profitability. Here, ESSs employing principles of modeling, analysis, and management control were initiated to drive and support the needed change in the thinking and behavior of the management teams.

The preceding illustrations strongly underscore the importance of clarity of purpose to the developments of ESSs that truly make a difference to an organization. An East-West system would have failed to respond to the needs of the floppy disk company, and North-South system would have failed to achieve the change in thinking and action needed by Du Pont. Unfortunately, we see this kind of mismatch all too often in the ESS effort under way in many companies today.

FAILURE TO INTEGRATE WITH MANAGEMENT PROCESSES

Management processes are the context in which management information of any kind is put to constructive work. A weekly operations review meeting is a management process. So is a master manufacturing schedule session, a pricing committee meeting, a quarterly budget update, the capital appropriation process, or the incentive compensation plan. Some management processes are informal, such as setting goals with a subordinate. Management processes that are poorly informed are next to worthless, and, by the same token, executive support systems that are disconnected from the basic management mechanisms of the business are of very limited value. In fact, it is the connection with management process that normally provides the executive with a solid reason to learn and keep using an ESS in the first place.

The senior executive who initiates an ESS without an eye to how it will support or change management processes – or the systems staff that allows this connection to be ignored – runs a serious risk of producing a system that will fail to achieve its potential. Ultimately, it is the executive sponsor who must take the lead here. Management process, after all, is the turf of the senior executive.

Executive support systems at Xerox Corporation were fairly benign and unevenly used until the CEO, the chief of staff, and the director of ESS conspired to completely re-engineer the corporation's planning process around the capabilities of the existing ESS. This single act, which required executives to make active use of the ESS to produce and negotiate their annual and long-range plans, raised the stakes on ESS and turned it from an informational/communication utility service into an essential management tool.[1]

TIPS FOR SUCCESS

Beyond the caveats issued previously, our experience over many years in the ESS field has left us with the following set of additional beliefs and keys to success:

- ESS applications that effect or enable change are the most worthwhile. Pure support-oriented efforts may be helpful discretionary investments of time and money, but should not be relied upon to make a significant impact.
- Take the time and effort to secure the right executive(s) to sponsor and lead the ESS effort. It is very hazardous for staff personnel (such as the information systems organization) to lead an ESS project, or to allow themselves to be delegated the task by a less-than-totally committed executive sponsor. As Ken Soha, director of executive support systems at Xerox, once said, "This stuff isn't for kids."
- Although the Critical Success Factors process is an excellent tool for achieving focus for an ESS, the simple elucidation of CSFs (the things that must go right for organizational success) will not necessarily point directly to the form and content of the needed ESS.
- Start with a prototype to understand and tackle the problem on a small scale, and to provide tangible and early proof of value.
- Never allow the executive sponsor to delegate the task of liberating from the organization the data needed by the ESS. We've seldom come across an ESS of any substance that has not generated some degree of organizational resistance to providing the often unconventional data these systems require. The executive sponsor must remain directly involved in the realities of securing the needed data; this person is the only one in a position to do the necessary negotiation, provide reas-

surance of fair use of the information, and make trade-offs between the value of the information and the cost and effort of routinely providing it.

- Finally, a note for the information systems professional: With executive support systems you get only one chance. When the opportunity comes, handle it with care.

SUMMARY

Executive support systems are becoming key tools in the executive arsenal. In the era of corporate reorganization, mergers and acquisitions, turbulent markets, and increasing competition, managers more than ever need more effective ways to understand their markets, their competition, and guide their operations and their people.

Executive support systems can be key to the effective executive. However, the building of these systems requires the utmost preparation, care, and understanding of the intended user's business problems, information needs, and management process. Only when the executive support system takes all of those into account, actually inducing change rather than merely supporting it, can the executive fully tap the power of information and information technology.

NOTES

[1]See *Business Week* article, "The Computer Age Dawns in the Corner Office," June 27, 1988.

33

The Knowledge Engineers

Eric Bender

When retiring experts walk out the door for the last time, a fortune's worth of undocumented experience may leave with them. Thanks to a new breed of PC software tools, however, a company can capture those intangible assets before they slip away forever. A firm can also tap the wisdom of experts with long careers still ahead, spreading their knowledge throughout the organization and freeing them from mundane tasks.

Software that successfully mimics aspects of human problem solving has been trickling out of the blue-sky artificial intelligence labs and into commercial use during the past decade (see "Experts on Call," *PCW,* September 1985). Known popularly as expert systems, the programs might be described more suitably as knowledge-based or advisory.

In the past year commercial knowledge-based systems have steadily infiltrated the offices and factories around us. Increasingly, these systems are available for PCs—a trend that will only accelerate as 80386-based machines proliferate. Now the challenge of building an expert system becomes how to capture the knowledge and experience of human experts, who are often elusive or expensive, or both.

ACQUIRING KNOWLEDGE

Among early commercial users, the Big Eight accounting firm Coopers & Lybrand tapped the expertise of dozens of its senior partners for ExperTax, an indepth tax adviser that runs on the AT. "The beauty of the system is that you don't have to know taxes to use it," says one employee. ExperTax can also dispatch updates quickly and unerringly through hundreds of Coopers & Lybrand offices.

Many other firms are creating somewhat less ambitious knowledge-based systems, narrowing the focus to matters such as technical-support phone calls. And

"The Knowledge Engineers" by Eric Bender, PC WORLD, September 1987, pp. 172–179. Reprinted by permission of PC WORLD, published at 501 Second Street, Suite 600, San Francisco, CA. 94107.

while small businesses are unlikely to devise seminal expert systems any time soon, Harvey Newquist, editor of *AI Trends,* a newsletter published in Scottsdale, Arizona, suggests boom times are ahead. By the end of 1987, Newquist predicts, "we'll probably start to see prepackaged systems—advisory systems—to perform inventory control, to create billing cycles, or to design manufacturing schedules."

Building moderately complex advisory systems is still likely to require considerable programming prowess, and familiarity with AI languages like LISP and Prolog will come in handy (see "A Prolog to the Future," *PCW,* December 1986). But rapidly evolving software tools are freeing developers to focus on picking the expert's brain. "The hard part of writing an expert system is knowledge engineering—finding out what the [given discipline's] rules are," says Eugene Wang, marketing vice president at Gold Hill Computers in Cambridge, Massachusetts.

"Knowledge acquisition is going to be the major bottleneck," agrees Leslie Porter of Index Systems, a management consulting firm also based in Cambridge. "People who have the ability to extract that knowledge are rare." And not surprisingly, a tension exists between expert and engineer, reflecting a clash between the expert's vernacular and the engineer's methodology.

"What we see is literally a whole new profession opening up," declares Karl Wiig, a principal with Coopers & Lybrand who is responsible for AI practice. "Five years ago I never would have believed I'd say that."

Other observers, however, downpay the call for a new breed of professional. "Developing an expert system is like developing any other computer system—almost," maintains Earl Sacerdoti, vice president for strategic projects at Teknowledge in Palo Alto, California. "We have a knowledge engineer, whom the rest of the world would call a systems analyst—and he sits down with the expert, whom the rest of the world would call a representative of the user community."

COVERING THE KNOWLEDGE BASES

At the lowest level, nontechnical PC users are employing inexpensive and reasonably powerful expert system shells. Such shells are simply high-level tools that provide a framework for assembling knowledge-based systems without the need to delve deeply into the vagaries of LISP or other AI languages.

These products are likely to earn their keep by solving small but nagging problems like how best to ship a package. A few shell-based systems easily subdue what appear to be daunting jobs and offer solid payoffs, available today.

But the true potential of expert system technology is demonstrated most impressively by the high-end systems built by teams of professionals—like those at Arthur D. Little's Artificial Intelligence Applications Center, where some staffers gather nuggets of information while others write software.

A classic advisory system begins with a business problem that an expert can solve in a single phone conversation. Teknowledge's Sacerdoti expands the list of criteria: Can the knowledge base (the information gathered) be encoded? Do your sources perform better than average, even if they're not world-class experts? Can the knowledge engineer translate the expert's sensory cues? (As Sacerdoti puts it, "The human expert can hear that the machine sounds funny or can smell the burning lubricant.") And, of course, does the problem have a solution?

"You're looking for a problem with a specific solution that the expert can articulate," says Sajnicole Joni, director of consulting at Gold Hill. "You can write a great expert system to support a sports training system, but it won't teach you to hit a tennis ball like Martina Navratilova."

SCOPING IT OUT

Like any software project, a fair-size knowledge-based system is built on estimates of goals, time costs, appropriate hardware, and impact on work habits. With this breed of software, it's particularly important that these estimates not be chiseled in stone.

Expert systems can be split into two components: the knowledge base, which holds rules and related information; and the inference engine, which provides the problem-solving mechanism (which in turn holds the underlying control structures). Control structures, in turn, can be either rule-based or frame-based.

Almost all PC systems are rule-based, linking a series of IF . . . THEN rules with forward-chaining or backward-chaining architectures. Forward chaining starts with a premise and chugs through the rules and the relevant information to find solutions; backward chaining starts with a hypothetical solution and then tries to justify that solution. Forward-chaining seems the more natural method of the two: You enter a mass of data and rules and see what happens. Backward chaining is less intuitive but often more efficient.

Frame-based systems are inherently more complicated. These systems rely on convoluted dependencies and generally run on specialized LISP machines or super-minicomputers.

In grappling with these technical issues, programmers work with diverse tools, including languages such as LISP, Prolog, and C, and shells such as Teknowledge's M.1 and Gold Hill's Gold-Works. Figure 33.1 shows a sample scheme for developing a prototype knowledge-based system.

A QUALIFYING SYSTEM

Gold Hill's Joni describes the design for a system that qualifies sales leads. The process begins with the acquisition of data on methods the sales force is currently using. "You get all the salespeople to write down what they do," she says. Then she selects roughly 20 representative scenarios of how the salespeople perform in the field.

She next analyzes that data and the process of obtaining it. "What's the salesperson's thinking process? You look for critical variables that allow the salesperson to make decisions very quickly."

Exhibit 33.1

Iteration Plus Interaction Equals Knowledge-Based Systems

Developing a prototype knowledge-based system, knowledge engineers
go through an iterative process (A). The overal development cycle for a
knowledge-based. system (B).

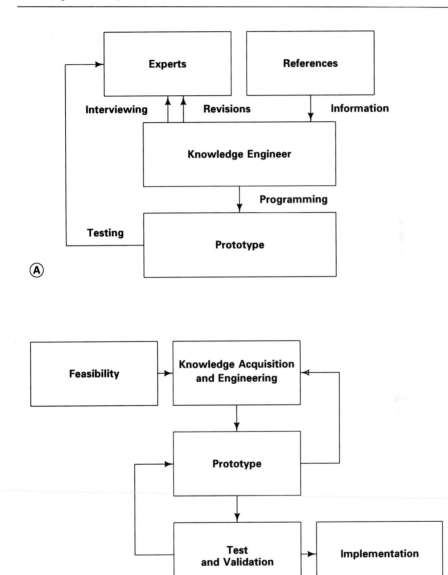

Although users often want to solve an array of problems, it's crucial that each system be confined to a single problem, such as targeting potential customers above a specified income level.

From there, Joni assembles the pieces of information that make up the knowledge base and then determines how to string the pieces together. A flexible, modular approach is essential to easily accommodate new categories of information. The system should be capable of incorporating details that are not necessarily part of any decision-making process. "Salespeople may want to include the customer's hobby or favorite drink," she explains. And the system should accommodate exceptions.

Next come architectural questions, addressing whether forward-chaining or backward-chaining controls are most appropriate for a given task. After the first attempt at a rule architecture, it's time to write the rules themselves. Joni then throws everything into a software prototype, tries it out, patches it here and there, and begins a long trial-and-error period with the experts: "You have to be prepared to hear your experts say, 'That's not how I do it.' "

As the knowledge engineers build systems, they must often sidestep company politics, turf battles, conflicts over information that employees want to keep to themselves, and similar traps. Gold Hill R&D vice president Gerald Barber emphasizes that the engineer must always keep the final user in mind.

EXPERT ADVICE (AND CONSENT)

Teknowledge, one of the more successful suppliers of knowledge-based system tools, adheres to a methodology closer to conventional software design than that followed at some expert system houses.

Although developing knowledge-based systems is an iterative process, Teknowledge's Earl Sacerdoti stresses the importance of identifying problems as far in advance as possible. "We try to map out the universe and the kinds of subproblems that will come up," he says. With this controlled approach, "the surprises tend to be conventional—things like choice of interface."

"In terms of pulling knowledge from people, we've adopted a few principles from clinical psychology," he says. "But that's not a critical issue. People succeed with wildly different efforts." Teknowledge advises against including the expert in the development team or pitting expert against expert in "knowledge games," although both approaches have paid off for other developers.

The key, Sacerdoti says, is to pair a cooperative expert with a knowledge engineer "who can operate in an egoless fashion and let the expert be the 'owner' of the system, and who can ask questions and listen to the answers." It's just as necessary that the knowledge engineer gain the expert's trust. "They will be dealing with each other in fairly intimate detail," says Harvey Newquist. Intimacy can, however, produce sparks.

"A crucial step in building a system is learning the expert's language," accord-

As a knowledge-acquisition interview rolls along, things are not proceeding smoothly. Increasingly irritated by the knowledge engineer's queries, the manufacturing expert throws up his hands and fumes, "OK, do it your way!"

According to knowledge engineers Helen Ojha and Susan Stafford, the scene is a textbook example of an approach to avoid.

"Over the years experts develop what appear to be odd ways of doing things," says Ojha, a former political scientist who worked at Arthur D. Little before joining Coopers & Lybrand. She describes knowledge engineers as "visitors to a culture they have not grown up in." At work, they're much like anthropologists, who are trained to be keen observers of things they don't fully understand.

Experts, she says, tend to generalize about experiences from fragments of actual events. "Our job can be to translate that knowledge into something that's more usable." Experts are often visual or kinesthetic, not verbal, and thus can't easily express what they know. A meteorologist who was superb at predicting the volatile weather at the Kennedy Space Center "would use his body to mime the evolution of clouds," she recalls. "We spend a lot of time thinking about the cognitive style of the expert," adds Stafford, a onetime philosophy professor.

The two engineers classify four types of experts. First is the professional practitioner, who's very procedural "and can give an apparently coherent verbal rendering of how it is," according to Ojha. "He or she has all the patina of logic." Doctors tend to fit that mold.

Next is the "practical knowledge worker," whom Ohja describes as one who cares more about the content of a problem than its structure. These experts are generally most articulate "if they have all of their artifacts with them," Stafford says.

The third type is a "performer, a primitive actor," says Ojha. "These experts tend to be people-oriented, and are exquisitely good" at relating to individuals. They spend much of their time preparing themselves to respond to a situation. Here you're apt to find stock-market traders, the folks who make all that noise on the exchange floor.

Fourth is the "communicating negotiator," Ojha says. "These people dance their way around things. They like to engage you in dialogue." The classic example is the sales professional.

Initially, experts cast a jaundiced eye on the knowledge engineering team. For one thing, says Ojha, "a lot of experts don't believe in their own expertise. They believe that, yes, they do a good job—but if a computer system used their methods, it would be flawed."

Based on their own experience, the knowledge engineering duo emphasizes that familiarity with experts breeds anything but contempt. "The more you look at this stuff, the greater your respect for what those people do," Stafford marvels.

ing to Susan Stafford, a Coopers & Lybrand staffer who specializes in debriefing experts (see the box "Elicit Work"). "Often, the first thing you hear is not what the experts actually said, and the first thing they say is often not what they meant."

All of this suggests that a hacker with a little spare time is not necessarily the best candidate to plumb for expertise. Someone with a less technical background is often better suited; those with strong communications skills—like teachers and journalists—seem to be particularly effective. Arthur D. Little's AI group includes computer scientists, anthropologists, linguists, philosophers, sociologists, and psychologists. However, others insist there's no need to raid the social sciences. Existing personnel can carry out most of the work on a corporate project, according to Index Systems' Thomas Davenport, who doubts that many company payrolls include linguists or philosophers.

Meanwhile, software gurus continue trying to build automated knowledge acquisition tools that can lighten the system development burden, particularly for maintenance tasks. William Brodie of Brodie Associates in Boston says that in some cases those tools can carry on moderately sophisticated interviews and can even "detect and tactfully pose likely exceptions to general rules the human expert provides."

EXPERTS IN THE FIELD

Expert systems that reach the field are often greeted with skepticism. Doubt issues in equal measure from those who think the software will never work or never earn its keep and those convinced it will simply demonstrate the lack of genuine expertise in the world. Even the foremost advocates of expert systems acknowledge a need to accept limitations: "An expert system, like an expert, does not guarantee the optimum result and does not guarantee correctness," says Index's Leslie Porter.

In addition, expert systems demand more fine-tuning than do most classes of software. That's because of the volume of information, its often rapid obsolescence, the inherent conflicts among experts, and the tendency of the rules themselves to change with new information. "There's a horrendous problem in maintaining knowledge bases," says David Pensak, a technical support professional at DuPont corporate headquarters in Wilmington, Delaware. "We're back to a form of knowledge representation that is at least as archaic as punch cards."

But Earl Sacerdoti insists that system upkeep is not overwhelming if the proper knowledge is available: "We have fielded many systems that are maintained by a fraction of one individual's time."

Within medium-to-large companies, information systems groups typically act as custodians for knowledge-based systems. Opinions vary on how well these groups handle the onslaught of computer-based advice. Many have actively pushed such technology as automated spreadsheets, but others "have enough problems with the COBOL side of the house without dealing with these Star Wars applications," notes Index's Porter.

What changes people's minds are the payoffs—not only in day-to-day operations but in the wealth of detail that knowledge-based systems can generate about how work gets done within an organization. "As part of integrating knowledge, these systems identify gaps where not only the computer but the organization lacks information," says Sacerdoti.

And the systems also pay off in personal satisfaction. Sacerdoti recounts the story of one industrial plant where an expert system was being tested with a thorny diagnostic problem. "The expert was showing me around, and a technician came up and told him, 'That was a tough problem—the repair manual was wrong and you were right!' The expert loved it."

34

Information Systems and Organizational Change

Peter G. W. Keen

1. INTRODUCTION

This paper discusses long-term change in organizations in relation to information systems. The aim is to explain why innovation is so difficult and to point towards effective strategies for managing the process of change. Many commentators have drawn attention to the problems of implementation that result in systems being technical successes but organizational failures [69, 23, 32, 19]. Their analyses stress the complexity of organizational systems and the social inertia that damps out the intended effects of technical innovations.

The growing body of research on implementation deals mainly with tactical issues: How to create a climate for changing, building and institutionalizing a specific system.[1] This paper focuses on strategic questions:

1. What are the causes of social inertia?
2. What are the main organizational constraints on change?
3. What are the mechanisms for effecting change?

Effective implementation relies on incremental change, small-scale projects, and face-to-face facilitation [22, 71, 36]. A strategy for long-term change and large-scale innovation requires a broader strategy; the conceptual and empirical work on implementation, both within MIS and OR/MS and in political science, provides a few guidelines and some very pessimistic conclusions. The main argument of this paper is that information systems development is an intensely political as well as technical process and that organizational mechanisms are needed that provide MIS managers with authority and resources for negotiation. The traditional view of MIS as a staff function ignores the pluralism of organizational decision making and the link between information and power. Information systems increasingly alter relationships, patterns of communication and perceived influence, authority, and control. A strategy for implementation must therefore recognize and deal with the politics of data and the likelihood, even legitimacy, of counterimplementation.

2. THE CAUSES OF SOCIAL INERTIA

"Social inertia" is a complicated way of saying that no matter how hard you try, nothing seems to happen. The main causes of inertia in relation to information systems seem to be:

1. Information is only a small component of organizational decision processes;
2. Human information-processing is experiential and relies on simplification;
3. Organizations are complex and change is incremental and evolutionary; large steps are avoided, even resisted;
4. Data are not merely an intellectual commodity but a political resource, whose redistribution through new information systems affects the interests of particular groups.

Computer specialists generally take for granted that information systems play a central role in decision making. Mintzberg's [51] and Stewart's [65] descriptive studies of managers' activities suggest this is often not the case [39]. In general, decision processes are remarkably simple [50]; what has worked in the past is most likely to be repeated. Under pressure, decision makers discard information, avoid bringing in expertise and exploring new alternatives [75]; they simplify a problem to the point where it becomes manageable. Almost every descriptive study of a complex decision process suggests that formal analysis of quantified information is, at best, a minor aspect of the situation [57, 7]. Negotiations, [67] habit, rules of thumb, and "muddling through" [46] have far more force. This may seem an extreme assertion but there is little if any empirical evidence to challenge it. The point is not that managers are stupid or information systems irrelevant but that decision making is multifaceted, emotive, conservative, and only partially cognitive. Formalized information technologies are not as self-evidently beneficial as technicians presume. Many descriptive models of decision making [46, 12, 28] imply that "better" information will have virtually no impact.

Simon's concept of bounded rationality stresses the simplicity and limitations of individual information processing.[2] There has long been a conflict between the normative perspective of OR/MS and MIS, which defines tools based on a rationalistic model of decision making, and the descriptive, largely relativistic position of many behavioral scientists who argue that that conception is unrealistic.[3] Mitroff's study of the Apollo moon scientists is perhaps the best supported presentation of this position [54]. Regardless of one's viewpoint on how individuals should make decisions, it seems clear that the processes they actually rely on do not remotely approximate the rational ideal. This gap between the descriptive and prescriptive is a main cause of inertia:

1. There is little evidence to support the concept of consistent preference functions [9, 31, 42];
2. Managers and students (the traditional subjects of experiments) have difficulty with simple trade-off choices [77];
3. Perceptions are selective [14];
4. There are clear biases and personality differences in problem-solving "styles" [30, 49, 16] that may even lead individuals to reject accurate and useful information [11, 17];
5. Even intelligent and experienced decision makers make many errors of logic and inference [68, 61];
6. Managers prefer concrete and verbal data to formal analysis [51, 65].

All in all, human information-processing tends to be simple, experiential, nonanalytic, and on the whole, fairly effective [8, 46]. Formalized information systems are thus often seen as threatening and unneeded. They are an intrusion into the world of the users who see these unfamiliar and nonrelevant techniques as a criticism of themselves.

Leavitt's classification of organizations as a diamond, (Exhibit 34.1) in which **Task, Technology, People,** and **Structure** are interrelated and mutually adjusting, indicates the complex nature of social systems [44]. When **Technology** is changed, the other components often adjust to damp out the impact of the innovation. Many writers on implementation stress the homeostatic behavior of organizations [60, 22, 76] and the need to "unfreeze the status quo." (This term is taken from the Lewin-Schein framework of social change, discussed below.)

Information systems are often intended as coupling devices that coordinate planning and improve management control [21]. Cohen and March's view of many organizational decision processes as a garbage can [12] and Weick's powerful conception of "loose coupling" [72] imply, however, that signals sent from the top often get diffused, defused, and even lost, as they move down and across units whose linkages are tenuous. The more complex the organization, the less likely the impact of technical change; homeostatic, self-equilibrating forces in loosely coupled systems are a major explanation for the frequency of failure of large-scale planning projects [29, 32, 25].

The characteristics of individuals and organizations listed above suggest that dramatic change rarely occurs in complex social systems. Lindblom's well-known concept of muddling through reinforces that view [46]. He points out the value of incremental, remedial decision making and rejects the "synoptic ideal." Wildavsky [74] similarly disdains formalized planning and recommends an avowedly political process based on partiality and incremental analysis. He contrasts political and economic rationality. The latter looks for optimal solutions through systematic metho-

Exhibit 34.1
The Leavitt "Diamond": Components of the Organization.

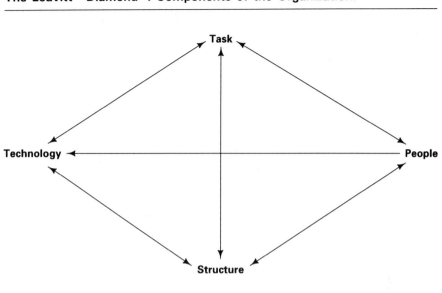

dologies. Compromise is pathological since by definition it represents a retreat from rationality (one might expect that few people would espouse this position in so pristine a form—until one listens to a faculty full of microeconomists). Political (or social) rationality looks only for feasible solutions and recognizes that utopian change cannot be assimilated by complex systems composed of individuals with bounded rationality. Only small increments are possible and compromise, far from being bad, is an essential aspect of the implementation process.

The final cause of inertia is less passive than the others. Data are a central political resource. Many agents and units in organizations get their influence and autonomy from their control over information. They will not readily give that up. In many instances new information systems represent a direct threat and they respond accordingly. We now have adequate theories of implementation. We have less understanding of counterimplementation, the life force of more than a few public sector organizations and a hidden feature of many private ones. This issue is discussed in more detail in Section 6.

All these forces towards inertia are constraints on innovation. They are not necessarily binding ones. Implementation is possible but requires patience and a strategy that recognizes that the change process must be explicitly managed. Only small successes will be achieved in most situations. These may, however, be strung together into major long-term innovations. "Creeping socialism" is an instance of limited tactical decisions adding up to strategic redirection; no one step appears radical.

3. OVERCOMING SOCIAL INERTIA: A TACTICAL APPROACH

There are several well-defined tactical models for dealing with inertia. They are tactical in the sense that they apply largely to specific projects. They recommend simple, phased programs with clear objectives [59] and facilitation by a change agent or a "fixer" [5], an actor with the organizational resources to negotiate among interested parties and make side payments. The Lewin-Schein framework and an extension of it, Kolb and Frohman's model of the consulting process [41], have been used extensively by researchers on OR/MS and MIS implementation,[4] both in descriptive studies [22, 76] and prescriptive analysis [48, 32, 69]. This conception of the change process (see Exhibit 34.2) emphasizes:

1. The immense amount of work needed prior to design; change must be self-motivated and based on a "felt need" with a contract between user and implementer built on mutual credibility and commitment;
2. The difficulty of institutionalizing a system and embedding it in its organizational context so that it will stay alive when the designer/consultant leaves the scene;
3. The problem of operationalizing goals and identifying criteria for success.

This tactical approach is "Up-and-In" rather than "Down-and Out". [45] DO is based on direction from the top, lengthy design stages, and a formal system for planning and project management. UI relies on small groups, with face-to-face involvement and participative management. The design evolves out of the Entry process [41].

Leavitt and Webb point out that UI works well for small projects. However, large-scale change requires an engineering approach to design that quickly encounters social inertia. The dilemma is that UI limits itself to feasible, incremental change while DO, the broader strategic process, is rarely successful. The tactical model needs extension; facilitation is not enough and social inertia is dangerously close to social entropy [5].

No formal effective strategic model exists. If it did, one might expect to find it in political science, which frequently reconstructs the processes underlying efforts to deliver major social, technical, or political programs [63, 59, 27, 15]. Political science deserves the label of the "dismal" science far more than economics, which after all believes in the eventual triumph of rationality; most studies in this field deal with failures. (Saplosky's analysis of the Polaris project is a rare example of a success.) They identify as forces impeding change not only social inertia but also pluralism and counterimplementation—overt moves, often made by skilled actors, to prevent a disruption of the status quo. Counterimplementation is most likely to occur when outsiders bring in threatening new technologies [55, 10]. Information systems are exactly that in many cases [3, 4, 25, 26].

4. PLURALISM: THE NEED TO MOBILIZE

Political science views organizations mainly as groups of actors, often with conflicting priorities, objectives, and values [1]. The management literature generally assumes far more commonality of purpose. The Down-and-Out approach relies on this. Up-

Exhibit 34.2
Tactical Model for Describing and/or Managing Change

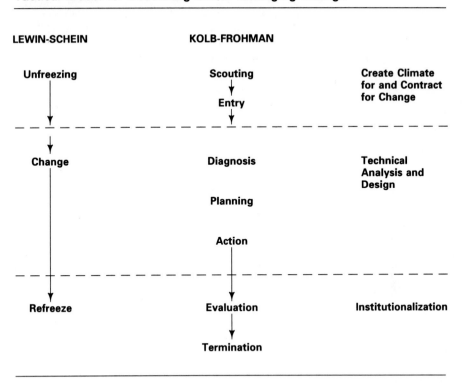

LEWIN-SCHEIN	KOLB-FROHMAN	
Unfreezing	Scouting → Entry	Create Climate for and Contract for Change
Change	Diagnosis / Planning / Action	Technical Analysis and Design
Refreeze	Evaluation → Termination	Institutionalization

and-In evades the problem by limiting the scope of the project and hence the number of actors involved; it fails completely if consensus is not impossible. The more the organization is viewed as a set of loosely coupled units [72] where joint action rests on negotiations [67], the more any strategy for implementation must emphasize the need to mobilize coalitions, to provide the necessary support for an innovative proposal. Obviously, that process is based on political rather than economic rationality. The corollary of this argument is that lack of attention to the constraints on change imposed by pluralism in organizations will result in failure.

Many writers who attack the rationalist tradition on which OR/MS and MIS are based stress the legitimacy of pluralism and hence of incremental decision making. Lindblom sees the use of social interactions instead of analysis and planning as analogous to reliance on a market system to simplify the process of resource allocation [47]. Strauss argues that "social order" and decision making in any organization are predominantly based on negotiations:

> . . . when individuals or groups or organizations work together to 'get things done' then agreement is required about such matters as what, how, when, where, and how much. Continued agreement itself may be something to be worked

at . . . negotiations pertain to the ordering and articulation of an enormous variety of activities.[5]

In many instances, pluralistic perspectives view formal information systems as either ethically dangerous in that they impose a false rationality [29], naive [74], or simply irrelevant [46]. They also deny their value as coupling devices that help coordinate planning and communication; pluralists see merit in disorder and redundancy [37]. Weiner and Wildavsky, commenting on federalism, summarize this argument: What is needed is ". . . planning with a different aim: to foster choice through careful structuring of social interaction."[6]

These viewpoints are obviously not shared by most proponents of analytic methodologies. Since they are mainly based on studies of public policy issues, one may argue that business organizations are more tightly coupled and less dominated by pluralism and incrementalism. This may be true in particular instances; there are many companies whose planning systems are effective in establishing and communicating goals, involving managers in the decision process, and creating a climate for innovation [70]. Even so, most case studies of complex decisions suggest that companies are far more pluralistic than we conveniently assume. Pettigrew's analysis of a decision to purchase a computer, for example, reveals innumerable territorial disputes, maneuvering for position, conflict over goals, and irreconcilable differences in perspective among organizational units [57]. Believers in pluralism do not find that surprising but most computer specialists do.

The point is not to justify pluralism. It seems clear, however, that it is a main cause of inertia. "Getting things done", whether Down-and-Out or Up-and-In, requires the careful building of coalitions based on complex negotiations. The larger the scope of a project and the more strategic its goals, the truer this will be, because of the ". . . geometric growth of interdependencies . . . whose implications extend over time." [59] Section 8 suggests some organizational mechanisms that can provide information systems developers with the authority and resources to resolve these complexities.

5. COUNTERIMPLEMENTATION

Believers in rationalism generally view resistance to change and protection of vested interests as faults to be ignored or suppressed. The tactical approach to implementation sees resistance as a signal from a system in equilibrium that the costs of change are perceived as greater than the likely benefits. The bringers and sellers of change — academics, computer specialists, and consultants — assume that what they offer is good. In practice, there are many valid reasons to go beyond passive resistance and actively try to prevent implementation. Many innovations are dumb ideas. Others threaten the interests of individuals and groups by intruding on their territory, limiting their autonomy, reducing their influence, or adding to their workload. While we all may try to act in the "corporate" interest, we often have very different definitions of exactly what that is. (Dearborn and Simon point out that even senior executives adopt the perspective of their department [14]).

Obviously there is a fine line between honest resistance to a project one feels is misguided and selfish sabotage of a necessary innovation. The difference is a matter for conscience and self-scrutiny. In both cases, the response is political, whether "clean" or "dirty" politics.

Bardach [5] defines implementation as a game and outlines some of the moves and countermoves by which actors: (1) divert resources from a project; (2) deflect its goals; (3) dissipate its energies. A central lesson to be learned from examples of successful counterimplementation is that there is no need to take the risky step of overtly opposing a project. The simplest approach is to rely on social inertia and use moves based on delay and tokenism. Technical outsiders should be kept outside and their lack of awareness of organizational issues encouraged. ("Why don't you build the model and we'll deal with the people issues later; there's no need to have these interminable meetings.") If more active counterimplementation is needed, one may exploit the difficulty of getting agreement among actors with different interests by enthusiastically saying, "Great idea—but let's do it properly!" adding more people to the game and making the objectives of the venture broader and more ambitious and consequently more contentious and harder to make operational.

This author has found examples of most of the tactics Bardach identifies, in an ongoing study of the implementation of information systems and models for educational policy analysis in state government. Before discussing them, it is important to examine what is perhaps the single most important cause of counterimplementation in information systems development—the politics of data.

The link between control over information and influence has often been noted. "Information is a resource that symbolizes status, enhances authority and shapes relationships." [74] "Information is an element of power." (Quoted in Greenberger et al. [24]) Computer systems often redistribute information, breaking up monopolies. Building a database then becomes a political move; sometimes it is equivalent to a declaration of war. The system designer needs to ask:

1. Who owns the data?
2. Who will share it?
3. What will be the perceived impact of redistribution on:
   a. evaluation;
   b. influence and authority;
   c. communication?

He or she should then get ready to deal with counterimplementation.

Dornbusch and Scott define evaluation as central to the exercise of authority [18]. In general, providing management (or outside agencies) with data that permits closer observation of subordinates' decision making or helps define additional output measures increases control and decreases autonomy. Many public sector agencies protect data on their operations as a means of maintaining their independence. Laudon's study of information systems in local government provides many illustrations of this point [43], i.e., police agencies protect their data from mayors and budget agencies. Information is control [58].

Evaluation and monitoring are often "improved" (from the manager's viewpoint) through the collection of routine operational data. An unanticipated side effect of information systems is an increase in the superior's ability to evaluate personnel. For example, telecommunications, office automation, and integrated databases provide and record simple access to information that may then be used to observe subordinates. The introduction to office automation has, for instance, led some managers to study "productivity" of clerical staff, measured in terms of lines typed or error rates. Hospitals similarly use computer-derived data to track nurses' performance; previously evaluation required interaction, some degree of negotiation and respect for the nurses' "professional" judgement. Some managers are concerned that trends in computer networking and database administration may similarly encourage their superiors to snoop.[7]

The link between evaluation and authority is recognized by many trade union leaders. Greenberger et al.'s discussion of the joint effort of Rand and the administration of Mayor Lindsay in New York to apply management science to city government provides several examples of their refusal to permit data to be gathered that might later be used to evaluate productivity [24]. Teacher unions similarly opposed efforts to introduce accountability programs. In at least one state, the Department of Education joined them in an elegant counterimplementation move, a variant of one Bardach [5] labels Pile On. Teacher accountability measures had been tacked into a school finance bill. The Department of Education suggested six comprehensive programs, all of which involved collecting and processing additional data. It then scheduled about 30 statewide meetings, open to parents, the press, school officials, and teachers and loftily entitled "The Search for Consensus". This generated 44 separate accountability measures. The program is, of course, now dead. This counterimplementation was overt and skilled, but puzzling to analysts who saw the need for "better" data as in the interests of all.

A corollary of the link between evaluation and authority is the relationship between ownership of information and autonomy. In some cases, departments or individuals have influence only because they have a data monopoly. (Cyert and March [13] comment that organizations are partly designed in terms of rules for filtering and channelling data. Particular units are given responsibility for collecting and interpreting data and other units may not challenge them.) Finance and Planning, for example, may own data on capital allocations. In state government agencies, budget officials often have a monopoly on the details of particular programs and expenditures which gives them great influence on the decision making process. Staff specialists, who often lack direct authority, rely on careful rationing of technical information on negotiations and on their ability to withhold data [58].

Information systems redistribute data and are sometimes intended to break up monopolies. This may be equivalent to redesigning parts of the organization, disrupting patterns of communication, and reallocating authority. Of course, this also means that they may be explicitly used to ". . . perpetuate or modify decision processes and social structures." (Bariff and Galbraith [6]) Information systems then become a tool for organizational development in the most literal sense of the term. The key point is that designers must recognize that far from being divorced from messy "politics", information technology has a major impact on a critical resource and source of power. It is hardly surprising then that teachers view a productivity reporting system as an outrage or that operating divisions oppose the efforts of Finance to coordinate planning through a budget tracking system. Computer specialists tend to be very surprised.

6. THE TACTICS OF COUNTERIMPLEMENTATION

A key step in the tactical approach to implementation is to convert the general impetus for change which is usually based on broad goals and rallying cries, into operational objectives and a specific contract [41, 22]. Any project is very vulnerable to counterimplementation until this is done. Programs that have unclear goals or ambiguous specifications and that rely on continuing high levels of competence and coordination are easy targets for skilled game players. Bardach [5] outlines a variety of games. (Table 34.1) Easy Money involves supporting a project because it can be used to finance some needed activity within the player's sphere of interest. The Budget game is played by managers as budget maximizers and Territory is similarly used to protect or extend control.

Table 34.1
Implementation Games (Bardach).

Diverting Resources	Sample Motivation
Easy Money	"Get a little more than we give back."
Budget	"We never turn down money."
Easy Life	"Make sure we're in charge and don't let outsiders cause trouble; take it slowly."
Pork Barrel	The elected official's version of Easy Money; "grab it while you can."
Deflecting Goals	
Pile On	"Let's do it right!—We have to make sure our interests are included in the project."
Up for Grabs	"If they don't know what they want, we'll take over."
Keep the Peace	"We're going to have to work closely with Marketing and make sure we're both happy."
Dissipating Energies	
Tenacity	"No." "One more time." "We're not happy about . . . ."
Territory	"This is *our* job." "We think we should run the project since . . ."
Not Our Problem	"Marketing really ought to handle this."
Odd Man Out	"We're certainly interested and we'll be happy to provide some inputs, but . . ."
Reputation	"I want an integrated-on-line-real-time-database-management-distributed-processing-planning system. My system will . . ."

Within a game, there are some predictable moves. Tenacity exploits social inertia and interdependencies: ". . . all it takes is the ability and the will to stymie the completion, or even the progress, of a program until one's own particular terms are satisfied."[8] Odd Man Out creates an option to withdraw if the project gets into trouble and then the chance to say "I told you so." This move is made easiest in projects where only the designer is accountable and no visible commitment is required from the game player. Up For Grabs is used to take over a program where the mandate is half-hearted or ambiguous.

All these moves are found in information systems development. There is an additional maneuver employed wherever computers are found — the Reputation game. Here, a manager gets credit as a bold innovator by sponsoring a new system — the closer to the state-of-the-art the better, since this increases his or her visibility and creates excitement. The Reputation gamer will have been transferred to a new position by the time the project collapses and can then ruefully say ". . . when I was in charge of things . . ." The short tenure of upwardly mobile managers and their need to produce fast results encourages this move, which is only possible however when the goals of the project are not made operational or specific commitments made to deliver phased outputs.

This analysis of implementation as a game may seem overcynical. However, it seems essential to ask at the start of the project:

1. Are people likely to play games?
2. Is the proposal proof against subversion?

These two simple questions provide the basis for a defensive strategy.

7. COUNTERCOUNTERIMPLEMENTATION: THE MANAGEMENT GAME

Most of the moves Bardach discusses exploit ambiguity and a lack of control mechanisms. The Reputation game player can get early credit and not be held accountable later. Easy Money is possible only because the goals of the project are too broadly stated. Odd Man Out occurs when technicians have to carry the venture (or choose to do so). Bardach suggests designers use "scenario-writing" (Table 34.2) and in essence ask "who can foul it up." The tactical approach to implementation makes the same recommendation, though more optimistically. At the Entry stage the implementer tries to identify and bring into the (facilitative) negotiations any party whose actions or inactions can affect the chances of success. Scenario-writing forewarns the designer and partially protects him or her against (1) monopoly and tokenism; (2) massive resistance; and (3) delays, deliberate or accidental. Bardach recommends a variety of responses to counterimplementation such as creating substitute monopolies (information systems personnel can use their specialized technical resources in this way for bargaining), co-opting likely opposition early, providing clear incentives {"If policy analysts carry bumper stickers, they should read 'Be Simple!

Table 34.2
Scenario-Writing (adapted from Bardach).

A. Basic Objectives:	—What exactly are you trying to get done? (not what does the system look like?) —What resources are needed? —Who controls them, directly or indirectly? —How can you minimize the effects of social inertia?
B. Dilemmas of Administration:	—What elements are critical? —Are any of them subject to monopoly interests? —Will their owners be uncooperative? —Can you work around them or buy them off? —Will they respond with delays or tokenism? —How will you deal with massive resistance?

C. Games:	—What games are likely to
	  (a) divert resources?
	  (b) deflect goals?
	  (c) dissipate energies?
	—How can you counteract or prevent them, if necessary by redesigning the project?

D. Delay:	—How much delay should you expect? —What negotiations are needed? —What resources do you have for negotiations and/or control? —Would it help to use project management, work around possible obstacles and delay or enlist intermediaries?
E. Fixing the Game:	—What senior management and staff aid do you need? —What resources do they have? —What incentives are there for them to play the fixer role? —Can you build a coalition to fix the game?

Be Direct' or 'PAYMENT ON PERFORMANCE',[9] (Pressman and Wildavsky [59]} and creating a bandwagon.

The Management game uses control mechanisms overlaid on others' games. By assigning priorities, developing project management procedures and above all, by keeping the scope of the project small and simple, which is often intellectually harder than designing a complicated system, the implementer can limit the range of moves actors can make. The Management game is difficult to play without a "fixer",[10] a person or group with the prestige, visibility, and legitimacy to facilitate, deter, bargain, and negotiate effectively. Information systems teams often lack this key support.

8. CONCLUSION: A STRATEGIC PERSPECTIVE ON CHANGE

Countercounterimplementation (CCI) is largely defensive, whereas the facilitative tactical approach is proactive. To an extent, CCI involves containing and doing the opposite of counterimplementers, whose strategy may be summarized as:

1. Lay low;
2. Rely on inertia;

3. Keep the project complex, hard to coordinate, and vaguely defined;
4. Minimize the implementers' legitimacy and influence;
5. Exploit their lack of inside knowledge.

The tactical model addresses some of these issues:

1. Make sure you have a contract for change;
2. Seek out resistance and treat it as a signal to be responded to;
3. Rely on face-to-face contracts;
4. Become an insider and work hard to build personal credibility;
5. Co-opt users early.

A strategic model for change needs to resolve some additional concerns:

1. What happens when consensus is impossible?
2. How can large-scale projects evade social inertia?
3. What authority mechanisms and organizational resources are needed to deal with the politics of data and counterimplementation?
4. What is the role of management?

Some points are obvious from the analysis so far. Whether we like it or not, we can only hope for incremental change [except, as Ansoff points out [2] in situations of mild crises, where the status quo is no longer satisfactory, and organizations rethink their goals and are more willing to think "rationally"]. This reality suggests that systems designers must always aim for simplicity of design and precise objectives. However, if they are to go beyond tactical innovations based on Up-and-In, they need Down-and-Out directional planning; they must establish the direction of change and evolve complex systems out of phased components. This requires nontechnical resources such as (1) a meaningful steering committee and (2) authority.

The analysis in this paper indicates that information development must be spearheaded by a general, not coordinated by aides-de-camp. It must be defined as part of the Information function of the organization, instead of being a staff service labelled data processing or management science. The issues of negotiations seem central (Kling and Gerson [40]). To position a system one must clarify objectives, respond to resistance, adjust other components of the Leavitt Diamond (**Task, Technology, People, Structure**) and block off counterimplementation. The politics of data (and of software engineering; see Keen and Gerson [35]) make it essential that negotiations be handled by a fixer, well-linked into senior managements' decision making. Large scale change is a process of coalition-building; this cannot be done by staff analysts, who are too easily caught in the middle with no formal powers.

The strategy for managing social change is based on acceptance of the political nature of information systems development and the need for suitable authority. Many organizations have moved in this direction. Neal and Radnor and their colleagues [56, 62] conclude that OR/MS groups with formal charters (budgets, senior job titles for their managers, and the right to turn down user requests) are more successful than ones that are a corporate service unit. The few Grand Old Men in the information systems field who have risen to senior positions in large companies have built up organizational mechanisms that provide them with authority and strong links with top level planning in the organization [66, 20]. There is perhaps an almost Darwinian process of natural selection, where the MIS group adopts a purely technical focus or cannot obtain authority for negotiations, it becomes merely a data processing service limited to routine applications and subject to all the forces of inertia and counterimplementation discussed here.[11]

It is not the aim of this paper to define a specific strategy for implementation. The outline seems clear:

1. A senior level fixer must head the Information function; he or she must have full authority and resources to negotiate with or between users and with those affected by information systems;

2. There must be some policy planning or steering committee which includes senior line managers; it will delegate to technical staff responsibility for projects that do not have significant organizational impact but will be actively involved with ones that are part of the politics of data (the policy committee also provides a negotiating table);

3. The planning process will require substantial time and effort in the predesign stages, where objectives are made operational and evolution of the larger system is defined by breaking it into clear phases;

4. Formal contracts will be needed, in which commitments must be clearly made and such games as Up for Grabs, Reputation, Easy Life, and Territory made illegal and ineffectual;

5. "Hybrid" skills must be developed in systems staff; they cannot dismiss organizational and political issues as irrelevant or not their responsibility, but must be able to operate in the manager's world and build credibility across the organization.[12]

6. With the umbrella provided by the fixer's authority and the steering committee, the tactical approach remains an excellent guide to managing the implementation process for a given project.

The simple, central argument presented here is that information systems development is political as well as, sometimes far more so than, technical in nature. When that is accepted, the organizational mechanisms follow naturally. Unfortunately, "politics" have been equated with evil, corruption and, worst of all, blasphemy in the presence of the Rational Ideal, but politics are the process of getting commitment, or building support, or creating momentum for change; they are inevitable.

The final comments to be made here concern research. There have been few studies of the political aspects of information systems development. The topic is rarely discussed in textbooks and even the literature on tactical implementation deals with it only peripherally. Yet when one tries to reconstruct or observe the progress of any major project, this is an obvious and important feature. It is absurd to ignore it or treat it as somehow an unsuitable subject for study or for training MIS specialists. There is some fragmented research available: Pettigrew's observation of a computer purchase decision, [57] Laudon's, *Computers and Bureaucratic Reform,* [43] and the work done by the Urban Information Systems Research Group at the University of California at Irving (Kling [38], [39]). Greenberger et al. [24] also provide some vivid illustrations of the political nature of computer models in public policy making. Most of this work is based on case studies. Politics are hard to study. They involve many hidden agenda (counterimplementers do not boast about their triumphs) and in most instances a skilled observer has to ferret out and interpret what has happened. In political science, the work on implementation is almost entirely narrative and descriptive. A political perspective on information systems is needed in research. It will of necessity be based on comparative field studies that illustrate theoretical concepts.[13] It will not fit the standard mold for behavioral research. It can immensely add to our understanding both of the implications of information technology and the dynamics of effective implementation. For a long time the word "implementation" was not included in the index to literature on OR/MS and MIS. It is to be hoped that "politics", "negotiations", and "authority" be increasingly found in the titles of papers on information systems. That the papers will often be case studies does not mean they are not "legitimate" research. We badly need more understanding of these issues which are of fundamental importance to the effective exploitation of computer technology.

NOTES

[1]See [34] for a critical evaluation of implementation research.

[2]See [64]. See also [13], and with a different flavor and very different conclusions, Lindblom [47] who argues that:

"The human condition is small brain, big problems. People then need help – devices, processes and institutions – to simplify problem-solving." (p. 66).

[3]See [33] for a historical summary of the (largely axiomatic) concept of optimality.

[4]Ginzberg [22] provides a useful summary of this perspective. See also [34].

[5][67], p. ix.

[6][73], p. 17.

[7]See [40]. [6] provides an excellent summary of power issues in relation to information systems, viewed mainly in terms of the accounting function.

[8][5], p. 148.

[9][59], p. 159.

[10][5], pp. 273–278. The concept of a fixer vastly extends the platitude in the implementation literature of the need for top management support.

[11]See [35] and [32], who argues that most MIS groups are locked into the "maintenance" activities of the organization which reinforces the status quo and emphasizes efficiency. They have little impact on the "adaption" functions, which involve innovation and strategic planning.

[12]See [36], Chap. 9.

[13]Mintzberg [52] provides a full discussion of the difficulties of studying phenomena which involve "soft" variables and need an integrating perspective. His own field research [51] is a striking example of how much we can learn from simple, imaginative observation, which often conflicts with complex over-narrow experimentation.

REFERENCES

1. Allison, G.T. *Essence of Decision.* Little Brown, Boston, Mass, 1971.

2. Ansoff, H.I., *Business Strategy.* Penguin, London, England, 1968.

3. Argyris, C. Resistance to rational management systems. *Innovation,* 10, (1970) pp. 28–35.

4. Argyris, C. Management information systems: The challenge to rationality and emotionality. *Management Sci. 17,* 6, (1971), pp. B275–292.

5. Bardach, E. *The Implementation Game: What Happens After a Bill Becomes a Law.* MIT Press, Cambridge, Mass., 1977.

6. Bariff, M.L. and Galbraith, J.R. Intraorganizational power considerations for designing information systems. The Wharton School, Univ. of Penn., Philadelphia, Penn., Jan. 1978.

7. Bower, J. *The Resource Allocation Process.* Irwin, New York, 1970.

8. Bowman, E.H. Consistency and optimality in managerial decision making. *Management Sci. 9,* 2, (Jan. 1963) pp. 310–321.

9. Braybrooke, D. and Lindblom, C.E. *A Strategy of Decision.* Free Press, New York, 1963.

10. Chesler, M. and Flanders, M. Resistance to research and research utilization: The death and life of a feedback attempt. *J. Appl. Behavioral Sci. 3,* 4, (Fall 1967), pp. 465–487.

11. Churchman, C.W. Managerial acceptance of scientific recommendations. *Calif. Management Rev. 7,* 1 (Fall 1964), pp. 31–38.

12. Cohen, M.R. and March, J.G. *Leadership and Ambiguity.* McGraw-Hill, New York, 1974.

13. Cyert, R.M. and March, J.G. *A Behavioral Theory of the Firm.* Prentice-Hall, Englewood Cliffs, N.J., 1963.

14. Dearborn, D.C. and Simon, H.A. The identification of executives. In *Administrative Behavior* (3rd ed.). H.A. Simon, Ed. Free Press, New York, 1976, pp. 309–314.

15. Derthick, M. New towns in-town. The Urban Institute, Washington, D.C., 1972.

16. Doktor, R.H. Developing and mapping of certain cognitive styles of problem-solving. Unpublished Ph.D. Dissertation, Stanford Univ., Stanford, Calif., 1969.

17. Doktor, R.H. and Hamilton, W.F. Cognitive style and the acceptance of management science recommendations. *Management Sci. 19,* 8 (April 1973), pp. 884–894.

18. Dornbusch, S. and Scott, W.R. *Evaluation and the Exercise Authority.* Jossey-Bass, San Francisco, Calif., 1975.

19. Drake, J.W. *The Administration of Transportation Modelling Projects.* Heath, Lexington, Mass., 1972, pp. 14–17.

20. Edelman, F. Four ways to oblivion—A short course on survival. *Interfaces* August, 1972, pp. 14–17.

21. Galbraith, J.R. *Designing Organizations.* Addison-Wesley, Reading, Mass., 1977.

22. Ginzberg, M.J. A process approach to management science implementation. Unpublished Ph.D. Dissertation, Sloan School of Management, M.I.T., Cambridge, Mass., 1975.

23. Grayson, C.J. Management science and business practice. *Harvard Business Rev. 51,* 4 (July–Aug. 1973), pp. 41–48.

24. Greenberger, M., Crenson, M.A., and Crissey, B.L. *Models in the Policy Process,* Russell Sage Foundation, New York, 1976.

25. Hall, W.K. Strategic planning models: Are top managers really finding them useful? *J. Business Policy 3,* 3, 1973, pp. 19–27.

26. Hall, W.K. Rationality, irrationality and the policy formulation process in large organizations. *Planning Rev. 4,* 6 (May 1976), pp. 22–26.

27. Hargrove, E.C. The missing link: The story of implementation process. The Urban Institute, Washington, D.C., 1975.

28. Hirschman, A.O. *The Strategy of Economic Development.* Yale Univ. Press, New Haven, Connecticut, 1958.

29. Hoos, I.R. *Systems Analysis in Public Policy,* Univ. of Calif. Press, Berkeley, Calif., 1972.

30. Huysmans, H.B.M. *The Implementation of Operations Research.* Wiley, New York, 1970.

31. Kahneman, D. and Tversky, A. Prospect theory: An analysis of decision under risk. *Econometrica 47,* (March 1979) p. 263.

32. Keen, P.G.W. Managing organizational change: The role of MIS. in *Proc. 6th and 7th Ann. Conf. of the Soc. for Management Infor. Syst.,* J.D. White, Ed. Univ. of Michigan, Ann Arbor, Mich., July 1976, pp. 129–134.

33. Keen, P.G.W. The evolving concept of optimality. In *Multi-Criteria Decision Making.* M.K. Starr and M. Zeleny, Eds., The Inst. of Management Sci. (TIMS), Studies in Management Sci., 6, 1977, pp. 31–57.

34. Keen, P.G.W. Implementation research in MIS and OR/MS: Description versus prescription. Stanford Business School Research Paper No. 390, Stanford, Calif., 1977.

35. Keen, P.G.W. and Gerson, E.M. The politics of software engineering. *Datamation 23,* 11 (Nov. 1977), pp. 80–86.

36. Keen, P.G.W. and Scott Morton, M.S. *Decision Support Systems: An Organizational Perspective.* Addison-Wesley, Reading, Mass., 1978.

37. Klein, B. and Meckling, W. Applications of operations research to development decisions. *Operations Res. 6,* 3, (May–June 1958), pp. 352–363.

38. Kling, R. Information systems in policy making. *Telecomm Policy, 2,* 1, (March 1978), pp. 3–12.

39. Kling, R. Social analyses of computing: Theoretical perspectives in recent empirical research. *Comptng Survey 12,* 1 (March 1980) pp. 61–110.

40. Kling, R. and Gerson, E.M. The social dynamics of technical innovation in the computing world. *Symbolic Interaction, 1,* 1 (Fall, 1977) pp. 132–146.

41. Kolb, D.A. and Frohman, A.L. An organizational development approach to consulting. *Sloan Management Rev. 12,* 1 (Fall 1970) pp. 51–65.

42. Kunruether, H. and Slovic, P. Economics, psychology and protective behavior. *Am. Econ. Rev.* Papers and Proceedings, May 1978.

43. Laudon, K.C. *Computers and Bureaucratic Reform: The Political Functions of Urban Information Systems.* Wiley, New York, 1974.

44. Leavitt, H.J. Applying organizational change in industry: Structural, technological and humanistic approaches. *Handbook of Organizations,* J.G. March, Ed. Rand McNally, Chicago, Ill., 1965.

45. Leavitt, H.J. and Webb, E. Implementing: Two approaches. Stanford Univ. Research Paper 440, Stanford, Calif., May 1978.

46. Lindblom, C.E. The science of muddling through. *Public Administration Rev., 19,* 2, (Spring 1959), pp. 79–88.

47. Lindblom, C.E. *Politics and Markets.* Basic Books, New York, 1977.

48. Lucas, H.C. and Plimpton, R.B. Technological consulting in a grass roots, action-oriented organization. *Sloan Management Rev. 14,* 1 (Fall 1972) pp. 17–35.

49. McKenney, J.L. and Keen, P.G.W. How managers' minds work. *Harvard Business Rev. 52,* 3 (May–June 1974) pp. 79–90.

50. Miller, R.B. Psychology for a man-machine problem-solving process. IBM Data Systems Division Laboratory, Rept TR00-1246, February 1965.

51. Mintzberg, H. *The Nature of Managerial Work.* Harper and Row, New York, 1973.

52. Mintzberg, H. Policy as a field of management theory. *Academy of Management Review,* January 1977. (Unnumbered paper).

53. Mintzberg, H. Beyond implementation: An analysis of the resistance to policy analysis. *Infor 18,* 2 (May 1980) pp. 100–138.

54. Mitroff, I.I. *The Subjective Side of Science: A Philosophic Enquiry into the Psychology of the Apollo Moon Scientists.* Elsevier, New York, 1974.

55. Munson, F.C. and Hancock, W.M. Problems of implementing change in two hospital settings. *AIIE Trans. 4,* 4 (Dec. 1977) pp. 258–266.

56. Neal, R.D. and Radnor, M. The relation between formal procedures for pursuing OR/MS activities and OR/MS group success. *Operations Res. 21,* (March 1973), pp. 451–474.

57. Pettigrew, A.M. *The Politics of Organizational Decision Making.* Tavistock, London, England, 1973.

58. Pettigrew, A.M. Implementation control as a power resource. *Sociology 6,* 2, (May 1972) pp. 187–204.

59. Pressman, J.L. and Wildavsky, A. *Implementations.* Univ. of Calif. Press, Berkeley, California, 1973.

60. Roberts, E.B. On implementing systems studies: Strategies for achieving organizational change in response to model-based analysis. Paper presented at the American-Soviet Conference Series on Methodological Aspects of Social Systems Simulation, Sukhumki, USSR, Oct. 17-23, 1973.

61. Ross, L. The intuitive psychologist and his shortcomings in *Advances in Experimental Social Psychology.* L. Berkowitz Ed. Academic, New York, 1964, pp. 173–220.

62. Rubenstein, A.H., Radnor, M., Baker, N., Heiman, D. and McCoy, J. Some organizational factors relative to the effectiveness of management science groups in industry. *Management Sci. 13,* 8, (April, 1967), pp. B508–518.

63. Saplosky, H.M. *The Polaris System Development.* Harvard Univ. Press, Cambridge, Mass. 1972.

64. Simon, H.A. A behavioral model of rational choice. In *Models of Man,* H.A. Simon, Ed. Wiley, New York, 1957, pp. 241–260.

65. Stewart, R. *Managers and Their Jobs.* McMillan, London, England, 1967.

66. Strassman, P. Managing the costs of information. *Harvard Business Rev., 54,* 5 (Sept-Oct 1976) pp. 133–142.

67. Strauss, A. *Negotiations: Varieties, Contexts, Processes, and Social Cries.* Jossey-Bass, San Franciso, Calif., 1978.

68. Tversky, D. and Kahneman, A. Judgment under uncertainty: Heuristics and biases. *Science, 185,* (Sept. 1974), pp. 1124–1131.

69. Urban, G.L. Building models for decision makers. *Interfaces 4,* 3, (May 1974) pp. 1–11.

70. Vancil, R. and Lorange, P. *Strategic Planning Systems.* Prentice-Hall, Englewood Cliffs, N.J., 1977.

71. Vertinsky, I.R., Barth, T., and Mitchell, V.F. A study of OR/MS implementation as a social change process in *Implementing Operations Research/Management Science,* R.L. Schultz and D.P. Slevin, Eds. American Elsevier, New York, 1975, pp. 253–272.

72. Weick, K. *The Social Psychology of Organizing.* Addison-Wesley, Reading, Mass., 1969.

73. Weiner, S. and Wildavsky, A. The prophylactic presidency. *Public Interest 52,* 52, (Summer 1978), pp. 3–19.

74. Wildavsky, A. *The Politics of the Budgetary Process.* (2nd Ed.), Little, Brown, Boston, Mass., 1974.

75. Wilensky, H.L. *Organizational Intelligence: Knowledge and Policy in Government and Industry.* Basic Books, New York, 1967.

76. Zand, D.E. and Sorenson, R.E. Theory of change and the effective use of management science. *Administrative Sci Quarterly, 20,* 4, (Dec. 1975), pp. 532–545.

77. Zionts, S. and Wallenius, J. An interactive programming method for solving the multiple criteria problem. *Management Sci. 22, 6,* (Feb. 1976), pp. 652–663.

PART FOUR

Managing Waves of Change

This section of the book provides "leading edge" thinking about the management of IT resources in a constantly changing business world. For instance, a major issue confronting many firms is deciding whether a corporate information systems department, a business unit, line managers, or some combination of these three should manage IT resources. Reading 35, "Changing Role of the Corporate Information Systems Officer," discusses the meaning of these changes to organizations struggling to manage IT resources effectively. The next four articles (Readings 36–39) continue to focus on this theme and provide both an appreciation for the complexities of the issue and a knowledge of possible management solutions.

The next five articles discuss ways of approaching several other key IT management challenges facing businesses today. In Reading 40, Brandt Allen and Andrew Boynton discuss critical concerns in designing an IT architecture that is effective in matching a firm's strategy, goals, and objectives. Effective approaches for managing end-user computing, an issue of increasing importance among managers and professionals in all organizations, is the topic of Reading 41. The next reading, "Managing the Data Resource: A Contingency Perspective," explores the nature of managing data and information, which are now recognized as important organizational resources. Despite the importance of data and information, few companies successfully "manage" them; Reading 42 thus serves as a valuable tool by providing practical information on different approaches to data management. Readings 43 and 44 offer important insights into one of the biggest hurdles in implementing effective IT applications—justifying the substantial financial investments that are often required.

The last two articles in this section are case studies that illustrate two proven methods for IT planning, a crucial management task for any firm wishing to use IT resources effectively. Reading 45 demonstrates how the "critical success factor" methodology can be used for IT planning, and Reading 46 shows how to link IT planning and business planning to identify strategic information systems.

35

Changing Role of the Corporate Information Systems Officer

Robert I. Benjamin,

Charles Dickinson, Jr., and

John F. Rockart

IS managers hardly need to be told that their world is changing. Change is everywhere—a harsher, more competitive business environment; rapidly evolving information technology; and increasingly knowledgeable, demanding, and diverse user constituencies. The problem for IS managers is not one of acknowledging change; it is one of adapting to it successfully. The purpose of this article is to report on a recent research effort that describes the adaptation made by corporate information officers (CIO's). The results of this research suggest that our sample of CIO's, working in very successful large corporations, are rapidly developing a new role for themselves—one that is radically different from the traditional role of the IS Manager.

In describing this new role of the CIO, we shall draw upon two types of material: first, a set of predictions about the new role itself, and second, findings from the CIO research.

Our research model was exploratory and designed to provide some validation for the conclusions reached in an earlier article by Rockart, Bullen and Ball [8]. Our sample was small but of very high quality. A questionnaire was sent to approximately 25 CIO's in a variety of large U.S. and Canadian corporations, of whom 20 (in a few instances their chief aides) responded. Because most of the CIO's have had a long term connection as sponsors of the Center for Information Systems Research (CISR) at the Sloan School, MIT, we were able to place high confidence in the care they took in responding to the survey. As a further step in eliminating ambiguities, the survey results were reviewed with most of the respondees at a CISR workshop in May of 1983.

The sample is clearly not a random one, and is not large enough for meaningful statistical analysis. The sample is representative of a number of business sectors (Table 35.1a), however the results must be viewed in the light of two built-in biases.

First, the respondents are from very large corporations with large IS budgets (Table 35.1b&c). Second, as CISR sponsors they have frequently been in contact with each other to discuss issues such as this one. From our many contacts outside of CISR we believe the respondee sample is reasonably representative of large corporations, and is at the leading edge in understanding the changing role of the corporate information officer.

THE CHANGING WORLD OF THE CIO: PREDICTIONS

While CIO's have coped, some more successfully than others, with the changes in their world during the last several years, researchers and consultants have attempted to understand and describe these changes. Some strong perspectives have emerged on the direction that leading-edge organizations have been taking. It is useful, therefore, to summarize the traditional view of IS as a backdrop to our research findings.

Traditional View of IS Role

In 1974, Davis [1] described the IS organization as consisting of an executive with three responsibilities; analysis, programming, and operations. In 1981, Gruber and Synott [4] describe an organization with four responsibilities; data processing,

Table 35.1
Basic Company Information

a. Industry		
Category	**Number**	**%**
Manufacturing	9	45
Banking	3	15
Insurance	2	10
Petrochemical	2	10
Government	1	5
Other	3	15
Total	20	100

b. Revenues		
Category	**Number**	**%**
More Than $5 Billion	10	50
$.5 to $5 Billion	9	45
N/A (Government)	1	5
Total	20	100

c. IS Budget		
Category	**Number**	**%**
More Than $100 Million	12	60
$10–50 Million	6	30
$50–100 Million	2	10
Total	20	100

telecommunications, methods, and systems development. Both of these traditional views of the IS organizational are functional in perspective, the latter one merely adding the telecommuniations function.

In 1982, Nolan [5] identified a number of critical IS issues based on interviews with senior managers; balancing the supply and demand for computing resources as well as rationalizing the managing of IS as a profit center, measurement of effectiveness, centralization, planning and control, project selection, leadership, and (in terms of future opportunities) forecasting and administrative costs. As in most writings to this point, the issues highlighted were almost all aimed at improving the delivery of current large data center-based paperwork processing services.

Current Perspectives

Nolan [6], has suggested that IS is currently in a period of "technological discontinuity" as it makes the transition from a traditional DP technology (characterized by mainframe computers and common software under the control of a centralized data processing organization) to a user-dominated technology. Just as the traditional DP technology has its own learning curve (which provided the basis for Nolan's original description of the stages of DP growth [7]), so does the new, user-dominated technology. The complexity of the current IS environment is caused by the discontinuity and change associated with the transition from one learning curve to another.

Nolan, and others who have participated in his research, identify several implications for IS management:

- The computer infrastructures of organizations are shifting dramatically to the new user-dominated technologies.
- Senior management is looking to corporate IS for leadership in making the transition across technologies.
- Companies are being forced to shift from narrow DP planning to enterprise-wide computer architecture planning.

As Nolan points out, a major issue for companies as they pass through this "window" of technological discontinuity is one of leadership — effective management of the transition from traditional technology to the user-driven technologies.

Benjamin [1] draws upon Nolan's framework, but is more specific about the types of changes or discontinuities that IS is experiencing as it moves from one technology to the other. He describes five trends:

- There is a powerful movement in the direction of greater distribution and complexity of processing environments in all major organizations today. This trend is increasing with the introduction of newer, lower cost, more powerful technologies.

- Unprecedented user demand for IS resources has been generated by the explosive growth in workstations, software packages, and easy-to-use languages. This demand is now driving IS resource management.
- New ways of developing systems, where the user can develop and operate many applications independently, are radically changing the power balance between the IS department and the user organizations.
- In contrast to the communications task of the 70's (the connection of workstations to specific applications on mainframes), the communications task of the 80's is much more complex. It consists of interconnecting a range of applications to a single workstation, interconnecting the hierarchy of processing environments, and making databases accessible wherever needed in the organization.
- In the long run, of most fundamental significance is the realization that IS has become a factor in business strategy. Today's information technologies, coupled with advances in data communications, have made information systems a weapon to be considered in the fight for competitive advantage. Accordingly, IS management must develop an outward business-strategy perspective, in addition to its traditional operational focus.

Rockart, Bullen, and Ball [8] emphasize this evolving staff orientation for IS management—in particular for the CIO. Drawing upon the combined thinking of a group of successful CIO's and established researchers in the field, they theorized about the evolving CIO role. (It should be noted that of the 18 respondents in their panel only four were respondents in the survey reported here.)

This new role, as Rockart, et al. envision it, contains a new set of requisite managerial attributes for the individual CIO. More specifically, they make three "predictions" regarding this emerging role:

1. Decentralization of line responsibilities to divisions and departments—The new management environment will make it impossible for the CIO to maintain direct line management control over computer-based technology throughout the company. Accordingly, "line management of local hardware and much of the software development will be thrust into divisions and departments" [8, p. 14].

    Nonetheless, the CIO will necessarily retain direct, line responsibility for several critical areas associated with the information infrastructure of the firm. These areas will include the communications network, corporate data management, common software development (including a changing array of start-up projects), and the corporate computing facility.
2. Staff orientation—The new emphasis on staff-oriented responsibilities will result in the need for organizations to have a focal point for planning and facilitating the organization's move into the information era (or, in Nolan's terminology, into the advanced stages of user-dominated technologies).

    The CIO will increasingly focus on strategies and planning. He/she will be oriented towards facilitating, guiding, and promoting change—but will not control it. Techniques utilized by the CIO to guide, facilitate, and promote will include: communication and education processes, standards (e.g., for data, communication, privacy and security), and other indirect controls (e.g., steering committees, policies, and guidelines, and individual persuasion). Rather than being the "owner" of a centralized IS technology, the CIO will become the "gatekeeper" and "integrator" of an increasingly diverse spectrum of technological resources which will be decentralized throughout the firm.

3. Corporate responsibility for information resource policy and strategy — Increasingly, the CIO will be a member of the top management team. He/she will have broad responsibility for developing policies and strategies for the information resources of the firm, just as the CFO (chief financial officer) has similar responsibility for the financial resources of the firm.

This clearly suggests that the CIO will not simply be the custodian of the data. Rather, he or she will be the corporate officer who truly understands the interconnection of the information flow to the business. The CIO will have "the responsibility of assuring that new opportunities presented by the technology are seized and that capital expenditures for information resources are ranked according to business needs" [8, p. 5].

If these predictions are true, Rockart, et al., suggest that the emerging role for the CIO will require a set of managerial skills and attributes which, though useful to the IS executive in the past, will become absolutely critical in the future. It will not be enough that the CIO have a considerable understanding of the technology. In addition, the CIO must be a general-business oriented manager with considerable political, organizational, and communication skills.

RESEARCH ON THE CIO ROLE

Research Model

The CIO model developed by Rockart, Bullen and Ball was developed to identify a range of issues associated with the transitional management of the IS function in the 1980's. In particular, the predictions about the emerging CIO role and the associated managerial attributes for this role were intended to assist practicing CIO's in adapting successfully to a radically changed environment.

Although these predictions may be helpful, their practical value is limited until tested and validated by the actual experiences of successful CIO's in a variety of corporate environments. Our research on the emerging role of the CIO was thus undertaken to determine whether these predictions are, in fact, borne out by the actual experiences of successful CIO's in large corporate environments.

Research Findings

Our research was undertaken to test the three predictions of Rockart, et al., to determine whether or not they are validated by the day to day experiences of practicing, successful CIO's. Accordingly, we will discuss the findings of this research in the context of each prediction.

1. Distribution of Line Activities to Subsidiary IS Units and User Management — Results from the CIO questionnaires indicate that a decentralization of the line activities is taking place. CIO's were asked to indicate the location of responsibility (corporate IS, subsidiary IS groups, or user management) for an extensive list of staff and line activities. These were grouped into four general IS management functions (planning, managing, internal services, and user services).

   Table 35.2a shows those activities where the CIO's were at least 60% agreed on whether they were centralized or distributed. The data shows clearly that major elements of line responsibility (development and operation of application systems, and line management of hardware and software) have been distributed to subsidiary IS groups and user management. It is generally agreed by the CIO's that subsidiary IS units are responsible for the operation of mainframe and minicomputer hardware, selection and maintenance of applications software, and implementation of the system life cycle, as well as implementation of end user support. In addition, they are seen as having the responsibility for such line planning functions as budgeting (multi-year and annual) and architecture design for applications.

   In spite of this significant pattern of decentralization, some key line activities are not distributed to subsidiary IS units and user management. Most of these activities are associated with developing and maintaining the information utilities that constitute the IS infrastructure for the firm. In addition, they identified line tasks in support of the corporate staff such as executive support systems.

   There were a number of activities that the data did not identify clearly as corporate or distributed (Table 35.2b). These activities are generally associated with new evolving technologies (telecommunications, personal computers and office systems) and activities where the transition to decentralized operations is still evolving (e.g., applications planning).

   The distribution of responsibilities is a general trend that has focused on movement between corporate and distributed IS. Some movement of responsibilities is taking place between subsidiary IS and user management as well. This is shown in Table 35.2c as activities that at least 30% of the CIO's perceived user management to be responsible for. They emphasize a heavy user management role in applications, office and personal computers, and external databases and timesharing.

2. IS Budget — CIO's were asked to indicate the percentage of the entire IS budget that is under their direct control, both at present and estimated for three years in the future. In addition, they were asked to indicate the percentage of their budget which is dedicated to service utilities such as data centers, corporate applications, systems programming, and voice or data telecommunications. The premise in asking for this budget information was that the size of budget, and the trend over the next three years, would corroborate or weaken the CIO's own stated perceptions of their line/staff relationships. The results of these budget-related questions are shown in Table 35.3.

Table 35.2a
Distribution of IS Activities Centralized vs. Distributed Greater Than 60% Consensus by CIO's

Activity	Corporate IS	Distributed IS
Planning the IS Function		
• IS Strategic Planning	72	
• IS Multi-year Budgets or Project Plans		67
• IS Annual Budgets or Project Plans		67
• Technology Scanning/Anticipation	87	
• Architecture Planning Applications		73
• Application Portfolio		
a. Plan		88
b. Prioritize		89
Managing the IS Function		
• Mainframes/Mini		
a. Approval	61	
b. Standards	83	
c. Operations		72
• Personal Computers		
a. Selection		67
b. Operations		88
• Telecommunications/Voice		
a. Approval	68	
b. Standards	61	
• Telecommunications/Data		
a. Approval	88	
b. Standards	83	
Managing the IS Function		
• Office Systems Operations		88
• Systems Life Cycle		
a. Standards	61	
b. Implementation		79
• Applications Software		
a. Selection		72
b. Approval		61
c. Standards		69
• National/Multinational Vendor Contracts	76	
• Security/Privacy Standards	70	
IS Internal Services		
• Consulting Services/Technical Expertise	71	
• Information Exchange	88	
IS User Services		
• IS Education		
a. Senior management	66	
b. Line users	61	
• End User Support		62
• Executive Support	72	
• External Databases		88
• Timesharing		
a. Internal	63	
b. External		82

Table 35.2b
Centralized vs. Distributed Activities
Without 60% Consenses by CIO's

Architecture Planning
  Hardware
  Database

Mainframe/Minis
  Selection

Personal Systems
  Approval
  Standards

Telecommunications/Voice
  Selection
  Operations

Telecommunications/Data
  Selection
  Operations

Office Systems
  Selection
  Approval
  Standards

Application Software
  Standards

IS Internal Services
  Personnel Management
  Education Training of IS

IS User Services
  Office Systems
  Implementation of
    Common Systems

The data suggests that corporate IS is playing a less dominant role than it has in the past in terms of overall expenditures, and that this trend will continue in the future. The average corporate-controlled IS budget in the 20 firms is only 48% of the entire IS expenditures in the firm. Additionally, in the next three years it is expected to drop to 44%. Even today corporate IS does not control the majority of IS expenditures for the firm. These figures are consistent with the specific line/staff trends discussed previously.

Increasing Staff Orientation   In order to test the prediction of increased staff orientation, CIO's were asked to describe their most critical responsibilities. An average of three responsibilities were provided by each CIO. In addition, they were asked to indicate how they felt these responsibilities would be different three years from now. Our concern in both of these questions was to determine whether these critical responsibilities were primarily staff- or line-oriented.

The CIO responses, summarized in Table 35.4 clearly indicate that staff responsibilities are predominant in both instances. Of the 62 responses for current critical responsibilities, 40 (or 66%) fall into categories that are staff-oriented; only 21 (or 34%) can be classified as line responsibilities. Furthermore, to the extent that the CIO's anticipated change in the next three years most CIO's responded in a manner that was even more heavily weighted in favor of staff-oriented categories (13 of 15 responses). For a more detailed description of the responses see Benjamin [2].

The current line responsibilities cited by the CIO's may be organized into three categories. The first, creating and maintaining information utilities, reflects the residual line activities that were identified earlier. Responsibilities cited by CIO's included managing the corporate-wide computing center, world-wide networks and data, and the like. The other two categories of line responsibility are associated with

Table 35.2c
User Management Responsibilities Greater
Than 30% Perception by CIO's

Application Portfolio
Plan 33%
Prioritize 78%

Personal Computers
Selection 50%
Approval 34%
Operations 84%

Telecommunications/Voice
Operation 33%

Office Systems
Selection 36%
Operations 76%

Applications Software
Approval 33%

External Databases 53%

External Time Sharing 64%

Table 35.3
IS Budget Distribution

Budget Responsibility	Current Budget	Budget in 3 Years
Corporate IS		
Service Utilities	28%	26%
Other Corporate	20%	18%
Other IS Functions	52%	56%

the direct provision of information services, either at the corporate level (e.g., operation of corporate systems, providing end user computing environment for corporate) or for the organization as a whole (e.g., develop and maintain administrative systems on a worldwide basis, total responsibility for data processing operations and systems development).

Within the current staff activities, planning responsibilities are particularly prominent. Over 40% of the staff-oriented responsibilities are associated with technology planning (e.g., information architecture, evaluating new technology) or IS strategic planning, (e.g., linking to the strategic plan of the corporation, providing support for corporate goals). Although the preponderance of responses in the strategic planning category reflect an emphasis on supporting business strategy, only two responses emphasized a responsibility to influence the strategy of the firm (e.g., influence product strategy, increase use of computer as tool to increase productivity/profitability of the corporation). This was inconsistent with the response of the CIO's to their

Table 35.4
Critical Line and Staff Responsibilities
of CIO's: Current and Future

Current Line Responsibilities	Current Frequency	Change
1. Create/Maintain Information Utilities	7	+2
2. IS Services, Organization-Wide	6	—
3. IS Services, Corporate	8	—
Total, Current Responsibilities	21 (34%)	
Total, Future Change (Projected)		23 (30%)
Current Staff Responsibilities		
1. Technology Planning	6	+1
2. IS Strategic Planning	12	+3
3. Literacy/Education on Information Technology	6	—
4. Human Resource Management	3	—
5. Consultation/Support	7	+9
6. Standards/Control	6	—
Total Current Responsibilities	40 (66%)	
Total Future Change (Projected)		53 (70%)

selected key initiatives (discussed later) where influencing corporate strategy was one of their three highest ranking initiatives.

In addition to the planning responsibilities, CIO responses also emphasized such traditional staff functions as consultation and support (e.g. providing consulting to CEO, establishing end user computing, advising on effective utilization of computer and telecommunications technologies). These comprise over a third of the staff-oriented responsibilities identified by the CIO's. In addition, the CIO's felt that the category of consultation and support was going to be significantly more important in the future.

The remaining critical responsibilities identified by the CIO's fall into the staff-oriented categories of human resource management (e.g., attract, retain, and develop talent, develop competent people for key jobs in affiliates) and literacy or education on IS technology (e.g., see to it that the company is trained in computer technology, educate key executives on possibilities). The human resource category of responsibilities represents a rather traditional staff function. However, the responsibilities associated with fostering a growing literacy and understanding of IS technology represents an emerging need to understand and communicate the rapidly changing potential of information systems.

The CIO's view of critical responsibilities three years from now is little changed from today with some additional emphasis on consulting and planning activities. The staff-oriented picture of the CIO's role that is developed out of the list of critical responsibilities is consistent with the data that describes the distribution of corporate IS activities to subsidiary IS and user management. Inspection of Table 35.2 shows that the residual activities left under Corporate line up well with the staff activities described above.

What emerges from this aggregated listing of critical responsibilities, both at present and as anticipated for the future, is a rather sharply defined picture of the CIO as a high-level manager who is primarily concerned with issues of long-range planning, consultation, and support to a broad set of constituencies throughout the organization.

Corporate Responsibility for Information Resource Policy and Strategy

1. Reporting Relationships – In order to gauge CIO standing in the corporate hierarchy, CIO's were asked to indicate their reporting relationship to other top managers, particularly the CEO. The results of this question are summarized in Table 35.5, and compared to a 1968 survey reported by Davis [3, pp. 374–375]. The table summarizes the response to both surveys in terms of absolute numbers of respondents and percentage of respondents, indicating the number of levels a CIO is removed from the CEO, and where the CIO reports; finance or another key function.

   These results suggest two significant findings. First, the CIO is becoming an integral part of the top management team. Sixteen of the 20 CIO's surveyed are positioned within two levels of the CEO – and four of them report directly to the CEO. This finding indicates that although only 4 of 20 CIO's reports to the CEO, the chief manager of the IS function is no longer buried mid-range on the organizational chart.

   Second, the CIO reporting relationship is outside the traditional reporting pattern for IS executives – that of finance. Sixteen of twenty of the CIO's report to an area other than finance (e.g., operations, engineering, chief of staff). These organizational reporting paths are very consistent with the culture of the organization. To cite one illustration, the CIO of a major chemical corporation with a strong research and engineering tradition reports to the senior vice president of research and engineering.

Table 35.5
Reporting Relationship of CIO

Levels from CEO	Reporting to Finance		Reporting to Other		Total	
	1983	1968	1983	1968	1983	1968
1	n/a	n/a	4/20%	12/12%	4/20%	12/12%
2	4/20%	19/20%	8/40%	12/12%	12/60%	31/32%
3	0	36/37%	4/20%	18/19%	4/20%	54/56%
Total	4/20%	55/57%	16/80%	42/43%	20/100%	97/100%

2. Importance of Selected IS Initiatives – CIO's were asked to rate the importance of selected IS initiatives (specific areas requiring concentrated attention) on a scale of 1 (little importance to me as CIO) to 5 (critical to my success as CIO), both now and 3 years in the future. The mean ratings for each of these initiatives and the standard deviation is shown in Exhibit 35.1

The three initiatives rated most important by the CIO's were end user services, telecommunications, and corporate strategy. CIO's have some confusion about the importance of end user services in the short term (note the large standard deviation), but little uncertainty about its importance in the long term. CIO's also place considerable importance on initiatives in the areas of office systems and personal computers, which are special forms of end user services.

Eleven out of the 20 companies surveyed are in industries where CAD/CAM is significant (manufacturing and petrochemicals); they give it considerable importance as an initiative.

Directional change in initiatives is consistent with the predictions in the first section of this article. Application selection will be of lower concern as the CIO distributes responsibility, and telecommunications and corporate strategy will be of increasing concern as the CIO moves into a staff role. It is interesting to note that the three year view of end user services, telecommunications, and corporate strategy initiatives have little dispersion, indicating that the CIO's have a consistent sense of where they are heading.

Conclusions and Future Research

This research survey, conducted with 20 CIO's from major companies, gives strong evidence that a changing role for the chief information officer is winning acceptance. This confirms the predictions made by Rockart, Bullen and Ball, and the more general predictions of Nolan and Benjamin. Of most importance to the IS executive and to senior management is that the pace of this change is faster than was anticipated. It was predicted to be transitional through the end of the decade but, in fact, describes reality for many leading companies today. Specifically:

- The distribution of corporate IS activities to subsidiary IS and user management is proceeding rapidly. Our research demonstrates this from both a budgetary and from a functional point of view. CIO's are concentrating their line activities where interconnection is required – corporate-wide applications, corporate data networks, and the like.
- The CIO, as evidenced by the responses received, accomplishes primary goals through staff activities.
- The CIO's are proactive executives who, in general, report to the CEO or one level below, and are aligned through their reporting relationships to the strategic and operational elements of the business. Their strongest personal initiatives are in areas of strategic importance: end user computing, telecommunications, and

Exhibit 35.1
Importance Ratings for Major IS Initiatives Current and in 3 Years

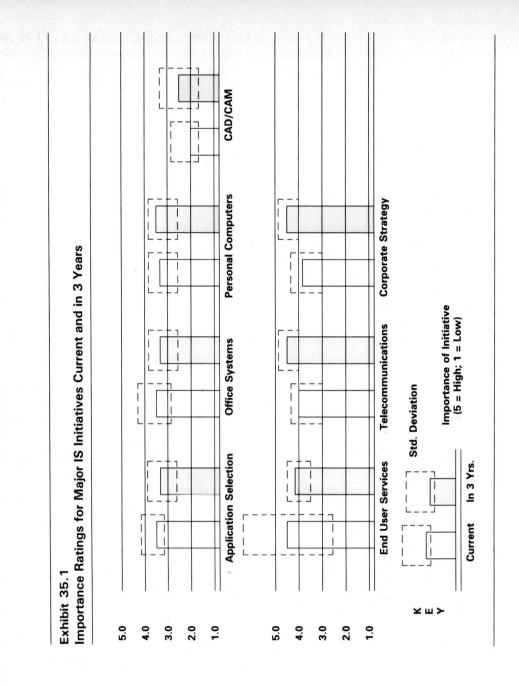

strategic planning (linking IS to the business, and gaining competitive advantage through use of information technology)

As with all research, the examination of the data and conclusions raises a number of interesting research questions.

- To what extent is the pattern of distribution of the IS function related to the size of the companies (which were very large in this sample), to the type of industry, and to organizational cultures?
- To what extent will the distribution of responsibility from subordinate IS to user management follow the pattern of distribution of responsibility from corporate to subordinate IS?

One final comment in concluding this report. The trends in leadership (large, sophisticated organizations) appear strong, and IS organizations that do not take them into account may encounter significant difficulty in coping with the transitional changes of the '80's.

REFERENCES

1. Benjamin R.I. "Managing Through a Decade of Discontinuity," *Information Systems News,* August 22, 1983, p. 20.

2. Benjamin R., Dickinson C., and Rockart J. *Changing Role of the Corporate Information Systems Officer,* Working Paper #113, Center for Information Systems Research, Massachusetts Institute of Technology, Cambridge, Massachusetts, March 1984, appendix 1.

3. Davis G.B. *Management Information Systems,* McGraw-Hill, New York, New York, 1974, p. 374.

4. Gruber W.H. and Synnott W.R. *Information Resource Management,* John Wiley & Sons, New York, New York, 1981, p. 183.

5. Nolan R.L. *Managing the Data Resource Function,* (2nd Ed.), West Publishing Company, St. Paul, Minnesota, 1982, pp. 346–360.

6. Nolan R.L. *Managing the Advanced Stages: Key Research Issue,* to be published as part of 75th Anniversary Colloquium papers; Harvard Business School, Cambridge, Massachusetts, July 1983.

7. Nolan R.L., and Gibson C.F. "Managing The Four Stages of EDP Growth," *Harvard Business Review,* January–February, 1974.

8. Rockart J.F., Bullen C.V., and Ball L. "Future Role of the Information Systems Executive," *MIS Quarterly,* Volume 6, Special Issue, December 1982, pp. 1–14.

36

A Rock and a Hard Place

Preston Gralla

Ask almost any head of information systems to list the primary corporate goals he or she is struggling to meet, and more likely than not, two will stand out: cutting costs and moving computing resources out into the company's business units and departments.

The need for the first is obvious—in today's business climate, streamlining is an absolute necessity as companies try to squeeze more and more profit out of existing resources. The second priority has equally clear benefits—if computing power is more directly tied to those parts of the company that actually do the business, then information systems can become a truly strategic force and not merely be confined to being record keepers and ciphers.

The problem, most managers will tell you, is that the two goals are often irreconcilable. The most efficient way to cut costs without also slicing services, say information executives, is to centralize the computing power of a company. If each division has its own electronic mail system, sales-tracking system, record-keeping system and the like, there is by necessity a duplication of services and personnel. Bringing back all computing resources under one roof will mean a decrease in hardware, software and personnel costs.

Doing that, however, goes against the grain of companies trying to align their computing power more closely with their business goals. The easiest way to do this, these companies have concluded, is to bring computing power out into the business units themselves.

Yet dispersing computing resources in this manner generally brings with it an increase in costs. So what's a manager to do? Faced with the Scylla of centralization and the Charybdis of decentralization, which course to steer?

The answers are as varied as the number of corporate cultures in today's business world. Some companies try to navigate a straight line between the two extremes, while others list more heavily to one side or the other. In fact, according to many corporate computing officers, most firms constantly swing between the two poles, centralizing when cost-containment is more important, and decentralizing when there is a greater need to put strategic resources into the hands of business units.

The reconciliation of these apparently opposite goals will continue to be high on the "must-do" list of anyone involved with information systems today. And the best way to understand how to resolve the apparently unresolvable is to look at those who have been struggling to come up with answers.

John Hammitt, vice president of information management with the Pillsbury Co. in Minneapolis, puts himself squarely on the side of those who believe the benefits of decentralization far outweigh any cost savings that centralization might bring.

"I'm a dyed-in-the-wool decentralist," he said. "I would have to be convinced there is a reason for centralization."

For the last five years, Hammitt has not merely talked a good line; he's overseen a basic restructuring of the information resources at Pillsbury, putting the responsibility for computing into the hands of the business units and taking it away from a central department.

The reason? "We needed to move the businesses closer to the systems," Hammitt said. "Rather than have IS as the experts who sell ourselves to the business units, we need people at the businesses themselves" responsible for overseeing information systems. Each business has "different strategic horizons," which must be taken into account, he said, adding that this is best done locally. Managers in the business units know far better than a central MIS department what their computing needs are, and so they should have the authority to set up and oversee those systems.

Decentralization has already led to measurable benefits at Pillsbury. "We can point with clarity to an improvement in business performance, with regard to profits and share of market," Hammitt said. "There's a direct link there. . . . If there's been a significant change [brought by decentralization], it's that we've found we can measure the productivity of systems now."

With the authority for information systems spread throughout the company, the question may arise whether this has led to a diminishment of Hammitt's power, authority or influence, and whether the same might be said for other CIOs who decentralize.

In each instance, he said, the answer is no. "I represent the position that suggests there's no loss in power as long as you continue to add value on your job, and as long as top management looks to you for advice and counsel on how to run the systems. . . . I want to measure my contribution by the value I've given to shareholders."

While Hammitt's changed role has not in his eyes diminished his authority, he believes it may be difficult for some CIOs to accept this new way of looking at their jobs. "It takes a special perspective to live in that ambiguous world where you don't manage a whole lot directly, but you influence everything," he said. "Some people who have grown up professionally owning it all are uncomfortable with this way of doing things. . . . Some people say that to have influence, you need to own something, but I don't think so. It's all a matter of personal style."

When Hammitt is a strong believer in decentralization, he recognizes that there are forces at work pushing for centralization as well. And he believes there are times

Is Cost-Consciousness Turning American Businesses Back Toward the Days of the Monolithic IS Fortress? Maybe Yes, Maybe No . . . While information executives say their companies often swing between centralization and decentralization, one consultant in the IS field sees things going in one direction only – toward centralization of MIS. And that, he said, bodes ill for American business.

James Kubeck, president of K4 Enterprises Inc., a management consulting and training firm in Whiting, Ind., said: "I see a lot of mouthing about decentralization, but I don't really see it in practice. More and more actions indicate [that companies are intent only on centralization of IS functions]. I see more and more [of it]; the words people speak are decentralization, but the behavior is toward centralization."

The great danger Kubeck sees in this is that individual initiative and the entrepreneurial spirit are crushed when information systems are centralized. A study done by his firm "shows that the strategic competitive advantage goes to those who decentralize MIS to make it more consistent with business operating strategies." Despite these benefits, he said, the trend in American business in general, and IS in particular, is clearly toward consolidation. "I have an inherent fear of centralization, that it's a euphemism for building up the bureaucracy," he said. "How do you measure the productivity lost when you centralize . . . ? At a time when childlike inquiry is essential, we're diluting the individual's passion and individual and group accountability. . . . When we talk about centralization we forget – in search of the almighty dollar sign – about the individual. It has an extremely negative effect on an MIS professional's vision, communications skills, entrepreneurial focus and judgment."

Kubeck also assailed the conventional wisdom that centralization brings about cost-cutting. "There's a school of thought that believes that keeping things central can cut costs, but I have not seen one iota of evidence to lead me to believe that centralized systems can save money," he said. "People can juggle the numbers any way they want."

Not all consultants in the field agree with Kubeck that information systems are being increasingly centralized. Irene Nesbit, president of Nesbit Systems Inc. in Princeton, N.J., said that "there is a corporate trend toward decentralization [of IS]; it's just the nature of the business today where you have many offices spread all over the country." In addition, more powerful personal computers and mini-computers have been developed that lend themselves to decentralized uses.

And while Nesbit agrees that decentralization is a worthy goal, she does see one possible drawback to it – "If you hand over [information systems] budgets to the divisions, they will always buy small machines, while centralized MIS will buy heavy-duty machines like mainframes and big lasers."

While such expensive machinery is not suited for every task, she said, there are some jobs that only they can do, and for which less-expensive computer equipment is not adequate.

when centralization may be necessary. "If you need to quickly turn around an organization and you have a newly focused market strategy, you may need to centralize" as a way of instilling efficiency in a diversified company, he said. And even companies that have decentralized, such as Pillsbury, may at times need to centralize again.

"It's relatively expensive to decentralize, for a large company such as us, because when you do it you build in redundant [computing] capacity with many data centers and staff. So you have to re-examine the reasons for decentralization. You have to ask, are there certain pieces—such as telecommunications—which you should bring back" to a central department as a way to cut costs.

"The systems world is caught in a crossfire of schizophrenic forces," he said. "Businesses need systems to have more of an impact, and so there's a strong force for decentralization. But almost all businesses face competitive pressures and are forced to cut costs, and so there are forces for cost-containment" and centralization as well.

In general, Hammitt said that the movement between centralization and decentralization is much like a pendulum swinging back and forth, and that "there will be a constant swinging; I don't think the pendulum ever stops moving. It's like the forces at work in the last 50 to 75 years of industrial history, with companies moving back and forth between the two. . . . We'll see the same thing in the systems world."

And in this constantly shifting world, he has one major piece of advice for others in a similar position: "The one lesson learned is that you must be more comfortable in an ambiguous world and be comfortable with change."

David Steele, manager of planning and technology for the Chevron Information Technology Company in San Ramon, Calif., has seen a shift at Chevron equal in magnitude to the one that occurred at Pillsbury—except that the movement went in the opposite direction. Chevron has been consolidating its resources by closing decentralized data centers since the early- to mid-1970s and is continuing the shift even today.

By the beginning of the 1970s, Steele said, Chevron had 18 or 19 data centers. By the end of the decade and the first wave of consolidation, that number had shrunk to six—four in the United States and two abroad. Chevron is now in the midst of its second wave of centralization, he said, and those six major centers will be reduced to two large centers and two very-scaled-down centers.

The reason for it all is simple economics. By concentrating resources in central locations and departments rather than having them spread across the country, "there are tremendous economies of scale and a tremendous productivity increase," Steele said. "We centralized for cost reduction, and to get central control over our information systems." This newest wave of centralization will mean a seven percent decrease in manpower, he said. "The biggest single benefit in it has been a reduction in the cost of doing business."

The move to consolidate, however, has not been without its pain. "There was a fair amount of user dissatisfaction" with the move, Steele said. "But it didn't get too bad, because our company has a history of central control," and so centralization fitted in very well with the existing company culture.

That fit may have been a key to success. The most recent move toward tighter centralization, which was initiated early this year, came neither solely from above nor from within MIS. Instead, a task force interviewed members of Chevron's business units on the pros and cons of further centralization. The results showed companywide interest in pursuing this option in more detail. Five study teams were then set up, with representatives from across the company (Steele was the IS rep on both the task force and the study teams). The study teams recommended a schedule and action plan for consolidation to top management, which approved the plan in May. Consolidation is now ongoing and should be completed by the end of the year.

In centralizing, Steele sees a chance for those who run information systems to do more than cut costs—they can also more easily create computer systems that will be used as strategic business tools. "A long time ago we realized information technology was a productivity tool as well as a strategic tool," he said. In having those tools in one central location, a kind of critical mass can be reached for creating even more useful applications.

For other managers going through a similar process, he had one primary piece of advice: "Our ability to consolidate was made possible by the use of strong standards and the global nature of the systems we were putting together. Because of this it was easier to move the workloads [from local data centers to central data centers]. Uniformity and strong standards are the key."

Even companies that opt strongly for one path or the other recognize that there are benefits to the alternate route as well. As a result, some corporations have attempted to take the best from both worlds. One such firm is the Corning Glass Works, in Corning, N.Y.

Harvey Shrednick, Corning's vice president of information services, said that while the company chose to centralize its resources, he determined that the only way it would work was if there were some way to maintain heavy local input into the control of the information systems. While centralizing may help cut costs, he noted, decentralized control may mean a greater responsiveness to local needs.

To nurture that local responsiveness, he came up with what he calls the "relationship manager" concept. Each local site has a manager whose job is to build a working relationship between the local business and the central information-systems people. The relationship manager, who has a staff of several people, helps develop a local information strategy, which is then implemented by the central office. In this way, central control is maintained over the systems (since the relationship manager reports to Shrednick), but there is a great deal of local input into the development of information strategy.

"The object is to manage the relationship rather than the technology," Shrednick said.

The centralization plan began a year and a half ago. The decision, as is often the case, was largely a matter of money, though Shrednick said that the issue of the quality of the information systems entered into it as well. Centralizing "allowed us to concentrate on sharable, quality systems at lower costs," he said. The strategy led to a 15 percent personnel decrease within the IS function companywide.

Prior to centralization, the central information systems organization had control over things such as corporatewide systems and telecommunications, but the business units had their own data centers and information systems staffs. "I sort of managed [local data-center personnel] on a dotted line," Shrednick said. "In reality, all I could do was influence and coerce them—carry a soft stick, so to speak."

Before centralization, it was often necessary for IS to resort to political maneuvering to get the job done. All in all, it was then "quasi-centralized, sort of halfway between the two." Shrednick did a study of what should be done and recommended a centralized approach, which was accepted by top management. But a recommendation is one thing, and putting a plan into effect is another, especially when it could be perceived by local people that their control and authority were being usurped.

To guard against that, a team approach to centralization was followed. "We didn't do it by fiat," Shrednick said. People in the divisions worked together with Shrednick's staff to create the new organization, focusing on the idea of the "relationship manager." In this way "we were able to centralize while still involving people at the local level," he said. "Rather than make it a takeover, I took the best of the division information system people and blended them with my staff so they weren't made to feel subordinate. It's not like we were conquerors."

A great deal of Shrednick's work was in "changing a culture," he said. A key to making it work was involving local people, "because then they buy into it." In the long run, he said, the plan will only work if "your people are an integral part of the business. The information system plan must be integrated into the business plan. There must be a direct link between the overall business strategy and the way you achieve it."

Another company attempting to blend the two approaches is the Quaker Oats Company of Chicago. Ron Brzezinski, vice president of information systems at Quaker Oats, has seen the pendulum swing more than once in the last three and a half years. Before that, the company was strongly centralized. Then it moved toward decentralization. Now it is moving again—this time modestly back in the direction of centralization. This constant movement between the two poles, he believes, is inevitable. "There's no right answer" as to which approach to use, he said. Rather, "the smart approach is to use a combination of the two."

Quaker Oats decentralized by moving minicomputers and desktop computers into remote locations. A degree of central control was maintained, however, since the standards for computer use and the direction it would take was dictated centrally. In Brzezinski's words, the company has "central direction, but decentralized location."

While there were many benefits from the move, there were also a few problems, particularly with a duplication of effort. So now the company is looking at pulling back a bit, and moving toward regaining a degree of centralization. "We're adjusting now because maybe we moved too fast" to decentralize, Brzezinski said. "But because of the importance of applications to the business, we wanted people in the businesses managing them. . . . Maybe we went too fast, but it accelerated the learning curve of how to do this. Had we not done what we did, we wouldn't have the knowledge and involvement of the client community which we now have.

"The importance of computing in most businesses has significantly increased in the last 10 years," he continued. "Ten years ago [computers] were used for record keeping; today they're an integral part of the decision-making process. . . . A need to weave computers into the business dictates a blending of the two approaches."

In the long run, said Brzezinski, hardware and software will be decentralized because the technology is moving in that direction. The advent of personal computers, local area networks and easier-to-use software makes decentralization possible, whereas years ago it may not have been. But he is not so clear on where the data itself will reside. On the one hand, data integrity needs to be maintained — which calls for a centralized approach. On the other hand, business units need instant access to that data — which means a more decentralized system.

But not knowing all the answers right away doesn't bother Brzezinski. In fact, if there is a single "answer" that he and the others interviewed agree on, it is that one must be constantly open to change. "Businesses are dynamic organizations, and it would be foolish to think that applications should not be as dynamic," he concluded.

In other words, the pendulum will keep swinging.

37

Leaving the IS Mothership

Kay Lewis Redditt and
Thomas M. Lodahl

Increasing pressure for systems that deliver competitive advantage is driving many companies toward "dispersed computing"—transferring control over computing resources to the hands of business unit managers.

For the first time, forces beyond the control of IS managers and professionals are fundamentally changing the role and the organizational structure of IS. External market forces require a continual jockeying for market share—through either real or perceived product or service advantages created or supported by IS systems. For a company in this market position, business-unit performance depends heavily on IS capability and responsiveness, and business-unit managers are demanding control over their own IS support.

In these companies, pragmatic business forces are pitted against the traditional IS professional fortress. The CIO's job is to mediate this struggle, translating for both sides and choosing moves for the overall good of the organization. With dispersion, as with most other IS strategies, it is possible to both go too far and go about it improperly. For example:

- Three years ago a large natural resources conglomerate began dispersing a major portion of its IS professionals into the business units. Within a year some of the business units had lost 50 percent of the dispersed professionals, who felt their careers were foreshortened or severely capped due to diminished opportunity for advancement.

- Ten years ago a large bank holding company dispersed almost all of its central IS functions. Four years later chaos caused by the proliferation of technology led the bank to re-establish central control of technology standards. Two years ago the necessity of integrating product services among all banks drove it to re-establish central control over data architecture and systems design standards as well.

Pressure for dispersion is mounting in companies where IS systems are essential for meeting competitive challenges or everyday operations. What should the CIO in such companies worry about? What should other senior managers know as they consider IS dispersion strategies? Where are some of the pitfalls, and how can they be avoided?

This article is based on a study of 20 companies that volunteered for our research. These companies ranged in size from $100 million to $10 billion in annual sales. Degrees of dispersion were measured by what organization levels had the most influence over various IS activities: The lower the organization level having the most influence, the more dispersion. Seven companies had at least one business unit where the most influence was at or below the departmental level; these were termed "high dispersion" companies. Detailed interview follow-ups with these seven companies helped to identify organizational problems and solutions in their combined 24 business units. These were then compared with data from a total of 24 business units in the 13 low-dispersion companies.

Before discussing what dispersion is, it should be made clear what it is not: IS dispersion is not the same as decentralization, which usually means taking the central IS fortress and replicating it as smaller fortresses in the separate divisions; decentralization may move formal control to a smaller unit, but the unit remains centralized. Nor is dispersion the same as distributed computing, which usually means networking processor power and peripherals out to users while IS retains central control of applications and architecture. It is also not the same as end-user computing, which generally refers to non-shared ad hoc applications developed by users on stand-alone systems or terminals.

What dispersion is, is the devolution of influence over IS activities, computer power and applications to user organizations. As technology consultant Joseph Izzo put it in his book, *The Embattled Fortress:* "[U]ser organizations can employ a dispersed computing technology in precisely the way it is best for them: creating their own systems, designing their own databases or setting task priorities to suit themselves."

The study found three main driving forces for dispersion: industry and company pressure for competitive systems, increasing availability of and familiarity with powerful desktop systems, and economic pressures to reduce IS expenses. Pressure for competitive-advantage systems is the most important of the three forces. Measured on a scale of 10, pressure for competitive-advantage systems was much higher in the high-dispersion companies than in low-dispersion companies. The high-dispersion companies were mainly in highly competitive industries such as pharmaceuticals, petroleum, high technology and financial services.

No matter where they are located or who uses them, business-critical information systems still require professional IS competence and management. So, both during and after dispersion, there is a role for the CIO to play. The problem for the CIO is how to ensure good management of IS in the dispersed environment. In passing influence over IS to the business unit, the CIO must decide what functions to pass on, whom to give them to and how quickly to make the transition. Many respondents were at a loss on these issues since there is no established body of knowledge on dispersion and since they are now immersed in improvising their own solutions.

One said he wakes up with "knots in his stomach" thinking about it. Managers fear that in giving up power to users, they lose the ability to enforce standards that ensure good IS work: clean code, good documentation, correct data and database architectures. And in the event of a major application disaster, IS people often feel they will still be held responsible.

On the business side, PCs and off-the-shelf software have somewhat demystified the technology black box and made some business managers sophisticated users. However, most business managers are not knowledgeable about technology capabilities, systems programming standards and management of IS professionals. One business manager in the study asked that the IS professionals dispersed into his organization be ". . . taken back by central IS because they are too difficult to manage."

For the CIO, there are two key issues here. One is to ensure that senior management understands the risks of dispersion and is willing to help in preparing for the transition. The other is to ensure that managers in the receiving organization are ready to accept this responsibility, and that they know what it entails. A great deal of education and readiness work is needed for both IS and business management. But when this is handled well and the overall environment is favorable, the CIO can actually gain influence and effectiveness while giving up formal power and control.

The basic culture of an organization is the key variable in managing the transition to a dispersed IS environment. The easiest transition is in companies with a decentralized organizational structure, a history of developing or "home-growing" their own professionals and managers, and a preference for hiring generalists straight from college (see Table 37.1). It is more difficult for companies with a centralized organizational structure, and for those that hire professionals and managers from the traditional markets to fill open positions.

A company with a decentralized organizational structure has, by and large, already struggled with the territorial issues around the distribution of power. Companies that have a centralized organizational structure are more likely to have a "kingdom culture" (particularly in the IS organization), where the redistribution of power will be a new and difficult struggle. In the words of one of the respondents, "If an organization with a kingdom culture is committed to dispersing IS resources, the IS king won't survive."

The CIO facing dispersion needs to assess his company's basic organizational culture before making the transition. Knowing that kings won't survive in the dispersed world, CIOs emerging from a kingdom culture can carve out for themselves productive roles of a more collaborative, less "kingly," nature. People with good business and interpersonal skills are needed to manage both the transition period and the ongoing dispersed IS environment.

There are two very different types of cultures for developing managers and professionals: one that is primarily technical and one that is primarily generalist in its emphasis. In the generalist-development culture, individuals with a predominantly generalist college background who seek a career with the company are hired at entry-level positions and moved among many jobs and different physical and reporting locations for a period of years before a specific career ladder is chosen. In these cultures, IS is one of the accepted entry-level positions.

Table 37.1

Organizational Characteristics

Various conditions can make the dispersion process either easier or more difficult.

Conditions	Easier to Disperse	More Difficult to Disperse
Source of Professionals and Managers	Homegrown	Traditional Markets
Type of Recruits	Generalists	Technologists
Source of Recruits	College	Traditional Markets
Organization Culture	Decentralized	Centralized
Length of IS Dispersion Process	8–10 Years	Now
Depth of Dispersion in Organization	Below Department	Business Unit
IS Turnover Response to Dispersion	Low	High

In the technical-development culture, managers and professionals come largely from traditional labor markets. These cultures tend to hire employees to fill higher-level positions based on their experience and technological skills. The company's development expectations and reward structures support a continuing refinement of their existing skill set. For IS recruits, this means a career path within the IS organization. Consequently, movement to positions reporting or physically located outside of the IS organizational structure is perceived as a failure at worst and an obstacle to career advancement at best. Such professionals have experienced a tougher time managing IS dispersion.

Once the CIO has assessed the IS development culture, he or she can identify individuals who have a broad base of experience in the organization, and prepare them well for the transition to the dispersed environment. Those with very technically oriented development experiences might better be retained to deal with key central issues such as architecture and standards. Those who fit neither requirement may not survive the transition, and would be better off moving to a more traditional setting in another company.

The dispersion of IS resources creates tough career dilemmas for IS managers and professionals. Managers fear they will lose power and make serious mistakes in coping with this trend, and professionals find their career mobility blocked and old career paths gone. Both must cope with strong new demands for business skills. The dispersed IS professionals are cut off from much of the central IS support infrastructure, such as human resources and professional development. In some dispersed environments there is a chaotic situation with inconsistent job descriptions and pay scales for IS professionals in the business units, which can lead to piracy of good people from one unit to another.

In highly dispersed companies, most systems-development activity takes place at the business-unit level of the organization or lower, with more than half of the IS professionals located in and reporting to these levels (though some still have a dotted-line relationship to central IS). Relocation to lower organizational levels means that the professional's career cap is lower (there aren't as many rungs on the ladder), and they have to learn new business skills and jargon. IS professionals are coming into a situation that calls for a broader base of skills. In effect, they have to learn a second profession—they are required to be not only technically proficient, but literate in business.

Training is a critical element in establishing a bridge to this new "business analyst" role. Many high-dispersion companies, finding that they can't provide the necessary variety of training to produce these hybrids, are turning to outsiders for training on business concepts and knowledge, communication and consulting skills. However, this market is not yet as well-developed as that offering traditional IS skill training.

These problems require extensive attention from human-resources professionals before and during the transition. Yet in most cases, the dispersed IS professional is cut off from human-resources support knowledgeable about the ongoing special needs of technical professionals. The transition problems are not addressed by the business-unit human-resources support group, which sometimes considers the IS professional to be a prima donna.

Thus it is up to the CIO to arrange for orderly new career pathways between IS and business, and to communicate to the IS staff before the transition the opportunity to augment purely technical with business expertise. This also requires careful planning of career pathing, career development, common job descriptions and pay scales—which means getting more human-resources support, not less.

Skill requirements for the IS professional have expanded to the extent that one company informally applied the term "Renaissance Man" to describe the person they are seeking. This remarkable person has a good general knowledge of business; good communication, technical and creative skills; and an aptitude for management. Finding such people is difficult, but they do exist in most organizations, having grown by chance through a succession of both business and IS positions. The challenge to the CIO facing dispersion is how to find and nurture such people, who may not be fully appreciated by either business or professional IS communities.

Recruiting criteria have also changed dramatically for highly dispersed companies. Such organizations, recruiting from the traditional IS labor market, seek individuals who have worked closely with business professionals. However, most are finding it difficult, if not impossible, to find such individuals in the market and are now recruiting directly at the bachelor's degree level from college campuses as well as "home-growing" their own IS professionals. These companies are gradually abandoning the highly technical computer departments and recruiting from computer-science departments that stress strong business content. Some are even recruiting primarily from business programs, finding it easier to teach technical skills to business graduates than business skills to the IS professional.

In addition to the complex human-resources challenges, there are systems issues to consider as well when implementing a dispersed approach. Both types of issues were mentioned among the hard-learned lessons of companies that judged in retrospect that they had gone "too far" in their dispersion efforts:

- Systems that cut across organizational boundaries, lines of business or profit centers must retain integration capability—some might say "interoperability." This normally means that they employ a common data architecture and networking capability. Most companies today face a chaotic situation in both arenas, with a mix of old and newer existing software and with IBM's Systems Application Architecture—which will require extensive revision of existing applications—coming around the corner. At a minimum, systems must be built in such a way as to enable eventual integration.

- Someone must perform a strong IS oversight role. Standards for maintainability and system documentation of business-critical systems must be promulgated, bought into by user units and regularly audited. It is not enough for the IS function to say, "It's their responsibility now. I'll wait for them to come to me."

- With dispersion, there is a clear risk of seepage out of the IS professional pool into business units; with this seepage could come a gradual lowering of the level of technical skill in the pool. A case can be made for some central oversight of the pool by IS management, with an eye to managing career paths, identifying extraordinary talent and maintaining appropriate menus of training options. In many companies, such a function would also manage outside contracting for large temporary projects.

- Mainframes have not disappeared in most high-dispersion companies. They are still used as development environments (perhaps inappropriately) and as utilities for large databases and high processing volumes. And they are still run by a centralized "operations" group.

Finally, there is a potential for a "pendulum effect" between dispersion and reconsolidation, much like the old "centralization-decentralization" pendulum. However, this can be avoided if the dispersion process is managed well. The trick is to move at the right pace and make the right moves at the right time. The key issues are: what to disperse, to whom, at what pace and with what sort of preparation for which players. The answers depend heavily on the culture and the unique circumstances in a particular company.

Organizations that are dispersed or in the process of dispersing won't tell you the goal is easy to achieve. But the companies surveyed indicated that they saw dispersion as the only alternative for competitive survival. The human-resources implications raised by this study are clearly food for thought, but more work is needed on other outcomes of dispersion, especially on its effectiveness in giving users what they need.

38

Managing Information Technology: Just Whose Responsibility Is It?

Andrew C. Boynton,

Gerry C. Jacobs, and

Robert W. Zmud

There is increased dispersion of information technology related management respon-sibilities to line managers. If properly managed this dispersion will enable a firm to best take advantage of information technology resources by placing management responsibilities for their use directly in the hands of those that know the business the best—the line managers. To effectively manage this dispersion, devising and negotiating an effective information technology management architecture is a criti-cal issue for senior managers wishing to position their firms to exploit opportunities through effective use of information technology. In this paper, we propose an ap-proach with which a firm can craft an effective information technology management architecture.

Devising and negotiating an effective information technology (IT) management strategy is a critical issue for senior general managers wishing to position their firms to exploit opportunities through the effective use of information technologies. It is also perhaps the single biggest issue facing senior information-systems managers today. The important, and common, question being asked by senior managers in many firms is:

> How should we, given our company's strategy and culture and the limitations im-posed by our skill and IT resource base, organize the management of IT resources?

Because of the importance of IT resources to many firms' competitive positions, establishing an effective IT management strategy is a policy issue that must be care-fully analyzed by senior management. To design and implement quick-fix solutions that follow simplistic battle cries for decentralization or centralization should be ignored. Our experiences with firms indicate that today's effective practices aimed at managing IT resources resemble neither centralized nor decentralized patterns of responsibilities, but rather a shared alignment of IT-management responsibilities carefully crafted to be appropriate for the firm. To determine the appropriate alignment for a firm, what is needed is an approach that is built upon an understanding of a company's administrative heritage, strategic thrusts, internal operations, technological resources, and managers' requirements for information.

THE RISE IN DISPERSAL OF IT MANAGEMENT RESPONSIBILITIES

Whether in response to line managers' demands for control of IT resources or in anticipation of such demands, there is an increased dispersion of IT-related management responsibilities to line managers (Gerrity & Rockart, 1986; Keen, 1985, Rockart, 1988; Zmud, Boynton, and Jacobs, 1986). The question managers are asking recognizes the fact that operating business units in many firms are assuming increasing responsibility for planning, building, and running the information systems that affect their operations and strategies. In particular, line managers are "taking charge" of the identification, design, and implementation of non-trivial information systems (Rockart, 1988). To carry out their new role effectively, line managers are pinpointing valuable opportunities for applying IT resources and actively leading efforts to conceptualize and implement information systems. In short, line managers are, de facto, taking on an increasing proportion of the IT-related management responsibilities required to identify successfully and then implement important information systems.

Factors Underlying the Dispersal of IT Management

Five factors associated with technological developments and related issues explain much of the dispersal of IT resources and IT-related management responsibilities. While the relative importance of each force varies among firms of different sizes, industries, and competitive postures, we believe that these forces are increasing in strength and irreversible in effect.

Technological forces have dramatically improved the capabilities (speed, capacity, ease of use) and significantly reduced the costs of IT resources. What was yesterday's mainframe computer is today's microcomputer-based workstation. Under these conditions, IT resources are less and less viewed as the domain of technical specialists; rather, they are considered core business resources to be applied and leveraged much in the same way as a firm's financial and human resources. This technological force is the single most important factor pushing the dispersion of IT. Simply put, as technological capabilities increase and costs decrease, dispersion will occur, because powerful ITs can be acquired at a cost that falls within many line managers' discretionary budgets.

Second, the explosion of information regarding the benefits of IT throughout the popular press, as well as the incorporation of IT courses within most executive education programs, has heightened IT literacy at all management levels. The result is a surging demand for IT capabilities by managers on all levels.

A third force is the demand for more applications, which is exacerbating the backlog that exists in many central operations for building new and maintaining existing information systems. When a line manager, after recognizing a critical information system opportunity, is informed that it will be one or two years before the application can be delivered, he or she no longer waits patiently. Facing such an intolerable situation and with less expensive, more powerful IT resources available, the line manager is likely to do what any effective manager is expected to do in such circumstance—"take charge" and acquire the needed IT resources to deliver the system in a timely fashion.

Fourth, advances in our abilities to operate IT resources remotely have also propelled dispersion of information technologies. The merging of computer and telecommunication resources has enabled non-trivial information systems to be managed locally within business units or remotely at customer or supplier locations. In addition, the management of technical computer operations (i.e., error checking, reliability and performance monitoring, and maintenance) no longer requires personnel to be located at the computer's physical location. Line managers can accept the responsibilities of dispersed IT management without bearing the overhead of maintaining redundant technical specialists. If remote operation was not possible, many firms simply could not recruit sufficient technical specialists to maintain IT resources located within line operations.

Fifth is a factor not specifically related to information technology. The U.S. business community has been attempting to become more responsive to the market by decentralizing decision making in an effort to get "closer to the customer." The driving down of profit centers to lower and lower levels in the firm illustrates this trend. As responsibility for managing other resources has been distributed in a decentralized fashion, so has the management of IT resources. As Exhibit 38.1 illustrates, regardless of a company's particular structure, the dispersion of IT management responsibilities can be carried out at any level within the firm.

Benefits and Drawbacks from Managed Dispersion

The appropriate distribution of IT management responsibility to functional managers is the best, and perhaps the only, way to link IT consistently to a firm's day-to-day core business activities. The link is unlikely to occur if an organization's central information systems function dominates the management of IT for at least two reasons.

In firms whose IT resources are the principal responsibility of and managed by a central information systems function, line managers are placing the fate of their operations, and their professional careers, in the hands of others. Under these conditions, line managers resist relying on IT resources that they neither control nor, most likely, fully understand. Due to the increasing importance of IT resources to most operating units' success, we believe that functional managers will increasingly (and appropriately) resist this extreme dependence on a central information systems

Exhibit 38.1

The Dispersion of IT Management (ITM)
Responsibilities in Different Company Structures

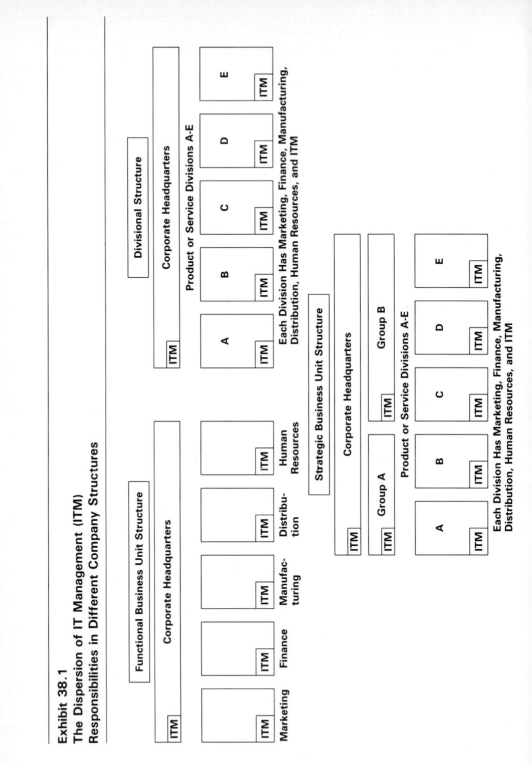

function, even if the information systems staff has been responsive to their needs in the past. The benefit of dispersion is that functional managers are given increased responsibility over the use of those technologies required to plan for, build, and maintain information systems that address business-unit tasks or strategies important in their area.

Second, in the long run, for the great majority of firms, we can find no substitute for merging line managers' in-depth insights into the firm's business processes, strategic direction, and competitive environment with a knowledge of the capabilities and limitations of IT resources. Functional managers' decision making, including strategic decision making, is often driven by opportunities and problems that arise in day-to-day management. By taking responsibility for managing IT resources, the functional managers themselves will dramatically increase their understanding of how these resources can be applied to current business problems and opportunities. Thus the increased responsibility and increased understanding of IT resources will benefit the firm by raising the quality of thinking regarding how and when to apply IT. Line managers, when faced with decisions that must be made quickly, will apply to those decisions those resources they understand and are responsible for managing.

Simply stated, functional managers know the business best. No techniques aimed at bridging the "knowledge" gap between information systems specialists and functional managers can substitute for synergistically uniting these areas of knowledge within a line manager's own understanding. In short, the effective application of IT resources to important business issues can occur best and most consistently when these resources are managed and understood by those who best know the business — functional line managers.

There is a risk, however, in giving line managers sole responsibility for determining how and when IT is to be applied within the firm. Because line managers tend to think short term, steps need to be taken to balance increased line-manager responsibility for managing IT resources with mechanisms to ensure that the long-term deployment of IT resources facilitates and is consistent with the strategic direction of the firm. What is needed is a balanced approach to IT management, where responsibilities for managing IT resources are appropriately shared among a firm's managers. The balance that is required to combine long-term and short-term perspectives can only be obtained by apportioning IT management responsibilities among a firm's managers based on the firm's specific (and, perhaps, unique) information-management requirements.

A PROVEN APPROACH FOR ASSIGNING IT MANAGEMENT RESPONSIBILITIES

A key question remains: how should an organization position itself managerially to achieve that balance? Two critically important issues arise in answering this question: (1) How should the "ownership" of IT responsibilities, as well as the resources required in carrying IT out, be apportioned among information systems and line managers? (2) What are the management responsibilities crucial to effective IT management?

If increased line-manager involvement in IT management is an emerging, beneficial, and perhaps inevitable trend, then a systematic approach to define the appropriate line-manager role is required. The approach we propose has proven to be successful in this regard. Exhibit 38.2 introduces our model by identifying four factors that have vital ramifications for the correct apportionment of IT-management among the different IT-management locations within a firm. The approach we propose calls for a four step process.

The first step is to evaluate the four factors for possible resource sharing across the business units within a firm. Each factor can be evaluated by asking key questions such as those illustrated on the worksheet provided in Table 38.1.

In many instances, we have found that how the questions are answered for a particular firm can be linked to the company's culture, management style, or strategy. For example, a company's strategy may call for strategic business units to act independently of each other, which would mitigate the need to share data across units. On the other hand, a company's strategy might be to have strategic business units access customers through one common distribution or marketing channel. Under those conditions, the need to share data and telecommunication facilities may be significant. The analysis of the four factors would vary in these two cases. Similarly, a company's culture, management style, and structure will drive how the four factors affect the apportionment of IT-management responsibilities.

Second, each of the four factors should be developed into an indicator (which we have labeled horizontal requirement indicator) on a worksheet (see Table 38.1). The composite horizontal requirement indicator is the combined view of the firm's requirement for sharing each resource. For example, if requirements for sharing the resources across business units specified by the four factors are extremely high, IT-management responsibilities should be maintained by a corporate or centralized information systems group. At the other extreme, if requirements for sharing resources across business units are very low, dispersing IT-management responsibilities to lower levels in the company is the appropriate strategy. The horizontal requirement indicator, therefore, is used to reflect the extent to which the need to share IT resources horizontally within a company exists, and a firm's position on the indicator is used to help construct an appropriate IT-management architecture.

Third, the four factors must be studied with two time perspectives in mind: today and 3–5 years into the future. Therefore, horizontal requirement indicators for each factor should be explicitly noted for both time frames. Because of inevitable changes in a firm's competitive environment, strategy, or structure, today's appropriate assignment of responsibility for IT-management is likely to be different from what will be most appropriate in the future.

The first three steps require extensive management involvement. It is critical that different levels of management—senior corporate managers, line managers, and information systems managers—be committed to and involved in evaluating each of the factors. We have found that the different managers often disagree on what are common information needs or requirements to share data among divisions. It is precisely the resolving of this disagreement among managers that leads to successful allocation of responsibilities for key IT-management processes.

Exhibit 38.2
Four Key Factors in Degrees of Resource
Sharing Across the Company's Structure

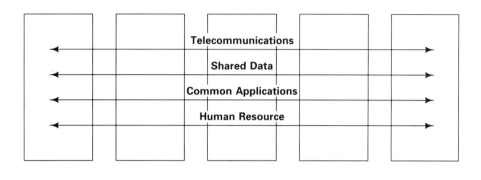

Finally, after the factors have been assessed, the process for assigning IT-management tasks can begin. Recent research has proposed several approaches to conceptualizing the IT-management processes that must occur for effective use of information technology (Allen, 1982; Cash, McFarlan, & McKenny, 1988; La Belle & Nyce, 1987; Rockart, 1988; Zmud, Boynton, & Jacobs, 1987, 1988). Drawing from this research and our own experience, we identify five key IT-management processes that must be given clearly defined management responsibility within a firm (see Table 38.2).

Each IT-management process must be viewed along two dimensions: (1) a "container" and (2) the container's "content." The container represents management responsibilities for how the IT-management process will be carried out within the firm. The content represents management responsibilities for what gets done with respect to each process. For example, consider a typical firm's budget process. That budget process is usually "owned" by the financial function, which determines when the budget is to be done, how often it is updated, what information goes in, and the format of that information. The financial function is responsible for communicating the correct process to each business unit. That aspect of the budget process, how it gets done, is conceptually analogous to container responsibilities. The financial organization, responsible for the container, is responsible for the quality of the budgeting process. The content in the budget-management process is supplied by each business unit, which is responsible for the quality of its input.

The identification and clear assignment of management responsibility by both container and content is key to successful IT balance—especially when dealing with IT that affects multiple business units within a firm. An analogy would be assigning shared management responsibility for the setting of strategic direction among different

Table 38.1
Worksheet for Evaluating the Four Factors and Assessing a Company's Position on the Horizontal Requirement Indicators

Telecommunications

Q1. To What Degree Do Any of Our Business Units Require Telecommunication Capabilities?
- Are there requirements to transport all forms of information: data, voice, video, text, graphics, and image internally or externally?
- Are there requirements to connect business units internally for electronic mail, access to data, etc.?
- Are there requirements to connect business units externally with business partners (i.e., electronic data interchange)?
- Are there requirements to reduce costs by sharing telecommunication resources?

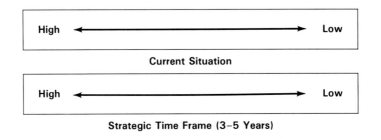

Current Situation

Strategic Time Frame (3–5 Years)

Shared Data

Q2. To What Extent Is Data Shared (e.g., Product, Marketing, Supplier Data) Across Any of Our Business Units?
- Are there requirements for standardized subject data bases?
- Are there requirements to share more than financial data across business functional areas? (i.e., customer, market, product, services, etc.)
- Are there requirements to share data with customers, suppliers, or buyers?

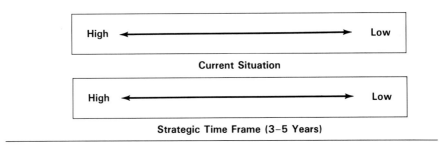

Current Situation

Strategic Time Frame (3–5 Years)

levels of management. Those levels may be corporate and divisional, or strategic business unit and divisional, or divisional and functional. Responsibility for managing the container surrounding the process of strategic direction setting may, for example, require a definition of such tasks as who will participate, how planning results will be communicated, what the planning format and time frame are, what informa-

Table 38.1   (cont.)

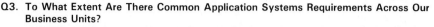

Common Application Systems

Q3. To What Extent Are There Common Application Systems Requirements Across Our Business Units?
- Are there requirements for consistent application architecture? Example; consistent office automation or electronic mail across the firm?
- Are there requirements for standardized presence or image with customers or suppliers?
- Are there requirements for high integration and coordination across business functional areas?
- Are there requirements for business process integration across business functional areas? (i.e., order entry, billing, customer service, etc.)

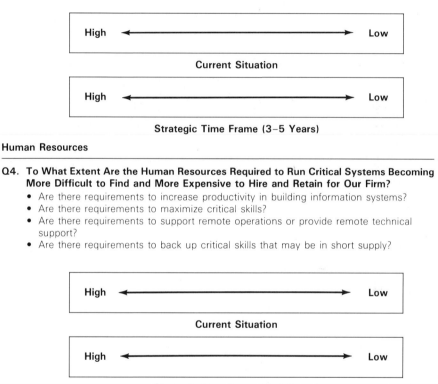

Human Resources

Q4. To What Extent Are the Human Resources Required to Run Critical Systems Becoming More Difficult to Find and More Expensive to Hire and Retain for Our Firm?
- Are there requirements to increase productivity in building information systems?
- Are there requirements to maximize critical skills?
- Are there requirements to support remote operations or provide remote technical support?
- Are there requirements to back up critical skills that may be in short supply?

High ← ──────────────────────────── → Low

Current Situation

High ← ──────────────────────────── → Low

Strategic Time Frame (3–5 Years)

tion is required for planning, how often plans will be updated, modified, or required, and a methodology or approach to resolving conflicts over scarce resources. The strategic planning content may be supplied by each unit within the framework defined by the container. That is, the business-unit manager is to follow the guidelines established by the container while putting in the content to the strategic-planning process.

Table 38.2
Key Information Technology Management Processes

1. **Strategic Direction**

   Responsibility for facilitating broad planning efforts regarding the strategic role of IT.
   —Requires engaging business-unit managers, senior-level managers, and IT professionals in ongoing dialogues aimed at identifying strategic uses of IT.

2. **Infrastructure Systems**

   (If required) Responsibilities for (1) establishing and communicating software and hardware standards, (2) planning, building, and running telecommunications highways with data access and delivery capabilities, including data-base managements (examples include inter-organizational information systems such as EDI or those aimed at channel blocking for "competitive advantage", (3) monitoring, and keeping an inventory of the base of application programs used in firms, and (4) coordinating the development of corporatewide or otherwise shared applications.

3. **Technology Scanning**

   Responsibilities for IT research and development efforts aimed at identifying, assessing, and experimenting.

4. **Technology Transfer**

   Responsibilities for IT-related education, specialized consulting, providing access to expensive, general-purpose IT (i.e., desk-top publishing, high-resolution graphics, data center), establishing and maintaining vendor relationships (i.e., service contracts, volume discounts), and establishing a strong, proactive marketing orientation to help line managers increase their awareness and literacy regarding the effective use of IT.

5. **Business Systems**

   Management responsibilities for planning for, building, and running specific application systems. Requires personnel proficient in systems design methodologies (e.g., life-cycle development approaches and prototyping), high-level programming languages or CASE technologies, business-process modeling, project management and implementation.

These four steps complete the approach that we have found effective in successfully apportioning IT-management responsibilities. The approach does not result in totally centralized or totally decentralized IT-management, but in a mixed or shared apportionment of responsibilities. In addition, because a company's position in the market varies dynamically, the process of apportioning IT-management responsibilities must occur on a regular basis to ensure the IT-management architecture is appropriately aligned with the current and planned strategic posture. Among the firms where we have introduced this approach, the examples provided in Table 38.3 seem to be representative of balanced approaches to IT-management responsibilities.

In these five firms, as in many others, the IT-management strategy that has emerged has resulted in sharing and dividing IT resources in a manner consistent with the strategic direction of the firm.

KEY CONDITIONS FOR SUCCESSFUL BALANCE OF IT-MANAGEMENT

This article has focused on describing the importance of and a process for establishing an effective IT-management strategy. The necessity for such strategies cannot be overemphasized. Key to developing an appropriate strategy is that an effective

Table 38.3
Different IT Management Architectures

Company One — Application Development Management Responsibilities
In a large East Coast insurance company, all application development to support products and services is the responsibility of business functional management. Corporate information systems is responsible for the development of core and common applications that are used by multiple functional units and transcend specific needs of product areas. This allocation of responsibility of the management of IT processes associated with business systems development is consistent with the firm's need for rapid introduction of new products into their marketplace.

Company Two — Human Resource Management Applied to Computer Operations
A large midwestern consumer products company with multiple business units and a heavy emphasis on innovation, based on scarce supply of human resources, has chosen to put mainframes and minicomputers physically into the business units. However, these computers are remotely operated and technically supported by the resources of a central information systems group. This is an example of a firm that has decided to allocate certain management responsibilities for IT processes associated with infrastructure systems to a corporate group because scarce human resources could not be cost-effectively duplicated in each of the firm's business units.

Company Three — Telecommunications Management Architecture
A large Midwestern financial services firm, as part of its overall corporate strategy, had a vision of a telecommunications system that would provide competitive advantage opportunities. The strategy was to have a single information-delivery system for multiple financial products and services. Therefore, a telecommunications utility was planned, built, and is run by corporate information systems' management. Management responsibilities for building business systems that interface with the corporate utility are allocated to business group managers. This is an example of a corporate group being responsible for a single information-delivery system with its economies of scale and standardization to ensure the shareability of data and client support. Using this single utility, business-unit managers are responsible for ensuring the developing of effective application systems that meet their particular strategic thrusts.

Company Four — A Management Architecture for Data Sharing
A West Coast manufacturing firm has a need for extensive data sharing. It has therefore allocated the management responsibilities for planning and building corporate data bases that transcend unique business-unit needs. The functional business managements are responsible for managing the planning and building of divisional or departmental data bases. Although in this firm specific divisional or departmental data does not need to be shared, today the view is that, in the long term, there will be a need to share the data throughout the firm. Therefore, although specific data requirements are determined at the business-unit level, the organization of data into data bases has to conform to the guidelines provided by the corporate information systems group.

---

technology platform must be in place. The technology platform consists of the configuration of hardware, software, personnel and telecommunication resources available for building information systems.

Without this technical platform, allocating management responsibilities for building information systems to line managers, for example, is impossible to carry out successfully. Regardless of the apportionment of IT-management responsibilities, building effective, non-trivial business applications can only occur if a carefully crafted, robust, technological base is in place for each business unit in the firm that hopes to take advantage of using IT resources. The base must allow high levels of data accessibility via well-organized data bases and communication capabilities so that functional departments can access the information they need, in a form they want, and in a timely fashion.

Whether single or multiple technology platforms must be established, operating units (or those management groups assigned responsibility for building information systems) must be provided a rich set of system-development tools and methodologies so that the desired information systems can be delivered to units in a timely, efficient, and cost-effective manner. In short, for the dispersal of IT-management responsibilities that are related to building information systems to be successful, line managers need ready access to appropriate technical resources to get the job done.

Finally, although establishing an IT-management structure must involve both line and information systems managers, responsibility for managing the change must be assigned to a single, high-level manager. This manager must receive the support and resources required to coordinate and bring about successful resolution and implementation of an effective IT-management organization.

CONCLUSION

The model we have proposed is intended to provide a framework for understanding the critical issues in building an appropriate IT-management structure, which inevitably will result in shared management responsibilities among line and central information systems managers. The increased dispersion of IT resources and management responsibilities over IT processes is the result of a number of forces largely beyond the control of any one management team. Moreover, trends indicate that the dispersal is inevitable. This dispersion should not be viewed as either threatening or dysfunctional. If management views it appropriately, it offers the best opportunity for firms to identify and then implement IT solutions that consistently and successfully address crucial business opportunities and threats.

REFERENCES

1. Allen, Brandt, "An Unmanaged Computer Can Stop You Dead," *Harvard Business Review,* November–December 1982, 77–87.

2. Cash, James I., McFarlan, F. Warren, and McKenny, James L., *Corporate Information Systems Management,* Homewood, Illinois: Irwin, 1988.

3. Dearden, John, "The Withering Away of the IS Organization," *Sloan Management Review,* Summer 1987, 87–91.

4. Gerrity, Thomas, and Rockart, John F., "End-User Computing: Are you a Leader or a Laggard?," *Sloan Management Review,* Summer 1986, 25–34.

5. Keen, Peter G.W., "Computers and Managerial Choice, *Organizational Dynamics,* Autumn 1985, 35–49.

6. La Belle, Antoinette, and Nyce, H. Edward, "Whither the IT Organization?," *Sloan Management Review,* Summer 1987, 75–85.

7. Rockart, John F., "The Line Takes the Leadership—IS Management in a Wired Society," *Sloan Management Review,* Summer 1988, 57–64.

8. Zmud, Robert W., Boynton, Andrew C., and Jacobs, Gerry C., "An Examination of Managerial Strategies for Increasing Information Technology," *Proceedings of the Eighth International Conference on Information Systems,* 1987.

9. Zmud, Robert W., Boynton, Andrew C., and Jacobs, Gerry C., "An Information Economy: A New Perspective for Effective Information Systems Management," *Database,* Fall 1988, 17–23.

39

Whither the IT Organization?

Antoinette La Belle and
H. Edward Nyce

One evening several months ago, on a commuter train heading back to the suburbs from New York City, two men who were both information technology managers for Fortune 500 firms happened to be seated next to one another and, in the way of such meetings, began to talk about their work. The conversation was not about hardware or software, not about the dearth of good programmers, nor about the latest news on packet-switching. It was about corporate policy. Organizational development. Strategic direction. Tactics. It was about what may be the most difficult and critical issue facing the information technology manager: how to structure the IT organization.

One of the commuters had been immersed for nearly a year in decentralizing his firm's information technology function. The other had been working just as hard and long managing an IT centralization in his firm. In one forty-minute train ride, the two commuters crystallized a debate—the centralization vs. decentralization debate—that has gone on in corporations for some thirty years, ever since computers first appeared on the corporate scene.

The decentralizing commuter is the coauthor of this article. Left alone to reflect on the conversation for two more stops after the centralizer had disembarked, I came to three realizations: First, that the centralization-decentralization debate is, like the Holy Roman Empire, not properly a debate and not really about centralizing or decentralizing. Second, that there is probably no more pressing or persistent a challenge for the IT manager than this misnamed issue. Third, that resolving the issue requires that skills and resources be brought to bear on a scope of concerns unheard of when I first went to work in information technology management.

In this article, we tell the story of more than a year of effort aimed at changing the way information technology is managed in a major financial services organization, Manufacturers Hanover Corporation (MHC). We believe the story illustrates the critical nature of such a change, as well as what is required to bring it off successfully. The "new" structure for information technology management at Manufacturers Hanover is only the latest in an evolutionary process, and further change will doubtless be required as the corporation's needs develop.

THE ARGUMENT ON THE TRAIN

To centralize or decentralize: Is that really the question? On the train rolling out of the city, our spirited debate revealed some interesting conclusions. I, the decentralizing manager, agreed with many of my companion's reasons for centralizing IT in his firm. And he quickly acceded to my goals and procedures for decentralization at Manufacturers Hanover. We were not, in fact, at cross purposes.

What he called centralization might more aptly be referred to as recentralizaiton. Having decentralized IT management some years before, the firm found that the decentralized applications were unable to communicate among themselves. A certain measure of control had been lost. Decentralization set up roadblocks along the path of data interchange, especially at the level of corporate data. Efforts to redo some major applications had stalled because of integration problems. Senior managers were beginning to feel stifled in their attempts to leverage information technology for competitive advantage. Hence the decision to "take back" some of the authority that had been diffused through decentralization. The issue he was grappling with was precisely what and how much to take back, and how to do it.

In our case, the issue was to decentralize resources to support a major corporate reorganization that gave each sector of our business maximum control of its operations. At the same time, we felt that certain IT responsibilities cut across all business operations, and therefore belonged at the core of the corporation, or were critical to senior management's broad overview of the business. Those responsibilities should remain, in some measure, centralized. The challenge facing our IT organization was—to what measure, and how to make it work.

Not so different, after all, from my fellow commuter's recentralization challenge.

The issue is ill served, we believe, by the label "centralization vs. decentralization." The game isn't tennis; it's a balancing act. Today there is probably no organization of any complexity where information technology management is either wholly centralized or wholly decentralized. The question is how to judge what to centralize and decentralize. Where is the point, somewhere between the centralization pole and the decentralization pole, at which information technology management is effectively meeting the organization's needs? This point will not remain static. As the organization changes, the balancing point will shift, moving up or down to "catch" the weight.

The IT manager's job is to determine the critical equilibrium; to manage up, down, and sideways to get the organization on track; and then to define a process for managing the equilibrium until the need for a new critical point makes itself felt.

Here's how we did it at Manufacturers Hanover.

THE IMPETUS OF CHANGE

On April 19, 1985, Manufacturers Hanover Corporation, the fifth largest commercial banking organization in the United States, announced a major reorganization. Five business sectors were created. Each was to be responsible for its own return on assets and equity, and each was to have direct management control over such support functions as financial reporting, planning, marketing, human resources, and operations. (The five sectors were Asset Based Financing, Banking and International, Corporate Banking, Investment Banking, and Retail Banking.)

"What we have now," said Chairman John McGillicudy, "is both a change in structure—clustering units according to the customer groups served—and a change in management style—decentralizing all management functions into five business sectors including staff and operational support groups. This will give the sector executive and his team control over costs and complete accountability for performance . . . Our new management process will make the corporation more responsive to customer requirements."

For information technology, the charter was to give each of the five newly created business sectors of the corporation "maximum control over all needed resources." Our IT organization had actually been moving toward that goal for some eight years, decentralizing steadily to move resources closer and closer to the end user. The corporate reorganization was simply a dramatic acceleration of IT management's natural evolution.

MHC first turned to computers in the 1960s in a drive to clean up the back office. Our first computers were large mainframe processors for high-volume batch applications. The aim was to cut down on paperwork and streamline processing. The management was entirely centralized, the operation functionally organized.

During the 1970s, on-line applications became preeminent. We were not just meeting processing needs anymore; we were also developing and integrating systems to enhance business operations. Since end-user requirements differed from operation to operation, we dedicated certain data centers to the major business operations. We called them Vertically Integrated Data Centers (VIDCs). For the wholesale business unit, for example, there was a Wholesale VIDC with dedicated computer resources, systems development resources, and transaction processing resources. Another VIDC served the retail business unit. A third served trust and securities. A fourth, Corporate VIDC, served the corporation's internal needs by providing systems such as payroll and personnel. The Corporate VIDC, though, unlike the others, was embedded in a larger organizational unit, Corporate Systems and Staff Services (CS&SS). This unit was additionally responsible for managing what we called "utilities"—such as a global telecommunications network, time sharing, and electronic mail—and was used where economics dictated a centralized, internal provider. Utility usage, though, was not mandated, which made it difficult for CS&SS to maximize ongoing investment and to be a "least cost provider" of service.

During the 1980s, we added tremendously to our total technology capability and expanded our use of technology. This expansion enhanced the corporation's competitive edge. The VIDCs were renamed VIOGs—Vertically Integrated Operating

Groups — to reflect their growth of technological capability and the increasing scope of their activities.

By the mid-1980s, we had gone about as far as we could go on the path of dedicating resources to major business units. The next step would have been to cede total control and accountability for information technology to a unit. From a senior management point of view, there is much in this that is attractive. As John Rockart and Thomas Gerrity have put it: "New product/market opportunities that yield real competitive advantage are generally spotted by professionals and managers who are 'on the firing line' — that is, close up to the markets and products — and who have a practical, working knowledge of new, enabling technologies. . . . Hence, we believe that those firms that seize the opportunity to effectively manage end-user computing are creating capabilities needed to gain the lead in tomorrow's marketplace."[1]

On the other hand, if the technology capability resides in multiple end-user areas, can the corporation-as-a-whole — that amorphous but very real entity — be assured that the technology will be used to its greatest advantage? Will the corporation-as-a-whole be reaping the full rewards of its collective investment? And — how will we know?

We had an answer to those questions, or at least a driving philosophy: While further decentralization or "disaggregation" of computer operations was desirable, it had to be coupled with the realization that technology must both disaggregate responsibility and institutionalize it. Only thus, we reasoned, could technological efficiencies be realized while technological advances were being leveraged against corproate goals.

The question then became: How do you implement this concept? How do you make it work in real life, every day, in an organization embracing thousands of functions, people, responsibilities, tasks, egos, and machines? Then came April, 1985, and the most sweeping organizational change in our history. Suddenly, for IT management, the meter was running.

GETTING STARTED

Our task was to rechart a giant corporation's approach to information technology management. By consensus agreement of the corporation's executive management, this was managed by the Corporate Systems and Staff Services Group. This group had both line and staff experience and had dealt with all business, operational, and technical components of the organization and, therefore, had a good, broad IT perspective.

The authors were intimately involved in the process. Edward Nyce had directed the CS&SS group for eight years and was in charge of redeveloping the IT management function and of implementing the change. Antoinette La Belle was responsible for coordinating the recharting process.

When we first sat down to consider how to organize the assignment, a number of concerns emerged. The first was simply the magnitude of the job before us. How would we deploy resources such as staff, time, and budget? What kind of timetable should we lay out, and what would we be able to deliver when we were finished?

The second concern was the analysis that would form the basis of our IT recharting. We had to begin with a clean slate; nothing, we realized, could be a foregone conclusion. Our direction was to give the new sectors maximum direct control of their support operations. If any centralized IT functions were required, they were to be established and/or maintained at the "essential minimum." We had to remember that "if"—there might not be a strong need for any centralized IT group. Or, if a need could be demonstrated, the benefits might not outweigh the costs. The VIOGs were inclined against any centralization. They were already less than satisfied with their interactions with CS&SS, so they wanted less central control, not more. The corporate reorganization looked like a perfect opportunity to achieve this goal.

This perception on the part of the VIOGs had some substance. During the time they had been growing, the centralized IT management group had been, too. The growth had proceeded rapidly and sometimes without coordination, often without a clear definition of roles and responsibilities. As key staff were brought in, as control of various functions shifted, organizational continuity was diluted. Individual agendas often supplanted, at least in part, the corporate philosophy of checks and balances. Existing checks and balances were often not codified. One example of a tug between the VIOGs and CS&SS was over office automation (OA) technologies. Initially, as OA was emerging, research and technology transfer was handled by a centralized OA unit under CS&SS. Ultimately portions of this function were moved out to the VIOGs, but they believed the move happened later than it should have. The still-centralized portion of research often caused some tripping up and redundancy as the VIOGs moved to extend their own capabilities. It is not surprising that the VIOGs were pushing for even greater automony.

The recharting team was left with a somewhat thorny problem. We had been asked to work out an IT infrastructure that complemented the new sectors. Thus part of the task would be to challenge our own existence. Another part would be to challenge the perceptions of others about our existence. Not an easy task, it was rendered more difficult by being politically charged.

We decided to call in a leading management consulting firm, both because its contribution would lend credibility to the initial analysis and because, while we might focus on the trees, an outsider could be relied on to see the forest. We asked them to assess where our management of it stood—in terms of corporate trends, our competition, and the latest thinking on the subject. Because the consultants had worked with other organizations that had gone through a similar centralization-decentralization evolution, they were able to provide us with models against which to measure ourselves. We wanted to know what lessons had been learned. If they could do it again, would these organizations do anything differently?

A third major concern was the need to create a process for reaching consensus. A new approach to IT management would touch so many areas of the corporation, affect so many people, that the approach would almost surely fail unless its creation included the involvement of those who would feel its impact. We needed to give everyone a stake in the results by ensuring that they participated in the process. It would be time-consuming—especially since the corporate reorganization virtually doubled the number of "stakeholders," as each new sector management team that assumed accountability over its IT function needed to be included. But we were convinced that it was critical to spend the time if we wanted to end up with an effective IT organization. In the end, the time we spent reaching consensus proved to be time well spent indeed.

RESULTS OF THE ANALYSIS

Our consultants helped us to assess our options and to create a model that would support the corporation's strategic goals. Four factors tend to drive the degree of centralization or decentralization of IT functions within an organization: business characteristics—the number of markets in which a firm operates and the environment in which it performs; business strategy—the approach to dealing with its business characteristics; scale economies—the level of affordability of an approach; and organizational maturity—the firm's readiness for either a centralized or decentralized approach. Reviewing Manufacturers Hanover's position and maturity, we jointly formed a premise that some centralization of information technology was necessasry and would complement, not work against, sectorization. But we didn't stop there.

For an independent check, we asked the consultants to evaluate the experiences of the model organizations, which were involved in manufacturing and distribution as well as in financial services. While a broad range of alternatives existed, they agreed that certain areas of IT should indeed remain centralized. And they were relatively consistent about the specific functions that required central management:

- Telecommunications. To ensure cost effectiveness and business coordination.
- Standard Hardware and Operating Software Architecture Methodologies. To ensure systems compatibility across business units, thus enabling staff transfers and data interface while helping to strengthen vendor relations. Applications architecture, however, should be the user's responsibility.
- Information Policy; Data Ownership and Sharing. To assess the need for and manage "corporate" ownership and sharing of data. This was an emerging issue for most models studied, especially given the onslaught of end-user data access.
- Risk Management. To protect the organization in the event of widespread computer failure. Most models used a third-party service or had no formal recovery plan.
- Shared Services. To achieve potential economies of scale and clout with vendors on services that can be shared across business units—for example, technology R&D, contract administration, procurement, and vendor tracking.
- Shared Utilities. To achieve cost economies on facilities that can be shared across business units—timesharing, for example.
- Human Resources. To ensure existence of IT career paths, appropriate compensation, fairness of job grades, rotation, training, etc.

Our own organizational approach already meshed reasonably well with this structure. We had shared utilities for telecommunications, interactive computing, and information center activities. We had established a computer risk management organization and a large contingency processing facility. The corporate personnel department was already coordinating IT human resource issues. We were only beginning to create centralized management philosophies for architecture and data administration, but at least we were on the way.

Our consultants pointed out that companies tend to reach a balance between degrees of central control and decentralized control of information technology resources. Reaching the balance or equilibrium point is rarely a smooth process, but failing to achieve it can invite chaos. As shown in Exhibit 39.1, a high degree of decentralization in an environment that tightly controls resources is perceived as "conflictive." Conversely, a low level of corporate control coupled with little centralized management of resources is perceived as "ineffective." In either case, the result is dysfunction.

When we applied this point to our own situation—where we had come from, where we were at that point, and our goal for the reorganization—we located an ideal equilibrium point, shown in Exhibit 39.1. Doing so provided a conceptual framework for planning and gave our task some sense of scale. It was more than just a useful exercise. It also directed us to the next essential task, designing the new IT management organization that would put us at the critical equilibrium point.

A NEW IT CONSTRUCT

The "equilibrium" model gave us an endpoint on a set of loosely defined coordinates. Our task now was to determine the components of an IT management organization. Once we had created this construct, which would include the functions that the models believed should be handled centrally, we would be in a position to identify which responsibilities should remain centralized and which should be given to end-user organizations.

We analyzed that issue by "breaking it down and building it up again." We looked at the IT organization for our group and for several representative VIOGs and listed all activities that occurred within them. We also looked for gaps—things that should be done but did not seem to be—and added these activities to the list. We rebundled those activities into logical, natural groupings. This synthesis, which was independent of organizational structure, became our working construct. The nine IT management components we arrived at are shown in Exhibit 39.2.

Before attempting to define an appropriate split in responsibilities for each component, we needed to clarify the mission of a centralized IT department. Eventually we reached this conclusion: In a decentralized environment, the central IT group's mission is to ensure the competitive use of technology and to provide cost-effective utilities, while minimizing operational and technical risks and facilitating organizational flexibility.

Exhibit 39.1
Decentralized vs. Centralized Information Technology:
The Essential Equilibrium

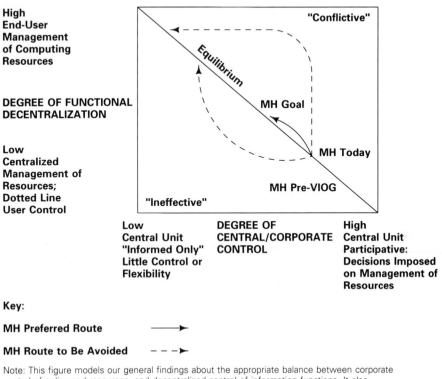

Key:

MH Preferred Route ———►

MH Route to Be Avoided – – –►

Note: This figure models our general findings about the appropriate balance between corporate control of policy and resources, and decentralized control of information functions. It also models Manufacturers Hanover's individual goal.

With that as a premise, we could proceed. Every function within a component that supported this mission belonged under a central umbrella; most belonged with a central IT group. (Exceptions would be human resources and risk.) Everything else belonged with a central IT group. (Exceptions would be human resources and risk.) Everything else belonged to the sector IT groups. Table 39.1 shows a breakdown of one component, Information Technology Architecture Management.

We broke down the remaining eight components following the same procedure. Broadly speaking, Exhibit 39.3 shows how each component is split between a centralized IT organization and sector IT organizations. The functions ceded to the centralized group tend to concern strategic management (technology research and

Exhibit 39.2
Information Technology Management Functions

Strategic

Strategic Planning and Control	**Marketplace Intelligence and Technology Research**	**Architecture Planning**
Establishing the end-point objectives and priorities for systems activities over five-to ten-year periods	Monitoring IT trends among vendors and competition assessing impact on MHC	Developing and maintaining architecture for information systems, databases, hardware, telecommunications, operating systems

Tactical

Resource Planning and Acquisition	**Systems Development**	**Computer and Telecommunications Operations**
Developing tactical plans for systems development, technical and human resources, funding aspects	Acquiring and managing resources necessary for satisfaction of applications needs	Controlling and supporting activities needed for functional data centers, corporate utilities, and end-user computing, and measuring performance of each

Infrastructure

Policy and Standards Management	**Human Resources Management**	**Risk Management**
Formulating, communicating, and monitoring technical, planning, and management standards	Recruiting, developing, and compensating skilled IT personnel, managing the systems associated with these activities	Developing and executing contingency plans—risk assessmant, recovery management, and the like—and managing all facilities dedicated to these activities

planning, standards and policies maintenance, data administration for corporation-wide data) or utility services including internal administrative systems such as payroll.

DESIGNING THE NEW IT ORGANIZATION

We restructured and renamed CS&SS to embody the IT construct philosophy. The group's broadened charter was reflected in its name: MH Information Technology Service (MHITS). Exhibit 39.4 shows the new group's structure.

The utilities were to be organized as two groups: telecommunications, and information systems and support. Neither one underwent any significant structural

Table 39.1
Division of Responsibility: IT Architecture Management

Function	Central IT Group	Sector Operations (VIOG)
• Develop and maintain information architectures	• Monitor process; provide assistance if requested	• Complete business architectures defining business (within sectors) by location • Complete translation of strategy into technology requirements • Define information architecture
• Develop and maintain applications architectures	• Set standards; monitor process • Review architectures and report on adequacy to MH Technology Committee • Ensure appropriate commonality	• Define requirements and develop architecture • Coordinate between sectors for common businesses
• Develop and maintain data architectures	• Coordinate development/ establishment of common database management processes • Create/maintain corporate databases	• Define requirements; develop in accordance with standards
• Develop and maintain hardware/ operating systems architectures	• Monitor development/implementation within sectors • Develop and maintain architecture for corporate users support operations	• Develop in accordance with corporate standards, business requirements • Request variances as appropriate; make change recommendations
• Develop and maintain telecommunications architectures	• Develop in accordance with standards and business requirements	• Define requirements • Report performance/responsiveness problems

Exhibit 39.3
IT Functions: Ideal Degree of Central Control, Sector Control

Strategic

Strategic Planning and Control	Marketplace Intelligence and Technology Research	Architecture Planning

Tactical

Resource Planning and Acquisition	Systems Development	Computer and Telecommunications Operations

Infrastructure

Policy and Standards Management	Human Resources Management	Risk Management

Notes: White areas represent degree of control exerted by central IT management: central Human Resources and Risk Management, though, reside in other parts of MHT.

Shaded areas represent degree of control exerted by sector IT groups (VIOGs).

change. The biggest proposed change was the formation of the Strategic Technology and Research (STAR) group. STAR's mission would be to support IT management through research and direction setting and to ensure that MHC maintained a competitive edge through the use of technology.

Exhibit 39.4
Central IT Management Group Structure

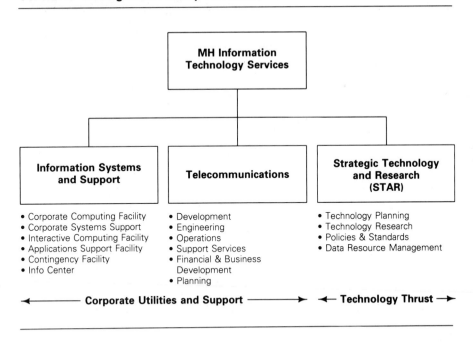

We also recommended a new hierarchical structure for IT management. First, we decided that the existing corporate management committee – made up of the chief executives of all sectors, as well as the corporation's chairman, president, and vice chairmen – should play a more pronounced role in technology decisions. Thus we recommended that their charter be expanded to include reviewing both our major technology planning and our technological competitive position, and approving technological policies.

Beyond this, we recommended the creation of a technology committee made up of the senior sector operations heads, the MHITS director, and the STAR director. This group would review strategy and policy issues, propose items for review by the management committee, and provide a forum for adjudicating technology issues between a sector and MHITS.

We also recommended establishing utility review boards to ensure that utility plans complemented and supported sector priorities, to review services for cost competitiveness, and to evaluate requests for alternative services. The recommended corporate infrastructure for information technology management is pictured in Exhibit 39.5

Exhibit 39.5
Corporatewide IT Management Infrastructure

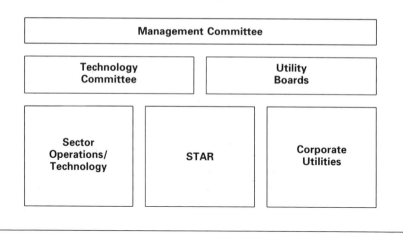

IMPLEMENTATION: GETTING CONCURRENCE

Our work had only just begun. We needed a strategy for the transition, but first we needed concurrence on the construct and infrastructure. We had been careful to touch base with operations staff and sector management throughout the analysis phase; now we wanted to draw these people into a formal review of our recommendations. This was not window-dressing; once the recommendations were accepted, we would invite the participation of these stakeholders throughout implementation.

We met with nearly 100 people to present our analysis and recommendations and to seek input. It took almost three months to do so, one month longer than the actual analysis phase. As a result of the review process, our work was better understood in important quarters of the corporation. We encountered no significant obstacles in the course of this review process, nor did we make any major modifications.

A STRATEGY FOR THE TRANSITION

We saw the transition as falling into two phases. First, we would need to flesh out roles and responsibilities and draft IT policies that would constitute a "code of conduct." Second, we would need to retool the central IT group.

Although the utilities would remain basically unchanged in structure, they would undergo a critical shift in approach: Staff would now "sell" quality service at competitive prices to the sectors. But all other units of the old CS&SS were subject to question. We reviewed twenty-one distinct units, one by one. Given the new mission, would the unit remain unchanged, would it remain but in a new form, or would it be eliminated?

For each unit, we plotted the nature of the change, as well as the timing, rationale, and actions required to implement that change. In addition, we developed interim management processes to create a bridge from the old CS&SS to the new MHITS.

The size of the task boggled our minds until we actually sat down and forced ourselves through it. Staffing emerged as the most difficult issue. We were aware that many of the problems between the VIOGs and the old CS&SS reflected a typical line-group to staff-area challenge. Its predictability, though, did not make it invalid. In order to ensure that MHITS was not seen as "old wine in new bottles," we developed a model of the technical, interpersonal, and consultative skill requirements. Based on that new model, we initiated both an internal and an external search for a STAR director and for other key personnel.

The "people factor" was significant throughout the transition process. Because of the stress created by the major changes, central IT group "churn" was at a high point. Though the broad outlines of the reorganization were generally known, some individuals—managers in particular—feared for their jobs or worried that the scope of their work might be narrowed. We were careful to communicate organizational changes and details when we could. Knowing that many eyes and ears were on us, we tried to be sensitive about what we said, and to whom. But our timetable often did not meet perceived needs for information. In the absence of hard facts, many staff members relied on the office grapevine for news of the reorganization. Rumors took on a life of their own. We tried to contain this problem by keeping an open door and by talking with individuals if they seemed overly concerned. We walked a fine line, though, because we had to deal with their concerns without compromising the reorganization or creating false expectations.

The bottom line in terms of actual impact on positions was this: approximately 25 percent of the positions within the core group were changed. Of those, approximately 5 percent were eliminated, but all the incumbent staff were relocated within the company. The remaining 20 percent of the positions (and respective staff) were either decentralized or moved to other areas of the corporation. Getting through this period, though, was very difficult for the staff.

Deliberate as we had been, the meter was still running; in fact, we now had only four months before the first VIOG was scheduled to move to its sector. In order to make this happen, we had to drive our broad recommendations down to the next level of detail, spelling out exactly how various units would interact.

To do so, we appointed a fulltime transition team of four people drawn from the VIOGs and the central IT group. This transition-team tactic was a new one for the corporation. The point was to ensure that the transition team would not be pulled away by day-to-day operating problems. We needed fulltime attention because the issues—particularly how different units interact—were typically not concrete; they were behaviorial and difficult to chart. Consequently careful codification was required. Without it, the tendency would have been to copy the past.

It was not easy to convince the VIOGs to relinquish talented staff for three months. Our persistence was as determined as was the VIOGs' reluctance. Ultimately, the team was staffed. It produced overview statements defining key philosophies, policies, and detailed roles and responsibilities for each component of the IT construct. To arrive at these, the team worked closely with VIOG operations managers and with central IT utilities managers to achieve agreement on the final statements.

This method put us in a good position to gain agreement on this level of detail. Indeed, the first VIOG moved to its sector on January 1, 1986—eight months after the corporatewide sectorization announcement—with full formal agreement from all participants on the key policies, operating concepts, and roles and responsibilities appropriate to each of the players. This first move was handled more formally than the subsequent ones would be, because it was intended to set the example in tone and content. Ultimately, all remaining moves went reasonably smoothly.

CRITICAL EQUILIBRIUM: THE IT MANAGER'S ROLE

Almost two years after the MHC chairman announced the corporate reorganization, our transition to the new IT construct is still evolving. The charting of roles and responsibilities, defining of policies, and shifts of structure, though complete, are not everything. To take hold, a change of this magnitude requires a change in mindset, which comes about gradually as people begin to work under the new structure and to understand what is expected of them.

Some overt tactics help to reinforce the change—the name change (to create a special identity), group meetings with executives around the corporation to articulate the changes, MBOs tied specifically to aspects of the change, and a program of internal communications reporting on progress, to name a few. But ongoing attention from IT management is perhaps the key ingredient in turning new expectations into well-worn patterns.

The transition process was a learning process, and our experience included some specific insights into the trials and tribulations of technology reorganization. For example:

- The analysis turned out to be the quickest and easiest part of the entire process. Planning and implementation were not easy, especially since we had few guidelines to follow.

- The involvement of those people and areas most affected by a reorganization is fundamental. While we did involve the operations and utility managers, even more of their time would have helped to build greater commitment. Each operations manager was also working on his own reorganization within the new sector during this period. Time priorities often conflicted.

- Staffing in key positions is vital to any major reorganization. We have been successful in this area—both in attracting and retaining some top-notch talent. In retrospect, though, it would have been helpful to bring key people on board sooner than we did.

- And finally, the key to our MHITS reorganization is and will continue to be follow-up. We have specific people and mechanisms to ensure that new patterns of behavior are sustained, supported, and reinforced.

For an IT manager who started out in data processing, managing such a transition is a major eye-opener. For along with the evolution of DP into IT, along with the demise of the centralization vs. decentralization argument and the impetus instead to find the critical equilibrium for effective organization—along with all this is the coming of age of the IT manager.

The IT manager today is—or must learn to be—a strategist. Information technology itself is an increasingly important tool in corporate strategy, and the manager must learn to assume a corporate viewpoint.

By the same token, the day-to-day work of an information technology group is increasingly strategic. More and more, utilities are being asked to lower costs and improve productivity, while IT staff are being asked to help shape a strategic competitive future in application development and product delivery.

Thus the essential tools of the job today are, inevitably, tools of strategy, policy, direction setting—with a major dollop of organizational development and human resources savvy. The IT manager who recognizes and embraces a new role as part of the strategic heart of the corporation becomes integral to its achieving competitive advantage.

NOTES

[1]T.P. Gerrity and J.F. Rockart, "End-User Computing: Are You a Leader or a Laggard?" *Sloan Management Review,* Summer 1986, pp. 25–34.

40

Restructuring Information Systems: The High Road and the Low Road

Brandt Allen and Andrew C. Boynton

Without doubt, information systems in most large corporations and their management must be restructured. The masses of old systems in many companies are both functionally and technologically obsolete for several reasons: the demands for electronic-data interchange (EDI) and other business-to-business links to customers and suppliers require new technical systems and equipment; the lines of responsibility for managing information systems are unclear and in a constant flux; and the technology itself is changing fast. Important as they are, however, reasons for restructuring are not primary. Businesses are overhauling their information systems to survive!

The successful organization of the 1990s will have to be dynamic and adaptive; it must be able to change continuously. Thus the competitive business will need the most flexible IT system it can find. But where are such systems? The reality is that IT has been anything but flexible in the past. IT efforts generally automate the status quo, freezing the organization into patterns of behavior and operations that resolutely resist change. Traditional systems don't bend; they won't change, and they can't adapt. The challenge for business is to break the rules of the past and structure IT to meet a variety of changing information requirements, some of which cannot even be fully known before the systems are built. The decisions managers make today about their IT architecture will determine their organization's ability to respond to environmental challenges and opportunities for many years to come. Organizational transformation and IT redesign are increasingly seen as a single task.

The change must come through revamped IT architecture—that set of policy and rules that govern an organization's actual and planned arrangements of data collection, computers, human resources, communication facilities, software systems, and management responsibilities. Architecture specifies how and why the pieces fit together as they do; where they go, when they're needed, why and how changes will be implemented. IT architecture presents many difficult choices: what data and applications must be companywide, what should be managed locally? What standards should be adopted, or vendors chosen? What rules should govern the decisions? What policies should guide the process?

Trends today suggest a move away from the centralized IT-management approach of the past toward a dispersal of all but the most essential, common or global, computing and telecommunications services. In this dispersed approach, data interchange and intra-company networks are the keys to integration. A decentralization, however, brings great dangers: it can become both the high-cost and least flexible option over the long run. On the other hand, the opposite approach—common systems, shared data collection, and central architectural control—also presents great risks. Thus the question arises: are there other choices? What is the preferred structure for information processing when the organization must continuously change?

THE CASE FOR CONTINUAL CHANGE

Few businesses will be successful in the decade ahead with organization structures that are just a little bit better than what they have now. In the words of Jack Welch, chief executive of General Electric,

> the '90's will be a white-knuckle decade for global business . . . fast . . . exhilarating . . . with sudden failures for many and victory for others.[1]

We can already see examples of far-reaching changes that support Mr. Welch's predictions. They include "fast cycle times," networked organizational structures, strategic business alliances, and a belief that people, not strategy, are the key to business success. Each of these trends places heavy demands on architectural flexibility.

Fast Cycle Time has become a competitive weapon for both manufacturing and service firms (Bower and Hout, 1988). Whether tracking customer attitudes, fine tuning manufacturing cycles, enhancing product design, or billing a customer—those companies that prosper will respond to changing demands and market conditions in an accelerated fashion. Because speed will be a hallmark of competitive success in the 1990s, an IT architecture that can respond rapidly will be a crucial ingredient in achieving "fast" organizations.

Networked Organizational Structures are seen as one key to fast-acting organizations. They depend upon temporary structures such as business teams and open communications channels for their strength and dynamism. The result is more decentralized, autonomous units linked by electronic networks. In this dynamic, network structure (Miles and Snow, 1986), devices other than plans and controls are used to provide the necessary coordination and integration. Such structures depend less on formal planning, coordination, and control mechanisms than on individual contributors and teams working together in a fluid, unstructured, yet harmonious, fashion. Networked organizations require easy access to information and to individuals with knowledge and talent wherever they may be in the corporation. What emerges are adaptive, "dual" organizations; in addition to the core activities of the business in which efficiency and productivity are key a second organization exists where information systems, people, decision processes, and culture are geared toward flexibility and change.

Strategic Alliances among companies will alter the competitive landscape by merging the strengths of various organizations into major roadblocks for competitors. For example, the alliance of EDS, Amdahl, and Anderson Consulting combines competencies in facilities management, computer-system development, and computer-system equipment to pose a direct challenge to IBM. These alliances extend the networked organization form across businesses, enabling organizations to share and increase their research, know-how, designs, people, and processing capacities. The IT architecture alliances use must provide the cross-organizational information "highway" on which cooperation and resource sharing among companies can travel.

Perhaps the most interesting trend we see is the increasing belief in people. The future decade may well be remembered as the decade where businesses discovered the importance to corporate success of every single employee. In a world where access to capital, markets, materials, technology, and information is open to all, where competitive advantage is often short-lived, an organization's distinctive competence will be found in the knowledge and ability of its employees — if the organization is structured to empower its people. Companies that invest in people and support them with a culture of trust and respect will often be more effective organizations than those based on the traditional distinctions of employee-manager-executive. People-based organizations face major IT structural challenges as they struggle to create, accumulate, and disseminate relevant information to empower employees.

These trends, singly and together, point to a need for fundamental restructuring of the organization's IT architecture. The demand is for a degree of flexibility in information processing that we've yet to see in large businesses.

IT ARCHITECTURE AND TECHNICAL TRENDS

Clearly, IT architectures must reflect the most important technology trends, but the direction of technology is not clear. Right now, there are many challenging questions: Will optical fibers win back the communications edge from land lines that satellites won away from copper wire? Will supercomputers and data-base machines edge out distributed processing and local networks? Will CASE (computer-assisted software engineering) methodologies substantially change the human costs of systems? Dozens of such key questions must be addressed by any large organization seeking to restructure its activities.

The best forecasts at the moment seem to be for evolutionary, not revolutionary, change in technology. At the level of architecture planning for a large organization and with a time frame encompassing the next decade, no real technological imperatives can be spotted. The favorable trends in computer processing costs and storage efficiency will probably continue for quite some time. The result will be a continuous spectrum of computing capacities with little if any scale economies. Technically, no compelling arguments can be made to favor large mainframes over distributed, local processing for the computers of the 1990s, or vice versa. In fact, the message from most mainframe and minicomputer vendors is that the products and services they offer today should form the platform for a stable but flexible IT architecture for the next 10 years. The biggest factors driving costs for IT will continue to be people and the growing use of telecommunications. Computer-hardware costs will continue to decline as a portion of the total cost of IT for the firm. In short, technical change will not be the decisive factor for corporations faced with a choice of IT structures.

TOWARD FLEXIBILITY AND EFFICIENCY

While there may be no technology forecasts of sufficient significance to cause an organization to adopt one type of architecture over any other, there are criteria of great importance that must be addressed. One is overall IT efficiency, and the second is flexibility. The former is a concern of long standing and one that will always be with us. The latter challenge is emerging as the critical architectural issue for large organizations in the coming years.

Of all the IT decisions senior managers are asked to make, the choice of IT structure or architecture is clearly the most important. The changing conditions facing organizations in the future will not allow the single, monolithic application system to reap competitive advantage for long. Rather, the key for organizations will be to build IT architectures that can rapidly respond to changing market conditions. Such architectures will provide the foundation for hosts of relatively short-lived systems aimed at yielding competitive advantage. These applications systems will extend from a relatively stable architectural base but be responsive to rapidly changing information requirements facing the organization.

TWO ARCHITECTURAL CHOICES

Which architecture will best achieve the twin goals of efficiency and flexibility? Two quite different solutions have emerged. We call them the "low road" and the "high road." Each scenario has its persuasive rationale, concrete advantages, and distinct weaknesses. Each has its own group of supporters, and many examples can be found of large organizations adopting one or the other approach. Each also has a fatal flaw.

THE LOW ROAD

IT can itself take a dynamic, network form. In this scenario, technology and its management are dispersed widely throughout the firm. IT becomes the responsibility of every operating manager. Data, computers, networks, applications, programming, and all the supporting resources are pushed as far down in the organization as possible. The structure is not just a one-step decentralization beyond the corporate IT organization but dispersion all the way down into the offices, plants, divisions, and subsidiaries of the organization.

Of course, the low road is more than just all-out decentralization; it ties critical units together with data-exchange conventions, inter-linked communications, and a philosophy of full access to information. The concept of "internal EDI" is to insure data exchange and integration. Just as external or electronic-data interchange (or electronic document interchange) is fast on its way to becoming a means of linking companies within an industry or across several industries for high-speed exchange of orders, invoices, payments, inquiries, so also can EDI be used internally. Intracompany or internal EDI uses the same concepts: telecommunications, networks, standardized data definitions, and common format standards. When they have agreed to a common set of standards and definitions for information exchange and have built a corporate network that links and bridges the dispersed work stations and data centers, divisions and headquarter departments linked by a corporate network can exchange product, vendor, customer, personnel, financial, and other types of information.

The policy of full access to information is one that seeks to open rather than restrict, access to data throughout the organization. The philosophy recognizes the need for data sharing by permitting business teams, task forces, and other units to gather information quickly, without having to seek approval through data "owners" or custodians. It is a concept based on trust; it acknowledges that ad hoc groups and special teams are a way of life, not exceptions. It does not mean that any individual in the organization may rummage through the corporate data collections on a whim, but it does mean that the "owners" of various data collections are expected to provide data access and interpretation to a growing array of teams and task forces.

The philosophy of full access presents an interesting challenge to the various organizational units compiling information. They must exercise care to insure the protection of often valuable and sensitive data, while at the same time assuring full access to bona fide data seekers. If low-road scenarios lead to restrictive access to information, the rationale for the dynamic organization will be compromised. The promise of flexibility afforded by the low road is critically dependent on internal EDI and full access to information. It is this uninhibited access to standardized data that is to support business needs.

In the low-road scenario, the role of any central IT organization is to insure the integrity of the internal data definitions and the networking standards and to provide full access. This approach has no room for an organizationally powerful, senior information-systems executive or chief information officer (CIO). Indeed, aside from a process for establishing a minimal set of data definitions and a means for data exchange, there may be no central IT organization at all. Organizations often use a centralized telecommunications-network function, but even this is not necessary. Some large multinationals have already adopted a low-road approach to telecommunications management by decentralizing responsibility for networks to their operating units. The only necessary central role is standard setting; a central means of bridging or linking networks is optional.

The role of standards in the low-road scenario is an important but limited one. Standards insure the integrity of the internal data-exchange process. Beyond that, there is no vital role for guidelines or other limitations over the IT activities of the operating units. In the classic low-road approach, a business unit pursues its IT destiny linked to the corporate parent only by imposed or agreed standards for data exchange and interoperability of networks. Of course, one might find substantial cooperation in IT affairs among business units in software development, purchasing arrangements, personnel management, training, and other activities, but the cooperation is not imposed on the units by some central group.

The low-road philosophy views most corporate technology standards as impediments to progress. Imposed standards for programming languages, data-base management, development methodologies, even computer hardware, are seen as unnecessary and constraining. Such standards only mean "old, outdated, and illsuited to our purposes" to low-road enthusiasts. They deny standards of this kind are necessary for integration or change. They demand to use the latest in technology, the best of the new development tools, and the most appropriate software for their particular application. Their prospects for change and adaptation rest on three elements: minimal data standards, corporatewide networks, and a policy of full access to information.

Many arguments exist for choosing the low road. The approach is considered:

A Natural Solution The dispersed-network structure for IT is a natural fit with many organizational structures. It is a structure that fully capitalizes on the benefits of decentralized responsibility and control. Using the low road, then, implies that data are collected, processed, and stored where they are used, by employees of the business units. Divisions, departments, and other units take responsibility for their own IT. This solution rejects the arguments that there is something "special" about IT, that it can only be managed successfully if managed centrally, or that economics or some other aspect of technology dictate central coordination or a centralized management structure.

Fast Dispersed and networked IT is the key to speedy implementation of new systems and rapid deployment of technology. Centralized solutions take an order of magnitude longer and often don't meet all the local needs.

Innovative The low road leads to innovative use of current technology and the adoption of newly emerging technology. New software, computers, and design and development methods can be adopted as soon as they hit the market. They needn't wait for committees, councils, standards bodies, advisory groups, impact studies from other divisions, or similar bureaucratic processes.

Effective Locally developed systems best meet local needs. In the low-road approach, technical solutions for local needs can be adopted without regard to the needs of other divisions or business groups. If UNIX, or a Sun work station, or a particular software package best meets that unit's needs, then it can be chosen. End of issue!

Efficient   The argument is frequently made that the low road will eventually become the overall low-cost scenario for IT. A networked IT structure capitalizes on the new economics of computing that the low-cost solutions to computing made through minis, micros, LANS, and low-cost software.

Strategic   Managers tend to use whatever resources are at their disposal when faced with market-place challenges or opportunities. If IT is part of their tool kit, it will get used along with the people, money, time, and other resources of the business unit. If IT is not a resource the manager can command, then it simply won't be used to the degree and with the same intensity as otherwise. Substantial evidence indicates that most strategic systems and so-called competitive-advantage applications are not the creations of CIOs or IT managers but are the brainchild of operating managers. Pushing technology control and responsibility far down in the organization is, therefore, much more apt to stimulate creative business-related applications than is vesting its future in a supposedly all-seeing, all-knowing CIO.

Group Oriented   The low road results in an IT architecture that is more supportive of business teams, temporary groups, task forces, and other change agents than is central IT control. Any new group can speedily assemble the technology it needs from the latest and best that is available. The group can collect whatever internal data are needed through open access to internal EDI facilities.

Drawbacks

There are many problems with the concept of dispersed, localized IT united by a common internal EDI. The biggest are:

Efficiency   Despite its proponents' arguments, the low road just can't help being a costly solution to IT structure in the long run. It leads to accumulation of more technology with lower utilization rates, more duplication, more people, more package purchases, more of everything than a centralized approach. Businesses that have adopted the low road strongly suspect that dispersed-technology management is more costly, but the costs are less visible.

Integration   The efforts necessary to link separate business entities' IT activities with each other and with headquarters are complex, no matter how effective the organization's internal networks and data-exchange mechanisms. The United States has many large corporations, especially manufacturing corporations, that have struggled with severe computing and communications problems as they've tried to adopt computer-integrated manufacturing, just-in-time, reduced-time-cycle planning, and other restructurings of operations. General Motors is perhaps the most prominent example of a company in which dispersed IT and an ineffective internal EDI became serious impediments to integration in the early 1980s. Today, many organizations are faced with similar problems as they attempt to participate in industry-wide EDI projects. They may suddenly discover that they can't combine their own customer, parts, or vendor data across the organization because of the myriad local, independent data structures fostered by the low-road scenario.

Integrity   Another casualty of dispersed IT is data integrity. Even under the best circumstances, standardizing and maintaining data or information standards are difficult. Words just don't mean the same thing from one unit to another, and over time, the differences tend to increase in large organizations. It's a bad situation when units of the same organization cannot exchange data without a lot of manual intervention because of missing data standards. It is an even worse situation when they exchange and use data they think has a commonly accepted meaning, but it doesn't.

Internal EDI   Only with a Herculean effort can a large, fast-changing organization actually achieve and maintain an effective internal data-exchange system. Change itself is an enemy here. Many large organizations decentralized a good portion of their IT in the 1980s, or found it becoming dispersed because of acquisitions and organizational restructurings, well before they had a standard set of data definitions. Internal EDI is usually an afterthought. Rarely does a large multi-business, multi-country corporation enjoy a set of core data definitions—one and only one part number for an item throughout the enterprise, for example, or one customer ID, one coding scheme for vendors, even one common general ledger.

Uneven Efforts   Another drawback to the low-road scenario is that it leads to uneven levels of accomplishment throughout the organization and, in time, uneven levels of effort within a single unit. There are inevitably going to be business segments that fall way behind in the deployment of IT.

Short-Run Focus   The planning horizons of operating managers are frequently much shorter than what executive officers, board members, and informed shareholders would like. Information system projects can have the longest lead times of any projects in an operating unit. It is sad but true that, in many companies today, a new plant can be built and a new product launched faster than the IT group can build the systems to support the new business. Infrastructure building such as IT projects often don't get the attention they should from local operating managers, who are under pressure to achieve immediate results.

The Fatal Flaw with the Low-Road Scenario

The biggest drawback of all, and the real risk in the low-road scenario, is simply that it may not work! Five or ten years from now, organizations that enthusiastically adopted this direction may discover to their horror that the structure can't cope with change, that unforeseen unknowns are overwhelming its ability to adapt. The company will try to absorb an acquisition, restructure its manufacturing or distribution networks, reassign products, markets, or plants and awake to a mess of incompatible technologies, systems, procedures, and data that simply won't support the new business requirements.

Many of the large, decentralized multinationals operating in Europe now face just such a predicament. They have had local systems in each country and diverse technology implemented in a dozen different languages and reflecting an enormous variety of governmental and cultural restrictions. Now comes 1992! They would like to adjust their operations to a European wide scale and rationalize their product lines, manufacturing, and distribution, but they find their dispersed computing blocking the way. For them, low-road IT has become an impediment to change.

THE HIGH ROAD

The structure that best addresses the weaknesses of the low-road approach is the high road. In this philosophy, many of the properties featured in the low-road solution are reversed: The role of the senior IT executive is expanded. The core IT activities of the business are centralized. Investments and IT infrastructure are built around the central precepts of corporatewide networks, central data collections, common business practices, common application systems, and standard hardware, operating systems, and data bases. Core applications are designed to be organizationally independent—that is, immune to the restructurings that so often plague the conventional MIS activities of corporations where applications are "owned" by user divisions and departments.

The key arguments for taking the high road are that it is:

A Catalyst for Change   Businesses that depend on IT cannot restructure themselves without a concurrent restructuring of their computing systems, communications, and decision processes. The great promise of the high road is that it permits change. Senior management can transform the organization beginning with the classic change questions: what businesses do we want to be in, how do we want to operate, what is the ideal structure for our corporation? Organizational design and IT system planning are done concurrently.

Integrative   Shared data is the key to integration. Carefully planned and managed data collections are the hallmark of the relational data structures made possible with the very large storage systems and advanced data-management software of the latest in large-scale computers. Large data stores can be managed effectively if centralized, and time-critical operations can be supported efficiently. Recent developments in software suggest we can expect continued improvement in storage capacities and speed and, within the next decade, distributed, but still coordinated and synchronized, data control.

Efficient   The high road is the most efficient structure for the long run—one set of data, one set of core application systems, minimal redundancy, and few people needed for maintenance.

Flexibility   Another key aspect of the high-road scenario is flexibility, which is provided by relational data systems and organizationally independent application systems for core, generic business activities. The problem with the old data system techniques was that it couldn't cope with unanticipated demands and didn't accommodate new data elements. Relational systems overcome these problems. The same is true for common application systems: they are designed to support change, because they are organizationally independent.

Strategic   The book on successful competitive-advantage IT is almost universally a story set on the high road. Otisline, SABRE, American Hospital Supply's ASAP system, USAA, the Cash Management Account system of Merrill-Lynch, Federal Express, Frito-Lay—all are centrally designed and managed, communications-oriented (that is, high-road) efforts.

A Top-Management Tool   The high road is the only approach that permits senior management to focus its time and attention efficiently on the IT structure of the firm.

Drawbacks

Unfortunately, the high road also has weaknesses. Perhaps, the greatest problem is "development risk." The history of computing in many large corporations is filled with expensive and painful failures, especially with attempts to build common systems and central data stores. The high road is especially high risk because of:

Customizing   The applications usually must be custom built. Package solutions aren't really feasible when one sets out to build a suite of organizationally independent applications. Not many packages are available, and not many new ones are under development. Few package options exist for large companies and mainframe-sized processors. In banking, insurance, manufacturing, distribution, airline reservations, and petroleum refining, there are one or two systems choices and they all have limitations and constraints. Too often one hears, "We looked at packages, but none met our needs. We'll have to write our own."

Management Dependency   The successful high-road solution depends heavily on senior management's ability to plan both the enterprise of tomorrow and the data and systems to support it. Many North American and European banks and insurance companies admit that they've been slow to recognize the importance of customer-oriented file structures, cross-functional selling, and integrated financial services. If asked why they were so slow, they give reasons that all seem to come back to a management that didn't see the need. They couldn't visualize the potential. Even when they had the vision, they often lacked the courage: many grand efforts at common systems in large financial institutions floundered and were scaled back.

Politics   The high road is fraught with political pitfalls because operating managers distrust central solutions, especially IT ones. Thus, common application systems and shared data collections frequently run counter to the culture of many large corporations.

Planning Techniques   Common system architectures built around central data collections place great stress on systems-planning methodologies. Advances in planning technologies have not kept pace with the size, complexity, or expectations of information systems. Unfortunately, as organizational size, geography, intra-organizational relationships, and inter-organizational relationships grow the demands they place on the planning process grow geometrically. Planning approaches such as IBM's BSP or Arthur Andersen's Method One simply are too complex to apply to a large entity such as General Motors or American Express.

The High-Road Fatal Flaw

Even if these problems can be overcome, the chief drawback to the high road is the same as for the low road: There is the very real likelihood that it won't work, that it won't adapt to the needs of a changing organization. The danger with the high-road strategy is that it will freeze the organization into a fixed structure, culture, decision-making process, and pattern of relationships both inside and outside the business.

There's no guarantee that common systems and centrally managed data structures built with relational data bases and fourth-generation programming languages, parameter-driven applications, reusable codes, or any of the other aspects of the high road will lead to what management demands — flexibility and efficiency. Indeed, the evidence so far has been just the reverse: the larger the organization, the more comprehensive the systems, the wider the scope of the data, the richer the relationships with vendors and customers, the faster the rate of organizational change, then the greater the chances that the high road will never be finished. Even if it is finished, moreover, it may never meet the changing expectations of the firm. Evidence was seen in the late 1960s and early 1970s when common systems and other high-road solutions were eagerly pursued; it is also what we see today.

THE MIDDLE ROAD

There must be a better way! If the low road eventually leads to a maze of expensive, incompatible efforts that are impervious to systemwide change, and the high road either never gets built or won't adapt when it does, what scenario will work? How do we get the benefits of both while minimizing the drawbacks? How do we get the efficiency and control provided by the high-road solution simultaneously with the low road's ability to respond to rapidly changing information-processing needs of operating managers throughout the organization?

So far, the architectural or structure choices have been presented at the extremes: the low road, distributed network, scenario assumes no central systems are needed, that integration and connectivity can be provided by Internal EDI, that there need be no CIO or broad set of standards and central administration. The high road was silent as to local computing, local data collections and local initiatives.

Obviously there is much to be said for a middle road. Companies must do both. Clearly some system tasks are global to the firm and require high-road, central solutions; the many tasks that are not global, however, are best done locally. Deciding what to manage centrally and what to disperse is really the key question. All organizations are different, and there can be no solution that will be ideal for everyone, but there are generic contingencies that everyone must respect.

A middle road would respect both the advantages of central solutions and the power of a networked approach. It would recognize that requirements for efficiency and economy of scale can only be met by high-road solutions, but that flexibility and speed are best achieved along the low road.

Organizations face certain constraints on what can be approached via a low road. By their nature, some data are common and cannot be decentralized with current technology; nor should they be. Some part of the IT structure of almost every large corporation should be accomplished with high-road solutions. This high-road structure would cover two parts of the corporation's IT architecture: the headquarters segment and the IT activities that pervade the rest of the corporation.

Hewlett-Packard is a good example of a large, diverse corporation that has taken a middle road after much management attention to the formulation of internal IT architecture. The company is an innovator and is organized with considerable decentralized responsibility throughout its 54 manufacturing sites and 375 sales and service offices. Following a low-road philosophy, IT is decentralized and IT management is considered a critical part of every manager's responsibility. Yet the corporation has concluded that high-road needs exist for companywide data and common systems in five key areas:

- sales and service
- procurement
- quality
- personnel
- accounting

These five global systems are tied to divisional manufacturing, product-design, inventory-management, and cost-accounting systems and to sales and service applications for customer and product information, credit administration, invoicing, accounts receivable, and service administration.

Digital Equipment Corporation is another example of a large corporation that is combining an element of high-road philosophy in an otherwise decentralized, low-road IT structure. Prior to 1980, the corporation had few central systems; most IT activities were organized along product lines, which were mostly autonomous. Finance and accounting systems were local, duplicative, costly, and implemented on a variety of different computers. Horizontal and vertical information flows were slow, complex, and costly, requiring many conversions and translations.

In the early 1980s, a decision was made by DEC to adopt a high-road solution for financial systems. The new structure entails:

- a common operating chart of accounts for the entire corporation
- common financial applications and data bases for the general ledger, accounts receivable, fixed assets, capital projects, purchasing, inter-company variances, project reporting, payroll, inventory, and revenue accounting

- organizationally independent processing centers for regional accounting and consolidations
- a common management reporting chart of accounts

Other IT activities, called the business cores, are the collection of data, applications systems, management and networking technology that are common to part, but not all of the organization's activities.

A key decision for any management is how many levels in the corporation have a distinct IT perspective? Some large corporations have chosen to focus their IT activities at an SBU or line-of-business level. Some banks organize their U.S. domestic systems in one core and their international systems in another; others divide the IT activities along retail vs. wholesale lines. A large multinational petroleum corporation has created distinct high-road solutions for IT in chemicals, upstream oil, downstream oil and several other units.

All IT activities that are not centralized along such high-road dimensions are then decentralized to become low-road, local solutions. An important element, however, is linking the organization horizontally and vertically with communications and data-exchange facilities—that is, the internal EDI, the internal information network of the firm, is critical to the middle road. Almost all large corporations have encouraged or permitted some degree of low-road IT activity. As a consequence, they have wrestled with the problems of data integrity, data exchange, and data access. Almost all sense the need for some high-road influence, with some minimal standard data definitions and mechanisms for data exchange. Unfortunately, the needs often become apparent only after a considerable investment in local technology or after changes bring new requirements that cannot be met. What's necessary is to establish a minimal set of standardized information that will stand up to unforeseen changes of the next 20 years.

Beyond the components of the corporation's IT structure that are naturally high road, managers should be convinced that an IT application meets three tests before concluding that it's to be a part of a high-road solution: synergy, feasibility, and fit.

Synergy

The default rule for writers, "when in doubt, leave it out," has a corollary in IT architecture: "when in doubt, let the businesses do their own." Managers must be convinced that pursuing the high road can add value; otherwise they had best stay with local solutions that can respond to local needs in rapid fashion.

Feasibility

Common systems, by their nature, are high risk. Corporate executives should be humble in their expectations for the success of common systems, especially those that cut across different businesses. The bank with 200 U.S. branches probably has no other choice than to standardize, and the differences from branch to branch are probably small (at least all are in one country, and all personnel speak a common language). The corporation that sets out to build common applications for manufacturing, distribution, sales, and accounting for multiple business lines across many countries is entertaining an entirely different degree of risk.

Fit

Besides the tests of synergy and feasibility, core IT activities must also pass the fit test. Fit has many dimensions. High-road solutions work best in stable environments; while low-road structures are best in volatile businesses. High-road solutions are easier to construct and maintain when the intra-unit relationships are limited and straightforward. When intra-company relationships (such as transfer pricing, technology exchanges, design and engineering) are complex and fast changing, low-road IT systems will be more likely to cope than high-road centralizing.

High-road solutions best fit businesses that are alike. When the products, processes, customers, suppliers, decision processes are diverse, common systems just don't work well. TOYS "R" US is a large U.S. toy store chain that is busily expanding to Japan, Hong Kong, England, Italy, West Germany, and the rest of Europe. These environments are quite different, but the stores are essentially the same in every country—as is IT. The computing systems in the foreign stores are the same as those in the U.S. Unilever NV, on the other hand, is not one business. Its worldwide activities span food, soap, chemical, and fats products from beer to tea and from margarine to cooking oil. It produces and sells products in over a hundred countries. Unilever could not hope to drive its businesses with a single set of systems.

A FINAL WORD

Low-roaders are betting that future flexibility and efficiency can best be met by dispersed technology under local management with a companywide set of minimal data-exchange standards; high-roaders believe that flexibility-but-efficiency can be met best by standardized technology, common systems that are independent organizational upheaval and data collections that are centrally directed. They are both wrong. Most companies need a mix of both.

NOTES

[1]"GE's Management Mission," *Washington Post,* Sunday, June 15, 1988.

41

End-User Computing: Are You a Leader or a Laggard?

Thomas P. Gerrity and
John F. Rockart

We are witnessing dramatic growth in the direct use of information technology as personal support tools by executives, managers, and professionals. These end users, not the traditional systems development staff, are now the key forces driving the acquisition and use of computer resources. In fact, current research indicates that the growth rate in end-user computing is at least five times that of conventional systems: a 50 to 100 percent growth rate per year has been the norm.[1]

The following examples illustrate how the focus of information technology is shifting rapidly in organizations.

- At Xerox over 40 percent of the corporation's total computer resources are now devoted to direct support of end users. Although traditional computer "paperwork processing" is continuing to grow, its proportional share of computer resources is steadily shrinking vis-à-vis the end user. It is estimated that end-user consumption at Xerox will grow 75 percent by 1990.[2]

- Major corporate investments in personal computers are growing exponentially. One automotive company recently ordered 25,000 personal computers. At least one insurance company, The Travellers, installed 2,000 personal computers, and there are several thousand more on order.

- Even top executives are getting into the act. The CEO of a national restaurant chain, along with his staff, interrogated an on-line system to analyze trends in customer preferences, simulated changes in menu items, and did "what-if" analysis of potential price changes. The chairman of Procter & Gamble also uses a personal computer to perform his own analysis of key business situations.

This new period, often referred to as either the "Third Era" or the Information Era, is an outgrowth of the First and Second Eras.[3] From its early accounting and clerical applications in the First Era (circa 1955–1964), the use of information technology expanded in the Second Era (1965–1974) to include direct support of many operational functions in the firm (e.g., manufacturing control, order entry). In the Third Era, the relevant technology now supports key staff and managerial needs. In other words, while the technology of the earlier eras served the paperwork- or data-processing needs of accountants and operational supervisors in a firm, the Third Era's end-user capabilities focus on information, problem-solving, and communication needs of a corporation's decision makers and their staff.

Unfortunately, despite the critical importance of end-user computing, the appropriate approach for managing it has not been developed in most companies. Although its benefits have been widely publicized, end-user managers are often still mired in the management techniques and processes developed during the first quarter century of the computer age—that is, techniques designed to support and control a very different set of computer uses.[4] Therefore, in this article, we will examine those factors that relate specifically to end-user computing:

- The strategic value and business impact of end-user computing activities;
- The pros and cons of three managerial approaches currently used to cope with end-user computing; and
- The five key elements that we believe underlie the development of a successful end-user computing strategy for the Third Era.

WHAT END-USER COMPUTING CAN DO

Increase Individual Performance

The benefits of end-user computing are not readily justified in terms of return on investment of traditional information systems. Instead, enhanced efficiency and effectiveness of an individual professional or manager are often the initial payoffs. This measurement is at least as great and full of qualitative judgment as is the performance appraisal process of that same individual.

Increase Learning

Beyond such individual payoffs, we also observed in company after company that the real long-term value of end-user computing lies in the accelerated learning on the part of the user about his or her job, about the discovery of innovative new approaches to tasks that actually can transform the nature of the job, and finally about the new opportunities and limits of the technology itself. The growing body of end-user computing experience is producing more sophisticated and effective "clients" of the central IS organization than has ever been witnessed. And despite some of the frictions associated with any major change, such a growing knowledge base will ultimately benefit all.

Moreover, it is through this expanded organizational learning via end-user computing that real leverage is brought to two other payoff areas for information technology: (1) a competitive advantage, and (2) improved internal organizational effectiveness.

Competitive Advantage

New product/market opportunities that yield real competitive advantage are generally spotted by professionals and managers who are "on the firing line"—that is, close to the markets and products—and who have a practical, working knowledge of new, enabling technologies. With the widespread development of end-user computing, practical uses of information technology are being discovered at the same time that such technology offers the greatest opportunities—and threats—in today's volatile marketplace. Some firms have used information technology to distinguish themselves from their competitors by locking up a distribution channel. American Hospital Supply, for example, posed a serious threat when it installed terminals in hospitals and thus allowed its customers to order directly. Hence, we believe that those firms that seize the opportunity to effectively manage end-user computing are creating capabilities needed to gain the lead in tomorrow's marketplace.

On the other hand, as critical as they are to corporate leadership or even to survival, major strategic competitive moves come only now and then. More often than not what leads to corporate excellence is the cumulative effectiveness of a vast number of minor organizational improvements made by many people, not just the "bold strategic stroke."[5] Task-related learning and exploration of end-user computing provides a strong base for making small improvements.

Improve Internal Organizational Effectiveness

There is a final managerial benefit. Virtually every business is living in increasingly turbulent and volatile marketplaces, and as the uncertainty increases, the value of manageable access to good information also increases. Those organizations that are further up the "learning curve" in end-user computing have cadres of managers at all levels who have greater expertise in getting, using, and disseminating good management information for improved organizational effectiveness. Also, to the extent that our nation's (and each firm's) workforce is composed of more and more "knowledge workers" and information handlers, the leverage is even greater.

We see the effective diffusion of end-user computing as a relatively low-risk endeavor kept in balance by normal budgetary controls. Therefore, it is of immense potential value to develop more effective information technology clients, enhance the prospects for achieving real competitive advantage, and contribute directly to improved organizational effectiveness. However, we also believe that time is of the essence: the leaders and laggards are being sorted out. Now is the time to select and implement effective management approaches to Third Era computing.

Dispelling Fears

Given that end-user managers of most organizations hardly even know all of the ways in which these tools are being used, it is not surprising that both information systems (IS) and senior managers are at least concerned, if not quite suspicious, that resources are being wasted on frivolous activities. For one thing, end-user professionals and managers are busy people—they have full-time jobs to do. Practically speaking, they make use of this technology only when it provides a direct, quick, and pragmatic benefit to getting their jobs done, usually by just doing some things faster and better.

Furthermore, most end users operate under normal budgetary constraints and are motivated to expend resources wisely. It is, therefore, startling to find some cases where a manager who has discretionary spending control over hundreds of thousands of dollars is held suspect for a considered purchase of a $3,000 personal computer.

Finally, we observed that another senior management fear—that personal computers will be bought and then left sitting idle on a manager's desk—is, in general, unfounded. Those managers whose planned use of a personal computer does not work out are usually quite quick to transfer it to someone who will make use of it. This is not to argue that there are not cases of wasted resources, or that some degree of standards, policies, and guidelines are not valuable. We simply find that, for the most part, end users can be trusted to make sound individual use of personal computers and similar tools to a much higher degree than is usually suspected in top management circles.

Overcoming Myopia

To a great extent, the rapid growth in end-user demand for information resources has "blind sided" many IS executives. This myopia is understandable given that for the past two decades IS managers have been struggling just to install each new wave of increasingly productive (and complex) hardware and software of First and Second Era computing. Faced by project backlogs ranging from two to four years, IS staffs have been tied down by developing or improving these paperwork-processing systems. Available managerial time has also been invested in creating better and more refined approaches to plan and control those applications, which are now a steadily shrinking portion of the total information systems "pie." Thus, despite their dramatic importance, the Third Era changes that are under way have not been given significant management time and attention because the demand for traditional systems has continued to grow.

As a result, many IS executives are entering the era of end-user dominance without having prepared for it. For the most part, managerial approaches to Third Era computer use have been superficial, diffuse, and reactive. Separate groups often have been set up to control the use of personal computers, time sharing, and office systems. Most, however, are merely responsive to user-initiated demand. What is more, many IS managers have discovered that most of their critical management tools and skills, developed so painstakingly over the past twenty-five years, are of little value in managing Third Era developments.

THREE COMMON MANAGERIAL APPROACHES

The prevailing question is, What are companies actually doing? Although the details may differ, management typically has taken one of three general approaches to end-user computing—monopolist, laissez-faire, or the information center.

Monopolist Approach

Often the initial approach in many firms is for the IS organization to attempt to maintain firm control over all end-user computing, usually by limiting it severely. One consumer products company, scarred by the painful and costly evolution of its traditional information systems over the past two decades, adopted a "go-slow" attitude toward the integration of computers into the management process. Not only did the firm choose as the company standard a complex programming language, which is inaccessible to all but the best-trained users, but it also created a set of policies that actively discourages managers from utilizing computer resources. Each personal computer, for example, must be fully and painstakingly justified. And personal computer users are denied any access to corporate databases.

There are several variations of the traditional monopolist view, but they all spring from a basic belief that the IS organization should control all information processing: systems should be developed by a professional data-processing staff to ensure efficient use of computer resources, good documentation, good controls on privacy and security of data, and strong financial controls over the use of the data-processing resource.

The monopolist approach, however, is breaking down in most of those companies that are using it. There are several key reasons for its failure.

- There is not sufficient IS staff available to develop all of the needed systems. Users, faced with a two-to-four-year backlog, are bypassing the "monopoly" by going to external time sharing or "bootlegging" in their own small computers.
- With the declining cost of computer hardware, it is becoming apparent that the monopolist's focus on control to maximize hardware efficiency is increasingly irrelevent.
- The documentation and controls necessary for development of large paperwork-processing systems are unnecessary for many Third Era applications, which may be used only by their authors on a one-time basis or for a very short time.
- An increasing number of computer-savvy managers and staff professionals feel, and rightly so, that they can directly develop many systems more quickly and cheaply, with less friction, and more specifically targeted at their needs than can the traditional monopoly. They refuse to place a system in the central development backlog, which they know they can develop by themselves and have available much sooner. "Why should I wait eight months and pay $50,000 when I can do this over a couple of weekends on my IBM PC?" is a typical user response.

Laissez-Faire Approach

The laissez-faire approach is almost the opposite of the monopolist's view. Here, user-managers, as long as they have their own budgets, are allowed to buy whatever resources they please — time sharing, microcomputers, and even minicomputers. This approach reflects beliefs similar to those stated by one IS manager: "No central organization can plan for end-user computing. Each user is an individual with differing needs. The sum of these needs is too big, too complex, and too diverse. No single central group can possibly understand or control them all." The key here is for each user to make creative, effective use of the tools. If the corporation allows "free-market" access to computation, users will spend their own budgets more wisely than a central authority could possibly do. Therefore, it is outside the role of the IS manager to worry about end-user computing.

As a result of this approach, almost half of the corporate computer resources at one of the world's largest electronics companies are now being consumed by management and staff who are developing and running Third Era systems. The corporation's posture of letting people "do their own thing" has led to a current forecasted requirement of acquiring an additional large mainframe computer every six months just to support end users. Not surprisingly, senior management recently demanded reassurance that comparable benefits are being received from the increased computer costs.

In addition to financial considerations, the total "laissez-faire" philosophy has several other major drawbacks. Some are subtle, some are obvious, but all are increasingly apparent.

- There are many diverse hardware and software tools available today. Much can be gained by having a corporate center or centers of expertise continually study the available tools and help users match their perceived needs with appropriate technology.

- The "invisible hand" in this case is often driven by immediate and tactical needs of operational managers. While such applications can be valuable and useful learning experiences, major opportunities may be missed if no one identifies end-user systems that may be strategically beneficial to the organization. In other words, a firm needs to work in both directions — top down and bottom up — toward productive and strategic uses of the technology. An example of a top-down application is American Airlines' Sabre system: the airline leases terminals to travel agents, who, in turn, use them for making reservations and ticketing online. American Hospital Supply's order-processing system is an example of a bottom-up application in that it resulted from user needs.

- Users value ongoing support. Having received advice and consulting concerning appropriate hardware and software, users need continual updates in the use of software and other aspects of end-user computing. It is also ineffective to let users slowly and arduously track down the location of data specifically valuable to them, manage the transfer of data to their own systems, worry about data security and privacy, or maintain their own databases if they are sizable. These are all matters best supported by information systems professionals.

- Efficient use of Information Era technology demands some corporate-wide standardization. Discounts are available from vendors for quantity purchases. Training programs, however, can be run for only a small set of machinery and software — not for each of the hundreds of personal computers and thousands of software packages now available. Transfer of software and know-how is easier among end users using the same underlying tools. Central leadership is necessary to create an appropriately effective and evolving efficient "network architecture" to meet changing needs.

- Finally, the laissez-faire approach makes no provisions for transforming ad hoc quickly developed support systems into formal, ongoing, often-used support systems. This is a task best performed by IS professionals and is increasingly seen as necessary for some Information Era systems as they gain widespread use throughout organizations.

Information Center Approach

Recognizing the difficulties of the monopolist approach and some of the obstacles of the laissez-faire one, some major computer vendors, most notably IBM, are focusing on an organizational approach most commonly known as the "Information Center" (IC). This initial attempt to provide a focused managerial approach to end-user computing has much to offer.

For one thing, the IC is a centrally located group of personnel, distinct from the rest of the IS staff, to whom users can come for guidance and support concerning the selection and use of appropriate hardware, software, and data. Strong "product" expertise, education, and ongoing training on each supported software language and user-oriented "package" (e.g., electronic mail, word processing, graphics, and statistical analysis systems) are available from various specialist members of the IC. In some cases, the IC is also in charge of ensuring that each application is "justified."

One such information center has been established in a major pharmaceutical company. The IC, staffed with IS support personnel, was chartered to provide assistance, upon request, for all of the twenty-three end-user software tools that the company owned. The center's manager, however, soon found that his small staff's attempts to support the multitude of diverse users and their applications interests were highly inadequate to meet the demand. Because it lacked sufficient resources, the center began to founder. Other centralized ICs, even with a more limited range of products, found it difficult to serve the vastly increasing number of users who desire help.

The IC is the newest of the three approaches, and it is closer to providing more effective results than the others. Many are quite successful. As usually practiced, however, the IC is an incomplete management solution for the Information Era. The information center focuses on support and, to an extent, control, of users. Both support and control are important, but there are several shortcomings to the usual IC implementation.

- The IC, as usually structured, is a centralized organization. Yet, users desire and need localized support.[6]
- Although strong on technological and software product knowledge, most IC personnel often do not have the functional and applications knowledge, which is the end user's primary concern.

- The IC is a creation of the central IS department. User influence on its design, procedures, and services can be minimal. In addition, it may not even have the full backing of IS management and, therefore, may be viewed as an experimental palliative to user demands.

- Often the IC will represent only one or two of the four major end-user computing technologies: time sharing, communications networking, personal computers, and office systems. For effective end-user support, all four must be managed in coordination.

- The IC is often only reactive to expressed user needs. Yet, Third Era technology presents many opportunities that may not be recognized by technologically unsophisticated users. Proactive managerial efforts to identify and rank high payoff opportunities have been extremely useful in the organizations with which we have worked.

- Finally and perhaps most important, the IC is a solution expressed in terms of organizational structure. And structure should reflect strategy. However, the majority of the firms we have observed have neglected the critical initial step, the development of a strategic direction for the exploitation of Third Era technology. In the absence of a clear strategic context, the IC "solution" produces less value.

A NEW APPROACH: MANAGED FREE ECONOMY

Given the potential strategic benefits to the firm, end-user computing has won "center stage" and, therefore, demands much more than either a laissez-faire, "take-what-you-get" approach or a limited, reactive management. Both approaches are patently inadequate because in the next few years increased end-user computing needs will cause many major companies to spend hundreds of millions of dollars in equipment, systems development, and user time.

What is needed to manage Third Era computing is a proactive and strategic approach called a managed free economy. This approach must balance two opposing but equally essential needs. Users must be allowed to create, define, and develop their own applications of the technology to fulfill their information needs. Yet, at the same time, some central authority must take responsibility to consult with users concerning what is feasible, to support users where special IS expertise can add value, and to ensure that the appropriate technical policy structure is in place.

The parallel to a regulated economy is clear. At the national level, the United States has such an economy. Fiscal and monetary policies, the legal systems, antimonopoly regulations, and many other government-imposed guidelines determine the "rules of the game." Working within this framework, private organizations and individuals strive to maximize their own gains. Yet, they are bounded by a set of constraints, which, while they inhibit individual actions, serve to ensure that the nation as a whole will prosper.

The same is true for end-user computing. There is a need for "regulations." For example, a central authority must develop policies to limit the number of types of personal computers that can be used. This ensures that the training courses, support systems, and network protocols that must be established for each different type of computer can be put in place. While it is impossible to develop these support services for 100 brands of personal computers, it can be done well for a few. In like manner, software standards must be established; otherwise, users, having learned a particular spreadsheet or word-processing package might, when transferred to another department, have to repeat an extensive learning process. In addition, a single electronic mail system should be established to allow communication across the organization.

Working within these few (although very significant) guidelines, computer users (like private U.S. citizens) are free to act in their own interest. They may select and program their own applications, maintain personal files, and do and act as they see fit with regard to purchasing and using computer software and hardware: within bounds, the regulated individual is free. Like the national economy, the end-user environment should be regulated just enough to ensure that the optimum balance is maintained between government control and individual freedom.

FIVE CRITICAL ATTRIBUTES

The three managerial approaches, including many variations and hybrids of those described, vary significantly from company to company. Some are markedly successful from both user and IS management viewpoints. Many are not. Although the exact implementations differ, those approaches considered to be successful by both users and IS exhibit all or most of the five critical attributes of the "managed free economy" approach:

1. A stated end-user strategy;
2. A user/IS working partnership;
3. An active targeting of critical end-user systems and applications;
4. An integrated end-user support organization; and
5. An emphasis on education throughout the organization.

Stated Strategy

Users continually ask the questions: "What is IS going to do to support me?" "What is the end-user strategy?" "What is IS management's view of the general directions of Third Era computing?" "What end-user hardware and systems will be supported by IS?" "Will the specific support mechanisms (e.g., education, hardware discounts, ongoing assistance) be provided?" In short, users desire a statement of strategic direction and knowledge of the key elements of its implementation.

The development of a strategy, therefore, requires both an assessment of the technology and a determination of user application needs. As new products are continually being introduced, the shape of end-user product direction becomes increasingly clear. Future user needs can be determined in large part by an analysis of staff department computer needs. After all, staffs are the major manipulators of information in the firm; they are the focus of 80 to 90 percent of all end-user computing.[7]

Working Partnership

Both the strategy and all programs growing out of the strategy must reflect user needs. In the past, the "rules of the game" in information systems were formulated by the IS organization to effect efficient implementation of paperwork-processing systems. Today, the "rules" regarding justification of systems, pricing of services, access to data, privacy, and security need to be reexamined. Because these rules so strongly affect end users, it is important that they be worked out in collaboration with end users and their IS management.

For example, at Gillette, a set of policies and guidelines very different from those previously governing the earlier eras have been developed to support end-user computing. The key to their development is a policy group including end-user departments and several senior managers from these departments. The policy committee is chaired by a user manager. While significant expertise is added to the committee's deliberations by IS, the policies that evolve are clearly seen to reflect the needs of users.

Targeting Critical Systems and Applications

Allowing ideas for uses of the new technology to merely "bubble up" from individual users is not enough. Individual managers are noticeably short range and "local" in their thinking. Systems with long-range benefits, which span multiple individuals or departments, or which require special technological expertise to envision and formulate, are not often generated from end users alone. Therefore, to ensure that limited IS resources are used well, leading companies are implementing broad strategic-minded scans of critical end-user applications now made possible by the new technology.

At Southwest Ohio Steel, the senior management team engaged in a Critical Success Factors-based study of corporate information needs.[8] What emerged from the study was the recognition that Third Era technology could be most effectively used to provide, among other things, an information marketing database. This database is now being accessed daily by officers and managers of the firm including Jacques Huber, marketing vice-president.

Integrated Support Organization

The skills necessary to assist end users are vastly different from the skills required to design and program systems in the IS organization. First, end-user support personnel must focus on end use, not on technology. Second, because support personnel provide expert advice, they must not only be knowledgeable of a wide spectrum of new tools and techniques, but they must also have the desire and the skills to teach and help, not to do. Working with users in this capacity requires patience and interpersonal skills not commonly found in traditional IS personnel.

Even more important than the skills requirements is the need for an organization to have a separate identity — that is, a central support organization. Much hard work is required to develop the elements of an end-user strategy. In addition, ongoing user support is essential. If user support is merely a secondary function of the regular IS organization, any crisis in conventional processing can steal significant resources away from the Third Era tasks. A focus on ongoing support must be maintained or users lose confidence. To maintain this focus, separate, dedicated organizations already have been formed in many leading companies. Although we expect that this organization will eventually evolve and merge with other parts of the information systems organization, its specialized role appears to demand organizational separation today.

At Gillette, for instance, all aspects of end-user computing are under the direction of one senior manager in IS. Policies, guidelines, and strategic directions are well thought out and advertised. Experts are available from this central staff to consult about time-sharing products, personal computers, and office systems.

Still, end users are busy people who require extensive support. Therefore, the support person must be local — physically close by, available, and able to speak the users' language about their business needs.[9]

At Owens Corning Fiberglas, Paul Daverio, vice-president for information systems, transferred special IS personnel to the staff departments that are responsible for finance, personnel, etc. This was done to provide on-site end-user consulting. Another case in point is Texas Instruments. Here, end users in each department or division can make use of three levels of support. First, and most effective, are the home-grown functional specialists in the department: finance, marketing, or other users who have become the local, available computing experts. They, in turn, are supported by IS computing consultants who have more overall computing knowledge and a set of guidelines on applications that should be executed by personal computers, time sharing, or office systems hardware and software. Referrals can be made, if necessary, to the appropriate specialty hardware of software experts. What is more, with a single IS person as a focal point for all the user specialists, knowledge about the entire end-user environment in each organization can be more effectively consolidated for shaping the evolving end-user computing strategy.

Education throughout the Organization

End-user technology is coming to market in extraordinary diversity. Yet, IS personnel are often uneducated. We find that less than one in ten of the IS systems analysts today have more than a cursory acquaintance with the new technology. Senior management, in general, is not adequately informed. And middle management, deluged with an extraordinary number of claims by vendors and confused about what moves to make, needs an increased understanding of the ways in which the technology can best be applied to particular tasks. A well-thought-out educational program, adapted to the needs of each type of "student" is absolutely necessary to allow an organization to make effective use of the technology.

ARCO met this challenge head-on. A ten-day program has been devised and instituted to reeducate 1,000 of the company's top IS personnel. The course centers on the concepts, tools, and techniques of the Third Era. In addition, short seminars are being given to the top senior management. The seminars stress both basic concepts and current, effective uses of the new technology within ARCO. Courses for middle management are being developed as well.

CONCLUSION: SHIFT THE FOCUS

This is an era when astute leadership in exploiting information technology will create a competitive edge in the marketplace. Yet, many managers, fearing that they will lose control over computing costs, hesitate to pursue the substantial benefits offered by this technology. Before the end-user era, an analysis of the costs and benefits of each major proposed application system or hardware purchase was possible through careful scrutiny of the IS budget. Today, however, such single-point control is no longer possible: usage is scattered widely throughout the organization—and in much smaller increments.

Still, adequate control over computer utilization is feasible. Ensuring that the five attributes are in place will produce a working partnership between user management and IS staff, who together can implement two quite different but complementary forms of "control" over the computing environment.

A first and vital step is to develop a set of policies, standards, and guidelines. This will ensure a standard technical and management environment, which can yield significant benefits: volume hardware and software discounts from vendors and education programs and assistance for a limited set of standard products will be made available. In addition, such policies will enable users to move freely from one part of the organization to another without having to learn a new set of hardware and software systems. All users will be assured that their personal computers "connect" to the network, which will allow access to one another and to remotely stored data.

After the guidelines are established, individual end-user projects of size must be scrutinized to ensure they have business value. The responsibility for this control belongs to the local unit's line management. Therefore, line management must be increasingly knowledgeable of the potential value of technology—at least to the extent necessary to determine whether expenditures on computers or communications make good business sense. Such knowledge requires, as we have already noted, that these managers receive an education in technology. An IS staff can and should be consulted for advice in specific instances, but the basic control over what is being done—in an era when virtually everyone in the corporation will soon have a terminal—has shifted from the staff experts to the line organization.

NOTES

[1] J.F. Rockart and L. Flannery, "The Management of End-User Computing," *Communications of the ACM,* October 1983, pp. 777–784.

[2] R.I. Benjamin, "Information Technology in the 1990s: A Long-Range Planning Scenario," *MIS Quarterly,* June 1982, pp. 11–31.

[3] J.F. Rockart and M.S. Scott Morton, "Implications of Changes in Information Technology for Corporate Strategy," *INTERFACES,* January–February 1984, pp. 84–95; J.F. Rockart, "The Role of the Executive in the New Computer Era," in *Global Technological Change: A Strategic Assessment* (Proceedings of A Symposium for Senior Executives, MIT Liaison Program, June 21–23, 1983).

[4] Rockart and Flannery (October 1983); J.C. Henderson and M.E. Treacy, "Managing End-User Computing for Competitive Advantage," *Sloan Management Review,* Winter 1986, p. 3; E. Arkush, "Beyond End-User Computing: Managing in the Third Era," *The Journal of Information Systems Management,* Spring 1986, p. 58; J.F. Rockart and M.E. Treacy, "The CEO Goes On-Line," *Harvard Business Review,* January–February 1982, pp. 82–88.

[5] T.J. Peters and R.H. Waterman, Jr., *In Search of Excellence* (New York: Harper & Row, 1982).

[6] Rockart and Flannery (October 1983), p. 783.

[7] Ibid., p. 779.

[8] J.F. Rockart, "Chief Executives Define Their Own Data Needs," *Harvard Business Review,* March–April 1979, pp. 81–93; J.F. Rockart and A.D. Crescenzi, "Engaging Top Management in Information Technology," *Sloan Management Review,* Summer 1984, pp. 3–16.

[9] F.G. Withington, "Coping with Computer Proliferation," *Harvard Business Review,* May–June 1980, pp. 152–164.

42

Managing the Data Resource: A Contingency Perspective

Dale L. Goodhue,

Judith A. Quillard, and

John F. Rockart

Today, corporations are placing increasing emphasis on the management of data. To learn more about effective approaches to "managing the data resource," case studies of 31 data management efforts in 20 diverse firms have been conducted. The major finding is that there is no single, dominant approach to improving the management of data. Rather, firms have adopted multiple approaches that appear to be very diverse in (1) business objective, (2) organizational scope, (3) planning method, and (4) "product," i.e., deliverable produced. The dominant business objective for successful action is improved managerial information; most data management efforts are "targeted" without a formal data planning process; and the dominant product was "information databases." In addition, several key organizational issues must be addressed when undertaking any data management effort.

INTRODUCTION

Although the literature presents both conceptual justifications for managing data as a resource [8, 10, 15] and approaches/methods that describe how to do so [16, 19, 21], it unfortunately contains little discussion of actual business problems caused by poorly managed data, of business successes made possible by well-managed data, or the data management actions that make a difference. The result may be the impression that data management is a technology-driven concept in search of a concrete business need.

The problems of unmanaged data are, however, quite real and exist in a broad range of organizations. A major bank seeking to shift its strategy toward a focus on customers finds that it cannot determine how profitable individual customers are, or even what its total business is with each customer, because its customer codes are not common across branches or lines of business. A manufacturing firm with nine plants cannot negotiate favorable purchasing agreements with its major suppliers, because it cannot pool inconsistent data from these plants to find out how much it buys from each supplier. An insurance company discovers it cannot check group health insurance claims against previous claims for the same individual participant, because the structure of the data precludes it. A company attempting to merge two divisions finds that incompatibilities in data definitions and systems provide one of the greatest obstacles to attaining this important strategic action.

These few examples might be dismissed as unfortunate abberations if similar problems were not found in so many organizations today. In fact, it is likely that management's demand for up-to-date information from many different sources at many different levels of aggregration will increase even further as the business environment becomes more competitive [11]. This makes it critical that businesses better appreciate the implications of poorly managed data, and understand the variety of ways in which they can improve the management of data. The three-year study described here attempts to address this need by looking at some thirty data management efforts in 20 firms.

The major finding from this study is that there is no single dominant approach to improving the management of data. Rather, firms have adopted multiple approaches, all of which need to be considered by any organization striving to leverage data as a valuable business resource. In addition, this study identifies a set of key organizational issues that should be addressed when undertaking any data management effort.

The rest of this section summarizes some current approaches to data management in the literature and describes the research method. The next section presents the major findings using a framework that represents the variety and contingency seen in the data management efforts studied. This is followed by a brief discussion of several key organizational issues that managers should explicitly address as they consider the options suggested by the framework. The article concludes with a discussion of the major lessons learned.

Current Approaches to Data Management

As the business need for information has increased, so has the technical capability to handle information. A rapidly growing amount of data is now available in electronic form—most of it designed and organized to meet the needs of specific applications, with little thought given to compatibility of data across applications or business functions. Managing this data in a manner that best contributes to business objectives has become a complex problem [11]. Various solutions that have been discussed in the existing data resource management (DRM) literature can be categorized into three types of approaches:

- *Approaches with a technical focus.* These include tools and techniques such as database management systems [6, 7], data dictionaries [2, 21], and data entity-relationship modeling [3, 4].

- *Approaches with a focus on organizational responsibilities.* These include the establishment of organizational units such as database administration and data administration [12, 13, 18], and the formulation of administrative policies and procedures covering areas such as data ownership, access, and security [1, 23].
- *Approaches with a focus on top-down, business-related planning.* These include planning processes and methods such as Martin's [19] strategic data planning, Holland's [14] strategic systems planning, and IBM's business systems planning (BSP) [16]. All of these approaches link the acquisition and use of data with business objectives.

It is increasingly evident that neither of the first two categories provides a completely adquate approach. Coulson [5] acknowledges that many efforts to solve data management problems through the implementation of a data dictionary have failed. Kahn [17] presents empirical evidence suggesting that most data administration groups have had little or no success in correcting key data management problems, and Tillman [22] discusses several reasons for the failure of data administration organizations to live up to management's expectations, such as insufficient management support.

The third type of approach has received great attention, because the ultimate goal of data resource management is not to put tools in place or to create organizational units but to provide data to support the needs of the business. Such planning approaches, however, require significant resource commitments and, as will be discussed later in the article, often are not easy to accomplish.

Research Approach

Given the limited general knowledge of firms' experiences with existing approaches to data management and the need to develop new ways of thinking about the area, exploratory case studies have been conducted across multiple firms and industries. One to six days of interviews with IS managers and user managers were carried out in each of 20 large corporations during 1985–86. The firms were from a range of industries, including electronics, consumer goods, insurance, banking, computers, and energy. The largest company was in the top 10 of the *Fortune* 500; the smallest had annual revenues of $500 million.

Table 42.1 provides brief descriptions of the firms (with disguised names) and their data management efforts. In each company, we focused on one to four data management projects, for a total of 31 data management efforts studied. Almost all of these efforts were viewed as successful by both information systems and user management.

In all, over 230 managers and other professionals were interviewed; approximately 70 percent were from IS departments and 30 percent from user departments. The interviewees discussed the data-related policies, processes, controls, standards, and tools that their firm had in place or had attempted. Also discussed were the factors that motivated each organization to take action and the results that were achieved. In addition, the interviews gathered opinions regarding the most important problems and issues concerning the management and use of data.

An initial assumption, supported by the present findings, was that similarities

Table 42.1
Firms and Data Management Efforts in the Study

Disguised Names	Description	Data Management Efforts
Financial Services		
Coolidge International	Financial services, over $3 billion in revenues	Operational SDABs to support core customer financial services
Dobbs Insurance	Among Top 10 insurance cos. in assets	Change in the basic business data collected by one division
Taft Insurance	Over $3 billion in revenues	Information database to support auto insurance business
Van Buren Bank	Over $50 billion in assets	Customer information database for top 1000 customers in corporate and government banking group
Manufacturing		
Blaine Corporation	Personal care products; Fortune 500	Data access services for end users
Crockett	Canadian subsidiary of Fortune 500 U.S. computer company	Operational SADBs for finance and administrative applications and managerial reporting
Eakins Corporation	Multibillion dollar international industrial and service company	1. Information database for consolidated financial data from subsidiaries 2. Information database for employee insurance claims
Foothill Computer	Fortune 250	1. Information centers providing data and data consulting 2. Set of standard data definitions established by corporate task force 3. Strategic data planning for the order flow function
Global Products, Inc.	Fortune 500 manufacturing	Subject area databases being gradually implemented
LDI Electronics	Over $2 billion in sales	1. Corporate information database for engineering specifications 2. Information database for product quality tracking 3. Information database for managerial analysis across product divisions in the components group

Table 42.1 (cont.)

Disguised Names	Description	Data Management Efforts
Matrac Corporation	Fortune 100 manufacturing	Data access services for end users
Spectrum Electronics	Fortune 100	Integrated manufacturing database in one division
Process Industries		
Derrick Energy Products	Largest Subsidiary of Fortune 100 company	1. BSP in Production Division 2. Six operational SADBs as part of its asset management program
Sierra Energy	Among top 10 energy companies	Information database for consolidated financial reporting
Waverly Chemicals	Fortune 500 diversified chemical company	1. Common manufacturing systems in largest division 2. Common accounting systems used by multiple divisions 3. Strategic data modeling done for IS planning in largest division 4. Set of standard data definitions established by corporate IS group
Windsor Products	Fortune 100	1. Several information databases built 2. "Data charting" effort
Other		
Consumer Publications	Over $1 billion in revenues	1. Strategic data planning for the corporation 2. Operational SADBs to support the promotion function
Diverse Conglomerate	Fortune 500	Information database for use by senior management
National Technologies	Over $5 billion in revenues	Strategic data planning for the corporation
Winslow	Aerospace division of a multi-billion dollar conglomerate	Data access to divisional data through fourth generation tools

in data management issues faced by large corporations outweigh differences among industry groups. In choosing companies to study, the goal was to find a range of firms that were actively trying to improve their management of data. The sample was drawn from firms known to have forward-thinking IS groups. This means that the sample is not random. However, because of the number and variety of firms studied, the findings should be generalizable to other large organizations that have recognized data management as an important issue.

A CONTINGENCY APPROACH TO DATA MANAGEMENT

The picture emerging from these case studies is that effective data management efforts fit no single clear pattern. In analyzing the cases, there is an interlinked set of choices that depend heavily on organizational considerations. Certainly, one must be careful in generalizing from a non-random sample of 20 companies, but, at least in these organizations, successful efforts appear to be diverse in terms of (1) business objective; (2) organizational scope; (3) planning method; and (4) "product," i.e., major deliverable produced.

As a starting point for visualizing the contingency approach to data management, Exhibit 42.1 presents a simple framework that reflects the variety of options found in the case studies. The four main elements of the framework represent the key components of the data management efforts studied. These elements are:

- The identification of a business objective. In the successful companies in the sample, data management actions were almost always justified not by conceptual or technical arguments, but by one of four compelling business needs: operational coordination, organizational flexibility; improved managerial information; or IS effectiveness.

- The scope of the data management project. The firms studied explicitly defined and limited the organizational scope of their efforts. Some focused on a functional area (such as finance), others on a division, while some were corporate-wide.

- The data planning method. Top-down, indepth strategic data modeling was not the only data planning process. In fact, there appear to be a number of obstacles to accomplishing a large-scale strategic data planning effort. The planning processes utilized varied widely in terms of their formality, their detail, and their emphasis on data models. The range of options varied from strategic data planning to more limited planning approaches to no planning whatsoever.

- The "product" of the data management effort. Much of the existing data resource management literature centers on the implementation of subject area databases [19]. In the case studies, however, were seen five distinct "products," which were the end results of the data management project team's work. These products are: subject area databases for operational systems; common systems; information databases; data access services; and architectures or standards for future systems.

The next four sections of the article discuss each of the elements in the framework. To facilitate the discussion, the elements are discussed in reverse order from

Exhibit 42.1

Framework of Data Management Choices

Note: The numbers in parentheses show how many data management efforts fell into each category.

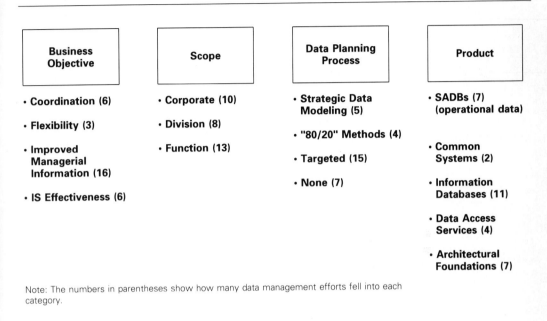

Business Objective	Scope	Data Planning Process	Product
• Coordination (6)	• Corporate (10)	• Strategic Data Modeling (5)	• SADBs (7) (operational data)
• Flexibility (3)	• Division (8)	• "80/20" Methods (4)	
• Improved Managerial Information (16)	• Function (13)	• Targeted (15)	• Common Systems (2)
• IS Effectiveness (6)		• None (7)	• Information Databases (11)
			• Data Access Services (4)
			• Architectural Foundations (7)

Note: The numbers in parentheses show how many data management efforts fell into each category.

that shown above, with the most tangible element, the "products," first, followed by planning processes, scope, and business objectives.

Five Data Management ''Products''

Any successful data management effort results in a product or deliverable such as a new system, service, or policy. The "product" most common in the existing data resource management literature is a set of subject area databases used by multiple operational systems. We also found, however, four other products. Like subject area databases, two of the other product types—common systems and information databases—require a systems development effort. The final two product types, which usually do not involve new systems or databases, were labelled data access services and architectural foundations.

Subject Area Databases for Operational Systems   Subject area databases (SADBs) contain data that is organized around important business entities or subject areas, such as customer and product, rather than around individual applications, such as order processing or manufacturing scheduling. Many different operational applications may share data (i.e., both access and update data) from a single set of SADBs. In seven of the 31 cases, the product can best be described as SADBs for operational data.

Consumer Publishing, Inc. (all company names have been disguised), does many direct mailings using its large customer base and other purchased lists in order to promote its books and magazines. To help support and control this important activity, Consumer Publishing has built a set of SADBs (including product, vendor, postal regulations, and promotion plan) that are used by three major applications: (1) an MRP-like system for planning and execution of mailings; (2) a purchasing system for mailing-related materials; and (3) an inventory system. The implementation occurred in several phases between 1981–84, and was the first time that Consumer Publishing's IS department took a data-focused approach to systems development. The SADBs and applications have helped to simplify and improve mailing-related operations, and have greatly reduced inventory costs.

Common Systems　A second type of data management product is the set of operational data files or databases that are developed for common systems. Common systems are applications developed by a single, most often a central, organization to be used by multiple organizational units. Physically, there can be one or multiple copies of the system. The concept of common systems is not new. They have often been developed not for data mangement purposes but rather to ensure common procedures or to lower IS costs. Common systems cannot be developed, however, without surfacing and resolving data definitional issues, since old systems (and old definitions) will be discontinued.

Waverly Chemicals is a major, diversified chemical company, and its largest division operates about a dozen plants. Since about 1980, this division has emphasized the development of common systems for manufacturing applications such as production scheduling and spare parts inventory. The availability of well-defined, standardized data has enabled the division to reduce inventory costs and to greatly improve coordination among the plants.

While only two of the companies studied developed new common systems, several of the other companies had a significant existing base of common systems. These firms often were able to use the standard data in their common systems to leverage other data management efforts.

Information Databases　A third new systems product is an information database, which can be defined as a subject area database intended for use by staff analysts and line management. Information databases are "secondary" databases, which periodically draw their contents from operational databases and (sometimes) external sources, and often store data in aggregated forms. Significantly, information databases can provide data without requiring major rewrites of current systems. Instead, "bridges" are built from the existing operational systems to provide the appropriate data to the new database.

Information databases were the most prevalent product in the sample, occurring in 11 (35 percent) of the 31 cases.

At Windsor Products, a consumer goods manufacturer, corporate management's demands for information led to the development of several new databases. Standard codes and definitions were defined for these databases; however, existing applications and the operational databases on which the transaction systems depend were left in place. Automated bridges from the existing systems populate the new "information-only" databases for customer, product, and shipment. These information databases are now widely used.

LDI Electronics is building an information database to contain data on key characteristics of the parts and materials the company uses in its electrical components, including specifications, availability, reliability, and cost. Most of the data is already collected, in various forms, by existing procurement, engineering, and manufacturing systems. Thus, bridges and translation routines are being built to the new database. A prototype is in use by engineers in nine product groups.

Data Access Services   The first three "products" discussed emphasize developing new databases or files with pertinent, accurate, and consistent data. Four firms in the study, however, focused mainly on improving managerial access to existing data, without attempting to upgrade the quality or structure of the data.

Data access services are usually provided by a small cadre of personnel, often part of an information center, whose goal is to better understand what data is available in current systems and to put in place mechanisms to deliver this data. These mechanisms include locating appropriate data, extracting data from production files, or training users in fourth generation languages. Such efforts are widely applauded by managers who now have help in "getting their hands" on existing data.

A multi-billion dollar manufacturing firm, Matrac Corporation, has put in place a "data service" for its corporate end users. The data service organization is a small group within the corporate IS organization that locates data, arranges for extracts, and delivers the data in the user's choice of formats. The group maintains copies of most of the data it provides and arranges for periodic updates.

Data access services are expected to be more helpful in companies where existing data is of reasonable quality. Where data is of poor quality, the process of delivering data in its current form to managers may spur action toward increasing data standardization and control mechanisms. Some firms are following up initial efforts to provide data access with the development of a data directory designed specifically to assist end users by listing and cross-referencing the available data.

Architectural Foundations for the Future   In most of the firms studied, managers focused on a limited set of data serving a portion of the corporation. However, there clearly is a danger in approaching data management function by function, business unit by business unit, or subject area by subject area. A company may find itself facing problems in the future if it desires to integrate data across these boundaries. To avoid these future incompatibility problems, some organizations have focused on developing "architectural foundations," which are policies and standards that force systems development efforts to conform to a well-structured, overall data plan.

One type of architectural foundation is a corporate-wide strategic data model designed to serve as an underlying blueprint for all future systems development. Martin's [19] Strategic Data Planning approach produces such a model as one of its products. IBM's BSP methodology [16] and Holland's [14] methodology are others that produce a data architecture.

Proponents of these approaches argue that a strategic data model provides an architectural foundation that will lead to consistency of data, more easily integrated systems, and improved productivity in systems development and maintenance.

Five of the firms studied developed a strategic data model primarily as an architectural foundation for future systems development.

Waverly Chemical's largest division began a strategic data modeling effort for the entire division after the successful implementation of common manufacturing systems. The model was used to help create a strategic IS plan that identified key business areas that had little systems support. Due to a downturn in the division's primary business, limited action has been taken based on the plan. The division, however, has shown its data model to other Waverly divisions; at least one other division has decided that the model fairly closely fits its business and has used it, with some modifications, as a basis for its IS plans.

A second, more limited approach to data architecture is the standardization of data definitions and codes. Most of the new system products developed by the firms in this study require that line management and IS technical personnel agree on the precise definitions of a specific set of data elements as a prerequisite to building the system. In two firms, however, a set of corporate-wide data definitions was developed solely as an architectural foundation to facilitate meeting future information requirements.

In 1984, Foothill Computer formed a task force, chaired by corporate IS, to identify and define key data elements being used in multiple areas of the business. There were no immediate plans to implement the agreed-upon definitions. Rather, it was assumed that future systems development work would conform to these definitions. In addition, it was established that any group supplying data to another group within the corporation would be required to deliver that data in conformance with the definitions, if asked. After coming to agreement on definitions for over 200 data elements, the task force has more recently refocused its efforts to concentrate only on defining those elements for which a specific business impact can be identified and pursued.

As these examples illustrate, either a widescope strategic data model or a set of standard data definitions can be a product in its own right. When data models or standards are enforced, an organization should gain a major asset of interpretable, shareable data. But usefulness of these architectural foundations can always be questioned, unless the data model is used to guide future systems development, or unless the definitions eventually become incorporated in either operational or managerial databases.

A Range of Data Planning Processes

This section focuses on the planning processes organizations use to identify the target for data management action, and to choose the action (or "product") to pursue. To many people, planning for data resource management is synonymous with a large-scale strategic data planning and modeling effort. There are, however, other less comprehensive planning approaches that can be extremely effective. This section categorizes the planning processes from the case studies into four types: strategic data planning; "80/20" approaches; "targeting;" and no explicit planning. These approaches represent a continuum of planning processes that ranges from global, well-defined, rigorous methods through more local, often less formal approaches, to no data planning at all.

Strategic Data Planning   Strategic data planning is the category that encompasses rigorous top-down planning approaches focused on understanding and modeling data in the context of business functions. The resulting plan defines an architecture of major subject area databases and prioritizes their implementation.[1] The diagram in Exhibit 42.2 adapted from Martin's [19] *Strategic Data-Planning Methodologies,* is representative of these approaches. The left side of the diagram shows a top-down planning approach, leading to the identification of logical subject area databases. In general, only selected portions of the plan are chosen for bottom-up design and implementation.

The underlying assumption of top-down data planning methodologies—that it is impossible to plan effectively if one does not know what the business is, what it does, and what data it uses—is difficult to contest. However, of the 31 data management efforts studied, only five used a strategic data planning approach. In general, these five firms undertook a strategic data planning effort to produce both a strategic data model (which we call an architectural foundation) and a plan of action.

None of these firms saw the kind of success envisioned in the literature—a master data architecture that identifies strategic opportunities and guides all new development. The outcomes of the five efforts varied, but in none did the plans directly lead to the implementation of new systems or subject area databases. In one case, although the clearest benefit was a better understanding of the data by those involved in the planning process, the effort was viewed as worthwhile. Two of the efforts were generally perceived as failures.

In 1982, the central IS planning staff at National Technologies, Inc., a large high technology firm with 20 divisions, began a comprehensive data planning effort in response to the complexity and variability in National Technologies' business environment. The goal was to link strategic IS planning with strategic business planning and to link a logical model of the business data with the development of physical databases and systems. The planning effort took about a year and involved eight people from IS planning and the user community. Although the strategic data model was completed and turned over to systems development teams, the model was not adhered to. The pressures of the operating environment took hold, and deadlines, not the global data model, became the significant driving force. Also, conflicts among the users about definitions and uses of data arose, despite the generally agreed upon data model. In addition, limitations in data-oriented design tools and relational database technology were noted.

In the other two of the five cases, while strategic data planning did not lead directly to an IS plan of action, it did provide an architectural base for subsequent data management efforts.

Exhibit 42.2
Strategic Data Planning²

A strategic data planning process begins with the development of an enterprise or business model (Box 1, below). The enterprise model depicts the functional areas of the firm, and the processes that are necessary to run the business. The next step is to identify corporate data entities and to link them to processes or activities (Box 2). Data requirements are thus mapped onto the enterprise model, leading to the identification of subject areas for which databases need to be implemented (Box 3).

In general only selected portions of the enterprise model and subject area databases are chosen for bottomup design. Building the logical data model is the first step. The data model (Box 5), results from a synthesis of detailed management and end-user data views (Box 4) with the results of the previous top-down entity analysis (Box 2). Database design and subsequent design of application programs (Boxes 6 and 7) proceed from the logical data model.

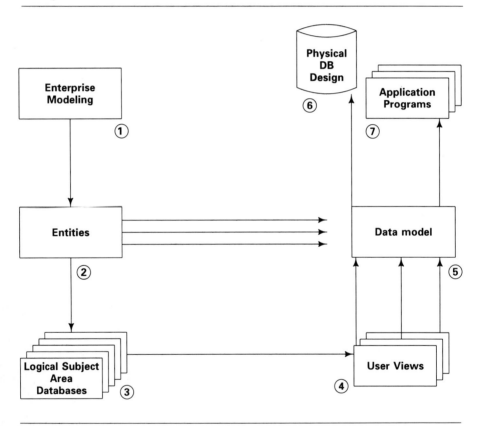

Derek Energy Products completed a business system planning effort for its production division in 1982. Shortly after the plan was complete, the division participated in a major reorganization, and the plan was shelved as no longer appropriate. In 1984, Derek formulated a new long-range IS strategy. The strategy identified a "target future state" for the division's information systems. Key user managers participated with IS personnel in the development of an implementation plan based on the "target future state," critical business objectives, and the current slate of system requests. As part of the planning effort, the business process/data model from the BSP was revived and modified by a small group of IS professionals. The BSP model was useful in categorizing 50 current project requests and in making it apparent that a third of these requests depended on the same six subject area databases. These six databases are now being developed.

In most of the data management efforts studied, the planning and implementation process did not proceed as suggested by strategic data planning methods. Ex-

Exhibit 42.3
The Planning Reality

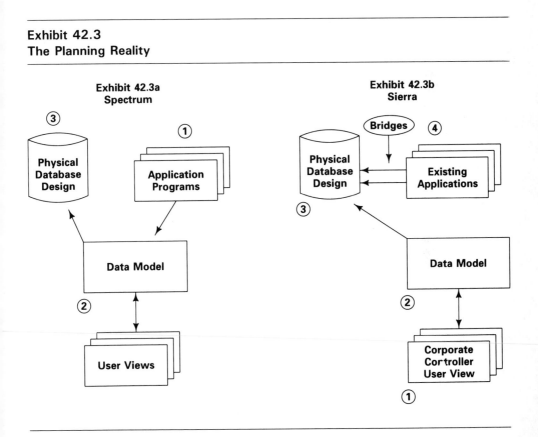

Exhibit 42.3a
Spectrum

Exhibit 42.3b
Sierra

hibit 42.3 illustrates the actual planning process for two companies that were typical of the other case study sites and, in contrast to Exhibit 42.2 shows an altered sequence of steps. In these two cases, as in most of the other firms studied, the companies skipped or abbreviated the "left side" or top-down portion of the top-down planning, bottom-up design process. In doing so, they followed the alternate planning processes to be discussed in the next sections.

As shown in Exhibit 42.3a, Spectrum Electronics chose to develop manufacturing systems without having used any top-down, data-oriented planning methodology to arrive at that decision. The company started with the objective of implementing a particular set of applications (1), then developed a logical data model (2) for this application set's data, and finally designed the physical database and the applications (3).

Sierra Energy (Exhibit 42.3b) started with a particular user's view (1)—that of the corporate controller—and designed a data model (2) and physical databases (3) from that perspective. Methods for "bridging" data from existing applications were then developed (4).

There appear to be a number of reasons that help explain why more firms are not successfully using strategic data planning methods. Table 42.2 lists some of the reasons why it is difficult to gain commitment to the process and to manage expectations regarding the outcome of the strategic data planning. The bottom line is that, for many firms, the approach is too expensive, its benefits are too uncertain, and it is organizationally difficult to implement.

Targeting High-Impact Areas   Most corporations that skip or abbreviate top-down planning methods do not act without a plan. There are a variety of alternative planning processes that can be used. The most common process (seen in 15 of 31 cases) is the "targeting" of a particular function or business area. In some companies, important problem or opportunity areas are evident without extensive analysis.

At Sierra Energy, the corporate controller knew from his experience that he needed, but did not have, consistent, accurate data for corporate reporting purposes. He initiated the development of an information database to be used by the company's many decentralized business units.

When top management at LDI Electronics made improved product quality a corporate priority, the only quality-related information easily accessible was warranty accounting data. It was clear that additional data needed to be collected and made available. A corporate-wide information database for product quality is being designed.

Neither Sierra nor LDI used a rigorous data planning method. But in both companies there were key line managers who could visualize the benefits of accessible quality data. In each case, the data management program was limited in scope but was effective and feasible.

"80/20" Planning Methods   In some firms, there is a desire to get the major benefits of global data planning without having to invest the resources necessary to carry out a fullscale strategic data planning process. The aim in these cases is to zero in quickly on the key "products" to be implemented (bottom-up), while reducing the amount of effort spent in a global planning (top-down) phase. This type of

Table 42.2
Why Strategic Data Planning Approaches Are Difficult to Implement

- The strategic data planning process, done in detail and with a wide scope, can be very time consuming and expensive. For the process to be successful, key operating managers must commit significant time and effort. This commitment is often difficult to obtain (and keep) from these busy individuals.

- Because of the up front effort needed, organizations face a longer and more expensive development process for the initial systems developed with data planning methods. Line managers do not like to see project schedules lengthened. Similarly, IS managers, who have incentives to deliver quickly and to contain costs, may resist the additional effort involved.

- The methodologies require new IS skills and, therefore, may not be easily adopted by IS personnel.

- Often the business will change while the plan is being developed and implemented.

- Total implementation of a wide-scope data planning effort can be extremely expensive. There is a tendency to avoid these new costs, especially if many of the existing systems, which represent a huge investment are still effective.

- When implementing only a subset of the plan, it can be difficult to bridge the gap from the top-down plan to bottom-up design. If proposed and existing systems interface along different boundaries, it may be hard to isolate and replace a subset of existing systems with a subset of proposed systems. The use of application packages also creates interface and boundary problems.

- It is not always clear to the planners or top management whether a strategic data model is being developed to produce a systems plan, create an architecture, or to design new databases. It is difficult to manage the expectations of those involved regarding the results and benefits of the process.

planning, found in four of the 31 cases, can be termed an "80/20" approach, after the adage that for many undertakings, 80 percent of the benefits can be achieved with 20 percent of the total work.

Windsor Products, having carried out its first round of data management in a quick targeted manner, found itself uncertain as to the next information databases to implement. Management decided, however, that a full strategic data model was not necessary for its purposes. It therefore developed its own abbreviated planning approach, which it calls "Data charting." This involved identification of about 100 major data aggregates (i.e., high-level data entities) and the groups in the corporation that used them. This method took less than six man-months of effort, and involved reviews by line managers in all parts of the business. The data chart is serving as the basis of planning for the next round of information databases.

The problem with strategic data planning approaches is the investment of time and dollars needed to obtain results. Drawbacks of "targeting" include the probable inconsistencies that will arise from multiple targeted projects and the fact that in some companies, the most important targets may not be evident. An 80/20 approach, while not providing the detail of strategic data planning or the quick hit of targeted approaches, does appear to offer the major benefits of both previous approaches.

No Planning Process   There are also data management actions that can be taken without any data-oriented planning. For example, if a decision is made to provide better access to existing data without addressing changes in the form of that data, then no data planning methodology is needed. Rather, data can be made available as it is requested. This was the case at Matrac, with its data services approach described earlier and at six other companies.

Bounded Scope

In this study, no firm attempted to manage all the data used by the corporation; all limited the focus of the effort in one or more ways. An important factor in the success of data management efforts is that the scope (i.e., the part of the organization to be included in the effort) be carefully selected. Although the scope of eight data management efforts was divisional, 13 cases, strikingly and logically, focused on a functional area such as manufacturing or finance. This limited scope was usually dominated by a single manager who was able to visualize the results of a data management effort in a segment of the business.

In 10 cases, the scope of the planning effort was corporate. In only three cases did the scope include all of the corporation's data; two of these were corporate-wide strategic data planning efforts for which the results were not as useful as the organization had expected. The third was Windsor Products' 80/20 planning effort to develop a corporate-wide data chart.

In the other seven cases, the effort involved a limited subset of the total data used by the corporation. For example, one effort focused on key corporate-wide subject areas, such as customer or product. Two focused on a small set of important data definitions. Others provided users with ad hoc access to existing data files.

In addition to functions and divisions, other suborganizations such as groups, geographic districts, and product lines exist within a firm. Some corporations may choose one or another of these units as a locus for data management efforts. As the next section will show, the scope of the data management effort is substantially determined by the business objective.

Business Objectives, Not Conceptual Justifications

The proponents of data management far too often base their arguments on either the conceptual soundness of viewing data as a resource or the rationale underlying data-centered systems design. They assert that processes change while data is relatively stable and that data should therefore be the key element in IS planning. Or they argue that global data management is essential because one needs a global plan before developing the individual pieces. While these arguments are appealing, they rarely engender action in the pragmatic, cost-conscious world of the business manager.

Most successful data management processes observed have been aimed at solving a clear and specific business problem or exploiting an opportunity. In some cases, the data management effort occurred because of a line manager's need to respond to changes, such as increased competition, in his or her environment. IS deparments have also had a key role in initiating many of the efforts and in educating line managers as to how improving the management of data can contribute to the business. This section discusses the business-related reasons why firms are motivated to consider more proactive management of data.

Operational Coordination   A major objective for data management action is to better coordinate operational activities, either within specific functions or business units, or across them. This objective often arises when competitive pressures cause a firm to focus on cost reduction. Improved coordination requires an enhanced ability to communicate within or among organizational units. In practical terms, this implies the ability to readily share data. There are six clear examples of coordination as a motivation in the case studies.

Both Spectrum Electronics and Waverly Chemicals felt the need to standardize their manufacturing systems so that many plants could be coordinated more effectively. In both cases, their efforts have meant significant benefits. For example, the standardization of data has led to reduced in-process and inter-plant inventories and to the coordination of spare parts availability, which has reduced downtimes. Common data has also facilitated coordinated purchasing, which has enabled special arrangements with vendors to be made.

Organizational Flexibility   A second type of objective for data management, seen in three cases, is the desire for greater organizational flexibility to allow either an internal restructuring of the organization, or a refocusing of the organization due to changes in the environment.

Waverly Chemicals has restructured its divisional organization several times over the past decade. It merged two large manufacturing divisions in the mid-1970s, and faced major problems with accounting systems that had been designed and implemented separately in the original divisions. In the late 1970s, Waverly combined five old divisions into two new ones. It was quite clear to senior management that there would be other reorganizations in future years. As long as each division had its own accounting systems with much incompatible data, the problems would persist.

Changing an organization's strategic focus can also require more effective data management. Several companies studied have been faced with important changes in the marketplace that put intense competitive pressures on them to change from a product focus to a market or customer focus. Organizational flexibility is often hindered by data structures that have been designed to support particular applications or suborganizations but which are not flexible enough to provide new strategically important "views" of the business.

In 1984, Dobbs Insurance Companies determined that the basic data structure used by its Group Insurance Division, while still appropriate for 90 percent of its current business, would not support its future needs. For example, the "flexible benefits" products the company was considering offering would require major changes in the way it kept data about policies and policy holders. Given the competitive pressures in the insurance industry, Dobbs felt it had no choice but to move to a more flexible data structure.

Improved Information for Managers   The dominant objective for more effective data management, seen in 16 of 31 cases, was to improve information for senior managers, middle managers, and key staff personnel. The need for better data is recognized, for example, when management wants to analyze changing market trends or more closely monitor profitability. These information consumers want two things: improved access to data and improved data quality.

Van Buren Bank wanted to manage customer relationships better, especially with its largest clients. Because each bank branch assigned its own customer identifier to each customer with whom it dealt, there was no easy way to aggregate data for a single customer across the entire bank. The bank has now spent over $1 million to develop a customer information database to allow account managers to retrieve information about the bank's 1000 largest customers.

When problems such as these become important enough to management, strong motivations arise to improve data quality and access.

IS Effectiveness   As information and information technology become more important to firms and information systems budgets grow, there is strong pressure on IS groups to not only develop systems faster (while controlling costs and improving quality) but also to be more proactive in addressing business needs. Improved data management can potentially contribute to the effectiveness of IS planning and delivery by linking the data requirements of the business with IS plans, by increasing systems development productivity, or by reducing systems maintenance costs. Data management actions may also be motivated by the recognition of a lack of integration among existing systems and the difficulties this causes as demand for multi-function or multi-organization systems or information grows.

In six of the 31 cases, the primary motivator for data management efforts seemed to be general IS effectiveness, without any more specific business goals. Four of these six were strategic data planning efforts, while two were efforts to identify and standardize key corporate data element definitions.

Many firms felt that the data management actions they were undertaking would involve greater, not lower, IS costs in the short run. On the other hand, two firms, acting with a clear business objective as the primary motivator, had IS effectiveness as a secondary objective and said that they had achieved reductions in development or maintenance costs.

Spectrum Electronics eliminated separate programs and programming staffs in its plants by centralizing all data processing and by using a centralized database and common software for all manufacturing systems. The company also claims to have reduced maintenance costs by eliminating not just redundant data, but the programs that updated redundant data and the programmers who maintained those programs.

Crockett, the Canadian subsidiary of a major American computer manufacturer, claims a 40 percent reduction in development costs because of a new development process focused on data, the use of an active data dictionary, and users' generation of their own reports.

Major Patterns in the Cases

The four critical components for data management action—business objectives, scope, data planning process, and "product"—provide a rough framework for thinking about the 31 data management efforts. By placing those efforts in the appropriate categories of the framework, as shown in Exhibit 42.4, we can see which choices predominate, and what combinations emerge as recurrent patterns. (Examining the patterns by industry group showed no major differences; see the Appendix.)

Three major patterns, shown by the arrows in Exhibit 42.4, emerge when the sets of choices made by the case study firms are analyzed. The most striking pattern (solid arrows), followed in six cases, represents firms that sought improved managerial information, in a functional area by targeting key business opportunities and by building information databases. Two other firms followed almost this same path, but with a corporate or divisional scope. Management's need to be able to see consolidated financial information, comprehensive data about its customers or profitability of products is a major impetus for data management action and can often be addressed through an information database.

The second prominent pattern (dashed arrows), with four cases, represents firms seeking better operational coordination in a functional area by targeting key business opportunities and building either operational SADB's or common systems. If operational coordination is the goal, then these two products are the most appropriate.

The third pattern (dotted arrows), also with four cases, is made up of firms seeking improved management information, at either a corporate or divisional level, which put in place improved data access services using no explicit data planning process. This is an important option, especially in companies with many common systems extensive data definition and coding standards. This approach rapidly places data where it is valuable—in the hands of end users—and does so at minimal cost.

Two of these three major patterns (and 11 of the 31 cases) involve functional scope and targeted planning. This reflects the importance of managers in specific functional areas who are able to see concrete ways in which better data can assist them in their areas of responsibility.

If we look at the numbers of occurrences in each box of Exhibit 42.4, it becomes apparent that for three of the components of data management action, one alternative dominates the others. Sixteen of the 31 efforts were motivated by a business need for better managerial information. Fifteen of the efforts addressed a targeted need without using a more formal planning process. Eleven of the 31 products were information databases. That these alternatives are well represented is not surprising, but the fact that they are so predominant suggests they are "high-action areas" that ought to be carefully considered by practitioners of data management.

Finally, even though there were only four instances of 80/20 planning processes in this study there is a need to emphasize the importance of this approach. In many corporations, after the more obvious targets are addressed, an important shift is expected toward 80/20 planning processes that identify strategic opportunities without the major investment of more rigorous strategic data planning approaches.

Exhibit 42.4
Major Patterns in the Framework

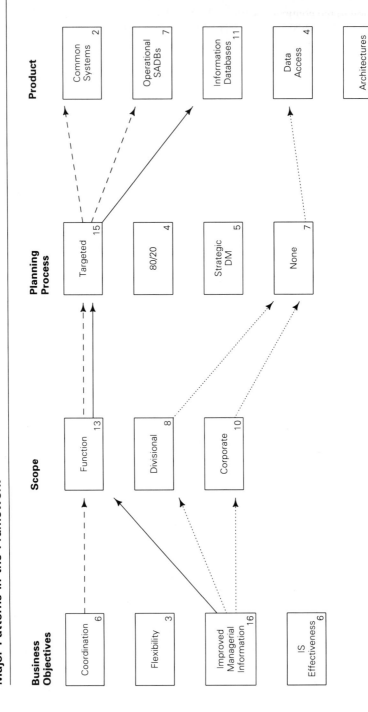

Note: The numbers show how many data management efforts fell into each category.

ORGANIZATIONAL ISSUES AFFECTING DATA MANAGEMENT IMPLEMENTATION

In addition to the contingency model of data management choices presented above, the interviews with IS and line managers have suggested five organizational issues that affect the ability of firms to implement data management efforts. This section briefly presents these issues.

Issue 1: Short-Term and Long-Term Trade-offs in Resource Allocation

Managers considering data management actions must decide how to allocate limited resources among activities that will produce immediate benefits and "infrastructure" efforts that often do not have a quick payback. This tension between long and short term is reflected in our framework. The framework's categories represent a continuum of data management actions that can be directed toward any of three aspects of a corporation's data: infrastructure, content, or delivery.

Infrastructure encompasses the standards that force systems development efforts to conform to a coherent data architecture. Actions to build a data infrastructure (e.g., developing a strategic data model) tend to be both difficult and expensive, and the benefits from such actions are most often realized only in the longer term.

Content refers to the choice of what data to maintain, and also to policies that address the accuracy of that data. Systems to capture new or more detailed data and decisions to purchase external data are examples of actions that affect data content. These efforts tend to be moderately expensive, with benefits in the middle term.

Delivery refers to making existing data available to managers who need it. Data consulting services, extract policies, and the provision of fourth generation reporting tools are examples of mechanisms to improve delivery. Actions in this area tend to be less expensive and have short-term benefits.

The choice of where a firm should best allocate its resources—among infrastructure, content, and delivery—depends very much on the willingness and ability of senior management to invest currently for future benefits. A characteristic of American businesses has been the short-term focus of line managers. Decisions to allocate resources to data architecture are in direct conflict with the pressures to achieve demonstrable results, near-term earnings per share, and this year's return on investment. Not surprisingly, most of the successful efforts reported in this article have tended toward the short-term end of the spectrum. On the other hand, firms that have put in place stronger data architectural foundations appear less likely to face problems integrating and sharing data across the organization.

Issue 2: The Centralizing Tendency of Data Management

Underlying any effort toward more effective data management is the reality that improved data management can lead to greater centralization of decision making in an organization. Increased standardization of data facilitates increased central control. For example, standard data definitions may be established as common systems are developed. If the resulting data is made accessible to senior executives, they will have an enhanced ability to compare operational details of business units under their jurisdiction. There is indeed a tendency to act on this kind of data; several of the systems described here were instituted to facilitate "central" coordination and control. Even where increased centralization is not a design objective, it may be a result.

Issue 3: Impact on the IS Culture

A third organizational issue is the impact of data management on the IS culture. As Durrell [9] points out, "data administration challenges the basic process-oriented approach that has been employed during the last 20 years. This can be disconcerting and sometimes insulting to many long-time DP professionals" [9, p. 1D/29].

The new data-centered system used at Crockett has had a major impact on the work of programmers and analysts. The major activity of these people now is working with business managers to define the business rules governing the meaning of data elements and entering those rules into the active data dictionary. Not surprisingly, this has had a significant impact on the attitudes and turnover of the programmer/analyst staff there. While the level of enthusiasm of current personnel is high, many programmers found their traditional skills of no value in the new environment and left during the transition period.

The problem is not only one of teaching information systems professionals new skills. There must also be changes in organizational processes and managerial policies to support the move toward data-oriented design. For example, incentive mechanisms must be changed to reward programmers for conforming to a corporate data model even if it involves additional time and resources. Without these changes, when system deadline pressures become high, programmers will have a strong tendency to develop their own local data structures rather than embark on negotiations with the data administrator for changes to the corporate data model.

Issue 4: New Responsibilities for User Management

If data is to serve business needs, to what extent must line managers, not only IS professionals, assume new responsibilities? In two firms studied user organizations assume almost complete responsibility for data management. At Sierra Energy, a group within the corporate controller's organization provides general policies and support for systems and data management actions related to the firm's financial functions. At Foothill Computer, a data management group within the corporate-level customer administration function is responsible for managing data subject areas such as customer and price. This group views itself as a data custodian, responsible for obtaining data from the appropriate source organization (e.g., price data from the product line managers), for maintaining the integrity of the data and for delivering data to the user organization's transaction or information systems.

Other firms focused on increasing user involvement in the process of managing data. At a minimum, many firms had task forces with user (and IS) representation to establish data definitions.

It seems obvious to say that the effective management of data as a corporate resource requires the participation of business managers. But the exact nature and scope of line management's responsibilities are not well defined.

Issue 5: The Process of Effectively Introducing Innovations into the Organization

The implementation of initial data management efforts can be usefully viewed as the process of effectively introducing innovations, i.e., new methods or tools of unproven value. Rogers [20] suggests that in general the diffusion of innovations is dependent on, among other things, five characteristics of the innovation. These are (1) the relative advantage of the innovation over its alternatives; (2) the observability of the results; (3) the compatibility of the innovation with existing values, past experience, and perceived needs; (4) the complexity of the innovation; and (5) its "trialability," or the extent to which the innovation can be experimented with on a small-scale, low-risk basis.

Rogers' [20] research can help explain why it has been difficult to implement data management actions, especially large-scale efforts, in many corporations. First, the relative advantage of most data management actions compared to current practice is not known. Also, in most organizations there have been few results to observe. Where results are available, it is extremely hard to separate and quantify the impact of data management from other related (or unrelated) actions.

As noted previously, a data-focused approach to systems is not compatible with the existing process-oriented focus, where the goal is to build individual systems to specification on time, rather than to create a data architecture to meet current and future needs. Certainly, data management involves a great deal of complexity as the walls between applications are torn down and the interrelationships between systems, functions, and organizational units are examined. Finally, very often data management actions have not been presented as testable, small-scale low-risk efforts. Instead, data resource management has been sold on the basis that a major financial investment and top-to-bottom commitment in the organization will be needed to achieve results.

Viewing data management as an innovation also helps to explain the successful efforts studied here. From Rogers' [20] perspective, successful implementation of data management efforts is more likely for more limited approaches where the relative advantage is clearer, the impacts are more observable, and the complexity is lessened. In addition, limited approaches can be viewed as trials or experiments. When the first trial is successful, the organization will probably be ready for a more ambitious second trial and ultimately for significant investment in data management.

CONCLUSION

These exploratory case studies in 20 organizations suggest that there is no single clear-cut approach to improving the management of the data resource. A wide range of options exists that can be selected to fit the needs of a particular business. The appropriate planning process to use and the best "product" to deliver depend heavily on the particular business objective and organizational scope. However, in spite of this variety in approaches, there are seven important conclusions that can be drawn from this research.

Business Benefits Can Result from Improvements in Data Management   Many of the companies studied have realized significant benefits in their attempts to improve the management of data, as reported by their own evaluations. To highlight a few of the benefits mentioned in the case vignettes: Waverly Chemical attributes a reduction of 20 percent in spare parts inventory to the fact that its dozen plants now use a common system; Sierra Energy has reduced the amount of effort it takes to consolidate financial reports from a six person effort taking two weeks to four people taking four days; Consumer Publications has reduced costly errors caused by the manual transcription of data and has simplified the process of managing a promotional mailing; management at Crockett, using its new operational subject area databases and a special query system, is now able to get previously unavailable answers to wide-ranging ad hoc questions, such as the actual effects of price changes on quarterly revenues. For the most part, the companies that realized major benefits were motivated by specific business goals rather than by conceptual arguments for data resource management or a desire to improve general IS effectiveness.

Lack of Data Standardization is a Key Managerial Problem Today   A great portion of the data maintained by corporations today was originally designed to meet the needs of isolated applications, developed in dispersed or autonomous suborganizations. The resulting lack of data standardizations is a major underlying problem with data, often making it difficult or impossible to share or interpret data across application system boundaries. In the study, most of the data-related problems encountered by business managers surfaced when they needed to combine data from several different functions or from several different organizational groups. Almost all of the successful data management efforts involved at least some improvement in data standardization (i.e., common definitions and common codes), even if the improvements were to only a few key data elements, such as customer, product, or vendor IDs.

Total Standardization is Not the Goal   Too great an emphasis on data standardization is a mistake. A detailed corporate-wide data model is probably premature in most companies today because of important hard-to-resolve differences in the way data is defined, stored, or used in different parts of the organization. These significant managerial and system differences are a major reason why strategic data planning approaches are so difficult to carry out. It is extremely costly to completely revamp three decades of embedded systems. Because of the expense, data standardization efforts should focus first on the obvious high payoff areas having a clear business impact. The question of whether, for example, standard customer or vendor identifiers are appropriate targets depends entirely on the business situation. The end goal is not total standardization but only as much standardization as makes sense from a business point of view.

"80/20" Processes Are Growing in Importance in Data Planning   In some situations, it is possible to quickly target the key business impact areas. Where these areas are not apparent, 80/20 planning processes provide an attractive alternative to larger scale strategic data planning methodologies. These 80/20 approaches lead quickly to the next targets for action and can provide a rough interim data model as a starting point for guiding and coordinating various data management efforts. Although this research notes far more "targeted" planning efforts, it is believed that the advantages of 80/20 approaches will, and should, lead to their growing use in the next several years.

Information Databases Will Remain the Dominant Product for the Foreseeable Future   Operational subject databases are not the only appropriate "product" for data management efforts. An information database can provide a standardized source of managerial data drawn from non-standardized applications. Building information databases is usually less expensive and can be done much faster than rewriting the existing non-standardized applications. They can be developed using technology (e.g., relational databases and fourth generation languages) most appropriate for managerial use. In addition, information databases can provide a significant element of a de facto architecture for future development work.

Resource Allocation Must Balance Long-Term and Short-Term Considerations   Organizations wishing to address data problems face a resource allocation choice between improvements to infrastructure (or data standardization), development of specific new databases, and enhanced delivery of the existing data resource. While there is a tendency in American business to opt for the near term payoff (for example, addressing delivery or implementing information databases), the long term appears to favor judicious investments in data architecture infrastructures that will ensure greater data standardization.

A Number of Difficult Organizational Issues Must Be Addressed   No matter which resource allocation choices are made, there are a number of organizational issues that must be addressed for successful implementation of data management efforts. The managerial predilection for short-term results, the centralizing tendency of data management, and the impact of data management on the IS culture, as well as on the responsibilities of line managers, all present issues that, if not managed well, will severely inhibit the effectiveness of data management efforts. Treating an initial foray into data management as a process of introducing innovation can help managers understand which efforts are practicable in their organizational environment.

APPENDIX

An important question is whether the type of data management problems experienced or whether the most effective approaches differ from one industry group to another. Given only 20 companies and 31 data management efforts, it is impossible to give a definitive answer. However, the different industry groups have been compared using the dimensions of the framework. Table 42.3, for example, shows the distribution of data management products for the four industry groups from Table 42.1.

With the possible exception of the process industry group, there are no clear differences among the groups. The process industry group had the only new common systems efforts and a higher incidence of efforts aimed at architectural foundations. These differences could easily be due to chance variations within the groups, to the smallness of the sample, or might reflect special problems or concerns for that group. A similar analysis of the distribution of the three overall patterns by industry group (shown by the arrows in Exhibit 42.4) also shows no clear differences.

Table 42.3
Appendix Table

	Product				
Industry	Operational SADBs	Common Systems	Information Databases	Access Services	Architectural Foundations
Financial Services	1	0	2	0	1
Manufacturing	3	0	5	3	2
Process	2	2	2	0	3
Other	1	0	2	1	1

NOTES

This research was supported by the MIT Center for Information Systems Research and the IBM Program of Support for Education in the Management of Information Systems.

[1] The word plan has two definitions: (1) a scheme of action or procedure; and (2) a representation drawn on a plan, e.g., a map, a model. Although the terms data planning and data modeling have often been used synonomously, it is helpful to distinguish between them. Data planning is used here to mean an effort to develop a "scheme of action." Data modeling refers to the preparation of a "representation" with predetermined scope and level of detail. The representation may be a useful aid in developing a scheme of action, or when done in great detail, may be the basis for a system design. Many strategic data planning methodologies aspire to produce both a model and a plan.

[2] Adapted from James Martin, *Strategic Data-Planning Methodologies*, 1982, p. 109. Used by permission of Prentice-Hall, Inc., Englewood Cliffs, N.J.

REFERENCES

1. Appleton, D.S. "Business Rules: The Missing Link," *Datamation* (30:16), October 1984, pp. 145–150.

2. Appleton, D.S. "The Modern Data Dictionary," *Datamation* (33:5), March 1, 1987, pp. 66–68.

3. Chen, P.P.S. "The Entity-Relationship Model – Toward a Unified View of Data," *ACM Transactions on Database Systems* (1:1), March 1976, pp. 9–36.

4. Chen, P.P.S. (ed.) *Entity-Relationship Approach to Information Modeling and Analysis,* North-Holland, Amsterdam, 1983.

5. Coulson, C.J. "People Just Aren't Using Data Dictionaries," *Computerworld* (16:33), August 16, 1982, pp. ID15–22.

6. Curtice, R.M. "Getting the Database Right," *Datamation* (32:19), October 1, 1986, pp. 99–104.

7. Date, C.J. *An Introduction to Database Systems,* 3rd edition, Addison-Wesley, Reading, MA, 1981.

8. Diebold, J. "Information Resource Management – The New Challenge," *Infosystems* (26:6), June 1979, pp. 50–53.

9. Durrell, W. "The Politics of Data," *Computerworld* (19:36), September 9, 1985, pp. ID25–36.

10. Edelman, F. "The Management of Information Resources: A Challenge for American Business," *MIS Quarterly* (5:1), March 1981, pp. 17–27.

11. *EDP Analyzer.* "Making Better Use of Your Data," (24:8), August 1986.

12. Gillenson, M.L. "Trends in Data Administration," *MIS Quarterly* (9:4), December 1985, pp. 317–325.

13. GUIDE International Corporation. "Establishing the Data Administration Function," Chicago, IL, 1977.

14. Holland, R.H. "Tools for Information Resource Management," presented at The GUIDE Conference, New Orleans, LA, November 9, 1983.

15. Horton, F.W., Jr. *Information Resources Management,* Prentice-Hall, Englewood Cliffs, NJ, 1985.

16. IBM, *Business Systems Planning,* IBM Manual #GE20-0527-3, July 1981.

17. Kahn, B.K. "Some Realities of Data Administration," *Communications of the ACM* (26:10), October 1983, pp. 794–799.

18. Kahn, B.K. and Garceau, L.R. "A Developmental Model of the Database Administration Function," *Journal of Management Information Systems* (1:4), Spring 1985, pp. 87–101.

19. Martin, J. *Strategic Data-Planning Methodologies,* Prentice-Hall, Englewood Cliffs, NJ, 1982.

20. Rogers, E.M. *Diffusion of Innovations,* Free Press, New York, 1962.

21. Ross, R.G. *Data Dictionaries and Standard Data Definitions: Concepts and Practices for Data Resource Management,* Amacon, New York, 1981.

22. Tillman, G.D. "Why Data Administration Fails," *Computerworld* (21:36), September 7, 1987, pp. 73–76.

23. Weldon, J.L. "Who Owns the Data?" *Journal of Information Systems Management* (3:1), Winter 1986.

43

Justifying New Manufacturing Systems: A Managerial Approach

Jack R. Meredith and
Marianne M. Hill

Bill Jones, manufacturing manager for Dacro Machinery, was having trouble meeting his firm's three-year payback criterion for new machine tools. The manufacturing system he was considering had numerous advantages over the current tools and equipment Dacro was using, but how could he quantify the cost savings resulting from shorter lead times, more consistent quality, better scheduling, and less hassle on the shop floor?

Although hypothetical, this scene is being played out over and over again in manufacturing offices across America. Manufacturers are facing ever more severe competition from abroad, yet we are slipping even further behind the competition in a number of industries.

Those who have studied America's ailing competitiveness often propose the adoption of currently available advanced manufacturing technologies, but numerous firms are still not pursuing what many experts feel is their best chance for long-term survival. While some firms have moved ahead in their automation programs, the majority seem to have floundered on the rocks of ROI and payback hurdles.

The need to upgrade our manufacturing abilities is illustrated by the following:

- More than 34 percent of U.S. machine tools are twenty or more years old, the highest proportion of any major industrialized nation.[1] The corresponding figures for England and Japan are 24 percent and 18 percent, respectively. Furthermore, in the U.S. only 31 percent are less than ten years old, while in Japan an astounding 61 percent are less than ten years old.

- In U.S. metal-cutting industries, only about 4 percent of all machine tools are numerically controlled, even though this technology has been commercially available for over a quarter of a century. Ninety-six percent are older vintage, manu-ally operated machines.[2] And within the last five years, 55 percent of Japan's new machine tools were computer numerically controlled, while only 18 percent of the United States' were.[3]

- The half-life of many products has decreased to the point that 50 percent of their sales occur within the first three years.[4] New products must thus be continually designed and manufactured, reducing the advantages of manufacturing economies of scale and increasing the need for flexible production systems that are economic at low volumes.

Though factory automation appears to be crucial to the survival of many firms, it is often significantly easier to justify an equal investment in a marketing program, a high-level personnel hire, office automation, or even an executive retreat.

In most firms, proposed investments in new manufacturing technology com-pete with other projects and potential expenditures on the basis of "best financial return." Forcing manufacturing managers to justify new manufacturing systems solely on the basis of financial formulas is, we feel, a misapplication of these techniques. The inappropriate use of financial justification approaches has resulted largely from two historical patterns of thinking.

The first is simply that manufacturing machinery has always been justified based on the labor savings it allowed. It was natural, therefore, to identify such manufac-turing techniques with the machinery instead of the use to which the machinery was being put. But the reasons for using machinery have been changing in the last few years. Now it is acquired for reasons far removed from pure labor savings—lead time reduction, quality, advanced capabilities, flexibility, safety, and numerous others.

This change in the use of machinery parallels the second trend in thinking about manufacturing. Historically, manufacturing has been the firm's productivity machine, a "can do" resource that executed strategic plans expediently, adding value to the product and simultaneously meeting marketing, financial, and regulatory constraints. A few firms, largely those employing the advanced manufacturing technologies, have moved past this stage toward the realization that manufacturing can be a highly com-petitive strategic weapon. It is simply incongruous to use a justification approach based on cost savings to make a decision about turning manufacturing into a strate-gic competitive weapon. Strategies are, by definition, oriented toward the long term, and any anticipated cost benefits simply may not materialize in the short-term finan-cial horizon.

The transitional nature of manufacturing today poses a number of familiar and well-publicized dilemmas for top managers:

- Having to "automate, emigrate, or evaporate" without fully understanding either the complete costs or the complete benefits of complex, expensive automated systems.
- Trying to decide which alphabet soup of technologies to choose, or which biased vendor or consultant to engage.
- Having a lack of in-house expertise, but being warned that turnkey systems are unacceptable.

- Facing a "you bet your firm" situation, or else incrementally adding incompatible "islands of automation."
- Needing to decide which systems should be interconnected and which can remain independent.
- Trying to determine if the new manufacturing systems are information or production systems, and if either one is worth the cost.

Some of these issues are extremely complex, and solutions should not be attempted without a thorough understanding of the technologies involved. Although we cannot address all these issues here, we do offer some structure for thinking about advanced manufacturing technologies that we believe will provide insights.

IDENTIFYING THE ACQUISITION PURPOSE

It is helpful for top management to focus on the reason for considering new manufacturing technologies. The critical factor to identify is the intended use of the new system. For example, it may be acquired because existing machines or systems are incapable of handling the volumes that will be required in the future. Then the firm is facing a straightforward capacity-addition situation and can handle it as such.

Similarly, the firm may be replacing one machine or system with another. Again, if the aim is simply to become more efficient, then the firm is facing a straightforward efficiency-improvement situation. An example of this was Cincinnati Milacron's replacement of welding teams with a robotic welder; the welding teams were transferred to other tasks within Milacron.[5] Not only were cost savings significant, but consistency and quality of welds were much improved also.

On the other hand, the acquisition may have little to do with increasing the efficiency of a particular operation. Long-, or even medium-, range planning may have forced the realization that drastic changes must be made in the firm's products—in their mix, their volume, or their design—that cannot take place using existing equipment and processes. Thus, the acquisition of technology is deemed necessary for the firm to achieve its goals. Note that the emphasis here is now on effectiveness, not efficiency, as has been the case with manufacturing in the past.

As one example, Illinois Tool Works' (ITW) managers knew they had to change their entire competitive approach for producing and distributing keyboards and other computer data-entry devices.[6] Using advanced manufacturing techniques such as group technology, the firm increased product variety and drastically cut product cycles. Three-year product development lead times were reduced to six months. ITW intentionally fractured its mass market into smaller minimarkets of sizes, models, and options that better provided what the customer needed and were also more resistant to entry from competitors. This change also eliminated a number of production costs, such as buffer stocks and work standards.

This situation was clearly not a straightforward replacement or capacity-addition decision, but rather a strategic change of major proportions. To sufficiently increase effectiveness, extensive changes were required, with concomitant organizational impacts and a substantial risk to the firm. It was not unlike the merger of two firms, when physical and organizational systems must be totally redesigned and integrated.

As a more detailed example, consider the case of Peerless Saw Company, a small sheet steel fabricator in Ohio that was reeling from the impact of foreign competition, escalating costs, and obsolete equipment.[7] Its steel blade markets were being taken en masse by foreign competition offering similar quality at lower prices for high-volume models of blades. The firm was at the point of being forced to replace its outdated punch presses, but management knew this would not blunt the impact of foreign competition. The only hope for long-term survival was to move into the custom-products market, where the chances of competing were better.

Top management considered replacing the punch presses with laser-cutting machines, but the technology was pushing the state of the art. The president envisioned a menu-driven computerized system that allowed the current high-school-educated employees to design the blades and download the design into the programmable controller-driven laser cutter. No such CAD/CAM software existed.

When all the projected costs — including programming the desired software — were added up, the system did not come close to being cost justified. Yet the president believed the technology was the only long-term hope for his firm and went ahead with the project. In retrospect, as the president now relates, the system still could not be justified on the basis of cost savings. What the system did do was to totally change the market in which the firm competed. It is now in the custom-designed, high-value blade market. Even this market has been altered by the new technology. Customers have found it so easy to alter blade designs, with such quick turn-around, that they are experimenting with new designs themselves in order to wring 1 and 2 percent speed improvements, or quality improvements, from the blades.

And last, the new technology was so creatively applied to fabricating other products that an entire new division, Peerless Laser Processors, Inc., was created to explore new markets. The firm is now the leader in the industry, an industry it created. Had the president relied on simple economic justification techniques to guide him in his decision about acquiring this technology, the firm would probably no longer exist. Instead, a strategic view was used, and the technology was applied in innovative ways to create an entire industry.

The two methods of applying advanced manufacturing technology described above — straightforward replacement for efficiency and complex integration for synergistic competitive advantage — are extremes on a continuum that can be placed on a scale based on the technology's level of integration.

LEVELS OF ADVANCED MANUFACTURING SYSTEMS

Exhibit 43.1 shows four relatively separate levels of technological integration. Level 1 is defined as stand-alone, or unitary, equipment such as machine tools or robots. A majority of U.S. manufacturing firms operate at this elementary level.

Level 2 consists of cellular groupings of equipment and materials for the production of families of parts. They may be computerized or not, as the various versions and implementations of group technology may be. Group technology, which originated in the Soviet Union, was largely adopted and promoted by the British. But most instances of this mode of production occur in Japan, where it is used exten-

Exhibit 43.1
Characteristics of Advanced Manufacturing Systems

	Level 1 Stand-alone	Level 2 Cells	Level 3 Linked Islands	Level 4 Full Integration
	NC Machine Tools	GT	MRP II	CIM
	Robot	FMS	CAD/CAM	
		CAE	AS/RS	
			GT/CAPP	

Purpose	Change
Objective	Effectiveness
Benefits	Intangible
Scope of Effects	Systemwide
Organizational Impact	Extensive
Risk	Substantial

sively. Relatively few U.S. manufacturers use Level 2 systems, though interest in the approach is growing.

The next level of integration is represented by the linked islands of Level 3 systems. These are virtually always computerized and either tie many pieces of a large functional area together (for example, manufacturing resource planning, or MRP II, ties various departments in the production area together) or else tie separate functional areas together (for example, engineering with manufacturing). Though not particularly common in U.S. firms yet, there is considerable activity in this area. Many firms are striving to implement MRP II systems, and General Motors has introduced the manufacturing automation protocol (MAP) system. Other countries are not particularly advanced in this level either, because they frequently have even less access to computer power than U.S. firms.

The fourth level of relatively full integration, or "computer integrated manufacturing" has been virtually achieved by a number of American, Japanese, and European firms. The widely publicized factories of Fanuc in Japan, GE Dishwasher in Louisville, Kentucky, and IBM Proprinter in Charlotte, North Carolina, are good examples of this level of integration.

Though worldwide statistics based on these definitions are not available, it is clear that the higher levels of integration are relatively rare, and that the first two levels characterize the overwhelming majority of worldwide manufacturing. However, the U.S. firms can largely be characterized by Level 1, while Japanese industry can more appropriately be characterized by Level 2—a more effective, as well as efficient, level.

It should be noted that two firms may buy identical equipment but have quite different purposes in mind, at least in terms of integration level. For example, a few robots and machining centers may be purchased to replace a number of different stand-alone machines or labor installations (Level 1), or to form into cells (Level 2), or to create linked islands (Level 3), or even to be part of a fully integrated plant (Level 4).

Since the purpose of acquiring new manufacturing technology varies so much, we should expect that the justification process would as well. Therefore, in describing the levels of technological integration below, we also address the difficulties of justification and suggest appropriate procedures for each level.

We do not mean to imply that only one justification method is appropriate for a particular level of technology, or that a method is inappropriate for other technologies. Rather, higher levels of technology have different purposes, so different justification approaches tend to be most applicable.[8]

Level 1: Stand-Alone

This level represents stand-alone hardware that is commonly controlled by self-contained computers, or possibly programmable controllers. Items likely to fail in this category include wire-guided vehicles, numerically controlled (NC) machine tools, robots, and other equipment with highly limited and local information requirements. Level 1 systems are everywhere; they are by far the most common form of manufacturing automation.

The sole purpose of the system, or hardware, is to replace an existing machine, or perhaps a group of machines and workers. The intent is to continue existing operations but to achieve better quality, or more efficiency, or higher speed or capacity. The replacement might thus create savings because of decreased inspections, lower levels of inventories, increased safety, reduced rework and scrap, less downtime, and so forth.

The stand-alone replacement ordinarily incurs minimal risk and usually will not affect the organization's structure. Effects are typically confined to the new equipment and its interfacing systems. If the equipment fails to perform as expected, the buyer contacts the vendor immediately, and the problem is usually corrected without incident. The user knows what the need is and what the new system is supposed to do. If any risk exists, the user knows what it is and how to ensure protection from failure.

Given the clear aims of Level 1 systems and hardware, common economic justification techniques are entirely appropriate. The relevant benefits and costs are identified and converted into measures that have well-known, predetermined criteria.

The economic techniques are primarily short term and financially oriented. These well-known approaches include payback (or payout), return on investment (ROI), net present value (NPV), and cash flow. Many other techniques are also used, but these are the most common ones. Since these measures are so well known, we will not define them further.

The advantages of purely economic justification techniques are their simplicity, clarity, and data availability. For strict equipment-replacement projects that aim to save costs, these measures are most appropriate. If the intent is direct labor savings, the expected reduction in man-hours can be estimated and the savings evaluated. Ancillary costs—increases or decreases in setup labor, scrap, work-in-process investment, floor space, and so on—can also be calculated.

When a heavy equipment manufacturer decided to install welding robots, for example, management was easily able to calculate the savings expected from reduced man-hours and decreased scrap. But they also needed to consider the cost of acquiring new fixturing to hold the workpieces in the right position for robotic welding, and the expense of replacing shears and brake presses upstream in the process so that the robots were presented with consistent pieces.

There are some dangers in using these simple justification approaches. One such danger is the use of an artificially inflated "hurdle" rate, typically mandated to encourage proposals that offer high returns. These high hurdle rates may discourage important, lower-return projects. Furthermore, these rates commonly assume "everything else equal." But if necessary replacements in equipment and systems are not made as needed, everything else may not remain equal, and the high hurdle rate will in reality never be achieved.

Second, all affected costs should be considered in the calculations. Cost savings in one area are nearly always offset by unexpected cost increases in other areas. It is much too common in U.S. industry for one department to implement a cost-reduction project that simply shifts the costs to another department, where they are much more difficult to identify. For example, a number of firms have found that advanced technologies can save machine-operator labor, but only at the expense of hiring additional, expensive software programmers.

Level 2: Cells

Systems at Level 2 have a higher level of interaction and communication. Typically, they consist of multiple pieces of individual, Level 1 equipment, placed or connected in a "cellular" configuration to perform multiple but ordinary tasks on a family of parts. This cell accomplishes a variety of functions, largely through the ability of the integrated information system.

At this second level, the purpose of the system is to facilitate some required change in the firm's product mix, capacity, lead time, or a combination of these factors. To an extent the production strategy is being altered. The objective is to make the system more "effective": to achieve higher quality, new products, improved customer responsiveness, and so on. Again, the organizational impact will be moderate, though the system will affect a larger area because of its interfaces. The risk is greater than with Level 1, since compatibility problems do exist and better coordination is required, but it is still low.

Examples of Level 2 systems are group technology (GT) lines where multiple cells are employed for producing product and part families; flexible manufacturing systems (FMSs) comprising a half-dozen or so NC machines with automated materials handling; and computer-aided engineering (CAE) for stress analysis, finite element modeling, and other engineering tasks performed on a computer model of the product. The FMS cells used by Ingersoll, Vought, FMC, Rockwell, and Mazak are the most publicized form of Level 2 technology. These cells cost millions of dollars and produce anywhere from a few to several thousand different parts, many only once. The most important benefits of Level 2 systems are probably the intangible ones: greater flexibility, reduced lead time, lower work-in-process, smoother work flows, and better quality.

Because Level 2 technologies are normally employed for their broader, less tangible benefits, a justification procedure that can recognize these benefits is needed. "Portfolio" models are well suited for the analysis of these broader issues and can help managers to choose among competing projects on the basis of multiple criteria. The economic justification techniques of Level 1 can be included as one element in the portfolio analysis, and can be weighted heavily, if desired.

The portfolio approach comprises a group of justification procedures for choosing which among a large number of competing projects will be funded.[9] The various projects' investment costs, on-going costs, and benefits are usually identified, as is some estimate of each project's risk. The manager selects several projects that together make up a portfolio, which must satisfy a set of minimum criteria concerning ROI, risk, strategic or tactical benefits, and so on. Normally, either benefits are maximized subject to capital investment and risk limitation, or risk or capital is minimized subject to an acceptable level of benefits returned. Three major types of portfolio techniques exist: programming models, scoring models, and growth options.

Programming Models   These algorithmic techniques include linear, integer, and goal-programming formulations. Almost every large firm has used one of these techniques (especially linear programming) at one time, and there are many microcomputer software programs that can solve these models. As an example, each project can be represented as a 0–1 variable in an integer program selecting projects that maximize a set of weighted scores (see equation below) subject to particular constraints, such as resource use.

Goal programming allows the manager to consider separate objectives independently – that is, without putting them all on the same weighted basis. The program can include resource constraints on capital, facilities, labor, and other such factors.

Scoring Models   These techniques, even more common than programming models, include many variations: weighted, unweighted, 0–1, linear, and so on. Essentially, the manager determines a set of relevant factors, then assigns each project a "score" (say s_1) for each factor. The factor scores are summed up to give that project a total score:

$$\text{Total Score} = s_1 + s_2 + \ldots .$$

The project with the largest total score (assuming larger is better) is deemed "best." Weights (w_i) can be included in the equation to derive a weighted total score. Virtually every manager has used the scoring approach for some decision.

Growth Options   Kester argues that the "soft" side of an investment argument can be hardened by considering future investment opportunities as analogous to call options on securities.[10] A project that creates opportunities to invest capital in productive assets at some future point is seen as a "growth option" and has a definite "expected value."

For instance, a firm that wants to acquire a manufacturing cell will gain more than the direct benefits of that system; it will also gain a link that can later be part of a more fully integrated system. Thus the option's value is the current value of expected cash flows from the cell, plus the expected value of new growth opportunities arising through the ownership and use of the asset. The firm must add the probability of additional use to the option's current value in order to determine its expected value.

An advantage of this approach is the explicit recognition that not investing leaves the firm in a weakened competitive position for the future — a recognition that is often ignored, at their peril, by executive committees. Determining the value of a technology option is a difficult subjective judgment for most managers, but assigning some definite value to strengthening the firm's future competitive position is important and can seriously affect technology decision making.

Level 3: Linked Islands

At the third level, some cells ("islands of automation") from Level 2 are connected to form linked islands, typically through computerized information networks. At this level of integration, multiple departments and functions are affected by the extensive change required; the changes may even affect the organizational structure. The linked islands' production flexibility offers competitive advantages: the ability to more easily and quickly generate new products and enter new markets, the opportunity to bring synergy to the production process, and, in general, the ability to provide a barrier to entry by competitors. The extensive integration and complexity of Level 3 systems add more risk, however, because the failure of any one element, or the lack of full coordination, can cause the entire network to fail, or at least compromise its effectiveness.

One example of Level 3 linked islands is computer-assisted design/computer-aided manufacturing (CAD/CAM). CAD includes shape, size, function, and, typically, drafting; CAM usually refers to automatic fabrication or generation of machining instructions. Other examples are automated storage and retrieval systems (AS/RS), group technology/computer-aided process planning (GT/CAPP), where CAPP constructs the routings and operations automatically, and even manufacturing resource planning (MRP II) — the set of information packages that includes forecasting, master scheduling, material-requirements planning, inventory, plan monitoring, maintenance, cost accounting, and so on. Well-known examples of MRP II systems include Black & Decker, Tennant Company, Twin Disc, and other "class A" firms. The primary advantages here are the synergistic benefits to the firm of everyone working toward the same goals, especially in terms of design lead time and customer specials that could open a new market or give the firm a competitive edge.

Level 3 systems require more intense analysis than Level 1 or 2, because they involve additional risks. The portfolio and economic analysis factors are still relevant and should be included; any possible uncertainty should be considered as well. There are two major techniques available for these more "analytic" requirements: value analysis and risk analysis. The former is more pragmatic, the latter more academic, but both methods can include subjective judgments and uncertainty. Because of this, and their ability to include difficult-to-quantify costs and benefits, these methods are more realistic for Level 3 systems.

Value Analysis   Keen proposes the use of value analysis to justify advanced, computerized systems.[11] The methodology involves two stages. In the first (pilot) stage the firm considers whether or not to build a complete but small-scale system. The decision is made by identifying (not necessarily quantifying) the pilot's benefits, then determining a cost threshold — what the firm would be willing to pay to receive those benefits. In this pilot stage the project is considered an investment in R&D rather than a capital investment in manufacturing.

If this stage is successful, the list of pilot benefits can be revised or extended, and the potential capabilities of the full system can be better assessed. The decision to build the full system is based on establishing its cost and on determining the benefit threshold necessary to justify the investment, and the likelihood of attaining that threshold.

Many firms grouping elementary part-families for more efficient design, purchasing, and manufacturing use this approach. They may not even relocate machinery at this stage, but focus instead on the gross, elementary benefits of group technology. If the benefits of this low-level investment appear worthwhile, they may then proceed to a full-scale effort with complete coding and classification, physical relocation of machines, and so on. Other firms experiment with cellular production involving only two or three machines before proceeding to larger cells.

Risk Analysis   This approach, popularized by Hertz, relies on simulation of probabilistic factors (costs, capacities, benefits, labor negotiations, and so on) to statistically or graphically describe outcomes.[12] The initial probability distributions can be obtained either from historical records of the data or from the subjective opinions of managers. The latter is appropriate if data is not historically tracked or cannot be easily measured (the likelihood of a new federal regulation being passed, or the chances of a strike).

Risk analysis is then used to produce a cumulative distribution function showing the likelihood of achieving various measures: profits, lead times, ROI, market share, and so on. Various policies or projects are tested; their cumulative distribution functions are compared vis-à-vis means and probabilities of exceeding (or perhaps not meeting) specific values assigned to the measures. Using the concept of "stochastic dominance," managers can identify superior projects or policies.

For example, Exhibit 43.2 illustrates the cumulative probabilities of market share being less than the values shown on the x-axis for three different projects involving linked islands. At a market share of 15 percent, for example, the probability that project A would have less than this share is 90 percent, whereas the probability for project C is only 10 percent. Reading the exhibit across a constant probability, 50

Exhibit 43.2
Risk Analysis Plot

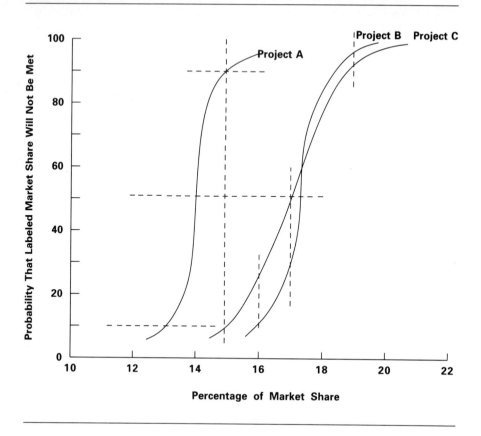

percent, we see that project A comes in at a 14 percent share and project C at a 17 percent share. Since project C has a better (lower) value of probability than project A for every value of market share, we say that project C "dominates" project A. More technically, project C dominates A by what is theoretically known as "first order stochastic dominance."

Of more interest is the comparison of project B with project C. At low levels of share, such as 16 percent, project B has a lower probability (10 percent versus 25 percent) of being less than this share and hence would tend to be preferred. But at higher levels of share, such as 19 percent, project C has the lower probability (92 percent versus 96 percent) and would tend to be preferred. That is, project C has more variability in its outcome than project B, offering more opportunity for a high share but also more risk of a low share. Even so, under certain not particularly restrictive conditions relating to "second order stochastic dominance," we can conclude that project B dominates project C, as well as project A.

Florida Power & Light Company used risk analysis to quantify the uncertainty of a $30-million new-technology project. Managers were particularly concerned about the possibility of cost over-runs, especially if adverse rulings occurred during the project. They were also particularly interested in the likelihood of schedule slippages, and in the interplay between schedule slippages and costs.[13] Air Products and Chemicals, Inc., used risk analysis for a computer facility project, predicting the possible costs of backup alternatives resulting from schedule delays in project completion.[14] The analysis allowed management to select a low-cost alternative, knowing the likelihood and impacts of a delay of a disaster.

Level 4: Full Integration

Full integration links the entire manufacturing function and all its interfaces through extensive information networks. This level includes all Level 3 systems, as well as transportation equipment, functional departments, top management, and so on. This level of integration is commonly known as computer-integrated manufacturing (CIM). We should differentiate between CIM and a system that ties the entire firm together, sometimes called computer-integrated business. We are focusing here only on how manufacturing interacts with other areas: forecasts and inquiries from marketing, cash needs to finance, costs to accounting, and so on.

Integration at Level 4 allows the new production strategy to become a true competitive weapon in the marketplace. Such extensive integration also, however, typically demands a major change in the way the business is run, including purchasing, finance, marketing, and even top management functions. That is, to utilize the benefits that integration brings requires major organizational changes in the firm. Of course, this involves major risk as well. Even in a greenfield plant, new workers are doing new jobs with new equipment to perform new operations. Everything is changing at once. It is a virtual "you bet your company" situation.

Examples are infrequent but do exist. General Motors' "factory of the future" project in Saginaw, Michigan, is one, as are Pratt & Whitney's showcase compressor blade plant in Columbus, Georgia, and Mazak's machine tool plant in Florence, Kentucky. In these cases the firms were committed to becoming fully competitive and focused on a mix of properties: quality, lead time, reliability, and other performance factors relevant to the specific market of interest. Whether they will succeed is still unknown.

Full integration adds a hefty increment of risk, but Level 4's primary additional element is the new manufacturing strategy based on these advanced technologies. The justification process, therefore, needs to recognize this change in strategy. The issues of economics, subjective benefits, risk, and uncertainty from Levels 1, 2, and 3 are not ignored at this level; rather, strategic benefits are now management's primary focus.

Based on our research, we typically see one of two general approaches. Very large firms seem to ask themselves whether this is a market they want to stay with, or one that they should get out of. If they decide to stay in, they agree to reinvest heavily to become (or remain) an industry leader. For example, GE spent nearly

$40 million to renovate its Louisville dishwasher plant. Based on its success, management plans to do the same at other appliance plants. And IBM spent approximately a third of a billion dollars to renovate its typewriter plant in Lexington.

In medium-sized and small firms, such as Peerless, the investment is examined very closely. Operations critical to improving competitive ability are identified for upgrading consideration. Then the benefits are evaluated, the costs are determined, the risks are weighed, and an intensive analysis is conducted before a decision is made.

The "strategic" techniques are generally less formal and technical than the other approaches and might therefore tend to be viewed as weaker. Yet they frequently play a commanding role. What top management must decide is whether a strategic shift overshadows any weaknesses in the other justification criteria. Many well-known implementations of these technologies were given the go-ahead based primarily on strategic factors, rather than on the criteria of the first three levels. It may seem unfortunate that the technologies could not be justified on "legitimate" grounds, but with new technologies there is often little hard data to go on. The firm, to stay at the forefront, must make decisions based on gut feeling. Four approaches are typical of this mind-set.

Technical Importance   The thinking in these cases is that the organization cannot move beyond its current stage without first introducing a given technical innovation—that is, it cannot "leapfrog" to another stage. The return may be negligible but the project is mandatory if, based on the innovation, more complex but also more desirable projects are to be implemented later on. Managers facing this situation commonly group this project with another favorable project and have them both approved at the same time; the second project requires the first project's existence.

All firms that have attempted material-requirements planning systems are aware that inventory records must be 95 percent accurate, and bill of material records 98 percent accurate, if the MRP system is to work. Clearly, a firm may have been operating fine without this level of accuracy, so the return on this investment would not seem to be significant, but it is necessary in order for the new technology to work properly. A similar example is the coding and classification that must precede group technology implementation.

Business Objectives   In this situation, the project contributes directly to the strategic objectives of the firm; monetary considerations may be almost irrelevant. For example, a primary business objective of the firm may be to stand out as a technological leader. A particular project may demonstrate, or build, this competence better than any other approach.

An example is the recent tendency of some machine tool manufacturers to install flexible manufacturing systems in their own production facilities, because they need to send the message that they use what they sell. This also allows them to experience the problems that their customers have and consequently to develop improved products.

Competitive Advantage   Here, the project may yield a significant competitive weapon. It is an opportunity the firm cannot afford to pass up. The project typically builds on a small competitive advantage the firm already holds, significantly strengthening it in the process. On occasion, a unique set of circumstances comes together, allowing the firm to take advantage of the benefits the project offers.

Peerless provides an example of this approach. Faced with dismal long-term prospects, the president forged a strategic approach to survival that yielded a weapon with significant competitive advantage—more than even the president realized at the time he made the decision. Subsequent technology decisions have all been based on the competitive advantage the laser system gave the firm in the first place.

Research & Development   The R&D approach is to treat the project as a high-risk endeavor with an improbable payoff. The strategy here is that one of many projects will eventually pay off and reimburse the firm for all the failures. Clearly, only projects in the mainstream of the business are considered for this treatment. The examples provided earlier under "value analysis" embody this approach in their first, pilot stage.

MATCHING JUSTIFICATION APPROACH AND MANUFACTURING TECHNOLOGY

The match between justification technique and integration level is illustrated in Exhibit 43.3. The conceptual basis for this diagram is that justification techniques appropriate for low-level systems are simply inadequate for higher-level systems. They can be useful supplements, but they do not critically measure the primary use for which the technology is being considered.

For example, a project that is synergistic with other ongoing projects and contributes in indirect ways to strategic business objectives, perhaps at high risk, simply cannot be reduced to a decision involving one or two numbers. And as more integration is required, the benefits and risks become potentially greater and must be considered more explicitly, which economic justification techniques fail to do.

Trying to use financial techniques to justify a strategic investment is, clearly, problematic. Purely economic justifications are inadequate at higher levels of integration for other reasons, as well. Numerous authors have warned of the dangers inherent in trying to justify these systems with horse-and-buggy economic techniques: cost accounting systems that track smaller and smaller percentages of direct labor in products, economies of scope rather than scale, and intangible benefits that far outweigh the tangible benefits, to name a few.[15]

Another danger is that when a technology is justified on the basis of cost savings, there is a tendency to employ it solely for that purpose and to ignore its other benefits and uses. With such flexible, powerful tools available, a company must not blind itself to the unique and creative uses of technologies, nor to the benefits that can be wrung from those uses.

It is important that the justification approach match the intended level of integration, rather than the equipment itself. It is the acquisition purpose that determines the justification process, not the type of equipment. The following passage illustrates this point:

Exhibit 43.3
Justification Approaches for Advanced Manufacturing Systems

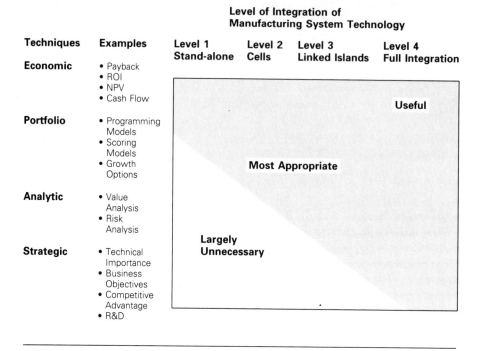

**Level of Integration of
Manufacturing System Technology**

Techniques	Examples	Level 1 Stand-alone	Level 2 Cells	Level 3 Linked Islands	Level 4 Full Integration
Economic	• Payback • ROI • NPV • Cash Flow				**Useful**
Portfolio	• Programming Models • Scoring Models • Growth Options		**Most Appropriate**		
Analytic	• Value Analysis • Risk Analysis				
Strategic	• Technical Importance • Business Objectives • Competitive Advantage • R&D	**Largely Unnecessary**			

Systems designed to take over performance of existing tasks can be evaluated on the basis of the cost of task performance; a successful system should reduce this overall cost. (Higher level systems) however are designed to enable the performance of new tasks. This cost displacement model cannot be used to accomplish an evaluation of a system which aims to make the organization more effective, as opposed to more efficient, by enabling it to do things it could not do previously.[16]

Again, the general match between justification approach and intended level of integration shown in Exhibit 43.3 does not imply that less sophisticated techniques have no value at higher levels. Indeed, the evaluations may very well constrain or even dictate the technology selected. But the major focus required for higher levels of integration is on the higher-level techniques, addressing, as they do, the critical needs of the firm for technological integration.

Similarly, the more sophisticated techniques may have value in the justification process for the lower-level technologies, but they are not usually considered worth the heavy investment of time and trouble. Stand-alone or cellular systems may very well contribute to strategic objectives, but this is not typically their purpose.

IMPLEMENTING HIGHLY INTEGRATED MANUFACTURING SYSTEMS

The key to strategic employment of advanced manufacturing technologies is integrating them with other operations to obtain a competitive advantage. These are not at all like the stand-alone accounting and payroll packages that firms installed in the past with only minor difficulty.

Just having the technology does nothing for the firm. The trick is to put it in the hands of creative, innovative people who will develop novel uses and applications that may never have been considered in the justification proposal. The learning curve for these technologies should itself be managed, with users constantly striving for further improvements in the manufacturing process.

A key to this effort is to fully capitalize on the vendors' knowledge of their product and its installation. The firm should work hand-in-hand with the vendor and involve the technologies' ultimate users—the accountants, the foremen, the operatives on the floor. It is paramount that these people be included in planning and implementation very early on.

It is also important to note that companies do not "leap" directly into Level 4 technologies. A firm should probably start at Level 1 and, as it becomes more knowledgeable about manufacturing technology, move into Level 2, then 3, and possibly, eventually, into Level 4. The firm must learn as it goes, and the learning cannot be limited to the manufacturing people. Everyone—accounting, marketing, top management—must become involved, or else there will be only "islands of knowledge." The whole firm will not be able to move forward, because the ignorance in one area will hold it back.

One of the most common reasons for the failure of advanced manufacturing systems is the lack of planning before the technology is acquired. These complex systems demand extensive preplanning. The manufacturing strategy they will support, and how this strategy relates to and facilitates the business strategy, should be understood by everyone in the firm.

But a warning! It is often said that a major "strategy" will be round-the-clock utilization of advanced manufacturing systems. High utilization is not a strategy. Extensive utilization may well be desirable, but to run the system continuously simply because it is expensive smacks of the "economies of scale" philosophy that dominated our manufacturing strategy for so many years. What good are a million items for which there is no demand? As Whybark so eloquently pointed out: If you have a car sitting in the company parking lot, a high-utilization strategy would mean you hired a chauffeur to drive it continuously around the plant while you were working, in order to keep it highly utilized.[17]

In all cases, if a pilot process can be attempted, it should be. In more than one firm the preparation for automation, usually known as systemization (correcting data records, simplifying production processes, redesigning the product for automated manufacture), was so effective that the automated equipment was not needed immediately. This allowed management to better plan and prepare for the eventual automation.

The point here is a sensitive one. Automation demands excellence of management—lacking that, it will not pay off. The greatest mistake a firm can make is to automate the production process that is in place—we have yet to find a firm whose existing manufacturing process could not be improved. Before automation, systemize.

Systemization offers another advantage. Change should be carefully controlled. The easiest way to fail is to change everything at once: the product, the process, the equipment. By systemizing first, each change can be carefully planned and controlled without the pressure of an enormous capital investment demanding immediate high utilization.

In conclusion, advanced manufacturing systems offer firms (particularly American firms, with their historic labor problems) tremendous advantages for competing in the world economy. But narrow perceptions of their benefits, outmoded justification techniques, and fear of the risks involved have brought the adoption of these systems to a stand-still. By better understanding the benefits the systems offer, the manner in which they should be implemented, and the way in which they should be employed, top management will be more receptive to automated manufacturing systems.

NOTES

[1]G. Bylinsky, "The Race to the Automatic Factory," *Fortune*, 21 February 1983, pp. 52–54.

[2]Ibid.

[3]R. Jaikumar, "Post-Industrial Manufacturing," *Harvard Business Review*, November–December 1986, pp. 69–76.

[4]J.D. Nichols, "How Customer Needs Are Shaping the 'Factory of the Future,' " *Management Review* 73 (1984): 29, 35.

[5]M.M. Hill, "Cincinnati Milacron Welding Robot Case Study," in *Management Issues in High-Technology Manufacturing Industries*, ed. J. Comer (Cincinnati: final grant report to the Cleveland Foundation, University of Cincinnati, 1985).

[6]J.D. Nichols (1984).

[7]J. Meredith, "Peerless Laser Processors," in *Management Issues in High-Technology Manufacturing Industries* (1985).

[8]For more information on details of justification techniques, see J. Meredith, *Justifying New Manufacturing Technology* (Norcross, GA: Industrial Engineering and Management Press, 1986); and J. Meredith and N.C. Suresh, "Justification Techniques for Advanced Manufacturing Technologies," *International Journal of Production Research* 24 (1986): 1043–1057.

[9]J. Meredith and S.J. Mantel, Jr., *Project Management: A Managerial Approach* (New York: Wiley & Sons, 1985).

[10]W.C. Kester, "Today's Options for Tomorrow's Growth," *Harvard Business Review*, March–April 1984, pp. 153–160.

[11]P.G.W. Keen, "Value Analysis: Justifying Decisions Support Systems," *MIS Quarterly*, March 1981, pp. 1–15.

[12]D.B. Hertz, "Risk Analysis in Capital Investment," *Harvard Business Review*, January–February 1964, pp. 95–106.

[13]"Information Systems: A Long Way from Wall Carvings to CRTs," *Industrial Engineering,* April 1978, pp. 24–36.

[14]H.W.R. Townsend and G.E. Whitehouse, "We Used Risk Analysis to Move Our Computer," *Industrial Engineering,* May 1977, pp. 32–39.

[15]B. Gold, "CAM Sets New Rules for Production," *Harvard Business Review,* November–December 1982, pp. 88–94; J. Goldhar and M. Jelinek, "Plan for Economies of Scope," *Harvard Business Review,* November–December 1983, pp. 141–148; W. Skinner, "Operations Technology: Blind Spot in Strategic Management," *Interfaces,* January–February 1984, pp. 116–125; S.C. Wheelwright and R.H. Hayes, *Restoring Our Competitive Edge: Competing through Manufacturing* (New York: John Wiley & Sons, 1984).

[16]M.J. Ginsberg, "A Redesign of Managerial Tasks: A Requisite for Successful Decision Support Systems," *MIS Quarterly,* March 1978, pp. 39–52.

[17]D.C. Whybark, "The Management of Manufacturing Technology," *Operations Management Review,* Fall 1985, pp. 1–9.

44

The Benefit of Quality IS

Edward Rivard and

Kate Kaiser

Since the late 1970s and 1980s, improvements in data structures, access methods, and telecommunications have spurred the evolution of systems that support decision processes and offer competitive advantage through improved customer service. These new systems have less-quantitative benefits than earlier systems that merely automated accounting and payroll.

Regardless, systems analysts and management still often ignore the significance of qualitative benefits when evaluating systems development project proposals. Typically, project proposals simply include checklists of intangible benefits, such as higher accuracy of data and improved customer service, with minimal description.

Qualitative benefits are seen as "icing on the cake" when projects have quantifiable economic impact, whether in the form of new earnings or savings, or early paybacks. On the other hand, qualitative benefits also may sell systems that do not have early paybacks and that management probably would have rejected otherwise.

The danger of excluding or not properly emphasizing qualitative benefits is the neglect or rejection of many potential new systems offering high returns from intangible benefits. Benefits such as improved decision-making, customer satisfaction, and employee productivity contribute significantly to most businesses. Each allows management to capitalize on opportunities not previously available.

To identify and measure intangible or qualitative benefits for systems development project proposals, they must first be distinguished from their quantitative cousins. Quantitative benefits directly reduce cost or increase revenue. Staff reduction typifies these benefits. Because they can be directly attributed to a particular system, they are easily identified, measured, and verified. Intangible benefits have an indirect relationship, if any, to cost reductions, and depend on several variables. For example, a system may contribute perhaps only one factor, such as better information, to improved decision-making. Other factors, such as decision-makers' capabilities and the circumstances, also contribute, and realizing improved decision-making depends on each of them. Each factor has associated probabilities that seldom recur and which makes them difficult to assess, resulting in cash flows that are difficult to assess.

Despite the importance of intangible benefits, systems analysts receive little help in identifying or presenting them. Increased employee productivity may have resulted from work measurement systems. Nevertheless, verifying the value of that productivity requires several things: that mechanisms measuring employee productivity under the new system are comparable to previous measures; that employees' work does not change; and that employees can accomplish another measurable task with the increased time available.

Some benefits may not have any cost savings associated with them. For example, an electric utility's major objective is to provide quality customer service at a low price. One measure of service quality might be customers' attitudes. A system might provide billing statements in an improved format that improves customers' attitudes. Assigning dollar figures to this benefit means little, however, as customers aren't likely to purchase more electricity as a result of the improved format.

The difficulty in assigning value to information in general exemplifies the problems in identifying and measuring qualitative benefits to systems. Computers can provide faster retrieval, improved accuracy, and better presentation of an increased volume of information, but the value of those capabilities depends on the value of the information itself. Information has an implied value if decisions would differ without it. Conversely, information has no value if it does not influence decisions. Methods for determining the value of information range from "theoretical utility" approaches to "expected value" approaches. Each depends on analysts' subjectivity. Similarly, the value of qualitative benefits depends on the subjectivity of analysts, users, and management.

IDENTIFYING QUALITATIVE BENEFITS

To successfully identify qualitative benefits, all members of the project team must understand the project's and the company's goals and objectives, management's attitude toward such benefits, and the industry.

Although the computer profession has not emphasized qualitative benefits, other professions have. Public administrators and marketers attempt to determine the "why" behind the numbers, allowing researchers to explore and identify the interrelationships of issues.

The computing profession would benefit from these approaches to evaluating verbal and behavioral data; they require key people to discuss their own priorities, problems, and perceptions.

Qualitative methods use various forms of unstructured and nondirective inquiry. Open-ended questions allow respondents to create their own framework of response. Analysts must upgrade their interviewer skill levels from asking yes/no questions. A broad range of business experience and the ability to ask "dumb" questions will assist in learning new insights by interpreting responses and not simply accepting them at face value.

Table 44.1
The Expected Value of Quality IS

Using the expected value method, one can compute the financial benefit of more timely information in reducing a utility company's annual downtime. The total annual cost of downtime is estimated at $8,000,000.

1 Possible Cost Reduction (%)* (Reduction in Downtime)	2 Probability of Occurrence (%)	3 Midpoint of Possible Cost Reduction (%)	4 Cost Reduction (Col. 3 × Total Cost)	5 Probable Savings (Col. 2 × Col. 4)
0	0	—	—	—
1–5	25	3.0	$240,000	$60,000
5–10	45	7.5	$600,000	$270,000
10–15	20	12.5	$1,000,000	$200,000
15–25	10	20.0	$1,600,000	$160,000
>25	0	—	—	—

Expected Value of Benefit: $690,000

*The 0% possible cost reduction is presented separately to show management some dollar savings associated with this benefit, which may not necessarily be true for all qualitative benefits.
Source: Kaiser and Rivard

BENEFITS METHODOLOGY

Methods used for identifying these benefits include focus groups, in-depth interviews, expert opinion, the Delphi technique, observation, benefit profile charts, and existing systems review.

Focus groups should consist of from eight to 10 people who delve into an issue for one to two hours. Analysts begin discussion with open-ended questions and act as moderators, providing direction and focusing discussion on the topic. An advantage of focus groups is the stimulation that respondents provide one another. When conducting focus groups, participants should have similar backgrounds or rank; otherwise, clients resist sharing their ideas. Assembling focus groups may prove less convenient than interviewing individuals, but it costs less than in-depth interviews because analysts can talk to several people at one time. The groups help identify benefits associated with systems that have large numbers of users from similar positions. For example, a proposed customer information system project might form a focus group of customer relations staff to aid analysts in identifying benefits.

In-depth interviews. These interviews provide the detailed thoughts and opinions of an individual rather than the general opinions of a group. Analysts see individuals in their environment, which helps them to understand the subjects' responsibilities.

The expert opinion and the Delphi technique. These assist when little or no data exists to assess the impact of future events. The expert opinion method uses interviews or surveys of experts to derive opinions. With this technique, analysts do not necessarily attempt to reach consensus among experts. The Delphi method surveys experts regarding the probability of occurrences and their likely effects. Analysts compute survey results, and experts review them independently and revise them accordingly until the group reaches consensus. The Delphi method attempts to reduce bias that occurs during face-to-face interviews or group discussions.

These two methods determine the likelihood of benefits. A compilation of both survey results would aid analysts in determining the validity of benefits, providing support for their presentation.

Observation. Analysts can use either random observance or "continuous shadowing." With the random method, analysts observe individuals who are unaware of being observed. By contrast, with the continuous shadowing technique, workers are aware of being observed and probably alter their behavior. Observation familiarizes analysts with user environments, allowing them to visualize the system's interaction with user functions. The disadvantage of observation is that analysts get no idea of the cognitive processes involved in observed work.

A benefit profile chart describes a comprehensive list of various benefits, such as greater reliability, more concise information, easier access, and better use of employee time, among other things. Probably the most popular method used by computer professionals today, benefit profile charts help assure analysts that they do not overlook any significant items.

A review of existing systems can identify benefits not realized until after implementation. This could help identify qualitative benefits for a proposed system. The review could ask users how the system affects their jobs, what new things it enables them to do, results of any additional capabilities, if they anticipate any additional future benefits, and which resources are required to accomplish existing work without systems.

FACTORS TO CONSIDER

Independent of any of the above methods, analysts should consider several factors when identifying benefits:

- User involvement. Most development methodologies emphasize user involvement in systems design. Although excluding users from systems design is a mistake, the other extreme—of assigning users responsibility, with minimal assistance from systems analysts—can also cause problems. Even though users know systems environments, they are not usually familiar with analysis methods.
- Users' critical success factors (CSFs). CSFs, as defined by J. Rockart in the *Harvard Business Review* (March–April 1979), are the areas in which satisfactory results ensure successful performance for the firm. For example, a financial manager's CSFs may include budget compliance for the overall organization and

return on investment. Identifying how systems can support users' CSFs can result in identification of potential benefits.

- Multiple user perspectives. Analysts must consider that people at different levels and departments in the organization have different sets of CSFs. What some consider intangible benefits, others consider intangible costs, especially with multiuser systems. For example, accounting and finance management are likely to perceive positively the implementation of an inventory system because of the financial benefits expected from improved control over inventory. Sales management, however, might assume a lack of product availability.
- Explicitness. Explicit identification is necessary when presenting benefits to management. Improved decision-making has minimal value for management if analysts do not identify those decisions affected, how systems affect decision processes, and the possible results.
- Assumption documentation. Successful benefit presentation depends upon explicitly documenting the assumptions that were made during benefit identification, allowing reviewers to evaluate the degree of subjectivity involved.

Several approaches measure and present qualitative benefits, including incremental analysis, value analysis, expected value, the excess tangible cost method, the worst/most-likely/best-case method, or a checklist approach. These also deserve exploration.

Incremental analysis calculates the cost to perform the work if systems didn't exist. The first step requires analysts to estimate maximum workloads for future time periods and assign probabilities to the likelihood of reaching those limits. Users and analysts identify alternative methods for accomplishing forecasted workloads, assigning costs to each and translating estimated costs into benefits by using corresponding probabilities.

Assume that state or federal regulations require utilities to carry out conservation programs and that analysts are considering the development of a system to aid in administering those programs. The proposed system would run on a mainframe. Analysts could ask future users, industry experts, and/or company management what volume of transactions they expect. The results of the analysts' survey might identify the expected transactions processed each year as follows:

.6 probability for 400,000 transactions

.3 probability for 800,000 transactions

.1 probability for 1.2 million transactions.

Multiplying each probability factor by its respective transaction load cost, it becomes possible to compare the costs of three different alternatives to implementing a new system. The alternatives might be these:

- Hire two $25,000-per-year clerks who can each manually process 200,000 transactions, for a total of 400,000 transactions at $50,000, 800,000 transactions for $100,000, and 1.2 million transactions for $150,000, for a total cost of $75,000.

Table 44.2
Proving the Cases for Quality IS

The worst/most-likely/best-case method presents management with three possible situations for accruing qualitative benefits.

One-Time Development Costs:		$(2,000,000)	

Annual Net-Tangible Benefits:

Year 1	$250,000		
Year 2	250,000		
Year 3	250,000		
Year 4	250,000		
Total	$1,000,000	$1,000,000	

Net Benefit/(Cost) Without Intangible Benefits: $(1,000,000)

Estimates Including Intangible Benefits:

	Pessimistic	Most Likely	Optimistic
Net Tangible Cost:	$(1,000,000)	$(1,000,000)	$(1,000,000)
Intangible Benefits:			
Year 1	$240,000	$600,000	$1,600,000
Year 2	$240,000	$600,000	$1,600,000
Year 3	$240,000	$600,000	$1,600,000
Year 4	$240,000	$600,000	$1,600,000
Total	$960,000	$2,400,000	$6,400,000
Net Benefit/(Cost) With Intangible Benefits:			
	$(40,000)	$1,400,000	$5,400,000

Source: Kaiser and Rivard

- Subcontract to a service bureau charging $55,000 for 400,000 transactions, $75,000 for 800,000 transactions, and $90,000 for 1.2 million transactions, for a total cost of $64,500.
- Implement the system on personal computers at a cost of $65,000 for 400,000 transactions, $70,000 for 800,000 transactions, and $85,000 for 1.2 million transactions, for a total cost of $68,500.

A benefit's value equals the least-cost alternative, which in this case is subcontracting to an outside service with a value of $64,500. This approach carries two disadvantages. First, since the least-costly alternative is considered the system's benefit, users and analysts likely won't identify other specific benefits or notice them when they are realized. The second disadvantage is that it is difficult to verify, during a post-implementation audit, benefits that were accrued through cost avoidance rather than cost reduction.

Incremental analysis, however, aids analysts in determining future processing and computing capacity requirements, and in evaluating alternatives or additional computing resources.

The value analysis method, also called adaptive design, uses three assumptions: that innovation is value driven and not cost driven; that intangibles can be identified and subjectively assessed but rarely measured accurately; and that an inevitable clash exists between those persons driven by cost and those driven by effectiveness.

A multistage iterative process begins with a prototype system. Rather than develop extensive specifications, analysts provide beginning models to expand and modify until a more complete design evolves. Users provide analysts with feedback on the prototype's value and limitations. The difference between incremental and value analysis is that the former method begins with a final solution while the latter uses an evolutionary process. The amount that users are willing to pay to obtain the benefits of prototyping over incremental analysis is called a cost threshold.

Analysts determine whether a prototype can be implemented within the cost threshold. If so, they design the prototype, measure its use and costs, obtain feedback from users, and modify the accrued benefits to reflect feedback. The next step identifies and estimates one-time or fixed costs for the more complete system that would evolve from the prototype. Examples of one-time and fixed costs include computer hardware and software, development labor, and computer usage costs incurred during development. Users provide judgments of benefits needed to justify an expanded system. If users justify new cost thresholds, analysts modify the prototype to meet users' needs. The process continues until users and analysts are satisfied that the best solution has been achieved.

This method has several disadvantages: some analysts do not have much prototyping experience; the method's lack of an initial estimate of final costs and benefits may commit management to unexpected future expenditures; without "final" systems requirements, existing program revisions can be significant; as with the incremental analysis method, benefits are based on cost avoidance and thus analysts cannot determine the actual amount of avoided costs; and specific benefits, as in the incremental analysis method, are not identified.

Advantages of value analysis include quick user requirement identification; improved communication between analysts and users; incremental evaluation of benefits and costs, which enables management to continue or stop; an evolutionary approach, which results in user-tailored systems, providing greater user satisfaction than traditionally developed systems; and the incremental identification and presentation of benefits associated with value analysis, which allows analysts to treat functions of systems as increments.

The expected value method differs from the previous two methods by using cost reduction rather than cost avoidance. Analysts segment benefits into various ranges of cost reduction. The total existing cost is then multiplied by the midpoint of the range to determine the cost reduction/benefit of a range. The cost reduction for the range is multiplied by probabilities of occurrence to arrive at a probable savings. The sum of the probable savings from each range is the expected value for that benefit.

For example, the average annual downtime for a power plant is four weeks. One week of downtime costs a utility $2 million. The availability of more timely and accurate information will result in improved decisions regarding power plant maintenance, which could reduce downtime (see "The Expected Value of Quality IS").

Analysts with limited knowledge concerning power plant maintenance could determine ranges of possible cost reduction and probabilities of occurrence by using the Delphi or expert opinion methods outlined above.

The advantages of this technique include benefit verification after implementation due to cost reduction; identification and measurement of specific benefits; and documentation of users' and analysts' subjectivity used in arriving at estimates.

The excess tangible cost approach, as previously defined in DATAMATION by researchers Steve Drummond and Charles Litecky, compares net tangible costs with various intangible benefits. It resembles break-even analysis, indicating the minimum value of intangible benefits necessary for a project to break even.

Litecky identified four assumptions for using this method:

- Tangible costs and benefits are relatively easy to estimate.
- Intangible benefits are most difficult to estimate.
- Tangible costs are much greater than tangible benefits.
- Intangible costs are insignificant.

Two advantages of presenting net tangible and intangible benefits/costs separately are that management can apply the value of intangible benefits subjectively; and it educates management, especially conservative management, on the importance of intangible benefits (see "The Excess Tangible Cost Method").

Table 44.3
The Excess Tangible Cost Method

For the same utility company, this approach compares net-tangible costs to various intangible benefits. (With this method, assume that management demands a payback period of less than four years.)

One-Time Development Costs:		$(2,000,000)
Annual Net-Tangible Benefits:		
Year 1	$250,000	
Year 2	250,000	
Year 3	250,000	
Year 4	250,000	
Total	$1,000,000	$ 1,000,000
Net Benefit/(Cost) Without Intangible Benefits:		$(1,000,000)
Annual Intangible Benefits:		
Year 1	$690,000	
Year 2	690,000	
Year 3	690,000	
Year 4	690,000	
Total	$2,760,000	$ 2,760,000
Net Benefit/(Cost) with Intangible Benefits:		$ 1,760,000

The minimum intangible benefits for this project to break even is $1,000,000, or $250,000 per year.

Source: Kaiser and Rivard

Worst/most-likely/best-case method. This method presents management with three situations for qualitative benefits: the most pessimistic view, the most likely case, and the most optimistic view. In addition to having the advantages of the excess tangible cost method, this method provides management with upper and lower boundaries.

Using the power plant maintenance system example, a presentation using the worst/most-likely/best-case method can be made in the excess tangible cost format (see "Proving the Cases for Quality IS").

The benefit profile chart approach is probably the most widely used method of presenting intangible benefits. The disadvantages of this approach include: analysts tend to use the checklist as the only method for identifying intangible benefits and therefore neglect benefits not on the list; benefits' descriptions are usually abbreviated so that reviewers' interpretations can result in misunderstanding or misperception; and checklists exclude identification of how a postimplementation audit can verify benefits.

The advantages of this approach include easy implementation; versatility to most applications; easy updates for new benefits; effective means of communication with explicit benefit descriptions; and assurance that no benefits are overlooked with a later checklist review.

PLACING PROPER EMPHASIS

Qualitative or intangible benefits constitute a larger portion of the benefits planned for development today than in the past. Because intangible benefits may have a significant impact on organizations, analysts need to place proper emphasis on identifying these benefits during analysis and need to present them to management in a manner that conveys their significance.

No single method identified here is best for all situations, but a combination of methods capitalizes on the advantages of each method used and minimizes the disadvantages of any one method.

45

Critical Success Factor Analysis as a Methodology for MIS Planning

Michael E. Shank,

Andrew C. Boynton, and

Robert W. Zmud

This article addresses the use and benefits of the Critical Success Factor (CSF) methodology in identifying corporate information needs and, subsequently, in developing a corporate information systems plan. The conclusions presented are drawn from an analysis of a CSF study conducted at Financial Institutions Assurance Corporation (FIAC). Interestingly, the initial purpose of this study was to evaluate the firm's existing data processing system in light of intermediate-term corporate objectives. However, the outcome of the CSF study has been a fundamental rethinking of the nature of the corporation, and its impact far surpassed the initial expectations of everyone involved. The case presented here, combined with information drawn from the CSF literature, can provide a number of meaningful insights on the use of the CSF methodology as a procedure for MIS planning and for building support for using information technologies throughout a user population.

INTRODUCTION

Historically, FIAC's operating posture, in regulating insured financial institutions through field work and cooperative efforts with state authorities and independent auditors, was reactive in nature. Through insights gained via the Critical Success Factors (CSF) study, the Corporation has become much more proactive in its relationships with member institutions. There has been a rethinking of FIAC's information infrastructure, an MIS Department has been created, and information technology is now regarded as a strategic tool with which to leverage corporate productivity and enhance FIAC's ability to compete in the marketplace. The CSF methodology

"Critical Success Factor Analysis as a Methodology for MIS Planning" by M.E. Shank and A.C. Boynton. Reprinted by special permission from the MIS QUARTERLY, Volume 9, Number 2, June 1985. Copyright © 1985 by the Society for Information Management and the Management Information Systems Research Center at the University of Minnesota.

has also been adopted as a continuing methodology for both departmental and strategic planning.

CORPORATE HISTORY

FIAC is a private deposit insurer created in 1967 pursuant to North Carolina law. The broad statutory purposes of the Corporation are: 1) to insure the deposits of member financial institutions, and 2) to assure the liquidity of its member institutions. More specifically, FIAC must protect the savings of depositors in its insured institutions by seeing that these institutions maintain an adequate net worth and cash flow. As a private deposit insurer, FIAC provides services similar to the services provided by the Federal Deposit Insurance Corporation (FDIC). FIAC competes with federal deposit insurers and other private deposit insurers for financial institutions' business.

FIAC's original base of eleven insured institutions had total savings of $50 million at the end of 1967. At the end of 1983, FIAC insured 65 institutions with total savings in excess of $2.8 billion. Early growth resulted from a lack of competition. When FIAC was created there was no national deposit insurance program for credit unions. Many savings and loan associations chose not to obtain Federal Savings and Loan Insurance Corporation (FSLIC) insurance or would not qualify for such coverage because of their small size or rural markets.

In the early 1970's the National Credit Union Administration (NCUA), a federal agency, was created to insure the deposits of credit unions. As the savings and loan industry grew, more institutions became eligible for FSLIC insurance. And as competition for consumers' deposits increased, financial institutions used federal deposit insurance as a competitive weapon to lure savings from uninsured or FIAC-insured institutions.

FIAC, however, worked with state financial regulators and legislators to reform laws and regulations which restricted the operation of state chartered financial institutions. These new laws and regulations allow FIAC insured, state chartered financial institutions to better serve consumers. Institutions with federal deposit insurance were restricted as to the types of loans they could make and the amount of interest they could pay on savings. These operating advantages contributed to the growth in size and number of FIAC insured institutions. The competitive advantages of state chartered, privately insured institutions was a contributing factor to the federal deregulation of financial institutions in the late 1970's and early 1980's.

The increased powers and rapid growth of FIAC insured institutions placed increasing demands on FIAC's ability to monitor these institutions. Manual analysis gave way to programmable calculators, and finally to an automated financial analysis system run as a monthly batch job on a minicomputer. The relative stability of the environment, the outdated computerized information systems of FIAC's competitors, and the small number of institutions being monitored by FIAC allowed the original computer system to remain in place for several years.

Financial institutions, like many other businesses, were rocked by record high interest rates in the early 1980's. Failures of financial institutions and payouts by deposit insurers occurred in historically high amounts. FIAC was able to withstand these fluctuations without incurring any losses. The corporation is very proud of its record of safety. Neither FIAC, nor any of its insured institutions, have ever had a loss from a deposit related claim. However, the pressures of maintaining this record led FIAC to adopt a very defensive corporate posture.

Deregulation essentially erased most of FIAC's competitive advantages. All institutions, not just those insured by FIAC or other private insurers, could pay market interest rates. All institutions enjoyed broad asset and investment powers. Recognizing the need to regain its marketing edge and bolster its ability to maintain its record of safety, FIAC's Board of Trustees decided in 1983 to pursue a strategy of geographic and institutional diversification in order to spread risk and increase the potential market. A change in its enabling legislation allowed FIAC to offer deposit insurance to any institution eligible for FDIC, FSLIC or NCUA insurance regardless of geographic location. Prior to this change FIAC could only insure credit unions and savings and loan associations in North Carolina. FIAC is now the only private deposit insurer authorized to insure all types of financial institutions (banks, credit unions, savings and loan associations, and others) throughout the United States.

THE CORPORATE CULTURE AND ENVIRONMENT PRIOR TO THE CSF STUDY

FIAC exhibited many of the traits of a small business which has experienced rapid growth. Management decisions were made by the Chief Executive Officer or were centralized in a small group of individuals. These individuals controlled all aspects of the corporation's operations. Planning and operations were approached with a short time horizon. More time was spent dealing with operational problems than anticipating them. The staff had excellent entrepreneurial spirit and was very flexible. Staff members were hard working "athletes" in keeping with the corporation's "lean and mean" culture. Monitoring insured institutions was characterized by a large amount of data gathering and a short analysis period before the data gathering cycle began again. Communication between staff members was informal and infrequent. Higher level managers were generalists with responsibilities in all areas and lower level staff members carried out narrowly defined functions with little direct knowledge of the Corporation's overall activities.

Analysis of insured institutions required a great deal of work by a small group of individuals who supplemented financial data with large amounts of soft information gathered through industry and regulatory sources, as well as visits to insured institutions. Individuals became responsible for certain institutions by default because of the large amount of undocumented information they personally maintained about those institutions. This necessity to rely on rather intimate client relations became troublesome when the corporation took supervisory action against several insured institutions. The staff contact person, long viewed as a friend of the insured institution, came to be seen as a potential threat, capable of initiating supervisory actions against the institution or its management.

FIAC's original minicomputer system was purchased with the understanding that customized, third party software would be developed over several months and purchased for $10,000. The development actually took 18 months and cost over

$40,000. Once installed, the system was maintained during a staff member's "spare time." A standard set of reports was produced on a monthly basis using insured institutions' financial statements and statistical summaries as input. There was no separate corporate budget for data processing.

With the installation of this first computer system, data processing was viewed as a necessary evil to relieve tedious "number crunching" on a monthly basis. The formal processes involved in retrieving and manipulating data were actually seen as dysfunctional by some staff members. Many staff analysts made extensive use of paper spreadsheets and hand held calculators both before and after the installation of this first system.

FIAC's entrepreneurial culture and the maintenance of private data by staff analysts had an adverse impact on initial data processing efforts. Information was viewed by some individuals as a critical source of power they could use to influence decisions. Other staff members argued that this centralized data processing activity was impairing the corporation's flexibility.

THE CSF PROJECT

The corporation's defensive posture, combined with a volatile economy, continuing deregulation, and planned corporate expansion led to a proposed review of FIAC's data processing system in 1983. Senior management conceived this as a technical review of system capacity in light of the corporation's expansion plans. Management also hoped to be able to improve the efficiency of the present system by increasing the computer's input, throughput, and output capabilities.

A consultant was hired to review the existing system's capacity and to recommend a plan for enhancing this capacity. The consultant felt that senior management had underrated the potential impact that data processing could have within the corporation. He approached senior management with the concept of critical success factors (CSF's). The CSF concept was intuitively appealing to senior management. Its potential to focus attention on vital organizational issues appeared useful in a number of areas within the corporation.

Capitalizing on the appeal of the CSF method, the consultant then suggested that FIAC adopt an information resource approach to the project rather than the initial information function approach [3]. An information resource approach to MIS planning uses an organization-wide perspective in addressing the management of a firm's information systems. An information function planning approach deals mainly with the technical activities involved in establishing and managing a firm's information systems.

The consultant educated the corporation's staff on the CSF concept, providing reading materials [4] and answering questions. Each staff member was asked to make a list of personal CSFs and a list of corporate CSFs in preparation for meeting with the consultant.

The consultant and a senior manager interviewed every member of the staff at all levels of the organization. The interviewee was asked to relate his individual and corporate CSFs. The ultimate purpose of the CSF project (that of information resource planning) was not revealed. The interviewee was not asked to discuss sources of information until he had described all of his CSFs and related ideas. The consultant and senior manager were careful not to lead the discussion in any direction. Staff members were encouraged to be open and to express their own opinions, not their perception of management's opinions. Nondirective counseling techniques and other measures were used to encourage creativity and free expression [2].

A chart of CSFs was developed by the consultant following the interviews. From this chart, an aggregated list was made for the corporation as a whole. This list grouped trends and eliminated repetitive responses. Similarities and differences within departments were noted. A list of corporate CSFs was then developed from the aggregated list.

A staff retreat was held to examine and discuss corporate, departmental, and individual CSFs. At this retreat, staff and management focused on organizational changes which internal growth and environmental change seemed to demand. By linking information resource planning, organizational redesign, and strategic planning through the CSF focus, information technology became a catalyst to discussions of desirable organizational changes. The corporation had been built on people; the most appropriate use of information technology by FIAC would be to leverage its staff through technology. Through these discussions it became clear that an information system mission directed toward the "efficient" processing of information would not meet FIAC's evolving organizational information needs.

The retreat characterizes the participative nature of the CSF process. This was particularly important at FIAC because of a gap which had arisen between senior management and staff. The methodology made formerly implicit corporate goals explicit, thus resulting in their specific inclusion in the planning process. Moreover, explicitly stated goals, shared by both staff and management, served to reduce conflict and increase cooperation.

The approach taken, and the results of the staff retreat, provided an excellent structure for the staff's annual strategic planning session. A cross section of the staff reviewed and critiqued the final CSF lists. A prioritized consensus list of CSFs was used to guide the development of a new organizational structure and as a template for the staff's annual planning session agenda. The final CSF list read:

1. Prevent losses through risk management,
2. Increase diversification of the customer base,
3. Increase professional staff productivity, and
4. Enhance the corporation's image with the firm's markets and the public.

Meetings were held with staff members, individually and in groups, to develop specific organizational information needs. These needs were used as input into the design of the corporation's new computer-based information system. Subsequent staff discussions were held to review specific hardware/software products and develop an implementation plan for moving to a new corporate information environment.

Exhibit 45.1 summarizes the process used in the CSF study. Steps 1 through 10, actual events, are highlighted by the accompanying interpretive remarks.

Exhibit 45.1
Processes in the CSF Study

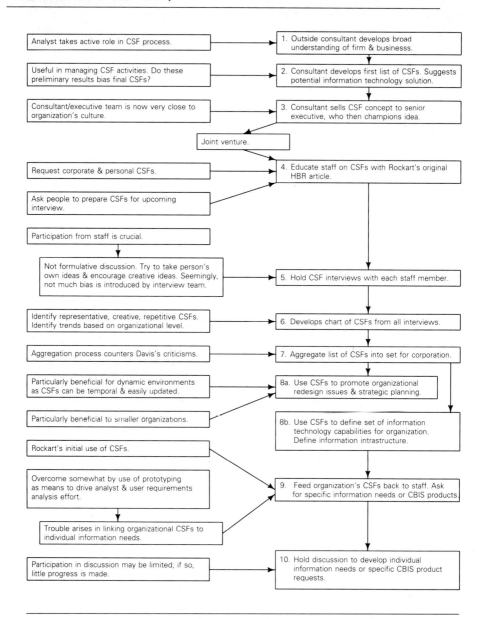

| Analyst takes active role in CSF process. | → | 1. Outside consultant develops broad understanding of firm & businesss. |

| Useful in managing CSF activities. Do these preliminary results bias final CSFs? | → | 2. Consultant develops first list of CSFs. Suggests potential information technology solution. |

| Consultant/executive team is now very close to organization's culture. | → | 3. Consultant sells CSF concept to senior executive, who then champions idea. |

Joint venture.

| Request corporate & personal CSFs. | → | 4. Educate staff on CSFs with Rockart's original HBR article. |

| Ask people to prepare CSFs for upcoming interview. | |

| Participation from staff is crucial. | |

| Not formulative discussion. Try to take person's own ideas & encourage creative ideas. Seemingly, not much bias is introduced by interview team. | → | 5. Hold CSF interviews with each staff member. |

| Identify representative, creative, repetitive CSFs. Identify trends based on organizational level. | → | 6. Develops chart of CSFs from all interviews. |

| Aggregation process counters Davis's criticisms. | → | 7. Aggregate list of CSFs into set for corporation. |

| Particularly beneficial for dynamic environments as CSFs can be temporal & easily updated. | → | 8a. Use CSFs to promote organizational redesign issues & strategic planning. |

| Particularly beneficial to smaller organizations. | → | 8b. Use CSFs to define set of information technology capabilities for organization. Define information intrastructure. |

| Rockart's initial use of CSFs. | |

| Overcome somewhat by use of prototyping as means to drive analyst & user requirements analysis effort. | → | 9. Feed organization's CSFs back to staff. Ask for specific information needs or CBIS products. |

| Trouble arises in linking organizational CSFs to individual information needs. | |

| Participation in discussion may be limited; if so, little progress is made. | → | 10. Hold discussion to develop individual information needs or specific CBIS product requests. |

Reprinted from "An Assessment of Critical Success Factors," by Andrew C. Boynton and Robert W. Zmud, *Sloan Management Review*, Volume 25, Number 4, pp. 17–27, by permission of the publishers. Copyright © 1984 by the Sloan Management Review Association. All rights reserved.

CORPORATE IMPACT

The CSF study has had a profound impact on FIAC's use of information technology and its corporate culture. Four distinct impact areas are described: the new information system plan, changes in the corporation's attitude toward data processing, increases in staff productivity, and the adoption of the CSF methodology as a continuing management tool.

The Information System Plan

The major result of the CSF was the redefinition of the corporation from an operations-driven deposit insurer to an information-driven risk manager. A three stage approach to redesigning the corporation's information infrastructure reflects this new orientation.

Stage One: Information Processing First, the corporation's present batch-oriented minicomputer will be replaced with a supermini to serve as a host to personal microcomputer workstations. The supermini will maintain a newly designed database that will allow access to information currently stored off-line, unavailable to staff analysts and managers.

The system will provide for the collection and retrieval of both hard and soft data. Information previously gathered in analyst's conversations and stored in their personal files or memories will now be available on-line. The host will also provide access to external databases. This new data will provide quantitative support for decisions which have historically been made based on individual perceptions. Financial analysts will have the ability to download both hard and soft data from the host to personal computers and to manipulate it using spreadsheet, query, and word processing packages.

Applications are currently being prototyped using personal computers and the corporation's present database. Current prototypes include decision support systems intended to reduce the amount of time spent by analysts reviewing standard reports. Time formerly spent using calculators and paper spreadsheets to crunch numbers will be used for information analysis, problem solving, and direct contact with insured institutions.

Stage Two: Office Automation In the second stage, data processing functions on the supermini will be integrated with an office automation system which includes shared logic word processing, integrated graphics, electronic mail, electronic filing, calendar management, and project tracking. This integration will enhance the efficiency and effectiveness of staff analysts in their efforts to monitor insured institutions. This integrated system will be accessed by field analysts using portable personal computers. This should enhance productivity outside of the office, bolster both intraorganizational and interorganizational communications, and make information resources available to all staff members at all times, regardless of their proximity to the home office. Initial production of prototype reports using graphics, word processing and customized spreadsheets have already enhanced information dissemination internally and with insured institutions.

Stage Three: Future Automation   The third stage will involve developing direct access to the information maintained by insured institutions on their in-house or time sharing systems. It is expected that pioneering such a client relationship within the industry will enhance the technological edge the corporation now holds over its major competitors.

Corporate Attitude toward Data Processing

In the past, data processing was seen as a confining operation which was unable to keep up with the changing environment in which the corporation operated. Management and staff at FIAC now view information technology as a driving force which provides the corporation with a vital competitive edge. Consider the evolution of one senior manager's attitude:

"We don't need a computer."

"What's wrong with the system we've got?"

"When do I get my PC?"

"When will the new database be operational?"

The corporate culture vividly reflects this attitude change. The only nonfinancial industry professional ever hired by the corporation is the new MIS Director. This individual, an MBA with previous MIS work experience, was hired more for his business sense than his technical competence. His position is intimately tied to FIAC's planning process and is expected to influence strategy in the new corporate organization. The new MIS Director oversees the expenditure of 10% of the Corporation's operating budget. These expenditures are projected to be more than equaled by increased revenues from expansion, new information-related customer services, and decreased expenses from better risk management.

The changes in corporate attitude toward information technology were aptly captured in a recent presentation by the CEO to a state legislative study commission. The CEO, once skeptical of the need for a commitment to information processing, used a portable computer linked to a wide screen television to present various spreadsheets and graphs on the financial services industry, the economic environment, and FIAC's financials. The CEO has requested that additional computer-based presentations be prepared for meetings with state regulators. The use of computers has added considerably to the effectiveness of presentations like these and has led to FIAC being perceived as a technological leader within the industry.

Staff Productivity

Access to databases and decision support systems using personal computers have contributed to increased information availability throughout the Corporation. This has increased the productivity of established staff members, allowed new staff members to become productive more rapidly than in the past, and contributed to the generation of new ideas by staff members at all levels of the Corporation. Management confidence in staff members has consequently increased. This increased confidence, along with an ability to track projects more closely using PC's, has increased the extent to which responsibilities are delegated. This, in turn, will hopefully enhance the Corporation's management development process.

Through the use of personal computers the Corporation has increased its ability to provide significant amounts of analyzed data to insured institutions. This has helped rebuild the intimate relationships which existed prior to the supervisory actions of the early 1980's. At the same time, these rebuilt relationships and the increased availability of information have expanded FIAC's control over insured institutions. The ability to rapidly analyze large amounts of data, calculate peer comparisons, and carry computing power into the field has given staff analysts more confidence and increased the respect that managing officers of insured institutions have for these analysts.

FIAC's confidence in its ability to use the CSF methodology and its enhanced information technology allows the corporation to cope better with uncertainty. The corporation has grown out of its defensive posture. In the past, uncertainty and rapid change were viewed as threats. Now they are seen as opportunities which FIAC can successfully exploit using its information resources. The difficulties of managing risk in an ever-changing and growing market now provide an opportunity for FIAC to outperform other deposit insurers who exhibit a more traditional approach to information systems.

CONTINUED USE OF THE CSF METHODOLOGY

FIAC now uses the CSF methodology in information resource planning, strategic planning, and individual goal setting as part of its performance appraisal and bonus systems. Use of this common methodology has narrowed the gap that previously existed between senior management and other staff members. All staff members have a better idea of the broad goals and activities of the corporation. Additionally, a common focus now exists throughout the organization and serves to align the goals of individuals and departments with the corporation's goals.

Broad conceptual planning and tactical concepts are more easily shared through a common information "map" of the corporation built through the CSF project. Staff members have redefined their jobs around the information processing nature of their tasks and are now more likely to document and disseminate "personal" information in order to increase corporate effectiveness at all levels. Senior managers now concentrate their attention on those areas identified as critical during the project. Concentration on critical areas rather than on less important operational matters has increased management's time horizon by freeing more time for planning, anticipating change, and formulating contingency responses.

EXPLAINING THE CSF PROJECT'S RESULTS

It is extremely difficult in a case study such as this to identify factors that led to a project's success or failure. The corporate context, the personalities involved, and environmental pressures cannot be controlled. Still, the behavioral dynamics that were observed during the CSF project strongly suggest three explanations for the project's success.

First, the CSF methodology is business-driven rather than technology-driven. This allowed a corporation which was not technically-oriented, nor very experienced with computer-based information systems, to commence an MIS planning effort without discussing technology at an early stage. Business strategies and tactics were translated into technological solutions only after consensus was reached regarding both the need to change and the direction for change.

Second, the business strategies and tactics that evolved from the CSF project followed a top-down design process. Once all staff members understood and accepted the organization's CSFs, it became possible to develop departmental and personal CSFs that were consistent with one another and with the organizational-wide CSFs. Once a common organizational map had been built, staff members readily accepted the information map from which the MIS plan was developed.

Third, and most important, the intuitively-appealing nature of the CSF concept prompted a FIAC senior manager to "buy-in" to the project at a very early stage. Without this individual championing of the project, it is unlikely that it would have been as successful. Not only did the senior manager's involvement testify to top managements' support of the project, but his enthusiasm overcame any reluctance on the part of other senior managers to involve themselves in, and otherwise support the project.

While we believe that these planning behaviors were induced through our application of the CSF methodology, similar behaviors might have been induced through the use of other MIS planning methodologies. The key is not which planning methodology is used but rather the planning behaviors that result.

It also seems appropriate to mention one problem that arose throughout the project. While the CSF methodology was well-received by FIAC staff members, only the firm's senior managers found the methodology useful in defining their individual reporting needs. A plausible explanation for this is the conceptual nature of CSFs. Lower level managers seemed to have considerable difficulty relating to the broad set of corporate CSFs and defining concrete information measures to represent their individual CSFs. However, the ability of these staff members to use the CSF methodology does seem to be improving over time.

GUIDELINES FOR USE IN OTHER ORGANIZATIONS

In some ways FIAC provided a unique opportunity to use the CSF methodology for MIS planning. The changing environment and evolving corporate culture responded well to a method which linked MIS planning with strategic corporate planning. The following guidelines gleaned from this case experience are offered to other organizations considering using the CSF methodology for MIS planning:

1. CSFs are very flexible and may entice some users to be too casual in their application. Casual application may provide false results. CSFs should be used with the precision of a more formal method.

2. The individual managing a CSF study should have a thorough understanding of the organization's business. MIS and the executive suite cannot speak the same language unless they both understand their common business endeavors.

3. It is very helpful to have a member of senior management champion the CSF project. A senior manager can motivate others in the corporation to be more receptive to the project in its early stages.

4. Education of staff members on the CSF method before the actual interview is helpful. A basic understanding of the concept and time to think before the first interview will make those interviews more productive.

5. CSFs should not be linked explicitly to information needs, computer applications, or anything else concrete during the initial set of interviews. Staff members can be more productive and creative in identifying CSFs if their attention is directed away from current information system realities.

6. We found it helpful to conduct interviews on several levels of the target group. Responses validated one another and led to a broader picture. We believe this led to a higher quality set of organizational CSFs.

CONCLUSION

The CSF methodology was a major force to corporate-wide MIS planning at FIAC. It provided a clear focus to structure the vital issues which were considered in MIS planning. The CSF methodology proved to be practical and intuitive. It provided a natural link between tactical and strategic planning. Use of the method provided assurance that critical information needs were explicitly addressed in the planning process by relating information resources to those areas of an FIAC's activity which must go well in order for the corporation to succeed. The CSF methodology developed a core of information technology proponents throughout the organization and enhanced the understanding of MIS by management. Finally, this organization-wide CSF study now provides an excellent vehicle for the new MIS Director to align his strategic plans with those of FIAC's top management.

REFERENCES

1. Boynton, A.C. and Zmud, R.W. "Critical Success Factors: A Case-Based Assessment," *Sloan Management Review*, Volume 25, Number 4, Summer 1984, pp. 17–27.

2. Bullen, C.V. and Rockart, J.F. "A Primer on Critical Success Factors," Working Paper No. 69, Center for Information Systems Research, Massachusetts Institute of Technology, Cambridge, Massachusetts, June 1981.

3. King, W.R. and Zmud, R.W. "Managing Information Systems: Policy Planning, Strategic Planning and Operational Planning," *Proceedings*, Second International Conference on Information Systems, K. Ross (ed.) December 1981, Cambridge, Massachusetts, pp. 299–308.

4. Rockart, J.F. "Chief Executives Define Their Own Data Needs," *Harvard Business Review*, Volume 57, Number 2, March–April 1979, pp. 81–93.

46

Information Systems for Competitive Advantage: Implementation of a Planning Process

Nick Rackoff, Charles Wiseman, and Walter A. Ullrich

As the pace of competition intensifies in the 80's, the use of information systems as competitive weapons is accelerating. Among the now classic cases are the computerized reservation system of American Airlines, the Cash Management Account of Merrill Lynch, and the order entry system of American Hospital Supply. These are examples of strategic information systems (SIS). The work that gave rise to this paper addresses the question, "How can an organization discover such SIS opportunities systematically?"

The authors developed and implemented a five-phase planning process to identify and evaluate SIS and to win top management support. Underlying their approach is a conceptual framework that views an enterprise's suppliers, customers, and competitors as the strategic targets of five strategic thrusts: differentiation, cost, innovation, growth, and alliance. Strategic thrusts represent the fundamental link between the firm's strategy and its use of information technology. Strategic information systems support and shape the organization's strategic thrusts.

GAINING COMPETITIVE ADVANTAGE

The principal role that information systems have performed in the past has been one of operational and management support. But recently companies have begun using information systems strategically to reap significant competitive advantage.

American Hospital Supply, being the first to install online order entry terminals in hospitals, now dominates the medical supply business. Merrill Lynch, with its Cash Management Account, dependent on database and laser printing technology, preempted the market with its innovative product. American and United Airlines, through their computerized reservation systems, Sabre and Apollo, established an edge that other air carriers have found impossible to overcome.

The significance of these computer-based products and services lies neither in their technological sophistication nor in the format of the reports they produce. Rather, it is found by examining the role they play in their firm's quest for competitive advantage. The cases just mentioned are instances of strategic information systems (SIS) — information systems used to support or shape an organization's competitive strategy, its plan for gaining and/or maintaining advantage.

American Hospital Supply's system yielded advantage by locking-in its customers. Sabre and Apollo gave priority listings to the two carriers when agents checked their screens for flights. The advantage has been so great that competitors have appealed to the government and the courts for relief. In addition, the systems have become vehicles for diversification and growth, propelling their developers into entirely new lines of business such as telemarketing. Merrill Lynch's Cash Management Account, an innovative product made possible by an SIS alliance with the enterprising Banc One of Columbus, Ohio (that processes CMA debit card and check transactions), enabled the brokerage house to sign up over one million customers (10 times its nearest rival) and reap more than $60 million annually in fees.

Although the use of information systems may not always lead to industry domination, it can serve as an important weapon in a firm's strategic arsenal. Up to now, companies have uncovered SIS in an ad hoc fashion, without the benefit of a planning methodology designed specifically for the purpose. But as the pace of competition accelerates in the 80's, competitive leaders must develop a more systematic approach for identifying SIS opportunities.

This article presents the approach developed and implemented at GTE. It is a comprehensive method for generating a multitude of SIS ideas and selecting the most promising prospects for yielding substantial competitive advantage.

FROM THE CONVENTIONAL TO THE STRATEGIC PERSPECTIVE

The dominant view on information systems planning has for decades focused exclusively on the internal functions of the business. But this conventional perspective, powerful as it is for some purposes, cannot account for the SIS examples cited above in which information technology was used to gain competitive advantage. To understand why the conventional perspective is unsuited for identifying SIS, we need first to examine its theoretical underpinnings.

In the conventional view, the targets of information system applications are the organization's planning and control processes. These processes, described by Robert Anthony in his classic book, *Planning and Control Systems* [1], include: strategic planning (processes related to the organization's objectives, resource allocation policies, etc.); management control (processes related to assuring that strategic objectives are attained); and operational control (processes related to assuring that tasks are executed efficiently).

Anthony's model provides the foundation for identifying conventional information systems. The model was first applied in the information management field by Zani [17]. His work spotlighted areas in need of more penetrating analysis. In the 1970's and 80's, academics, and others working on conceptual frameworks for information systems, explored in greater depth topics merely mentioned in pasing by Zani. Gorry and Scott Morton [2] and Keen and Scott Morton [4] focused on systems designed especially for managerial decisionmaking. Nolan [7, 8, 9], IBM planners [3], King [5, 6], and Rockart [12, 13] concentrated on information systems planning topics. Rockart and Treacy [10, 11] specialized in systems targeted for top managers.

While the conventional perspective based on Anthony's model has served well to identify opportunities to improve internal business functions, it does not lead directly to the discovery of competitive uses of information technology. To uncover SIS opportunities, we need a new foundation for information systems planning, a foundation based in the world of competitive strategy, rather than in the arena of planning and control. This new foundation draws on some of the concepts developed by Porter in his book, *Competitive Strategy* [14].

Porter views business as being pressed by five competitive forces: the threat of new entrants, the intensity of rivalry among existing firms, the pressures from substitute products, the bargaining power of buyers, and the bargaining power of suppliers. He further proposes three generic strategies with which to combat these forces: differentiation (distinguish your company's products and services from others in all market segments), cost (become the low cost producer in all market segments), and focus (concentrate on a particular market segment and then either differentiate or become the low cost producer in that segment).

While Porter's model is helpful in thinking about the firm's competitive environment and the generic strategies a firm may follow, we have found it necessary to develop a more comprehensive framework, which we call the theory of strategic thrusts, for identifying SIS opportunities (see Exhibit 46.1).

Strategic thrusts are major competitive moves (offensive or defensive) made by the firm. It is our contention that the multitude of such moves reduce to five basic thrusts:

1. Differentiation—Achieve advantage by distinguishing your company's products and services from competitors, or by reducing the differentiation advantage of rivals.

2. Cost—Achieve advantage by reducing your firm's costs, supplier's costs, or customer's costs, or by raising the costs of your competitors.

3. Innovation—Achieve advantage by introducing a product or process change that results in a fundamental transformation in the way business is conducted in the industry.

4. Growth—Achieve advantage by volume or geographical expansion, backward or forward integration, product-line or entry diversification.

Exhibit 46.1
Framework for Identifying SIS Opportunities

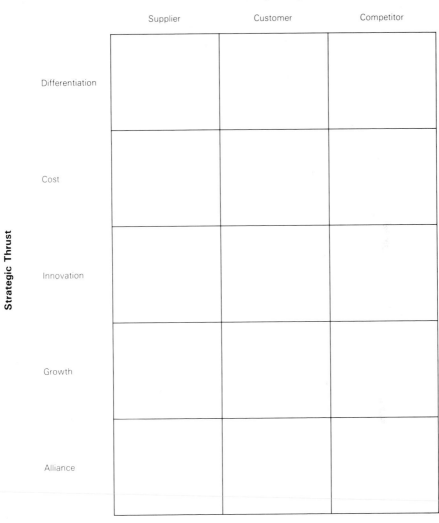

5. Alliance – Achieve advantage by forging marketing agreements, forming joint ventures, or making acquisitions related to the thrusts of differentiation, cost, innovation, or growth.

Information technology can be used to support or shape the firm's competitive strategy by supporting or shaping strategic thrusts. Strategic thrusts, therefore, constitute the mechanisms for connecting business strategy and information technology. The theory of strategic thrusts is developed in detail in Wiseman's book, *Strategy and Computers: Information Systems as Competitive Weapons* [16].

These thrusts strike at three classes of strategic targets:

1. Supplier targets – Organizations providing what the firm needs to make its product, for example, those providing materials, capital, labor, services, and the like.
2. Customer targets – End users as well as organizations (e.g., middlemen, physical distributors, financial institutions, etc.) purchasing the firm's product for its own use or for sale to end users.
3. Competitor targets – Organizations selling (or potentially selling) products judged by customers to be the same as, similar to, or substitutable for the firm's products.

THE SIS PLANNING PROCESS AT GTE

Description of GTE

GTE, a diversified, international telecommunications and electronics company with 185,000 employees and revenues over $14 billion, provides local telephone service in 31 states, two Canadian provinces, and the Dominican Republic. GTE Sprint operates the third largest long-distance telephone system in the U.S., and GTE Telenet runs a nationwide, packet-switched data communication network. In addition, GTE manufactures and markets a complete line of communication equipment, systems, and services, more than 6,000 types of Sylvania lamps and other lighting products, and precision metal, plastic, and ceramic materials used in electrical and electronic devices.

The largest business division, domestic telephone operations (TELOPS), contributes revenues of more than $9 billion, almost 90% of GTE's income. It consists of a corporate group, seven telephone companies, and a data services organization – GTE Data Services (GTEDS) – which provides information systems and services to the TELOPS units. Headquartered in Tampa, GTEDS has its own president who is also a TELOPS' corporate vice president. The methodology described below has been applied principally at TELOPS and the results discussed refer to this group. Preliminary efforts are underway to apply the SIS planning process at other GTE business units.

Overview of SIS Planning Process

GTEDS' information management (IM) planning staff realized the importance of the strategic perspective on information systems and took on the challenge of developing and implementing a planning process based on this point of view. They saw the task as two-fold:

1. Introduce management to this new perspective and secure its support
2. Create a mechanism for generating and evaluating SIS proposals.

To accomplish these ends, they designed a five-phase SIS planning process (see Table 46.1) that moved from an initial dissemination of SIS ideas and identification

Table 46.1
SIS Planning Process

Phase	Activity	Content	Purpose
A	Introduce IM Chief Executive to SIS Concepts	Overview of SIS concepts; cases of SIS applications in other companies	Gain approval to proceed with SIS idea-generation meeting for IM group
B	Conduct SIS Idea-Generation Meeting for IM Middle Management	Execute SIS idea-generation methodology; evaluate SIS ideas	Test SIS idea-generation methodology; identify significant SIS ideas for executive consideration
C	Conduct SIS Idea-Generation Meeting for IM Executives	Execute SIS idea-generation methodology; evaluate SIS ideas	Identify SIS ideas and evaluate these together with ideas from previous meeting
D	Introduce Top Business Executive to SIS Concept	Overview of SIS concept and some candidate SIS ideas for the business	Gain approval to proceed with SIS idea-generation meeting for business planners
E	Conduct SIS Idea-Generation Meeting for Corp. Business Planners	Execute SIS idea-generation methodology; evaluate SIS ideas	Identify SIS ideas and evaluate these together with ideas from previous meetings

of opportunities to a final acceptance by members of the TELOPS' senior management team. The last step in the process resulted in a portfolio of SIS applications (not described here for reasons of confidentiality) earmarked for implementation.

SIS Planning Process

In phase A, the head of TELOPS' information management planning function introduced GTEDS' president to the SIS concept through a series of informal meetings and memoranda on the subject. The purpose here was to win top-level support for the project and approval for the next two phases.

In phases B and C, GTEDS' information management planning staff ran offsite idea-generation meetings aimed at developing the strategic perspective on information systems and identifying SIS opportunities. These sessions involved two groups of information systems professionals. In phase B, participants were drawn from the data processing company's cadre of middle managers; in phase C, attendees were the top information management executives within the local telephone companies and GTEDS.

The successful completion of phases A–C led to a meeting (in phase D) between GTEDS' president and TELOPS' top business executive. The latter was introduced to the SIS concept and told of the opportunities already discovered at the previous two brainstorming sessions. This meeting set the stage for phase E, an SIS idea-generation meeting with TELOPS' corporate business planners, those responsible for initiating the business' strategic thrusts.

The idea-generation meetings, which occurred at phases B, C, and E of the SIS planning process, consisted of seven explicit steps (see Table 46.2) designed to introduce the strategic perspective on information systems, stimulate the systematic search for SIS opportunities, and evaluate and select a set of projects expected to secure the greatest competitive advantage for the firm. A description of each of the steps follows:

Step 1. Present Tutorial on Competitive Strategy and SIS   The tutorial was led by a consultant expert on the theory of strategic information systems. The tutorial emphasized the concepts of strategic targets and strategic thrusts and covered the role of information systems in supporting or shaping the competitive strategy of the firm. More importantly, it provided attendees with an analytical framework with which they could identify SIS opportunities and threats.

Step 2. Apply SIS Concepts to Actual Cases   Following the tutorial, participants solidified their understanding of the concepts presented by analyzing a set of actual SIS microcases drawn from a variety of industries. Working through about 20 examples selected from a prepared list of 50, they learned how to identify strategic targets and thrusts.

Table 46.2
SIS Idea-Generation Meeting Steps

Step	Activity	Purpose
1	Present Tutorial on Competitive Strategy and SIS	Introduce the concepts of strategic thrusts, strategic targets, and competitive strategy
2	Apply SIS Concepts to Actual Cases	Raise consciousness about SIS possibilities and their strategic thrusts and targets
3	Review Company's Competitive Position	Understand competitive position of the business and its strategies
4	Brainstorm for SIS Opportunities	Generate SIS ideas in small groups
5	Discuss SIS Opportunities	Eliminate duplication and condense SIS ideas
6	Evaluate SIS Opportunities	Evaluate competitive significance of SIS ideas
7	Detail SIS Blockbusters	Detail each SIS blockbuster idea, its competitive advantage, and key implementation issues

Step 3. Review Company's Competitive Position This step acquainted participants with the competitive realities facing the business. It was presented by the information management planning staff and covered such topics as markets, products, customers, suppliers, competitors, strengths, weaknesses, and business strategies. By understanding these elements, one is in a position to consider the question: "How can information technology be used to support or shape strategic thrusts aimed at the firm's strategic targets?"

Step 4. Brainstorm for SIS Opportunities In this step the group divided into teams of 5–8 participants and each brainstormed for different kinds of SIS opportunities. Some teams focused on leveraging existing information management assets, while others explored the possibility of creating new assets. Some concentrated on opportunities related to suppliers (providers of raw materials, capital, or labor) by addressing such questions as:

1. Can we use information systems to gain leverage over our suppliers?
   - Improve our bargaining power?
   - Reduce the supplier's bargaining power?
2. Can we use information systems to reduce buying costs?
   - Reduce our labor costs?
   - Reduce our supplier's costs?
3. Can we use information systems to identify alternative sources?
   - To locate substitute products and services?
   - To make versus to buy?
4. Can we use information systems to improve the quality of products and services we receive from our suppliers?

Other teams looked for SIS opportunities related to customers (those who retail, wholesale, warehouse, distribute, or use the firm's products) by responding to such questions as:

1. Can we use information systems to reduce our customer's telecommunication's costs?
2. Can we use information systems to increase a customer's switching costs (make it difficult for the customer to change suppliers)?
3. Can we make our databases available to our customers?
4. Can we provide administrative support to our customers? (billing, collection, inventory management, etc.)
5. Can we use information systems to learn more about our customers and/or discover possible market niches?
6. Can we use information systems to help our customers increase their revenues?

And still other teams searched for SIS opportunities related to competitors by answering such questions as:

1. Can we use information systems to raise the entry cost of competitors into our markets?

2. Can we use information systems to differentiate our products and services?
3. Can we use information systems to make a preemptive strike (e.g., to offer something they can't because we have the data) against our competitors?
4. Can we use information systems to provide substitutes before the competition does?
5. Can we use information systems to improve or reduce distribution costs?
6. Can we use information systems to form joint ventures to allow entry into new markets?
7. Can we use information systems to match an existing competitor's offering?
8. Can we use a new information technology to establish a new market niche?
9. Can we use our knowledge of the information industry and markets to find new markets or better ways of doing business?

To aid in the development of an SIS idea, each team completed a short form describing the idea, the intended strategic target, the basic strategic thrust, and the specific competitive advantage. The ground rule in these SIS idea-generation sessions is that criticism or evaluation of ideas must be suppressed so that creativity is not inhibited or stifled in any way.

Step 5. Discuss SIS Opportunities　　Each team reported its SIS ideas to the entire group and a scribe posted them on a flip chart for all to see. Group discussion encouraged clarification, elimination of duplicate proposals, and identification of overlapping suggestions. But again, as in the previous step, criticism was prohibited.

Step 6. Evaluate SIS Opportunities　　The purpose here was to rate and rank each of the SIS proposals generated. Participants were to apply the following evaluative criteria when making their judgements:

- degree of competitive advantage,
- cost to develop and install,
- feasibility (from technical and resource points of view), and
- risk (understood as the probability of reaping and sustaining the competitive advantage promised by the SIS idea).

Applying these criteria, SIS proposals were classed into four categories:

1. blockbuster (potential for strategic dominance),
2. very high potential (but not blockbuster),
3. moderate potential (worthy of further consideration), or
4. low potential (not worthy of further consideration).

Step 7. Detail SIS Blockbusters　　Here the group concentrated on refining and recording the SIS blockbuster ideas. This refinement details the technology employed, customer benefits, competitive advantage, responsibilities, and implementation concerns that aid in the process of transforming the idea into reality.

Meeting Dynamics   The SIS idea-generation meetings lasted for two full days. Each step took about two hours, with the exception of the tutorial and the exercise (Steps 1 and 2), which together needed about five hours from an outside consultant to convey the concepts. Step 4, the brainstorming session, unlike typical workshop breakouts whose effectiveness usually lasts between 45 and 90 minutes, required more time. In our meetings the teams of 5–8 were very lively and needed a solid two hours to develop their ideas.

RESULTS

Identification of SIS Opportunities

Each of the three brainstorming meetings generated over 100 SIS ideas. At each meeting about 10 were considered real winners. Many proposals overlapped across meetings, and there was consensus on the blockbuster suggestions. This consensus was fortunate since it validated the top ideas and built support and commitment for them from a variety of constituencies: corporate management, information management, and local telephone companies.

The SIS opportunities discovered by each group were combined after the final idea-generation meeting. Of the top 11 proposals, six were rated as blockbusters and five were classed as having very high potential. When one considers that most stories about the strategic use of information systems concern only one primary SIS idea, the process at GTE was prolific indeed. We would have scored our process a success had we uncovered one or two top ideas in this first pass, but instead we uncovered 11 worthy of implementation.

Impact on GTE

The development of a strategic perspective on information systems and the specific ideas generated in the SIS planning process resulted in several major managerial changes at TELOPS. For the first time, members of top management focused their attention on SIS opportunities. They now believe that information systems can play a critical role in shaping business strategy. Proof of this comes in management's immediate allocation of resources to implement the three best blockbuster ideas.

To insure that their new strategic vision about the role of information systems is made part of the fabric of the organization and not just a passing fancy, top management elevated the information management function in the corporate hierarchy. They created senior information systems positions at headquarters and at the telephone operating companies. These senior positions report directly to the chief operating officer of the unit instead of to the chief financial officer as they did in the past. (The positions are very much like the chief information officer function described by Synnott and Gruber [15]). Information management has finally become an equal partner in setting the strategic direction of the company.

Executives at GTE's local telephone companies agreed to implement similar SIS planning processes in their operating units. These will address the unique competitive environments, threats, and opportunities confronting each. The units also agreed to champion one of the original 11 SIS ideas.

To emphasize the importance TELOPS attaches to the strategic perspective on information systems, TELOPS information management function formally added a new SIS strategy to its long-range plan, which previously focused only on operational improvements.

Impact on Other GTE Businesses

TELOPS, GTE's largest division was the first to implement the SIS planning process outlined above. Its success prompted other GTE units, in widely different competitive environments, to initiate similar projects.

CONCLUSION

The SIS planning process described above resulted in the identification of many ideas to provide GTE Telephone Operations with significant competitive advantage. Some SIS ideas require investment in new information-based assets, while others leverage existing information resources. The continued application of the SIS planning process within TELOPS will ensure that the idea pipeline is full and that quality ideas will be implemented. Beyond TELOPS, the methodology is being used by other GTE units to identify SIS opportunities. We believe the methodology can be used by other firms whose vision extends to using information systems as competitive weapons in their quest for advantage.

REFERENCES

1. Anthony, R.N. *Planning and Control Systems: A Framework for Analysis,* Harvard University Press, Boston, Massachusetts, 1965.

2. Gorry, A. and Scott Morton, M. "A Framework for Management Information Systems," *Sloan Management Review,* Volume 13, Number 1, Fall 1971, pp. 55–70.

3. IBM *Information Systems Planning Guide: Business Systems Planning,* (4th Ed.), New York, New York, 1984.

4. Keen, P. and Scott Morton, M. *Decision Support Systems: An Organizational Perspective,* Addison-Wesley, Reading, Massachusetts, 1978.

5. King, W. "Achieving the Potential of Decision Support Systems," *Journal of Business Strategy,* Volume 3, Number 3, Winter 1983, pp. 84–91.

6. King, W. "Strategic Planning for MIS," *MIS Quarterly,* Volume 2, Number 1, March 1978, pp. 27–37.

7. Nolan, R. and Gibson, C. "Managing the Four Stages of EDP Growth," *Harvard Business Review,* Volume 52, Number 1, January–February 1974, pp. 76–88.

8. Nolan, R. "Managing the Crises in Data Processing," *Harvard Business Review,* Volume 57, Number 2, March–April 1979, pp. 115–126.

9. Nolan, R. "Plight of the EDP Manager," *Harvard Business Review,* Volume 51, Number 3, May–June 1973, pp. 143–152.

10. Rockart, J. and Treacy, M. "Executive Information Systems," *Center for Information Systems Research,* CISR Working Paper Number 65, Massachusetts Institute of Technology, Cambridge, Massachusetts, 1981.

11. Rockart, J. and Treacy, M. "The CEO Goes On-Line," *Harvard Business Review,* Volume 60, Number 1, January–February 1982, pp. 82–88.

12. Rockart, J. and Bullen, C. "A Primer on Critical Success Factors," *Center for Information Systems Research,* CISR Working Paper Number 69, Massachusetts Institute of Technology, Cambridge, Massachusetts, 1981.

13. Rockart, J. "Chief Executives Define Their Own Data Needs," *Harvard Business Review,* Volume 57, Number 2, March–April 1979, pp. 81–92.

14. Porter, M.E. *Competitive Strategy: Techniques for Analyzing Industries and Competitors,* Free Press, New York, New York, 1980.

15. Synnott, W. and Gruber, W. *Information Resource Management: Opportunities and Strategies for the 1980s,* John Wiley & Sons, New York, New York, 1981.

16. Wiseman, C. *Strategy and Computers: Information Systems as Competitive Weapons,* Dow Jones-Irwin, Homewood, Illinois, 1985.

17. Zani, W. "Blueprint for MIS," *Harvard Business Review,* Volume 48, Number 6, November–December 1970, pp. 95–100.

PART FIVE

Information Technology Management: In Depth Studies

One of the best ways to understand the key issues in applying and managing IT resources is to examine case studies. Thus we have selected five extended case studies that cover many of the topics addressed throughout this book. These studies are not meant to illustrate effective or ineffective approaches to applying or managing IT resources, but to provide a backdrop for the thoughtful analysis of these important issues.

The first two cases provide rich descriptions of IT applications in two distinct organizational contexts. Reading 47 illustrates some of the critical issues that arise in designing an information system to provide operational and decisional support of a manufacturing firm's core activities. Reading 48, "The House of Games," chronicles the impact that IT resources have on the financial-services community and on the stock market's operation and volatility.

The final three cases focus on the complexities of the systems-development process. Reading 49 discusses the design, development, and implementation of an information system that managed the complex communication requirements of the 1984 Olympic Games. Reading 50, illustrates how a variety of systems analysis and design methods can be applied in developing a sophisticated decision support system. The final reading, "Alcon Laboratories: Information Technology Group," describes a company's effort to radically change the manner in which it develops new IT applications. The Alcon Lab case also illustrates the changes occurring in the organizational roles of information systems professionals.

47

An Integrated Decision Support and Manufacturing Control System

M. T. Hehnen, S. C. Chou, H. L. Scheurman, G. J. Robinson, T. P. Luken, and D. W. Baker

A successfully implemented manufacturing decision system is used to maximize the return achieved by a forest products mill from the raw material flowing to it. The system integrates real-time decision making and control with a concurrent simulation capability. This combination was extremely successful in gaining operations and management acceptance of new technology and enhancing its economic benefit. The return on capital investment exceeds 40 percent, and the integration and system-wide economic perspective have proved extremely important.

For a number of years we have been developing and implementing systems to extract maximum value from the stream of raw material flowing to forest products conversion facilities. This broad class of operations research problems covers a spectrum from long-range strategic questions to immediate operational problems such as how to cut a long log into smaller logs for maximum value. This latter activity, called merchandising, is discussed here along with several generic problems associated with implementing real-time decision and control systems.

SYSTEM OVERVIEW

In 1979, the Weyerhaeuser Company began planning a new small log mill at Raymond, Washington. The mill is a stand-alone facility which processes wood, taking it from stems through to dried and packaged lumber. The mill design includes a merchandiser directly coupled to the front end of the mill. Long logs, those over 22 feet long, are referred to as stems. Because the longest log that the mill can handle is 20 feet, a stem requires at least one cross cut (buck). The merchandiser at Raymond is a large machine center which conveys stems, debarks them, feeds them to a bank of saws, and bucks them to various lengths. The resulting saw logs are conveyed to the mill, and residual pieces are fed to a chipper. The chips are trucked to nearby pulp mills.

The process of merchandising is quite simple and does not require much precision. Superficially, the decision about where to cut the stem appears easy. However, making good decisions about how to cut stems is a sophisticated problem in optimization. Recognizing this was the original stimulus for developing merchandising decision systems (MDS), a key technology in Timberlands R&D.

Essentially, the technology implemented at Raymond contains two parts: the real-time decision and control system proper (MDS) and a concurrent simulation system (COMPASS). The MDS consists of a data acquisition device which acquires information about the stem's geometry, a processor to compute an optimal decision, and control system interfaces for interacting with the operator and the saws. COMPASS is a decision support system to help mill management determine the effects of the decision system's logic and explore alternative merchandising strategies.

The MDS receives stems in a random manner from an inventory. Individual bucking decisions for each stem are based on the physical characteristics of each possible saw log in the stem, the potential profit contribution to the system of each such log, and constraints imposed by the physical limits of the merchandiser and saw mill. These decisions and their execution must take place in real time; that is, bucking should not be the bottleneck in the lumber making process.

PROBLEMS

In retrospect, the technical issues associated with implementing a sophisticated real-time optimization system were relatively easy to deal with by applying sound methodology. The hard problem was this: user acceptance requires understanding of system objectives and agreement on performance against those objectives. It turns out to be far more difficult to understand and evaluate a system which controls a particular machine center but whose objective is to maximize overall system profits, than it is to understand a control system whose purpose is simply to automate that particular machine center. In the latter case, the objective is to make the machine center do the same thing faster with minimal emphasis on the decision making. The former type of control system, which we will call a manufacturing decision system, is primarily concerned with influencing total system profits through the decisions being made at the particular machine center. Clearly, we are oversimplifying, but we do so to make a point; getting everyone to understand the real objective is a critical determinant of implementation success.

Another significant problem is the difficulty of measuring performance against a system-wide profit objective by simply observing the one machine center where the decisions are being made. In contrast, it is fairly straightforward to determine if you are processing 20 percent more logs in an hour. This is one of the reasons people measure things like logs per hour or board feed per shift. They are surrogate measures for final profit, which is less easy to measure. Hence, the forest products' Peter Principle of Measurement: "One measures what is easy to measure, not necessarily what is relevant."

SOLUTION

Thus, as we struggled to implement the MDS technology, we discovered that a manufacturing decision system project such as the MDS starts with a significant handicap in terms of end user understanding and acceptance. We spent countless hours trying to explain the opportunity, the benefit, and how the system works with little success. The missing piece was reaching agreement on a comprehensive economic context or model on which to base system design and performance criteria. Developing and communicating this model became the key to overcoming end users' profound resistance and confusion about the technology. The real end users of these systems are mill managers and their management teams, not the merchandiser operators. What we discovered after several years of grappling with this problem and many false starts is that creating a decision support system jointly with the user can very effectively resolve this communications problem. Exhibit 47.1 outlines the economic model that provided a framework for the simulation. Serendipitously, integrating the decision support system (COMPASS) with the decision system (MDS) increases profit contributions as well.

The COMPASS system operates as an "on line" simulation, that is, concurrent with the operation of the MDS. While the MDS is processing stems, COMPASS can simulate merchandiser operations for a large number of stems previously captured in its files. COMPASS then provides the user, typically the mill manager or his industrial engineer, with the ability to change the basic parameters of the economic model; lumber prices, processing rates, operating costs, and so on. Having done so, the COMPASS system recalculates log values and then simulates the merchandising of the selected set of stems using the same logic as the actual decision system. The output is a set of reports which describes the end products that result as well as financial statements. This enables the management team to carry out the sort of "what if" analyses for which simulations (or, decision support systems) are so well suited.

Most important to the problem of implementation, however, is the synergy that occurs when the two pieces, MDS and COMPASS, are used together. Each reinforces the utility and success of the other. For example, in order to understand and hence use the decision system to full advantage, the user and designer must understand the economic context. However, in order to build and use COMPASS in the first place, you have to construct a model of this context, then gather the relevant data. This data is precisely what is needed to run the MDS! This synergy was evident in a number of areas.

- The COMPASS system was very useful for developing concepts in that it first forced the designers and then the users to tackle the key problem, that of developing a correct view of the mill's economic environment. This development work was undertaken jointly by R&D and operations and served to communicate ideas and objectives in both directions, increasing learning by both groups. Then, as the model took shape, data needs became clearer, not only for COMPASS, but for the MDS itself.
- It became easier for the end user to visualize the results of the decisions being made since the results displayed by COMPASS are for a sufficiently long period

Exhibit 47.1

The simulation model at the heart of the COMPASS integrates both an economic model and a process simulation. The decision on how to buck a stem into logs affects eventual system profits through both product mix, hence revenue, and downstream processing costs. Their contribution can be computed as final product revenue minus variable processing costs, raw material costs being fixed at the merchandiser.

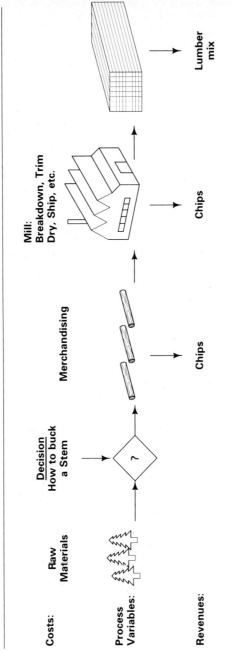

Costs: **Raw Materials**   **Decision How to buck a Stem**   **Merchandising**   **Mill: Breakdown, Trim Dry, Ship, etc.**

Process Variables:

Revenues: **Chips**   **Chips**   **Lumber mix**

of time; for example, a shift or a day. The alternative is to sit on the merchandiser deck and watch the stems being bucked one by one. In this myopic manner, it is nearly impossible to evaluate the decisions being made. In fact, since the decisions are often different from what conventional wisdom would dictate, it is easy to walk away from the saws thinking that this new computer system is goofy (a view we often heard prior to developing COMPASS). But, once we had agreed on a system-wide economic model for COMPASS, it was easy to see and believe the results of bucking decisions made over large numbers of stems.

- The integrated system proved effective in explaining the operation of the merchandiser decision system. By exploring individual bucking decisions and the way they change or don't change as a result of changing the parameters that go into the log valuation calculations in COMPASS, the operations staff developed an understanding of how the MDS works and the rationale which lies behind individual stem decisions.

- Once user and developer had worked their way through concept development, the economic modeling details, and an understanding of the objectives and effects of the system, it became much easier to visualize applications, not only for the decision support system (COMPASS) but for ways in which to use the decision system (MDS) to achieve mill objectives.

- Finally, the existence of a common system economic model enhances communications between the decision maker and other members of the mill staff and crew.

The essence of implementation, particularly for a technology which involves changing the way you think about things, is to achieve user acceptance and comfort. This jointly developed, well-understood simulation made it easier for the mill staff to understand the benefits of the decision system, the decisions that were being made, and the results of those decisions in terms they found meaningful.

THE MERCHANDISER DECISION SYSTEM

The Merchandiser Decision System (MDS), as implemented at the Raymond facility, includes not only the electronic equipment, such as the scanners and computers used to suggest decisions, but also the merchandiser operator, who accepts or corrects the decisions, and the electro-mechanical equipment, such as saws and conveyors, which put the decision into effect. These three elements function as a unit to buck stems into the logs and fiber segments which, when processed, will yield the best (maximum margin) finished product mix.

A key point here is that the operator has the final say as to how a particular stem is bucked; most of the time he accepts the suggested decision, but he may "override" the logic and supply his own solution. An override may be necessary when the suggested solution is not consistent with the visual characteristics (knots or rot, and so forth) of the stem or when a temporary materials handling problem is present, such as a downstream machine center becoming plugged up with 20-foot logs.

In discussing the MDS, we will concentrate on the components of the system that work together to supply the "suggested bucking solution" for each stem to the operator. The three major components of the real-time system are the Data Acquisition Subsystem (DAS), the Decision Logic and Control Subsystem (DLCS) and the Execution Subsystem (EXS).

Perhaps the quickest way to understand the system is to follow a typical stem through the process.

As the leading end of the stem enters the scanning zone, the DAS begins to collect raw stem geometry. The scanning zone is comprised of a longitudinal conveyor, a pair of photo-electric light curtains (one horizontal and one vertical), and an absolute position encoder mounted on the headspool of the conveyor. Data collection continues for numerous points along the stem, until its trailing end exits the scanning zone. The stem reaches the bucking station about 30 seconds later.

The raw stem geometry is filtered and smoothed by the DAS, producing a stem model which is transmitted to the DLCS. The DLCS accepts the stem model and places it at the end of the stem queue, which may consist of as many as eight stems. When the decision logic task has completed solving all the stems ahead of ours in the queue, it begins to compute a "suggested" solution. This solution is saved as part of our stem queue entry.

When our physical stem enters the bucking station, the EXS requests its "suggested" bucking solution from the DLCS. The DLCS retrieves this solution from the stem queue (now the top entry in the queue) and transmits it to the EXS where it is immediately displayed to the operator. Since the "suggested" solution matches the stem's visible characteristics, the operator accepts the solution and the EXS executes it. The EXS transmits a record of the stem's demise (our "asbucked" solution) to the DLCS. The DLCS appends this "as-bucked" data to our stem queue entry, writes the complete stem queue entry to the shift archive file, and then deletes the entry from the queue.

The DLCS also houses the mill management user interfaces. At the end of each shift (three times a day), a shift summary report is automatically generated and complete stem histories for the shift are made available to COMPASS. At any time during the shift, the foreman can call up shift-to-date status displays, and the industrial engineer can activate a new value base derived from his COMPASS work.

The decision logic task is an implementation of a single-state, multi-stage dynamic program where the objective is to maximize net return per stem. It is a cpu-limited (that is, no input or output operations) program with solution time proportional to stem length (longer stems take more time than shorter stems). As a cpu-bound program, the decision logic was implemented as a low priority real-time task, utilizing "spare" cpu cycles not needed by the other real-time tasks. This, in conjunction with the fact that a stem takes at least 30 seconds to travel from the scanning zone to the bucking station, has given us sufficient cpu time on the system processor, a Harris H80, for the decision logic task to function.

THE MDS/COMPASS INTERFACE

Since COMPASS shares a common cpu with DLCS, the interface between them is necessarily soft (that is, defined in software with some shared files). The two major functions across this interface are both controlled from the COMPASS side. The COMPASS user may extract some or all of the stem history records from the previous shift's archive file or he may choose to activate a new log value data base, which the decision logic will then use in determining "suggested" bucking solutions (Exhibit 47.2).

COMPASS, A CONCURRENT DECISION SUPPORT SYSTEM

As we mentioned earlier, during the early stages of MDS implementation at the Raymond mill, a significant problem that the project team had to constantly face was that the merchandiser operator, and mill management for that matter, would not accept some of the bucking decisions made by the decision logic of the MDS. For example, the logic may propose to cut the first 20 feet from a 24-foot stem into a saw log and throw the remaining four feet away as a fiber segment. In a situation like that, the operator, traditionally trained to maximize volume throughput, would most likely override the MDS with his own 16', 8' bucking decision—sending two logs instead of one into the mill, even though that particular eight-footer is marginal since the cost of processing it is greater than its revenue.

Tired of defending MDS bucking solutions with pencil and paper, the project team developed a set of computer programs to produce hard evidence (such as total margin, total variable cost, margin per mill hour, log mix, lumber mix, and so forth) which would show that over a period of time (a shift or a day), the MDS decisions did produce a greater profit. This decision support system was used extensively by the project team to monitor the on-line decision system (MDS) and to educate mill management and operators as well as themselves. We called this package COMPASS for COmputerized Merchandising for Premium ASSortment.

COMPASS consists of three major components: the database, simulation models, and interfaces.

The database is made up of stem models, prices, costs, log values, lumber yield data, control parameters, and various merchandiser production files. COMPASS provides extensive data management capabilities which allow the user to interactively view, edit, receive, and transmit data.

The simulation models accurately reflect the mill's manufacturing processes and economic context, generate log value data needed by the decision logic, and answer questions such as:

- What happens if the price of 2 x 4s changes?
- Can I alter my operating posture to make more money?
- When am I sending marginal logs to the mill?

The heart of this simulation is the prediction of the lumber that can be extracted from a log of a given geometry. This predictive model is also used downstream in the process control system for lumber breakdown at Raymond. Consequently, it has been extensively tested and validated. In addition, an extensive postimplementation test was conducted to evaluate the economic benefit of MDS at Raymond, and it demonstrated that the MDS/COMPASS combination improves mill profitability enough to pay for itself in one to two years.

Interfaces allow the user to invoke COMPASS functions and facilitate commu-

Exhibit 47.2

This high level overview of MDS and COMPASS shows the major data
flows. The key interactions between MDS and COMPASS are stem
descriptions captured by MDS and changes in log values passed on by
COMPASS as the result of "what if?" simulations by management.

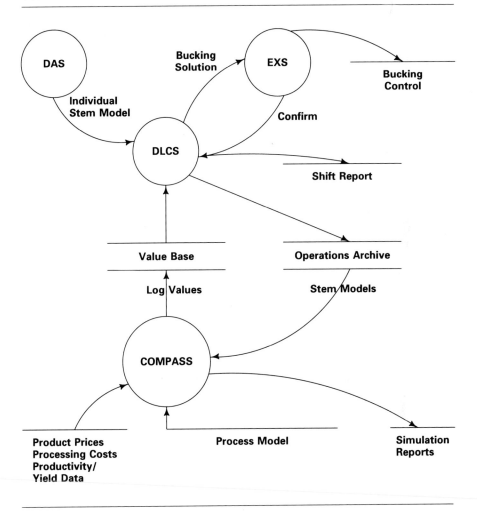

nications between COMPASS and MDS. We spent considerable effort on the interaction between user and COMPASS, to assure its acceptability.

To appreciate how COMPASS works, consider the following example: Suppose the sawmill superintendent wants to decide whether or not to discontinue making 1 x 4 lumber from the center portion of saw logs. The mill's industrial engineer
would go through the following sequence with COMPASS (Task numbers refer to
the system's menu for task selection [Table 47.1].):

- Select a set of stems from the COMPASS database (task 9) which resembles the
  raw material the mill would expect to process in the next three months.

- Prepare two sets of log values (task 4), one for making 1 x 4s from the center, the other not. Based on changes to lumber sawing factors entered by the industrial engineer (task 3), these log values are computed by an internal process model which simulates the lumber manufacturing process.
- Generate the data needed to evaluate the alternatives by setting up two merchandising simulations (task 7). In this process, an optimization model bucks the selected set of stems under the control of each set of log values and collects data on the predicted end products and costs.
- Evaluate the alternatives by comparing simulation results (task 8). Comparisons such as margin per mill hour and margin per unit of raw material provide mill management with valuable information on which to base the decision.
- Control the future results of the MDS by activating the log value database which corresponds to the preferred alternative (task 13).

Other uses are fairly evident from the menu (Table 47.1). COMPASS supports mill management by providing a window into the decision process through which mill management can maintain data and receive information, and a tool by which mill management can explore alternatives, test assumptions and hypotheses, build a mental image on which to base judgment, and activate control parameters.

SUMMARY

It is not enough to recognize a significant profit opportunity in applying operations research to an industrial problem. Even though focusing development resources on solving the technical problems is important, selling the concept often proves to be a major obstacle. We found that involving the users in developing a real-time decision and control system integrated with a concurrent decision support system was the key to successful implementation. It provided the needed synergy to create positive acceptance of the technology. We learned (or relearned)

- The importance of first having and then communicating a system-wide economic view,
- The value of providing a straightforward decision support system which is integrated with the decision system,
- The importance of developing the system using an evolutionary approach in close cooperation with the ultimate user, and
- The usefulness of decision support systems such as COMPASS in manufacturing applications as well as in the traditional financial and data-base situations.

A letter from Paul G. Goebel, Wood Products Manager, Twin Harbors Region, and Bill R. Norman, Mill Manager, Raymond Sawmill, attests that: "Weyerhaeuser

Table 47.1
The possible uses of COMPASS are clearly laid out in its task selection menu.

SELECT to

1. Examine COMPASS files
2. Edit lumber prices
3. Edit lumber sawing factors
4. Generate log segment values and lumber yields
5. Edit decision logic parameters
6. Edit COMPASS parameters
7. Set up merchandising simulations
8. Compare simulation results
9. Create stem files
10. Browse lumber yield tables
11. Examine merchandiser shift production data
12. Display current MDS shift production summary
13. Activate values and parameters to be used by the real time system
14. Exit from COMPASS

has used the merchandiser decision system as the primary decision and control system for our log bucking since May 1982. In a comprehensive test which we designed and conducted jointly with Weyerhaeuser research, we were able to quantify to our satisfaction the annual profit increment attributable to using the system. While we consider the specific results to be proprietary information, these test results indicate an investment pay back period of slightly more than one year, equivalent to a return on investment in excess of 40 percent under reasonable assumptions."

48 The House of Games

David Kull and

Lee Keough

Ask the American in the street what computers and the people who administrate them have done for the country lately. Chances are that the response will include some reference to the stock market collapse of October 19, 1987 – Black Monday.

Responsibility for the sickening plummet in stock prices that day has widely been assigned to a single primary influence: computer-triggered trading schemes, commonly known as program trading. In the intervening period, the use of program trading has been curtailed both voluntarily and through rule changes – although not nearly so much as the public has been led to believe – primarily as a means of restoring investor confidence in the New York Stock Exchange.

With program trading under control, then, is Wall Street's house in order? Not by any stretch of the imagination. In fact, months after the crash, Nicholas Brady, chairman of the Presidential task force – the Brady Commission – convened to study the crash, continued to warn of residual danger in market mechanisms. "We are looking down the barrel of a gun," Brady said, "and it's still loaded."

The immediate post-crash indictment of program trading by the vested interests on Wall Street, including the same brokerage firms that have continued to execute massive program trades every day on behalf of institutional clients, has since evolved into one of the biggest diversionary maneuvers since public opinion was first manipulated.

It has been manifest in some rather strange gimmicks, like the New York Stock Exchange's "express lane" service. That service, announced with much fanfare in July, stands to have no profound effect on trading dynamics. Under the rule, slated to be in effect by year's end and officially dubbed the Individual Investor Express Delivery Service, whenever the Dow Jones Industrial Average moves 25 points from the previous day's close, the NTSE's Designated Order Turnaround (DOT) processing system will give priority to the routing of simple market orders (those submitted

The Myth of High-Tech Access

Remember October [1987] when you reached for the phone, hoping to get your stockbroker to sell before your bull market earnings evaporated? Perhaps you were one of the many unfortunates told they had been beaten to the punch by somebody who got to "the computer" first.

More likely, you lost out to large institutional investors who transmitted their sell orders the only sure way—verbally—and had them executed manually. During Black Monday at the New York Stock Exchange, the only successful strategy was based on old-fashioned personal contact; otherwise, you could find yourself way back in an impossible computer queue.

The interface technology available today is not much help when a broker wants to execute a significant trade, says Thomas Doyle, managing director of Rochdale Securities Corp., a member of the NYSE. Doyle's firm deals only with large institutional clients; it uses no in-house automated trading, relying on links to an outside service bureau for transactions involving something less than 2,000 shares of stock. Larger trades are always handled manually via independent floor brokers.

"Whether you deal with a high-tech or low-tech brokerage doesn't make much difference for an individual," says Haim Mendelson of the University of Rochester (NY). "But when you are dealing with large quantities of stock, you have to worry whether your own trade will impact the stock price. At that point, faster access is essential."

On Wall Street, faster access doesn't necessarily mean high technology. "Once you're dealing with a trade of significant size," says Doyle, "you want to assess what the current supply and demand situation is."

"The specialist has the most information," says Junius Peake, an Englewood, NJ-based consultant, "so if the trader is on the floor of the exchange, he can go there and pick up gossip or get involved in an auction market." It can take 15 seconds for a clerk to mark down a trade, notes Peake; during that time, a broker who is physically present has plenty of opportunity to offer a better price.

For program trading, however, fast access to stock quotations is essential—even if the quotations don't reflect the limit orders in a specialist's book. "Some people look at tapes that are 15 minutes late," says Bruce Collins, a vice president in the equity arbitrage group at Shearson Lehman Hutton. "That's not acceptable if a client wants to execute a program trade."

Shearson's program trading systems—a combination of software on micros and mainframes are developed in concert with a client's own goals. For instance, the program may call for the client to sell 10 percent of its holdings in the market if the Dow Jones Industrial Average drops 20 points. When a drop in the market nears 20 points, and the client gives the go-ahead, the Shearson trader just pushes a button. The program selects which stocks to sell, and the order will be transmitted to the NYSE's Designated Order Turnaround system. That's fine on a normal day, but when DOT gets choked, program trades hit the floor via shoe leather.

Even if small investor orders get "express lane" priority through the DOT system when trading heats up, institutional

The Myth of High-Tech Access (cont.)

traders will still have the benefit of the verbal auction market, plus their information resources, to work with. They know what their clients plan to buy or sell, and for what price, and can parlay this information.

Does this leave the small investor a day late and more than a dollar short? Maybe, but many Wall Streeters—when

not on the public relations stump—protest its relevance. Who are institutional clients, they ask, if not the pension and mutual funds comprising many thousands of individual investors?

Besides, says Collins, stock is priced like anything else: Volume buyers can always get it wholesale.

for execution at whatever the current price) submitted by individuals over those submitted by institutions. The new rule, however, applies only to market orders of 2,000 shares or fewer, and these orders will still have to compete, at the conventional disadvantage, with those of insiders on the trading floor (see box "The Myth of High-Tech Access").

The overriding irony is that while rampant automation, on the traders' side, has been made the scapegoat for the market's woes, it is the inadequacy of its own information processing systems that keeps the 19th-century New York Stock Exchange from effectively participating in late 20th-century market dynamics. Consider the following evidence.

In its report on the crash, the Securities and Exchange Commission, the body charged with regulating the securities markets, called program trading "a significant factor in accelerating and exacerbating the declines." The SEC pointed out that such trading accounted for 20 percent of the volume in Standard & Poor's 500 stocks on Black Monday. That figure may not sound impressive. It means, after all, that 80 percent of the trading in those stocks came from sources other than program trades. The SEC pushed the point, however, by demonstrating that program trading "totaled more than 60 percent of S&P 500 stock volume in three different 10-minute periods" on October 19.

To a number of expert observers, that statement borders on flimflammery. Franklin Edwards, Arthur Burns professor of free and competitive enterprise at Columbia University in New York, observes that any analyst can easily pick an arbitrary, small time interval that shows an individual trader accounting for any proportion of trades that the analyst wants it to account for—even 100 percent. "Evidence drawn from discretionary short intervals of time is so arbitrary that its meaningfulness is open to serious question," Edwards says.

The New York Stock Exchange imposed—then voted to withdraw—a "collar" barring the use of DOT for program trades whenever the Dow Jones Industrial Average moves 50 points during a single trading session. The public and press applauded, but market insiders told DECISIONS that the collar—which should expire by the end of this year—affects only those brokerages that don't have enough employees on the trading floor of the exchange. For those that do, it's merely an inconvenience, forcing them to distribute their orders for program trades manually. For instance, when traders for Shearson Lehman Hutton see the Dow's movement approach 49 points, according to John Baker, executive vice president of equity trading systems at the firm, "we load up a bag with preticketed orders and just send it down to the floor." Baker calls the NYSE's DOT collar "silly," but at the same time he stresses that his firm executes program trades only for its institutional customers, and voluntarily abstains from using them for its own account.

Richard Grasso, NYSE president, defends the collar as an "experiment" in dealing with price volatility. "The process of going manual does in fact slow the [program trading] strategy down," Grasso says. "And in some people's minds, it changes the economics of the transaction, widening the cost of operations."

How serious was this experiment? In early July, Grasso told DECISIONS that the collar had been used four times (including at least once when the market went up too fast). "The responses I've heard have been generally positive," he said, while noting that there was "not a sufficient body of knowledge from which to draw any definitive conclusions." Less than a week after Grasso tentatively endorsed the collar, the NYSE's board of directors decided to eliminate it.

The most drastic official response to the October crash took nine months to materialize, in the form of an agreement by the NYSE and Chicago Mercantile Exchange to coordinate a "circuit breaker" that would stop trading in the NYSE and related markets for an hour whenever the Dow Jones Industrial average moves 250 points during a session. A fall of another 150 points on reopening would trigger a two-hour halt. An equivalent movement of the Chicago Mercantile Exchange's Standard & Poor's 500 Index would set off similar halts.

The circuit breaker will go into effect upon final approval from both the SEC and the Commodities Futures Trading Commission. Approval is seen as likely since the same circuit breaker had been advocated in an earlier Congressional hearing by both market and regulatory body leaders, through the so-called Presidential Working Group.

However, members of the group openly acknowledged the risks in such a mechanism: As the breaking point nears, traders could panic into selling before the chance is gone, driving prices to the breaking point whether they would have gone there or not. Their decision: programmed stoppages are worth the risk.

Even if they are, there remains the question of why the advocates selected the kind of circuit breaker they did. Working group members cited a similar Brady Commission recommendation as buttressing their proposal; what they did not say, however, was that the Brady Commission made no stipulation that the halts be triggered by price swings.

Robert Wood, director of the institute for security market studies at Pennsylvania State University and a Brady Commission member, says the commission actually favored a circuit breaker pegged to imbalances in buy and sell orders, not price swings. Wood publicly pointed that out to Richard Ketchum, the SEC's director of market regulation, at a recent New York University seminar on technology and the markets. Ketchum responded that the working group had assumed the Brady Com-

Three Minutes at the NYSE

1) It's 2 p.m. EST on the floor of the New York Stock Exchange. The specialist trading in XYZ Corp. stock has just executed an order to sell 1,000 shares of XYZ for $25 a share. This specialist's electronic order display—his "book"—currently shows the following: one bid for 50,000 shares of XYZ at $25; one bid for 30,000 shares at $24¾; one bid for 20,000 shares at $24½; and one bid for 2,000 shares at $24.

2) John Smith, an investor, meets with his broker, Karen Moms, at her Denver office. Precisely at 2 p.m. EST, they check the price of XYZ and find it trading at $25 per share. Smith places an order to sell 200 shares at the market price; Moms enters it into a system maintained by an outside service bureau, which sends it to the NYSE's Designated Order Turnaround system. The DOT system relays it to the floor, where it appears on the specialist's display. Elapsed time: 1.5 minutes. The specialist executes the order at the current price, now $24. Before brokerage fees, Smith's proceeds are $4,800—$200 less than the expected.

3) Also precisely at 2 p.m. EST, David Connelly, a Chicago broker, takes a call from a client who wants to sell 2,000 shares of XYZ stock. Acting on instructions, Connelly places a "day limit" order to sell 2,000 shares at $25. The broker enters the order directly into a terminal connected to DOT; it appears on the XYZ specialist's book. Elapsed time: 1.5 minutes. Since it is received after two large block trades cause the stock's price to fall, Connelly's order is never executed.

4) Boston broker Ben Snow gets a call from a client at 2 p.m. asking to buy 200 shares of XYZ stock at $25. The order is relayed to a trading system maintained by the brokerage house, which sends it to DOT, which routes it to the specialist's dis-

mission meant for price swings to trip the circuit breaker because, he claimed, "We don't know how to preset a halt based on imbalances."

That was in mid-May; less than two months later, the NYSE announced it would use its current computer system to track order imbalances in the 50 most valuable stocks and would temporarily halt trading in any of those stocks that experience an order imbalance of 50,000 or more shares.

Many observers see far more fundamental weaknesses in the market's information system than can be dealt with by overlaying it with express lanes, collars, and circuit breakers. Haim Mendelson, a professor at the University of Rochester (NY) School of Business Administration, compares today's related, but dissimilarly automated, financial markets to an automobile whose four wheels are powered by separate, unsynchronized motors: At low speeds, this vehicle appears to run smoothly, he says; at high speeds, it tears itself apart. Mendelson points out that these interactive financial markets—the New York Stock Exchange, regional exchanges that trade NYSE stocks, the Chicago-based futures markets pegged to those stocks, and options markets pegged to the stocks and futures—all vary greatly in the degree of effective automation they have in place. This lack of coordination has come about, play. Elapsed time: 1 minute. The special- ist sells 200 shares of XYZ from his portfolio. The purchase costs Snow's cli- ent $5,000 plus brokerage fees.

5) Having received a report detailing negative prospects for XYZ Corp., New York trader Donald Baker, who works directly with institutional clients "upstairs" – off the floor of the exchange – calls one of his largest clients, pension fund manager Katherine Moore. At 2 p.m., Moore tells Baker to sell about 50,000 shares of XYZ.

6) Baker immediately calls Keith Robert- son, a trader on the floor of the exchange, and tells him to sell 50,000 shares of XYZ at $23 or above. Robertson heads for the XYZ specialist's booth. Elapsed time since the order was placed: 30 seconds.

7) Robertson is barely beaten to the booth by another trader, who sells 50,000 shares of XYZ at $25. That trade is executed at

2:01 p.m. When Robertson gets his turn, he will sell 30,000 shares of XYZ at $24¾ and 20,000 shares of XYZ at $24½, thereby satisfying the orders on the specialist's book. The specialist executes those trades shortly after 2:01. The cost to Moore's fund for the delay: $17,500.

8) Also at 2 p.m. EST, Napa Valley broker Jeff Jones gets a call from a client wishing to sell 25,000 shares of XYZ for $24½ or more, and places a limit order with a Pacific stock exchange floor broker, but the best bid there is only $23. The floor broker then places the order on the inter- market Trading System, an electronic sys- tem that transmits regional orders to other U.S. stock markets. At 2:01 p.m., the or- der appears at the NYSE specialist's booth, but he is too busy executing local orders to notice it. The bid automatically expires at 2:03 p.m.

Mendelson says, because rather than developing an integrated system, most mar- kets have merely automated components of their manual systems.

For example, the DOT system automates the initiation of trades on the New York exchange, but it does nothing to automate the execution of trades, which re- mains largely a manual procedure.

When record volumes drove the markets at record speeds on October 19 and 20, there was plenty of evidence that they were tearing themselves apart. The Inter- market Trading System that links regional markets and the New York exchange came to a virtual standstill. By using ITS, traders in the member markets are supposed to be able to find the other side of a deal by broadcasting commitments to buy or sell a given stock at a given price. Theoretically, ITS's broadening of the markets is a good thing for everyone – potential buyers and sellers alike. These benefits re- main largely hypothetical, however, because ITS operates under limitations that re- strict its usefulness, under the best of circumstances, and actually paralyzed it when its market-broadening effects were needed most – during the crash.

Under ITS rules, the commitments to trade sent to the New York Stock Ex- change expire two minutes from the instant they're broadcast. Orders sent from New

York to the regional exchanges are good for just one minute. While they're still active, commitments are displayed on terminals at trading specialists' posts. The specialist decides whether to accept the commitment and execute a trade for the broker in the regional exchange, or offer a better price and execute a trade locally. In either case, the specialist must make the decision and manually execute the trade.

Even during normal times, specialists can find it difficult to track local bidding and simultaneously monitor the ITS screen. During especially active trading, local traders often won't even wait the minute or so it takes to execute an ITS order on a remote market, and will deal at a lower local price rather than trust the system. Thus, on an average day, 1.3 percent of ITS commitments sent to the New York Stock Exchange expire unexecuted. On October 19, 14 percent of them expired. According to the SEC, NYSE specialists never had the opportunity to accept some commitments "because the orders had expired before they arrived at the post" due to computer delays. ITS problems might have been even worse during the October crunch had a number of regional users not disregarded the system altogether.

The New York exchange wasn't the only ITS member with computer difficulties. According to the SEC, the Midwest Stock Exchange experienced 15- to 45-second delays in its ITS computer interface, leaving specialists as little as 15 seconds to get an NYSE-initiated trade executed.

Think of Haim Mendelson's vibrating, four-wheel drive automobile while reading this SEC description of the ITS system as the system operated at October's high speeds: "The lack of flexibility of ITS fragmented further the markets, reduced substantially the market-making capability of the regional exchanges, and caused [NYSE off-floor brokers] to place even more pressure on [the DOT system]. The unavailability of ITS . . . contributed to decisions by certain regional exchanges to reduce their volume guarantees . . . which, in turn caused [local brokerage] firms to reroute more orders to the New York Stock Exchange, placing even more pressure on its order handling system."

Junius Peake, an Englewood, NJ-based financial consultant, is a developer of the Peake, Mendelson, Williams (PMW) system—an automated, electronic trading system used at several securities exchanges, including those in Toronto and Paris. (His partners are Morris Mendelson of the University of Pennsylvania's Wharton School, and R.T. Williams, a Parsippany, NJ-based consultant.) Peake contends that the division of orders and executions into separate processes keeps ITS from being anything more than inefficient electronic mail.

"Think what might have happened," Peake proposes, "if the people who started the Pony Express had held a monopoly over communications when the telegraph was invented. Since they'd have wanted to protect their investment in horses and waystations, they might have said, 'Sure, set up the telegraph, but we're only going to use it to check on the progress of our messengers.' That, in effect, is what happened with ITS." While the system could have brought real efficiency to the market by executing matched orders entered through it, Peake points out, those with a monopoly on trading at the NYSE—the specialists—made sure ITS was endowed with only limited functionality.

The NYSE's Grasso concedes that ITS encountered "pockets of performance we were unhappy with" in October. But he argues that, while the system effectively links the markets, automatic execution of trades through ITS is neither feasible nor desirable. The delay between the broadcast of the ITS commitment and the order's execution gives additional traders the opportunity to offer better prices, Grasso believes.

Peake points out that only those on the trading floor are in a position to make better offers—by shouting them out. If a remote execution system were open to all traders, many more would be in a position to offer better prices. "Let's substitute computer power for lung power," Peake proposes.

The strength or weakness of ITS will grow as an issue in the next few months in light of the fact that it was originated in response to a mandate in the Securities Reform Act of 1975. That act called for the SEC to "facilitate the establishment of a national market system for securities." The U.S. Government Accounting Office, the investigatory arm of Congress, has begun looking into the SEC's compliance with the 1975 act to determine whether there should be a full investigation.

Perhaps the most significant single breakdown in market mechanisms last October was the "delinking" of the New York Stock Exchange and the Chicago Mercantile Exchange, where the S&P 500 futures are traded. In theory, futures prices should relate directly to the prices of the underlying securities. This allows trading in futures instead of the actual stocks; thus, an investor who decides his stock holdings are too risky can then hedge his position by selling a futures contract equivalent to the amount of stock he'd otherwise have to unload. Portfolio insurance is a term applied to a complicated set of methodologies involving the use of hedges.

Because they are traded separately, however, futures and stock prices don't always exactly match. These fleeting variances present an opportunity to the index arbitrageur, a trader who seeks to lock in instant profits by simultaneously buying in one market and selling in the other. Because they can jump on the spread the instant it materializes, arbitrageurs can win no matter which way the markets move. Their ultimate profits, however, depend on their ability to execute trades in hundreds of stocks—a program trade—before prices change and erase the opportunity. The net effect of this activity on the markets is to bring the prices of both futures and stocks back into line. Thus, the arbitrageurs provide a material link between the two markets.

In a nutshell, here's what happened to the arbitrage (program trading) that would have linked the markets on October 19: As trading on the NYSE became chaotic, arbitrageurs didn't dare venture in—even though a substantial spread occurred between futures and stock prices—because they couldn't be sure of executing their programs on time. The spread had opened in the first place largely because practitioners of portfolio insurance, seeking to reduce the risk of holding securities, had tried first to sell in the futures market. Ordinarily, the arbitrageurs, performing their linking function, would then have transferred such a sell-off to the stock market. But the arbitrageurs were out of the game, and the markets were delinked; the portfolio insurance investors were forced to go straight to the stock market to unload their securities in massive program selling.

In effect, the NYSE's collar on program trades would also tend to delink the markets by making it somewhat harder for arbitrageurs to operate. Thus, by dropping the collar and agreeing to coordinate the circuit breaker with the Chicago Merc,

The Lessons of October

The phenomenal stock trading volumes of October 1987 exposed a number of unanticipated information systems problems. There was plenty of simple queuing as volume exceeded capacity, but more subtle glitches also emerged during the chaos.

For example, ADP, the large financial services bureau, could not provide stock quotation information for about half an hour on October 19 because its system had been programmed to reject such enormous price swings as impossible. According to the Securities and Exchange Commission, another information vendor's system was shut down for 45 minutes because of a nine-minute outrage in a communications line from SIAC, the information support service of the New York Stock Exchange and a number of other markets. When the line came back up, ID numbers on the messages did not resume in sequence, causing the provider's system to reject them.

Here's a sampling of other problems that complicated trading at the NYSE; studies of the crash by the SEC, the U.S. Government Accounting Office, and the Brady Commission provide a multitude of similar examples.

• On October 19 and 20, the exchange's automated Designated Order Turnaround system processed 471,513 and 584,992 orders, respectively, compared with the previous month's daily average of 138,600 orders. The main bottleneck occurred at the printers that delivered many of those orders to the specialists. According to the SEC, during peak trading periods the exchange "reported that the printers created delays of 45 to 75 minutes in both market and limit orders."

The NYSE has since accelerated installation of the electronic workstation displays that replace the specialists' loose-leaf binders and the slow printers. In October, there were about 250 display books covering 600 stocks. Today, there are some 400 books covering more than 1,300 stocks.

• According to the GAO, the system for

the NYSE finally conceded last month that the two markets function as one. Still, it did nothing to address the underlying cause of the two markets' unraveling in October – the inability of its own specialists to execute orders on time.

What was the holdup? Failure of the operational systems supporting the market certainly played a part (see box "The Lessons of October"). The NYSE has since increased its computer system's capacity, but many observers see the NYSE's specialist trading structure as the real crux of the problem. It is these brokers who must execute each and every trade, and who, therefore, stood fast at the bottleneck on Black Monday.

The Securities Industry Automation Corp. (SIAC), the NYSE's data processing service, is in the process of equipping specialists with "electronic books," display terminals that help them manage the incoming order information that they previously received via slow printers and actually scribbled into loose-leaf binders. The electronic book is a prime example of automating the status quo: While it makes routing limit orders came to a halt on three separate occasions on October 20 because its storage capacity had been exceeded, delaying delivery of the orders by 20 minutes. The exchange has since increased the system's capacity by 40 percent.

- A system for advising specialists on their own holdings also failed, delaying delivery of reports due Monday afternoon for an entire day. Some specialists were thus forced to open trading in certain stocks on Tuesday without actually knowing how many shares they held. According to the GAO, this eventually led to odd-lot orders that totaled some 320,000 shares going unexecuted.

What of the future? Robert Van Kirk, a vice president at SIAC, says that the system has now been upgraded to handle an isolated 600-million-share day. Plans are to be able to accommodate occasional peak volumes greater than last October's within a few months, and a billion-share day by December of 1989. Long-range plans call for development of a new system architecture. "We're committed to looking at things in new ways," says Van Kirk.

As the exchange develops its new architecture, it might well look outside for guidance. Leo Lo, a capacity planning specialist at McDonnell Douglas Corp. in St. Louis, points out that a distributed system is the most efficient way of handling applications that must occasionally face very high peak demands. With a distributed architecture, processing can be moved anywhere there is available capacity, Lo says. He cites the telephone system as a prime example. "On Mother's Day, your call from New York to Washington may be routed through San Francisco, if that's where the available switching capacity is," he says.

If the lessons of October teach enough about the risks inherent in hierarchical systems — whether composed of computers or stock traders — Wall Street may finally move closer to Main Street.

the specialist's job somewhat easier and eliminates the printers that helped drag the system down on Black Monday, it does nothing to address the complex of problems the specialists faced that day or to effect any real change. The specialist still stands at his post at the climax of a trade, putting together orders coming from the electronic system and from traders on the floor, bargaining with the "crowd," determining a price and, finally, okaying the trade. Not only does this take time, but it also limits the number of players in the auction. Those on the floor can adjust their orders based on floor information, including information on orders coming through the DOT system; those on the outside don't have access to the floor information and, therefore, don't really compete.

This limitation on participation in the market relates to the second, perhaps more fundamental, weakness in the specialist system: the question of liquidity, the speed at which securities can be turned into cash.

A specialist firm holds a monopoly franchise to execute trades in a given stock in return for its pledge to provide a continuous, orderly market for it. This means that if there is no immediate bidder for a sale, the specialist is supposed to buy and hold the stock until one can be found. Even in normal times, this function carries some risk, and the specialists extract a price for assuming it. According to an unnamed government source quoted in *The New York Times,* the 54 NYSE specialists netted $369 million in earnings in 1987, despite losing $166.7 million in October.

Yet on a day like October 19, with lots of sellers and almost no buyers, the specialists simply stopped accepting that risk. That is, they temporarily halted trading in some stocks while they looked for buyers. Few observers blame them for this. To have done otherwise would have been to commit financial suicide; as it was, the October losses were not insignificant. Even if the specialists had continued buying when no other buyers could be found, it may not have made any difference. "No matter how much capital you threw in front of that speeding train on October 19," claims Richard Grasso, "the results would have been the same."

Even Junius Peake, a critic of the specialist system, doesn't fault the specialists' performance on Black Monday. But the true providers of liquidity to the market, Peake argues, are not the specialists but the buyers and sellers. A fully automated trading system could amplify that liquidity by bringing buyers and sellers together much more quickly and efficiently.

The system Peake would like to see implemented would allow traders to enter bids to buy and offers to sell stocks into a computer system that would automatically execute them against each other on a strict price-time priority. That is, the highest bids and lowest offers would always have priority for a trade, and among equal bids or offers, those submitted first would have priority. The computer would keep an unmatched bid or offer on the system until the opposite side matched it or until the trader withdrew all or part of it.

The New York Stock Exchange, as well, says specialists must give price-time priority to orders on their books. But an order has no priority standing at all until the specialist makes a bid or offer based on it. Once a trade has been executed at the bid or offer price, clearing some or all of the orders at those prices, the next bid or offer takes priority. Thus, a bid shouted by a trader at the specialist's post can immediately seize priority of execution based on price, even though any number of prior orders are on the books.

By the time news of an initial trade reaches those ordering from outside — only a matter of seconds via conventional information systems on a normal day — and they can respond with a new order, the active trader on the floor will always win the second trade. Further, that floor trader today is also likely to have the advantage of a good look at the specialist's book. Rules still say the book is confidential, but, in practice, specialists routinely show their books to traders on the floor.

According to Grasso, the NYSE is now arranging to disseminate, through information vendors, the specialists' "supply-demand equations," which are based on "the orders on the book, what the specialist is willing to do, and what the crowd is willing to do." Broadcasting the supply-demand equations, however, will not be accompanied by any change in the way specialists conduct auctions.

Under Peake's PMW system, everyone logged on can watch trades as they execute and see all bids and offers as they enter the system. On a day like October 19, Peake says, potential buyers could test for bottom prices by setting out bids for small amounts at various levels and watching the way the market reacts. Traders located across the country would themselves provide the liquidity. Direct access would be limited only by proof of ability to fulfill a trader's financial obligations, a requirement any market would enforce.

At the University of Rochester, Haim Mendelson has also designed an alternative, fully automated market system. Along with Yakov Amihud of the New York University School of Business Administration, Mendelson has proposed a hybrid market composed of a continuous auction component, similar to that used on the NYSE, combined with a clearinghouse, or "call" market. In the clearinghouse procedure, traders continuously enter orders, and, periodically, the computer generates a price that matches the greatest number of buy and sell orders. Those orders are then executed at the clearing price, as are all orders at better prices.

Some markets already use a clearinghouse procedure for market openings only or for single securities at a time. The Amihud-Mendelson system, called by its two designers the Integrated Computerized Trading System (ICTS), would clear all securities in the market simultaneously. This would allow traders to enter sophisiticated orders contingent on market conditions—for example, "if the price of Ford stock rises above $40 and that of GM falls below $60, sell 10,000 shares of Ford and buy GM." Today, because of the potential lag in executing the different components of such orders and because just entering the order can move a price away from the target, this kind of trading is complicated and difficult.

What if this simpler methodology had been available to traders on October 19? Mendelson believes traders would not have been afraid to enter the market because their orders could have been made contingent on an optimal scenario. What actually happened, of course, was that a lack of information kept almost all potential buyers out of the market that day.

An important feature of ICTS is that it would retain a specialists' role. Under ICTS, specialists would still operate a continuous auction market; traders could choose to lodge orders either there or in the clearinghouse market. The continuous market would give traders a shot at immediate floor trading, for which they would pay the specialists their price, just as they do today.

One of the ways specialists charge for their services is through the bid-ask spread, a difference between the price to the seller and the price to the buyer (see box "Portrait of a Specialist," on page 444). The specialist determines the size of the spread according to an assessment of the risk of holding the stock during the time it takes to find a buyer, among other factors. Consequently, the specialist's bid-ask spread is an indication of the stock's liquidity.

Liquidity adds value, no matter what kind of item or instrument it is associated with. Consider the different returns on certificates of deposit: Investors are willing to take lesser returns on—pay more for—certificates with an earlier expiration date. Mendelson applies the same principle to stocks: The faster and easier it is to sell a given stock, the more an investor should be willing to pay for it.

Indeed, a study of the NYSE's listed securities by Amihud and Mendelson found a direct correlation between bid-ask spreads and issue prices over a 19-year period. For example, a stock trading at $50 with a spread of 2 percent would typically increase in value, if the spread were reduced to 1 percent, to $56. Thus, by making it easier for traders to enter and use the markets, Mendelson believes, applied infor-

Portrait of a Specialist

Acting as auctioneer, trader, dealer, and information source on the trading floor, the specialist must execute each and every trade in the NYSE-listed stocks for which he is responsible. In many instances, this is done today as it has been done for about 100 years—somebody makes a mark on a piece of paper.

The specialist's charter is to ensure orderly trading as well as render service to other NYSE members by acting as their agent. The opening Automated Report Service pairs buy and sell orders received after the close of the previous day's trading, and presents the imbalance to the specialist. These are the only trades that are matched without him. Armed with this information, as well as his knowledge of the inventory in his own portfolio, the specialist strikes an opening quote, represented by a spread between the buy and sell prices.

This is one way the specialist makes money—he will offer to buy a stock at $20 and sell it at $20 1/8. The spread is never less than an eighth of a dollar per share, but depending on how actively traded the stock is, the spread can be larger, reflecting the specialist's risk.

The specialist also buys and sells stock from his own portfolio throughout the day when there is a temporary imbalance between buy and sell orders. About 15 percent of all NYSE trades involve the specialist on one side of the transaction. This is a second way the specialist can make money—by trading on his own account.

Like all investors, the specialist aims to buy low and sell high. As consultant Junius Peake points out, however, the specialist has more knowledge upon which to act on given stocks than any other investor. Although a specialist may risk substantial capital in a protracted bear market, it is difficult for him to lose when the bulls hold sway.

A specialist will usually accommodate small orders from his own account when there are no orders on the other side of a trade. When an intolerable imbalance accrues, it is the specialist who halts trading.

Peake notes that this aspect of the specialist's role is often confused with the provision of liquidity. If Black Monday demonstrated nothing else, Peake says, it proved that specialists can neither supply liquidity nor ensure an orderly market in the face of a barrage of sell orders.

The specialist's role as auctioneer subordinates his interests to those of traders representing the public. During trading hours, the specialist determines which orders to execute by looking at the activity displayed in his book and listening to bids and offers from the floor. Given orders of the same quantity and price, the specialist must execute trades on a first-come, first-served basis. Nonspecialist orders must always be facilitated before specialist orders are accommodated.

In this milieu, however, there is always room for negotiation, and simple logic says if you know what the best offer is, you can better it. When orders are presented to a specialist, he looks at his book — now often a terminal display — which shows the volume of buy and sell orders as well as a ledger-like listing of stock limit orders.

Automation of the display book is making a vast difference in the efficiency and accuracy of trades on the NYSE, says Bill Johnstone, a specialist with Agora Securities, which handles 41 stocks. Certain trades can now be confirmed electronically by typing those transactions into the specialist's terminal.

Johnstone notes, however, that the persistence of manual operations still contributes to inefficiency under a heavy load. Even today, not every specialist uses an electronic display book. Some refuse to enter any electronic confirmations; instead, they mark a computer card, which is fed into a wooden slot and sent to a printer. Even simple "market" orders — buy or sell at the going price — are confirmed by the specialist.

Although Johnstone insists it is a good idea to have a third party — the specialist — verify each trade, he sees no reason to do so manually. "It takes a lot longer to do it manually than on the display," he says.

Nevertheless, Johnstone doesn't expect the NYSE to eliminate manual procedures anytime soon. The actual manual confirmation process, he points out, is usually done by the specialist's clerk. Translation: the union representing NYSE's clerical employees has nothing to gain from automation.

A third function of the specialist is that of agent for other traders. When a trader on the floor of the exchange wants to execute a limit order, but does not want other traders to know his price until a deal can be struck, the trader can empower the specialist to act as his agent. Rather than wait for a buyer or seller himself, the trader leaves a confidential order with the specialist. Once an offer satisfactory to the trader is delivered to the booth, the specialist will execute it. In return for this service, the specialist gets a slice of the brokerage fee.

The specialist's role as information hub and facilitator of price negotiation is key. By talking to the specialist, a trader can get a feel for where a stock price is heading. "A trader's going to ask me what my perception is of the depth of the market," says Johnstone, who in most cases will tell him. "I'm in a service business," he says.

It's a service, however, provided for members of the New York Stock Exchange, and not necessarily the interests of investors at large.

mation technology could raise the overall value of the stock market by some $70 billion.

Say he's only half right—that's still enough to pay for the most sophisticated computer system imaginable and get back a nice piece of change. But who is capable of taking the lead? Judging from the fate of ITS, an effective government mandate seems unlikely. The markets themselves have always resisted fundamental change.

Some say only increased competition from other domestic and overseas securities markets can spur innovation on Wall Street. The London and Toronto stock exchanges are often cited by experts as being far ahead of U.S. markets in their use of technology. So far, the newer electronic markets, such as Instinet and the regional Cincinnati Exchange, have made only modest inroads on the New York Stock Exchange's business. But the hundreds of thousands of individual investors scared out of town on Black Monday remain leery of action on the Big Board. Given a basic education in the essential advantages, they could begin to move in larger numbers to the guaranteed execution and higher liquidity of the automated, open markets.

An old market adage has it that orders attract orders. One day, the alternatives may achieve enough critical mass to at least force the stock trading establishment to stop playing games with information technology.

49

The 1984 Olympic Message System: A Test of Behavioral Principles of System Design

*John D. Gould, Stephen J. Boies,
Stephen Levy, John T. Richards, and
Jim Schoonard*

This study is a comprehensive research effort aimed at evaluating a computer system design methodology. It reports on the 1984 Olympic Message System (OMS), a voice mail system that was developed according to three behavioral principles. It describes a project from start to finish—from design and development to actual use by the customer. This research is unique in that part of its purpose was to carry out a case study of system design methodology. Consequently, the research effort involved keeping a diary; recording observations, results, and personal feelings; retaining early versions of materials; and building a usage analysis recording system in the final product and carrying out the analyses later.

Fifteen behavioral methodologies used to achieve good usability are described. The dates, times, methodologies used, and numbers of people involved, as well as results, explain how the system development actually proceeded. All aspects of usability evolved in parallel and under one focus of responsibility. We also mention some mistakes made and how the behavioral methodologies allowed us to identify and recover from them. This makes it possible for the reader to learn when and how a particular methodology contributes to the design process, and how long it may take to carry out.

PRINCIPLES OF SYSTEM DESIGN

In the past decade, we have been trying to arrive at procedures that could be used to develop computer-based systems that are reliable, responsive, easy to learn, useful, and desirable. We have recommended three principles [10, 11] to test this research:

1. Early focus on users and tasks. Designers must first understand who the users will be. This understanding is determined in part by directly studying their cognitive, behavioral, anthropometric, and attitudinal characteristics, in part by studying the nature of the expected work to be accomplished, and in part by making users part of the design team through participative design or as consultants.

2. Empirical measurement. Early in the development process, intended users' reactions to printed scenarios and user manuals should be observed and measured. Later on they should actually use simulations and prototypes to carry out real work, and their performance and reactions observed, recorded, and analyzed.

3. Iterative design. When problems are found in user testing, as they will be, they must be fixed. This means design must be iterative: There must be a cycle of design, test and measure, and redesign, repeated as often as necessary. Empirical measurement and iterative design are necessary because designers, no matter how good they are, cannot get it right the first few times (see [11]).

SO WHAT? FIRST IMPRESSIONS

When we describe these principles, we often hear the following reactions:

- "They're obvious. Everybody says that." This reaction is simply incorrect. Of 450 system designers and developers who were asked to write down the steps they recommend in the design of an office system, 26 percent of them mentioned none of the three, and another 35 percent mentioned only one of the three principles [11].

- "Everybody does these things." We pay close attention to talks describing the development of one system or another, and find major differences between what we recommend and what actually happens. Often designers tell us that they intended to follow these principles, but for one reason or another, they were prevented from following them. Occasionally designers think they are following these principles when they are not (see [11]). Some design approaches are milestone oriented (e.g., project reviews, phase reviews), some are specification oriented or document oriented (e.g., functional descriptions, chart talks), and some are characteristics oriented (e.g., the system should be consistent, have a desktop metaphor). Our design principles are process oriented; that is, they specify an empirical approach to design, regardless of the type of system.

- "Human factors is just fine-tuning." Clayton Lewis has characterized this view as the "peanut butter" theory of usability: You can spread it on at the end, like peanut butter. However, like lukewarm chicken soup, it is bland and not curative. Gloss does not fix design defects.

- "In real life, you can't follow them." We often hear this reaction from designers who insist that following them takes too long. They say that the principles do not work on big projects or that they cannot test a system before it exists. On several occasions we have heard descriptions of development projects in which the initial intention was to follow these principles, but for various practical reasons, the developers discovered they could not follow them.

- "You can't measure usability." This is not correct. You can measure usability by (1) having in mind at the outset some behavioral criteria that your system should meet—for example, the system should be easy to use; (2) putting these criteria into specific, testable terms; and (3) testing against these specifications as development proceeds. For example, with a point-of-sale terminal a file clerk from a temporary agency with 30 minutes of training should be able to process customers' purchases with either credit cards, checks, or cash in 1.5 minutes per customer. This should be accomplished by asking no more than an average of 0.3 questions of a supervisor per instance. These specifications then become design goals, analogous to other design goals, for example, memory swap time, installation time, expected service calls, expected cost, and selling price.

THE IMPORTANCE OF THE STUDY

Building OMS was particularly difficult because of the high risk involved and the need for extremely good usability. The Olympics were in the public eye, and OMS could be used by anyone in the world. It was very visible and had the ability to handle sensitive information (personal communications). It was potentially subject to sabotage and abuse, and could have failed in many different and public ways. OMS had to work right and well when the gates opened. The dates could not slip. There would be no second chance to improve it.

This case study demonstrated that by following these principles a large system (a network of over 35 computers scattered over the Los Angeles area) can be rapidly designed, developed, tested, and changed (eight months) by a small group of people with a successful outcome for users.

THE OLYMPIC MESSAGE SYSTEM

There were approximately 10,000 Olympic athletes and officials in Los Angeles. The athletes lived in dormitories in two villages on the large university campuses of USC and UCLA. As was true of previous Olympic games, the athletes lacked support groups in the villages. Their families, friends, and personal coaches did not live there, and many did not travel to Los Angeles. It was estimated that over 50 different languages could be heard in Los Angeles during the games.

What Was the Olympic Message System?

OMS was built upon the IBM Audio Distribution System (ADS) code base [8, 9] and ran on six connected IBM S/1 computers. It allowed Olympians (the main user group) to send and receive voice messages among themselves. They could hear a message in the sender's own voice—as soon as it was recorded and exactly as he or she said it. They could use OMS from almost any push-button telephone in the world. People from around the world could send messages to the athletes and officials.

Table 49.1 is an example of a parent in Ireland leaving a message for his competing son. Over half of the messages Olympians received came from parents, friends, former coaches, etc., who could not come to Los Angeles (see [4] for a usage summary). Table 49.2 is an example of an American Olympian listening to a message sent from his father. OMS had an entirely prompted user interface. Table 49.3 is an example of an American Olympian leaving a message for an Olympian from Australia.

Since many people around the world who might wish to leave a message for an Olympian would not have access to a push-button telephone, OMS had to work with dial telephones as well. Non-Olympians called their own country's National Olympic Committee (NOC) office in Los Angeles. This ensured they would speak to someone who understood their language. A staff member, using a push-button telephone, connected the caller to OMS, aided the caller in any other way, and then got off the line. The caller spoke his or her message and hung up. The voice message was immediately in the new message box of the appropriate Olympian. If the NOC office was not staffed, the call was forwarded to a central group of telephone operators who connected the caller to OMS for that Olympian.

It was impossible to train non-Olympian callers. In order for them to become familiar with OMS, we prepared a one-page "Family and Friends User Guide" for the International Olympic Committee to send to each country's NOC. In turn, they would send them to each Olympian who could then give them to anyone he or she chose. Each pamphlet contained the telephone number of that country's NOC office in Los Angeles. As a backup, each Olympian was given postcards, printed in the appropriate language, upon arrival in Los Angeles. These postcards explained how to use OMS to send a message to an Olympian. There was also room for a personal

Table 49.1
Example of a Parent Leaving a Voice Message (for an Olympian)

Caller:	(Dials 213-888-8888.)
Operator:	Irish National Olympic Committee. Can I help you?
Caller:	I want to leave a message for my son, Michael.
Operator:	Is he from Ireland?
Caller:	Yes
Operator:	How do you spell his name?
Caller:	K-E-L-L-Y.
Operator:	Thank you. Please hold for about 30 seconds while I connect you to the Olympic Message System.
Operator:	Are you ready?
Caller:	Yes.
OMS:	When you have completed your message, hang up and it will be automatically sent to Michael Kelly. Begin talking when you are ready.
Caller:	"Michael, your Mother and I will be hoping you win. Good luck." (Caller hangs up.)

Table 49.2
Example of You (a User) Listening to a Message

You: (Dial 740-4560.)

OMS: Olympic Message System. Please keypress your three-letter Olympic country code.

You: U S A

OMS: United States, Etats-Unis. Please keypress your last name.

You: J O N E

OMS: John Jones. Please keypress your password.

You: 4 0 5

OMS: New messages sent by Message Center. "John, good luck in your race. Dad." End of message. Press 1, listen again; 2, leave a message; 3, hang up.

You: 3

OMS: Good-bye.

Table 49.3
Example of You (an Olympian) Sending a Message

You: (Dial 740-4560.)

OMS: Olympic Message System. Please keypress your three-letter Olympic country code.

You: U S A

OMS: United States. Etats-Unis. Please keypress your last name.

You: J O N E

OMS: John Jones. Please keypress your password.

You: 4 0 5

OMS: No new messages. Press 1, leave a message; 2, listen to an old message; 3, hang up.

You: 1

OMS: Please keypress the country code of the person you want to leave a message for.

You: A U S

OMS: Australia, Australie.

You: B R O W

OMS: Jane Brown. Press 1 when you have completed your message. Begin talking when you are ready.

You: "I'll meet you tonight at 8:00." 1

OMS: Press 1, listen to this message; 2, send it; 3, do not send it.

You: 2

OMS: Messge sent to Jane Brown. Press 1, leave a message; 2, listen to an old message; 3, hang up.

You: 3

OMS: Good-bye.

note. After the postcard was filled out, IBM filled in the telephone number of the Olympian's own NOC office and mailed it by express mail. Olympians sent over 20,000 postcards.

OMS worked in 12 languages. To the best of our knowledge, it was the first computer system to work in several national languages simultaneously. The languages were Arabic, English, French, German, Italian, Japanese, Korean, Mandarin, Norwegian, Portuguese, Russian, and Spanish. OMS kiosks were located in about 25 places in the Olympic villages, as well as at other important locations. These kiosks provided a visual presence for OMS. Each contained a PC-driven visual display of the names of Olympians who had new messages, an electronic bulletin board that displayed news items of interest, and a videodisc of a mime demonstrating how to use OMS. Olympians could press 1 of 12 buttons on the kiosk to select the appropriate language to hear the associated audio. Kiosks also contained copies of the "Olympic Message System User Guide" printed in 12 national languages.

All signs on kiosks were in English and French—the two official languages of the Olympics. Kiosks identified a Help Line number that Olympians who were having trouble could call. If need be, the person who answered could add on OMS, as a third party, and press the keys for the Olympian, thus helping him or her, for example, to sign on. This outreach program was much broader and more integrated than most training programs.

THE SUCCESS OF OMS

In evaluating the merits of our principles of design, one must ask if OMS was successful. It was. It was reliable and responsive. It ran 24 hours per day for the four weeks the Olympic villages were open. The system was never down entirely. We worked in the villages everyday and observed that the Olympians liked the system. Also, as shown in Table 49.4, it was used a lot. Forty percent of Olympians used it at least once. It was used an average of 1–2 times per minute, 24 hours per day (see [4] for a full description of usage, including by country and by language).

CARRYING OUT THE BEHAVIORAL PRINCIPLES OF DESIGN

We followed the three behavioral principles mentioned above. We discovered that the extra work these principles initially require greatly reduces work later on. It is not always easy, however, to follow the principles. At times it was psychologically difficult to break away from the terminal or leave the lab. There were also personal conflicts, for example, deciding whether to spend time programming a simulator or get on with the "real work" of programming the system.

How Did We Follow Them?

Printed Scenarios At the outset, in December 1983, we prepared printed scenarios of exactly how we envisioned the user interface would look. They were similar to Tables 49.1–49.3. These scenarios contrast with the more typical approach

Table 49.4

Summary of OMS Usage

Note that the data are based on 4,601 Olympians who used OMS from around July 14 to August 13. An additional 1,648 messages were sent to Olymipans who either did not use OMS or did not arrive at Los Angeles. The means are for each of these 4,601 Olympians.

	Totals	Means per Olympian
Number of Olympian sign-ons	31,407	6.83
Number of non-Olympian sign-ons	11,778	
Total number of usages	43,185	9.39
Messages sent from		
Same country	4,035	0.88
Other countries	1,678	0.36
Self	1,151	0.25
Non-Olympians	11,778	2.58
Total messages sent	18,642	4.05
Messages listened to	17,213	3.74

of preparing a list of functions that a new system will contain. They provided the first definition of system function and the user interface. In ways that are hard to imagine, they powerfully determined deep system organization. They identified conflicts that a list of functions could not do. They allowed people to see, comment, and criticize at a time when their comments could have the most impact. They gave an existence to the system. They were in a form that behavioral rationale for each step could be carefully examined—by designers, prospective users, and management. The Olympic Committee was clearly impressed by this behavioral orientation in our status presentations.

The scenarios provided the opportunity to make changes to the potential user interface, and accompanying function, before any code was written. In particular, they helped to define the sign-on procedure. They drove significant system organizational considerations; for example, we dropped the message verification function whereby after sending a message a user could learn if and when it was heard by the recipient. We dropped the ability to send the same message to a distribution list of users, as well as the function of OMS calling Olympians who had new messages. These scenarios saved time, because, on the basis of people's feedback, code was never written for functions that otherwise would have been implemented. Later, when working at various depths of coding and preoccupied with details at a microlevel, these printed scenarios provided a useful high-level reminder of exactly what we were trying to do.

Early Iterative Tests of User Guides   There were two main user groups: Olympians, and family and friends. Writing user guides early provides a portable way to bring the essence of a new system to the attention of potential users in a form that they can react to. It is a useful elaboration to user scenarios. Based on feedback from various tests of people using OMS, we iterated over 200 times on the English version of the user guide for Olympians, called the "Olympic Message System User Guide," and over 50 times on the English version of the "Family and Friends User Guide." How could we do this many iterations? Requests and negotiations with others were not required. The "Family and Friends User Guide" was finalized in April so that it could be sent to the Olympic Committee in time to be mailed to the homes of Olympians. Testing and modification of the "Olympic Message System User Guide" continued throughout June.

Early versions of the two guides were also written before coding began. They served to identify issues and problems in system organization. For example, the user interface for family and friends would require trained intermediaries who would have to work very fast so as to minimize the expensive long-distance telephone charges callers would incur when calling from outside the United States. Another example was the realization that OMS operators needed to be able to change the national language that an Olympian heard OMS in if he or she wanted a different one than was selected by his or her NOC, for example, a French-speaking Canadian.

The brief user guides became the definitive OMS documents. This has happened before, for example, in the 1970s with early versions of IBM's ADS [8], at Wang with a text editor, and at Digital Equipment Corporation with the VAXstation (personal communication from R. Rubenstein, 1984; see also [13]).

An unanticipated consequence of testing and iterating is that they prevent well-intentioned but counter-productive changes later on. On more than one occasion before the Olympics started, a powerful person proposed a significant, but poor, rewrite of the "Olympic Message System User Guide." Each time, we encouraged the person to do the proposed rewrite or have one of his people do it, and then test it out on 25 or so users, comparing the results with those we had already obtained. Our proposals had significant impact. There was more appreciation of and respect for the empirical steps that had led to the existing version.

Early Simulations   A few weeks after the project started, we ran simulations of the English version of OMS on an IBM VM system, using IBM 3277 and 3279 terminals. The PF keys on these terminals are laid out in the same 3-by-4 arrangement as push-button telephone keys. Participants pressed these instead of telephone keys to give commands. They would speak their brief messages, and the experimenter would type them. OMS prompts and feedback were displayed on the CRT screen. The experimenter would read the prompts and messages aloud, so participants would hear (rather than see) them.

This was more involved than a typical simulation. The program written on VM formed a real OMS, but a displayed version rather than an audio version. The code could be transferred in a matter of minutes, exactly "as is," to the harder-to-program-and-debug IBM S/1 computer. There it ran with no modification and provided the audio version of OMS. This VM approach was originally developed for ADS (see [8] and [9]). It was possible to use quickly because the table-driven ADS interface was easy to modify, and we were able to use much of the ADS code base in the simulator. This Voice Toolkit (see [12]) allowed us to debug the user interface, conduct informal user experiments for the interfaces for both major user groups (Olympians, and family/friends), and provide demonstrations to elicit people's comments.

We aimed at getting novices characteristic of both user groups to be able to read a one-page description of OMS and then carry out simple test problems. As usual, the approach was to test OMS with experimental participants, modify it, and test it again. In the early stages, laboratory personnel and visitors were sufficient to get rid of bugs and crude edges, and identify some poor judgments we were making about how the interface should behave. We learned (once again) that four audio alternatives on an audio prompt were unacceptable, for example, "Press 1, listen again; 2, listen to another new message; 3, send a message; 4, hang up." In this example, we dropped the "4, hang up" alternative, but in other cases we had to reorganize the user interface.

These simulations were used to define the help messages. When participants were confused or stuck, they either volunteered what they wished they knew at the point (i.e., what information would help them), or we asked them. This methodology of asking people what they wish they knew when they are stuck has general value. The help messages were of two types: user requested and system initiated. If the user wanted help, he or she pressed the space (#) key, and a helpful message played out: "When in doubt, pound it out." At every point in the system, if the user paused beyond a specified time, we assumed that the user was having some difficulty. OMS automatically played a "time-out" message about what to do. The delay time for each of these messages was individually specified in the OMS interface description tables, and the initial values were determined in these simulations.

Unlike printed scenarios, live simulations or prototypes indicate how much a user must know to use the system. The designer cannot just slough off a usability problem with the platitude "We have a help system to take care of this." Simulations provide early tests as to whether the help system actually takes care of a problem — or introduces new problems since the user must now know how to use it also.

The need for consistent "escapes" was also identified in these simulations. "The escapes take subtly different forms," we wrote in our diary on February 5, "which the short printed scenarios that we have been using [described above] do not identify the need for." For example, in signing on (Table 49.2), an Olympian might keypress a wrong (but valid) country code. This had jolting consequences. Instead of hearing "United States. Please keypress your last name," the user might hear "USSR" followed by a message in Russian that the American user did not understand. To address these problems, users pressed the backup (*) key, which "undid" their last action. Solutions like this require users to learn additional functions such as pressing the * key to backup. Designers often do not acknowledge the additional learning burdens that various help and error-correcting approaches place on learners.

Early Demonstrations   By February we were demonstrating audio versions of OMS to many people, with special emphasis on people from outside the United States who did not know much about computers. Here we received regular and strong emphasis to reduce function to the minimum. For example, in the family/friends interface it was recommended that we eliminate the ability for them to review a message before sending it. In the Olympian interface, it was recommended that we eliminate the ability to insert anywhere in a message. These functions, and others we dropped, were already smoothly accommodated into the user interface. The recommendations to drop them were made because additional function in a prompted interface comes at the price of additional prompts.

An Olympian on the Design Team Throughout development we consulted with an ex-Olympian who competed for Ghana at the Olympics in Mexico City and Munich, and had participated in a large number of other international track meets. We received some insight into the content of messages Olympians might receive and send (e.g., he emphasized the joy of receiving "good luck" messages), how Olympians spent their time at previous Olympics (an important consideration in selecting kiosk sites, for example), and appropriate functions to provide. As it turned out, these periodic conversations tended to be brief, but very helpful. Perhaps that is the nature of "participative design."

Tours of Olympic Villages The two Olympic villages were the large university campuses of USC and UCLA. Because of the many requests that vendors were making of the university people and the Los Angeles Olympic Organizing Committee (LAOOC), we were encouraged to stay away from these sites. We were told that we could look at maps or that the "appropriate people" could tell us what we needed to know. (But of course we would not know some of the important questions to ask until we saw the villages.) In the hectic world of system development, where key individuals have too much to do, this is, understandably, enough to discourage most system designers from going any further.

Walking around convinced us that it was not feasible to use classroom training for the Olympians. The campuses were large, and hilly (in the case of UCLA), and there was a chance the weather might be hot and smoggy. Living quarters were spread over many blocks, and large meeting rooms were unavailable.

Interviews with Olympians We spoke with international competitors and officials from many countries, including some from previous Olympic games and likely candidates for the Los Angeles games. They encouraged us, telling us we were on the right track toward supplying a needed and very useful system for the Olympics. We learned how Olympians spend their time and how seriously the bus schedules to practice and competition can drive their personal schedules. We learned that more pointed systems questions could be asked of Olympians in later interviews—questions that we did not envision at first. For example, would Olympians want to send messages to Olympians in the other village? The answer to this question had serious systems implications.

Overseas Tests of the Family/Friends Interface The audio prototype running in February gave us an opportunity to test, iterate, retest, etc., the family/friends interface from any telephone in the world (see Table 49.1). There was no difficulty in getting participants with the right characteristics. We studied people in their homes and offices, at social gatherings, and at schools. They would read the "Family and

Friends User Guide" (a pocket-sized card) and send a message to a specific person on the prototype system.

We also tested the family/friends interface from six South American countries to eliminate any unanticipated surprises due to overseas telephone systems. As so often happens, the emphasis in users' comments was on keeping things simple. This contributed to our eliminating several functions that were then running. Letting family or friends listen to a message they just recorded, or revise it before sending it if they had push-button telephones was dropped. We learned that the pamphlet should contain an example of how to use OMS, even though this would make it longer.

Hallway and Store Methodology   Visits to the villages startled us into the realization that we had to develop an Outreach Program — one that did not involve classroom training or was not people intensive in any other way. We decided that OMS kiosks would be the center of this program. They would give OMS a visual presence and provide a place for users to learn about OMS. They would reflect our philosophy of how people learn to do things. We believe people learn to do things not by reading about how to do them, but by observing and going. Kiosks combined the traditional historic features of people gathering together around a bulletin board to get the news with today's electronic technology.

The kiosk ultimately contained a CRT display of the names of Olympians having new messages, a push-button telephone, an instructional and entertaining videodisc of a mime demonstrating how to use OMS, and copies of the "Olympic Message System User Guide." The four-minute demonstration showed Olympians how to sign on, listen to a message, and send a message. They could see the demonstration and listen to it in their own language by pressing 1 of 12 buttons on the kiosk. (Readers can make a videotape copy of this demonstration by contacting us.) The user guides were also in 12 languages.

We started the design of these kiosks in early March 1984 following our return from visiting the villages. We put an 8-foot high, 45-inch diameter hollow cylinder in the front hallway of the Yorktown Research Lab in March. First, we simulated by pasting on this big cylinder CAD/CAM drawings of the two displays, the telephone, user guide holders, and instructional signs. Immediately we began to get comments and helpful suggestions from passersby, and their enthusiasm rubbed off on us. We were no longer just another five-person group. After a month we settled on the heights and locations of the displays, telephone, and user guide holders. This was done through several iterations of relocating the drawings and continuing to listen to comments. After these simulations we began the carpentry work of cutting holes in the prototype kiosk and making shelves. Hundreds of people viewed the (always interim) results and gave us useful comments. The wording of the English signs on how to use OMS and the translation into French were improved. Labeling the user guide holders in the wording and alphabet of the appropriate country, rather than in English, was suggested — for example, Deutsch rather than German. Aesthetic aspects were improved with suggestions, and a 72-inch crown was added to the kiosk for appearance sake.

We taped 12-foot wide, detailed CAD/CAM drawings of the kiosk on the wall in the hallway. These drawings elicited many comments also, often from craftsmen and construction workers. When it came time to manufacture kiosks, these plans and the working prototype were what the manufacturer followed.

By April we had a running OMS interfaced to the prototype kiosk. We put names of Yorktown people on the display in the hallway, together with a sign asking visitors whether their names were among those scrolling down the screen. People's comments helped determine the layout, scanning rate, and color of the display of Olympain names. The hallway kiosk provided an invitation for passersby to use OMS, which allowed us to receive even more comments. People volunteered to help us in other ways, for example, to do some initial language translation or spend the summer in Los Angeles.

Hallway methodology is an easy way to get participants for informal experiments. Besides being very useful, this methodology is exciting and personally rewarding. We wrote in our diary on April 4 that the "main feedback was how attractive, fun, useful" the kiosk and project are. "People really like looking for their names on the display. It gives our work an exposure and status out of proportion to only a five-person effort. It makes the project seem really important." Hallway methodology gives a project a visibility and existence that it would not otherwise have—especially in the early stages. This technique distinguishes a project from other projects. It accelerates beyond intuition the rate of progress. Other group members get a better feel for where their work fits in.

Yorktown Prototype Test   In preparation for a pre-Olympic field test, we conducted an intensive prototype test with about 100 participants. The use of prototypes can create several changes. Alavi [1], in analyzing 12 recent information systems projects that used prototyping, found that design managers felt it was harder to plan, control, and manage systems development when prototypes were involved, because they had to depart somewhat from fixed plans. At this point, OMS worked in four national languages. This test served mainly to debug the system and user interfaces. At the same time, it identified what we considered "trivalities," but in fact were not: for example, a system prompt we ultimately intended to change. It further identified what some of the help messages should be. It led to the tuning of the amount of time that should expire before a time-out message played out. It led us to create a "speech flow meter," whereby we could detect when a user, while recording a message, had stopped talking.

Win-a-Teddy Bear Contests   We offered free coffee and doughnuts to anyone (of about 65 people) who would, for example, be the third person to change his or her password, or send the fifth new message to John Richards, or answer a message from Jim Schoonard. These tests were typically brief and done in a spirit of fun. We would quickly announce on everyone's time-sharing visual terminal who had won. If a person uncovered a particularly pernicious bug, we would find a suitable reward. Olympic pins were one of these.

Such tests heighten the general awareness of usability—for the developers, the participants (who in turn may become more conscious of usability in their own projects), and management. They can give management an early and quick view of likely customer reaction. They sure catch bugs.

Try-to-Destroy-it Tests   These tests were conducted periodically through the end of June, following a major modification to OMS. On one occasion we had 10 people in the same room, each using OMS from a different telephone while we watched the computer console. Just prior to the Olympics, we had computer science students from a local college dorm try to crash OMS in the evening. They needed no motivation beyond trying to bring down the system. In Los Angeles we once had 24 students call OMS at exactly the same moment, pressing keys in unison. All these tests contributed to the reliability of the system.

Having outsiders try to crash your system eliminates the unconscious tendencies of system designers to gently avoid the soft spots in their own systems while conducting such tests. Conducting these tests requires courage and humility because people will find problems with your system. But it is in this test arena that these battles should be fought – not subsequently on a customer's territory. As can be seen, our several types of iterative testing were informal, rather than controlled formal experiments [2, 5].

Pre-Olympic Field Test   By early April we had a user interface and the "Olympic Message System User Guide," which we felt were excellent, based on user tests using the methodologies already discussed. OMS was installed in Los Angeles to be used at a pre-Olympic event with competitors from 65 countries. We quickly learned, to our concern, frustration, and sadness, that our interface was not as good as we had thought. The problems were small, but cumulative. At the end of the five-day event, we had a list of 57 usability items that had to be addressed before the Olympics (see the box on page 462 for a discussion and solution to a few of these).

The study introduced us, firsthand, to an international reality that we intellectually knew existed, but had not personally experienced. We had already decided that OMS should work in more than the two official languages of the Olympics (English and French), but we now learned just how correct that judgment was. The delegations of competitors from Oman, Columbia, Pakistan, Japan, and Korea were unable to use our system, due to language barriers. Watching this helplessness and hopelessness had far greater impact than reading about it. It was embarrassing to us. Had we not been able to modify all usability aspects of OMS as a result of this international field study, we would not have been as successful at the Olympics.

Yorktown Final Prototype Test   In this test, we joined 2800 people to OMS. It was done primarily to check system reliability with a large number of users, with subsets assigned to different countries.

LAOOC Final Prototype Test   In parallel with the above test, we joined 1000 people to another prototype OMS running in Los Angeles. These people used OMS in their work for several weeks prior to the Olympics. This was particularly useful in learning how to interface OMS with the Los Angeles telephone network (which involved three telephone companies).

DISCUSSION OF THE PRINCIPLES

The Basic Principles Were Reinforced

The three basic principles worked. One must focus on users early to learn the type of system required. Empirical measurement and iteration are musts if a system is to be reliable, responsive, useful, learnable, usable, and desirable. Our experience is that anyone who has tried any of these principles believes in them afterwards. In contrast to the vast majority of systems on which designers have little to say about the methodologies used, designers actually boast about using this methodology. At the very minimum, by following these principles a reliable, responsive system can be achieved.

Sometimes we are asked when, in this method, iteration finally ends. One answer is that, with testable behavioral specifications, you know when you have reached your goal. We did not formally specify the criterion values for these specifications at the outset of OMS, which is not what we recommend to others. Another answer is that it never really ends—the test site just shifts. With many systems new releases are already being planned when the present one is announced.

Integrated Usability Design: A Fourth Principle

Based on our OMS experience, we raise "integrated usability design" to the level of a principle. There are two aspects to this principle: We believe that all usability factors must evolve together, and responsibility for all aspects of usability should be under one control. The box on page 462 provides an example of why integrated design is necessary.

Usability Factors Should Evolve Together Usability is even broader than we had originally thought. Language translation of the user interface and reading materials was a much larger task than we envisioned (cf. [4] for a description of our behavioral approach to language translation). Another component has to do with user groups in addition to end users. In OMS there were several groups of operators, representatives, and runners who were responsible for day-to-day operations. Their jobs had to be defined and organized. For example, the system operator had to join 15,000 potential Olympians to OMS, which required recording their names in audio form. Assuming it took one minute to do this for each Olympian, this would require 30 person-days. Efficiency and correct pronunciation of names were critical. People fluent in all 12 languages needed to be selected and trained (see [4] for further discussion). Another usability component was the maintenance plan and people responsible for it, all of whom had to be recruited, trained, and supplied with reading materials. OMS had to be staffed by all these groups 24 hours a day.

Usually the major components of usability are developed sequentially, even though they jointly interact and affect each other. In OMS they were developed concurrently. We believe this was critical to our success. In this parallel evolution, all components were refined based on the same methodologies of testing and redoing.

Within each main component, usability is made up of many details. A few examples in OMS included the decision to use original or established music in the mime's demonstration; the balance between entertainment value and instructional value in the mime's demonstration; the type of paper to be used in the "Olympic Message System User Guide" (glossy paper might be subject to glare or might be hard to write on, whereas a light bond might disintegrate in sweaty back pockets); and the placement of page breaks in the example-of-use scenarios in the user guides. Once all of this was decided for English, the other 11 languages had to be considered. For example, which way should the Arabic user guide fold? Also, other features of the kiosks such as air conditioning, rain proofing, and the type of phone cord to use all had to be decided.

Responsibility for Usability under One Focus   It is impossible for all aspects of usability to develop in an integrated way when responsibility for it is spread over several groups, some of whom do not begin their work until others have nearly completed theirs. There is too much to remember, too much to negotiate, and too much to do. If responsibility for usability is fractionated, even the simplest changes are routinely difficult and require negotiation. It is vastly simpler to make changes yourself than to request others to make them, and live with the uncertainty of which ones will be made. Iterative design means lots of drudging work. No secretary would willingly retype the reading material as often as we did. How could a designer explain to anyone that he or she made so many mistakes that a user guide had to be modified 200 times?

Why Could We Follow the Principles?

Why were we able to follow these principles when few other designers do and when management often says it is impossible? First, we had good tools. The layered ADS architecture on which OMS was built was designed for iterative design (see [12]).

Table 49.5
Sign-On Sequence Used in the April Pre-Olympic Field Test, with Later Amendments in Italics

User: (Dial 8540.)

OMS: Olympic$ Message System. Please keypress your *three-letter Olympic* country code. ~~Systeme de Messages Olympique: Tapez le numer de votre pays, s'il vous plait.~~

User: U S A

OMS: United States. Les Etats-Unis. Please keypress your last name.

User: ~~goul~~ *G O U L*

OMS: *John Gould. Please keypress your password.*

User: *3 1 9*

OMS: ~~Welcome to the Olympics Message System.~~ *New Message from Stephen Boies.*

A Field Test Identified Required Changes

In April 1984 we conducted a field study at a pre-Olympic event in California with international competitors from 65 countries. We discovered serious problems based on non-English-speaking users—problems we were aware could crop up, but whose seriousness we did not fully appreciate. The following example illustrates three points: (1) You cannot get it right the first few times, (2) different behavioral methodologies yield different types of information, and (3) integrative design is necessary to achieve good usability.

Prior to the field test, we felt we had a good Olympian sign-on sequence. It had gone through much behavioral analyses and several iterations of testing and redesign—all on English-speaking participants. Table 49.5 shows the sign-in sequence as it was for this field test. Unfortunately, it did not work well. The parts of Table 49.5 with a line through them or in italics show changes that were made for the Olympics as a result of this study.

Country Code

When a user called, OMS greeted and asked the user, first in English and then in French (the two official Olympic languages) to keypress his or her country code. Three problems came to light at this point. First, European users sometimes confused their Olympic country code with the concept of an international dialing code prefix. Inserting the phrase "three-letter Olympic" in the message, as shown in Table 49.5, reduced this problem. This seemingly modest change had to be done in the interface, the help system, the reading materials, and the translations. Another help message was also added to reduce or eliminate this problem for the Olympics.

Second, playing the first message in both English and French (see Table 49.5) was too wordy. New users typically wait until an audio system becomes silent before beginning keypressing. They do not interrupt a message and start keypressing (as do experienced users). The switch in national languages was confusing. To remedy this for the Olympics, the first message played out in English only. Users could request the French version by pressing the asterisk (*) key. The user guide was suitably modified, and a mime demonstration and kiosk signs were developed to reflect this change. The solution to these two problems was possible because all aspects of usability were under one person's control and could be so integrated.

Third, the "time-out" help messages had been tuned for English. But, since the prompts were of different lengths in different languages (generally longer than in English), the tunings were good for English only. There was no way to make different tunings for different languages. So an algorithm was developed to start the time-out clock at the completion rather than the beginning of a time-out message, and this worked well for the Olympics. This was possible because the user interface, system functions, and system messages were each separate from each other.

Name

There were five main problems when users were asked to keypress their last name. First, some Middle Eastern and Far Eastern users were not sure whether to keypress their first name or their last name. This was solved for the Olympics by emphasizing, with a picture in the user guide, in the time-out help messages, in the user-requested help messages, and in the mime's demonstration, that users should spell their names exactly as spelled on their badges. Again, this demanded an integration of four usability components—user interface, help systems, reading material, and training or outreach.

Second, in 5 of the 12 languages—Arabic, Chinese, Japanese, Korean, and Russian—user names had to be transliterated into the English alphabet. We observed in our April field test that some of these users were cavalier about how their names might be spelled on OMS. This problem was solved by referring them to the spelling on their badges, thus demanding an integration of the user interface, help systems, reading material, and demonstration.

Third, from the previous problem we anticipated that users might not know how to spell the name of an Olympian, especially from another country, from whom they had received a message and wanted to send a message in return (a very likely possibility we were told in interviews). We added a prompted "Reply" function (something we had previously dropped in the printed scenario stage) that eliminated the spelling requirement under these circumstances.

Fourth, users were required to press only enough characters in a last name to distinguish it from other Olympians from that same country. This was a feature that we had learned users wanted in ADS [8, 9]. In signing on, it caused serious prob-lems in the field test. If a user pressed more than the minimum required characters in his or her last name, OMS considered them to be the first characters in his or her password (since the user's name had already been sufficiently specified from the system's point of view). Users became confused, particularly those who had no experience with "logging on" to a computer with the typical user id-password sequence. The problem was remedied for the Olympics by our creation of a "smart sponge," a part of the program that "soaked up" extra keypresses in a user's name. Once the user diverted from this string, OMS considered the characters to be the user's password. This algorithm worked better than earlier ones we developed based on interkeypress timings. The important metapoint here is that system resources must be used to solve usability problems.

Lastly, we had 4 national languages running for this field test. According to statistics from the Olympic Committee, about 80–90 percent of Olympians could be expected to speak 1 of these 4 languages. We decided that this was not enough, and went on to make OMS work in 12 national languages. This had implications for several aspects of usability—user interface, reading materials, and mime demonstration.

Password

The key problem here was that users did not always know their password. We solved this for the Olympics by initially assigning as a password the last three digits of each user's badge number. The mime demonstration and the user guide emphasized this point. Users could change their passwords, as shown in the user guide.

Some non-English speaking users told us that it was confusing to answer some prompts by entering characters (i.e., country code and name) and all others by entering digits. "You have to read the telephone keys differently," one explained. Although we kept this approach, we did change the typography of the user guide to help reduce this confusion. For example, as shown in Table 49.5, we switched to uppercase characters (because the telephone keys have these) to show that the user was keypressing characters, and we put spaces between the characters, as several users suggested.

Additional Usability Considerations

This field study convinced us that we needed an enhanced Outreach Program and an even more streamlined user interface than we had already developed. We settled on the notion of using a mime demonstration for instruction. The contents of the demonstration particularly addressed the sign-on sequence. We added the concept of a Help Line, with the ability to add on OMS to a conversation between a user who needed help and a helper. We emphasized this in the signs on the kiosk and in the user guide. This Help Line was used frequently in the Olympics, and it guaranteed that, no matter where an Olympian was, he or she could get help in sending or receiving messages. In streamlining the user interface further, we dropped the ability for a user to send the same message to more than one person. Only through a design philosophy where all aspects of usability are integrated could we have addressed the problems illustrated in this example so fast and so successfully. Simply modifying a couple of messages in the already existing user interface or a couple of lines in the already written user guide would not have done it.

There was a separation of user interface and function. The table-driven ADS user interface was easy to change. The VM "simulator," used two years earlier, was relatively easy to update.

Second, we committed ourselves to follow these principles, using OMS as a test case. We deeply believed that usability should drive system design. Arguments about how to proceed were settled by an appeal to the principles (e.g., see [4]).

Third, we were a small communicative group, and this reduced the need to formalize and freeze important usability characteristics very early. It made living with change possible and relatively easy.

We can exclude some reasons. The complexity of the system and probably the knowledge of the application do not seem to determine whether one can follow these principles. It is not sufficient to have human-factors people on the project. We can observe in our own backyard projects that do not follow these principles, even though they have human-factors people in key roles.

The data of this study are correlational—one system was developed with one design method. In this sense they are similar to other valuable case histories discussing systems development methodologies; for example, IBM's ADS [8], Tektronix's Graphic Input Workstation [16], Boeing's banking terminal [6], Digital Equipment Corporation's VAX Text Processing Utility [7], Xerox's Star system [14], Apple's Lisa system [17], and Swezey and Davis's [15] report on trying to apply existing human-factors guidelines in developing a graphics system.

Our study does not prove that the design principles used here are better than others. To do this would require a comparative study of several design methodologies (as the independent variable) with all other variables held constant. This scientific approach is possible only with problems of a much smaller scale (see [3] for comparison of two design approaches, prototyping versus specifying).

We have tried to assess honestly the value of the design principles used here. In our opinion the principles were necessary, but not sufficient, for the success of OMS. There were three other general factors that also contributed critically: first, the people themselves. We had a powerful, dominant leader, Stephen J. Boies, who understood most everything and drove everything. We were the ones who had done much of the design and programming of the prototypes (see [9]) that became IBM's ADS product—the system OMS was built upon. We had the right skill mix—of telephony, systems, application, and human-factors expertise. We had tremendous self-imposed pressure for success. We had no intention of failing—but we feared it (see [4] for a description of some of our fears and conflicts, and what it was like to work at the Olympics).

Second, we had outstanding support—both people and facilities. Without the variety of skills and facilities at Yorktown, OMS would not have been as good. When we needed somebody, we got the right person—and right away.

Third, the Olympics itself contributed. It greased the wheels in getting us what we wanted. The absolute certainty of the begin and end dates, and the certainty that we would be completely finished by the end of the summer, allowed us to work at the pace we did. In retrospect, we have not been able to identify another event—personal, national, or international—that generates comparable enthusiasm and inspiration.

What We Would Do Differently   In retrospect, there is no major aspect of OMS that we would change. Elsewhere, we have mentioned five minor things we would do differently [4].

What Is Exportable?

We learned four general points that can be applied to other systems. First, the principles of design are exportable. They are needed so you know what you are doing. In telling developers about the success of following these principles in developing OMS, we have occasionally noticed an attitude to trivialize OMS. It is worthwhile to remember that, although OMS was built by a few people in a short time, it was a large system (network of over 35 computers), contained a significant new function, and worked reliably and successfully. Furthermore, it was a high-risk system in the sense that it was very visible, handled sensitive information (personal communications), was potentially subject to abuse and sabotage, and could have failed in many different and public ways.

Second, the notion of layered system design is exportable. This is needed so you can make changes.

Third, the concept of tools for interface designers, as implemented in the Voice Toolkit or User Interface Management System used here [12], is exportable. They allow implementers to code and debug much more rapidly. They allow human-factors people to compose, test, modify, refine, and control the user interface — without having to be systems programmers. The mind-set remains in the right perspective. Tools enhance individual productivity and, more importantly, alow you to have smaller groups. Separating the organization and details of the user interface from the functions it calls provides a useful division of labor and adds greatly to the ultimate system goodness.

Fourth, the commitment to living in a sea of changes — and making them — is exportable. You need this to make a good system happen.

CONCLUSIONS

There were remarkable aspects to OMS: Planning and development were done over a short time by a small number of people, and second, it worked well and was a success. OMS was used more than once a minute, 24 hours a day during the Olympics. The project demonstrated that behavioral principles of design could be, and were, followed.

Rather than impede the development process, as is sometimes suggested, following these principles speeds up the development process by identifying right and wrong directions early, and by making change easy. Extra effort in the early stages, which these principles seem to require, leads to much less effort later on and a good system at the end. The project demonstrated that following these principles can be done, does not take too long, and does not cost too much. The principles made possible an integration of all aspects of usability. They led to a reliable, responsive, easy-to-learn system containing the right functions.

Acknowledgments   We received help from many people at IBM's Thomas J. Watson Research Center in Yorktown Heights and at IBM Corporate Headquarters. We especially thank Bill Bennett, Nils Bruun, Rich Finn, Walt Gray, Marilyn Hoppe, Ann Hubby, Linda Klapp, Bill Lewis, Clayton Lewis, Peggy Lohr, Jack McMahon, Angela Minuto, Mike Odierna, Michael O'Sullivan, Michael Starks, and Linda Tetzlaff. The IBM Los Angeles Olympic Project Office was managed by Brian King. Sue Blair had responsibility for OMS. We thank them, and their directors Paul Barton and Gene Fairfield, who provided so much help and expertise when it was needed. Jack Kesselman and Cliff Lau very effectively managed OMS installation and operations in the villages.

REFERENCES

1. Alavi, M., An assessment of the prototyping approach to information systems development, *Commun. ACM* 27.6 (June 1984), 336–383.

2. Bennett, J., Managing to meet usability requirements: Establishing and meeting software development goals, In *Visual Display Terminals: Usability Issues and Health Concerns*, Bennett, J., Case, D., Sandelin, J., and Smith, M., Eds. Prentice-Hall, Englewood Cliffs, N.J., 1984, pp. 161–184.

3. Boehm, B.W., Gray, T.E., and Seewaldt, T., Prototyping versus specifying: A multi-project experiment, *IEEE Trans. Softw. Eng. SE-10*, 3 (1984), 290–302.

4. Boies, S.I., Gould, J.D., Levy, S.E., Richards, J.T., and Schoonard, J.W., The 1984 Olympic Message System—A case study in system design, Res. Rep. RC-11138, IBM, Yorktown Heights, N.Y., 1985.

5. Bury, K.F., The iterative development of usable computer interfaces, in *Proceedings of INTERACT 84—First IFIP Conference on Human-Computer Interaction* (London, Sept. 4–7), Elsevier Science Publishers, Amsterdam, 1984, pp. 343–348.

6. Butler, K.A., Connecting theory and practice: A case study of achieving usability goals, in *Proceedings of CHI 85 Human Factors in Computing Systems* (San Francisco, Calif., Apr. 14–18), ACM, New York, 1985, pp. 85–88.

7. Good, M., The use of logging data in the design of a new text editor, in *Proceedings of CHI 85 Human Factors in Computing Systems* (San Francisco, Calif., Apr. 14–18), ACM, New York, 1985, pp. 93–98.

8. Gould, J.D., and Boies, S.J., Human factors challenges in creating a principal support office system—The speech filing system approach, *ACM Trans. Off. Inf. Syst., 1*. 4 (Oct. 1983), 273–298.

9. Gould, J.D., and Boies, S.J., Speech filing—An office system for principles, *IBM Syst., J. 23,* 1 (1984), 65–81.

10. Gould, J.D., and Lewis, C.H., Designing for usability—Key principles and what designers think, in *Proceedings of CHI 83 Human Factors in Computing Systems* (Boston, Mass. Dec. 12–15), ACM, New York, 1983, pp. 50–53.

11. Gould, J.D., and Lewis, C., Designing for usability: Key principles and what designers think. *Commun, ACM 28,* 3 (Mar. 1985), 300–311.

12. Richards, J.T., Boies, S.J., and Gould, J.D., Rapid prototyping and system development; Examination of an interface toolkit for voice and telephony applications, Res. Rep. RC-11433, IBM, Yorktown Heights, N.Y., 1985.

13. Rubenstein, R., and Hersh, H., *The Human Factor—Designing Computer Systems for People,* Digital Equipment Press, Burlington, Mass., 1984.

14. Smith, D.C., Irby, C., Kimball, R., and Verplank, B., Designing the Star user interface, *Byte 7,* 4 (Apr. 1982), 242–282.

15. Swezey, R.W., and Davis, E.G., A case study of human factors guidelines in computer graphics, *IEEE Comput. Graph. Appl., 3,* 8 (Nov. 1983), 21–30.

16. Weiner, H., Human factors lessons from the design of a real product, TEK Tech. Rep. Tektronix, Wilsonville, 1984. (Can be obtained from the author at Tektronix, Box 1000, Wilsonville, Oreg. 97070.)

17. Williams, G., The Lisa computer system, *Byte 8,* 2 (Feb. 1983), 33–50.

50

Decision Support Planning and Analysis: The Problems of Getting Large-Scale DSS Started

C. Lawrence Meador, Martin J. Guyote, and William L. Rosenfeld

Developing a large-scale institutional DSS designed to serve multiple managers in different business functions can be a more challenging task than that of developing the much more common one-user, one-function DSS that have evolved over the past few years. In this article, we review some of the evidence suggesting that extra effort and rigor in the early planning and analysis stage of large-scale DSS development is worthwhile. We attempt to identify those characteristics of DSS that require different treatment than those available in traditional structured techniques. We then present, in the form of a case study, a hybrid technique which we refer to as DSA (Decision Support Analysis) which has been used effectively in developing large-scale institutional DSS. Finally, we discuss some of the positive and negative experiences that have emerged from using DSA.

INTRODUCTION

Decision support systems (DSS) are computer-based information systems designed to help managers solve problems in semi-structured decision-making areas. Successful DSS applications have addressed problems and decisions in a broad range of managerial and policy environments [1, 2, 9, 11, 15, 26]. By definition, semi-structured decision-making environments are those not well enough understood to permit complete analytical description. This implies the need (and opportunity) to combine managerial experience and judgement with quantitative computer-based approaches.

Planning and analysis are critical tasks in the development of large, complex DSS environments, especially those designed to support several different business functions. Differences between DSS and traditional MIS and DP applications however, oblige developers to use different analytic methods for DSS. In this article we approach these differences from an applications perspective rather than from a theoretical perspective, though in many regards DSS lacks both theoretical and empirical underpinnings.

The early stage of large scale institutional DSS development, here called the Decision Support Analysis (DSA) stage, includes planning, end user needs assessment, problem diagnosis, management orientation and priority setting.

Five elements incorporated into the DSA approach include structured interviews, decision analysis, data analysis, technical analysis, and management orientation. The use of this approach is illustrated by a case study that analyzes the decision support needs of multiple business functions within the marketing organization of a large manufacturing firm.

DEVELOPMENT OF DSS VS. TRADITIONAL MIS SYSTEMS

Analysis in Traditional Systems Development

The importance of analysis in the development of traditional MIS and DP applications is well established. For example, Boehm [4] has shown that more errors are introduced into a new system through failures in analysis than through failures in design, construction, or implementation. Shooman and Bolsky [23] found that errors in analysis are more costly to correct and have greater impact upon system effectiveness than errors in design and construction. McKeen [12] found that additional time spent in front-end analysis led to less overall development time and cost, and greater user satisfaction with the delivered system. Developers of traditional systems — recognizing the importance of analysis — now give increased time and effort to front-end analysis. Their objective is a detailed prespecification of the full system. However, DSS development typically follows a different approach.

Analysis in DSS Development

DSS development follows a plan that lays out specific tasks to be performed, and the proper order of performance. Recent research on DSS applications suggests that planning is perceived by DSS users and developers to be a very important activity. However, it is often performed less effectively than is desired [13]. Exhibit 50.1 shows a typical DSS development plan that might be suitable for large-scale institutional DSS (sometimes referred to as an organizational support system). The first step in this process, Decision Support Analysis, involves the identification of:

1. high priority applications,
2. high level function requirements for those applications,

3. information characteristics and requirements,
4. appropriate fundamental approaches to addressing user needs, including system architecture and detailed technical requirements, and
5. orientation of users to DSS concepts and their relevance to supporting users' jobs.

The first four areas are used to guide software evaluation and selection, prototype design, and prototype construction. The decision support analysis stage provides initial direction to the entire DSS development process. In addition, management orientation to DSS that occurs during this stage helps to avoid organizational problems during implementation. It does this by fostering realistic expectations and generating commitment from users.

Traditional Systems Analysis Methodologies

Many methodologies for analyzing requirements of data processing applications have been developed during the last several years. They include IBM's Business Systems Planning [8], Yourdon's Structured Analysis Techniques [5], SofTech's Structured Analysis and Design Techniques [21, 22], and others.

These methodologies generally share the following characteristics.

1. They are typically used to analyze information flows and data structures for large, structured applications where the scope of the application is fairly well defined in advance.
2. The primary objective is to provide a detailed specification of data flows and structures that can be directly translated into system designs. Designs are then frozen prior to the construction phase. This construction method subdivides large projects among many programmers, thereby requiring greatly detailed specifications in order to avoid massive coordination problems.
3. Given the size of these applications, a second basic objective is to facilitate the translation of the detailed specifications into efficiently designed systems.
4. These methodologies require extensive investments in time and resources to achieve the level of detail required.

Requirements analysis is costly and may be hard to justify for DSS. Thus traditional methodologies may have to be scaled down and modified to be acceptable to DSS users for the following reasons:

1. Many DSS applications are smaller in scope than traditional MIS or DP applications.
2. The benefits of many DSS applications are hard to quantify.
3. DSS users have difficulty prespecifying their decision support needs without a concrete system to which they can react.
4. The decision support needs of DSS users change frequently.

Exhibit 50.1
A Tactical Plan for DSS Development

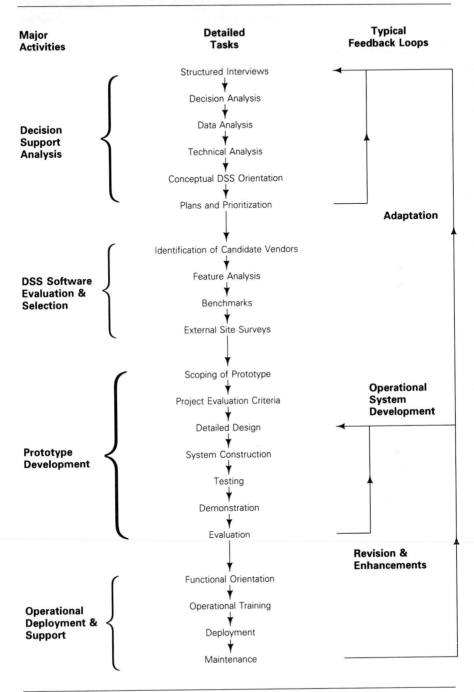

Major
Activities

Detailed
Tasks

Typical
Feedback Loops

Structured Interviews

Decision Analysis

Data Analysis

**Decision
Support
Analysis**

Technical Analysis

Conceptual DSS Orientation

Plans and Prioritization

Adaptation

Identification of Candidate Vendors

**DSS Software
Evaluation &
Selection**

Feature Analysis

Benchmarks

External Site Surveys

Scoping of Prototype

**Operational
System
Development**

Project Evaluation Criteria

Detailed Design

**Prototype
Development**

System Construction

Testing

Demonstration

Evaluation

**Revision &
Enhancements**

Functional Orientation

**Operational
Deployment &
Support**

Operational Training

Deployment

Maintenance

5. It is more important that DSS be effective than efficient (although efficiency is also, of course, an important goal).
6. Problems to which DSS are applied must often be addressed quickly relative to traditional system development timeframes.

These factors have led many authors to argue for an evolutionary approach to DSS development using prototypes and rapid development tools such as fourth generation languages [3, 17]. However, it is often still taken for granted that evolutionary application development must be preceded by a precise and detailed requirements analysis. This article supports an evolutionary approach for requirements analysis as well.

DSS Analysis Methodology

Procedures for DSS analysis and design should exhibit the following characteristics.

1. Minimal elapsed time prior to prototype development. Users need a concrete system to which they can react.
2. Robustness—given the preceding constraint, analysis will often be incomplete and fragmentary. The analytic method must compensate for less than perfect data by quickly focusing on the highest priority applications, and on those functional requirements for each application that warrant more detailed analysis.
3. Ability to evolve along with the DSS—the same methodology should be capable of being used to discover initial DSS opportunities, establish initial functional requirements, and evaluate existing systems to identify directions for further growth.
4. The analytic methodology must have user involvement as an important by-product.
5. There should be an orientation toward managerial users and their decision making activity. This implies designing the systems with special emphasis on the user interface(s), and providing procedures and data representations that fit well with specific managers' established activities.
6. At the same time, there should be an emphasis on prescription as well as description. The methodology should capture managers' decision processes and should establish priorities to improve these processes. This includes pinpointing potential applications with the biggest impact on managerial effectiveness and the highest priority functions needed for these applications. To do this well, the analysis of managers' activities should be tied to individual goals plus the overall goals of the organization, that is, to managers' critical success factors [20]. The analyses should explicitly surface information on improving specific business activities, satisfaction with current performance, perceived costs of improvement, and the amount of technological and organizational risk associated with proposed alternatives.

DECISION SUPPORT ANALYSIS APPROACH

Decision Support Analysis is designed to get DSS started quickly and to achieve the results described previously. There are five basic components of the DSA approach: structured interviews with management, decision analysis, data analysis, technical analysis and management orientation. These processes and their intended results are illustrated in Exhibit 50.2.

A case study is presented to show the overall flow of the process. The approach presented here is primarily oriented toward planning large-scale institutional DSS in settings where the user community includes multiple managers in different business functions. In other settings, however, it has been tailored to the needs of single business functions and smaller organizations, to the technological sophistication of

Exhibit 50.2
Decision Support Needs Assessment Process and Results

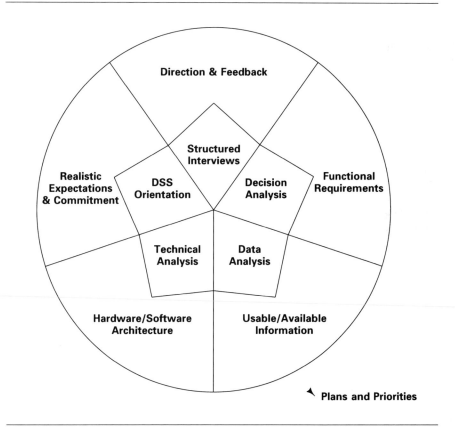

the organization, and the scope of the DSS. In such cases, specific tasks may be de-emphasized or eliminated in order to proceed more quickly and at lower cost.

The case study organization, which we will refer to as Image Technology Corporation (Imagtec), is a Fortune 100 manufacturer of consumer and industrial products. The corporation has a 500-person sales force in its U.S. and overseas subsidiaries. This sales force is managed from a central line organization supported by staff functions that perform forecasting, sales analysis, promotion analysis, market research, end consumer sales audits, product development, strategic planning and advertising. The marketing function was being supported by a marginally functional set of transaction processing systems but had very little decision support. A number of sophisticated software development tools had been acquired at various times but at the time of this study they were poorly utilized, and the resulting applications suffered from poor integration. The planning effort described here was initiated to develop a "blueprint" for a worldwide marketing information and decision support system (WMIS) and to obtain the necessary management support. The analysis and planning described was conducted by a team of five analysts over a three month period.

Structured Interviews

The process begins with interviews that allow managers to identify their critical needs, objectives, and priorities. When possible, interviews are conducted with senior management, systems management and staff analysts.

The interview process at Imagtec included one to two hour interviews with more than forty line executives and staff professionals in the above categories, all of whom were involved with the production and use of marketing information. Given the time constraints, two things are key to maximizing the usefulness of the interviews. The first is the use of interview checklists to focus interviews.

Interview checklists should be designed in consultation with one or two key user managers to ensure that all important areas of activity are covered. Broad areas of coverage should include:

1. a brief description of the objectives, scope, and plan of the project;
2. a description of the project methodology;
3. major business objectives/priorities/decisions;
4. areas for improved decision support (manual or automated);
5. interfaces with other groups and organizations (internal and external);
6. projections of future needs;
7. policy issues such as authority, accountability, and degree of direct use;
8. feedback on the interviews.

The checklists should be used in short preliminary sample interviews with a few selected managers, and then revised based on feedback received. By necessity, these interviews will gather impressionistic data, and techniques such as rating scales and semantic differentials are useful in structuring managers' reports of their preceptions and preferences. Aside from making quantitative analyses possible, the use of rating scales facilitates comparison of results from different respondents.

A useful technique in helping to establish priorities is to have the respondents rate lists of issues and/or functional features on two separate dimensions: perceived importance and perceived performance or satisfaction. High priority issues and features are those that are given high importance but low performance/satisfaction ratings.

We have found that "generic" lists of issues and features are often of limited usefulness, since such lists necessarily include many extraneous items and omit many important ones for any specific application. Further, they usually have to be reworded to conform to the internal terminology of the organization. However, there may be some classes of applications that lend themselves well to such checklists. One example would be organizational cost management and budget analysis systems, which for most large firms would have similar characteristics, including large, multi-user systems with substantial hierarchical consolidations, financial modeling, automated forecasting, alternative scenario analysis, and flexible reporting. In most cases, however, the issues and functional features must be developed by the team conducting the decision support analysis along with sponsoring senior managers.

The second key to the usefulness of the interview results is the experience and skill of the interviewer. The interviewer should go into the interview with a clear understanding of those characteristics that mark a particular task or decision making activity as a prime candidate for decision support. Examples of these characteristics include:

1. labor intensive calculations are involved;
2. frequent iterations of the calculations are needed to reach consensus on plans;
3. multiple scenarios are required to evaluate uncertainty and form contingency plans;
4. a process that is highly judgemental and cannot be completely programmed;
5. coordination among numerous individuals, so that the DSS can provide structure and a common language to enhance consistency and communication;
6. a task or decision process that has senior management involvement, and thus high visibility and potential impact;
7. a task or decision process that is compartmentalized. This facilitates a phased implementation plan using prototypes;
8. an environment that involves situations of clarification;

The ability to quickly spot high potential DSS applications is important in directing interviews along fruitful paths. This helps uncover as much useful information as possible in the allocated time. The interviewer must walk a fine line, however, between direction that facilitates the manager's identification of needs and putting words into the manager's mouth. The interviewee should be allowed to deviate from the interview checklist to discuss issues and features that may be of particular importance in his or her situation which were not anticipated.

In the early stages of interaction with Imagtec management, the interview process found that important decisions in advertising, promotion, pricing, and distribution were often made without determining the interrelationships among these areas. Such decisions were often made without an assessment of competitive actions along these same dimensions. Some of these deficiencies were apparent to the Group Vice President for Marketing. The senior manager who had approved the decision support planning and analysis activity initially was himself skeptical and unwilling to go through the structured interview process. Gentle but persistent pressure by the DSS development team eventually convinced him that he should participate in the process as well. Once he became committed through personal involvement in the process, his apparent understanding of it and appreciation for its value increased dramatically.

Significant deficiencies surfaced in the process by which market research impacted product development and strategic competitive positioning decisions. Five separate, independent and typically disparate forecasting processes operated in parallel to, and in competition with each other. No process existed to rationalize the discrepancies for senior management. These findings suggested that decision process integration was to be a major objective of the proposed DSS. Feedback on the overall interview results was provided to each participating manager as soon as analysis had been completed by the DSS development team. Each manager was asked to critique the assessment derived from the interview process for his or her area of responsibility.

Decision Analysis

At the conclusion of the structured interviews, we develop a conceptual framework to guide the identification of DSS opportunities, system design, project management, and communication of priorities between users and system developers. We call the development of this conceptual framework Decision Analysis, and it is the next step in Decision Support Analysis. (Please note that our use of the term "Decision Analysis" does not refer to the narrow — though well entrenched — view which applies Bayesian stastistical theory to analysis of decision problems.) The conceptual framework consists of the output from three tasks which are described below.

Business Area Analysis   The first step in Decision Analysis is completion of a business area analysis. This process studies representative business units to determine their decision support functional requirements. The analysis is closely tied to the existing organizational structure (as is the definition of the term "business area"). In one client situation, it might refer to corporate divisions, and in another, functional departments or even offices. This lets managers appreciate the extent to which each business unit has unique needs. It also allows for different levels of sophistication in the use of information technology. The result is a set of business area specifications that identify each group's mission, system objectives, basic functions, shared data, internal data, and reports/analysis needed. These specifications are critiqued and approved by each manager before proceeding to the next step.

Description of Logical Functional Flow   Once the business area specifications have been developed from an organizational perspective, they are converted to functional flow diagrams. This involves hierarchical decomposition of the decision making activities of the business areas. The purpose of the hierarchical decomposition is the description of the logical relationships among the business functions. Any of a number of analytic methodologies may be used for this purpose (the Structured Analysis and Design Technique (SADT) developed by Softech is illustrative in this regard — see [5, 21, 22]). The primary objective of the functional flow diagrams is to quickly provide a structure for the more detailed analyses that follow, so that only one or two levels of detail are necessary.

One of the functional flow diagrams developed for the Imagtec marketing function is shown in Exhibit 50.3. This is an SADT style diagram. A business function is defined as a group of logically related activities (decisions or tasks) required to manage the resources of the business. Thus, at the highest level, four major business functions were identified for the Imagtec marketing functions: planning, forecasting, sell-in, and sell-through. Manufacturing is shown on the diagram because of its interface with the marketing function at a central point in the ongoing process. The planning function is responsible for directing all of the marketing functions. The forecasting function is responsible for developing the shorter term, more quantitative plans that direct current operations. Manufacturing converts the plan into product. The sell-in process is concerned with moving inventory from Imagtec warehouses to the dealers' warehouses (i.e., "selling into" the dealer network). Finally, sell through is concerned with moving the product from the dealer to the customer (i.e., "selling through" the dealer network to the consumer marketplace).

The logical relationships among functions may be of two kinds. One type of relationship is the subordinate relationship which identifies the specific activities that make up a higher level function. In looking down the hierarchy from any given function, the subfunctions describe how to accomplish the function. On the other hand, looking up the hierarchy from any given function shows why that function is performed. Thus, in Exhibit 50.3, the overall forecasting function is broken down into three subprocesses: sales analysis, estimation of sales potential, and sales/production review.

The second type of relationship among functions is shown in Exhibit 50.3 by arrows denoting major information flows. These are used both to indicate the major information needs and outputs of any given function and also to establish sequential dependencies among functions.

The discipline behind the techniques used to develop the diagram may have a further purpose. It may highlight development opportunities that will emerge in the future. Such hierarchical descriptions may eventually be the requisite inputs to computer aided software engineering systems (sometimes referred to as automatic programmers). These can produce at least "first draft" computer code directly from the graphical descriptions. The CAD/CAM (computer aided design/computer aided manufacturing) tradition is now spawning a whole new prototypical generation of these systems development capabilities.

The functional flow diagrams also provide a context for other types of analysis and user communication. In combination with priority ratings given by managers,

Exhibit 50.3

Overall Context

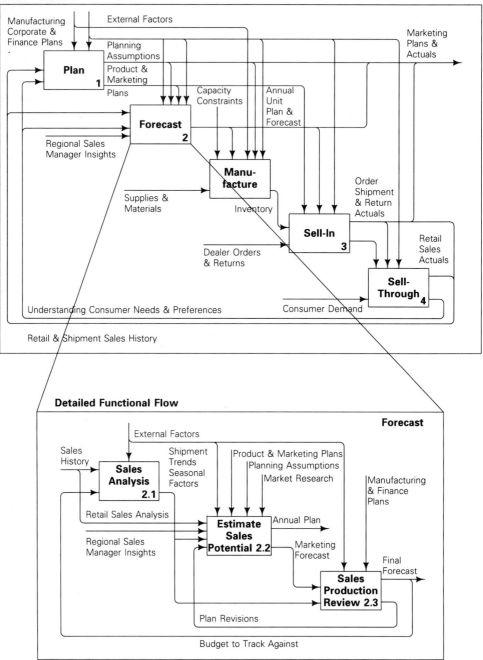

Detailed Functional Flow

they can be used to highlight the most important functions to support first. The diagrams are also used to classify and categorize information needs, and to guide system design and project management.

Specification of Detailed Decision Areas   The final step of Decision Analysis is decision identification and classification. Understanding decision domains allows us to effectively plan decision support. This simple observation is occasionally forgotten. A solid basis is developed for prioritizing DSS development by undergoing a formal process to identify the organization's major regular and ad hoc decisions. Decisions can be analyzed in terms of their complexity, frequency, level of detail, time horizon, accuracy requirements, information sources, and the scope of their information requirements.

One result of the functional flow diagrams is the identification, at the lowest level of the hierarchy, of detailed business functions or decision areas that offer distinct opportunities for decision support. As mentioned above, these lowest level functions should be specified so that they can serve as potential candidates for prototype systems. This means that each should describe a relatively modular task of modest scale that nevertheless has significant impact upon the success of a higher level function.

For the marketing function at Imagtec, a list of 16 detailed functions was derived; three of these are shown in the bottom diagram in Exhibit 50.3. A list of sample questions is then derived for each decision area (see Table 50.1) that reflects the highest priority information needs. These questions are later used as objectives to guide system design.

Data Analysis

The next step in DSA is the identification and description of the classes of data used by the functions. This is done through analysis of the functional flow diagrams. The purpose of Data Analysis is to identify commonalities in information requirements and usage among the decision areas. It also allows us to derive design requirements for application databases. These purposes are accomplished through: (1) data classifications to categorize variables of interest for the managers' interviews (e.g. product pricing, inventory levels, competitors' market share), and (2) dimensional representations developed to structure different views of these variables by time, product, market, etc.

For the Imagtec marketing function, 31 different classes of data were identified and described. Detailed elements were documented for each class of data. One of the outputs from this stage was a chart detailing the relationship between the data classes and the decision area. The Data and Function Usage Chart for the Imagtec marketing function is shown in Table 50.2. For each data class and decision area the chart shows whether the function uses (U), creates (C), or both uses and creates (B) the data. This chart provides insight into the most frequently used data and the most data intensive decision areas (e.g. estimation of sales potential in forecasting). In this case the chart clearly suggests the need for an integrated database—all of

Table 50.1
Examples of Key Questions for Sales Production Review

2.3 Hold Sales Production Review

1. Compare Alternative Forecasts
- How does marketing's forecast compare to manufacturing's estimate of sales?
- How does marketing's forecast compare to finance's estimate?
- Is there a consensus on the underlying assumptions?
- How does the current forecast compare to the annual unit plan?

2. Issue identification/Resolution
- Does manufacturing have the appropriate level and mix planned?
- Is there a consensus on the forecast?
- Are there products for which we have excessive or insufficient inventory to meet expected demand?
- Are there capacity constraints that will limit sales? If so, time/cost to increase capacity?

3. Risk Evaluation
- What is the range of sales potential and where do the marketing and manufacturing sales forecasts fall within that range?
- What are the consequences of various levels of over/under forecasting?
- What can be done to minimize the risk?

the data is used by more than one decision area. Thus, a central set of management data should be used to eliminate the need to re-enter or recreate data for different applications.

At Imagtec, the marketing function managers had grown weary of a data processing system which overwhelmed them with their own data. The marketing managers participating in this study came to realize the magnitude and complexity of the data resources needed to perform their functions—and thus understood why they currently had little or no reasonable basis for effective quantitative analysis. The prior existence of sophisticated DSS software was of little help. A few well positioned prototypes demonstrating some interactive database retrieval capabilities as well as analysis of sales accounts resulted in a broad management-end user support base.

One of the key elements in effective DSS is a set of well designed, multidimensional data structures that allow alternative views of important business variables. Research confirms that end users perceive the need for such capabilities [10]. Different responsibilities imply different views of strategic and operational information. At the same time, effective communication between managers requires consistent procedures for structuring and aggregating information across several dimensions. Some of the keys to effective design of the multidimensional data structure include:

1. Easy multidimensional access—Each manager and analyst must be able to access information at different levels using consistent procedures and commands.

2. Easy restructuring of information—Dimensions change over time. Product lines and markets are combined, added, and dropped, as are entire businesses and subsidiaries. The user should have the ability to restate and/or recalculate historical and forecasted information in terms of new dimensions or new values on existing dimensions.

3. Manageable dimensionality—Humans can only handle a certain level of complexity in information. Although computers can be made to deal with unlimited dimensionality in a database, we find that for managers using the database, an upper limit on the number of usable dimensions may be in the range of five to seven in a single data structure. A typical example would include the dimensions of time, product, market, division, and geographical region for actual and forecast data. Managers sometimes find it useful to picture multidimensional databases in terms of a series of information "cubes."

4. Use of "information bases" rather than databases whenever possible—We distinguish between information bases and transaction-processing databases in the following ways. (1) Information bases are relatively small, and usually highly aggregated, reflecting the fact that managers usually overestimate the amount of transaction detail required to satisfy their query and analysis needs. (2) Information bases have a much greater orientation toward future time periods than transaction-processing databases, which tend to focus on recent history. (3) Information bases provide value-added information through the addition of appropriate external data. (4) Information bases are optimized for efficient access and analysis, rather than for efficient updating and storage. (5) Information bases emphasize multiple scenarios and alternative views rather than consistency and completeness. (6) Information bases are constantly evolving.

For most DSS applications it is more cost effective to provide managers with interactive access to several small, highly summarized extracts providing alternative views of the data, rather than to provide access to large transaction files. This also helps to ensure the security and integrity of transaction files and databases. The information bases will satisfy 90–95% of user's queries, and the remainder can be processed via batch procedures.

The ultimate architecture for the integrated marketing databases at Imagtek took on the following characteristics. Using "inverted list" technology, simple databases were constructed. A series of databases were implemented, the largest of which contained relevant sales information for every product/customer combination in the prior 24 to 26 months. This file was accessed only on an exception basis, after higher level summary files (i.e., information bases) had enabled an area of interest to be identified.

The basis for constructing these critical summary files came from the decision and data analyses conducted with each marketing manager. Thus, the manager's own perspectives on his or her business was exactly the view they utilized to access their sales data. Finally, menu-based dialogues were constructed and data dictionaries were built to ensure ease of use and flexibility in building and accessing these critical tools (see Exhibit 50.4).

Table 50.2
Data and Function Usage

Legend: C = create
U = use
B = both

Phase	Function	Geography					Actuals						
		Sales Organization	Dealer	Channel	End User	Country	Orders	Shipments	Retail	Returns	Shelf Inventory	Company Inventory	Promotion History
Plan	Assess Market and Industries			B		U							
	Set Product/Marketing Direction	U		U		U	U	U					U
	Research New Concepts/Products				U								
	Develop Long Range Plans	U	U	U		U	U						
Forecast	Sales Analysis	U	U	U	U	U	U	U	U	U		U	B
	Estimate Sales Potential	U	U	U	U	U	U	U	U	U	U	U	U
	Hold Sales/Production Review					U							
Sell-in	Maximize Sales Effectiveness	C	C	U		U	U	U		U			
	Define Promotions and Programs					U							U
	Sell to Dealer	U	U	U		U	C	U		B	C		
	Distribute Product	U	U	U		U	U	C	U		B	U	
	Track the Sales Force Program	U	U	U		U	U	U		U			
Sell-through	National Dealer/Co-op Advertising	U	U	U	U	U	U	U	U	U	U		U
	Sell to Consumers				C	U			C				
	Retail Market Analysis		U	U		U	U	U	B			U	U
	Conduct Market Research		U	U	U	U							

Technical Analysis

Technical Analysis translates needs identified in the previous stages into a proposed system design with technical requirements for hardware and software. The results of this process will, of course, vary for each application. However, we have found that many issues appear time and again. These are described below in the context of the Imagtec environment:

There are a number of technical performance issues relative to the design, implementation, deployment, and operational use of the Imagtec systems. Some of the

Table 50.2   (cont.)

	External Plans and Data				Product					Predictions/Directions					Plans				
	Census/Demographics	Psychographics	Econometrics	Manufacturing/Finance Plans	Price	Features	Margin	Consumer Demand	Related Products	Long Range Plans	Annual Unit Plan	Forecasts	Quotas	Competitive Assessments	Marketing Plan	Product Plan	Pricing/Positioning	Promotions	Advertising Plans
Assess Market and Industries	U	U	U	U				U	U					U					
Set Product/Marketing Direction	U	U	U	U	B	B	B	U	B	U	U	U			B	B	B	U	C
Research New Concepts/Products	U	U	U	U	U	U		C	U					U					
Develop Long Range Plans	U	U	U	U	U	U	U	U	U	C				U	U	U	U		
Sales Analysis	U	U													U	U			
Estimate Sales Potential	U	U	U	U	U	U	U	U	U	U	B	B		U	U	U	U	U	U
Hold Sales/Production Review			U									U	U	U					
Maximize Sales Effectiveness	U					U		U	U	U				C	U	U	U		C
Define Promotions and Programs	U	U	U		U	U	U	U	U	U	U				B	U	U	C	B
Sell to Dealer	U										U	U						U	
Distribute Product																			
Track the Sales Force Program								U			U	U							
National Dealer/Co-op Advertising	U	U	U									U	U	U	U	U	U	U	U
Sell to Consumers					U	U		U	U										
Retail Market Analysis	U	U	U		U	U		B	U					U	U	U	U	U	U
Conduct Market Research	U	U	U		U	U		B	U						U	U	U	U	U

technical issues are functional in nature; many of them have important performance implications. The Imagtec marketing DSS had to provide considerably expanded functional capabilities over existing systems with acceptable performance parameters; achieving adequate performance turned out to be both complex and resource consuming.

A number of these technical requirements included:

- Increased access to information, including ability for multiple users to remotely and interactively review and analyze information.

Exhibit 50.4
Imagtec DSS Architecture Summary

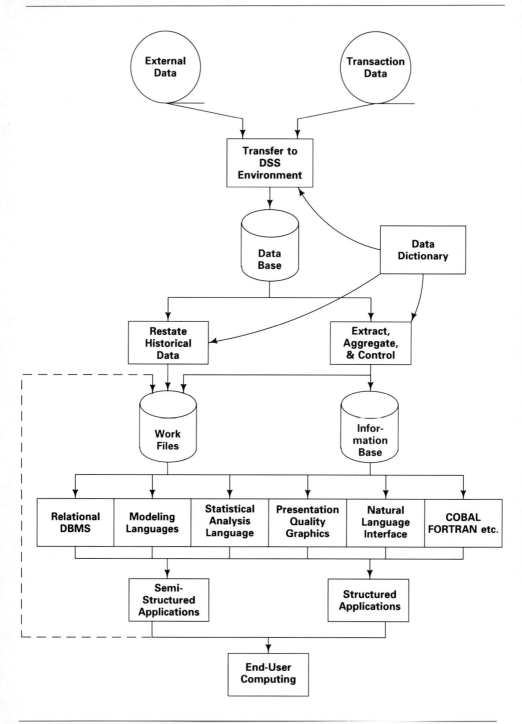

- More timely delivery of information from operational systems to DSS end users; this capability, of course, depends upon the originating source of the data and its ready availability to the DSS.
- Improved modeling and simulation capabilities to fully support expanded modeling, "what-if" and statistical analysis.
- Interactive development of ad hoc database and information base extracts and reporting.
- A high degree of overall systems reliability, including that of the host hardware, telecommunications, and support software, as well as that of the DSS support routines and application modules.
- Comprehensive security and integrity mechanisms which are effective to protect individual and group activities without being unduly awkward to use or generating excessive system overhead.
- Dual modes of DSS user interface – to enable novice users to operate in a fully prompted mode and enable expert users to bypass unneeded prompts and operate in a concise prompt or command driven mode.
- Display of data/information in a variety of formats: on screen, hard copy from screen, batch system or multi-copy, multi-destination routing, and routing to remote devices such as local area networks (LAN), "gateways," intelligent terminals, and personal computers.
- Choice of terminal devices to include on-line access via either full screen video/keyboard device or line by line hardcopy device, at user option, leased line and dial up methods of access.
- Flexible and convenient access to personal databases for personal experimentation, with ease of creating, modifying, deleting, and/or sharing the personal database.
- Appropriate use of batch processing, rather than online interactive processing, where the amount of processing, cost factors, and user response requirements dictate.

Once an initial system design architecture has been chosen, it must be translated into a set of requirements to guide software evaluation and selection. A summary list of features to consider in a DSS development language, for example, is shown in Table 50.3. The requirements drawn up must address technical issues relative to the design, implementation, deployment, and operational use of the DSS. Many of the technical issues are functional in nature, and have important performance implications. Some of those listed in Table 50.3 for the Imagtec DSS explicitly appeared in the user needs assessment (e.g., "what if" analysis capabilities), whereas others had to be inferred (e.g., the need for multidimensional data access). In addition to functional features, the important issues of implementation and ongoing support of any DSS should be reflected in characteristics such as the syntactic complexity and readability of the command language (which affects end user orientation and programmer productivity), security considerations [16], and the types of training and support offered by the vendor. A fuller discussion of other software features relevant to Technical Analysis of DSS is given in [14].

Table 50.3
Sample Criteria for Evaluating DSS Tools

A. Functions and Features

1. Modeling—able to calculate with the information in the system, do optimization, "what-if" analysis
2. Procedurality—ability to solve equations independent of their ordering, symbolic reference of data
3. Data Management—number of dimensions, handling of sparse data, ad hoc inquiry
4. Report Generator—ability to produce high quality formal reports quickly and easily
5. Graphics—line, pie, bar, quality of output
6. Statistics & Analysis—descriptive statistics, regression, significance tests
7. Project Management—PERT/CPM, multi-level work breakdown structure
8. Operations Research—linear, integer, dynamic programming
9. Forecasting & Econometrics—time series, analysis, seasonalization, smoothing
10. External Databases & Interfaces
11. Security—database, file, model, class of user

B. Ease of Use

1. End User—analysis performed directly by person who needs the information
2. Programmer/analyst—interested in the quality of the editor, data management, report writer, etc.
3. Ad Hoc Inquiry—end user answering questions for which no standard report is available

C. Facilities

1. Documentation—for user, programmer, operations
2. Training—novice/advanced, systems/user
3. Support—consultant, hot line
4. Host Hardware—computers supported
5. Operating Environment—operating systems, disk requirements, etc.
6. Availability In-House & On Timeshare

D. Market Posture

1. Pricing—lease, rent, purchase
2. Installations—number of users, length of use
3. Target Market—type of business actively pursued by the vendor
4. Plans—commitment to DSS as a business area, amount of R&D
5. User Perceptions—degree of use and support, functions used
6. Vendor Viability—size of company, revenues, etc.

Management Orientation

User needs assessment should serve to educate the DSS developer about the types of systems to build and how they will be used. The needs assessment process, along with Management Orientation, helps to educate potential users and other managers about the concept of DSS and what they can realistically expect the proposed system to do for them. Further, Management Orientation should indicate how the DSS should be effectively used. The educational needs of users depends upon their previous experience with computers and how they plan to use the proposed system (either directly or through intermediaries). Regardless of the exact topics covered, the basic objectives of the Management Orientation process are to promote:

1. information sharing among developers and users,
2. attitude change among users and developers,

3. skill building among the DSS development team members, and

4. actions motivated to ensure commitment to development and use.

The Management Orientation process at Imagtec took place in three steps. First, the managerial community (about 40 line managers and staff professionals) was briefed in detail on the specific design characteristics and utilization implications for each of their functional areas. Second, senior marketing management and information systems management were briefed on the organizational impacts and benefits and costs of implementation of the system. These two sets of orientations were conducted by the development team. Finally, afer an indepth briefing, the Chief Operating Office of Imagtec presented implementation recommendations for final approval to the Board of Directors. The Board accepted the plan and implementation was begun.

DISCUSSION

By following an effective Decision Support Analysis process, the organization can more quickly and confidently proceed with DSS development. Management priorities are known. User needs have been analyzed, documented, and structured in an overall framework. Data requirements are understood and integrated within that framework. Technical plans have been developed to create an appropriate environment for system development, and criteria have been established to guide appropriate technology selection. Most importantly, manager involvement and education provide direction, build support, encourage the acceptance of appropriate responsibilities, and create realistic expectations.

These results of Decision Support Analysis guide the DSS development process through detailed design, prototype development, and full-scale operational deployment. The plans and priorities established in these initial stages, together with careful project management during construction and implementation, help to guarantee a system that will effectively support users in high priority tasks.

In the Imagtec case study, a DSS development plan was created for 16 major business functions within 10 functional areas of the marketing organization in three months (less detailed planning, using the same DSA approach for smaller organizations, has been completed in six weeks). The identification of priority projects proved, in this case, to be critical because funding only allowed development to proceed in certain areas.

The DSS development manager at Imagtec used the overall plan to identify potential high payoff projects for development, to place them in context, and to ensure integration of the separate efforts. The use of this particular approach to analysis and design at Imagtec also served other very practical purposes. The marketing information systems organization was initially viewed as a group of systems engineers whose job it was to analyze, design and implement systems. DSA allowed that role to be expanded into a partnership with key marketing managers in the identification of critical areas of improvement in the decision making process. This was initiated at the middle management level, not as a top executive Critical Success Factors study, but simply as a user needs assessment aimed at producing more useful information to marketing managers.

The process was able to identify critical needs, achieve a consensus on priorities, and ultimately received funding from senior management. It was even able to withstand some fairly critical organizational changes. Shortly after the DSS planning process was completed, the senior manager who sponsored the study was reassigned to an entirely different project activity. This might have led to complete abandonment of the DSS development project were it not for the then existing shared perspectives and goals of Imagtec marketing managers as well as careful documentation of objectives, approach, benefits and impacts.

The resulting architecture and individual project plans have continued with varying degrees of success. The implementations of prototypes for marketing managers most closely associated with the project have been by far the most successful. The overall objective of marketing data integration has suffered due to the discontinuity of management sponsorship. However, a marketing organization once overwhelmed with data has some useful information and increased confidence in an information systems organization and its new technologies and methodologies. Most importantly, it has a plan and an architecture that in time can bring more information to bear on its critical marketing decisions.

These benefits, of course, have their associated costs. The decision to perform Decision Support Analysis adds up-front costs to the development effort, and delays the development of prototypes. In the case of Imagtec, for example, four man-months of effort over three calendar months were required. This may seem antithetical to the DSS philosophy of quick prototype development. However, we observe in many cases that large-scale, institutional DSS such as the Imagtec application resemble large scale transaction processing applications in that the costs of initial analysis are usually more than offset by a reduced risk of project failure, and by lower costs in all other phases of development. Large-scale, institutional DSS represent a hybrid case somewhere between personal DSS and large transaction processing systems, and the approaches to analysis and design should reflect this. In the Imagtec setting, it was possible to start implementation of prototypes in some areas before Decision Support Analysis was completed.

CONCLUSION

It has been suggested that there are natural stages of evolution and maturity in the use of organizational information systems. Some suggestive anecdotal evidence for such conclusions has been presented. It has often been observed (or at least argued) in biology that "ontogeny recapitulates phylogeny"—that is, particular organisms, in their development, go through stages that resemble some of their ancestral forms [24]. Perhaps DSS development methodology will (or should) recapitulate some of its own predecessors by implementing some of the lessons learned and techniques invented by those innovators who have contributed to the improvement and relevance of information systems development and utilization for a wide range of earlier, larger and more traditional application domains.

We note that many instances of important evolutionary progress in new fields have arisen from a combination of judicious use of good ideas from prior disciplines and a willingness to abandon those ideas that don't apply to the new endeavors. We don't necessarily advocate the particular approach to Decision Support Analysis that has been described in this article for all large-scale DSS development efforts, but we do believe that the use of an explicit, consistent, and repeatable methodology has value in structuring specific development projects as well as institutionalizing successful practices. Improvements from an established baseline may be easier and more relevant, as well as more effective, than always starting from scratch.

Acknowledgment

The methodology presented and the case cited are based on client activities at Research and Planning Inc.

REFERENCES

1. Alter, S.L. *Decision Support Systems: Current Practice and Continuing Challenge,* Addison-Wesley, Reading, Massachusetts, 1980.

2. Bennet, J.L. *Building Decision Support Systems,* Addison-Wesley, Reading, Massachusetts, 1983.

3. Berrisford, T. and Wetherbe, J. "Heuristic Development: A Redesign of Systems Design," *MIS Quarterly,* Volume 3, Number 1, March 1979, pp. 11–19.

4. Boehm, B. "Quantitative Assessment," *Datamation,* Volume 19, Number 5, May 1973, pp. 49–57.

5. Constantine, L. and Yourdon, E. *Structured Design,* Prentice-Hall, Englewood Cliffs, New Jersey, 1979.

6. Donovan, J.J. and Madnick, S.E. "Institutional and Ad hoc Decision Support Systems and Their Effective Use," Working Paper CR14-27, Massachusetts Institute of Technology, Cambridge, Massachusetts, 1977.

7. Hamilton, M. and Zeldin, S. "The Functional Life Cycle Model and Its Automation: USE.IT," *Journal of Systems and Software,* Volume 3, Number 1, March 1983.

8. International Business Machines Corporation. "Information Systems Planning Guide," White Plains, New York, 1978.

9. Keen, P.G.W. and Scott Morton, M.S. *Decision Support Systems: An Organizational Perspective,* Addison-Wesley, Reading, Massachusetts, 1978.

10. Kuhn, T.H. *The Structure of Scientific Revolutions,* The University of Chicago Press, Chicago, Illinois, 1962.

11. Little, J.D.C. "Models and Managers: The Concept of a Decision Calculus," *Management Science,* Volume 16, Number 8, April 1970, pp. B466–485.

12. McKeen, J.D. "Successful Development Strategies for Business Applications Systems," *MIS Quarterly,* Volume 7, Number 2, September 1983, pp. 47–59.

13. Meador, C.L., Guyote, M.J. and Keen, P.G.W. "Setting Priorities for DSS Development," *MIS Quarterly,* Volume 8, Number 2, June 1984, pp. 117–129.

14. Meador, C.L. and Mezger, R.A. "Selecting an End User Programming Language for DSS Development," *MIS Quarterly,* Volume 8, Number 4, December 1984, pp. 267–281.

15. Meador, C.L. and Ness, D.N. "Decision Support Systems: An Application to Corporate Planning," *Sloan Mangement Review,* Volume 14, Number 2, 1974, pp. 51–68.

16. Meldman, J.A. "SMR Forum: Educating Toward Ethical Responsibility in MIS," *Sloan Management Review,* Volume 23, Number 2, Winter 1982, pp. 73–75.

17. Ness, D.N. "Interactive Systems: Theories of Design," paper presented at the Wharton Office of Naval Research Conference on DSS, University of Pennsylvania, Philadelphia, Pennsylvania, November 4–7, 1975, pp. 1–24.

18. Nolan, R.L. "Managing the Crisis in Data Processing," *Harvard Business Review,* Volume 57, Number 2, March–April 1979, pp. 116–118.

19. Nolan, R.L. and Norton, D.P. "Recharter DP to the Advance Stages," *Stage by Stage,* Volume 2, Number 3, 1984, pp. 1–5.

20. Rockart, J.F. "Chief Executives Define Their Own Data Needs," *Harvard Business Review,* Volume 57, Number 2, March–April 1979, pp. 81–93.

21. Ross, D.T. and Schoman, K.E. "Structured Analysis for Requirements Definition," *IEEE Transactions on Software Engineering,* Volume SE3, Number 1, January 1977, pp. 6–15.

22. Rudkin, R.I. and Sheve, K.D. "Structured Decomposition Diagram: A New Technique for System Analysis," *Datamation,* Volume 25, Number 11, October 1979, pp. 130–146.

23. Shooman, M.L. and Bolsky, M.I. "Types, Distribution, and Test and Correction Times for Programming Errors," *International Conference on Reliable Software Proceedings,* Los Angeles, California, 1975, pp. 347–357.

24. Simon, H.A. *The Sciences of the Artificial,* Massachusetts Institute of Technology, Cambridge, Massachusetts, 1969.

25. Sprague, Jr., R.H. and Carlson, E.D. *Building Effective Decision Support Systems,* Prentice-Hall, Inc., Englewood Cliffs, New Jersey, 1982.

26. Urban, G.L. "Building Models for Decision Makers," *Interfaces,* Volume 4, Number 3, May 1974, pp. 1–11.

27. Zmud, R.W. "Management of Large Software Development Efforts," *MIS Quarterly,* Volume 4, Number 2, June 1980, pp. 45–55.

51

Alcon Laboratories: Information Technology Group

David K. Goldstein

In April 1985, Dennis Beikman was concluding his third year as manager of the Information Technology (IT) group at Alcon Labs in Fort Worth, Texas. He had supervised a major turnaround in the IT group, creating a state-of-the-art information systems shop. The 1970s' vintage batch COBOL systems had been replaced by a combination of on-line COBOL systems, software packages, and systems developed in RAMIS—a fourth-generation language.

Beikman's success, however, had become a source of concern to him. Users who previously had relied on the IT group to develop information systems to meet their needs, were now using RAMIS to develop the systems themselves. Hence, the backlog for new information systems had almost disappeared. Since Beikman's current organization was designed to develop and maintain application systems effectively, he became concerned that these tasks might no longer require IT professionals. If this were the case, he would have to decide what the IT organization's role should be in this new systems development environment. As he saw it, the key question was: How does the successful exploitation of software packages and fourth-generation languages affect the role and structure of Alcon's IT organization?

ALCON LABORATORIES

In 1947, two Texas pharmacists, Robert D. Alexander and William C. Conner, had founded Alcon Laboratories in order to develop in a large-scale manufacturing facility more accurate, sterile, and stable specialty pharmaceutical entities than could be developed in a retail drug store. In its early years, Alcon concentrated on manufacturing and marketing ophthalmological drugs (drugs used in the treatment of diseases of the eye). At the time the company was founded, 85% of all eye-care drugs were being compounded in drug stores.

As doctors became familiar with the company's products and their quality, they prescribed them more frequently, and Alcon prospered. Its sales grew from $1.3 million in 1958 to $68 million in 1976. In 1976, Alcon manufactured pharmaceuticals in 22 plants in the U.S., Puerto Rico, and overseas, and sold them in 100 countries. Although over 50% of Alcon's sales were ophthalmic pharmaceutical products, the company also sold ophthalmic surgical products and dermatological, urological, and pediatric products.

In 1978, Alcon was acquired by Nestle S.A., the $12.7 billion Swiss-based food company. This acquisition allowed Alcon to expand its research and marketing efforts, and by 1984 sales had risen to $375 million (see Table 51.1).

ORGANIZATION AND CORPORATE CULTURE

In spite of its rapid growth, Alcon still had the feel of a small company: it was not uncommon to see Ed Schollmaier (the current president) and several of Alcon's vice presidents having lunch together, alongside research scientists and factory workers, in the company cafeteria. The friendliness of the employees, coupled with the large amount of research that took place at the company, created a collegial corporate culture.

Alcon was organized into three product divisions — ophthalmic, surgical, and international. The three division senior vice presidents, and the senior vice presidents in charge of finance and administration, legal, and science and technology activities reported to Ed Schollmaier (Table 51.2). Most of the senior managers were

Table 51.1
ALCON LABORATORIES: Information Technology Group

Alcon Sales 1973–1984	
Year	Sales (in $ millions)
1973[a]	40
1974	49
1975	58
1976	68
1977	82
1978[b]	116
1979	166
1980	205
1981	250
1982	274
1983	289
1984	375

[a]1973–1977 sales from Alcon Laboratories Annual Reports.

[b]1978–1984 sales in Swiss francs converted to U.S. dollars. (From Nestle, S.A. Annual Reports.)

in their early 50s, with over 20 years' experience at Alcon. The majority had started out as salespeople and had worked their way up through sales and marketing. Ed Schollmaier had joined Alcon as a salesperson directly after receiving his MBA from Harvard in 1958, and had moved up through the marketing ranks to assume the corporate presidency in 1972.

MARKETING

One key to Alcon's success was its marketing efforts. The company continued to focus its efforts in the prescription ophthalmic-drug market. Alcon controlled about 20% of the $650 million U.S. ophthalmic-drug and contact lens-care market. It also sold dermatological drugs and contact lenses. It faced competition from other specialty pharmaceutical companies, such as Allergan (a subsidiary of SmithKline Beckman), Barnes Hines (a subsidiary of Revlon), Coopervision and, to a lesser extent, from the larger pharmaceutical companies (e.g., Merck and Pfizer).

Alcon's strategy with respect to prescription ophthalmic drugs was to develop and market a broad range of high-quality products that met the needs of ophthalmologists. Individually, the products did not account for large sales volume, but in aggregate, they created Alcon's significant market share. Product quality was essential for maintaining the company's favorable reputation among ophthalmologists.

The direct sales force was Alcon's principal tool for marketing its prescription pharmaceutical products, and its two distinct activities were creating demand and distribution. To create demand the salesperson called directly on the ophthalmologist to "detail" (describe) a few of Alcon's products and to try to convince the doctor to prescribe them. The detailing of products involved a great deal of nonproductive time since the salesperson might wait half an hour to see an ophthalmologist for 5 minutes between appointments. The products being detailed by the sales force would also be featured in advertisements in medical journals and at conventions.

The distribution effort involved sales calls on pharmacies, hospitals, and wholesalers. Salespeople visited the 10% of pharmacies that sold a large amount of prescription ophthalmic drugs. In their distribution-related sales calls, the salespeople mentioned the products they were detailing and tried to ensure that sufficient supply of all Alcon products were in stock.

Alcon sold its nonprescription products through optical retail, drug, supermarket, and discount chains, and through wholesalers. These sales efforts were supplemented by selective mass media advertising and special promotions.

RESEARCH AND DEVELOPMENT

The showpiece of Alcon's corporate headquarters was the new $30 million research and development facility, one of the largest ophthalmological research facilities in the world. It housed 300 employees, including 78 Ph.D. chemists, biologists and statisticians, who developed and tested new ophthalmic drugs.

The development of new products was important for ensuring the future profitability of Alcon since new products usually are very profitable once they get to

Table 51.2
Alcon Laboratories: Information Technology Group—Organization Chart for Alcon Labs

Nestle

President & CEO
Ed Schollmaier

Sr. VP International Tim Sear	Sr. VP Ophthalmic Dick Sisson	VP General Manager Surgical John Spruill	Sr. VP Science & Technology George Leone	Sr. VP Finance & Administration R. Montgomery	VP General Counsel J. McIntyre

VP Research & Development D. Raval

VP Information Technology D. Beikman

market. Within the pharmaceutical industry, only one in 10,000 compounds makes it through the development process, which typically lasts between ten and fifteen years. Approximately 27% of Alcon's 1984 sales came from products released in the past five years.

THE MANAGEMENT INFORMATION SERVICES GROUP IN EARLY 1982

In early 1982, just prior to Dennis Beikman's arrival, the Management Information Services (MIS) group consisted of 48 people involved in systems development, data entry, data center operations, and technical services. It was responsible for Alcon's corporate data center in Fort Worth. The group operated an IBM 4341 computer that was running at approximately 40% of its capacity. The major systems developed by the group were accounting systems (e.g., accounts payable, accounts receivable, and general ledger), a domestic and an international order entry system, and a sales analysis system. These applications were all batch COBOL systems developed by the MIS group.

The systems under the control of the MIS group were not, however, the only computer systems at Alcon. The research and development area had several of Digital Equipment's PDP 11 series computers used for statistical analysis and laboratory data gathering. In addition, each of Alcon's four major manufacturing plants had an IBM system/34 computer. There were six programmer/analysts and operators in R&D and three operators in manufacturing. Several users developed their own systems using time-sharing service bureaus.

There was a great deal of dissatisfaction with the systems development and operations functions among information system users and their managers. Robert Montgomery, then the controller in the International Division, summed up the user attitude toward the MIS group in 1981:

> If you wanted to do something, you did it yourself. The MIS group couldn't meet the company's changing technological needs. They were ready to go under.

Nick Tsumpis, then manager of technical services in the MIS group, expressed similar sentiments:

> The MIS group wasn't supplying the services that the users wanted. That was why we were losing end users to time-sharing.

CHANGES MADE BETWEEN 1982 AND 1985

Dennis Beikman came to Alcon in February 1982 with a background in chemistry and 20 years of experience working in information systems groups at pharmaceutical companies, starting out as a programmer on an IBM 1401. In his previous job, he had been the information systems manager for the division of a large pharmaceutical company.

Beikman's first task was to assess the state of affairs in the MIS group. He asked Tom Caraway, who had just been made manager of systems development, to bring him up-to-date on the problems he faced. Caraway reported that the systems development group had lost all its personnel with expertise in the billing, sales, and quota systems. Moreover, these systems were poorly designed and needed to be replaced (see Table 51.3). The problems described by Caraway were not limited to those three systems. Of the eleven major applications supported by the MIS group, Beikman rated four as acceptable, one as marginal, and six as unacceptable in a presentation he made to senior management shortly after his arrival.

The group faced problems in one other area. It was converting its operating system from DOS/VS (a system designed for smaller IBM installations) to the more powerful OS/MVS operating system. This conversion was behind schedule, a problem documented in the memo from Beikman to Montgomery (who had by this time been promoted to vice president for finance and was Beikman's boss) found in Table 51.4.

Table 51.3
Alcon Laboratories: Information Technology Group

Date: March 8, 1982
From: Tom Caraway
Dept. or Terr: MIS
Subject: Daily Billing, Sales, and Quota Systems
To: Dennis Beikman

During the past few weeks we have, as you know, lost all of our personnel with expertise in the Daily Billing and Sales Systems. It has been a priority for us to re-establish this knowledge quickly. In doing this we have discovered several deficiencies in the systems highlighted by the following points.

A. The systems contain no edit programs. Editing is by data entry verification. This is a very inefficient and dangerous practice. I have no idea why this was allowed. It must be corrected with the addition of edit programs in the systems.

B. There are no reliable audit trails in any of these systems.

C. There are no control reports in these systems.

D. The systems design is very poor. I feel that no real overall design was followed, rather a series of programs were produced following a disjointed (if any) plan.

E. Interface with other systems i.e., inventory was very poorly planned. An example of this is the creation of an additional perpetual inventory file. The sole purpose of this file is to report inventory quantities. It, however, is an exact duplicate of the perpetual inventory master and appears to have been created for the same purpose. I can only guess that no interface took place with the inventory programmer/analyst at design time. This file will be eliminated.

F. The systems are very inefficient, requiring an average of three hours a night for each processing cycle.

In short this newly developed series of programs are the most unreliable, ineffectual and costly I have ever seen. It is in Alcon's best interest that we repair or replace as soon as practical.

After assessing the situation at Alcon, Beikman developed a plan, and he discussed his proposed changes in a presentation to Ed Schollmaier and several senior vice presidents in June 1982:

1. Accelerate the implementation of on-line interactive application systems to replace old batch-oriented operational systems, utilizing packaged software whenever possible.

2. Increase user personnel awareness and direct participation in systems development, by providing direct access to appropriate databases utilizing advanced "user friendly" software.

3. Decentralize the data entry function to user departments by providing on-line, interactive data entry capability.

4. Provide appropriate software capability and ongoing training and support to user personnel to begin addressing decision support applications.

5. Integrate more fully MIS applications development personnel into Alcon's business operations.

Table 51.4
Alcon Laboratories: Information Technology Group

Date:	February 8, 1982
From:	Dennis Beikman
Dept. or Terr:	MIS
Subject:	Management Information Services Update Status
To:	R. R. Montgomery

It has been one month today since assuming responsibilities of Director, Management Information Services. My assessment of the department's overall status is essentially optimistic but with a few, serious reservations. Namely:

- The billing, sales, and quota systems are in a catastrophic state. See Attachment A. (Exhibit 50.3)
- The MVS conversion has not been properly managed or controlled. We are still facing an estimated three months full time effort of nine Programmer/Analysts to complete this task. The justification or rationale to convert to MVS seems to me to have been very poorly thought out, if at all. The only basis that I can determine for this decision is that "future growth and capability" mandated the conversion. It will be a costly effort for Alcon. However, in the long run Alcon should be able to recover this cost by providing user oriented support capabilities that would not otherwise have been available under DOS/VS. I believe that it is in Alcon's best interest to continue with the conversion effort despite the lack of planning and the cost incurred to date.
- No backup exists for the Manager of Software Systems. All of the conversion support expertise rests with one individual. Alcon is at great risk with its dependence on one individual.
- All applications software is being converted as is from DOS/VS to OS/MVS. Therefore, if the design quality was poor under DOS it will remain equally poor under OS/MVS.

I have taken the following measures to address these problems as well as other issues not mentioned. . . .

Over the next three years, Beikman acted on his five points. His first priority was to replace the unacceptable batch applications with on-line systems that met the needs of Alcon.

The first application that the MIS group replaced was the accounts receivable system: Alcon was collecting its receivables up to nine months late. A project team led by the credit manager, with participants from both the accounting and MIS areas, developed the systems requirements and considered alternative systems development approaches: an Alcon-developed accounts receivable system and several software packages. Rejecting an in-house systems-development effort, the team selected a system from a major software vendor. The development process, from requirements definition to package installation, took six months. The implementation was a success, and receivables were brought down to a more reasonable level.

A similar process was used to purchase packaged software for accounts payable and purchasing. The MIS group is currently installing a general ledger package and will be installing a centralized manufacturing package later this year. The only major system that was rewritten in-house was the order entry system.

The MIS group, in an effort led by Beikman and Tom Caraway, selected RAMIS as its "user friendly" software to increase direct access to information by end users. RAMIS is a fourth-generation language that can be used by trained users and MIS personnel to answer database queries and to write reports.

The major application for RAMIS involves sales data analysis. Data on customer orders is taken from the order entry system each night and is placed in a RAMIS database that contains sales data for all the company's products and customers. Both scheduled (e.g., weekly or monthly) and ad hoc reports are then written using RAMIS. To insure the success of RAMIS, a major user training effort was implemented.

Another major change made by Beikman was the introduction of Business Systems managers (BSMs). The BSMs act as liaisons between user groups and the Information Technology group. They have a matrix reporting relationship and report to both Beikman and to the controller of the user group for which they work. The BSMs work with users and MIS personnel in defining systems requirements, in systems design, and in providing support for existing systems. In describing his strategy for hiring BSMs, Dennis Beikman stated, "I was not looking for traditional information systems people. I wanted people with a general business background and an interest in technology."

STATUS OF THE INFORMATION TECHNOLOGY GROUP IN 1985

The Information Technology group contained 48 people who reported directly to Beikman or to one of his subordinates and nine people who had a matrix reporting relationship to Beikman (Table 51.5). The 48 direct reports were divided into two groups: the Corporate Communications and Technical Services group, and the Systems Development and Administration group.

The Corporate Communications and Technical Services group was headed by Nick Tsumpis, who joined Alcon in 1978 as a programmer/analyst after four years

Table 51.5
Alcon Laboratories: Information Technology Group

Vice President, Finance

Vice President Information Technology
D. Beikman

Secretary
D. Abernathy

Corporate Director Systems Development Administrator
T. Caraway (Acctg.)

- **Manager Sys. Development**
  T. Caraway
  - Secretary
    R. Willis
  - Int'l & Mfg.
    D. Russell
    T. Harmon
    M. Williamson
    M. Blevins
    Vacancy
  - Corp. Fin.
    J. Glass
  - Order Entry Bill & Mkt.
    B. Martin
    S. Box
    E. Finley
    M. Cook
    B. Keeth
    P. Chee
    C. Lucas
  - N. Gilliam
    T. Self
    J. Rollins
    L. Voshalike

- **Manager Admin.**
  D. Dureau
  - Secretary
    P. Grace
  - Education Training
    K. Bice
    J. Campbell

Matrix

- Corp. Records Manager
  B. Maxwell[a]
  L. Baker[a]
  Clerk/Typist
- BSM Reports
  H. Walti
  P. Kruger
  B. Kling
  J. Stafford
  R. Eckols[a]
- Mgr. R&D Automation
  N. Stample
- Dir. QA Automation
  S. Singhal

Corporate Director Corporate Comm. & Technical Supervisor
N. Tsumpis (Acctg.)

- **Mgr. Tech. Services**
  N. Tsumpis
  - Secretary
    C. Ballard
  - Sec. Admin.
    C. Crocker
  - CICS Software
    P. Duran
  - SYS Software
    C. Fulkerson
    Vacancy
  - Corp. Comm. Mgr.
    T. King
    - Comm. Spec.
      C. Woods
    - Comm. Spec.
      D. Pierce
    - PBX
      J. Rhoades
      C. O'Neal
      N. Miller

- **Manager Operations**
  C. Ramirez
  - Computer Operations
    W. Dunnam
    S. Doty
    R. Robbins
    R. Gilley
    D. Daniel
  - Production Cont/Sched
    G. Vick
    R. Hyde
    S. Regester
    M. Norrell
    Vacancy
    J. Moore
    L. Oxford
  - Data Space Analyst
    B. Brauer

---

[a]Included in VP Information Technology Headcount and Expense Budget.

Alcon Laboratories: Information Technology Group **499**

in technical services. The group performed three main functions — technical services, computer operations, and communications. Nick Tsumpis described the major responsibilities of the group:

> The group has a strong service orientation. Availability of the computer is very important. The technical services people work with both the applications area and with the operations area in diagnosing and resolving systems problems. The group is also responsible for hardware capacity planning, installing and maintaining the current operating system, operating the voice and data communication network, and administering the data security function.

The Systems Development and Administrative group was managed by Tom Caraway, who had a degree in computer science and worked as a programmer and project leader before joining Alcon in 1976. The group had two main functions: systems development and maintenance, and user training.

The systems development and maintenance function was performed by 13 programmers and systems analysts and three project leaders. They had the responsibility for developing new interactive COBOL systems and for supporting the COBOL systems, the RAMIS systems, and the software packages. They worked with users to define systems requirements, to choose new software packages, and to develop RAMIS databases and write reports. Four of the programmer/analysts were working primarily on COBOL applications, three were supporting software packages, four were supporting RAMIS applications, and two were working on both COBOL and RAMIS applications.

The systems development area was divided into three project groups — international and manufacturing systems, corporate financial systems, and order entry, billing, and marketing systems. Two of the three programmer/analysts in the international and manufacturing systems group were working on the development of a centralized on-line COBOL system in the manufacturing area. The centralized COBOL system will replace the System/34-based system in the four largest manufacturing plants. This system, in turn, will be replaced by a software package being developed by Martin Marietta (the parent company of Mathematica — the maker of RAMIS) to be run on Alcon's mainframe. This package will provide easy links with RAMIS for inquiries and report writing. In addition, it will utilize RAMIS' new and more powerful database management system. The third programmer/analyst was providing RAMIS support to the international and manufacturing areas.

The four programmer/analysts in the corporate financial area were supporting three software packages: the accounts/payable and purchasing package, the accounts/receivable package, and the general ledger package (which is currently being installed).

B.J. Martin, project leader in the order entry, billing, and marketing area described the work carried out by his group:

> The group's responsibilities are the support of the order entry, billing, sales and marketing areas. When I took over in 1982, the order entry system looked like it contained converted IBM 1401 (an early 1960s vintage computer) code. This system was replaced with an on-line order entry system written in COBOL.

In addition, a RAMIS-based sales and marketing system was developed. The system's databases contain sales information for each division. They also contain customer product information, inventory, sales quota, and sales forecast data.

Of the six people who work for me, two are out in the divisions working with users. (Almost all of the other programmer/analysts are located in the IT area.) They support people in getting the results they want with RAMIS, IFPS (a financial modeling package), and DYNAPLAN (a spreadsheet package). They'll answer questions from users and work with users to develop new programs. Some of the users are very good at RAMIS. Users come from many areas including Science and Technology and corporate accounting. A third person supports sales and marketing applications that use both RAMIS and COBOL.

The three other programmer/analysts work on order entry, customer service, and billing applications. They develop and maintain on-line COBOL applications and RAMIS reports. The applications themselves are written in COBOL. Each night the data files from the applications are added to the RAMIS database. All reports are then written in RAMIS.

The order entry process had recently changed with Alcon's participation in the ORDERNET system. The system was operated by a time-sharing service bureau and was used by pharmaceutical wholesalers and distributors to place orders with their suppliers. Wholesalers and distributors, using computer terminals, dialed up the ORDERNET system and simultaneously placed orders with all their suppliers. All orders for Alcon were stored in computer-readable form in an Alcon "mailbox." These orders were transferred daily to Alcon's order entry system. About 40% of Alcon's dollar volume of orders, mostly those for consumer products, were received through ORDERNET.

The second major function carried out by the Systems Development and Administration group was user training. Two trainers have taught the basic RAMIS course to 215 Alcon employees. The nine-hour class developed by Mathematica has been given to personnel ranging from clerks to middle managers. Of those trained in RAMIS, about 45% used it at least once in the third quarter of 1984. Tom Caraway estimated that between 20 and 30 of those are "hard-core users"—people who use RAMIS several times a week.

There were also four advanced RAMIS courses that have had a combined attendance of 104 employees. The most popular of these was a records management course designed for workers who want to build their own databases. According to Kathylin Bice, one of the trainers, Alcon employees were using RAMIS to build many small databases that were previously handled manually. These included databases of doctors' names and addresses, project control information, mailing lists, distribution lists for internal reports, and the Alcon internal phone book. Two other popular courses taught DYNAPLAN (a spreadsheet package) and GDDM (a graphics package). Both packages were available in the mainframe.

Another function of the IT group was technology assessment. This task was carried out by Nick Tsumpis and Tom Caraway. Tsumpis estimated that they each spent seven or eight days a month examining new technologies and assessing the feasibility of introducing the technologies at Alcon. The latest outcome of this endeavor was a voice mailbox system used by the field sales force.

THE ROLE OF THE BUSINESS SYSTEMS MANAGERS

There were five Business Systems managers at Alcon. Each reported both to Dennis Beikman and to the controller of the user division for whom he worked. All five were located in the user area. Four of the five were part of the headcount for the user division.

Brad Kling, the BSM for the ophthalmic products division, was one of the first BSMs, having been hired in August 1982. His previous work was with a public accounting firm and as a controller in a small company. He had an interest in personal computing, but no formal information systems background. He described his role at Alcon:

> I view my role as primarily one of providing direction by working with the Information Technology group and with users in information systems planning and in application definition.
>
> Currently, I spend about 70% of my time on planned projects and 30% handling ad hoc requests from users. During the past year, I have spent three-fourths of my planned time working on the new manufacturing system. The manufacturing plants were using IBM System/34 computers, but they had difficulty integrating the manufacturing systems with other systems that were run on our mainframe.
>
> Our first step in this process involved reassessing manufacturing systems requirements. We found that inventory concepts used by other companies, such as "just-in-time," were not used at Alcon. We decided to look for a centralized system to fill our needs. A project team was formed that was led by me and made up of members of the Information Technology group and one person from each plant. We made plant visits, developed a requirements document, and selected Martin Marietta's MAS-E system.
>
> This system will not be available until later this year. In the meantime, we have converted the decentralized system to a centralized system written in COBOL and RAMIS. This was completed in mid-March. Manufacturing has traditionally lagged behind in end user computing and now, with access to RAMIS databases, they have the opportunity to catch up.
>
> The other planned projects that I'm working on are a sales forecasting system, an office automation equipment upgrade, and the billing and order entry systems. My nonplanned time consists of answering user questions and working on administrative items, such as obtaining users IDs.
>
> One problem I have found is that there is some confusion as to who is the primary user contact. Now if users have a question or want information, they can go to their BSM, a programmer/analyst or their project manager. I would like the IT group to formalize their support role with respect to users and BSMs. The BSMs need a central source of technical assistance on a variety of issues.
>
> I found that the job offers lots of opportunities and lots of freedom to pursue my own direction. Sometimes, however, I ask myself, "Am I spending my time productively?"

Rick Eckols provided another perspective on the role of the BSM. Before becoming a BSM in October 1984, he had been a senior programmer/analyst, working on the development of the order entry, pricing, and customer service systems (all interactive COBOL-based applications). Eckols was the BSM working with the corporate staff functions—human resources, corporate accounting, treasurer, tax, legal, and auditing. He described his role:

> Two of my tasks are writing RAMIS procedures and designing RAMIS databases. I made some enhancements to our RAMIS-based executive compensation system and transferred the Science and Technology compensation system to RAMIS. I am also working on writing reports in RAMIS for our new general ledger system. The system has a poor report writer. It would take about 500,000 lines of code to produce the reports we wanted using the general ledger's report writer. Only 100 to 200 lines are needed to write the reports using RAMIS.
>
> Currently, my main responsibility is getting users in the human resources group started using RAMIS. They have RAMIS databases, but few end users are producing their own reports. If they want to do something in RAMIS, I do it. My goal is to train them so they can do it themselves. The human resources users were all trained in RAMIS, but they had the training before they had data to work with. Of the eleven RAMIS users whom I work with, four can write their own reports.
>
> I also have a role as a technical reference for users. I help them understand what technology they should use. In addition, I help coordinate and make recommendations for computer terminals, personal computers, and workstations, etc. I also work with users to develop hardware and software plans and serve as a liaison between users and the IT group.
>
> The users see me as their advisor. I have always viewed myself as a user advocate.
>
> This job is very different from my previous job as a senior programmer/analyst. I work more on my own with much less direction from management.

END USER PERSPECTIVE

User satisfaction with the work of the Information Technology group can be examined in two ways. The questionnaire results in Table 51.6 indicate a high degree of user satisfaction with the projects on which the IT group worked in 1984.

Another perspective on user attitude to the changes made in the IT group was obtained from Dick Hedlund, manager of sales services for the lens care and ophthalmic division. Hedlund, a pharmacist by training who became a salesperson for Alcon, moved into his current job in 1977. He reported to the national sales manager for the ophthalmic division.

The sales services group consisted of 27 people who provided sales district managers with reports, and with information on customer bids and on government contracts. They also provided sales management with summary reports on sales data.

Table 51.6
Alcon Laboratories: Information Technology Group
User Evaluation of 1984 IT Projects

	Excellent (4)	Good (3)	Fair (2)	Poor (1)	No Response	Mean
Overall Satisfaction with Project	76	64	3	0	16	3.5
Quality of Documentation	54	46	4	0	55	3.5
Satisfaction with Assigned MIS Personnel	87	53	0	1	18	3.6
Satisfaction with Requested Deliverable	73	59	1	0	26	3.6

Hedlund, who had no previous computer experience or training, was an experienced and knowledgeable RAMIS user. He described the use of RAMIS in his group:

At first users were very reluctant to use RAMIS to create their own reports. Once the users understood the advantages of creating their own reports and controlling their own data, their attitude completely turned around. Now the users are using RAMIS extensively. Of the 27 people who work for me, 15 are RAMIS users and 8 have their own RAMIS databases. Further, we plan to add four more individual databases in the near future.

About 25% of my time involves working with RAMIS—10% answering ad hoc queries from management or field sales and 15% writing RAMIS programs. We are working to get all the sales service production programs converted to RAMIS. We are working closely with four people in the IT group to convert these programs. They provide help mostly in converting external files to RAMIS databases and in writing the file descriptions in RAMIS. We write our own reports and modify existing reports.

We are now working on converting our bid system to RAMIS. It was a mixture of COBOL and RAMIS. We are getting advice from the IT group, but we are writing and testing the programs ourselves.

The IT group estimated it would take them 9 to 10 months to convert the bid system. We can do it in 60–90 days. Knowing the system, I have a much better feel for what I want and how I want it to look. If the IT group was developing the system, I would have to explain to them what I wanted and we would go through a lengthy trial and error period. Being able to adjust the results immediately is a real plus for me.

Using RAMIS has allowed us to take on additional responsibilities without hiring more people. We get more and better reports, better data, and we have more control over our data. I have no idea how many people we'd need if we didn't have RAMIS.

We currently have 15 people handling customer service and hospital charge-backs (transactions between Alcon, the wholesaler, and the hospital). When all the changes have been made, we'll only need 10 or 11 people to handle chargebacks and customer services.

Our goal is to get all applicable data in our RAMIS system so that we can have control of our reporting.

COMPUTING IN RESEARCH AND DEVELOPMENT

Among the organizational changes that have occurred since 1982, both the R&D and the Quality Assurance computing facilities reported to Dennis Beikman (and also to the directors of the R&D and QA functions, respectively).

The R&D computing facility was managed by Norm Stemple, a Ph.D. chemist, who joined Alcon R&D in 1975 with 15 years' experience in laboratory automation. Six people worked for him — two in operations and four in systems development and maintenance. R&D had systematically upgraded its hardware between 1975 and 1985 and had added some new packaged software. In addition to two PDP 11 series computers used for data gathering, there were three of DEC's VAX series computers in R&D. One was used for statistical analysis of data from drug tests; the second was used for centralized word processing, serving 30 secretaries and word processing specialists; the third was used for drug design.

Interactive computing had always been the key objective in R&D computing systems. In 1985 there were about 170 terminals serving the 300 R&D scientists and staff. Almost all employees used the computer for part of their daily work. The digital data network in R&D permitted any user (given proper password authorization) to access any of Alcon's computers (including the corporate IBM system).

To accommodate special reporting and file storage and retrieval needs the fourth-generation language DATATRIEVE was installed in 1982. It has provided R&D users with capabilities similar to those provided to corporate users through RAMIS. For some applications, data were transferred between RAMIS and DATATRIEVE. DATATRIEVE was only one of several software packages used by R&D personnel. At the request of the chemists, the R&D organization purchased a large software package to do chemical modeling to aid in drug design. The system was developed by a company that specializes in software for the chemical and pharmaceutical industries. The request was reviewed by Stemple's group before the purchase was approved.

Stemple's group was examining other software packages including a system that facilitated the presentation of data from the testing of drugs on animals. Norm Stemple commented on the changes in R&D computing:

Originally (1976) most of our software consisted of small systems developed in-house. Now the emphasis is on purchased software. The push for this software is coming from the users. They know what's out there (through going to conferences and talking with their colleagues) better than us. The growth in computer usage has been phenomenal, from 15 terminals in 1981 to the current 170.

FUTURE DIRECTIONS FOR THE IT GROUP

One of the major short-term problems facing the Information Technology group was the shrinking backlog of new systems projects. The systems development group was working on three major projects – the manufacturing system, the general ledger system, and the order entry system. These three projects employed 6 of the 13 programmer/analysts. When these were completed (later in 1985) there would be no new major projects on which the programmer/analysts could work. Much of the demand for new applications was being satisfied by the users themselves with the aid of RAMIS.

There were, however, two technological changes that would be introduced into Alcon through the IT group. A new more user friendly version of RAMIS called RAMIS/ENGLISH was being tested at Alcon. This language should make the RAMIS databases more easily accessible to users. Alcon was also planning to upgrade its RAMIS database manager. The upgraded system would have more capabilities than the current system, and would permit Alcon to write more of its applications in RAMIS and further reduce its dependence on COBOL.

Several of the people at Alcon had ideas about the future role of the IT group:

Tom Caraway   The systems development staff should shrink in size over the next three years. By that time it should be split into two groups. A development group that supports the packaged software and does maintenance and small development requests in COBOL, and an information resource center that supports end user software (e.g. RAMIS and IFPS), personal computer software, training, and database administration.

There will have to be a change in outlook on the part of our managers. While the number of people who report to them is important now, in the future, the number of functions they support should be important.

We have a staff that's done a great job, but they will have to be retrained. We will need more product specialists than we have now.

Nick Tsumpis   There are several big issues that we will have to handle in the future. We are growing in CPU usage at 100% per year. Our biggest challenge is to handle the growth by ensuring that new CPUs perform properly and are cost effective. We will also need to install a local area network and a digital PBX in the next few years. People are also starting to get personal computers and I'm starting to hear them say, "If I only had the data on my PC. . . ." Data access and security is an issue now and will be a bigger issue in the future.

I don't think there will be any growth in either the data center or in technical services. I would like to set up a help desk so that there is a central place for users to call if they have a problem. There's a need to supply better services to the end user.

Bob Montgomery   Alcon's strategy for the future is to be the most successful specialty pharmaceutical company we can be. Our success will depend on our ability to develop significantly technologically advanced products in the ophthalmological area. We must also successfully manufacture and market these products in the U.S. and worldwide. With larger companies entering the ophthalmic market, we must be preemptive in our development of new products.

The IT group must become more user oriented so that it can provide the best tools to aid the company in implementing its strategy. We need people with a high degree of product sensitivity who are able to interface with operations managers. The members of the IT group need to have a better sense of where Alcon makes its money.

One area where an information system could be used is the improvement of our relationships with ophthalmologists. Each year we sponsor a visit to Alcon by ophthalmological interns from several leading hospitals. The purpose of the visit is to familiarize the interns with our products and our research efforts. Providing a database system containing our latest research and product information would allow us to maintain contact with the doctors. This type of system could provide Alcon with an important strategic advantage over our competitors.

Dennis Beikman was aware that his organization was designed to develop and maintain application systems. It appeared that these tasks might not be the responsibility of the IT group in the future. He wanted to set new goals for the IT group and to reorganize the group to meet these goals. As he contemplated how he would do this, he decided the best starting point would be to develop a vision for the future. What functions would the IT group at a typical company perform in 1990? How would that group be structured? Determining the answers to these questions would help Beikman decide what actions he should take between 1985 and 1990 to prepare for these future requirements.

BIBLIOGRAPHY

Harvard Business School Case Studies on Selected Topics

To obtain copies of the following case studies, write Harvard Business School Publishing Division, Operations Department, Boston, MA, 02163, or phone (617) 495-6117. Please refer to the case title and number provided below. The availability of case studies is subject to change.

Telecommunication for a Competitive Edge

Manufacturers Hanover: Worldwide Network, 9-187-015 (video available)

Ivans, 9-187-188

Building Information Systems

Massachusetts Mutual: The Strategic Technology Initiative, 9-188-056

Northwestern Mutual Life Insurance, 9-188-007

Managing End-User Computing

McGraw-Hill Book Company, 9-187-150

Air Products and Chemicals, Inc.: MIS Evaluation of End-User Systems, 9-182-005

Air Products and Chemicals, Inc.: Personal Computers, 9-183-014

Mead Corporation, 9-185-078

Project Management

Concordia Casting Company, 9-187-029

The Manufacturing Integrated Control System, 9-188-151

Strategic Use of IT Resources

Otisline, 9-186-304 (video available)

McGraw-Hill: New Information Products, 9-187-170

Pacific Pride Commercial Fueling, (A) 9-189-153; (B) 9-189-154; (C) 9-189-155; Teaching Note, 5-189-158

Capital Holding Corporation, 9-187-169

Batterymarch Financial Management: Information Systems and Technology, 9-188-013

Emery Worldwide, 9-184-019

Volvo Cars of North America, Inc., (A) 9-188-109; (B) 9-188-110

Frito-Lay: Strategic Transition, 9-187-065

Strategic Use of IT Resources: Evolution in the Health Care Industry

American Hospital Supply Corporation: The ASAP System, 9-186-005

Johnson & Johnson, (A) 9-364-053; Policy Perspective, 9-364-054

Baxter Healthcare Corporation, 9-188-080

IT Management Issues

Manufacturers Hanover: The New Information Technology Organization, (A) 9-189-037; (B) 9-189-038; (C) 9-189-039; Teaching Note, 5-189-060

Child World Planning, Inc.: Information Technology Planning, 9-188-002 (video available)

Frito-Lay: Funding for IS, 9-187-012

Executive Information Systems

Phillips 66: EIS, 9-189-006

The Grumman Corporation, 9-680-032

Lockheed-Georgia Company, 9-187-135

Selecting Hardware and Software

Budd Services, Inc., 9-189-150

Artificial Intelligence and Expert Systems

Texas Capital Investment: Expert System, 9-188-050

Boeing Computer Services, 9-187-105

Managing Change and Information Systems

Tiger Creek, 9-485-057

Hercules, Inc., 9-186-305 (tape available)

Manufacturing and Information Technology

Gleason Components Group, 9-189-136

Deere & Company: CIM Planning at the Harvester Works, 9-687-093

Office Automation

IBM Europe Headquarters, 9-187-025

IBM Computer Conferencing, 9-188-039

International Orientation

Finnpap/Finnboard Fin Project, (b) 9-188-103

Finnpap/Finnboard, 9-186-130

Data Administration in Citibank Brazil, 9-486-109